Group Policy
Fundamentals, Security, and Troubleshooting

D1198584

Group Policy
Fundamentals, Security, and Troubleshooting

Jeremy Moskowitz

Wiley Publishing, Inc.

Acquisitions Editor: Allegro Editorial Services
Development Editor: Lisa Bishop
Technical Editor: Jakob Heidelberg
Production Editor: Elizabeth Campbell
Copy Editor: Judy Flynn
Production Manager: Tim Tate
Vice President and Executive Group Publisher: Richard Swadley
Vice President and Executive Publisher: Joseph B. Wikert
Vice President and Publisher: Neil Edde
Book Designer: Bill Gibson and Judy Fung
Compositor: Craig Woods, Happenstance Type-O-Rama
Proofreader: Amy McCarthy
Indexer: Nancy Guenther
Cover Designer: Ryan Sneed

Cover Image: © Polka Dot Images/Jupiter Images

Library of Congress Cataloging-in-Publication Data

Moskowitz, Jeremy.

 Group policy fundamentals, security, and troubleshooting / Jeremy Moskowitz. -- 1st ed.

    p. cm.

 ISBN-13: 978-0-470-27589-4 (paper/website)

 ISBN-10: 0-470-27589-8 (paper/website)

 1. Microsoft Windows (Computer file) 2. Operating systems (Computers) 3. Software configuration management. 4. Computer security. I. Title.

 QA76.76.O63M69677 2008

 005.8--dc22

                                   2008009609

Dear Reader,

Thank you for choosing *Group Policy Fundamentals, Security, and Troubleshooting*. This book is part of a family of premium quality Sybex books, all written by outstanding authors who combine practical experience with a gift for teaching.

Sybex was founded in 1976. More than thirty years later, we're still committed to producing consistently exceptional books. With each of our titles we're working hard to set a new standard for the industry. From the paper we print on, to the authors we work with, our goal is to bring you the best books available.

I hope you see all that reflected in these pages. I'd be very interested to hear your comments and get your feedback on how we're doing. Feel free to let me know what you think about this or any other Sybex book by sending me an email at nedde@wiley.com. Or, if you think you've found a technical error in this book, please visit http://sybex.custhelp.com. Customer feedback is critical to our efforts at Sybex.

Best regards,

Neil Edde
Vice President and Publisher
Sybex, an Imprint of Wiley

To everyone I've ever had the chance to meet in "real life." Your energy and excitement make it all worthwhile.

—Jeremy

Acknowledgments

We've changed the title (again), moved some of the best stuff to its own book (don't worry, it's happier in the companion book, *Creating the Secure Managed Desktop*), but I like to think of this as the 5th edition of "the Big Green Group Policy Book" (as we've come to call it).

First, I want to thank my assistant, Margot Cullen, for clearing the path necessary for me to write this book. You do a great job, even when I'm heads down and in "can't talk now!" mode. Thank you.

Next, I want to thank Jakob Heidelberg for joining on as the book's technical editor. You did a fantastic job, and I know I picked the right guy for the job. I positively couldn't have done it without you. If there are still any technical problems with the book, blame me, not him. He was great.

I want to thank Elizabeth Campbell, who has been editing my works for more than seven years now. We joke that she's "…been making Jeremy sound like Jeremy since 2001." And it's mostly true. Thank you.

Eric Johnson started out as "a regular guy" on www.GPanswers.com and helped in both the last edition of the book and this edition of the book with some of the "triple-checking on stuff Jeremy was 99.98 percent sure was right but didn't have the time to re-re-check." Not to mention that Eric Johnson is one heck of a SoftGrid propeller-head and also wrote two chapters in the companion book, on—what else—SoftGrid!

When I tell you that an army of people have contributed in some fashion to this book, it would be a huge understatement. I want to thank the Sybex and Wiley magicians, especially Tom Cirtin, Peter Gaughan, and Lisa Bishop who helped me shape the book into two books to better focus the content. To Judy Flynn, for getting the kinks out of the text. To Jay Lessandrini, Dave Mayhew, and Neil Edde: Once again, your dedication to my book's success means so much to me. You take everything I create and deal with it so personally, and I really know that. Thank you, very sincerely.

A special thanks to Mark Gray from the Group Policy team at Microsoft. Mark is new to the Microsoft team, but he hacked and slashed through my tortuous questions one after another. A simple "Thanks!" simply isn't enough to convey my appreciation.

Thanks to Brandon Shell, PowerShell MVP, who helped me write the new chapter on Group Policy and PowerShell, Chapter 11. Read that guy's name again. It's Brandon *Shell*. He's got Shell in his name. It's like if my name were Jeremy Policy. I know I picked the right guy for the job; thanks Brandon.

Thank you to the other folks on the Group Policy team who always support me: Mark Lawrence, Erik Vosukil, Mike Stephens, David Power, Craig Marl, John Kaiser, Judith Herman, Dilip Radhakrishnan, and Jason Leznek (who isn't on the Group Policy team but is awesome nonetheless). Thank you also to the other members of the Group Policy team who support me directly and indirectly and help me out whenever you can. A special thank you to lead Group Policy Program Manager Kevin Sullivan for his foreword and support.

To my girlfriend, Laura (who was only listed as "friend" in the last edition). We've come a long way since that first chapter in our lives; here's to what's next for us. (Note: She didn't even flinch when I had to put our big vacation plans on hold so I could finish the book. Even my *girlfriend* is dedicated to your Group Policy success! She's really the best.)

To my parents and the people I'm proud to call my friends: Jill, Alisa, Tom, Jennifer, Chris, and everyone else.

Thank you Mark Minasi, for asking me to be a part of your series those many years ago. You're a trusted friend and have been a great inspiration to me personally and professionally.

Finally, I want to thank all the readers of the previous editions who believed in Group Policy and have used it daily to make their administration experiences even better. And a heartier thanks to those folks on www.GPanswers.com who ask questions, help others, and help me make this book the best it can be.

About the Contributors

Jakob H. Heidelberg, our technical editor, currently works as an IT specialist for Interprise Consulting A/S, a Microsoft Gold Partner based in Denmark. He is also a writer for www.windowsecurity.com (see www.tinyurl.com/ypar82) and takes on freelance teaching and public speaking when possible.

Jakob is very engaged as a contributor at the largest online Microsoft community for Danish IT Pros, www.it-experts.dk, and spends a great deal of time in the www.GPanswers.com forum too. He also writes on his own blog, heidelbergit.blogspot.com (www.tinyurl.com/2mctjf), and likes to catch up on as much new stuff as possible within the Microsoft world. He currently specializes in Group Policy, scripting, and security.

To my wonderful wife—the better half who was and is always on my mind.—Jakob

Eric Johnson started his career in IT over a decade ago and has run the gamut of IT jobs, from answering technical support calls, teaching technology classes, network administration, Citrix administration, server engineering, and systems analysis to his current role as an infrastructure project manager at a nonprofit health system in Idaho. His current focus involves implementing a suite of Microsoft applications and tools including Windows Deployment Services (WDS), Systems Management Server (SMS), Group Policy, and Microsoft Application Virtualization (SoftGrid). Eric wrote two chapters on SoftGrid for the companion book.

To my three wonderful girls: Sharon, Lexus, and Shelby. Your never-ending optimism and support inspires me to do things I never thought possible.—Eric

Brandon Shell has been in the IT industry since 1994. He spent the early years as a PC tech and general fix-it guy for numerous companies. He started a consulting company in 1999 building, designing, and supporting networks and Windows infrastructure. He joined Microsoft in 2002 as a full time rapid response field engineer doing mostly Directory Service support for companies in the Northeast. In 2006 he fell in love with PowerShell, he spread the love by starting his blog, www.bsonposh.com, and spending night and day on the news groups. He continues to spread his passion by speaking and designing cmdlets to fill the gaps. He is happy to bring you his chapter on leveraging PowerShell with Group Policy technology.

Contents at a Glance

Contents

Introduction

If you've got Active Directory, you need Group Policy. Group Policy has one goal: to make your administrative life easier. Instead of running around from machine to machine tweaking a setting here or installing some software there, you'll have ultimate control from on high.

Turns out that you're not alone in wanting more power for your desktops and servers. Managing user desktops (via Group Policy) was the top-ranked benefit of migrating to Active Directory according to 1,000 members who responded to a 2003 poll from www.TechTarget.com. You can find the study at http://tinyurl.com/47wrg.

Like Zeus himself, controlling the many aspects of the mortal world below, you will have the ability, via Group Policy, to dictate specific settings pertaining to how you want your users and computers to operate. You'll be able to shape your network's destiny. You'll have the power. But you need to know exactly how to tap into this power and exactly what can be powered, and what can only *appear* to be powered.

In this introduction and throughout the first several chapters, I'll describe just what Group Policy is all about and give you an idea of its tremendous power.

Group Policy Defined

If we take a step back and try to analyze the term *Group Policy*, it's easy to become confused. When I first heard the term, I thought it was an NT 4 System Policy that applied to Active Directory groups. But, thankfully, it's much more exciting. Microsoft's perspective is that the name *Group Policy* is derived from the fact that you are "grouping together policy settings." Group Policy is, in essence, rules that are applied and enforced at multiple levels of Active Directory. All policy settings you dictate must be adhered to. This provides great power and efficiency when manipulating client systems.

When going though the examples in this book, you will play the parts of the end user, the OU administrator, the domain administrator, and the enterprise administrator. Your mission is to create and define Group Policy using Active Directory and witness it being automatically enforced. What you say goes! With Group Policy, you can set policies that dictate that users quit messing with their machines. You can dictate what software will be deployed. You can determine how much disk space users can use. You can do pretty much whatever you want—it is really up to you. With Group Policy, you hold all the power. That's the good news.

The bad news is that this magical power only works on machines running Windows 2000 or later. That includes Windows 2000, Windows XP, Windows Server 2003 (as a client), Windows Vista, and Windows Server 2008 (as a client).

That's right; there is no way—no matter what anyone tells you—to use the magic that is known as Group Policy in a way that affects Windows 95, Windows 98, or Windows NT workstations or servers. But, since this is 2008, you likely don't have many of these kicking around anymore.

The application of Group Policy does not concern itself with the mode of the domain. Windows 2000, Windows 2003, or Windows Server 2008 domains need not be in any special functional mode.

If the range of control scares you—don't be afraid! It just means more power to hold over your environment. You'll quickly learn how to wisely use this newfound power to reign over your subjects, er, users.

Group Policy vs. Group Policy Objects

Before we go headlong into Group Policy theory, let's get some terminology and vocabulary out of the way:

- *Group Policy* is the concept that, from upon high, you can do all this "stuff" to your client machines.

- A *policy setting* is just one individual setting that you can use to perform some specific action.

- *Group Policy Objects (GPOs)* are the "nuts-and-bolts" contained within Active Directory Domain Controllers, and each can contain anywhere from one to a zillion individual policy settings.

- The Group Policy *preference*, or *preference item*, is new to the Group Policy world. It's like a policy setting, except it doesn't always act like one. These come from the new Group Policy Preference Extensions (which we cover in excruciating detail in Chapter 10).

It's my goal that after you work through this book, you'll be able to jump up on your desk one day and declare, "Hey! Group Policy isn't applying to our client machines! Perhaps a policy setting is misconfigured. Or, maybe one of our Group Policy Objects has gone belly up! I'd better read about what's going on in Chapter 4, 'Group Policy Processing Behavior Essentials.'"

This terminology can be a little confusing—considering that each term includes the word *policy*. In this text, however, I've tried especially hard to use the correct nomenclature for what I'm trying to describe.

> Note that there is never a time to use the phrase "Group Policies." Those two words together shouldn't exist. If you're talking about "multiple GPOs" or "multiple policy settings" these are the preferred phrases to use.

Where Group Policy Applies

Group Policy can be applied to many machines at once, or it can be applied only to a specific machine. For the most part in this book, I'll focus on using Group Policy within an Active Directory environment where it affects the most machines.

A percentage of the settings explored and discussed in this book are available to member or stand-alone Windows machines—which can either participate or not participate in an Active Directory environment.

However, the Folder Redirection settings, discussed in Chapter 3 of the companion book, *Creating the Secure Managed Desktop*, and the Software Distribution settings, discussed in Chapter 4 of the companion book, are not available to stand-alone machines (that is, computers that are not participating in an Active Directory domain). In some cases, I will pay particular attention to non–Active Directory environments. However, most of the book deals with the more common case; that is, we'll explore the implications of deploying Group Policy in an Active Directory environment.

Most of the screen shots in the book are of Windows Vista and Windows Server 2008, with some Windows XP thrown in, but most of the book is still applicable for domains with Windows 2000 clients. However, note that the material in Chapter 10, covering the new Group Policy Preference Extensions, is not valid for Windows 2000 machines as clients.

With that in mind, you should not be scared off even if you're stuck with 100 percent Windows 2000 Domain Controllers or a mix of Windows 2000, Windows Server 2003, and Windows Server 2008 and various client types (Windows 2000 and above). Where appropriate, I've noted the differences between the operating environments.

This Book and Beyond

Group Policy is a big concept with some big power. This book is intended to help you get a handle on this new power to gain control over your environment and to make your day-to-day administration easier. It's filled with practical, hands-on examples of Group Policy usage and troubleshooting. It is my hope that you enjoy this book and learn from my experiences so you can successfully deploy Group Policy and manage your desktops to better control your network. I'm honored to have you aboard for the ride, and I hope you get as much out of Group Policy as I do from writing and speaking about it in my hands-on workshops.

As you read this book, it's natural to have questions about Group Policy or managing your desktops. To form a community around Group Policy, I have a hugely popular community forum that can be found at www.GPanswers.com. My technical editor, Jakob Heidelberg has his own blog at heidelbergit.blogspot.com (www.tinyurl.com/2mctjf).

I encourage you to visit our websites and post your questions to the community forum or peruse the other resources that will be constantly renewed and available for download. For instance, in addition to the forum at www.GPanswers.com, you'll find the full scripts for Chapter 11 and additional ADM and ADMX templates and Group Policy Preference Extensions XML files to download, tips and tricks, a third-party Group Policy Solutions Guide, and more!

If you want to meet me in person, my website at www.GPanswers.com has a calendar of all my upcoming appearances at various conferences, events, and intensive training and workshop classes. I'd love to hear how this book met your needs or helped you out.

What's New (in Vista and Windows Server 2008 Group Policy and in This Book)

If you're like me, you just want to get right to the good stuff and find out what's new. Many people have upgraded their technology (and this book!) over many years, and I'm very thankful for that.

If you're one of those folks who buys every edition and you're just looking for where the updates are, this section will help you quickly find the new stuff.

I'm also anticipating a lot of people upgrading from the 3rd edition of *Group Policy, Profiles, and IntelliMirror*, having skipped over the 4th edition, named *Group Policy: Management, Troubleshooting, and Security*, which had updated coverage for Vista. So I'll give pointers on what was added in the 4th edition and what's new in the 5th edition.

And perhaps by now, if you've perused the table of contents, you've noticed we have expanded coverage in some areas and other areas seem to have vanished. That really isn't the case. What is true is that we've really *expanded everything*! But to do that we had to make two books.

There isn't *officially* a volume 1 and a volume 2 (but if there were, this would be volume 1), but in practice, you might find it best to get both.

The idea is this: Learn Group Policy using this book, and then take what you know, build on it, and do even more stuff with it in the companion book, named *Creating the Secure Managed Desktop: Group Policy, SoftGrid, Microsoft Deployment Toolkit, and Management Tools.* You can find out more about this book at www.GPanswers.com/books.

In the "What's Kept, What's New, What's Moved, and What's History" section, I'll break down which chapters moved where and to which book; that way, you've got a feel for what's ahead.

For newcomers to Group Policy, I suggest that you start with the introduction and read all the way through. What's new in Windows Server 2008 (and Vista) Group Policy won't matter much to you at this point.

Again, *this* whole "What's New" section is for people who are already accustomed to Group Policy and are just looking for pointers to the updates. So, if you're not accustomed to Group Policy, you might find some areas of this section a little obtuse. I promise in the rest of the book, I'll ensure that everything is well spelled out to give you a clear understanding of all of the topics.

What's Kept, What's New, What's Moved, and What's History

Even though the book's title has changed (again), you could think of this book as the 5th edition of the original Group Policy book I started work on back in 2000.

- The 3rd edition introduced the GPMC.

- The 4th edition introduced the huge array of changes in Windows Vista.

- This edition introduces the GPMC 2.0, the Group Policy Preference Extensions, Windows Server 2008, the Advanced Group Policy Management tool, and more.

I assure you, for administrators with modest goals, as well as the "Power Administrator," there's lots of great stuff to discover.

What's Kept from the 4th Edition (In Other Words, What Was New in Vista Group Policy)

Group Policy is, to me, is a two-headed animal. There's stuff that makes up the Group Policy engine, and there's stuff you do with Group Policy. In the 4th edition, both areas of coverage were expanded. That coverage is maintained in this book (though some chapters may be moved around, or, again, moved to the companion book).

Under-the-Hood Changes

The under-the-hood changes are numerous and should be discussed so we can get a handle on where things are going. Let's take a tour of what's new in the Group Policy nuts and bolts.

Group Policy Becomes a Client Service   Prior to Vista, the "moving parts" of Group Policy were contained within a process called WinLogon. Winlogon had a lot of responsibility, including getting people logged on and doing the Group Policy chores. Now Group Policy has been designated as its own Windows Service. And what's more, it's hardened. That is, it cannot be stopped, nor can an administrator take ownership of the permissions on it and turn it off. These changes enhance the overall reliability of the Group Policy engine. Read more about this in Chapter 4.

GPMC Built In   The Group Policy Management Console, or GPMC, which was previously only available as a download, is now just built into Vista. Except it disappears when you install SP1. Confused? Then read both Chapter 1 and Chapter 3 (GPMC 2.0).

Updated Network Awareness   The Vista Group Policy engine has a new way to determine if the link is truly fast or not. It also determines if there's a Domain Controller available to deliver Group Policy. Read more about Network Location Awareness (NLA 2.0) in Chapter 6.

Multiple Local GPOs   This is a big, new feature in Vista. In addition to a GPO that affects everyone on the machine, additional GPOs can be layered at the local level. That is, you can now have additional multiple local GPOs—one that affects mere-mortal accounts and one that affects administrator accounts. Read more about this in Chapter 1.

Error Messages and Troubleshooting   Windows Vista has a whole new Event log system (which could be a whole article in and of itself). However, in short, the Group Policy engine now leverages this new event system and splits up events into two particular logs. Read more about this in Chapter 6.

ADM vs. ADMX Files   ADM files are the underlying definitions for what's possible in Group Policy. But Vista brings a new format—ADMX. The ADMX files are replacements for ADM, and with them come new management techniques and things to watch out for. We'll spend a great deal of time on ADMX files in Chapter 7.

New Stuff to Control

Windows Vista brings about 700 new policy settings to the table. Covering *all* of these settings would make this book too huge. Our goal is to cover the settings that most help you manage your world.

There are already categories of settings that you know and love. And Vista brings some new categories to the table that lacked any Group Policy controls, or simply hadn't existed.

Enhanced areas in Group Policy:

- Wired and Wireless policy (covered in Chapter 9)
- Windows Firewall and IPsec (covered in Chapter 9)
- Desktop Shell (covered in various places)
- Remote Assistance (not specifically covered)
- Tablet PC (not specifically covered)

New areas in Vista Group Policy:

- Removable Storage Device management (covered in Chapter 10 of the companion book)
- Power Management (not specifically covered)
- User Account Control (covered in Chapter 9)
- Network Access Protection (covered in depth in Chapter 9 of the companion book)
- Windows Defender (not specifically covered)

Microsoft has a nice concise document about what's new for Vista with expanded discussion here: `http://tinyurl.com/ffelo`.

What's New in This Edition?

This new edition is updated for Windows Server 2008 and covers the new GPMC 2.0. This section describes what's new for this book and where to find it.

Group Policy Management Console Is Unloaded with Vista + SP1   Don't panic. It's a free download to get the GPMC (again). Read all about in Chapter 1 and Chapter 3.

Comments, Search, and Starter GPOs   It's all new with the GPMC 2.0. Learn more in Chapter 3.

Group Policy Diagnostics Best Practices Analyzer (GPDBPA)   It's a tool to help you create a baseline of what's going on in your Group Policy universe and report on any well-known errors. Read all about it in Chapter 5.

Windows Server 2008 Auditing Changes   There's a gaggle of new settings that are available to audit on Windows Vista and Windows Server 2008. I missed covering this in the 4th edition because it technically was available with Vista, but it's in here now for both Windows Vista and Windows Server 2008. The only problem is that these new features aren't enabled directly using Group Policy. Grr. I cover it anyway in Chapter 8.

Windows Server 2008 Fine-Grained Password Policy (FGPP)   Another interesting feature that's not specifically controlled using Group Policy. But I'll tell you what you need to know about it and how to make the best of it (using a little Group Policy magic!). Also in Chapter 8.

Security Configuration Wizard   This was introduced in Windows Server 2003 and is updated in Windows Server 2008. Check it out in Chapter 8.

PowerShell Your Group Policy World   Group Policy + PowerShell = Awesomeness. Check it out in Chapter 11.

Group Policy Preference Extensions   This might be the reason you picked up this book. Microsoft bought a company called DesktopStandard, and out of that acquisition came 21 new Group Policy toys to play with. All in Chapter 10.

Advanced Group Policy Management (AGPM) Tool   Another tool to come out of the Desk-topStandard acquisition, it enables you to put a real "change management" system around your Group Policy deployment. You have to pay extra for it, but it may be just what the doctor ordered. Read all about it in Chapter 12.

What's Moved Since the 4th Edition

In short, all the IntelliMirror/Managed Desktop components have been moved to the companion book, *Creating the Secure Managed Desktop: Group Policy, SoftGrid, Microsoft Deployment Toolkit, and Management Tools.*

Here's a breakdown of where they were in the 4th edition and where they are now in the new book.

RIS, WDS, BDD, and WSIM   RIS was excised in the 4th edition to make way for WDS. If you need to spawn new machines from scratch, check this chapter out. It's the first chapter in the companion book.

Managed Desktop Part I: Profiles   The popular "final word" on profiles has moved from this book to the companion book. Everything changed with Vista, and this chapter was fully updated when Vista came out. It's in Chapter 2 of the companion book.

Managed Desktop Part II: Redirected Folders and Offline Files   Everything changed here with Vista and now you can manage your users' data better. Chapter 3 of the companion book will show you how.

Managed Desktop Part III: Group Policy Software Installation   This is how you plunk applications down on desktops. Not much has changed since Windows Server 2003. This one has moved to Chapter 4 of the companion book.

Printers and Shadow Copies   This material was in the final chapter of the 4th edition book. It's been moved to Chapter 10 of the companion book.

Other Material in the Companion Book (Or Why You Want to Run Out and Buy That Book Too)

The fun doesn't stop when you learn Group Policy. That's when it begins. That's where the companion book, *Creating the Secure Managed Desktop: Group Policy, SoftGrid, Microsoft Deployment Toolkit, and Management Tools,* really takes off.

We assume a decent level of Group Policy knowledge at that point. We then craft the desktop's experience, applications, and security using the knowledge you already have, plus additional knowledge you can't get anywhere else.

The previous section described the material that was moved to the companion book, and here are the other goodies:

WDS Updates for Windows Server 2008   Did someone say "multicast?" You're gonna love it. It's in Chapter 1 of the companion book.

SoftGrid Essentials   If you've invested in SoftGrid, learn how to get started using it. I'll share some tips and tricks that you won't find anywhere else to get you jumpstarted quickly with your investment. Get started in Chapter 5 of the companion book.

SoftGrid Advanced Techniques   Take what you learned in SoftGrid essentials to the next level. Again, you're positively going to love this stuff, and it continues through Chapters 6 and 7 of the companion book.

WSUS 3.0 Manage your patches with style. In Chapter 8 of the companion book.

MBSA Figure out where you need patches. In Chapter 8 of the companion book.

Using Group Policy to Keep the Bad Guys off Your Network Leverage Windows Server 2008, Group Policy, and Network Access Protection to keep the bad guys out of your network (and out of your hair). In Chapter 9 of the companion book.

Finishing Touches to the Managed Desktop with Group Policy Did someone say printers? How about ensuring that your people don't plug USB sticks into your computers? And quickly restoring files? Yeah, I thought you might want to check out the Finishing Touches in Chapter 10 in the companion book.

Total Lockdown with Windows SteadyState Group Policy can implement some security settings, but it can't necessarily prevent users from loading evil software and taking down your system. But this can. Get it together in Chapter 11 of the companion book.

So, with all that new goodness awaiting you in the new book, why wait? Get started with Group Policy today, then expand your "way of life" with *Creating the Secure Managed Desktop: Group Policy, SoftGrid, Microsoft Deployment Toolkit, and Management Tools.*

You can learn more at www.GPanswers.com/book.

What's History

The Disk Quota section that's been in the book since basically Windows 2000 has been killed. If you need it, it's still in the 3rd and 4th editions (updated slightly in the 3rd edition if I remember correctly).

1

Group Policy Essentials

In this chapter, you'll get your feet wet with the concept that is Group Policy. You'll start to understand conceptually what Group Policy is and how it's created, applied, and modified, and you'll go through some practical examples to get at the basics.

The best news is that the essentials of Group Policy are the same in all versions of Windows 2000 onward. This includes server products (Windows 2000 Server, Windows Server 2003, and Windows Server 2008) and all client versions of Windows including Windows 2000, Windows XP, and Windows Vista.

Group Policy isn't really a server-driven technology. As you'll learn in depth a little later, the magic of Group Policy happens (mostly) on the target (client) machine, say Windows XP or Windows Vista. So, if your Active Directory Domain Controllers are a mixture of Windows 2000 and/or Windows 2003 and/or Windows Server 2008, nothing much changes. And it doesn't matter if your domain is in Mixed, Native, or another mode—Group Policy works exactly the same in all of them.

 There are some enhanced bits you get with upgraded domain types. With the Windows 2003 schema, you'll get something neat called WMI filters (described in Chapter 5). And, it also should be noted that in a Windows 2008 Functional mode domain level, the replication of the file-based part of a Group Policy Object can be enhanced to use DFS replication instead of SYSVOL replication.

Regardless of what your server architecture is, I encourage you to read and work through the examples in this chapter.

The last time I revised this chapter, I said the following:

> When Longhorn server [Windows Server 2008] is released, the good news is that there won't be a lot of new stuff to learn. You already have the right book you need until the next "big iteration" of Windows comes out.

Yikes! I was wrong. Well, kind of. I was right in one way, and wrong in another. That's why we have a new book! Books, actually, since there's also a companion book to this one named *Creating the Secure Managed Desktop: Group Policy, SoftGrid, Microsoft Deployment Toolkit and Management Tools* (Sybex, 2008). Together these books give you a foundation in Group Policy and what to do with Group Policy to make the most of it.

Learn more about the companion book, including opportunities to download e-chapters, at www.GPanswers.com/book.

Let's start with why I was wrong. I was wrong in my prediction because I didn't know that something big was about to happen between the last edition of the book and this edition of the book. And that big thing is, or was, that Microsoft bought out a company named DesktopStandard and integrated its technology into the Group Policy ecosystem. That means there's more to love (see Chapters 10 and 12).

But I was also right. That is, the *essentials* of Group Policy didn't change. The stuff people learned years ago is still as valid today as it ever was.

So, in this chapter, there are not a lot of Windows Server 2008–specific updates. That's because this chapter focuses on essentials, and most of the new "essentials" stuff that comes with Windows Server 2008 could be categorized as extras or light updates.

But then there are the features that came out of the DesktopStandard acquisition. They're definitely more than just "extras." It's like a new rocket turbo-boost! In a nutshell, Windows Server 2008 (and an available add-on for Windows XP, Windows Vista, and Windows Server 2003) increases Group Policy's reach immensely. Additionally, Microsoft added a new way to add change control management around Group Policy creation and deployment. Again, for more information on these new features, stay tuned for Chapters 10 and 12.

So, let's get started and talk about the essentials.

Getting Ready to Use This Book

This book is full of examples. And to work through these examples, I'm going to suggest a sample test lab for you to create. It's pretty simple really, but in its simplicity we'll be able to work though dozens of real-world examples to see how things work. Here are the computers you need to set up and what I suggest you name them (if you want to work through the examples with me in the book):

DC01.corp.com   This is your Active Directory Domain Controller. It can be a Windows 2000 Server, Windows Server 2003, or Windows Server 2008 Domain Controller. For this book, I'll assume you've loaded Windows Server 2008 on this computer and that you'll create a domain called Corp.com.

In real life you would have multiple Domain Controllers in the domain. But here in the test lab, it'll be okay if you just have one.

I'll refer to this machine as DC01 in the book. We'll also use DC01 as a file server and software distribution server and for a lot of other roles we really shouldn't. That's so you can work though lots of examples without bringing up lots of servers.

XPPRO1.corp.com   This is some user's Windows XP machine and it's joined to the domain Corp.com. I'll assume you've loaded Windows XP's SP2 (though SP3 might be available by the time you read this). Sometimes it'll be a Sales computer, other times a Marketing computer, and other times a Nursing computer. To use this machine as such, just move the computer account around in Active Directory when the time comes. You'll see what I mean. I'll refer to this machine as XPPRO1 in the book.

Vista1.corp.com   This is some user's Windows Vista machine and it's joined to the domain Corp.com. I'll refer to this machine as VISTA1 in the book. Like XPPRO1, this machine will move around a lot to help us "play pretend" when the times arise. Windows XP works a little differently than Vista, so having both a Vista machine and a Windows XP machine in your environment will be good for testing.

Vistamanagement.corp.com   This machine is yours—the IT pro who runs the show. You could manage Active Directory from anywhere on your network, but you're going to do it from here. This is the machine you'll use to run the tools you need to manage both Active Directory and Group Policy. I'll refer to this machine as VISTAMANAGEMENT. As the name implies, you'll run Windows Vista from this machine.

Figure 1.1 shows a diagram of what our test network should look like if you want to follow along.

You can build your test lab with real machines or with virtual hardware. I use VMware Workstation (for-a-fee tool) and VMware Server (free tool) for my testing. However, Microsoft's tools, like Virtual Server 2005 and Virtual PC 2007 (both free), are great choices as well. That way, if you don't have a bunch of extra servers and desktops around, you can follow along with all the examples.

FIGURE 1.1   Here's the configuration you'll need for the test lab in this book. Note that the Domain Controller can be 2000 or above, but 2008 is preferred to allow you to work through all the examples in this book.

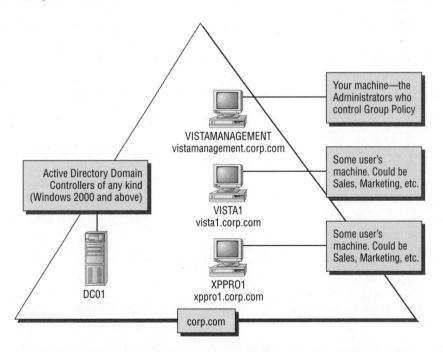

Because Group Policy can be so all-encompassing, it is highly recommended that you try the examples in a test lab environment first before making these changes for real in your production environment.

Note that from time to time I might refer to some machine that isn't here in the suggested test lab, just to illustrate a point. However, this is the minimum configuration you'll need to get the most out the book.

Some Group Policy History

If you've done any work at all with Group Policy and Active Directory before Windows Vista came out, you're likely familiar with the usual Group Policy interface, which was "in the box." Microsoft then went on to provide the free downloadable tool called the GPMC, or Group Policy Management Console. The GPMC is an add-on for Windows XP (or Windows Server 2003) machines to make the task of managing Group Policy easier. Windows Vista comes with the GPMC preloaded, so there's nothing to download. And—you already know this, but it's good to repeat anyway—you can manage your entire Active Directory from any computer on your network. Therefore, for the majority of tasks in this book, we're going to be using our Windows Vista machine (named VISTAMANAGEMENT) to perform the majority of Active Directory and Group Policy tasks.

So the goal of the GPMC is to give us an updated, refreshing way to view and manage Group Policy; indeed, this tool enables us to view and manage Group Policy the way it was meant to be viewed and managed. The new GPMC interface provides a one-stop shop for managing nearly all aspects of Group Policy in your Active Directory.

With the GPMC tool, it doesn't matter if your entire Active Directory (or individual domains) has Windows 2000, Windows 2003, or Windows Server 2008 Domain Controllers. And it doesn't matter what kind of Windows clients you have (from Windows 2000 onward). It just matters that you have Active Directory.

However, one thing you'll quickly learn here and in future chapters is that you'll want to create and edit everything surrounding Group Policy using newer operating systems, like Windows Vista and Windows Server 2008.

And it's free for downloading if your management station machine is the following:

- Windows 2003

- Windows XP

And, here's something strange:

- The GPMC is in the box for Windows Vista RTM (in other words, it ships from the factory, in the box).

- But the GPMC gets removed when you install Windows Vista + SP1.

- And it's available as a free GPMC 2.0 download for Windows Vista + SP1 in what's known as the Remote Server Administration (RSAT) package.

- But it's also already in the box for Windows Server 2008.

Confused? You won't be. I talk more about how this wacky situation came to be at the beginning of Chapter 3 where we talk more about the GPMC 2.0.

Stay tuned, dear reader. We'll get to that exciting new and free stuff right away in this first chapter. I don't want to keep you in suspense for too long.

Getting Started with Group Policy

Group Policy is a big, big place. And you need a road map. Let's try to get a firm understanding of what we're about to be looking at for the next several hundred pages.

Group Policy Entities and Policy Settings

Every Group Policy contains two halves: a User half and a Computer half. These two halves are properly called *nodes*, though sometimes they're just referred to as either the *User half* and the *Computer half* or the *User branch* and the *Computer branch*.

A sample Group Policy with both the Computer Configuration and User Configuration nodes can be seen in Figure 1.2. Don't worry, we'll show you how to get there in just a second.

Group Policy Object Editor vs. Group Policy Management Editor

The screen that enables us to actually manage the Group Policy itself goes by two names, depending on the revision of the editing tools and the situation in which the tools are being used.

Confused? You can safely ignore this if you're just getting started with Group Policy; it's just here for completeness anyway.

In short, here's the scoop:

- The editor will always be named Group Policy Object Editor when the GPMC edition is 1.0 (download for Windows XP for 2003) or 1.5 (built into the shipping version of Windows Vista).

- The editor will be named Local Group Policy Object Editor or Group Policy Object Editor when you're editing local GPOs on Windows Vista or Windows Server 2008.

- The editor will be named Group Policy Management Editor when you're editing Active Directory GPOs using the GPMC 2.0 (either built into Windows Server 2008 or when using Windows Vista + SP1 + GPMC 2.0 within the RSAT download).

But in the end, it doesn't really matter. For the remainder of this book, I'll assume you're using the updated tools and we'll mostly be editing Active Directory GPOs. So, appropriately, I'll call it the Group Policy Management Editor (GPME). However, if I slip up and say the GPOE (Group Policy Object Editor), you'll still know what I mean.

The first level under both the User and the Computer nodes contains Software Settings, Windows Settings, and Administrative Templates. If we dive down into the Administrative Templates of the Computer node, underneath we discover additional levels of Windows Components, System, Network, and Printers. Likewise, if we dive down into the Administrative Templates of the User node, we see some of the same folders plus some additional ones, such as Shared Folders, Desktop, and Start Menu and Taskbar.

In both the User and Computer halves, you'll see that policy settings are hierarchical, like a directory structure. Similar policy settings are grouped together for easy location. That's the idea anyway; though, admittedly, sometimes locating the specific policy you want can prove to be a challenge.

When manipulating policy settings, you can choose to set either computer policy settings or user policy settings (or both!). You'll see examples of this shortly. (See the section "Updated GPMC Filters" in Chapter 3 for tricks on how to minimize the effort of finding the policy setting you want.)

 Most policy settings are not found in both nodes. However, there are a few that overlap. In that case, if the computer policy setting is different from the user policy setting, the computer policy setting generally overrides the user policy setting. But to be sure, check the Explain text associated with the policy setting.

Wait... I Don't Get It. What Do the User and Computer Nodes Do?

One of the key issues that new Group Policy administrators struggle with is, What the heck is the difference between the Computer and User nodes?

Imagine that you had a combination store: Dog Treats (for dogs) and Candy Treats (for kids). That's right, it's a strange little store with seemingly two types of incompatible foods under the same roof. You wouldn't feed the kids dog treats (they'd spit them out and ignore the treat), and you wouldn't feed a dog the kids' candy (because the dogs would spit out the sour candy and ignore the treat).

That's the same thing that happens here. Sure, it looks tempting. There are lots of treats on both sides of the store, but only one type of customer will accept each type of treat.

So, in practical terms, the Computer node (the first part of the policy) contains policy settings that are only relevant for computers. That is, if there's a GPO that contains computer-side settings and it "hits" a computer, these settings will take effect. These computer-side settings could be items like Startup Scripts, Shutdown Scripts, and how the local firewall should be configured. Think of this as every setting relevant to the *computer itself*—no matter who is logged on at that moment.

The User node (the second part of the policy) contains policy settings that are relevant only for users. Again, if there's a GPO that contains user-side settings and it "hits" a user, these settings will take effect for that user. These user-side items only make sense on a per-user basis, like Logon Scripts, Logoff Scripts, availability of the Control Panel, and lots more. Think of this as every setting relevant to the currently logged-on user—and these settings will follow the user to every machine they pop on to.

Feeding users dog treats, er, computer settings doesn't work. Same thing with feeding computers user-side settings. When a GPO hits user objects with computer policy settings or computer objects with user policy settings, it simply will *not* do anything. You'll just sit there and scratch your head and wonder why it doesn't work. But it's not that it's not working; this is how it's designed.

Computer settings are for computer objects, and User settings are for user objects. If this is bad news for you, then there is an advanced technique called *loopback processing* that can help you out. Look for more information on loopback processing in Chapter 5.

The 18 (Original) Categories of Group Policy

In this section, you'll learn how to gain access to the interface, which will let you start configuring these categories.

Now, as you're following along working through these examples (or you read Table 1.1 and want to get started right away), you might start to think to yourself, "Jeremy's screen shots don't look like what I have on my screen." There's an answer for that.

If you're already using Windows XP, Windows Vista, or Windows Server 2003 as the place you manage Group Policy, your screens are going to look different than mine.

That's because something big and new is ready for you to start using. But you only get it if you can manage your Group Policy world from Windows Server 2008 or from a Windows Vista + SP1 machine with a set of tools called the RSAT tools installed. I'll show you how to do this in the section "Implementing the GPMC on Your Management Station" coming up a little later in this chapter, so don't worry about it for now.

When you start using Windows Server 2008 (or Windows Vista + SP1 + RSAT), the Computer Configuration and User Configuration parts of the Group Policy Objects are split into *two* additional subnodes: Policies and Preferences.

Local policies are *not* split into two subnodes though—that is because the Preferences node is only available within Active Directory GPOs.

 So, if you're missing the Policies and Preferences nodes within User Configuration and Computer Configuration right now, don't panic. You'll learn how to get those nodes introduced.

In this book, you'll learn about the 18 major categories of Group Policy. Here's a table that should be helpful if you're looking to get started working right away with a category. Again, your Group Policy editor might not show the Policies nodes unless you're using the GPMC 2.0 and you're editing an Active Directory GPO.

TABLE 1.1   The 18 Major Categories of Group Policy

Group Policy Category	Where in Group Policy Interface	Which Operating Systems Support It	Where to Find Information in the Book	Notes
Administrative Templates (also known as Registry Settings)	User or Computer ➤ Policies ➤ Administrative Templates	Windows 2000+	Many examples throughout the book	
Security Settings	Computer or User Configuration ➤ Policies ➤ Windows Settings ➤ Security Settings	Windows 2000+	Chapters 8 and 9	
Wired Network (802.3) Settings	Computer Configuration ➤ Policies ➤ Windows Settings ➤ Security Settings ➤ Wired Network (IEEE 802.3) Policies	Windows Vista only	Chapter 9	Be sure to read Chapter 9 before attempting to use these settings.
Wireless Network (802.11) Settings	Computer Configuration ➤ Policies ➤ Windows Settings ➤ Security Settings ➤ Wireless Network (IEEE 802.11) Policies	Windows XP and Windows Vista (set independently)	Chapter 9	Be sure to read Chapter 9 before attempting to use these settings for Windows Vista.

TABLE 1.1   The 18 Major Categories of Group Policy *(continued)*

Group Policy Category	Where in Group Policy Interface	Which Operating Systems Support It	Where to Find Information in the Book	Notes
Scripts	Computer Configuration ➢ Policies ➢ Windows Settings ➢ Scripts (Startup/Shutdown) and User Configuration ➢ Policies ➢ Windows Settings ➢ Script (Logon/Logoff)	Windows 2000+	Chapter 8	
RIS (Remote Installation Services)			We cover RIS's upgrade called WDS in Chapter 1 of the companion book, *Creating the Secure Managed Desktop: Group Policy, SoftGrid, Microsoft Deployment Toolkit and Management Tools.*	RIS has been deprecated in lieu of Windows Deployment Services (WDS). However, WDS can run in Mixed mode where it can emulate a RIS setup. These settings are not available in Windows Vista and are only accessible when you're editing GPOs on previous versions of Windows. If you want to specifically control RIS, it is suggested you manage the machine directly, without GPOs. I won't cover the RIS aspects in this book. For RIS information, see previous editions of the book.

TABLE 1.1 The 18 Major Categories of Group Policy *(continued)*

Group Policy Category	Where in Group Policy Interface	Which Operating Systems Support It	Where to Find Information in the Book	Notes
Group Policy Software Installation (also known as Application Management)	Computer or User Configuration ➤ Policies ➤ Software Settings	Windows 2000+	I cover this topic in Chapter 4 of the companion book.	
Folder Redirection	User Configuration ➤ Policies ➤ Windows Settings ➤ Folder Redirection	Windows 2000+; some additional options for Windows XP; many additional options for Windows Vista	I cover this topic in Chapter 3 of the companion book.	
Disk Quotas	Computer Configuration ➤ Policies ➤ Administrative Templates ➤ System ➤ Disk Quotas	Windows 2000+	I don't cover that subject in this book. That content has been removed to make room for other material. Disk Quotas have been covered in previous editions.	There is a brief article on disk quotas here: http://support.microsoft.com/kb/183322. There is another article here: http://tinyurl.com/35mvny.
Encrypted Data Recovery Agents (EFS Recovery Policy)	Computer Configuration ➤ Policies ➤ Windows Settings ➤ Security Settings ➤ Public Key Policies ➤ Encrypting File System	Windows 2000+	Chapter 8	
Internet Explorer Maintenance	User Configuration ➤ Policies ➤ Windows Settings ➤ Internet Explorer Maintenance	Windows 2000+	Chapter 9	

TABLE 1.1   The 18 Major Categories of Group Policy *(continued)*

Group Policy Category	Where in Group Policy Interface	Which Operating Systems Support It	Where to Find Information in the Book	Notes
Software Restriction Policies	Computer or User ➤ Policies ➤ Windows Settings ➤ Security Settings ➤ Software Restriction Policies	Windows XP+	Chapter 8	
Quality of Service (QoS) Packet Scheduler and Policy-Based QoS	Computer or User Configuration ➤ Policies ➤ Windows Settings ➤ Policy-based QoS	Windows XP+; Policy-based QoS is Vista-only.	Not covered	You can start your Windows Vista QoS journey here: http://tinyurl.com/yxg1pp.
IPSec (IP Security) Policies	In XP: Computer Configuration ➤ Policies ➤ Windows Settings ➤ Security Settings ➤ IP Security Policies	Windows 2000+	Chapter 9	In Vista, this is now part of the Windows Firewall with Advanced Security section located under Computer Configuration ➤ Policies ➤ Windows Settings ➤ Security Settings.
Windows Search	Computer Configuration ➤ Policies ➤ Administrative Templates ➤ Windows Components ➤ Search	Windows Vista	Not covered	http://www.microsoft.com/windows/desktopsearch
Deployed Printer Connections	Computer or User Configuration ➤ Policies ➤ Windows Settings ➤ Deployed Printers	Technically, Vista only; workaround available for Windows 2000+	I cover this topic in Chapter 9 of the companion book.	

TABLE 1.1   The 18 Major Categories of Group Policy *(continued)*

Group Policy Category	Where in Group Policy Interface	Which Operating Systems Support It	Where to Find Information in the Book	Notes
Offline Files	Computer or User Configuration ➢ Policies ➢ Administrative Templates ➢ Network ➢ Offline Files	Different Group Policy "moving parts" to make this technology work in Vista and Windows Server 2008 than in previous operating systems; feature available in Windows 2000+	We cover this topic in Chapter 3 of the companion book.	
Group Policy Preference Extensions	Computer or User Configuration ➢ Preferences (not available in local policies, only domain policies)	Group Policy Preference Extensions built in to Windows Server 2008 but are an additional download and installation for Windows XP and Windows Vista; not supported on Windows 2000 machines	Chapter 10	This is one of the big things Microsoft got when it bought out DesktopStandard. These used to be called Policy Maker Standard Edition and PolicyMaker Share Manager.

Group Policy is a twofold idea. First, without an Active Directory, there's one and only one Group Policy available, and that lives on the local Windows XP or Windows 2000 workstation (note that this changes in Windows Vista, and technically in Windows Server 2008, but we'll discuss that later). Officially, this is called a *local policy*, but it still resides under the umbrella of the concept of Group Policy. Later, once Active Directory is available, the nonlocal (or, as they're sometimes called, *domain-based* or *Active Directory–based*) Group Policy Objects come into play, as you'll see later. Let's get started and explore both options.

While you're plunking around inside the Group Policy Object Editor (also known as the Group Policy Management Editor), you'll see lots of policy settings that are geared toward Windows 2000, Windows XP, Windows Vista, Windows 2003, and/or Windows Server 2008. Some are only for Windows Vista, and others are only for Windows 2003, and so on. If you happen to apply a policy setting to a system that isn't listed, the policy setting is simply ignored. For instance, policy settings described as working for Windows XP will not typically work on Windows 2000 machines. Each policy setting has a "Supported on" field that should be consulted to know which operating systems can embrace which policy setting.

Understanding Local Group Policy

Before we officially dive into what is specifically contained inside this magic of Group Policy or how Group Policy is applied when Active Directory is involved, you might be curious to see exactly what your interaction with Local Group Policy might look like.

Local Group Policy is best used when Active Directory isn't available, say either in a NetWare environment or when you have a gaggle of machines that simply aren't connected to a domain.

Local Group Policy is different for Windows Vista versus the other Windows operating systems. Let's explore Local Group Policy on pre-Vista machines first and then move on to the Vista-specific features.

Local Group Policy on Pre-Vista Computers

The most expeditious way to edit the local Group Policy on a machine is to click Start ➢ Run and type in **GPEDIT.MSC**. This pops up the Local Computer Policy Editor.

You are now exploring the Local Group Policy of this Windows XP workstation. Local Group Policy is unique to each specific machine. To see how a Local Group Policy applies, drill down through the User Configuration ➢ Administrative Templates ➢ System ➢ Ctrl+Alt+Del Options and select **Remove Lock Computer** as seen in Figure 1.2. Once it's selected, click Enabled and select OK.

FIGURE 1.2   You can edit the Local Group Policy using the Local Group Policy Editor. (GPEDIT.MSC)

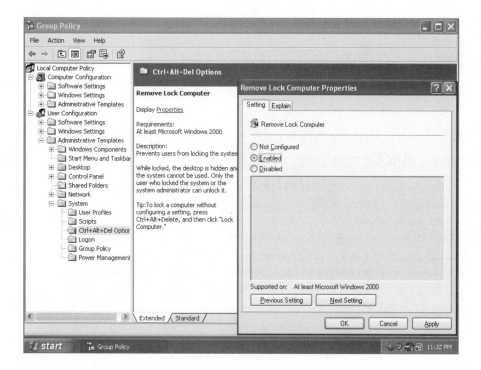

When you do, within a few seconds you should see that if you press Ctrl+Alt+Del, the Lock Computer option is unavailable.

To revert the change, simply reselect Remove Lock Computer and select Not Configured. This reverts the change back to the way the operating system works by default.

 You can think of Local Group Policy as a way to perform decentralized administration. A bit later, when we explore Group Policy with Active Directory, we'll saunter into centralized administration.

This Local Group Policy affects everyone who logs onto this machine—including normal users and administrators. Be careful when making settings here; you can temporarily lock yourself out of some useful functions. For instance, frequently administrators want to remove Run from the Start menu for Windows XP machines. Then, the first time they themselves want to go to a command prompt, they can't choose Start ≻ Run. It's just gone!

 To get that Run command back, you'll have to click the MMC.exe icon in Explorer (or via command line/batch file) and manually load the Group Policy Snap-in.

As I stated in the introduction, most of the settings we'll explore in this book are available to workstations or servers that aren't joined to an Active Directory domain. However, many functions, like Folder Redirection settings (discussed in the companion book), the Software Distribution settings (also discussed in the companion book), and others are not available to stand-alone machines without Active Directory present.

 You can point toward other computers by using the syntax gpedit.msc /gpcomputer:"targetmachine" or gpedit.msc /gpcomputer:"targetmachine.domain.com"; the machine name must be in quotes.

Local Group Policy on Vista and Windows Server 2008 Computers

It's true that you can also type **GPEDIT.MSC** at the Vista command prompt and get the same Local Computer Policy Editor you just saw in Windows XP. However, Windows Vista takes Local Group Policy to the next level.

Remember how, not more than three paragraphs ago, I stated this:

> This Local Group Policy affects everyone who logs onto this machine—including normal users and administrators. Be careful when making settings here; you can temporarily lock yourself out of some useful functions.

True: for pre-Vista machines. On Vista, the superpower is that you can decide who gets what settings at a local level. This feature is called Multiple Local GPOs, or MLGPOs for short.

This is most often handy when you want your users to get one gaggle of settings (that is, desktop restrictions) but you want to ensure that your access is unfettered for day-to-day administration.

Now, in these examples, we're going to use Windows Vista. But, this same feature is available on Windows Server 2008. It's just not all that likely you'll end up using it on a Windows Server 2008 server.

Understanding Multiple Local GPOs

The best way to understand MLGPOs is by thinking of the end product. That is, when we're done, we want our users to embrace some settings, and we'll want us (administrators) to potentially embrace some settings. Or, perhaps you want just one specific user to embrace a particular combination of settings.

When you type `GPEDIT.MSC` at a command prompt, it's just as if you did it on Windows XP: you're affecting all users—mere mortals *and* administrators.

However, with just a little bit of extra knowledge you can tap into one of Vista's "secret features." That is, Windows Vista actually has three "layers" that can be leveraged to ensure that some settings affect regular users and other settings affect you (the administrator).

Let's be sure to understand all three layers before we get too gung-ho and try it out. When MLGPOs are processed, Windows Vista checks to see if the layer is being used and if that layer is supposed to apply to that user.

Layer 1 (lowest priority) The Local Computer Policy. You create this by running `GPEDIT.MSC`.

- The settings you make on the Computer Configuration side are guaranteed to affect all users on this computer (including administrators).
- The settings you make on the User Configuration side may be trumped by Layer 2 or Layer 3 (see below).

Layer 2 (next highest priority) Is the user a mere-mortal user *or* a local administrator? (One account cannot be both.) This layer cannot contain Computer Configuration settings.

Layer 3 (most specific) Am I a specific user who is being dictated a specific policy? This layer cannot contain computer configuration settings.

You can see this graphically laid out in Figure 1.3.

If there are no conflicts among the levels, the effect is additive. For instance, let's imagine the following:

- Layer 1 (the Local Computer Policy level): The wish is to **Remove Lock Computer** from the Ctrl+Alt+Del area.
- Then, at Layer 2: We say "All local users" will have "Search" gone from the Start menu.
- Then, at Layer 3: We say Fred, a local user, will be denied access to the Control Panel.

The result for Fred will be the sum total of all edicts at all layers.

But what if there's a conflict between the levels? In that case, the layer that's "closest to the user" wins (also known as "Last Writer Wins"). So, if at the Local Computer Policy the wish is to **Remove Lock Computer** from the Ctrl+Alt+Del area, but that area is expressly granted to Sally, a local user on that machine, Sally will still be able to use the Lock command. That's because we're saying that she is expressly granted the right at Layer 3, which "wins" over Layers 1 and 2.

Trying Out Multiple Local GPOs on Windows Vista

Just typing **GPEDIT.MSC** at the Vista Start Search prompt doesn't give you the magical "layering" superpower. Indeed, just typing **GPEDIT.MSC** performs the exact same function as it did in Windows XP. That is, every edit you make while you run the Local Computer Policy affects all users logged onto the machine.

FIGURE 1.3   A block diagram of how Multiple Local GPOs (MLGPOs) are applied to a system

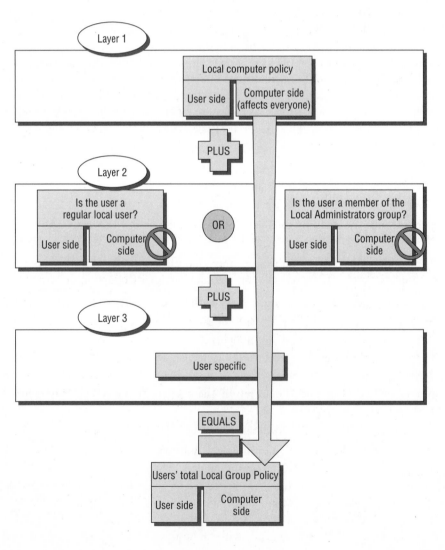

To tell Vista you want to edit one of the layers (as just described), you need to load the Group Policy Object Editor by hand. We'll do this on VISTA1.

On VISTA1, to load the Group Policy Object Editor by hand, follow these steps:

1. Click Start, and then in the Start Search box (which will run things), type **MMC**. A "naked" MMC appears. Note that you will have to approve the User Access Control (UAC) message (UAC is discussed in detail in Chapter 9).

2. From the File menu, choose Add/Remove Snap-in to open the Add/Remove Snap-in dialog box.

3. Locate and select the Group Policy Object Editor Snap-in and click Add (don't choose the Group Policy Management Snap-in, if present—that's the GPMC that we'll use a bit later).

4. At the "Select Group Policy Object" screen, note that the default Local Computer Policy is selected. Click Browse.

5. The "Browse for a Group Policy Object" dialog appears. Select the Users tab and select the layer you want. That is, you can pick Non-Administrators or Administrators, or click a specific user, or the Administrator account as seen in Figure 1.4.

In the Group Policy Object Exists column in the Users tab, you can also tell whether or not a local GPO layer is being used.

6. At the "Select a Group Policy Object" dialog, click Finish.

7. At the "Add or Remove Snap-ins" dialog, click OK.

You should now be able to edit that layer of the local GPO. For instance, Figure 1.5 shows that I've chosen to edit the Non-Administrators portion of the GPO (which is on level 2).

To edit additional or other layers of the local GPO, repeat the previous steps.

Here's an important point that bears repeating: Layers 2 and 3 of the MLGPO cannot contain computer settings. That's why in Figure 1.5 you simply don't see them—they're not there. If you want to introduce a computer-side setting that affects everyone on the machine, just fire up **GPEDIT.MSC** and you'll be off and running. That's Layer 1, and it affects everyone.

Local GPOs Final Thoughts

You can think of Local Group Policy as a way to perform desktop management in a decentralized way. That is, you're still running around, more or less, from machine to machine where you want to set the Local Group Policy.

The other strategy is a centralized approach. Centralized Group Policy administration works only in conjunction with Active Directory and is the main focus of this book.

For more information, check out the article "Step-by-Step Guide to Managing Multiple Local Group Policy" from Microsoft. At last check, the URL was http://tinyurl.com/e4e9k, but it could change by the time you read this.

FIGURE 1.4   Edit specific layers of Windows Vista's MLGPOs by first adding the Group Policy Object Editor into a "naked" MMC. Then browse for the Windows Vista Local Group Policy by firing up GPEDIT.MSC.

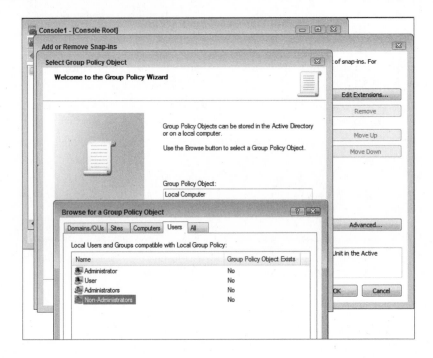

FIGURE 1.5   Below the words Console Root, you can see which layer of the local GPO you're specifically editing.

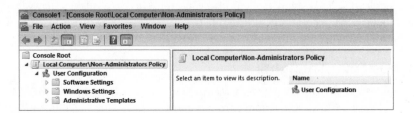

In case you're curious, Local Group Policy is stored in the `C:\windows\system32\grouppolicy` directory. The structure found here mirrors what you'll see later in Chapter 6 when we inspect the ins and outs of how Group Policy applies from Active Directory. Windows Vista and Windows Server 2008 store Local User Policies (level 3) below `C:\windows\system32\grouppolicyusers`.

You will notice one folder per user policy you have created, each named with the Security ID (SID) of the relevant user object.

Active Directory–Based Group Policy

To use Group Policy in a meaningful way, you need an Active Directory environment. An Active Directory environment needn't be anything particularly fancy; indeed, it could consist of a single Windows 2000, Windows 2003, or Windows Server 2008 Domain Controller and perhaps just one Windows XP or Windows Vista workstation joined to the domain.

But Active Directory can also grow extensively from that original solitary server. You can think of an Active Directory network as having four constituent and distinct levels that relate to Group Policy:

- The local computer
- The site
- The domain
- The organizational unit (OU)

The rules of Active Directory state that every server and workstation must be a member of one (and only one) domain and be located in one (and only one) site.

In Windows NT, additional domains were often created to partition administrative responsibility or to rein in needless chatter between Domain Controllers. With Active Directory, administrative responsibility can be delegated using OUs.

Additionally, the problem with needless domain bandwidth chatter has been brought under control with the addition of Active Directory sites, which are concentrations of IP (Internet Protocol) subnets with fast connectivity. There is no longer any need to correlate domains with network bandwidth—that's what sites are for!

Group Policy and Active Directory

When Group Policy is created at the local level, everyone who uses that machine is affected by those wishes. But once you step up and use Active Directory, you can have nearly limitless Group Policy Objects (GPOs)—with the ability to selectively decide which users and which computers will get which wishes (try saying that five times quickly). The GPO is the vessel that stores these wishes for delivery.

 Actually, you can have only 999 GPOs applied to a user or a computer.

When we create a GPO that can be used in Active Directory, two things happen: we create some brand-new entries within Active Directory, and we automatically create some brand-new files within our Domain Controllers. Collectively, these items make one GPO.

You can think of Active Directory as having three major levels:

- Site
- Domain
- OU

Additionally, since OUs can be nested within each other, Active Directory has a nearly limitless capacity for where we can tuck stuff away.

In fact, it's best to think of this design as a three-tier hierarchy: site, domain, and each nested OU. When wishes, er, policy settings, are set at a higher level in Active Directory, they automatically flow down throughout the remaining levels.

So, to be precise:

- If a GPO is set at the site level, the policy settings contained within affect those accounts within the geography of the site. Sure, their user account could be in one domain and their computer account could be in another domain. And of course, it's likely that those accounts are in an OU. But the account is affected only by the policy settings here because the account is in a specific site. And logically, when a computer starts up in a new site, the User object will also get its site-based Group Policy from the same place. This is based on the IP subnet the user is a part of and is configured using Active Directory Sites and Services.

- If a GPO is set at the domain level, it affects those users and computers within the domain and all OUs and all other OUs beneath it.

- If a GPO is set at the OU level, it affects those users or computers within the OU and all other OUs beneath it (usually just called child or sub OUs).

By default, when a policy is set at one level, the levels below *inherit* the settings from the levels above it. You can have "cumulative" wishes that keep piling on.

You might wonder what happens if two policy settings conflict. Perhaps one policy is set at the domain level and another policy is set at the OU level, which reverses the edict in the domain. The result is simple: Policy settings further down the food chain take precedence. For instance, if a policy setting conflicts at the domain and OU levels, the OU level "wins." Likewise, domain-level settings override any policy settings that conflict with previously set site-specific policy settings. This might seem counterintuitive at first, so bear with me for a minute.

Take a look at the following illustration to get a view of the order of precedence.

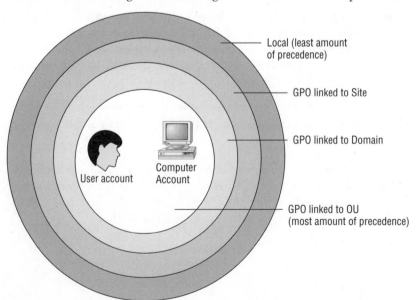

The golden rule with Group Policy is truly "Last writer wins."

However, don't forget about any Local Group Policy that might have been set on a specific workstation. Recall that for pre-Vista machines, everyone logging onto that workstation is affected by that policy setting. You just learned how Vista's MLGPOs add up to three layers (where Windows XP's local GPOs has just one).

Regardless, once that local policy is determined, only *then* do policy settings within Active Directory (the site, domain, and OU) apply. So, sometimes people refer to the *four* levels of Group Policy: local workstation, site, domain, and OU. Nonetheless, GPOs set within Active Directory always trump the Local Group Policy should there be any conflict.

If this behavior is undesirable for lower levels, all the settings from higher levels can be blocked with the Block Inheritance attribute on a given OU. Additionally, if a higher-level administrator wants to guarantee that a setting is inherited down the food chain, they can apply the Enforced attribute via the GPMC interface (or No Override attribute in the old-school parlance). (Chapter 2 explores both Block Inheritance and Enforced attributes in detail.)

Don't sweat it if your head is spinning a little bit now from the Group Policy application theory. I'll go through specific hands-on examples to illustrate each of these behaviors so that you understand exactly how this works.

Linking Group Policy Objects

Another technical concept that needs a bit of description here is the "linking" of GPOs. When a GPO is created at the site, domain, or OU level via the GUI (which we'll do in a moment), the system automatically associates that GPO with the level in which it was created. That association is called *linking*.

Linking is an important concept for several reasons. First, it's generally a good idea to understand what's going on under the hood. However, more practically, the Group Policy Management Console, or GPMC, as we'll explore in just a bit, displays GPOs from their linked perspective.

You can think of all the GPOs you create in Active Directory as children within a big swimming pool. Each child has a tether attached around their waist, and an adult guardian is holding the other end of the rope. Indeed, there could be multiple tethers around a child's waist, with multiple adults tethered to one child. A sad state indeed would be a child who has no tether but is just swimming around in the pool unsecured. The swimming pool in this analogy is a specific Active Directory container named Policies (which we'll examine closely in Chapter 6). All GPOs are born and "live" in that specific domain. Indeed, they're replicated to all Domain Controllers. The adult guardian in this analogy represents a *level* in Active Directory—any site, domain, or OU.

In our swimming pool example, multiple adults can be tethered to a specific child. With Active Directory, multiple levels can be linked to a specific GPO. Thus, any level in Active Directory can leverage multiple GPOs, which are standing by in the domain ready to be used.

Remember, though, unless a GPO is specifically linked to a site, a domain, or an OU, it does not take effect. It's just floating around in the swimming pool of the domain waiting for someone to make use of it.

I'll keep reiterating and refining the concept of linking throughout these first four chapters. And, in Chapters 2 and 4, I'll discuss why you might want to "unlink" a policy.

This concept of linking to GPOs created in Active Directory can be a bit confusing. It will become clearer a bit later as we explore the processes of creating new GPOs and linking to existing ones. Stay tuned. It's right around the corner.

An Example of Group Policy Application

At this point, it's best not to jump directly into adding, deleting, or modifying our own GPOs. Right now, it's better to understand how Group Policy works "on paper." This is especially true if you're new to the concept of Group Policy, but perhaps also if Group Policy has been deployed by other administrators in your Active Directory.

By walking through a fictitious organization that has deployed GPOs at multiple levels, you'll be able to better understand how and why policy settings are applied by the deployment of GPOs.

Let's start by taking a look at Figure 1.6, the organization for our fictitious example company, Example.com.

This picture could easily tell 1,000 words. For the sake of brevity, I've kept it down to around 200. There are two domains, Example.com and Widgets.example.com. Let's talk about Example.com first:

- The domain Example.com has two Domain Controllers. One DC, named EXAMPLEDC1, is physically located in the California site. Example.com's other Domain Controller, EXAMPLEDC2, is physically located in the Phoenix site.

- As for PCs, they need to physically reside somewhere. Sally's PC is in the California site; Brett's PC and Adam's PC are in the Delaware site. JoesPC is in the Phoenix site.

- User accounts may or may not be in OUs. Dave's and Jane's account is in the **Human Resources** OU.

- Computer accounts may or may not be in OUs. FredsPC is in the **Human Resources** OU. Adam's PC is specifically placed within the **High Security** OU. JoesPC, SallysPC and BrettsPC aren't in any OUs.

Using Active Directory Sites and Services, a schedule can be put in place to regulate communication between EXAMPLEDC1 located in California and EXAMPLEDC2 located in Phoenix. That way the administrator controls the chatter between the two Example.com Domain Controllers and it is not at the whim of the operating system.

Another domain, called Widgets.example.com, has an automatic transitive two-way trust to Example.com. There is only one Domain Controller in the Widgets.example.com domain, named WIDDC1, and it physically resides at the Phoenix site. Last, there is MarksPC, a member of the Widgets.example.com domain, and it physically resides in the New York site and isn't in any OU.

FIGURE 1.6 This fictitious Example.com is relatively simple. Your environment may be more complex.

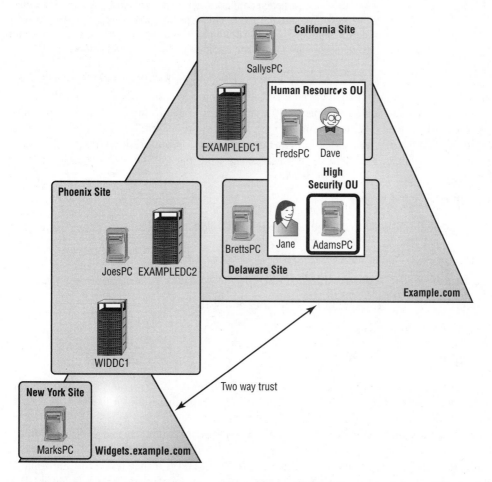

Understanding where your users and machines are is half the battle. The other half is understanding which policy settings are expected to appear when they start logging onto Active Directory.

Examining the Resultant Set of Policy

As stated earlier, the effect of Group Policy is cumulative as GPOs are successively applied—starting at the local computer, then the site, the domain, and each nested OU. The end result of what affects a specific user or computer—after all Group Policy at all levels has been applied—is called the *Resultant Set of Policy*, or *RSoP*. This is sometimes referred to as the *RSoP calculation*.

Throughout your lifetime working with Group Policy, you will be asked to troubleshoot the RSoP of client machines.

> Much of our dealings with Group Policy will be trying to understand and trouble-shoot the RSoP of a particular configuration. Getting a good, early understanding of how to perform manual RSoP calculations on paper is important because it's a useful troubleshooting skill. In Chapter 4 and Chapter 6, we'll also explore additional RSoP skills—with tools and additional manual troubleshooting.

Before we jump in to try to discover what the RSoP might be for any specific machine, it's often helpful to break out each of the strata—local computer, site, domain, and OU—and examine, at each level, what happens to the entities contained in them. I'll then bring it all together to see how a specific computer or user reacts to the accumulation of GPOs. For these examples, assume that no local policy is set on any of the computers; the goal is to get a better feeling of how Group Policy flows, not necessarily what the specific end-state will be.

At the Site Level

Based on what we know from Figure 1.6, the GPOs in effect at the site level are shown below.

Site	Computers Affected
California	SallysPC, EXAMPLEDC1, and FredsPC
Phoenix	EXAMPLEDC2, JoesPC, and WIDDC1
New York	MarksPC
Delaware	AdamsPC and BrettsPC

If we look at the graphic again, it looks like Dave, for instance, resides in California and Jane, for instance, resides in Delaware. But I don't like to think about it like that. I prefer to say that their accounts reside in OUs.

But, users are affected by site GPOs *only* when they log onto computers that are at a specific site.

In Figure 1.6, we have Dave and Jane's account in the Human Resources OU. And that's great. But they're only affected by California Site-Level GPOs if they travel to California. It doesn't matter where they usually reside; again, they're only affected by the Site-Level GPOs when they're physically present in that site.

So, don't think that user accounts *reside* at the site level. Rather, they reside in the OU level but are using computers in the site and, hence, get the properties assigned to all users at that site.

> Sites are defined using the Active Directory Sites and Services tool. IP subnets that constitute a site are assigned using this tool. That way, if a new computer turns on in Delaware, Active Directory knows what site the computer is in. For more information, check out http://tinyurl.com/b5mbn.

At the Domain Level

Here's what we have working at the domain level:

Domain	Computers/Users Affected
Example.com Computers	SallysPC, FredsPC, AdamsPC, BrettsPC, JoesPC, EXAMPLEDC1, and EXAMPLEDC2
Example.com Users	Dave and Jane
Widgets.example.com Computers	WIDDC1 and MarksPC

At the OU Level

At the organizational unit level, we have the following:

Organizational Unit	Computers/Users Affected
Human Resources OU Computers	FredsPC is in the **Human Resources** OU; therefore, it is affected when the **Human Resources** OU gets GPOs applied. Additionally, the **High Security** OU is contained inside the **Human Resources** OU. Therefore, AdamsPC, which is in the **High Security** OU, is also affected whenever the **Human Resources** OU is affected.
Human Resources OU Users	The accounts of Dave and Jane are affected when **the Human Resources** OU has GPOs applied.

Bringing It All Together

Now that you've broken out all the levels and seen what is being applied to them, you can start to calculate what the devil is happening on any specific user and computer combination. Looking at Figure 1.6 and analyzing what's happening at each level makes adding things together between the local, site, domain, and organizational unit GPOs a lot easier.

Here are some examples of RSoP for specific users and computers in our fictitious environment:

FredsPC	FredsPC inherits the settings of the GPOs from the California site, then the Example.com domain, and last, the **Human Resources** OU.
MarksPC	MarksPC first accepts the GPOs from the New York site and then the Widgets.example.com domain. MarksPC is not in any OU; therefore, no organizational unit GPOs apply to his computer.

AdamsPC	AdamsPC is subject to the GPOs at the Delaware site, the Example.com domain, the **Human Resources** OU, and the **High Security** OU.
Dave using AdamsPC	AdamsPC is subject to the computer policies in the GPOs for the Delaware site, the Example.com domain, the **Human Resources** OU, and finally the **High Security** OU. When Dave travels from California to Delaware to use Adam's workstation, his user GPOs are dictated from the Delaware site, the Example.com domain, and the **Human Resources** OU.

> At no time are any domain GPOs from the Example.com parent domain automatically inherited by the Widget.example.com child domain. Inheritance for GPOs only flows downward to OUs within a single domain—not between any two domains—parent to child or otherwise, unless you explicitly link one of those parent GPOs to a child domain container.

If you want one GPO to affect the users in more than one domain, you have four choices:

- Precisely re-create the GPOs in each domain with their own GPO.

- Copy the GPO from one domain to another domain (using the GPMC, as explained in the appendix).

- Use a third-party tool that can perform some magic and automatically perform the copying between domains for you.

- Do a generally recognized no-no called *cross-domain policy linking*. (I'll describe this no-no in detail in Chapter 6 in the section "Group Policy Objects from a Domain Perspective.")

Also, don't assume that linking a GPO at a site level necessarily guarantees the results to just one domain. In this example, as in real life, there is not necessarily a 1:1 correlation between sites and domains.

At this point, we'll put our example Example.com behind us. That was really an on-paper exercise to allow you to get a feel for what's possible in Group Policy land. From this point forward, you'll be doing most items in your test lab and following along.

Group Policy, Active Directory, and the GPMC

Active Directory administrators already somewhat familiar with Group Policy will tell you that finding what you need and understanding what's going on under the hood can sometimes be confusing. The interface used to create, modify, and manipulate Group Policy in the original iteration of Active Directory on Windows 2000 has led to numerous missteps and head scratching when people try to figure out why something isn't going the way it should.

Occasionally, the folks at Microsoft have recognized that the first iteration of a product release has missed the mark a little in the way the product works, acts, or interfaces. They often request additional customer feedback, embrace it, regroup, and return a new and improved version of the product.

To make optimal use of Group Policy in an Active Directory environment, the Group Policy team at Microsoft introduced a free, downloadable tool for managing Group Policy in Active Directory in a meaningful way. It's called the Group Policy Management Console, or GPMC, as mentioned earlier. The GPMC isn't part of the Windows 2000, Windows 2003, or Windows XP operating systems; you need to fetch it and install it. It is, however, part of the shipping version of Windows Vista and Windows Server 2008, so no extra effort is required.

Except it should be noted that the GPMC is uninstalled with Windows Vista when SP1 is installed. And to reinstall it, you have to fetch what's known as the Remote Server Administration Tools, or *RSAT*. Inside RSAT is the updated GPMC.

I know, I know. This is all weird, right? I promise a detailed explanation of why in Chapter 3.

Kickin' It Old School

Out of the box, the tools built into Windows 2000 and Windows 2003 domains use the old-style interface. This interface is built into Active Directory Users and Computer and Active Directory Sites and Services.

If you've never seen the old-style interface, you can do so right now before we leave it in the dust for the new GPMC in the next section.

To see the old-style interface and create your first GPO at the domain level, follow these steps:

1.   Log onto the Domain Controller DC01 as the Administrator account (which is a Domain Administrator).

2.   Choose Start ➢ All Programs ➢ Administrative Tools and select Active Directory Users and Computers. Alternatively, select Start ➢ Run and select dsa.msc to open up Active Directory Users and Computers.

3.   Right-click the domain name and choose Properties from the shortcut menu, as shown in Figure 1.7, to open the Properties dialog box for the domain.

4.   Click the Group Policy tab.

There is a Default Domain Policy GPO, but you won't modify it at this time. (I'll talk about it in Chapter 7.)

5.   Click the New button to spawn the creation of your first GPO.

6.   For this first example, type **My First GPO**, as shown in Figure 1.8.

7.   Highlight the policy and click Edit to open the Group Policy Management Editor.

FIGURE 1.7   Right-click the domain name and choose Properties.

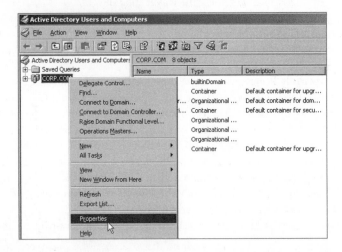

At this point, things should look familiar, just like the Local Group Policy Management Editor, with the user and computer nodes. For example, if you drill down into the Administrative Templates folder in the User Configuration ➢ Policies folder, you can make a wish at the domain level and all your computers will obey.

For now, don't actually make any changes; just close the Group Policy Management Editor and read on.

FIGURE 1.8   You've just created your first GPO in Active Directory.

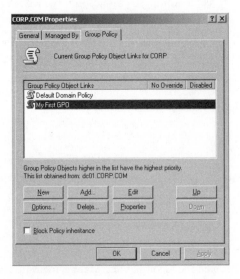

GPMC Overview

The Group Policy Management Console (GPMC) was created to help administrators work in a "one-stop-shop" place for all Group Policy management functions. Since 2003, it was freely downloadable as an add-on to either Windows XP or Windows Server 2003 systems. In Windows Vista, it's included in the box! That is, until you load Windows Vista's SP1, when the GPMC is uninstalled until you fetch the RSAT tools.

The best part is, it doesn't matter if your Active Directory or domains or Domain Controllers are Windows 2000, Windows 2003, or Windows 2008; it just matters that you have Active Directory.

Why Abandon Old School?

In Figure 1.8, we were able to create our first GPO (even though we didn't actually place any policy settings in there). The interface seems reasonable enough to take care of such simple tasks. And, heck, this interface is already part of the operating system, so why move away from it?

The old-school way of viewing and managing Group Policy just isn't scalable over the long haul. This interface doesn't show us any relationship between the GPO we just created and the domain it's in. As you'll see in this chapter, the new interface demonstrates a much clearer relationship between the GPOs you create, the links it takes to use them, and the domains where the GPOs actually "live."

The old-style interface also provides no easy way to figure out what's going on inside the GPOs you create. To determine what changes are made inside a GPO, you need to reopen each GPO and poke around. I've seen countless administrators open each and every GPO in their domain and manually document their settings on paper for backup and recovery purposes.

Indeed, backup and recovery is a really, really big deal, and the old-school mechanism (via NTBACKUP) provided no realistic way to back up and recover GPOs without copious amounts of surgery. The GPMC makes it a snap.

With that in mind, I encourage all of you—those currently using the original Windows 2000 old-school way and those who haven't even yet been to school—to step up and try the new way of doing things, the GPMC.

 Even though you cannot load the GPMC on a Windows 2000 Domain Controller or a Windows 2000 Professional machine, it's still capable of controlling Windows 2000 domains.

About the GPMC

The GPMC's name says it all. It's the Group Policy Management Console. Indeed, this will be the MMC snap-in that you use to manage the underlying Group Policy mechanism. The GPMC just helps us tap into those features already built into Active Directory. I'll highlight the mechanism of how Group Policy works throughout the next four chapters.

One major design goal of the GPMC is to get a Group Policy–centric view of the lay of the land. Compared with the old interface, the GPMC does a much better job of aligning the user interface of Group Policy with what's going on under the hood.

The GPMC also provides a programmatic way to manage your GPOs. In fact, the GPMC scripting interface allows just about any GPO operation (other than to dive in and create or modify actual policy settings). We'll explore scripting with the GPMC in Chapter 11. So, if you're interested in scripting, you'll need to have the GPMC bits loaded on the Windows XP, Windows Vista, or Windows Server 2008 systems you want to script.

> The GPMC scripts, which were previously part of the downloadable GPMC package, are not included in Windows Vista or Windows Server 2008. You have to specifically download them from the GPMC scripting center at http://tinyurl.com/23xfz3 or search for "Group Policy Management Console Sample Scripts" in your favorite search engine.

There are lots of ways you *could* manage your Group Policy universe. Some people walk up to their Domain Controllers, log onto the console, and manage their Group Policy infrastructure there. Others use a *management workstation* and manage their Group Policy infrastructure from their own Windows XP or Windows Vista workstations.

I'll talk more about the use and best practices of a Windows Vista management workstation in Chapter 7.

Implementing the GPMC on Your Management Station

As I mentioned, the GPMC isn't part of the standard Windows 2003 or Windows XP package out of the box. And, it's already installed into Windows Vista and Windows Server 2008

That's right—at first there's nothing to download, nothing to install, and nothing to worry about. That is, until Windows Vista + SP1 is installed, at which time the GPMC is uninstalled.

Don't panic. It's a quick hop, skip, and jump to get the latest GPMC from Microsoft's website. I'll show you how to do this in a minute.

Remember earlier I stated that you could manage your Active Directory from anywhere. And this is true. You *could* walk up to a Domain Controller, you *could* install the GPMC on a Windows XP or Windows Server 2003 server, or you *could* use Terminal Services to remotely connect to a Domain Controller.

But in this book, you won't be. Your ideal management station is a Windows Vista + SP 1 + RSAT machine, or a Windows Server 2008 machine (which is ready to go, no downloads needed).

If you must use something else (Windows XP, Windows Server 2003, or Windows Vista RTM), I provide some advice for those. But you'll really want to use the recommended set to get the most out of this book.

Upgrading from NT 4 to Active Directory: Cleaning Up Old GPOs

If you have any remaining Windows 2000 Domain Controllers, you should have at least SP2 and preferably SP4 applied to them. This is because most Windows 2003 tools, including the GPMC, use LDAP (Lightweight Directory Access Protocol) signing for all communication. For more information, see the Microsoft Knowledge Base article 325465 at `http://support` `.microsoft.com/kb/325465`.

After you run the GPMC, you may be prompted to "clean up" older GPOs the first time you touch one. You should do so. Under the hood, the GPMC is adjusting some key security descriptors in Active Directory.

The precise error message you'll get is, "The permissions for this GPO in the SYSVOL folder are inconsistent with those in Active Directory." It is recommended that these permissions be consistent. To change the SYSVOL permissions to those in Active Directory, click OK."

By allowing this, you can do some fancy footwork later, as you'll see in the section "Advanced Security and Delegation with the GPMC" in Chapter 2. You will see this message if your Windows 2000 PDC-Emulator domain was upgraded from anything prior to SP4.

Using a Windows Vista or Windows Server 2008 Management Station

In this book, and in real life, I'm going to recommend that you use what's known as a Windows Vista management station. And, ideally, that Windows Vista management station would have SP1 with the updated (downloadable) GPMC installed on it.

You could also use a Windows Server 2008 machine as your management station, but it's not likely you're going to install that puppy on your laptop or desktop.

So, just to be clear, the following two ways to create and manage GPOs are equal:

- Windows Vista + SP1 + newly downloadable GPMC (contained within the RSAT tools)
- Windows Server 2008 with built-in GPMC

I'll usually just refer to a Windows Vista management station, and when I say that, I mean what I have in that first bullet point. Just remember that you can use a Windows Server 2008 machine as your management station too.

I delve into this in serious detail in Chapter 7, but here's the CliffsNotes, er, Jeremy's Notes version:

- Always use Windows Vista (or Windows Server 2008) as your management station and you'll always be able to control all operating systems' settings: Windows Vista, Windows Server 2008, and all earlier editions.
- If you have even one Windows Vista client machine (say in Sales, Marketing, etc.), you're going to need to manage it using a Windows Vista or Windows Server 2008 management station.

- If you create a GPO using Windows Vista or Windows Server 2008 but then edit it using an older operating system, you might not be able to "see" all the settings. And what's worse, some might actually be set (but you wouldn't see them!).

> What if you're not "allowed" to load Windows Vista on your management station? Well, you've got another option. Perhaps you can create a Windows Vista or Windows Server 2008 machine to act as your management station, say in the server room. Then set up Terminal Services or Remote Desktop to utilize the GPMC remotely.

Again, in our examples we'll call our machine VISTAMANAGEMENT, but you can use either a Windows Server 2008 or Windows Vista + SP1 + RSAT for your best management station experience.

Using a Windows Server 2008 Machine as Your Management Station

The latest GPMC is available in Windows Server 2008, except by default, it's not immediately usable. You need to install it or you won't be able to use it. There are two ways to install the GPMC: using Server Manager and also by the command line.

To install the GPMC using Server Manager:

1. Click Start, then point to Administrative Tools and select Server Manager.

2. In the Server Manager's console tree, click Features and then select Add Features.

3. In the Add Feature Wizard dialog box, select Group Policy Management Console from the list of features.

4. Click Install.

Close Server Manager once you're done.

You can also install the GPMC using the command line:

1. Open a command prompt as an Administrator.

2. In the command prompt, type **ServerManagerCmd -install gpmc**.

3. Close the command prompt when the installation has been completed.

Using a Windows Vista + SP1 + RSAT Machine as Your Management Station

The first step on your Windows Vista management-station-to-be is to install Windows Vista SP1. Next, you'll need to install RSAT. RSAT installs like a hotfix, and you may or may not need to reboot after installation.

Then, on Windows Vista, go to Control Panel and select Programs. Select "Turn Windows features on or off." Locate the Feature Administration Tools and Role Administration Tools nodes. Select Group Policy Management Tools and Active Directory Domain Services Tools, as seen in Figure 1.9.

Once you're done, close the Windows Features window and, if prompted, reboot your Windows Vista machine. The next time you boot, you'll have Active Directory Users and Computers, the GPMC, and other tools available for use in the rest of the book.

FIGURE 1.9   The RSAT tools install like a hotfix but then must be individually selected using Control Panel ≻ Programs ≻ Turn Windows features on or off.

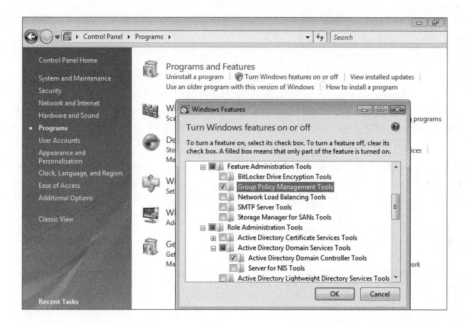

Other Management Station Options

If you positively cannot use a Windows Vista + SP1 + RSAT machine to be your management station, and you must limp along with Windows Vista RTM, Windows XP, or Windows Server 2003 machine, you can.

But know that you won't get the full experience, and your screen might look different than my screenshots.

If you must use a Windows Vista RTM machine   On your Windows Vista machine, click Start, and in the Start Search prompt, type the **gpmc.msc** command. With Windows Vista RTM, the GPMC will just fire right up. I strongly encourage you to get to a Windows Vista + SP1 + RSAT machine as soon as possible. However, you can also perform the steps in the sidebar entitled "Adminpak on a Windows Vista RTM Management Station" to make the most of your situation.

If you must use Windows XP or Windows Server 2003 management station   Now, what if you really, really cannot use a Windows Vista or Windows Server 2008 management station? Well, then, sounds like you're stuck with Windows XP or Windows Server 2003. With that in mind, you can check out the sidebar titled "If You Must Use a Windows XP or Windows Server 2003 Management Station."

If You Must Use a Windows XP or Windows Server 2003 Management Station

Again, I recommend against using the GPMC on Windows XP or Windows 2003 if you've even got just one Windows Vista machine to use. Read Chapter 7 for the full rundown about why.

However, if you feel you must continue to use Windows XP or Windows Server 2003 as your management station, you can download the older GPMC for free from www.microsoft.com/grouppolicy. To be honest, I don't know how much longer they'll maintain the original GPMC. I wouldn't be surprised if, sometime soon, the only GPMC available is the updated edition (contained within RSAT), which runs on Windows Vista (and is built into Windows Server 2008).

Click the link for the Group Policy Management Console to locate the download. Once it's downloaded, the GPMC is called GPMC.MSI. You can install this on either Windows 2003 or Windows XP with at least SP1, but nothing else. That is, you cannot load the GPMC on Windows 2000 servers or workstations; but, as I noted before, the GPMC can manage Windows 2000 domains with Windows 2000 and Windows XP clients as well as Windows 2003 domains with Windows 2000 or Windows XP clients.

Installing the GPMC does require certain prerequisites, which must be loaded in the order listed here.

Loading the GPMC on Windows XP

If you intend to load the GPMC on a Windows XP machine to manage Group Policy in your domain, follow these steps:

1. At least Windows XP Service Pack 1 is required. If you are unsure whether SP1 (or later) is installed, run the WINVER command, which will tell you whether a service pack is installed. So, if your Windows XP system doesn't have at least SP1 installed, you should install the latest service pack.

2. The GPMC requires the .NET Framework 1.1 to run properly. Note that if you only have the newer .NET Framework (2 or higher), it won't work. It simply must be .NET Framework 1.1. If it's not installed, you'll need to download and install it. At last check, the .NET Framework download was at a URL I've shortened to http://tinyurl.com/7vshz. If it's not there, Google ".NET Framework 1.1."

    After downloading .NET Framework 1.1, double-click the install to get it going on your target Windows XP/SP1 (or greater) machine. It isn't a very exciting or noteworthy installation.

3. To install the GPMC, double-click the GPMC.MSI file you downloaded. If you're running Windows XP with SP1, the GPMC installation routine will report that a hotfix (also known as a QFE) is required and then proceed to automatically install the hotfix on-the-fly. This hotfix (Q326469) is incorporated into Windows XP's SP2. So, if installing on a Windows XP/SP2 machine, you won't be bothered to install it.

Technically the GPMC runs fine on .NET 2.0 only, but the MSI installer chokes when checking .NET versions. If you have the skills to get around that, you're theoretically good to go with just .NET 2.0.

Loading the GPMC on a Windows 2003 Domain Controller

If you intend to load the GPMC on a Windows 2003 Domain Controller or a member server, there are just a couple of things to do:

1. Although there aren't any Windows 2003 prerequisites, it's a good idea to install the .NET Framework 1.1. If the GPMC installation doesn't complain, you're good to go. Otherwise, load it up.

2. To install the GPMC, double-click the GPMC.MSI file you downloaded.

The Results of Loading the GPMC on Windows XP

After the GPMC is loaded on the machine from which you will manage Group Policy (the management workstation), you'll see that the way you view things has changed. If you take a look in Active Directory Users and Computers (or Active Directory Sites and Services) and try to manage a GPO, you'll see a curious link on the existing Group Policy tab (as seen below).

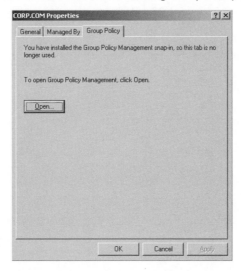

Additionally, you'll see a Group Policy Management icon in the Administrative Tools folder in the Start Menu folder.

Creating a One-Stop Shop MMC

As you'll see, the GPMC is a fairly comprehensive Group Policy management tool. But the problem is that right now the GPMC and the Active Directory Users and Computers snap-ins are, well, separate tools that each do a specific job. They're not integrated to allow you to work on both Users and Group Policy at the same time.

Often, you'll want to change a Group Policy on an OU and then move computers to that OU. Unfortunately, you can't do so from the GPMC; you must to return to Active Directory Users and Computers to finish the task. This can get frustrating quickly. The GPMC does allow you to right-click at the domain level to choose to launch the Active Directory Users and Computers console when you want, but I prefer a one-stop-shop view of my Active Directory management. It's a matter of taste.

As a result, my preference is to create a custom MMC that shows both the Active Directory Users and Computers and GPMC in a one-stop-shop view. You can see what I mean in Figure 1.10.

FIGURE 1.10 Use the MMC to create a unified console.

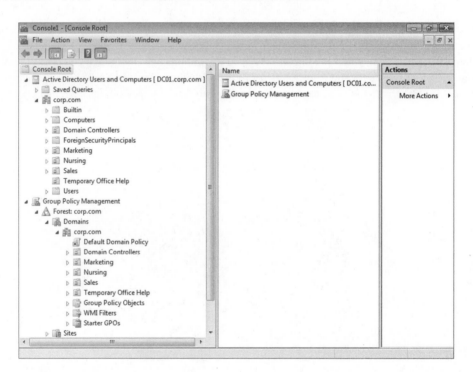

You might be wondering at this point, "So, Jeremy, what are the steps I need in order to create this unified MMC console you've so neatly described and shown in Figure 1.10?"

By the time you read this, Microsoft will have hopefully released the RSAT tools, which are the Windows Vista equivalents to the Windows XP Administration Pack tools. By using these tools, you can have a management station with both Active Directory Users and Computers and the GPMC (both included in the RSAT tools).

Just click Start and type **MMC** at the Search prompt. Then add in both the Active Directory Users and Computers and Group Policy Management snap-ins, as shown in Figure 1.11.

You won't need the Group Policy Management Editor (which allows you to edit one Group Policy Object at a time), the Group Policy Object Editor (for Local Group Policy), or the Group Policy Starter GPO Editor (which we use later in Chapter 3).

FIGURE 1.11   Add Active Directory Users and Computers and Group Policy Management into your custom view.

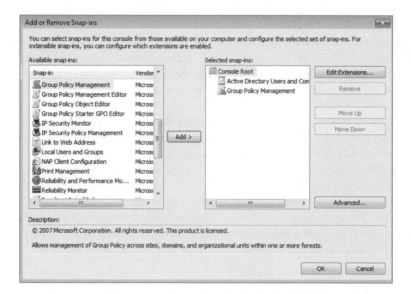

However, if the RSAT tools aren't available by the time you read this, there's another option that will work. See the sidebar "Adminpak on a Windows Vista RTM Management Station" for more information.

Adminpak on a Windows Vista RTM Management Station

Hopefully, by the time you read this, the equivalent of the Adminpak tools (to be known as RSAT tools) will be available as a regular, good ol' fashioned installation for Windows Vista. But if not, you'll need a workaround to get the old tools to work on your updated machine.

If you want to run the Windows Server 2003 Adminpak on your Windows Vista RTM management station, check out `http://support.microsoft.com/default.aspx/kb/930056` for the gory step-by-steps and gotchas.

> Get the latest version of the Windows Server 2003/SP1 Adminpak here: `http://tinyurl.com/9f2wm`.
>
> Ultimately, going through the pain will be worth it, because you'll then have both the Active Directory Users and Computer (from the Adminpak) and the GPMC (pre-loaded with Windows Vista) in one place.
>
> Then, you can just fire up `MMC.exe` and add in the two snap-ins you need, and it'll look just like Figure 1.9 (except it'll be on your Windows Vista management station).
>
> Again, this pain is only necessary if for some reason you cannot use a Windows Server 2008 or Windows Vista + SP1 + RSAT machine for your management station.

Once you have added both snap-ins into your console, you'll really have a near-unified view of most of what you need at your fingertips. Both Active Directory Users and Computers and the GPMC can create and delete OUs. Both tools also allow administrators to delegate permissions to others to manage Group Policy, but that's where the two tools' functionality overlap ends.

The GPMC won't show you the actual users and computer objects inside the OU, so deleting an OU from within the GPMC is dicey at best because you can't be sure of what's inside!

You can choose to add other snaps-ins too, of course, including Active Directory Sites and Services or anything else you think is useful. The illustrations in the rest of this book will show both snap-ins loaded in this configuration.

You can launch the GPMC from either the new link in Active Directory Users and Computers (or Active Directory Sites and Services) or directly from the new icon in the Start menu. However, clicking Open in the existing tools has a slight advantage of telling the GPMC to "snap to" the location in Active Directory on which you are currently focused.

Using the GPMC in Active Directory

For the examples in this book, I'll refer to our sample Domain Controller, DC01, which is part of my example Corp.com domain. For these examples, you can choose to rename the Default-First-Site-Name site or not—your choice.

Let's start with some basics to ensure that things are running smoothly. For most of the examples in this book, you'll be able to get by with just the one Domain Controller and one or two workstations that participate in the domain, for verifying that your changes took place.

Again, I encourage you to try these examples in your test lab and not to directly try them on your production network. This will help you avoid a CLM (Career-Limiting Move).

For our examples, we'll assume you're using VISTAMANAGEMENT as your management station, which is a Windows Vista + SP1 + RSAT.

Active Directory Users and Computers vs. GPMC

The main job of Active Directory Users and Computers is to give you an Active Directory object–centric view of your domain. Active Directory Users and Computers lets you deal with users, computers, groups, contacts, some of the Flexible Single Master Operations roles (FSMO roles), and delegation of control over user accounts as well as change the domain mode and define advanced security and auditing inside Active Directory. You can also create OUs and move users and computers around inside those OUs. Other administrators can then drill down inside Active Directory Users and Computers into an OU and see the computers, groups, contacts, and so on that you've moved to those OUs.

But the GPMC has one main job: to provide you with a Group Policy–centric view of all you control. All the OUs that you see in Active Directory Users and Computers are visible in the GPMC. Think about it—it's the same Active Directory behind the scenes "storing" that OU.

However, the GPMC does *not* show you users, computers, contacts, and such. When you drill down into an OU inside the GPMC, you'll see but one thing: the GPOs that affect the objects inside the OU.

In Figure 1.10, you were able to see the Active Directory Users and Computers view as well as the GPMC view—rolled into one MMC that we created earlier. The Active Directory Users and Computers view of **Temporary Office Help** and the GPMC view of the same OU is radically different.

When focused at a site, a domain, or an OU within the GPMC, you see only the GPOs that affect that level in Active Directory. You don't see the same "stuff" that Active Directory Users and Computers sees, such as users, computers, groups, or contacts.

The basic overlap in the two tools is the ability to create and delete OUs. If you add or delete an OU in either tool, you need to refresh the other tool by pressing F5 to see the update. For instance, in Figure 1.10, you could see that my Active Directory has several OUs, including one named **Temporary Office Help**.

WARNING   Deleting an OU from inside the GPMC is generally a bad idea. Because you cannot see the Active Directory objects inside the OU (such as users and computers), you don't really know how many objects you're about to delete. So be careful!

If I delete the **Temporary Office Help** OU in Active Directory Users and Computers, the change is not reflected in the GPMC window until it's refreshed. And vice versa.

Adjusting the View within the GPMC

The GPMC lets you view as much or as little of your Active Directory as you like. By default, you view only your own forest and domain. You can optionally add in the ability to see the sites in your forest as well as the ability to see other domains in your forest or domains in other forests, although these views might not be the best for seeing what you have control over.

Viewing sites in the GPMC   When you create GPOs, you won't often create GPOs that affect sites. The designers of the GPMC seem to agree; it's a bit of a chore to apply GPOs to sites. To do so, you need to link an *existing* GPO to a site. You'll see how to do this a bit later in this chapter.

However, you first need to expose the site objects in Active Directory. To do so, right-click the Sites object in GPMC, choose Show Sites from the shortcut menu (see Figure 1.12), and then click the check box next to each site you want to expose.

In our first example, we'll use the site level of Active Directory to deploy our first Group Policy Object. At this point, go ahead and enable the Default-First-Site so that you can have it ready for use in our own experiments.

Viewing other domains in the GPMC   To see other domains in your forest, drill down to the Forest folder in Group Policy Management, right-click Domains, choose Show Domains, and select the other available domains in your forest. Each domain will now appear at the same hierarchical level in the GPMC.

Viewing other forests in the GPMC   To see other forests, right-click the root (Group Policy Management), and choose Add Forest from the shortcut menu. You'll need to type the name of the Active Directory forest you want to add. If you want to add or subtract domains within that new forest, follow the instructions in the preceding paragraph.

FIGURE 1.12   You need to expose the Active Directory sites before you can link GPOs to them.

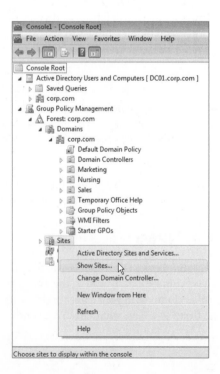

You can add forests with which you do not have a trust. However, GPMC defaults will not display these domains as a safety mechanism. To turn off the safety, choose View ➢ Options to open the Options dialog box. In the General tab, clear Enable Trust Detection and click OK.

Now that we've adjusted our view to see the domains and forests we want, let's examine how to manipulate our GPOs and GPO links.

The GPMC-centric View

As I stated earlier, one of the fundamental concepts of Group Policy is that the GPOs themselves live in the "swimming pool" that is the domain. Then, when a level in Active Directory needs to use that GPO, there is simply a link to the GPO.

Figure 1.13 shows what our swimming pool will eventually look like when we're done with the examples in this chapter.

FIGURE 1.13   Imagine your about-to-be-leveraged GPOs as just hanging out in the swimming pool of the domain.

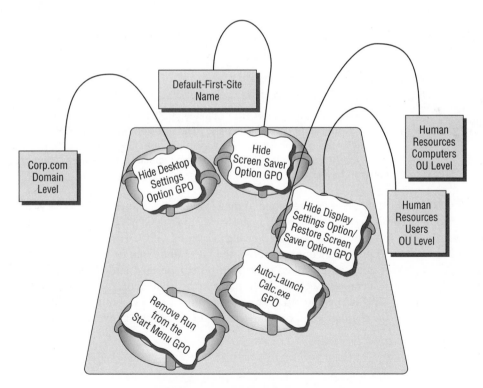

The Corp.com GPO Swimming Pool

Our swimming pool will be full of GPOs, with various levels in Active Directory "linked" to those GPOs. To that end, you can drill down, right now, to see the representation of the swimming pool. It's there, waiting for you. Click Group Policy Management ➤ Forest ➤ Domains ➤ Corp.com ➤ Group Policy Objects to see all the GPOs that exist in the domain (see Figure 1.14).

FIGURE 1.14   The Group Policy Objects folder highlighted here is the representation of the swimming pool of the domain that contains your actual GPOs.

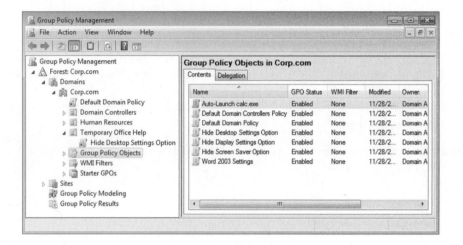

If you're just getting started, it's not likely you'll have more than the "Default Domain Controllers Policy" GPO and "Default Domain Policy" GPO. That's OK. You'll start getting more GPOs soon enough. Oh, and for now, please don't modify the default GPOs. They're a bit special and are covered in great detail in Chapter 8.

All GPOs in the domain are represented in the Group Policy Objects folder. As you can see, when the **Temporary Office Help** OU is shown within the GPMC, a relationship exists between the OU and the "Hide Desktop Settings Option" GPO. That relationship is the tether to the GPO in the swimming pool—the GPO link back to "Hide Desktop Settings Option." You can see this linked relationship because the "Hide Desktop Settings Option" icon inside **Temporary Office Help** has a little arrow icon, signifying the link back to the actual GPO in the domain. The same is true for the "Default Domain Policy," which is linked at the domain level, but the actual GPO is placed below the Group Policy Objects folder.

Our Own Group Policy Examples

Now that you've got a grip on honing your view within the GPMC, let's take it for a quick spin around the block with some examples!

For this series of examples, we're going after the users who keep fiddling with their display gadgets in Windows Vista, Windows XP, and Windows 2000.

If you want to see these examples in action using Windows XP, first start out on XPPRO1 by checking out the default Display Properties dialog box. Just right-click the Desktop and choose Properties from the shortcut menu. You'll see several tabs, including Screen Saver, Appearance, and Settings, as shown in Figure 1.15 (left screen).

If you want to see these examples in action using Windows Vista, first start out on VISTA1 by looking at the "Personalize appearance and sounds" page, which is located by right-clicking the Desktop and choosing Personalize. You'll see several entries, including Screen Saver, Windows Color and Appearance, and Display Settings, as shown in Figure 1.15 (right screen).

FIGURE 1.15 In Windows XP, all the tabs in the Display Properties dialog box are available by default (left screen). In Windows Vista, we can see lots of available areas in the Personalization screen, shown on the right.

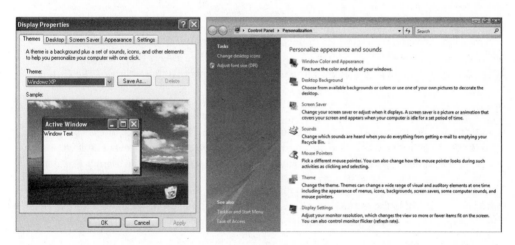

Since they're called tabs in Windows XP and entries or options in Windows Vista, I'll just generally call them options from here on out.

For our first use of Group Policy, we're going to produce four "edicts" (for dramatic effect, you should stand on your desk and loudly proclaim these edicts with a thick British accent):

- At the site level, there will be no more ability to change screensavers.
- At the domain level, there will be no Desktop Settings option in the Windows Vista Personalization page (or Desktop tab in the Display Properties dialog box for Windows XP).

- At the **Human Resources Users** OU level, there will be no Display Settings option in the Windows Vista Personalization page (or Settings tab in the Display Properties for Windows XP). And, while we're at it, let's bring back the ability to change screensavers!

- At the **Human Resources Computers** OU, we'll make it so whenever anyone uses a Human Resources computer, `calc.exe` automatically launches after login.

Following along with these concrete examples will reinforce the concepts presented earlier. Additionally, they are used throughout the remainder of this chapter and the book.

Understanding GPMC's Link Warning

As you work through the examples, you'll do a lot of clicking around. When you click a GPO link the first time, you'll get this message:

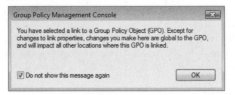

This message is trying to convey an important sentiment; that is, multiple levels in Active Directory may be linked back and use the exact same GPO. The idea is that multiple levels of Active Directory could use the exact same Group Policy Object contained inside the Group Policy Objects container—but just be linked back to it.

What if you modify the policy settings by right-clicking a policy link and choosing Edit from the shortcut menu? All instances in Active Directory that link to that GPO embrace the new settings. If this is a fear, you might want to create another GPO and then link it to the level in Active Directory you want. More properties are affected by this warning, and we'll explore them in Chapter 5.

If you've squelched this message by selecting "Do not show this message again," you can get it back. In the GPMC in the menus, choose View ➤ Options and select the General tab, select "Show confirmation dialog to distinguish between GPOs and GPO links", and click OK.

More about Linking and the Group Policy Objects Container

The GPMC is a fairly flexible tool. Indeed, it permits the administrator to perform many tasks in different ways. One thing you'll do quite a lot in your travels with the GPMC is to actually create your own Group Policy Objects. Again, GPOs live in a container within Active Directory and are represented within the Group Policy Objects container (the swimming pool) inside the domain (seen in Figure 1.13, earlier in this chapter). Any levels of Active Directory—site, domain, or OU—simply link back to the GPOs hanging out in the Group Policy Objects container.

To apply Group Policy to a level in Active Directory (site, domain, or OU) using the GPMC, you have two options:

- Create the GPOs in the Group Policy Objects container first. Then, while focused at the level you want to command in Active Directory (site, domain, or OU), manually add a link to the GPO that is in the Group Policy Objects container.

- While focused at the level you want to command in Active Directory (domain or OU), create the GPOs in the Group Policy Objects container and automatically create the link. This link is created at the level you're currently focused at *back* to the GPO in the Group Policy Objects container.

Which is the correct way to go? Both are perfectly acceptable because both are really doing the same thing.

In both cases the GPO itself does not "live" at the level in Active Directory at which you're focused. Rather, the GPO itself "lives" in the Group Policy Objects container. The link back to the GPO inside the Group Policy Objects container is what makes the relationship between the GPO inside the Group Policy Objects container swimming pool and the level in Active Directory you want to command.

To get the hang of this, let's work through some examples. First, let's create our first GPO in the Group Policy Objects folder. Follow these steps:

1. Launch the GPMC. Again, click Start, and then in the search box, just type **GPMC.MSC**.

2. Traverse down by clicking Group Policy Management ➢ Forest ➢ Domains ➢ Corp.com ➢ Group Policy Objects.

3. Right-click the Group Policy Objects folder and choose New from the shortcut menu as shown in Figure 1.16 to open the New GPO dialog box.

4. Let's name our first edict, er, GPO, something descriptive, such as "Hide Screen Saver Option."

5. Once the name is entered, you'll see the new GPO listed in the swimming pool. Right-click the GPO, and choose Edit as shown in Figure 1.17 to open the Group Policy Management Editor.

6. To hide the Screen Saver option, drill down by clicking User Configuration ➢ Policies ➢ Administrative Templates ➢ Control Panel ➢ Display. Double-click the **Hide Screen Saver tab** policy setting to open the Hide Screen Saver Tab Properties screen, as shown in Figure 1.18. Select the Enabled setting, and click OK.

7. Close the Group Policy Management Editor.

Note how the policy setting name is called **Hide Screen Saver Tab**. However, in Windows Vista, there isn't a "tab" as there is in either Windows 2000 or Windows XP. It's more like an option on the Personalization page. You'll see this later. Just note that not all policy settings have a 100 percent direct meaning sometimes, in rare occurrences like this.

FIGURE 1.16 You create your first GPO in the Group Policy Object container by right-clicking and choosing New.

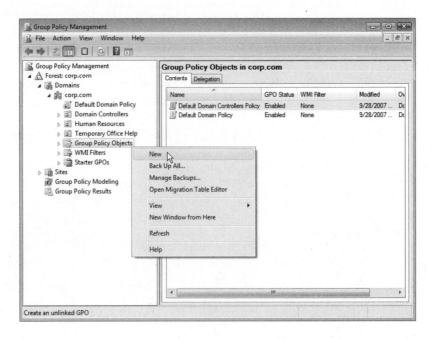

FIGURE 1.17 You can right-click the GPO in the Group Policy Objects container and choose Edit from the shortcut menu to open the Group Policy Management Editor.

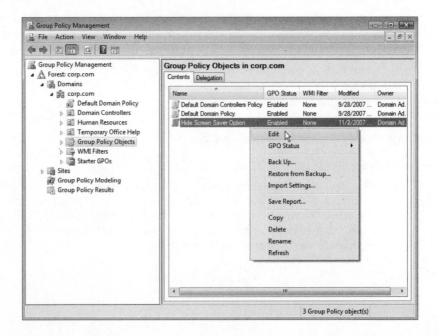

FIGURE 1.18   Double-click the policy setting and "Enable" it.

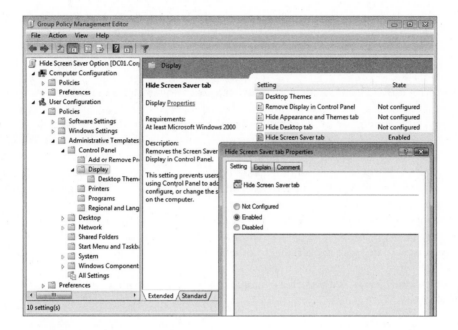

Understanding Our Actions

Now that we have this "Hide Screen Saver Option" edict, er, GPO floating around in the Group Policy Objects container—in the representation of the swimming pool of the domain—what have we done? Not a whole lot, actually, other than create some bits inside Active Directory and upon the Domain Controllers. By creating new GPOs in the Group Policy Objects folder, we haven't inherently forced our desires on *any* level in Active Directory—site, domain, or OU.

To actually make a level in Active Directory accept our will, we need to link this new Group Policy Object to an existing level. Only then will our will be accepted and embraced. Let's do that now.

Applying a Group Policy Object to the Site Level

The least-often-used level of Group Policy application is at the site. This is because it's got the broadest stroke but the bluntest application. And more and more organizations use high-speed links everywhere, so it's not easy to separate computers into individual sites because (in some organizations) Active Directory is set up to see the network as just one big site!

Additionally, since Active Directory states that only members of the Enterprise Administrators (EAs) can modify sites and site links, it's equally true that only EAs (by default) can add and manipulate GPOs at the site level.

When a tree or a forest contains more than one domain, only the EAs and the Domain Administrators (DAs) of the root domain can create and modify sites and site links. When multiple domains exist, DAs in domains other than the root domain cannot create sites or site links (or site-level GPOs).

However, site GPOs might come in handy on an occasion or two. For instance, you might want to set up site-level GPO definitions for network-specific settings, such as Internet Explorer proxy settings or an IP security policy for sensitive locations. Setting up site-based settings is useful if you have one building (set up explicitly as an Active Directory site) that has a particular or unique network configuration. You might choose to modify the Internet Explorer proxy settings if this building has a unique proxy server. Or in the case of IP security, perhaps this facility has particularly sensitive information, such as confidential records or payroll information.

Therefore, if you're not an EA (or a DA of the root domain), it's likely you'll never get to practice this exercise outside the test lab. And, note that in the upcoming chapters I'll show you how to delegate these rights to other administrators, like OU administrators around the bend.

For now, we'll work with a basic example to get the feel of the Group Policy Management Editor.

 Implementing GPOs linked to sites can have a substantial impact on your logon times and WAN (Wide Area Network) traffic if not performed correctly. For more information, see Chapter 6 in the section "Group Policy Objects from a Site Perspective."

We already stood on our desks and loudly declared that there will be no Screen Saver options at our one default site. The good news is that we've already done two-thirds of what we need to do to make that site accept our will: we exposed the sites we want to manage, and we created the "Hide Screen Saver Option" GPO in the Group Policy Objects container.

Now all we need do is to tether the GPO we created to the site with a GPO link.

To remove the Screen Saver option using the Group Policy Management Editor at the site level, follow these steps:

1. Inside the GPMC snap-in, drill down by clicking the Group Policy Management folder, the Forest folder, and the Sites folder.

2. Find the site to which you want to deliver the policy. If you have only one site, it is likely called Default-First-Site-Name.

3. Right-click the site, and choose Link an Existing GPO, as shown in Figure 1.19.

4. Now you can select the "Hide Screen Saver Option" GPO from a list of GPOs in the Group Policy Objects container in the domain.

FIGURE 1.19   Once you have your first GPO designed, you can link it to your site.

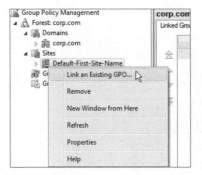

Once you have chosen the GPO, it will be linked to the site. You can also view it in the Linked Group Policy Objects tab in the right pane.

 Did you notice that there was no "Are You Sure You Really Want To Do This?" warning or anything similar? The GPMC trusts that you set up the GPO correctly. If you create GPOs with incorrect settings and/or link them to the wrong level in Active Directory, you can make boo-boos on a grand scale. Again—this is why you want to try any setting you want to deploy in a test lab environment first.

Verifying Your Changes at the Site Level

Now, log onto any workstation or server that falls within the boundaries of the site to which you applied the sitewide GPO. If you didn't change any of the defaults, you should be able to log onto any computer in the domain (say, XPPRO1 or VISTA1) as any user you have defined—even the administrator of the domain.

By right-clicking the Desktop and selecting Personalize (for Vista) or Properties (for Windows XP), you'll see that the Screen Saver option is gone, as shown in Figure 1.20.

 Don't panic if you do not see the changes reflected the first time you log on. See Chapter 4, in the section "Background Refresh Policy Processing," to find out how to encourage changes to appear. To see the Screen Saver tab disappear on Windows XP or Windows Vista machines right now, log off and log back on. The policy should take effect.

This demonstration should prove how powerful Group Policy is, not only because everyone at the site is affected, but more specifically because administrators are not immune to Group Policy effects. Administrators are not immune because they are automatically members in the Authenticated Users security group. (You can modify this behavior with the techniques explored in Chapter 4.)

FIGURE 1.20 The Screen Saver tab in Windows XP (shown on the left) is missing because the site policy is affecting the user. In Vista (shown on the right), the Screen Saver entry on the Personalization page is missing.

Applying Group Policy Objects to the Domain Level

At the domain level, we want an edict that says that the Desktop Settings option in the Windows Vista Personalization page (or Desktop tab in the Display Properties dialog box for Windows XP) should be removed.

Active Directory domains allow only members of the Domain Administrators group the ability to create Group Policy over the domain. Therefore, if you're not a DA (or a member of the EA group), or you don't get delegated the right, it's likely that you'll never get to practice this exercise outside the test lab.

To apply the edict, follow these steps:

1. In the GPMC, drill down by clicking Group Policy Management ➤ Forest ➤ Corp.com.

2. Right-click the domain name to see the available options, as shown in Figure 1.21.

"Create a GPO in this domain, and Link it here…" vs. "Link an Existing GPO"

In the previous example, we forced the site level to embrace our "Hide Screen Saver Option" edict. First, we created the GPO in the Group Policy Objects folder, and then in another step we linked the GPO to the site level. However, at the domain level (and, as you're about to see, the OU level), we can take care of both steps at once via the "Create a GPO in this domain, and Link it here" command. (Note, in previous versions of the GPMC, this was confusingly called "Create And Link A GPO Here." Being a grammar snob, this was a personal wish of mine to have clarified, and I'm happy to see Microsoft agreed and corrected it.)

This command tells the GPMC to create a new GPO in the Group Policy Objects folder and then automatically link the new GPO back to this focused level of Active Directory. This is a time-saving step so we don't have to dive down into the Group Policy Objects folder first and then create the link back to the Active Directory level.

So why is the "Create a GPO in this domain, and Link it here" option possible only at the domain and OU level and not the site level? Because Group Policy Objects linked to sites can often cause excessive bandwidth troubles when the old-school way of doing things is used. With that in mind, the GPMC interface makes sure that when you work with GPOs that affect sites, you're consciously choosing from *which* domain the GPO is being linked.

I'll talk more about this concept and how it's rectified with the GPMC way of doing things at the top in Chapter 4.

FIGURE 1.21   At the domain level, you can create the GPO in the Group Policy Objects container and then immediately link to the GPO from here.

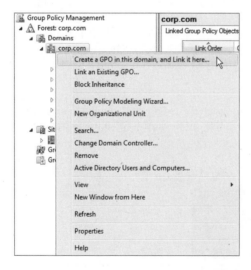

Don't panic when you see all the possible options. We'll hit them all in due time; right now we're interested in the first two: "Create a GPO in this domain, and Link it here" and "Link an Existing GPO."

Since you're focused at the domain level, you are prompted for the name of a new Group Policy Object when you right-click and choose to "Create a GPO in this domain, and Link it here." For this one, type a descriptive name, such as "Hide Desktop Settings Option." Your new "Hide Desktop Settings Option" GPO is created in the Group Policy Objects container and, automatically, a link is created at the domain level from the GPO to the domain.

Take a moment to look in the Group Policy "swimming pool" for your new GPO. Simply drill down through Group Policy Management ➢ Forest ➢ Domains ➢ Corp.com and locate the Group Policy Objects note. Look for the new "Hide Desktop Settings Option" GPO.

Right-click the link to "Hide Desktop Settings Option" (or the GPO itself) and choose Edit to open the Group Policy Management Editor. To hide the Desktop Settings option in the Windows Vista Personalization page (or Desktop tab in the Display Properties dialog box for Windows XP), drill down through User Configuration ➢ Policies ➢ Administrative Templates ➢ Control Panel ➢ Display, and double-click **Hide Desktop Tab**. Change the setting from Not Configured to Enabled, and click OK. Close the Group Policy Management Editor to return to the GPMC.

Verifying Your Changes at the Domain Level

Now, log on as any user in the domain. You can log onto any computer in the domain (say, XPPRO1 or VISTA1) as any user you have defined—even the administrator of the domain.

In Vista, right-click the Desktop and click Personalize. In Windows XP, right-click the Desktop and click Properties.

You'll see that the Desktop Settings option in the Windows Vista Personalization page (or Desktop tab in the Display Properties dialog box for Windows XP) is missing, as in Figure 1.22.

Once again, administrators are not immune to Group Policy effects. You can change this behavior, as you'll see in Chapter 4.

FIGURE 1.22   The Desktop tab is now also missing because the user is affected by the domain-level policy (left). In Vista, the "Desktop Background" entry is gone from the Personalization page (right).

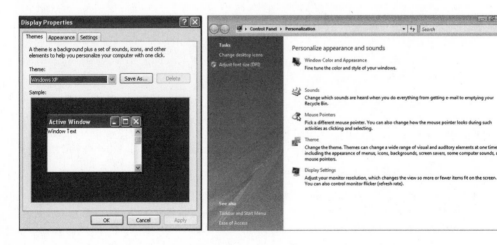

Applying Group Policy Objects to the OU Level

OUs are wonderful tools for delegating away unpleasant administrative duties, such as password resets or modifying group memberships. But that's only half their purpose. The other half is to be able to apply Group Policy.

You'll likely find yourself making most Group Policy additions and changes at the OU level, because that's where you have the most flexibility and the OU is the most refined instrument to affect users. Once OU administrators become comfortable in their surroundings, they want to harness the power of Group Policy.

Preparing to Delegate Control

To create a GPO at the OU level, you must first create the OU and a plan to delegate. For the examples in this book, we'll create three OUs that look like this:

- Human Resources
  - Human Resources Users
  - Human Resources Computers

Having separate OUs for your users and computers is a good idea—for both delegation of rights and also GPO design. Microsoft considers this a best practice. In the **Human Resources Users** OU in our Corp.com domain, we'll create and leverage an Active Directory security group to do our dirty work. We'll name this group HR-OU-Admins and put our first users inside the HR-OU-Admins security group. We'll then delegate the appropriate rights necessary for them to use the power of GPOs.

To create the **Human Resources Users** OU using your VISTAMANAGEMENT machine, follow these steps:

1. Earlier, you created a "unified console" where you housed both Active Directory Users and Computer and the GPMC. Simply use Active Directory Users and Computers, right-click the domain name, and choose New ➢ Organizational Unit, which will allow you to enter in a new OU name. Enter **Human Resources** as the name.

2. Inside the **Human Resources** OU, create two more OUs—**Human Resources Computers** and **Human Resources Users,** as shown in Figure 1.23.

> Alternatively, you can create the OU in the GPMC. Just right-click the domain and choose New Organizational Unit from the shortcut menu.

To create the HR-OU-Admins group, follow these steps:

1. In Active Directory Users and Computers, right-click the new **Human Resources Users** OU and choose New ➢ Group.

2. Create the new group HR-OU-Admins as a new Global Security group.

FIGURE 1.23   When you complete all these steps, your Human Resources OU should have a Human Resources Users OU and Human Resources Computers OU. In the users' side, put Frank Rizzo and the HR-OU-Admins.

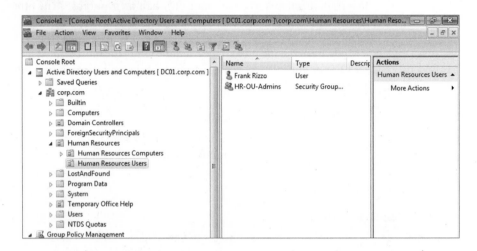

To create the first user to go inside HR-OU-Admins, follow these steps:

1. In Active Directory Users and Computers, right-click the **Human Resources Users** OU and choose New ≻ User.

2. Name the user Frank Rizzo, with an account name of **frizzo,** and click Next.

3. If you've established a Windows 2003 domain, you must now enter a complex password for a user. My suggested password in all my books is p@ssw0rd. That's a lowercase *p*, the at sign, an *s*, an *s*, a double-*U*, a zero, then *r*, and *d*.

4. Finish and close the wizard.

    If you're following along, Frank Rizzo's login will be `frizzo@corp.com`.

Easily Manage New Users and Computers

The Computers folder and Users folder in Active Directory Users and Computers are not OUs. They are generic containers. You'll notice that they are not present in the GPMC view of Active Directory. Because they are generic containers (and not OUs), you cannot link Group Policy Objects to them.

These folders have two purposes:

- If an NT 4 domain is upgraded, the User and Computer accounts will wind up in these folders. (Administrators are then supposed to move the accounts into OUs.)

- The two folders are the default location where older tools drop new accounts in when creating new users and computers. These older tools are in the Windows NT 4 User Manager (which still works in Active Directory domains). Additionally, command-line tools, such as the net user and net group, will add accounts to these two folders. Similarly, the Computers folder is the default location for any new client workstation or server that joins the domain. The same goes when you create computer accounts using the net computer command.

If you execute one of these commands, the objects you create will wind up in either the Users folder or the Computers folder. But really, you don't want your users or computers to be in these folders—you want them in OUs. That's where the action is because you can apply Group Policy to OUs, not to these folders! Yeah, sure, these users and computers are affected by site- and domain-level GPOs. But really the action is at the OU level, and you want your computer and user objects to be placed in OUs as fast as possible—not sitting around in these generic Computers and Users folders.

To that end, domains which are at least at the "Windows 2003 functional level" have two tools to redirect the default location of new users and computers to the OUs of your choice. For example, suppose you want all new computers to go to a **NewComputers** OU and all new users to go to a **NewUsers** OU. And you want to link several GPOs to the **NewUsers** and **NewComputers** OUs to ensure that new accounts immediately have some baseline level of security, restriction, or protection. Without a little magic, new user accounts created using older tools won't automatically be placed there.

In Windows 2003 Active Directory, Microsoft has provided REDIRUSR and REDIRCMP commands that take a distinguished name, like this:

```
REDIRCMP ou=newcomputers,dc=corp,dc=com and/or
REDIRUSR ou=newusers,dc=corp,dc=com
```

Now if you link GPOs to these OUs, your new accounts will get the Group Policy Objects dictating settings to them at an OU level. This will come in handy when users and computers aren't specifically created in their final destination OUs.

To learn more about these tools, see the Microsoft Knowledge Base article 324949 at http://support.microsoft.com/kb/324949.

To add Frank Rizzo to the HR-OU-Admins group, follow these steps:

1. Double-click the HR-OU-Admins group.

2. Click the Members tab.

3. Add Frank Rizzo.

When it's all complete, your OU structure with your first user and group should look like Figure 1.23, shown previously.

Delegating Control for Group Policy Management

You've created the **Human Resources** OU, which contains the **Human Resources Users** OU and the **Human Resources Computers** OU and the HR-OU-Admins security group. Now, put Frank inside the HR-OU-Admins group, you're ready to delegate control.

Performing Your First Delegation

You can delegate control to use Group Policy in two ways: using Active Directory Users and Computers and using the GPMC.

For this first example, we'll kick it old school and do it the Active Directory Users and Computers way. Then, in Chapter 2, I'll demonstrate how to delegate control using the GPMC.

To delegate control for Group Policy management, follow these steps:

1. In Active Directory Users and Computers, right-click the top-level **Human Resources** OU you created and choose Delegate Control from the shortcut menu to start the "Delegation of Control Wizard."

2. Click Next to get past the wizard introduction screen.

3. You'll be asked to select users and/or groups. Click Add, add the HR-OU-Admins group, and click Next to open the "Tasks to Delegate" screen, as shown in Figure 1.24.

4. Click Manage Group Policy Links, and then click Next.

5. At the wizard review screen, click Finish.

FIGURE 1.24   Select the Manage Group Policy Links task.

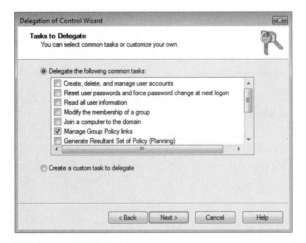

You might want to click some or all the other check boxes as well, but for this example, only Manage Group Policy Links is required. Avoid selecting Generate Resultant Set of Policy (Planning) and Generate Resultant Set of Policy (Logging) at this time. You'll see where they come in handy in Chapter 4.

The Manage Group Policy Links task assigns the user or group Read and Write access over the gPLink and gPOptions properties for that level. To see or modify these permissions by hand, open Active Directory Users and Computers and choose View ➤ Advanced Features. If later you want to remove a delegated permission, it's a little challenging. To locate the permission that you set, right-click the delegated object (such as OU), then click the Properties tab, click the Security tab, choose Advanced, and dig around until you come across the permission you want to remove. Finally, delete the corresponding access control entry (ACE).

Adding a User to the Server Operators Group (Just for This Book)

Under normal conditions, nobody but Domain Administrators, Enterprise Administrators, or Server Operators can walk up to Domain Controllers and log on. For testing purposes only, though, we're going to add our user, Frank, to the Server Operators group so he can easily work on our DC01 Domain Controller.

To add a user to the Server Operators group, follow these steps:

1. In Active Directory Users and Computers, double-click Frank Rizzo's account under the **Human Resources Users** OU.

2. Click the Member Of tab and click Add.

3. Select the Server Operators group and click OK.

4. Click OK to close the Properties dialog box for Frank Rizzo.

Normally, you wouldn't give your delegated OU administrators Server Operators access. You're doing it solely for the sake of this example to allow Frank to log on locally to your Domain Controllers.

Testing Your Delegation of Group Policy Management

At this point, log off as Administrator and log in as Frank Rizzo (frizzo@corp.com).

Now follow these steps to test your delegation:

1. Choose Start and type in **GPMC.MSC** at the Start Search prompt to open the GPMC.

2. Drill down through Group Policy Management, Domains, Corp.com, and Group Policy Objects. If you right-click Group Policy Objects in an attempt to create a new GPO, you'll see the shortcut menu shown in Figure 1.25.

As you can see, Frank is unable to create new GPOs in the swimming pool of the domain. Since Frank has been delegated some control over the **Human Resources** OU (which also contains the other OUs), let's see what he *can* do. If you right-click the **Human Resources** OU in the GPMC, you'll see the shortcut menu shown in Figure 1.26.

FIGURE 1.25   Frank cannot create new GPOs in the Group Policy Objects container.

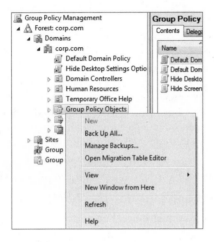

FIGURE 1.26   Frank's delegated rights allow him to link to existing GPOs but not to create new GPOs.

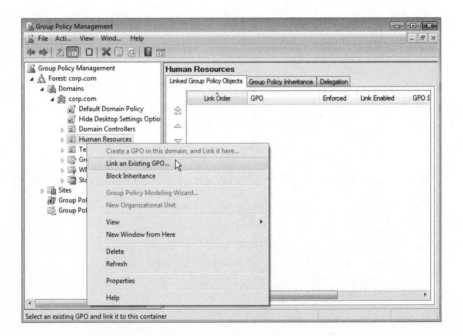

Because Frank is unable to create GPOs in the swimming pool of the domain (the Group Policy Objects container), he is also unable by definition to "Create a GPO in this domain, and Link it here." Although Frank (and more specifically, the HR-OU-Admins) has been delegated the ability to "Manage Group Policy links," he cannot *create* new GPOs. Frank (and the other potential HR-OU-Admins) has only the ability to *link* an existing GPO.

Understanding Group Policy Object Linking Delegation

When we were logged on as the Domain Administrator, we could create GPOs in the Group Policy Objects container, and we could "Create a GPO in this domain, and Link it here" at the domain or OU levels. But Frank cannot.

Here's the idea about delegating the ability to link to GPOs: someone with a lot of brains in the organization does all the work in creating a well-thought-out and well-tested GPO. Maybe this GPO distributes software, maybe it sets up a secure workstation policy, or perhaps it runs a startup script. You get the idea.

Then, others in the organization, like Frank, are delegated just the ability to *link* to that GPO and use it at their level. This solves the problem of delegating perhaps too much control. Certainly some administrators are ready to create their own users and groups, but other administrators may not be quite ready to jump into the cold waters of Group Policy Object creation. Thus, you can design the GPOs for other administrators; they can just link to the ones you (or others) create.

When you (or someone with the right to link GPOs) selects "Link an Existing GPO," as seen in Figure 1.26, you can choose a GPO that's already been created—and hanging out in the domain swimming pool—the Group Policy Objects container.

In this example, the HR-OU-Admins members, such as Frank, can leverage any currently created GPO to affect the users and computers in their OU—even if they didn't create it themselves. In this example, Frank has linked to an existing GPO called "Word 2003 Settings." Turns out that some other administrator in the domain created this GPO, but Frank wants to use it. So, because Frank has Manage Group Policy Links rights on the **Human Resources** OU (and OUs underneath it), he is allowed to link to it.

But, as you can see in Figure 1.27, he cannot edit the GPOs. Under the hood, Active Directory doesn't permit Frank to edit GPOs he didn't create (and therefore doesn't own).

In Chapter 2, I'll show you how to grant specific rights to allow more than just the original creator (and now owner) of the object to edit specific GPOs.

Giving the ability to just link to existing GPOs is a good idea in theory, but often OU administrators are simply given full authority to create their own GPOs (as you'll see later). For this example, don't worry about linking to any GPOs. Simply cancel out of the Select GPO screen, close the GPMC, and log off from the server as Frank Rizzo.

FIGURE 1.27 The GPMC will not allow you to edit an existing GPO if you do not own it (or do not have explicit permission to edit it).

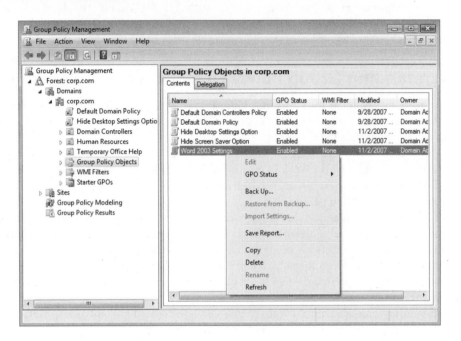

Granting OU Admins Access to Create New Group Policy Objects

By using the Delegation of Control Wizard to delegate the Manage Group Policy Links attribute, you performed half of what is needed to grant the appropriate authority to Frank (and any additional future HR-OU-Admins) to create GPOs in the Group Policy Objects container and link them to the **Human Resources** OU, the **Human Resources Users** OU, or the **Human Resources Computers** OU. (Though we really don't want to link many GPOs directly to the **Human Resources** OU.)

You can grant the HR-OU-Admins the ability to create GPOs in the Group Policy Objects container in two ways. For now, I'll show you the old-school way; in Chapter 2, I'll show you the GPMC way.

One of Active Directory's built-in security groups, Group Policy Creator Owners, holds the key to the other half of our puzzle. You'll need to add those users or groups whom you want to have the ability to create GPOs to a built-in group, cleverly named Group Policy Creator Owners. To do so, follow these steps:

1. Switch-User back to Domain Administrator.

2. Fire up Active Directory Users and Computers.

3. By default, the Group Policy Creator Owners group is located in the Users folder in the domain. Double-click the Group Policy Creator Owners group and add the HR-OU-Admins group and/or Frank Rizzo.

> If you just created a new Windows 2003 domain or upgraded your domain from NT 4, you will not be able to add the HR-OU-Admins group until the domain mode has been switched to Windows 2000 Native or Windows 2003 Functional level. Switch the domain by using Active Directory Domains and Trusts (or Active Directory Users and Computers). Switching the domain mode is a one-way operation, which shuts out older Domain Controllers. If you are not prepared to make the switch to Native mode, you'll only be able to add individual members—such as Frank Rizzo—and not a group.

> In Chapter 2, you'll see an alternate way to allow users to create GPOs.

Creating and Linking Group Policy Objects at the OU Level

At the site level, we hid the Screen Saver option. At the domain level, we chose to get rid of the Desktop Settings option in the Windows Vista Personalization page (or Desktop tab in the Display Properties dialog box for Windows XP). At the OU level, we have two jobs to do:

- Hide the Display Settings option for Windows Vista (or Settings tab in Windows XP).
- Restore the Screen Saver option that was taken away at the site level.

To create a GPO at the OU level, follow these steps:

1. Since you're on VISTAMANAGEMENT, log off as Administrator and log back on as Frank Rizzo (`frizzo@corp.com`)

2. Choose Start and type **GPMC.MSC** in the Start Search prompt.

3. Drill down until you reach the **Human Resources Users** OU, right-click it, and choose "Create a GPO in this domain, and Link it here" from the shortcut menu to open the New GPO dialog box.

4. In the New GPO dialog box, type in the name of your new GPO, say "Hide Display Settings Option/Restore Screen Saver Option." This will create a GPO in the Group Policy Objects container and link it to the **Human Resources Users** OU.

5. Right-click the Group Policy link and choose Edit from the shortcut menu to open the Group Policy Management Editor.

6. To hide the Display Settings option in the Windows Vista Personalization page (or Settings tab in the Display Properties for Windows XP), drill down through User Configuration ➤ Policies ➤ Administrative Templates ➤ Control Panel ➤ Display and double-click the **Hide Settings Tab** policy setting. Change the setting from Not Configured to Enabled, and click OK.

7. To restore the Screen Saver setting for Windows Vista (or Screen Saver tab in Windows XP), double-click the **Hide Screen Saver Tab** policy setting. Change the setting from Not Configured to Disabled, and click OK.

8. Close the Group Policy Management Editor to return to the GPMC.

By disabling the **Hide Screen Saver Tab** policy setting, you're reversing the Enable setting set at a higher level. See the sidebar "The Three Possible Settings: Not Configured, Enabled, and Disabled" later in this chapter.

Verifying Your Changes at the OU Level

On your test Windows XP or Windows Vista machine in the domain (XPPRO1 or VISTA1), log back on as Frank.

On XP, right-click the Desktop and choose Display from the shortcut menu to open the Display Properties dialog box. Note that the Display Settings Option (on Windows Vista) or Settings tab (on Windows XP) is missing but that the Screen Saver option is back, as shown on the left in Figure 1.28.

On Windows Vista, right-click the Desktop and choose Personalize. Note that the Windows Vista behavior is somewhat different this time: the Display Settings field is still available, but clicking on it yields an access error due to Group Policy enforcement. And, because of our edict, note that the Screen Saver entry has returned and is clickable (as seen in the right screen of Figure 1.28).

This test proves, once again, that even OU administrators are not automatically immune from policy settings. Chapter 4 explains how to change this behavior.

Group Policy Strategy: Should I Create More or Fewer GPOs?

At times, you'll want to lock down additional functions for a collection of users or computers. For example, you might want to specify that no users in the **Human Resources Users** OU can use Control Panel.

At the **Human Resources Users** OU level, you've already set up a GPO that contained a policy setting to hide the Display Settings option in the Windows Vista Personalization page (or Settings tab for Windows XP). You now have a decision to make. You can create a new GPO that affects the **Human Resources Users** OU, give it a descriptive name, say "No One Can Use Control Panel," and then drill down through User Configuration ➤ Policies ➤ Administrative Templates ➤ Windows Components ➤ Control Panel and enable the policy setting named **Prohibit Access to Control Panel**.

Or you could simply modify your existing GPO, named "Hide Display Settings Option/Restore Screen Saver Option," so that it contains additional policy settings. You can then rename your GPO to something that makes sense and encompasses the qualities of all the policy changes, say "Our Human Resources Users' Desktop Settings."

Here's the quandary: The former method (one policy setting per GPO) is certainly more descriptive and definitely easier to debug should things go awry. If you have only one policy set inside the GPO, you have a better handle on what each one is affecting. If something goes wrong, you can dive right into the GPO, track down the policy setting, and make the necessary changes, or you can disable the ornery GPO (as discussed later).

The second method (multiple policy settings per GPO) is a teeny-weeny bit faster for your computers and users at boot or logon time because each additional GPO takes some miniscule fraction of additional processing time. But if you stuff too many settings in an individual GPO, the time to debug should things go wrong goes up exponentially. Group Policy has so many nooks and crannies that it can be difficult to debug.

So, in a nutshell, if you have multiple GPOs at a particular level, you can do the following:

- Name each of them more descriptively.

- Debug them easily if things go wrong.

- Disable individually misbehaving GPOs.

- Associate that GPO more easily to a WMI filter (explored in Chapter 5).

- More easily delegate permissions to any specific GPO (explored in Chapter 4).

If you have fewer GPOs at a particular level, the following is the case:

- Logging on is slightly faster for the user (but really only slightly).

- Debugging is somewhat more difficult if things go wrong.

- You can disable individually misbehaving GPOs or links to misbehaving GPOs. (But if they contain many settings, you might be disabling more than you desire.)

So, how do you form a GPO strategy? There is no right or wrong answer; you need to decide what's best for you. Several options, however, can help you decide.

One middle-of-the-road strategy is to start with multiple GPOs and one lone policy setting in each. Once you are comfortable that they are individually working as expected, you can create another new GPO that contains the sum of the settings from, in this example, **Hide Settings Tab** and **Prohibit Access to Control Panel** and then delete (or disable) the old individual GPO.

Another middle-of-the-road strategy is to have a single GPO that contains only the policy settings required to perform a complete "wish." This way, if the wish goes sour, you can easily address it or disable it (or whack it) as needed.

Here's yet another strategy. Some Microsoft documentation recommends that you create GPOs such that they affect only the User half or the Computer half. You can then disable the unused portion of the GPO (either the Computer half or the User half). This allows for policy settings affecting one node to be grouped together for ease of naming and debugging and allows for flexible troubleshooting. However, be careful here because after you disable half the GPO, there's no iconic notification, and, in my opinion, troubleshooting can become harder if not performed perfectly and consistently. In all, I'm not a huge fan of disabling half the GPO.

FIGURE 1.28 On Windows XP, the Settings tab is missing along with the Desktop tab, but the Screen Saver tab has returned (left). The Windows Vista Personalization page is a bit different. It continues to show the Display Settings entry but denies access. And, the Screen Saver entry has return as expected (right).

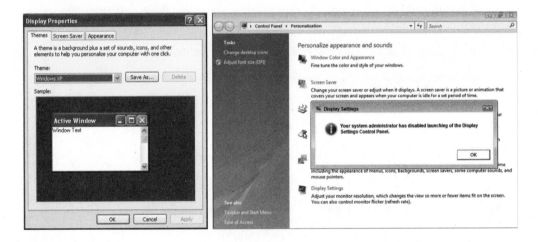

 Note that the policy changes we are making to the Windows Vista clients in the domain also take effect on Windows Server 2008 machines.

Creating a New Group Policy Object for Computers in an OU

For the sake of learning and working through the rest of the examples in this section, you'll create another GPO and link it to the **Human Resources Computers** OU. This GPO will auto-launch a very important application for anyone who uses these machines: calc.exe.

 The setting we're about to play with also exists under the User node, but we'll experiment with the Computer node policy.

First, you'll need to create the new GPO and modify the settings. You'll then need to move some client machines into the **Human Resources Computers** OU in order to see your changes take effect.

To auto-launch `calc.exe` for anyone logging into a computer in the **Human Resources Computers** OU, follow these steps:

1. If you're not already logged in as Frank Rizzo, the **Human Resources** OU administrator, do so now on VISTAMANAGEMENT.

2. Choose Start and type **GPMC.MSC** in the Start Search prompt.

3. Drill down until you reach the **Human Resources Computers** OU, right-click it, and choose "Create a GPO in this domain, and Link it here" from the shortcut menu.

4. Name the GPO something descriptive, such as "Auto-Launch calc.exe."

5. Right-click the GPO, and choose Edit to open the Group Policy Management Editor.

6. We want to affect our client computers (not users), so we need to use the Computers node. To auto-launch `calc.exe`, drill down through Computer Configuration ➢ Policies ➢ Administrative Templates ➢ System ➢ Logon, and double-click **Run these programs at user logon**. Change the setting from Not Configured to Enabled.

7. Click the Show button, and the Show Contents dialog appears. Click Add and in the "Add item" dialog, enter the full path to calc.exe as `c:\windows\system32\calc.exe` then click OK as shown in Figure 1.29. Click OK to close the Show Contents dialog, and click OK again to close the "Run these programs at user logon" policy setting.

8. Close the Group Policy Management Editor to return the GPMC.

Be aware of occasional strange Microsoft verbiage when you need to enable a policy to *disable* a setting. Since Windows 2003, most policy settings have been renamed to "Prohibit *<whatever>*" to reflect the change from confusion to clarity.

Moving Computers into the Human Resources Computers OU

Since you just created a policy that will affect computers, you'll need to place a workstation or two inside the **Human Resources Computers** OU to see the results of your labor. You'll need to be logged on as Administrator to DC01 to do this.

Quite often computers and users are relegated to separate OUs. That way, certain GPOs can be applied to certain computers but not others. For instance, isolating laptops, desktops, and servers is a common practice.

In this example, we're going to use the Find command in Active Directory Users and Computers to find a workstation named XPPRO1 and the Windows Vista workstation named VISTA1 and move it into the **Human Resources Computers** OU.

FIGURE 1.29 When this policy setting is enabled and calc.exe is specified, all computers in this OU will launch calc.exe when a user logs in.

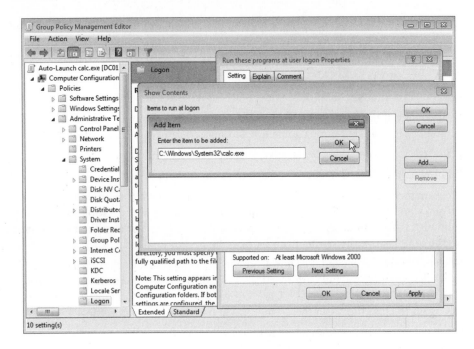

To find and move computers into a specific OU, follow these steps:

1. In Active Directory Users and Computers, right-click the domain, and choose Find from the shortcut menu to open the Find Users, Contacts, and Groups dialog box.

2. From the Find drop-down menu, select Computers. In the Name field, type **VISTA1** to find the computer account of the same name. Once you've found it, right-click the account and choose Move from the shortcut menu, as shown in Figure 1.30. Move the account to the **Human Resources Computers** OU.

   Repeat these steps for XPPRO1 and all other computers that you want to move to the **Human Resources Computers** OU.

3. Now that you've moved VISTA1 (and maybe also XPPRO1) into the new OU, be sure to reboot those client computers.

After you move the computer accounts into the **Human Resources Computers** OU, it's very important to reboot your client machines. As you'll see in Chapter 4, the computer does not recognize the change right away when computer accounts are moved between OUs.

As you can see in this example (and in the real world), a best practice is to separate users and computers into their own OUs and then link GPOs to those OUs. Indeed, underneath a parent OU structure, such as the **Human Resources** OU, you might have more OUs (that is, **Human Resources Laptops** OU, **Human Resources Servers** OU, and so on). This will give you the most flexibility in design between delegating control where it's needed and the balance of GPO design within OUs. Just remember that for GPOs to affect either a user or computer, that user or computer must be within the scope of the GPO—site, domain, or OU.

FIGURE 1.30   Use the Find command to find computers in the domain, then right-click on the entry and select Move to move them.

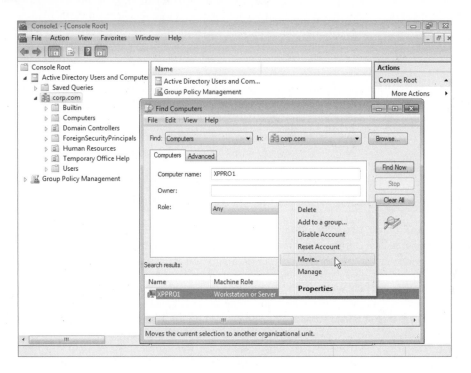

Verifying Your Cumulative Changes

At this point, you've set up three levels of Group Policy that accomplish multiple actions:

- At the site level, the "Hide Screen Saver Option" GPO is in force for users.

- At the domain level, the "Hide Desktop Settings Option" GPO is in force for users.

- In the **Human Resources Users** OU, the "Hide Display Settings Option/Restore Screen Saver Option" GPO is in force for users.

- In the **Human Resources Computers** OU, the "Auto-Launch calc.exe" GPO is in force for computers.

At this point, take a minute to flip back to Figure 1.13 (the swimming pool illustration) to see where we're going here. To see the accumulation of your policy settings inside your GPOs, you'll need to log on as a user who is affected by the **Human Resources Users** OU and at a computer that is affected by the **Human Resources Computers** OU. Therefore, log on as Frank Rizzo on XPPRO1.

If you're using Windows XP, right-click the Desktop and choose Display from the shortcut menu to open the Display Properties dialog box. Note that the Settings tab is still missing from the previous exercise (and the Screen Saver tab is restored). You should also see Windows Calculator jumping at you as soon as you log on (because your computer GPO told it to).

If you're using Windows Vista, right-click the Desktop and choose Personalize. Note that the Desktop Settings option is still missing from the previous exercise (and the Screen Saver entry is restored). And, when you logged in, did the computer GPO auto-launch Windows Calculator?

These tests prove that even OU administrators are not automatically immune from GPOs and the policy settings within. Under the hood, they are in the Authenticated Users security group. See Chapter 4 for information on how to modify this behavior.

The Three Possible Settings: Not Configured, Enabled, and Disabled

As you saw in Figure 1.18 earlier in this chapter, nearly all administrative template policy settings can be set as Not Configured, Enabled, or Disabled. These three settings have very different consequences, so it's important to understand how each works.

Not Configured   The best way to think about Not Configured is to imagine that it really says, "Don't do anything" or even "Pass through." Why is this? Because if a policy setting is set to Not Configured, then it honors any previously set setting (or, the operating system default).

Enabled   When a specific policy setting is enabled, the policy will take effect. In the case of the **Hide Screen Saver Tab** policy setting, the effect is obvious. However, lots of policy settings, once enabled, have myriad possibilities *inside* the specific policy setting! (For a gander at one such policy setting, use the Group Policy Management Editor and drill down to User Configuration ➤ Policies ➤ Administrative Templates ➤ Windows Components ➤ Internet Explorer ➤ Toolbars and select the policy setting named **Configure Toolbar Buttons**.) So, as we can see, Enabled really means "Turn this policy setting on." Either it will then do what it says or there will be more options inside the policy setting that can be configured.

Disabled   This setting leads a threefold life.

- Disabled usually means that if the same policy setting is enabled at a higher level, reverse its operation. For example, we chose to enable the **Hide Screen Saver Tab** policy setting at the site level. If at a lower level (say, the domain or OU level), we chose to disable this policy setting, the Screen Saver tab will pop back at the level at which we disabled this policy.

- Additionally, Disabled often forces the user to accept the administrator's will. That is, if a policy setting is disabled, some default behavior of the policy setting is enforced and the user cannot change it. To see an example policy setting like this, use the Group Policy Management Editor and drill down through User Configuration ➢ Policies ➢ Administrative Templates ➢ Control Panel and select the policy setting named **Force classic Control Panel Style**. Once this policy setting is disabled, the policy forces Windows XP users to use the Control Panel in the new task-based style. The point here is that the Disabled setting is a bit tricky to work with. You'll want to be sure that when you disable a policy setting, you're doing precisely what you intend.

- Disabled sometimes has a special and, typically, rare use. That is, something might already be hard-coded into the Registry to be "turned on" or work one way, and the only way to turn it off is to select Disabled. One such policy setting is the **Shutdown Event Tracker**. You disable the policy setting, which turns it off, because on Windows 2003 and Windows Server 2008 it's already hard-coded on. In Windows XP and Windows Vista, it's already hard-coded off. Likewise, if you want to kill Windows XP/SP2's or Windows Vista's firewall, you need to set **Windows Firewall: Protect All Network Connections** to Disabled. (You can find that policy setting at Computer Configuration ➢ Policies ➢ Administrative Templates ➢ Network ➢ Network Connections ➢ Windows Firewall ➢ Domain Profile (and also Standard Profile) while editing GPOs on Windows XP/Service Pack 2 and above.)

So, think of Not Configured as having neither Allow nor Deny being set. Enabled will turn it on and possibly have more functions. Disabled has multiple uses, and be sure to test, test, test to make sure that once you've manipulated a policy setting, it's doing precisely what you had in mind.

Final Thoughts

The concepts here are valid regardless of what your domain is running. It doesn't matter if you have a pure or mixed Active Directory domain with Windows 2000, Windows 2003, or Windows Server 2008 Domain Controllers. The point is that to make the best use of Group Policy, you'll need an Active Directory.

You'll also need a Vista management station to do the work. Again, we talk more about why you need a Windows Vista management station in Chapters 3, 7, and 10.

I know it's a little confusing to hear that the GPMC is built into Windows Vista only to be taken away with Windows Vista + SP1. But don't worry; you can grab it again from Microsoft within the RSAT tools in a jiffy.

The more you use and implement GPOs in your environment, the better you'll become at their basic use while at the same time avoiding pitfalls when it comes to using them. The following tips are scattered throughout the chapter but are repeated and emphasized here for quick reference, to help you along your Group Policy journey:

GPOs don't "live" at the site, domain, or OU level. GPOs "live" in Active Directory and are represented in the swimming pool of the domain called the Group Policy Objects container. To use a GPO, you need to link a GPO to a level in Active Directory that you want to affect: a site, a domain, or an OU.

GPOs apply to Active Directory sites, domains, and OUs.   Active Directory is a hierarchy, and Group Policy takes advantage of that hierarchy. There is one local GPO that can be set, which affects everyone who uses that machine. Then, Active Directory Group Policy Objects apply: site, domain, and then OU. Active Directory GPOs "trump" any local policy settings if set within the Local Group Policy.

Avoid using the site level to implement GPOs.   Users can roam from site to site by jumping on different computers (or plugging their laptop into another site). When they do, they can be confused by the settings changing around them. Use GPOs linked to the site only to set up special sitewide security settings, such as IPsec or the Internet Explorer Proxy. Use the domain or OU levels when creating GPOs whenever possible.

Implement common settings high in the hierarchy when possible.   The higher up in the hierarchy GPOs are implemented, the more users they affect. You want common settings to be set once, affecting everyone, instead of having to create additional GPOs performing the same functions at other lower levels, which will just clutter your view of Active Directory with the multiple copies of the same policy setting.

Implement unique settings low in the hierarchy.   If a specific collection of users is unique, try to round them up into an OU and then apply Group Policy to them. This is much better than applying the settings high in the hierarchy and using Group Policy filtering later.

Use more GPOs at any level to make things easier.   When creating a new wish, isolate it by creating a new GPO. This will enable easy revocation by unlinking it should something go awry.

Strike a balance between having too many and too few GPOs.   There is a middle ground between having one policy setting within a single GPO and having a bajillion policy settings contained within a single GPO. At the end of your design, the goal is to have meaningfully named GPOs that reflect the "wish" you want to accomplish. If you should choose to end that wish, you can easily disable or delete it.

As you go on your Group Policy journey...   Don't go at it alone. There are some nice third-party independent resources to help you on your way. I run www.GPanswers.com, which has oodles of resources, downloads, a community forum, downloadable eChapters, video tutorials, links to third-party software, and my in-person hands-on training seminars. Think of it as your secret Group Policy resource.

My pal (and technical editor for the previous edition) Darren Mar-Elia runs www.GPOguy.com.

My pal (and technical editor for this edition of the book) Jakob Heidelberg has a lot of great articles (mostly on Group Policy topics) at http://www.windowsecurity.com/Jakob_H_Heidelberg (http://tinyurl.com/ypar82).

There's also Microsoft's independent Group Policy Wiki at http://grouppolicy.editme.com/. All of these locations are here to help you get more advanced with Group Policy as you progress.

2

Managing Group Policy with the GPMC

In the last chapter, you got to know how and when Group Policy works. We used Active Directory Users and Computers to create and manage users and computers, but we used the GPMC to manage Group Policy. We got a little workout with the GPMC when creating new GPOs and linking them to various levels in Active Directory.

And, for just a moment, we went back to the old-school way to delegate control to Frank and the HR-OU-Admins group to link existing GPOs to their **Human Resources** OU structure.

In this chapter, I'll cover the remainder of the daily tasks you can perform using the GPMC. As a reminder, the GPMC is for all implementations of Active Directory. That is, you can use the GPMC to manage your Active Directory—whatever the Domain Controllers are that constitute it.

- You just need the GPMC loaded up on some machine. Now, in the previous chapter, I put a pretty fine point on it: you want this machine to be a Windows Vista machine or a Windows Server 2008 machine. Here's the breakdown of the GPMC editions:

  - GPMC 1.0: A download that you installed on Windows XP or Windows Server 2003.

  - GPMC 1.5: Built into the shipping version of Windows Vista. Automatically removed when Windows Vista's SP1 is installed.

  - GPMC 2.0: Built into Windows Server 2008 and also a download that can be installed on Windows Vista + SP1.

So, ideally, your management station shouldn't just be any ol' Windows Vista machine, but rather one with Windows Vista + SP1 and the newly downloadable GPMC 2.0.

In short, if you don't use a Windows Vista machine (or Windows Server 2008 machine) as your management station, you won't have access to all the latest awesome power. In this chapter, you're going to be working, again with your VISTAMANAGEMENT machine where you've already loaded the updated GPMC.

In Chapters 3 and 7, I delve into deep detail about why you want to ensure that your management station is a Windows Vista machine.

I'll tackle most of the core remaining features the GPMC has to offer in this chapter. But in the next chapter, I'll go into some of the newest features that are only available with the GPMC 2.0. (Again, the GPMC 2.0 ships with Windows Server 2008 and can be downloaded for Windows Vista + SP1.) And, of course, if we don't cover something in this chapter or the next, we'll be sure to tackle the remaining GPMC features in other chapters as the occasion arises.

 One of those remaining features is the ability to migrate GPOs between domains. For additional information, see the appendix.

With that in mind, let's get to know the GPMC a bit better.

If you're not already logged into your VISTAMANAGMENT machine, go ahead and do so now. Again, Vista out of the box has the GPMC loaded, but if you've got Vista + SP1 installed, you'll need to download the GPMC 2.0 from www.Microsoft.com/grouppolicy. Be sure to get the link that specifies that the download is valid for Windows Vista.

Once it's ready to go, just click Start, and in the Start Search box, type **GPMC.MSC**.

Common Procedures with the GPMC

In the last chapter, we created and linked some GPOs, which we can see in the Group Policy Objects container, to see how, at each level, we were affecting our users. In this section, we'll continue by working with some of the more advanced options for applying, manipulating, and using Group Policy.

Clicking a GPO itself (or a link) lets you get more information about what they do. For now, feel free to click around, but I suggest that you don't change anything until we get to the specific examples.

Various tabs are available to you once you click the GPO itself or a link. For instance, let's locate the GPO that's linked to the **Human Resources Users** OU. We'll do this by drilling down to Group Policy Management ➤ Forest ➤ Domains ➤ corp.com ➤ Human Resources ➤ Human Resources Users and clicking the one GPO that's linked there: "Hide Display Settings Option/Restore Screen Saver Option." With that in mind, let's examine each of the tabs you can flip through to get more information about the GPO you just found.

The Scope Tab   Clicking a GPO or a GPO link opens the Scope tab. The Scope tab gives you an at-a-glance view of where and when the GPO will apply. We'll examine the Scope tab in the sections "Deleting and Unlinking Group Policy Objects" and "Filtering the Scope of Group Policy Objects with Security" in this chapter, and "GPO Targeting with WMI Filters" in Chapter 5. For now, you can see that the "Hide Display Settings Option/Restore Screen Saver Option" GPO is linked to the **Human Resources Users** OU. But you already knew that.

The Details Tab   The Details tab contains information describing who created the GPO (the owner) and the status (Enabled, Disabled, or Partially Disabled) as well as some nuts-and-bolts information about its underlying representation in Active Directory (the GUID). We'll examine the Details tab in the sections "Disabling 'Half' (or Both Halves) of the Group Policy Object" and "Understanding GPMC's Link Warning" in this chapter.

Should you change the GPO status here by, say, disabling the User Configuration of the policy, you'll be affecting all other levels in Active Directory that might be using this GPO by linking to it. See the section "Understanding GPMC's Link Warning" as well as the sidebar "On GPO Links and GPOs Themselves" a bit later in the chapter.

The Settings Tab   The Settings tab gives you an at-a-glance view of what's been set inside the GPO. In our example, you can see the Enabled and Disabled status of the two policy settings we manipulated. You can click Hide (or Show) to contract and expand all the configured policy settings.

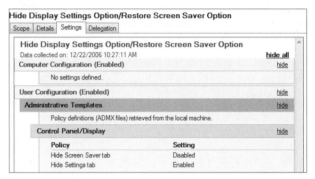

- Clicking Hide at any level tightens that level. You can expose more information by clicking the inverse of Hide when available, which is Show.

- Clicking the actual policy setting name, for example, **Hide Settings Tab,** displays the help text for the policy setting (but note that this is only applicable to Administrative Template settings). This can be useful if someone set up a GPO with a kooky name and you want to know what's going on inside that GPO.

- If you want to change a setting, you can right-click the settings area and select Edit. The familiar Group Policy Management Editor will appear. Note, however, that the Group Policy Management Editor will not "snap to" the policy setting you want to edit. The editor always starts off at the root.

- Additionally, at any time, you can right-click over this report and select Save Report, which does just that. It creates an HTML or XML report that you can then email to fellow administrators or the boss, and so on. This is a super way of documenting your Group Policy environment instead of writing down everything by hand.

I've said it before, but it bears repeating: you can also edit the settings by clicking the GPO or any GPO link for that object and choosing Edit. However, you *always* affect all containers (sites, domains, or OUs) to which the GPO is linked. It's one and the same object, regardless of the way you edit it. See the sidebar "On GPO Links and GPOs Themselves" a bit later in the chapter to get the gist of this.

If you chose to run the GPMC on a Windows 2003 or Windows Server 2008 machine, you may run into an initial problem when clicking the Settings tab. That is, certain aspects of the GPMC, such as the Settings tab, tap into Internet Explorer. Since Internet Explorer is hardened on Windows 2003 and Windows 2008 machines, you will have limited access to the whole picture. If you're presented with a warning box, simply add security_mmc.exe as a trusted website. This should make your problems go away. You can also turn off Internet Explorer Enhanced Security Configuration in Windows 2003 in Add/ Remove Programs. In Windows Server 2008, use Server Manager, and on the main screen within the "Security Configuration" section, click Configure IE ESC, where you'll be able to enable or disable. This is recommended in test labs but not really recommended on production servers.

The Delegation Tab The Delegation tab lets you set the security for who can do what with GPOs, their links, and their properties. You'll find the Delegation tab in a lot of places, such as when you do the following:

- Click a GPO link or click a GPO in the Group Policy Objects container
- Click a site
- Click a domain
- Click an OU
- Click the WMI Filters node
- Click a WMI filter itself
- Click on the Starter GPOs section (We'll talk about this in the next chapter.)

At each of these locations, the tab allows you to do something different. I'll discuss what each instance of this tab does a bit later in the section "Advanced Security and Delegation with the GPMC."

WMI, which stands for Windows Management Instrumentation, is discussed in Chapter 6.

Kickin' It Old-School: Filtering 1.0 with the Original GPMC

Imagine you were just given the task of preventing all your users from accessing the Control Panel. Where do you start to look for that policy setting?

The direct answer to that question is the GPMC 2.0, which ships with Windows Server 2008 and is an available download once your machine is Windows Vista + SP1 (this is discussed further in the next chapter).

You really should be using one of those two operating systems as your management station because you get so much more. Indeed, we're going to go into all of what you get in Chapter 3 and Chapter 7.

However, if you're still stuck using the GPMC 1.0 for some reason (the one that's downloadable for Windows Server 2003 or Windows XP) or the GPMC 1.5 (which is the in-the-box version that shipped with Windows Vista), then you might still need to know how to do something similar to what we're going to do in Chapter 3. That is, you'll need to know how to find policy settings and limit just how many darned settings you're looking at at any given time.

Again, ideally, you won't need the information in this section; that's because you're hopefully going to use a Windows Server 2008 or Windows Vista + SP1 + GPMC 2.0 management station. But, again, in case you're not able to, let's explore what your options are.

It can be a daunting place. Sometimes, you just don't know where to start clicking inside the Group Policy Object Editor (or, what's now known as the Group Policy Management Editor). You could be in the editor for a variety of reasons. Perhaps you want to locate a new policy setting to enable. With more than 1,800 possible settings in Windows 2003, 1,200 in Windows XP/Service Pack 2, and 2,400 in Windows Vista (and still a few more for Windows Server 2008), finding the specific policy setting you want can sometimes be a challenge.

To that end, the older GPMC 1.0's and GPMC 1.5's Group Policy Object Editor has a way to filter the view. The good news is that this feature has some usefulness. But the bad news is that this feature works only while you're browsing the Administrative Templates branch.

While you're in the Group Policy Object Editor, choose either User Configuration ➤ Administrative Templates or Computer Configuration ➤ Administrative Templates to examine the filtering option. Then, choose View ➤ Filtering to display the window shown here, which is described in the following sections.

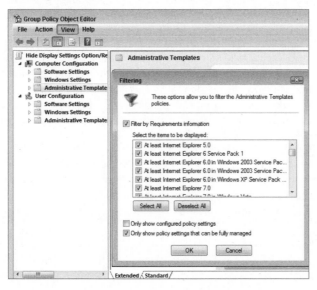

The Filter settings are independent on each of the User and Computer nodes. Additionally, should you close the Group Policy Object Editor and come back into it, those filters are not preserved.

Filtering doesn't specifically help you "find" a GPO, per se. For instance, you can't find policy settings based on names and Explain text, at least not in the GPMC 1.0 or GPMC 1.5. As you'll learn in Chapter 3, when you upgrade to the GPMC 2.0, you will be able to do a true search.

The "Only show configured policy settings" Setting   If you want to modify a policy setting that has something configured, you needn't click every branch in one of the Administrative Templates folders to hunt-and-peck. Once the "Only show configured policy settings" option, as seen in the above screen shot, is selected, you will see only policy settings that have been enabled or disabled within either User Configuration ➢ Administrative Templates or Computer Configuration ➢ Administrative Templates.

By default, the "Only show configured policy settings" check box is not checked, and therefore you can see policy settings that are enabled, disabled, and not configured. The "Only show configured policy settings" check box is independent for both the Computer and User node settings. Additionally, when you close the editor, the check box is always reset.

Policy Setting Filtering Based on Operating System and Service Pack   As you learned in the introduction, policy settings are specific to the operating system. For instance, a Windows XP policy setting such as **Turn off creation of System Restore Checkpoints** makes no sense to a Windows 2000 machine. This is because Windows 2000 doesn't have the System Restore feature. There are times when you want to search for policy settings specific to the computers you want to target. Simply click the "Filter by Requirements information" check box as seen in the above screen shot, and then proceed to check the items on which you want to filter.
You have a huge variety of criteria to choose from, including operating system, service pack, and even unique items such as Internet Explorer level and Windows Media Player.
Here's a quick tip: if the description of the filter is too long to read, simply hover the mouse pointer over the description (don't click) to display the entire description in a floating ToolTip-style window.

Using the "Only show policy settings that can be fully managed" Option   As we'll explore in Chapter 7, there's a difference between true policies and preferences. Here's the deal: some settings are "bad" because they don't modify the "correct" portion of the Registry. In general, this is highly undesirable because in this way they won't act like Group Policy. That is, these settings usually permanently "tattoo" the target machine until the settings are explicitly removed.
For more on the distinction between policies and preferences with respect to Group Policy settings, see the section "Policies vs. Preferences" in Chapter 7.

This check box is checked by default, as seen in the screen shot above.This gives a gentle persuasion to avoid the importation of old-school preferences instead of true policies.
You can choose to ensure that this check box is permanently checked by using the **Enforce Show Policies Only** policy setting as described Chapter 4, in the section "Using Group Policy to Affect Group Policy."
Again, all these GPMC 1.0 and GPMC 1.5 filter goodies are replaced with a true filtering and search mechanism in the GPMC 2.0. So, if you haven't upgraded to the GPMC 2.0, you might want to consider it right away. And that's what the next chapter is all about!

Locating Specific Policy Settings

I get tons of emails that ask the following question: "Jeremy, do you know if there's a policy setting that does <insert crazy thing here>?" My typical answer is, "I don't know. I'll have to look it up." Then I do. That's because there are more than 2,400 policy settings, each contained within some nook or cranny.

To that end, you can (hopefully) hunt down your own policy setting that does what you want in several ways.

GP.CHM   GP.CHM is part of the Windows 2000 Resource Kit. It's a CHM file, which means it's a compiled HTML file, and that basically means it's a help file like other help files. The good news is that it mirrors the hierarchy of the Windows 2000 Group Policy Object Editor. That is, it has both User and Computer nodes and then all the levels of Group Policy nooks and crannies underneath in a beautiful hierarchical manner. Best of all, you can search within the text file for the policy setting's help text and get what you want. The bad news is that it's getting kind of old. Many policy settings have been renamed since Windows 2000, but GP.CHM is still useful.

hh <*admtemplate*>.chm (not for Windows Vista or Windows Server 2008)   This one is most easily explained if you just go ahead and try it. Open a command prompt on your Windows 2003 machine and type **hh system.chm** or **hh inetres.chm** or **hh <*name_of_any_other_adm_template*>.chm** and out pops a searchable help file with the stuff contained within the corresponding ADM file. Keen!

hh SPOLSCONCEPTS.CHM (not for Windows Vista or Windows Server 2008)   This CHM file is built into Windows XP and Windows 2003 Server. To open it, choose Start ➤ Run to open the Run dialog box and enter **hh spolsconcepts.chm** in the Open box. You'll then see another help file that discusses only the security-related settings, such as the meaning of each of the User Rights Assignments, what each of the Audit Policies is, and all the Security Options. This is truly a nice built-in resource.

PolicySettings.XLS and VistaGPSettings.XLS   If you want a definitive list of all Administrative Template policy settings that can affect Windows 2000 and Windows 2003 Server, XP, and Vista machines, you can download a spreadsheet from Microsoft from my website at www.GPanswers.com. Note, however, that Microsoft's spreadsheet doesn't go into much detail beyond the Explain Text setting for each policy setting. But they're all there and searchable, and you can sort by which operating systems will embrace which policy settings. It's quite good. Also, if you've got an older version, you should note that these are always updated whenever a service pack comes out. And, starting with Windows XP/SP2, they've started to document some of the Security settings as well. And the Windows Vista version tries to express when a specific policy setting requires a logoff or a reboot. Nice touch! So, even though the GPMC 2.0 (which comes built in to Windows Server 2008 or as an add-on download for Windows Vista + SP1) has killer Find and Filter features, the spreadsheet still has some superpowers that are not available in the interface.

Raising or Lowering the Precedence of Multiple Group Policy Objects

You already know that the "flow" of Group Policy is inherited from the site level, the domain level, and then from each nested OU level. But, additionally, *within* each level, say at the **Temporary Office Help** OU, multiple GPOs are processed in a ranking precedence order. Lower-ranking GPOs are processed first, and then the higher GPOs are processed.

In Figure 2.1, you can see that some administrator has linked two GPOs to the **Temporary Office Help** OU. One GPO is named "Enforce 50MB Disk Quotas," and another is named "Enforce 40MB Disk Quotas."

FIGURE 2.1   You can link multiple GPOs at the same level.

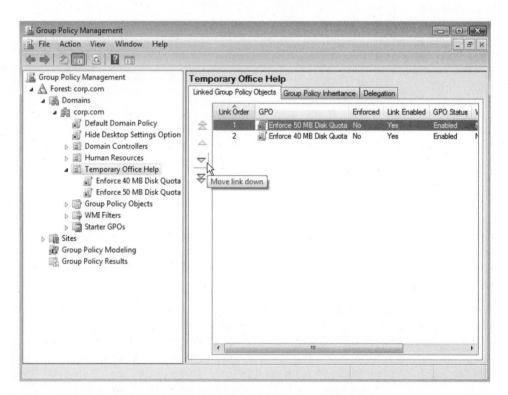

If the policy settings inside these GPOs both adjust the disk quota settings, which one will "win"? Client computers will process these two GPOs from lowest-link order to highest-link order. Therefore, the "Enforce 40MB Disk Quotas" GPO (with link order 2) is processed before "Enforce 50MB Disk Quotas" (link order 1). Hence, the GPO with the policy settings to dictate 50MB disk quotas will win.

So, if two (or more) GPOs within the same level contain values for the same policy setting (or policy settings), the GPOs will be processed from lowest-link order to highest-link order.

Each consecutively processed GPO overlays (and perhaps overwrites) overlapping policy settings. This could happen where one GPO has a specific policy setting enabled and another GPO at the same level has the same policy setting disabled.

Changing the order of the processing of multiple GPOs at a specific level is an easy task. For instance, suppose you want to change the order of the processing such that the "Enforce 40MB Disk Quotas" GPO is processed after the "Enforce 50MB Disk Quotas" GPO. Simply click the policy setting you want to process last and click the down arrow icon. Similarly, if you have additional GPOs that you want to process first, click the GPO and click the up arrow icon. The multiple arrow icons will put the highlighted GPO either first or last in the link order—depending on the icon you click.

Again—the last applied GPO wins. So the GPO with a link order of 1 is always applied last and, hence, has the final say at that level. This is always true unless the Enforced flag is used (as discussed later).

Understanding GPMC's Link Warning

In the previous chapter, I pointed out that anytime you click a GPO link, you get the informational (or perhaps it's more of a warning) message shown in Figure 2.2.

FIGURE 2.2   You get this message anytime you click the icon for a link.

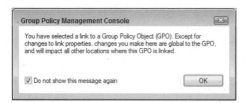

This message is trying to convey an important sentiment: no man is an island, and neither is a Group Policy Object. Just because you created a GPO and it is seen swimming in the Group Policy Objects container doesn't mean you're the only one who is possibly using it.

As we work through examples in this chapter, we'll manipulate various characteristics of GPOs and links to GPOs. If we manipulate any characteristics of a GPO we're about to play with, such as the following, then all other levels in Active Directory that also link to this GPO will be affected by our changes:

- The underlying policy settings themselves
- The security filtering (on the Scope tab)
- The WMI filtering (on the Scope tab)
- The GPO status (on the Details tab)
- The delegation (on the Delegation tab)

For instance, imagine you had a GPO linked to an OU called **Doctors** and the same GPO linked to an OU called **Nurses**. If you edit the GPO, or click on the link to the GPO and click

Edit, you're doing the same thing. Any changes made within the GPO affect both the **Doctors** OU and the **Nurses** OU.

This is sometimes a tough concept to remember, so it's good to see it here again. You can choose to squelch the tip if you like. Just don't forget its advice.

 The difference between the GPO itself and the links you can create can be confusing. Be sure to check out the sidebar "On GPO Links and GPOs Themselves" a bit later in the chapter.

Here's another way to see this principle in action by locating the "Auto-Launch calc.exe" GPO. In either the link upon the **Human Resources Computers** OU or the object itself with "GPOs," go to the Details tab and change the GPO status to some other setting. Then, go to the link or the actual GPO and see that your changes are reflected. You can even create a new OU, link the GPO, and see that the change is still there. This is because you're manipulating the actual GPO, not the link. If you choose to squelch the message, you can get it back by choosing View ➤ Options ➤ General and selecting "Show confirmation dialog to distinguish between GPOs and GPO links."

Stopping Group Policy Objects from Applying

After you create your hierarchy of Group Policy that applies to your users and computers, you might occasionally want to temporarily halt the processing of a GPO—usually because some user is complaining that something is wrong. You can prevent a specific GPO from processing at a level in Active Directory via several methods, as explained in the following sections.

Preventing Local GPOs from Applying

Before we get too far down the path with Active Directory–based GPOs, let's not forget that you might also want to stop a local GPO from applying. For instance, you might have walked up to 50 Sales computers and created a local GPO that prevents access to the Control Panel. However, now you want to reverse that edict. Instead of walking around to those 50 computers, you can just zap a Group Policy to those computers to inhibit the processing of local GPOs. Here's the trick though: This technique only works for Windows Vista (or Windows Server 2008 if you happen to have any local GPOs on your servers)—not for earlier versions of the operating system.

To do this trick, you'll use the policy setting found at Computer Configuration ➤ Administrative Templates ➤ System ➤ Group Policy, and it's called **Turn off Local Group Policy objects processing**. Just remember to ensure that your computers are in the OU where this GPO is targeted to take effect.

Disabling the "Link Enabled" Status

Remember that all GPOs are contained in the Group Policy Objects container. To use them at a level in Active Directory (site, domain, or OU), you link back to the GPO. So, the quickest way to prevent a GPO's contents from applying is to remove its "Link Enabled" status. If you right-click a GPO link at a level, you can immediately see its "Link Enabled" status, as shown in Figure 2.3.

FIGURE 2.3   You can choose to enable or disable a GPO link.

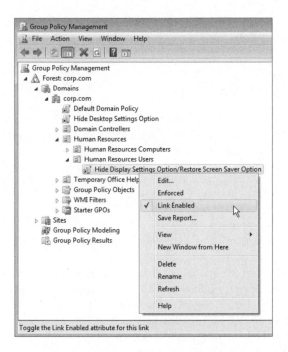

To prevent this GPO from applying to the **Human Resources Users** OU, simply click Link Enabled to remove the check mark. This will leave the link within the OU back to the GPO but disable the link, rendering it innocuous. The icon to the left of the name of the GPO will change to a scroll with the link arrow dimmed. You'll see a zoomed-in picture of this later in the section "GPMC At-a-Glance Icon View."

Disabling "Half" (or Both Halves) of the Group Policy Object

The second way to disable a specific GPO is by disabling just *one-half* of a Group Policy Object. You can disable either the User half or the Computer half. Or, you can optionally disable the entire GPO.

You might be wondering why you would want to disable only half of a GPO. On the one hand, disabling a GPO (or half of a GPO) actually makes startup and logon times a teeny-weeny bit faster for the computer or user, because each GPO you add to the system adds a smidgen of extra processing—either for the user or the computer. Once you disable the unused portion of the GPO, you've shaved that processing time off the startup or logon time. Microsoft calls this "modifying Group Policy for performance."

Don't go bananas disabling your unused half of GPO just to save a few cycles of processing time. Trust me, it's just not worth the headaches figuring out later where you did and did not disable a half of a policy.

Disabling half of the GPO makes troubleshooting and usage quite a bit harder, as you might just plumb forget you've disabled half the GPO. Then, down the road, when you modify the disabled half of the policy for some future setting, it won't take effect on your clients! You'll end up pulling your hair out wondering why once things *should* change, they just don't!

Why Totally Disable a Group Policy Object?

One good reason to disable a specific GPO is if you want to manually "join" several GPOs together into one larger GPO. Then, once you're comfortable with the reaction, you can re-create the policy settings from multiple GPOs into another new GPO and disable the old individual GPOs. If there are signs of trouble with the new policy, you can always just disable (or delete) the large GPO and reenable the individual GPOs to get right back to where you started.

You might also want to immediately disable a new GPO even before you start to edit it. Imagine that you've chosen "Create and link a new GPO here" for, say, an OU. Then, imagine you have lots of policy settings you want to make in this new GPO. Remember that each setting is immediately written inside the Group Policy Management Editor, and computers are continually requesting changes when their Background Refresh interval triggers. The affected users or computers might hit their Background Refresh cycle and start accepting the changes before you've finished writing all your changes to the GPO! Therefore, if you disable the GPO before you edit and re-enable the GPO after you edit, you can ensure that your users are getting all the newly changed settings at once.

This tip works best only when creating new GPOs; if you disable the GPO *after* creation, there's an equally likely chance that critical settings will be removed while the GPO is disabled when clients request a Background Refresh. We'll discuss the ins and outs of Background Refresh in Chapter 4.

To disable an unused half of a GPO, follow these steps:

1. Select the GPO you want to modify. In this case, select "Auto-Launch calc.exe" and select the Details tab in the right pane of the GPMC.

2. Since the policy settings within the "Auto-Launch calc.exe" GPO modify only the Computer node, it is safe to disable the User node. Select the "User configuration settings disabled" drop-down box, as shown in Figure 2.4.

3. You will be prompted to confirm the status change. Choose to do so.

Here are some additional items to remember regarding disabling portions of a GPO:

- It is possible to disable the entire GPO (both halves) by selecting the GPO, clicking the Options button, and selecting the All Settings Disabled option. If you select All Settings Disabled, the scroll icon next to the name of the GPO "dims" a bit to show that there is no way it can affect any targets. You'll see a zoomed-in picture of this later in the section "GPMC At-a-Glance Icon View."

FIGURE 2.4 You can disable half the GPO to make Group Policy process a weeee bit faster.

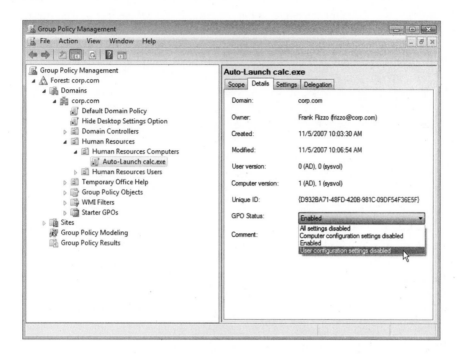

- As I stated in the section "Understanding GPMCs Link Warning," changing the GPO Status entry (found on the Details tab) will affect the GPO—everywhere it is linked—at any level, anywhere in Active Directory! You cannot just change the GPO status for the instance of this link—this affects all links to this GPO! The only good news here is that only the person who created the GPO itself (or anyone who has permissions to it) can manipulate this setting. To get the full thrust of this, be sure to read the sidebar "On GPO Links and GPOs Themselves" a bit later in this chapter.

- The GPMC does not have any indication, other than this GPO status, that the link has been fully or half disabled. However, the old-school "Active Directory Users and Computers" interface in Windows 2003 will alert you to a GPO that is half disabled. You'll see a yellow triangle warning icon next to the name of the GPO.

Deleting and Unlinking Group Policy Objects

As you just saw, you can prevent a GPO from processing at a level by merely removing its "Link Enabled" status. However, you can also choose to remove the link entirely. For instance, you might want to return the normal behavior of the computers such that `calc.exe` isn't launched whenever someone uses that machine. You have two options:

- Delete the link to the GPO
- Delete the GPO itself

Deleting the Link to the Group Policy Object

When you right-click the GPO link of "Auto-Launch calc.exe" in the **Human Resources Computers** OU, you can choose Delete. When you do, the GPMC will confirm your request and remind you of an important fact, as shown in Figure 2.5.

FIGURE 2.5   You can delete a link (as opposed to deleting the GPO itself).

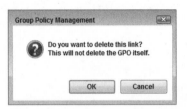

Recall that the GPO itself doesn't "live" at a level in Active Directory; it really lives in a special container in Active Directory (and can be seen via the Group Policy Objects container in the GPMC). We're just working with a link to the real GPO. And, in Chapter 6, you'll see where this folder relates directly within Active Directory itself.

When you choose to delete a GPO link, you are simply choosing to stop using it at the level at which it was created but keeping the GPO itself alive in the representation of the swimming pool—the Group Policy Objects container. This leaves other administrators at other levels to continue to link to that GPO if they want.

Truly Deleting the Group Policy Object Itself

You can choose to delete the GPO altogether—lock, stock, and barrel. The only way to delete the GPO itself is to drill down through Group Policy Management ➢ Domains ➢ Corp.com, locate the Group Policy Objects container, and delete the GPO. It's like plucking a child directly from the swimming pool. Before you do, you'll get a warning message as shown in Figure 2.6.

FIGURE 2.6   Here, you're actually deleting the GPO itself.

This will actually remove the bits on the Domain Controller and obliterate it from the system. No other administrators can then link to this GPO.

Once it's gone, it's gone (unless you have a backup).

If you delete the GPO altogether, there's only one problem. There is no indication sent to the folks who are linking to this GPO that you've just deleted it. You might be done with the "Auto-Launch calc.exe" GPO and don't need it anymore to link to *your* locations in Active

Directory, but what about other administrators? In this case, while I was out to lunch, Freddie, the administrator for the **Temporary Office Help** OU, has already chosen to link the "Auto-Launch calc.exe" GPO to his OU, as shown in Figure 2.7.

What if I had deleted the "Auto-Launch calc.exe" GPO? I'm pretty sure I would have received an angry phone call from Freddie. Or, maybe not—if Freddie didn't know who created (and owned) the GPO.

FIGURE 2.7   The "Auto-Launch calc.exe" GPO (lowest circle) is linked at both the Temporary Office Help OU (middle circle) and this Human Resources Computers OU (topmost circle).

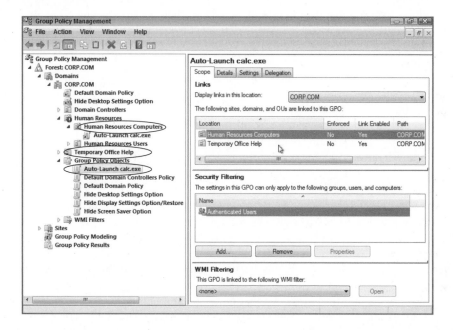

Since we only have a handful of OUs, this link back to the GPO was easy to find. However, once you start getting lots of OUs, locating additional links back to a GPO will become much harder. Thankfully, the GPMC shows you if anyone else is linked to a GPO you're about to delete. I call this ability "look before you leap." You can just look in the Scope tab under the Links heading as indicated in Figure 2.8 by the mouse pointer. There you can see that both the **Temporary Office Help** OU and the **Human Resources Computers** OU are utilizing the GPO named "Auto-Launch calc.exe."

If you're confident that you can still continue, you can delete the GPO contained within the Group Policy Objects container. However, for now, let's leave this GPO in place for use in future examples in the book.

The Scope tab shows you the links to the GPOs from your own domain. It is possible for other domains to leverage your GPOs and link to them. When you delete a GPO forever, you're deleting the ability for other domains to use that GPO as well. Note that there is a drop-down in the

Scope tab labeled "Display links in this location." If you want, you can show "Entire Forest." That way, if a GPO is being leveraged by doing a no-no like Cross Domain Linking, you can see if this GPO is linked to other areas you might not have intended it to be.

For now, don't delete the GPO. We'll use it again in later chapters. If you want to play with deleting a GPO, create a new one and delete it.

Block Inheritance

As you've already seen, the normal course of Group Policy inheritance applies all policy settings within GPOs in a cumulative fashion from the site to the domain and then to each nested OU. A setting at any level automatically affects all levels beneath it. But perhaps this is not always the behavior you want. For instance, we know that an edict from the Domain Administrator states there will be no Desktop Settings option in the Windows Vista Personalization page (or Desktop tab in the Display Properties dialog box for Windows XP).

This edict is fine for most of the OU administrators and their subjects who are affected. But Frank Rizzo, the administrator for the **Human Resources** OU structure, believes that the folks contained within his little fiefdom can handle the responsibility of the Desktop Settings option for Windows Vista (or Desktop tab for Windows XP) and the Screen Saver option, and he wants to bring them back to his users. (But he's not ready to give back the Display Settings option in the Windows Vista Personalization page or Settings tab for Windows XP.)

In this case, Frank Rizzo can prevent GPOs (and the policy settings within them) defined at higher levels (domain and site) from affecting his users, as shown in Figure 2.8. If Frank chooses to select Block Inheritance, Frank is choosing to block the flow of *all* GPOs (with all their policy settings) from *all* higher levels.

When Frank does this, the **Human Resources** OU icon changes to include a blue exclamation point (!) as seen in Figure 2.8. Once the check is present and the GPOs are reprocessed on the client, only those settings that Frank dictates within his **Human Resources** OU structure will be applied.

If you want to see the effect of Block Inheritance, ensure that the check is seen as shown in Figure 2.8. Then, log on as any user affected by the **Human Resources** OU—say, Frank Rizzo. You'll notice that the Desktop Settings option in the Windows Vista Personalization page (or Desktop tab in Windows XP) has reappeared. But you'll also notice that the Display Settings option in the Windows Vista Personalization page (or Settings tab in Windows XP) is still absent because that edict is contained within a GPO that's explicitly defined at the **Human Resources Users** OU level, which contains Frank's user account.

The Enforced Function

Frank Rizzo and his Human Resources folks are happy that the Screen Saver and Desktop Settings options in Vista (or Screen Saver and Desktop tabs for Windows XP) have made a triumphant return. There's only one problem: The Domain Administrator has found out about this transgression and wants to ensure that the Desktop Settings option in Vista (or Desktop tab in Windows XP) is permanently revoked.

FIGURE 2.8 Use the Block Inheritance feature to prevent all GPOs (and the policy settings within them) from all higher levels from affecting your users and computers.

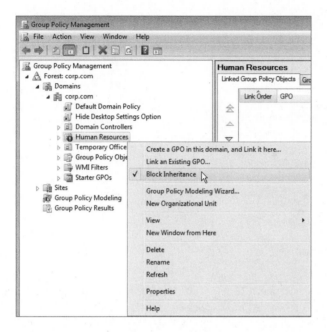

The normal flow of inheritance is site, domain, and then OU. Super. If you've set a Block Inheritance on an OU (say, the **Human Resources** OU), then *all* settings to that OU are null and void.

But, shouldn't there be some power to allow "bigger" administrators to get their wills enforced? Enforced! Heck, what a great term. I should patent that. To trump a lower level's Block Inheritance, a higher-level administrator will use the Enforced function.

Enforced was previously known as No Override in old-school parlance.

The idea behind the Enforced function is simple: It guarantees that policies and settings within a specific GPO at a higher level are always inherited by lower levels. It doesn't matter if the lower administrator has blocked inheritance or has a GPO that tries to disable or modify the same policy setting or settings.

In this example, you'll log on as the Domain Administrator and set an edict to force the removal of the Desktop Settings option in the Windows Vista Personalization page (or Desktop tab in the Display Properties dialog box for Windows XP).

To use Enforced to force the settings within a specific Group Policy Object setting, right-click the "Hide Desktop Settings Option" GPO link and select Enforced, as shown in Figure 2.9.

FIGURE 2.9   Use the Enforced option to guarantee that settings contained within a specific GPO affect all users downward via inheritance.

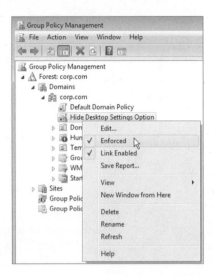

Notice that the GPO link now has a little "lock" icon, demonstrating that it cannot be trumped. You can see this in the "Hide Desktop Settings Option" GPO link icon in Figure 2.9. You'll see a zoomed-in picture of this later in the "GPMC At-a-Glance Icon View" section.

To test your Enforced edict, log on as a user affected by the **Human Resources** OU—Frank Rizzo. In the Display Properties dialog box, the Desktop Settings option in the Windows Vista Personalization page (or Desktop tab in Windows XP) should be absent because it is being forced from the Enforced edict at the domain level even though Block Inheritance is used at the OU level.

On GPO Links and GPOs Themselves

The GPMC is a cool tool, but, in my opinion, it actually shows you a bit *too* much. Sometimes, it can be confusing what can be performed on the GPO's link and what can be performed on the GPO itself. Remember that GPOs themselves are displayed in the GPMC via the Group Policy Objects container. The links back to them are shown at the site, domain, and OU levels. So here's a list of what you can "do" to a GPO link and what you can "do" to a GPO *itself*.

You can only do three things on a GPO link that applies to a site, a domain, or an OU:

- Link Enable (that is, enable or disable the settings to apply at this level).

- Enforce the link (and force the policy settings).

- Delete the link.

Everything else is always done on the *actual* GPO itself:

- Change the policy settings inside the GPO (found on the Settings tab).

- Apply security filters, rights (such as the "Apply Group Policy" privilege), and delegation (such as the "Edit this GPO" privilege) discussed in the section "Advanced Security and Delegation with the GPMC."

- Enable/disable the Computer and/or User half of the GPO via the GPO status (found on the Details tab).

- Place a WMI filter upon the GPO (discussed in Chapter 5).

If this seems clear as mud, consider this scenario:

- Fred and Ginger are the two Domain Administrators. By definition, they can create GPOs.

- Imagine that Fred designs the "Desktop Settings" GPO, which contains policy settings that affect both users and computers. Perhaps one user policy setting is **Remove Run off Start Menu**. Perhaps one computer policy setting is **Enforce disk quota limit**. And Fred sets the quota limit to 50MB.

- Fred links the "Desktop Settings" GPO to the **Dancers** OU as well as the **Audition Halls** OU.

- Ginger gets a phone call from the folks in the **Audition Halls** OU. The users in the **Audition Halls** OU report that the 50MB disk quotas are too restrictive. "Can they just turn off the computer-side settings for us Audition Halls folks?" one of them cries.

- Ginger goes to the "Desktop Settings" GPO link (which is linked to the **Audition Halls** OU), clicks the Details tab, and disables the computer settings using the "GPO Status" setting drop-down box.

- Fred then gets a phone call that the **Dancers** OU no longer has disk quotas being applied.

Why did this happen?

Because the Group Policy engine has certain controls on the GPO *itself* and has other controls on the Group Policy *link*. Because Fred and Ginger are both Domain Administrators, they jointly have ownership of the ability to change the GPO and the GPO link.

Whenever Ginger modifies any characteristic in the previous bulleted list, she's changing it "globally" for any place in Active Directory that might be using it. That's what the warning in Figure 2.2, earlier in this chapter, is all about.

If you'll allow me to get on my soap box for the next 10 seconds, the level of finite control over what Ginger can and cannot do to the GPO itself is fairly limited. In the future, I'd love to see the Group Policy engine extended so that we can delegate more aspects of control about the GPO link, not just about the GPO itself.

In any event, delegating what we can control over the GPO itself is precisely what the next section is about, specifically the "Granting User Permissions on an Existing Group Policy Object" section.

Advanced Security and Delegation with the GPMC

Mere mortals' access to Group Policy can be and, indeed, should be controlled. Users' access to all things Group Policy related is judged in many forms. However, the first question you'll want to answer and understand well is basic: To whom should Group Policy be applied, and to whom should it not be applied?

Once we can answer that, we can move on to some more advanced topics:

- What kind of access can I grant to mere mortals to manipulate the GPO itself? That is, can a user read or modify the GPO's settings or security?

- How can I grant a mere mortal access to create GPOs in the domain?

- Can a user perform special Group Policy–related stuff, such as the creation and management of WMI filters or access to RSoP tools?

- Who can create Starter GPOs? (We'll tackle this in the next chapter.)

You can answer all these questions by determining what security is placed on certain Active Directory locations and also on specific GPOs. Let's tackle these questions one at a time to locate all the places users' access touches our Group Policy infrastructure and where that access can be managed.

Filtering the Scope of Group Policy Objects with Security

The normal day-to-day Human Resources workers inside the **Human Resources** OU structure are fine with the facts of life:

- The Enterprise Administrator says that no one at the site will have the Screen Saver option.

- The Domain Administrator says that no one will have the Desktop Settings option in the Windows Vista Personalization page (or Desktop tab in the Display Properties dialog box for Windows XP). He is forcing this edict with the Enforced option.

- Frank Rizzo, the **Human Resources** OU Manager, says that for the **Human Resources Users** OU, he will remove the Display Settings tab but restore the Screen Saver option. For the **Human Resources Computers** OU, he'll want to make sure that calc.exe launches whenever someone uses a Human Resources computer.

- Additionally, at the top-level **Human Resources** OU, he will enable the Block Inheritance setting to give back the Screen Saver option removed by the Enterprise Administrator at the site level. But Frank is forced to live with the fact that he won't be able to return the Desktop Settings option in the Windows Vista Personalization page (or Desktop tab in the Display Properties dialog box for Windows XP) to his people. The Domain Administrator has taken this away and that's that.

But Frank and other members of the HR-OU-Admins security group are getting frustrated that they cannot access the Display Settings tab. And they're also getting a little annoyed that every time they use an Human Resources machine, calc.exe pops up to greet them.

Sure, it was Frank's own idea to make these two policy settings—one that affects the users he's in charge of and one that affects the computers he's in charge of. The problem is, however, it also affects Frank (and the other members of the HR-OU-Admins team) when they're working, and you can see where that can be annoying.

Frank needs a way to filter the *Scope of Management (SOM)* of the "Hide Display Settings Option/Restore Screen Saver Option" GPO as well as the "Auto-Launch calc.exe" GPO. By scope or SOM, I mean how far and wide the GPOs we set up will be embraced.

 Occasionally you will see references to SOM in your travels with Group Policy. An SOM is simply a quick-and-dirty way to express where and when a GPO might apply. An SOM can be nearly any combination of things: linking a GPO to the domain, linking a GPO to an OU, and linking a GPO to a site. However, if you start to filter GPOs within the domain, that's also an SOM. In essence, an SOM indicates when and where a GPO applies to a level in Active Directory.

In our case, the idea is twofold:

- Frank and his team are excluded from the "Hide Display Settings Option/Restore Screen Saver Option" GPO edict.

- The specific computers that Frank and his team use are excluded from the "Auto-Launch calc.exe" GPO edict.

Recall from Chapter 1 that, despite the wording of the term *Group Policy*, Group Policy does not directly affect security groups. You cannot just wrap up a bunch of similar users or computers in a security group and thrust a GPO upon them. There's nowhere to "link" to. You need to round up the individual user or computer accounts into an OU first and then link the desired GPO on that OU.

Here's the truly strange part: Even though you can't round up users in security groups and apply GPOs to them, it's the security group that we'll leverage (in most cases) in order to enable us to filter Group Policy application!

In order for users to get GPOs to apply to them, they need two under-the-hood access rights to the GPO itself:

- Read
- Apply Group Policy (known, in shorthand, as the AGP rights)

These permissions must be set on the GPO in question. By default, all Authenticated Users are granted the Read and Apply Group Policy rights to all new GPOs. Therefore, anyone who has a GPO geared for them will process it.

The following two things might not be immediately obvious:

- Administrators are not magically exempt from embracing Group Policy; they, too, are members of "Authenticated Users." You can change this behavior with the techniques described in the very next section.

- Computers need love, too. And for computers to apply their side of the GPO, they need the same rights: Read and Apply Group Policy. Since computers are technically Authenticated Users, the computer has all it needs to process GPOs meant for it.

With this fundamental concept in mind, let's look at several ways to filter who gets specific GPOs.

If you want to filter GPOs for either specific users or specific computers, you have three distinct approaches. For our three examples (which will all do the exact same thing), we want the "Hide Display Settings Option/Restore Screen Saver Option" GPO to "pass over" our heroes in the HR-OU-Admins security group but to apply to everyone else who should get them. We also want the "Auto-Launch calc.exe" GPO to pass over the specific computers our heroes use at their desks.

How Is a Computer an Authenticated User?

I was shocked to learn that a computer falls under the category of an Authenticated User. It's true: the computer account has the Authenticated User's SID in its access token. I was skeptical, but über-guru Bill Boswell proved it to me. And you can prove it to yourself by following these steps on a Windows XP machine (they won't work on Windows Vista):

1. Use the at command and specify a time at least one minute ahead of the current time to open a system-level console:

    at *<one minute in the future>* /interactive cmd

2. Use WHOAMI to verify that the cmd has run as System. Now use WHOAMI /ALL to verify that you have the Authenticated Users group in the access token.

Note that the System does not have domain credentials. When it touches another machine, it uses the Kerberos ticket issued to the local computer. You can take advantage of this for this experiment.

1. Set the NTFS permissions on a folder in a shared volume on another machine to deny access to Authenticated Users but allow access by Everyone.

2. Map a drive from the system console to the share point and try to access the contents of the protected folder. You'll be denied access.

Because Deny for Authenticated Users comes before Allow for Everyone, you've proved that the computer account has the Authenticated Users group in its access token.

Group Policy Object Filtering Approach #1: Leverage the Security Filtering Section of the Scope Tab in GPMC

In the first approach, you'll round up only the users, computers, or security groups who should get the GPO applied to them. To make things easier, let's first create two Active Directory security groups—one for our users who will get the GPO and one for computers who will get the GPO. Good names might be

People-Who-Get-the-Hide-DisplaySettingsOption-GPO

and

Computers-That-Get-the-Auto-Launch calc.exe-GPO.

Go ahead and do this in Active Directory Users and Computers as seen in Figure 2.10.

Next, add all user accounts that you want to embrace the GPO into the first security group.

You would then add all computer accounts that you want to get the GPO into the security group named Computers-That-Get-the-Auto-Launch calc.exe-GPO.

FIGURE 2.10   Create a new Active Directory security group to which you want the GPO to apply. Create security groups for both users and computers based on the GPO you want to filter.

Because we don't want these GPOs to apply to Frank or Frank's computer (XPPRO1 or VISTA1), don't add Frank to the first group (which contains users) and don't add XPPRO1 or VISTA1 to the second group (which contains computers).

Next, click the link to the "Hide Display Settings Option/Restore Screen Saver Option" GPO found in Group Policy Management ➢ Forest ➢ Domains ➢ Corp.com ➢ **Human Resources** OU ➢ **Human Resources Users** OU. In the Security Filtering section, you can see that Authenticated Users is listed. This means that any users inside the **Human Resources Users** OU will certainly get this GPO applied.

However, now we're about to turn the tables. We're going to click the Remove button to remove the Authenticated Users in the Security Filtering section; then we're going to add the People-Who-Get-the-Hide-DisplaySettingsOption-and-Restore-GPO security group, as shown in Figure 2.11.

Next, click the "Auto-Launch calc.exe" GPO link (which is under the **Human Resources Computers** OU). In the Security Filtering section of the Scope tab, you'll remove Authenticated Users and add the Computers-That-Get-the-Auto-Launch calc.exe-GPO security group.

In both cases, what we're really doing under the hood is giving these new security groups the ability to Read and Apply Group Policy. You'll see this under-the-hood stuff in a minute.

FIGURE 2.11 When you remove Authenticated Users, no one will get the effects of the GPO. Add only the users or groups you want the GPO to affect.

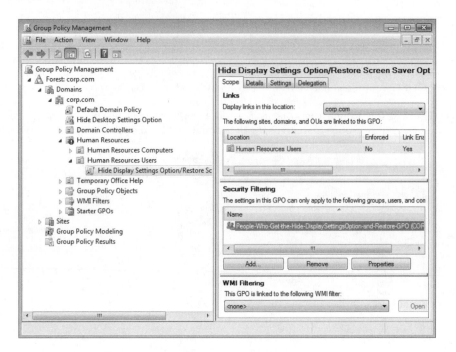

Testing Your First Filters

To see if this is working, log on XPPRO1 or VISTA1 as Frank (frizzo). Even though the GPO applies to the **Human Resources Users** OU, the GPO will pass over him and anyone else not explicitly put into that security group since Frank is not a member of the People-Who-Get-the-Hide-DisplaySettingsOption-GPO security group.

For another test, add a new user account or two to the **Human Resources Users** OU (via Active Directory Users and Computers). Then, log on as one of these new users (in the OU) and verify that they, indeed, do not get the GPO. This is because the GPO is only set to apply to members of the security group. Then, add the user to the security group and log on again. The GPO will then apply to your test users (inside the security group) as well. In fact, you can add users to the security group by simply clicking the Properties button in the Security Filtering section. Doing so opens the Security Group Membership dialog, in which you can add or delete users or computers.

Repeat your tests by adding XPPRO1or VISTA1 into the security group named Computers-That-Get-the-Auto-Launch calc.exe-GPO. When the computer is in the group, it will apply the GPO. Now, try removing XPPRO1 or VISTA1 and see what happens. When the computer is out of the group, the GPO will pass over the computer.

 You will have to reboot the machine to immediately see computer-side results.

What's Going on under the Hood for Filtering

As I implied, when you add security groups to get the GPOs in the Security Filtering section, you're really doing a bit of magic under the hood. Again, that magic is simply granting two security permissions: Read and Apply Group Policy to the users or security groups upon the GPOs linked to the OU.

To see which security permissions are really set under the hood for a particular GPO (or GPO link, because it's the same information), click the Delegation tab and select the Advanced button as shown in Figure 2.12.

FIGURE 2.12   Selecting Advanced in the Delegation tab for the GPO (or GPO link) shows the under-the-hood security settings for the GPO.

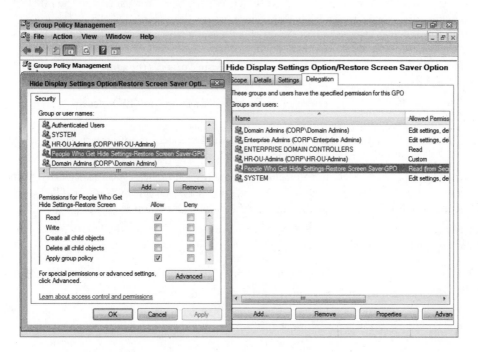

When you do, you can see the actual permission on the GPO itself. You can easily locate the security group named People-Who-Get-the-Hide-DisplaySettingsOption-GPO and see that they have both the Read and Apply Group Policy access rights set to Allow. This is why they will process this GPO.

Filtering Approach #2: Identify Whom You Do Not Want to Get the Policy

The other approach is to leave the default definition in for the GPO such that the Authenticated Users group is granted the Read and Apply Group Policy. Then, figure out who you *do not* want to have the policy applied to, and use the Deny attribute over the Apply Group Policy right.

When Windows security is evaluated, the designated users or computers will not be able to process the GPO due to the Deny attribute; hence, the GPO passes over them.

NOTE See the sidebar "Positive or Negative?" later in this chapter before doing this in your real environment.

For our examples, we want the "Hide Display Settings Option/Restore Screen Saver Option" GPO to pass over our heroes in the HR-OU-Admins security group but to apply to everyone else by default. We also want the "Auto-Launch calc.exe" GPO to pass over the specific computers our heroes use at their desks.

To use this second technique, we'll use the Deny permission to ensure that the HR-OU-Admins security group cannot apply (and hence process) the "Hide Display Settings Option/Restore Screen Saver Option" GPO. We'll also prevent Frank's computer, XPPRO1 or VISTA1, from processing the "Auto-Launch calc.exe" GPO.

Again, you'll do this on the GPO (or the GPO link, because it's the same information); click the Delegation tab, and then click the Advanced button. Follow these steps:

1. Locate the People-Who-Get-the-Hide-DisplaySettingsOption-GPO security group and remove it.

2. Locate the Authenticated Users group, select the Read permission, select Allow, select Apply Group Policy permission, and select Allow.

3. If you used Frank's account to originally create this GPO, he is specifically listed in the security list. You want to remove Frank and add the HR-OU-Admins group. Click Frank, and then click Remove. Click Add, and add the HR-OU-Admins group.

4. Make sure the Apply Group Policy check box is set to Deny for the HR-OU-Admins group, as shown in Figure 2.13.

FIGURE 2.13   Use the Deny bit on the Apply Group Policy right to prevent Group Policy from applying.

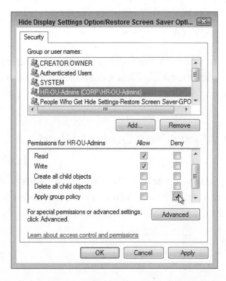

Do not set the Deny check box for the Read or Write attributes from the HR-OU-Admins (the group you're currently a member of when logged in as Frank). If you do, you'll essentially lock yourself out, and you'll have to ask the Domain Administrator to grant you access again.

1. Click OK to close the Group Policy Settings dialog box. In the warning box that tells you to be careful about Deny permissions, click Yes.

2. Click OK to close the OU Properties dialog box.

To test your first filter again, log onto XPPRO1 or VISTA1 as Frank Rizzo. Note that the Settings tab has returned to him because he is part of the HR-OU-Admins group. The "Hide Display Settings Option/Restore Screen Saver Option" GPO has passed over him because he is unable to process the GPO.

To bypass the "Auto-Launch calc.exe" GPO on XPPRO1 or VISTA1, you'll perform a similar operation. That is, you'll modify the security on the GPO to pass over the computers our heroes use by denying those specific computer accounts the ability to Apply Group Policy. You can then test your second filter by logging on as anyone to XPPRO1 or VISTA1. You should then see that calc will not launch when a user uses that machine.

Turns out, however, there's a major problem in using the aforementioned method. That is, if you performed the previous exercise and used the Deny attribute to pass over the HR-OU-Admins group using the Security on the GPO, you've got a small problem. Sure, it worked! That's the good news. The bad news is that GPMC isn't smart enough to interpret quite what you did back on the Scope tab in the Security Filtering section shown in Figure 2.14.

FIGURE 2.14 The Security Filtering section on the Scope tab will not show you any use of Deny bits under the hood.

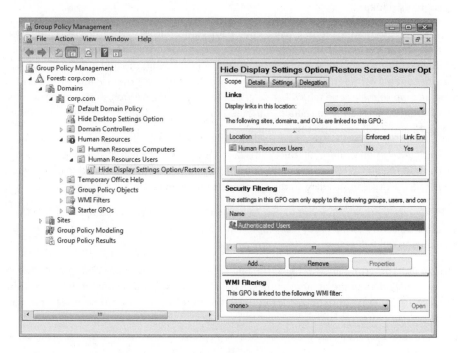

Yes, it's technically true what the Security Filtering section says: Authenticated Users will apply this GPO. However, it doesn't tell us the other important fact: that the HR-OU-Admins group *will not* process this GPO because they were denied the ability to Apply Group Policy (AGP).

The only way to get the full, true story of who will actually get the GPO applied to them is to look back within the GPO (or GPO link, because it's the same information), select the Delegation tab, and click the Advanced button to see who has Read and Apply Group Policy; then also see who is denied access to process the GPO via the Deny attributes.

 With the GPMC 2.0 (see next chapter), you can leave a comment inside the GPO for others to read regarding who has been specifically denied AGP access. The only problem is someone might not read it.

The moral of the story? Always consult the Advanced tab to get the whole truth as to the security on the GPO.

Positive or Negative?

Now that you can see the two ways to filter users from processing GPOs, which should you use? Approach 1 (adding only those you want to get the GPO) or Approach 2 (denying only those you don't want to get the GPO)? The data reflected within the GPMC's Scope tab clearly wants you to take the first approach. However, many Active Directory implementations I know take the second approach (and, in fact, it was my advice to do so in the first several editions of this book).

Now, you and your team need to make a choice for your approach. As you saw, when you create new GPOs, you can choose to filter via the Scope tab or the Advanced Delegation. So which do you choose? If you're going to be religious about using the first approach, you can then be reasonably confident that only the users, groups, and computers listed in the Security Filtering section of the Scope tab will, in fact, be the only users, groups, and computers who will get the GPO. You can then reduce your need to dive into the Security Editor as seen in Figures 2.12 and 2.13, earlier in this chapter.

However, if you (or other administrators) occasionally choose to use the Deny attribute on users, computers, and groups to keep them from getting the GPO, you'll need to additionally inspect the Security Editor dialog in the Delegation tab as in Figures 2.12 and 2.13.

The GPMC clearly encourages you to use Approach 1 for filtering. If you have older GPOs in your Active Directory that already use Approach 2 for filtering, consider changing it so that GPMC's Scope tab will actually reflect who will get the GPO.

There's no right or wrong answer here. The challenge is simply that the GPMC will not show who is expressly denied the ability to process the GPO. If you've got some in-house system to compensate for that shortcoming (or you use the new GPMC 2.0 Comment feature), you might be able to better make use of Approach 2.

Granting User Permissions on an Existing Group Policy Object

You already know the three criteria for someone to be able to edit or modify an existing GPO:

- They are a member of the Domain Admins group.
- They are a member of the Enterprise Admins group.
- They created the GPO themselves and hence are the owner. (We saw this in Figure 1.25 in Chapter 1 when Frank couldn't edit the GPOs he didn't create.)

But sometimes, you also want to add rights to a user on a GPO so that they can modify it. As we foreshadowed, the Delegation tab for a GPO (or GPO link, which reflects the same information) has a second purpose: to help you grant permissions to groups or users over the security properties of that GPO. If you click Add on the Delegation tab, you can grant any mere mortal user or group (even in other domains) the ability to manipulate this GPO, as seen in Figure 2.15.

FIGURE 2.15 You can set permissions of "who can do what" upon a GPO.

Once the permissions settings have been applied, the user has that level of rights over the GPO, as seen in Table 2.1.

TABLE 2.1 GPMC vs. Genuine Active Directory Permissions

Permissions Option	Actual Under-the-Hood Permissions
"Read"	Sets the Allow permission for "Read" on the GPO.
"Edit settings"	Sets the Allow permission for "Read," "Write," "Create Child Objects," and "Delete Child Objects." See the note regarding "under the hood" attributes.
"Edit settings, delete, modify security"	Sets the Allow permission for "Read," "Write," "Create Child Objects," "Delete Child Objects," "Delete," "Modify Permissions," and "Modify Owner." This is near-equivalent to full control on the GPO, but note that "Apply Group Policy" access permission is not set. (This can be useful to set for administrators so they can manipulate the GPO but not have it apply to themselves.)

TABLE 2.1 GPMC vs. Genuine Active Directory Permissions *(continued)*

Permissions Option	Actual Under-the-Hood Permissions
"Read (from Security Filtering)"	This isn't a permission located in the ACL Editor (see Figure 2.13); rather this is only visible if the user has "Read" and "Apply Group Policy" permissions on the GPO. This is a reflection of what is on the Scope tab.
"Custom"	Any other combinations of rights, including the use of the Deny permission. Custom rights are only added via the ACL Editor but can be removed here. They can be removed using the Remove button as in the Delegation tab.

 If you look really, really closely at the under-the-hood attributes specifically granted to the user when they are given "Edit settings" or "Edit setting, delete, modify security" rights, you'll note that "Write" isn't expressly listed. However, the ability to perform writes is granted because other subattributes that do permit writing are granted on the entry. To see those attributes for yourself, click the Advanced button while looking at the properties of the security on a GPO (like what we see in Figure 2.13).

Granting Group Policy Object Creation Rights in the Domain

As you learned in Chapter 1, a user cannot create new GPOs unless that user is a member of the Group Policy Creator Owners group. Dropping a user into this group is one of two ways you can grant this right.

However, the GPMC introduces another way to grant users the ability to have Group Policy Creator Owner–style access. Traverse to the Group Policy Objects container as seen in Figure 2.16, and click the Delegation tab. You can now click Add and select any user, including any user in your domain, say a user named Joe User, or users across forests, such as Sol Rosenberg, who is in a domain called bigu.edu. As you can see in Figure 2.16, both users have been added.

This can be handy if you have trusted administrators in other domains that you want to allow to create GPOs in your domain. You might want to round them up into a group (instead of just listing them individually as Sol is listed here), but that's your option.

Special Group Policy Operation Delegations

You can delegate three special permissions at the domain and OU levels, and you can set one of those three special permissions at the site level. Clicking the level, such as an OU, and then clicking the Delegation tab for that level shows the available permissions, as seen in Figure 2.17.

FIGURE 2.16   You can choose to delegate to users in your domain, in other domains, or in domains in other forests.

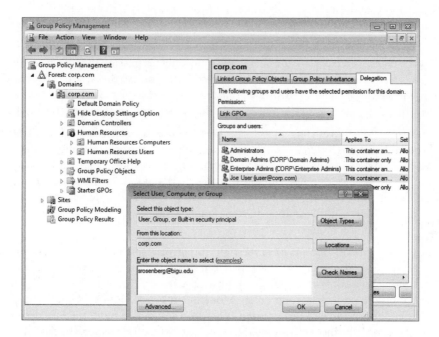

FIGURE 2.17   These operations are equivalent to the Active Directory Users and Computers Delegation Wizard.

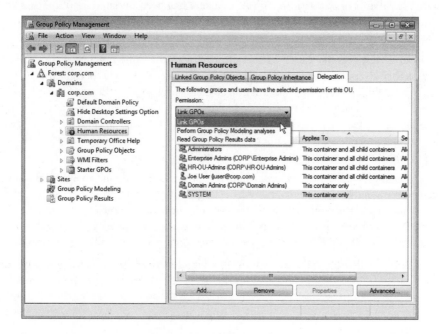

The interface is a bit confusing here. Specifically, you must first select the permission from the drop-down box. This lists the current users who can have permissions to use the right. You can then click the Add, Remove, or Advanced button to make your changes.

There are three permissions that may be selected from the drop-down box, as seen in Figure 2.17:

Link GPOs   Of the three permissions here, this is the only permission that can be configured at all levels: site, domain, and OU. Recall in Chapter 1 that you ran the Active Directory Users and Computers Delegation of Control Wizard (see Figure 1.24). Instead of using Active Directory Users and Computers to perform that task, the GPMC can do the same job—right here.

"Perform Group Policy Modeling analyses"   This right performs the same function as if we had used the Active Directory Users and Computers Delegation of Control Wizard to grant the Generate Resultant Set of Policy (Planning) permissions, as seen previously in Figure 1.24. The next section describes how to get more data about what's happening at the client. You'll see how to use this power in the section "What-If Calculations with Group Policy Modeling" later in this chapter. Group Policy Modeling lets you simulate what-if scenarios regarding users and computers.

By default, only Domain Admins have the right to perform this task. Domain Admins can grant other users or groups the ability to perform this function, such as the Help Desk, HR-OU-Admins, or your own desktop-administrator teams. You can choose to grant people the ability to perform Group Policy Modeling analyses on this specific container or this specific container and child containers. When you assign this right, the user performing the Group Policy Modeling analysis must have the delegated right upon the container containing the what-if user and also the container containing the what-if computer. If you don't grant rights in both containers, only half the analysis is displayed.

This right is available only if the domain AD schema has been updated for Windows 2003. Additionally, the Group Policy Modeling analyses function only when at least one Windows 2003 Domain Controller (or later) is available in the domain.

"Read Group Policy Results data"   This right performs the same function as if we used the Active Directory Users and Computers Delegation of Control Wizard to grant the "Generate Resultant Set of Policy (Logging)" permission (which isn't shown in Figure Figure 1.24 but it would be there if you scrolled down a little.). You'll see how to use this power in the section "What's-Going-On Calculations with Group Policy Results" later in this chapter. However, if you want to grant this power to others, you can. Again, a typical use is to grant this right to the Help Desk or other administrative authority.

When you assign this right, the user performing the Group Policy Results analysis must have the delegated right upon the container containing the target computer. Or this right can be applied at a parent container and the rights will flow down via inheritance. The user or group must also have this right delegated upon any container containing any users who have logged onto the machine you want to analyze. If you don't grant rights in both containers, no analysis is displayed.

This right is available only if the domain AD schema has been updated for Windows 2003 and later.

In Chapter 6, I have some additional notes on how to fully take advantage of the "Perform Group Policy Modeling analyses" and "Read Group Policy Results data" rights. Be sure to read the section entitled "RSoP for Windows Server 2008, Windows Vista, Windows 2003, and Windows XP."

Who Can Create and Use WMI Filters?

Okay, okay, okay. I know the subject of WMI filters has come up about 3,000 times already, and every time I refer you, the poor reader, to Chapter 5. Once you've read what they are and how to create them in Chapter 5, please come back here and read how to manage them.

Two types of people are involved in the management of WMI filters:

- Those who can create them
- Those who can use them

Delegating Who Can Create WMI Filters

By default, only the Domain Administrator can create WMI filters. However, you might have some WMI whiz kid in your company (and it's a good chance this isn't the same person as the Domain Administrator). With that in mind, the Domain Administrator can grant that special someone the ability to create WMI filters. To do this, drill down to the domain ➤ WMI Filters node, and then select Delegation in the pane on the right. You can now grant one of two rights, as shown in Figure 2.18.

FIGURE 2.18   These are controls over the creation of WMI filters.

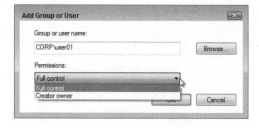

In Figure 2.18, we can see the two rights that appear in the drop-down box:

- Once a user has "Creator owner" rights here, they can create and modify their own WMI filters, but they cannot modify others' WMI filters. Note that members of the Group Policy Creator Owners security group have this right by default.

- A user with "Full control" rights here can create and modify their own WMI filters or anyone else's.

These rights to create WMI filters are available only if the domain AD schema has been updated for at least Windows 2003.

Delegating Who Can Use WMI Filters

Once WMI filters are created (again, see Chapter 5), you'll likely want to assign who can apply them to specific GPOs. To do this, drill down to the specific WMI filter, as shown in Figure 2.19. Then click Add, and you'll see that two rights are available for the user you want.

In Figure 2.19, we can see the two rights that appear in the drop-down box:

- Once a user has "Edit" rights here, they can edit and tailor the filter, as we do in Chapter 4.

- A user with "Full control" rights here can edit the filter as well as delete it and modify the security (that is, specify who else can get "Edit" or "Full control" rights here).

The rights to use WMI filters are available only if the domain AD schema has been updated for at least Windows 2003.

FIGURE 2.19 These are controls over the WMI filters themselves.

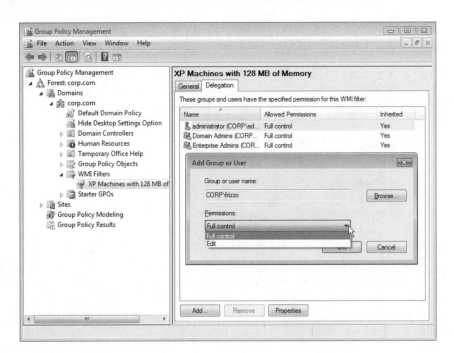

Performing RSoP Calculations with the GPMC

In Chapter 1, we charted out a fictitious organization's GPO structure on paper. We looked and saw when various GPOs were going to apply to various user and computers. Charting out the RSoP (Resultant Set of Policy) for users and computers on paper is a handy skill for basic understanding of GPO organization and flow, but in the real world, you'll need a tool that can help you actually figure out what's going on at your client desktops.

The GPMC has a handy feature to show us all the GPOs that are going to apply for the users and computers at a specific level in Active Directory. In Figure 2.20, when you click the **Human Resources Users** OU and then click the Group Policy Inheritance tab, you can see a list of all the GPOs that should apply to the **Human Resources Users** OU.

The site level is not shown in this Group Policy Inheritance tab. Because computers, particularly laptops, can travel from site to site, it is impossible to know for sure what site to represent here.

As I said, this tab in Figure 2.20 should really tell you what's going to happen. The operative word here is *should*. That's because a lot can go wrong between your wishes and what actually happens on the client systems. For instance, you already saw how to filter GPOs using security groups, which would certainly change the experience of one user versus another on the very same machine. And in Chapter 5, you'll learn about WMI filters, which limit when GPOs are applied even more.

FIGURE 2.20   The Group Policy Inheritance tab shows you which GPOs should apply.

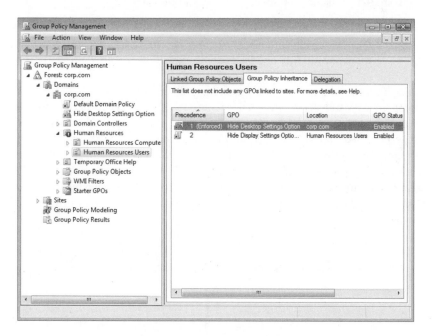

The point of all this RSoP stuff is to help us know the score about what's going on at machines that could be many hundreds of millimeters, meters, or kilometers away. When users freak out about getting settings they don't expect or when they freak out about lacking settings they do expect, the point is to know which setting is causing the stir and which GPO is to blame for the errant setting.

We know one thing's for sure: users do freak out a lot if anything changes, and it's our job to track down the problem (but not the user or computer). So the point of performing an RSoP calculation is to help you know what is going on and why it's going on that way. The GPMC can help with that.

What's-Going-On Calculations with Group Policy Results

If someone calls you to report that an unexpected GPO is applying, you can find out what's going on via the GPMC. You can find out what's going on if the machine in question is a Windows XP machine or higher. Sorry, Windows 2000 computers are left in the dust. Windows 2000 computers are not left in the dust for the what-if calculations with Group Policy Modeling in the next section.

Once the user with the problem has logged onto the machine in question, you can tap into the WMI provider built into all editions of Windows since Windows XP. Without going too propeller-head here, the upshot of this magic is that the GPMC (and the GPRESULT command, as you'll see in Chapter 6) can query any particular user that has ever logged on locally. It's then a simple matter to display the sexy results within the GPMC.

Once the results are displayed, you can right-click over the report and save them as an HTML or XML report.

The magic happens when the computer asking "What's going on?" (in this case, the computer running the GPMC) asks the target client computer. The target client computer responds with a result of what has happened—which GPOs were applied to the computer side and to the user side (provided the user has ever, at least once, logged on).

Let me expand on this important point: This Group Policy Results magic only works if the target user has ever logged onto the target machine. They only need to have ever logged on once, and here's the amazing part: They don't even need to be logged on while you run the test. But if the target user has *never* logged onto the target machine, the Group Policy Results will not allow you to select that user.

You can run your what's-going-on calculations inside the GPMC by right-clicking the Group Policy Results node at the bottom of the GPMC's hierarchy as shown in Figure 2.21. When you do, you can select the user and the computer and see their interaction.

FIGURE 2.21 The Group Policy Results Wizard performs what's-going-on calculations.

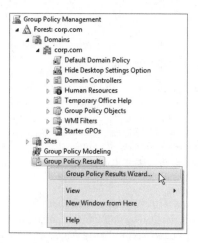

You need to remember the following before trying to run the Group Policy Results Wizard to figure out what's going on:

- The target computer must be Windows Vista, Windows XP, Windows Server 2003, Windows Server 2008, or later. Again, Windows 2000 machines are left out of the fun here.

- The target computer must be actually turned on and on the network. If this is not the case, you'll get an error to this effect. It will state that it cannot contact the WMI service via RPC.

- If the target machine is Windows Vista, Windows XP/Service Pack 2, or Windows 2003/Service Pack 1, the Windows Firewall must be disabled. Alternatively (in advance), you can open up ports 135 and 445 on the target machine. See the sidebar entitled "Understanding Windows XP/SP2 and Windows Vista's Firewall Settings (and Dealing with Group Policy Results)" for some ideas on how to mitigate this. If the machine is unreachable because the firewall is blocking access to port 135 or port 445, you'll get the same "RPC Error" as if the computer was off.

- The Windows Management Instrumentation service must be started.

- The user's local profile cannot be deleted. If the user has logged on but the administrator later whacks the local profile (or a Windows Vista–specific policy setting is enabled to auto-whack the local profile), WMI data will not be available.

Remember: The user you want to find out about must have logged onto the target computer *at least once* to be eligible to perform a Group Policy Results calculation.

The output generated from the GPMC version when performing Group Policy Results RSoP calculations is quite powerful, as shown in Figure 2.22.

Similar to the Settings tab, you can expand and contract the report by clicking Show and Hide. Inside, you can clearly see which GPOs have been applied and any major errors along the way. At a glance, you can see which GPOs have Applied and which were Denied (passed over) for whatever reason, such as filtering or that one-half of the GPO was empty.

Understanding Windows XP/SP2 and Windows Vista's Firewall Settings (and Dealing with Group Policy Results)

Once SP2 is loaded upon Windows XP (or you load Windows Vista, and for that matter, Windows Server 2008), the Windows Firewall is automatically engaged.

Now, regular, everyday Group Policy stuff works just fine when the firewall is on. That's because the Group Policy client requests what he wants, then the results are returned through the requested ports.

But, as you just learned, the ability to get Group Policy Results is effectively disabled when the Windows Firewall is engaged. That's because firewalls reject unrequested stuff when engaged. So, it feels like the target computer is turned off.

There was always a firewall built into Windows XP, but with Windows XP/Service Pack 2, Windows Vista, and Windows Server 2008, the firewall is turned on by default. To boot, it's now much more controllable via Group Policy. The policy settings used to control the Windows Firewall can be found in two locations: Administrative Templates ➤ Network ➤ Network Connections ➤ Windows Firewall ➤ Domain Profile and Administrative Templates ➤ Network ➤ Network Connections ➤ Windows Firewall ➤ Standard Profile.

You can see that the exact same policy settings are listed for both the Standard Profile and Domain Profile nodes. The Domain Profile settings are what will take effect when users are inside your corporate network; that is, when they're actively logged in by a Domain Controller. The Standard Profile, on the other hand, is used for when users are out of the office (perhaps in a hotel or other public network where they cannot reach your company's Domain Controllers for authentication).

Once a Windows Vista, Windows XP/Service Pack 2, or Windows Server 2008 computer receives the policy settings for both the Domain Profile and Standard Profile, that computer is ready to travel both in and out of the office. You can be sure that machine is embracing your company's firewall security policy both in the office and on the road.

If you're interested in learning more about how a computer makes a determination of whether it is supposed to use Domain Profile or Standard Profile policy settings, be sure to read Microsoft's document titled "Network Determination Behavior for Network-Related Group Policy Settings" at www.microsoft.com/technet/community/columns/cableguy/cg0504.mspx (shortened to http://tinyurl.com/cao73).

You have three options if you want to restore the Group Policy Results functionality when you have Windows XP/SP2 or Windows Vista (or Windows Server 2008) clients. Note that if you cannot locate the following policy settings to control the Windows XP/SP2, Windows Vista (and Windows Server 2008) firewalls, be sure to read Chapter 7, which explains ADM and ADMX Template management.

Approach 1: Kill the Windows XP/SP2, Windows Vista, or Windows Server 2008 Firewall
Now that you understand how to control Windows XP's, Windows Vista's, and Windows Server 2008's firewall settings, one approach is to kill the firewall completely. If you do this, you understand that you're giving up any of the protection that Windows Firewall affords. However, by doing so, you will restore communication to the target Windows XP/SP2, Windows Vista, or Windows Server 2008 computer. To kill the firewall, drill down to Administrative Templates ➢ Network ➢ Network Connections ➢ Windows Firewall ➢ Domain Profile and select **Windows Firewall: Protect all network Connections**. But here's the thing. You don't Enable this policy to kill the firewall. You Disable it. Yes, you read that right, you Disable it. Read the Explain text help inside the policy for more information on specific usage examples.

Approach 2: Poke Just the Required Holes in the Firewall   Instead of killing the firewall dead, you can simply open up the one port you need. Again, the idea is that if the target computer responds on port 135, you're golden. Windows Vista has a policy setting you can enable named **Windows Firewall: Allow Inbound Remote Administration Exception** (**Windows Firewall: Allow Remote Administration Exception** on Windows XP/Service Pack 2), which is located in Computer Configuration ➢ Administrative Templates ➢ Network ➢ Network Connections ➢ Windows Firewall ➢ Domain Profile. Again, when you do this, you're opening up the necessary port 135 (RPC). Note, however, that enabling this policy setting also opens up port 445 (SMB), which might be more than you need.

Approach 3: Keep the Firewall Engaged, and Don't Use Group Policy Results   You might opt for this third approach. That is, you really, really want to keep the firewall enabled and all ports closed on that target Windows XP or Windows Vista machine. If so, how will you find out "what's going on" on a target machine? There are two ways, both explored a bit later. One way is to trot out to the machine (or take remote control of it somehow) and run the GPRESULT command, which will tell you what's going on. Or, you can use a tool called GPMonitor (which we explore in the appendix). The idea is to have the target machines periodically push their Group Policy Results data to a location of your choosing. So, even if they're behind a firewall, you're still periodically able to see what's going on.

    The WMI filters category (shown in Figure 2.22) will not display data unless the target machine is running Windows XP with SP2 or higher.

If you click the Settings tab here, you get an extra bonus. That is, if there are conflicts along the scope of the GPO, you can see which other GPOs won in the contest for the ultimate Group Policy smackdown! Indeed, you can see this in Figure 2.23. Note, however, that the GPMC doesn't show you which GPOs lost when there was a conflict. This can sometimes mean more troubleshooting to determine other GPOs with conflicting settings. In Chapter 6, you'll learn how to locate losing GPOs.

FIGURE 2.22   The Group Policy Results report shows lots of useful information.

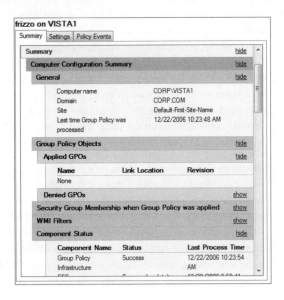

FIGURE 2.23   If specific settings conflict, you can quickly determine which GPO wins.

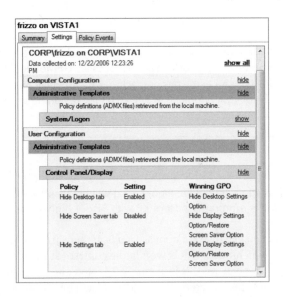

There are one or two caveats about Group Policy Results data. Specifically, when you produce a Group Policy Results report, some data simply isn't reported! Depending on the circumstances, you might not see some of the following data in a report:

- IPsec policies
- Wireless policies
- Disk quotas policies
- Third-party client-side extension add-ins

Note, however, that after the report runs, you can right-click the entry for the report (located right under the Group Policy Results node, as seen in Figure 2.24) and select Advanced View. When you do this, you'll see an alternate view of the report. The report runs in an MMC snap in, so it's not HTML. But the advantage of this Advanced report is that it can usually show extra attributes that are not always shown in the HTML report. But, since the report is within an MMC, and isn't HTML, it's not really "portable" and you can't print it or send it in an email.

Additionally useful here is the Policy Events tab, which will dive into the target machine's Event Viewer and pull out the events related to GPOs, as shown in Figure 2.24. Just double-click the event to open it. Talk about handy!

FIGURE 2.24   The Policy Events tab shows you events specific to this target computer.

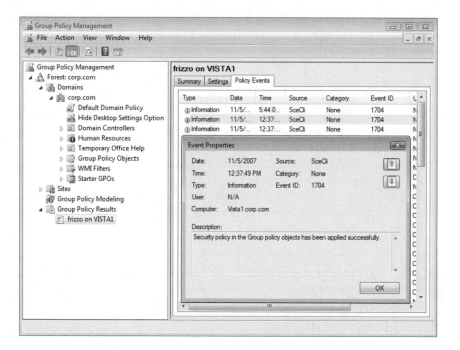

The GPMC will also save the query so you can reuse it later if you want to retest your assumptions. For example, you might want to retry this after you've corrected your software installation failure, added a new GPO to the mix, or moved a machine from one OU to another.

If you move a computer from one OU to another, you might not get the correct results right away because the computer may not immediately recognize that it has been moved. If you move a computer from one OU to another, you might want to synchronize your Domain Controllers and then reboot the target machine to get accurate results right away. This is discussed in more detail in Chapter 4.

What-If Calculations with Group Policy Modeling

Finding out what's going on is useful if someone calls you in a panic. However, you might also want to plan for the future. For instance, would you be able to easily determine what would happen to the users inside the **Human Resources Users** OU if a somewhat indiscriminately named GPO called "Desktop Settings" was linked to it? Maybe or maybe not. (With a horribly named GPO like that, likely not.)

Or, what might happen if Frank Rizzo took a trip to another site? Which GPOs would apply to him then? Or which GPOs would apply if the HR-OU-Admins were granted different security rights (or had them revoked)? The Oracle, er, the Group Policy Modeling Wizard found in the GPMC can answer a million of these questions. Its job is to answer "What happens if?"

This function is available only if the domain schema has been updated for Windows 2003 and you have at least one Windows 2003 Domain Controller available. This is because a Windows 2003 Domain Controller (or higher) runs a service that must be running for the calculation to occur.

The best news about what-if calculations is that Windows 2000 computers aren't left out of the picture. But the bad news is that the calculations shown for Windows 2000 machines are likely inaccurate. Modeling will happily tell you that your Windows 2000 machines will apply things only available for Windows XP and Windows Vista, such as Wireless policy (when it's not possible for Windows 2000 machine to get these at all).

Again, the only catch to this magic is that when you want to run what-if modeling calculations, the processing of the calculations must actually occur on a Windows 2003 or Windows 2008 Domain Controller. Even if you have the GPMC loaded on a Windows Vista or Windows XP management station, you'll still have to make contact with a Windows 2003 Domain Controller (or higher) to assist in the calculations.

WARNING This is the biggest warning icon the publisher gives me, but it isn't big enough for this message. If your Windows 2003 domain has been upgraded from Windows 2000 and you want to perform Group Policy Modeling between domains, it will likely not work without some manual attention. There are ACL permission problems on GPOs caused by performing a domain upgrade. To fix the problem in a flash, you run the `GrantPermissionOnAllGPOs.wsf` script that is included with the GPMC, or available on Microsoft's website. Specifically, you run `cscript GrantPermissionOnAllGPOs.wsf /FullEdit "Enterprise Domain Controllers"`. This will "touch" all GPOs in SYSVOL, which will force replication to all Domain Controllers and, hence, may cause a lot of network traffic. This could be an issue with environments with many GPOs.

You can kick off a modeling session by right-clicking the domain or any OU (as well as the Group Policy Modeling node) and selecting Group Policy Modeling Wizard. When you do, you'll be presented with the Group Policy Modeling Wizard Welcome screen.

You then choose which Domain Controller (2003 or 2008) will have the honor of performing the calculation for you. It doesn't matter which Domain Controller you choose—even those in other domains. Just pick one. Just note that it does need to be a Windows 2003 or 2008 Domain Controller and not anything less.

You'll then get to play Zeus and determine what would happen if you plucked a user and/or computer out of a current situation and modified the circumstances. In the wizard screens, you get to choose the following:

- Which user and/or computer (or container) you want to start to play with
- Whether to pretend to apply slow-link processing (if not already present on the target)
- Whether to pretend to apply loopback processing (if not already present on the target)
- The site in which you want to pretend the object is starting
- Where to move the user (if the user account moves at all)
- Where to move the computer (if it moves at all)
- Whether to pretend to change the user's security group membership
- Whether to pretend to change the computer's security group membership
- Whether to pretend to apply WMI filters for users or computers (if not already present on the target)

Now, to be clear: you don't have to tweak *all* of these settings—maybe just one or two. Just whatever applies to your situation.

Also note that you will likely get inaccurate results if you try to do something that isn't really possible. For instance, you can force the wizard into seeing what happens if Frank Rizzo's account is moved to another domain. But, since there isn't a way to actually move Frank's account, the displayed results will be cockeyed. You'll learn more about some of the additional concepts, such as slow-link processing and loopback processing, in Chapter 5. You'll also learn more about WMI filters in Chapter 5.

The output in Figure 2.25 shows what would happen if Frank Rizzo were removed from the **Human Resources Users** OU (and plopped into the root of the domain).

What to Expect from the Group Policy Modeling Wizard

When you first use the Group Policy Modeling Wizard, you may be surprised to see that it has Loopback, WMI Filters, and Slow Links options. At first, I was curious about why these were options in the wizard—if the wizard's whole job is to figure out what will be at the end of the simulation.

In a nutshell, the Group Policy Modeling Wizard allows you to simulate these additional items as if they all were *actually* going to be true. This way, you don't have to create an OU and/or a GPO with the specific policy settings (Loopback, and so on) *just* to turn it on. This makes sense: if you enable these options on the real OU, you change the live environment.

The point of the Group Policy Modeling Wizard is to let you just simulate *what if* you did this on the target. When using the wizard and selecting Loopback, Slow Links, or WMI Filters, don't expect it to tell you that any of these things *are* true in the target. The simulation demonstrates what would happen *if* these properties came into the mix.

Note that the Group Policy Modeling Wizard is unable to take into account any Local Group Policy Object settings on the potential target workstation. That's because this wizard never actually queries a target computer. The calculations all happen on a Windows 2003 or Windows Server 2008 Domain Controller and are then outputted in the GPMC.

FIGURE 2.25   Here, the Group Policy Modeling summary screen shows you what you're about to simulate. For instance, you can simulate moving a computer and/or a user to other locations.

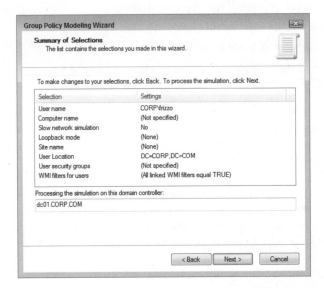

When the calculations are complete, you'll get a results dialog that looks quite similar to Figures 2.22 and 2.23. There, you can see how results will be displayed in both the Summary and Settings tabs. As a reminder, the Summary tab shows you which GPOs were applied; the Settings tab shows you which policies inside the GPOs will win if there's a conflict. Present only in Group Policy Modeling output (not shown) is another item, called the Query tab, which can remind you of the choices you made when generating the query.

Backing Up and Restoring Group Policy Objects

Inadvertently deleting a single GPO can wreak havoc on your domain. Imagine what happens when a bunch of GPOs are inadvertently deleted. Let's just say that the users are suddenly happy because they can do stuff they couldn't normally do, and you're not happy because now *they're* happy. Ironic, isn't it?

It's not just the errant Group Policy deletion that could cause an issue. Another administrator could inadvertently delete a portion of the SYSVOL container on one Domain Controller, which will replicate to all Domain Controllers and quickly damage your GPOs.

In both of these example cases, you'll need a way to restore.

The Backup and Restore functions for GPOs are only meant to work within the same domain. However, you'll see in the appendix how the GPMC can be used to back up and import a GPO to get the same effect *between* domains.

In our cases, if the policy settings inside the "Auto-Launch calc.exe" GPO were wiped out, the name of the GPO can surely help us put it back together. But the name alone might not be an accurate representation of what's really going on inside the GPO.

Then, there are still other questions: Where was this GPO linked? What was the security on the GPO? Who owned it?

All said and done, you don't want to get stuck with a deleted or damaged GPO without a backup. Thankfully, the GPMC makes easy work of the once-laborious task of backing up and restoring GPOs.

These techniques are valid for both all types and all configurations of Active Directory, Windows 2000 domains, and higher. So, back up those GPOs today with the GPMC regardless of your domain structure!

Backing Up Group Policy Objects

When you back up a GPO within the GPMC, you also back up a lot of important data:

- The settings inside the GPO.
- The permissions upon that GPO (that is, the stuff inside the Delegation tab).
- The link to the WMI filter—however, the actual filter itself is not preserved. (Again, I'll talk about WMI filters in Chapter 5.)

However, it's also important to know what won't be backed up:

- Any WMI filters contained within Active Directory. You must back them up separately. You can see one way to do this in the section "Backing Up and Restoring WMI Filters" later in this chapter.

- IPsec settings themselves aren't backed up via the GPMC Backup and Restore function. They are backed up during a Domain Controller's System State backup. But discussing backing up and restoring them is a bit beyond the scope of this book. My best suggestion: Manually document any GPOs with IPsec settings.

- GPO links aren't specifically backed up. Yes, you read that right. But before you panic, let me first explain how this is for your own protection. We'll examine this phenomenon in a little bit and try to make you a believer in why this is a good thing.

As you'll learn in Chapter 6, there are two parts of GPOs: the GPT (Group Policy Template) from Active Directory and the GPC (Group Policy Container) from within the SYSVOL. When a backup is performed, the GPT and GPC are wrapped up and placed as a set of files that can be stored or transported.

What's additionally neat is that contained within the backup is a report of the settings inside that GPO you just backed up. So, if someone backs up a GPO named "Desktop Settings" (again, a horrible name), you can at least see the report of just what is inside the GPO before you restore it to your domain.

To back up a GPO, you need Read access to that GPO, as shown earlier in an example back at Figure 2.15. You can start by locating the GPO node in the GPMC and right-clicking it. Select either Back Up All or Manage Backups. For this first time, select Back Up All.

You then select the location for the backup (hopefully some place secure) and click Backup. You'll then see each GPO being backed up to the target location as shown in Figure 2.26. When you're finished, you can rest easy (or at least easier) that your GPOs are safe.

FIGURE 2.26 You can back up all your GPOs at once, if desired.

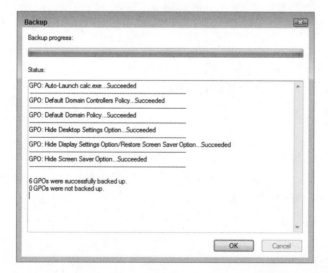

You can inspect the directories the backup produced if you like. You'll see a directory for each GPO, the XML file representing the GPT, and an XML report showing the settings. In the next section, you'll learn how to view the report (easily) by utilizing the View Settings button (as shown a bit later in Figure 2.27).

> In Chapter 6, we'll learn more about the underlying nuts and bolts of GPOs. Specifically, you'll learn that the underlying name of a GPO relies on a unique GUID name being assigned to the GPO. What isn't immediately obvious here is that the directory names produced by the backup (which take the form of GUIDs) are *not* the same GUIDs that are actually used for the underlying identification of the GPO. These are additional, unique, random GUID directory names generated just for backup. This seemingly bizarre contradiction becomes useful when you read the next paragraph.

The backup is quick, painless, and rather reasonably sized. The best part about the backup facility is that it's flexible. When you choose to run your next backup, you can keep your backups in the same directory you just chose, and you'll keep a history of the GPOs, should anything change. It's the underlying random and unique GUID names for the directories that allow you to keep plowing more GPO backups right into the same backup directory—there's no fear of overlap. Or you can keep the backups in their own directory; it's your choice.

If you dare, go ahead and delete the "Hide Display Settings Option/Restore Screen Saver Option" GPO. You'll restore it in the next section (I hope).

Now that you've backed up the whole caboodle, it should also be noted that you can back up just a solitary GPO. Right-click the *actual* GPO (which is located only in the Group Policy Objects container) and choose Backup. In Chapter 11, you'll find some scripts that enable you to automate your backups.

Be sure the place where you back up your GPOs is secure. You don't want the knowledge stored within the GPOs to possibly be used as an attack against you.

Restoring Group Policy Objects

The restore process is just as easy. It works for GPOs that were backed up in the same domain. Note that it's also possible to back up and restore between domains, but this is called a GPO Migration (see the appendix).

When you restore a GPO, the file object you created in the backup process is "unrolled" and placed upon Active Directory. As you would expect, the following key elements are preserved:

- The settings inside the GPO
- The friendly name (which comes back from the dead)
- The GUID (which comes back from the dead)
- The security and permissions on that object (which come back from the dead)
- The link to WMI filters (which comes back from the dead)

Whomping a GPO doesn't delete any WMI filters associated with a GPO itself. Any WMI filters are stored in a separate place in Active Directory. It's sort of like the Jacuzzi next to the swimming pool.

The GPO does not have to be deleted to do a restore. For instance, if someone changed the settings and you want to simply restore the GPO to get an older version of the policy settings, you can certainly restore over an existing GPO to put a previously known "good" version back in play.

Restoring GPOs requires the following security rights:

- If you want to restore on top of a GPO that already exists, you need Edit, Delete, and Modify rights, as seen back in Figure 2.15.

- If you want to restore a deleted GPO, you need to be a member of the Group Policy Creator Owners (or Domain Admins or Enterprise Admins) security group.

Warning: A Deleted GPO's Links Are Not Restored!

Assuming you went ahead in the last example and deleted the "Hide Display Settings Option/ Restore Screen Saver Option" GPO and are now ready to restore it, there is something you need to know before proceeding. That is, one critical item is missing: the Group Policy links to the GPO are *not* restored in this operation. The location of links is backed up, but during a restore, the links are *not* restored. You might be scratching your head wondering why this is.

Let's examine a theoretical timeline.

- On Day 0, a GPO named "Desktop Settings" is linked to two OUs named **Doctors** and **Nurses**.

- On Day 1, the GPO is backed up.

- On Day 2, a fellow administrator unlinks the GPO from **Doctors**. Now, the GPO is linked only to **Nurses**.

- On Day 3, someone deletes the whole GPO (and hence its links).

- On Day 4, someone recognizes this deleting and restores the GPO.

Here's the $50,000 question: Upon restore, where should the links be restored to?

Should the links be restored back to the last way it was *just before* the catastrophe on Day 3? Sure, that would be ideal, but how would the system know what happened between Day 2 and Day 4? As it is, on Day 4, the GPO is now linked *only* to **Nurses**, but how could the system know that now?

Should it link the GPO back to the *original* locations, as it was on Day 1? On Day 1, it was linked to **Doctors** and **Nurses**? But restoring those links back to the same location could be a catastrophic mistake. Clearly, on Day 2 an administrator unlinked it from **Doctors** for some good reason! Restoring the link back upon the **Doctors** could be detrimental to their health!

Instead of restoring the links, the GPMC does the smartest thing it can do during a restore: it doesn't restore the links. That's right—by not restoring the links, it ensures that you're not inadvertently relinking the GPO back to some location in Active Directory that shouldn't have it anymore.

However, as stated, the backup process does record where the links were at the time of backup. To that end, you can easily see where the links were at the time of backup, and if desired, you can manually relink the GPO back to the locations you want. To see where a GPO had links at backup time, here's what to do:

- Right-click over the Group Policy Objects node and select Manage Backups.

- In the Manage Backups dialog, ensure that you're looking at the directory with the contents of the backup.

- Locate, then select the GPO that was deleted.

- Then click the View Settings button (as seen in Figure 2.27).

A report will be generated that, among other things, shows you where the GPO was linked. Then, once the GPO is restored, you can manually relink it where you need it to be linked.

You can start a restore by right-clicking the Group Policy Objects container and choosing Manage Backups. You'll be able to select a location that will house your GPO backups; you might have multiple locations.

If you've chosen to keep backing up the GPOs into the same backup directory, you can select the "Show only the latest version of each GPO" option, which shows you only the last backed-up version. If you've forgotten what is contained in a backup, simply click the backup name and choose View Settings. You can see these options in Figure 2.27.

When you're ready, click the GPO to restore, and then click Restore. It's really that easy.

You can also right-click the GPO itself (found only in the Group Policy Objects container) and choose Restore from Backup, which in fact performs the same function. (See Chapter 11 for a script that will enable you to automate your restores.)

FIGURE 2.27   You can see all backups or just the latest versions.

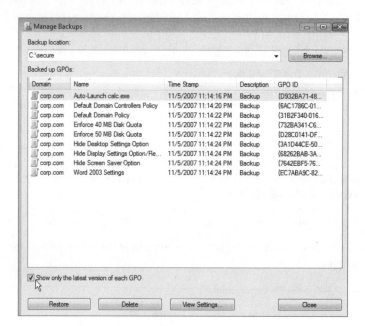

Backing Up and Restoring WMI Filters

As you read about WMI filters in the next chapter and learn what a pain in the tush they are to create, you'll be thankful that there's a mechanism that can back up and restore them. They are not backed up or restored in the process we just used. Rather, you must individually back up each WMI filter. Simply right-click the filter and choose Export. To restore, right-click WMI Filters node and choose Import. Sometimes restoring a WMI filter adds excess and invalid characters to the query. Simply re-edit the query and clean up the characters and you're back in business.

In the previous section, you saw that GPO links are not restored when the GPO is restored. The same is true for WMI filters: The WMI filter links are not restored when the WMI filter is restored. Again, for information on how to automatically document this information, see Chapter 6.

Searching for Group Policy Objects with the GPMC

As your Active Directory grows, so will your use of GPOs. However, sometimes remembering the one GPO that you used to do some magic a while ago can be difficult. To that end, the GPMC has some basic searching functionality.

With the search feature, you can search for GPOs with any (and all) of the following characteristics:

- Display name (that is, friendly name)
- GUID
- Permissions on the GPO itself
- A link, if it exists (used in conjunction with the name, and so on)
- WMI filters used
- Specific client-side extensions if they were used for either the user or computer side

 To be clear, I'm talking about finding a specific GPO itself, not finding the settings *within* a GPO. To learn how to find specific settings contained within GPOs, see the next chapter.

To search for a GPO that matches the characteristics you're after, right-click the domain and choose Search. In the Search Item dialog box, enter your criteria in the condition fields. The Value field will change based on the Search Item field. In Figure 2.28, I'm searching Corp.com for all GPOs with the word *Hide* in the name.

 The one thing *this* search engine cannot do is poke through each and every GPO to see where you enabled some policy setting. Again, check the next chapter for that added feature in the GPMC 2.0.

FIGURE 2.28 You can locate GPOs with lots of characteristics.

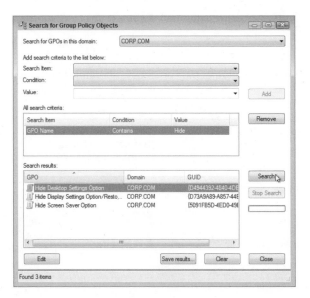

GPMC At-a-Glance Icon View

Because the GPMC contains so many icon types, it can be difficult to know specifically what an icon represents. That's what Table 2.2 is all about.

TABLE 2.2   GPMC Icon List

Icon	Description	What the Icon Means
	Scroll.	A GPO itself. You'll only see this in the Group Policy Objects container.
	Scroll with arrow.	A link to an actual GPO.
	Scroll with arrow. Just the arrow is dimmed.	GPO link that has Link Status disabled.
	Scroll with arrow. The whole icon is dimmed.	A link to a GPO whose status (on the Details tab) has been set to "All settings disabled."
	Scroll. Whole icon is dimmed.	The GPO whose status (on the Details tab) has been set to "All settings disabled."
	Scroll with arrow; additional lock icon.	Enforced link to this level.
	Blue exclamation point.	Block inheritance at this level.
	Folder with scroll.	Group Policy Objects container that actually holds the GPOs themselves.
	Folder with filter.	WMI Filters node.
	Filter.	A WMI filter.

The GPMC At-a-Glance Compatibility Table

You learned a lot in this chapter. Sometimes it can be confusing to know just when a feature is compatible with your setup in the office or the test lab. Hopefully, Table 2.3 will clear things up.

TABLE 2.3   Group Policy Functionality Compatibility Table

Function	Requirement	Where Discussed
Create and link GPOs and apply them to client systems.	Any Active Directory domain with Group Policy–capable clients (Windows 2000, Windows XP, Windows Server 2003, or Windows Vista).	Chapter 1
Back up and restore GPOs.	Any Active Directory domain plus GPMC console.	This chapter
Back up and restore Starter GPOs.	Any Active Directory with Windows 2008 schema plus GPMC 2.0.	Chapter 3
Transfer (migrate) GPOs between same forest.	Any Active Directory domain plus GPMC console.	Appendix
Run Group Policy Results reports.	Any Active Directory domain plus GPMC console. Targets must be Windows XP or higher. Target user must have logged on to target machine at least once.	This chapter
Run Group Policy Modeling reports.	Any Active Directory domain plus GPMC console. Must have at least one Windows Server 2003 or 2008 Domain Controller available to run the calculations. Targets may be Windows 2000, but you might get inaccurate results with Windows 2000 clients.	This chapter
WMI filters.	Windows 2003 domain or Windows 2000 with an updated Windows 2003 schema via the ADPREP /Domainprep command. Additionally, XP clients or above required. Windows 2000 clients ignore WMI filters.	Chapter 5

TABLE 2.3 Group Policy Functionality Compatibility Table *(continued)*

Function	Requirement	Where Discussed
Delegate Group Policy Results ability.	At least Windows 2003 forest or Windows 2000 updated schema via ADPREP /forestprep. Use Active Directory Users and Computers or GPMC to delegate rights.	This chapter
Delegate Group Policy Modeling ability.	At least Windows 2003 forest or Windows 2000 updated schema via ADPREP /forestprep. Use Active Directory Users and Computers or GPMC to delegate rights.	This chapter

Final Thoughts

While using the GPMC throughout this chapter, you ran queries and created several reports. What you possibly didn't know is that all that time you were creating HTML reports you can use to document your environment.

Back when you were first exploring a GPO's settings (see the screen shot in the section "Common Procedures with the GPMC" earlier in the chapter) and when you were creating RSoP reports (that is, Figures 2.23 and 2.24 and what would result after Figure 2.26), you were really generating HTML reports. Anytime you create those reports, you can right-click anywhere in the report and choose Save Report. Since these are standard HTML, you have an incredibly easy way to document just about every aspect of your Group Policy universe.

Backing up and restoring with the GPMC is simply awesome. But as you'll recall, when you restore a deleted GPO, you don't restore the links. You'll have to bring them back manually. Having good backups and good documentation about where each GPO is linked will always be your ace in the hole.

I stopped short in this chapter of demonstrating all of the GPMC's major additional functions, although in the next chapter, you'll learn what the GPMC version 2.0 brings to the table. That is, it brings filtering, comments, and Starter GPOs.

Something else not described here is that the GPMC provides a scriptable interface for many of our day-to-day GPO functions—including backups, creation, and management. You'll see that in Chapter 11. Additionally, you can use the GPMC to migrate GPOs from one domain to another. I'll tackle that in the appendix.

Remember that the GPMC is now built into Windows Vista and Windows Server 2008. Note that when you install SP1 on top of Windows Vista, the GPMC is uninstalled. To get it back, you'll need to install the GPMC 2.0 downloadable update.

Here are some parting tips for daily Group Policy Object management with the GPMC:

Check out these Microsoft documentation links.   Microsoft GPMC documentation is available at `http://tinyurl.com/2yhrej`.

Use Block Inheritance and Enforced sparingly.   The less you use these features, the easier it will be to debug the application of settings. Figuring out at which level in the hierarchy one administrator has Blocked Inheritance and another has declared Enforced can eat up days of fun at the office. The GPMC makes it easier to see what's going on, but still, minimize your use of these two attributes.

Remember what can only be applied at the link.   Three and only three attributes are set on a GPO link: Link Enable (Enable or Disable the settings to apply at this level), Enforce the link (and force the policy settings), and Delete the link.

Remember what can be applied only on the actual GPO itself.   The following attributes must be set on the GPO itself: the policies and settings inside the GPO (found on the Settings tab), Security filters, permissions (as in the Apply Group Policy permission), delegation (as in the "Edit this GPO" permission), Enabling/Disabling half (or both halves) of the GPO via the GPO status (found on the Details tab), and WMI filtering (discussed in Chapter 5).

Remember that Group Policy is notoriously tough to debug.   Once you start linking GPOs at multiple levels, throwing in a Block Inheritance, an Enforced, and a filter or two, you're up to your eyeballs in troubleshooting. The best thing you can do is document the heck out of your GPOs. The GPMC helps you determine what a GPO does in the Settings tab, but your documentation will be your sanity check when trying to figure things out.

Use Microsoft's spreadsheet.   Microsoft has an Excel spreadsheet of all the administrative templates for Windows 2000, Windows XP, and Windows 2003 and another for Windows Vista. (You'll learn more about why this is when you read Chapter 7.) My suggestion is to leverage this file every single time you create a new GPO and keep it in a common place for all administrators to reference to see what anyone else did inside a GPO. Be religious about it, and keep these files updated within your company. To locate the spreadsheet, go to `www.GPanswers.com`, in the "Microsoft Resources" section where I always have a link to it that's easy to find.

## 3

GPMC 2.0—Filtering, Comments, and Starter GPOs

In the Chapter 2, you learned how to do most of the important daily tasks with the GPMC. In this chapter, we'll explore the new features that you'll get with the GPMC 2.0.

As a quick refresher from Chapter 1, you can get the GPMC 2.0 in one of two ways:

- It's built into Windows Server 2008 machines.

- It's available for download and installation if your machine is already a Windows Vista + Service Pack 1. That download is called the Remote Server Administration Tools, or RSAT.

You should already have the GPMC 2.0 if you followed the directions in Chapter 1, where I showed you how to load it within Windows Server 2008 or, with Windows Vista + SP1, how to get the RSAT tools that contain the GPMC 2.0.

The three big topics we'll spend time on in this chapter are the new GPMC-specific features filtering, comments, and Starter GPOs. There are some additional little goodies in GPMC 2.0, but we'll cover those in other areas of the book.

With the new GPMC, you can also see Settings and RSoP reports for the new Microsoft Preference Extensions. We'll be exploring those reports later in Chapter 10 when we explore the Group Policy Preference Extensions.

Once You Install SP1 for Vista, Say Bye-Bye to the GPMC... Temporarily

In the previous chapters, we explored how Windows Vista (out of the box) already has the GPMC installed. Just type GPMC.MSC in the Start box, and voilà, the GPMC is instantly ready to manage your Active Directory. But, if you install Vista's Service Pack 1, the GPMC is uninstalled.

Yes, uninstalled.

Why?

Because uninstalling the GPMC allows for something that I've personally advocated for. That is, when the Group Policy team at Microsoft is ready to launch new Group Policy goodies, they can make the necessary changes and quickly get the updated GPMC out the door and into your hands.

Indeed, this is the way it was originally. When the GPMC was first released, it was a simple download and install. When bugs were found in the GPMC, they rounded up the fixes and reposted the download for the GPMC, calling it GPMC with Service Pack 1.

But as we learned in the previous chapter, the GPMC is a built-in part of the Windows Server 2008 and Windows Vista operating systems. Is this good? Well, yes, because it's already there and makes for one less thing to download and install. But what if some new whizbang feature is suddenly available? At best we'd have to wait for the next operating system service pack to see it; at worst we'd wait for a full operating system revision until we got to play.

But it seems that, going forward, the team has decided that the GPMC will "break free" from the operating system. This is both good and bad. It's good because bug fixes and updates will most certainly happen more quickly. It's bad because the GPMC is so great it just feels like it *should* be part of the OS. It's also bad because the poor Group Policy team at Microsoft has to wrap up their own changes (called out-of-band changes), whereas before, they could rely on different Microsoft build teams to keep the GPMC updated inside the operating system.

So, it's a little more work for the Group Policy team, but in my opinion it's a really good change. So now, once you load Vista SP1, no more GPMC; that is, until you download and install the RSAT tools, which contain the GPMC 2.0 (which has more features anyway). We'll explore its features in this chapter, and also in Chapter 10 when we talk about the new Group Policy Preference Extensions.

Now, here's the tricky part: Windows Server 2008 ships with the GPMC built in. It's currently unclear if Windows Server 2008's SP1 will uninstall the GPMC and therefore require a download, but I doubt it.

In this chapter, we'll assume your management station is running either Windows Vista with SP1 and the GPMC 2.0 (from RSAT) or Windows Server 2008 with the built in GPMC 2.0.

Updated GPMC Filters

How many individual Group Policy settings are there? Lots. There are now more than 2,400 with Windows Vista and Windows Server 2008. Sometimes it feels like you're trying to find a needle in a haystack.

Until now, the best way to discover particular policy settings was to consult a special Microsoft Excel spreadsheet listing all of the Group Policy settings. Since it was just a simple Excel spreadsheet, you could do a quick Find for what you were looking for, say, entries related to the Control Panel. But now, things are better.

We'll discuss more about the downloadable spreadsheet in Chapter 7, so stay tuned. You might still want use the spreadsheet in some rare cases. For instance, if you know the name of the Registry key that the policy happens to modify, you can still search for the Registry key name in the spreadsheet. Besides, because the GPMC 2.0's updated filtering doesn't cover security settings, this is still the best way to find them.

Where Did Filtering Come From?

The good news is that (finally!) Search is available within the Group Policy Management Editor (GPME). The bad news is that not every area within the GPME is searchable (boo!). Before we go into what is and is not available for the new search function, let's take a look at the historical archives for the Group Policy Filtering feature.

If you'll recall, the original Group Policy Editor (contained in the GPMC 1.0 and GPMC 1.5) has always had a View ➢ Filtering option, seen in Figure 3.1.

Note that the View ➢ Filtering option was available in the older GPMC only when you clicked Administrative Templates and then clicked the View menu.

FIGURE 3.1   The pre–Windows Server 2003 GPMC Filtering option

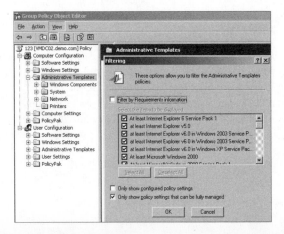

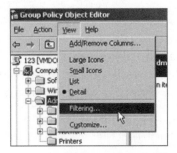

This filtering option had simple abilities. You could check "Filter by Requirements information" and filter for policy settings that would, for example, only work on Windows XP or newer computers.

When you use the GPMC 2.0, you get a new Filter On and Filter Options in the View menu (as seen in Figure 3.2), which replaces the View ➢ Filtering option.

FIGURE 3.2   The new GPMC 2.0 Filter Options selection

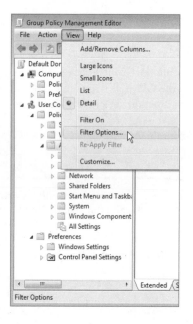

 The new GPMC 2.0 filter settings "stick around," meaning that the last filter you use is remembered the next time you apply a filter. This is an advantage if you are searching for a specific setting through different GPOs. Sure, you still need to open each GPO one by one, but the last filter specified will be utilized.

What's Available to Search

The good news is that Search is available. The bad news is that only the Administrative Templates Group Policy settings are available to search. So, if you're looking to find that security policy setting that will set **Accounts: Rename guest account** or **Devices: Restrict CD-ROM access to locally logged in user only,** well, you're out of luck. These lie within Computer Configuration ➢ Windows Settings ➢ Security Settings ➢ Local Policies ➢ Security Options. Really, anything that's within Computer Configuration ➢ Windows Settings or User Configuration ➢ Windows Settings is off-limits to the Search feature.

To get to the filter options, click anywhere within the User Configuration ➢ Policies ➢ Administrative Templates or Computer Configuration ➢ Policies ➢ Administrative Templates windows, then click View ➢ Filter Options, as seen in Figure 3.2. Once you do this, you'll get the Filter Options dialog, seen in Figure 3.3. You could also right-click within Administrative Templates and also select Filter Options.

FIGURE 3.3   The new GPMC 2.0 Filter Options dialog

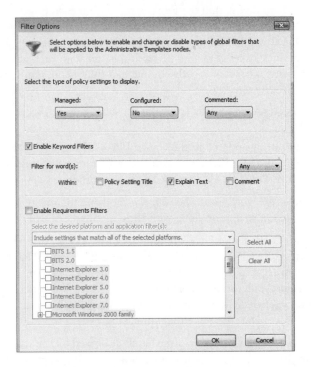

We'll discuss the dialog in three parts: top (type of settings to display), middle (keyword filters), and bottom (requirements filters). We'll start in the middle with keyword filters, then move to the top, then finally the bottom.

There are lots and lots of reasons you might want to use the Filter Options dialog. For instance, you might want to show only the policy settings that have been changed from their defaults. You can absolutely do that. Or, you might want to show the policy settings that affect only Windows Server 2008. You can also absolutely do that. But the most common reason for using the Filter Options dialog is to hunt down settings you think (or hope) might be there. For instance, you already know there are some settings that do something to the Control Panel, but you may not know the exact setting names. You can use this dialog to find the policy setting you seek.

We'll go through all the options in the Filter Options dialog, but keep in mind that the most common use is to hunt down settings you want to muck with, er, *experiment* with inside your test lab.

Keyword Filters

Arguably the most useful part of the dialog, the Keyword Filters option lets you type in something you know you want to do, then see which policy settings match that keyword. You can choose to search in the following three places:

Policy Setting Title: Searches text in the name of a policy setting, like **Remove Display in Control Panel.**

Explain Text: Searches the help text within the Explain tab within each policy setting. Note that all policy settings that ship in the box have Explain text (though some policy settings from ADM or ADMX templates that you get on the Internet might not). It should also be noted that the Explain text keeps getting better and better with each new edition of Windows. Even the Security entries are mostly commented (but again, remember that we cannot filter based on Security entries).

Comment: We'll talk about comments a little later. But, in short, you can search for any text in comments.

Let's say you wanted to find settings related to the Control Panel. Next to the "Filter for word(s)" line, you can see the default modifier Any, with All and Exact hiding underneath. Here's how the search for *Control Panel* would work with each modifier:

Any   Returns results where either the word *Control* or *Panel* or both are found. So, results like **Network control service type** would also appear along with **Hide specified Control Panel items.**

All   Returns results where both *Control* and *Panel* are found, but would not display settings that contain only one or the other. Results would include **Hide specified Control Panel items, Prohibit access to the Control Panel,** and **Show only specified Control Panel items.** If there were a setting called **Control a Panel of Experts to use Group Policy More,** it would return that too, because both *Control* and *Panel* are in the name, even though they don't appear right next to each other. (Oh, if only there were a setting like that—but I digress.)

Exact   Returns results where the word *Control* is immediately followed by the word *Panel.* If those two words weren't in that exact order, that setting would not show up.

Note that all of these modifiers, including Exact, ignore case. So *Control Panel* is the same as *CoNTrol PANel.*

Type of Settings to Display

Part of this section of the dialog can be seen in the following image. Here you'll be able to select three possible options: Managed, Configured, and Commented.

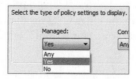

Managed   You'll learn more about Managed (blue dot/list icon) versus Unmanaged (red dot/down arrow icon) policy settings in Chapter 7. The quick summary in 100 words or fewer is that *Managed* policies act like true Group Policy settings and *Unmanaged* policies will "tattoo" the Registry. For more information about tattooing, read Chapter 7.

I'm not quite sure why, but the default here is set to Yes. That would mean the results will be *only* Managed policy settings. Just to be on the safe side, selecting Any is likely a better bet because that way, you'll get back both managed and unmanaged policy settings. Again, I'll talk about this more in Chapter 7.

Configured   As you learned in Chapter 2, Administrative Templates policy settings can be set to Enabled, Disabled, or Not Configured. The default for Configured is No, which means the results will show only policy settings that haven't been configured. If you select Yes, the results will show only Enabled or Disabled policy settings. If you choose Any, the results will show Enabled, Disabled, or Not Configured. Selecting Any here seems to be your best bet for finding a policy setting you might want to experiment with.

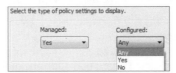

Commented   You'll learn about comments later on in this chapter, so stay tuned. The default here is Any, which means it will look for commented or uncommented policy settings within this GPO. Selecting Yes will show only commented policy settings within this GPO. Choosing No will show only those policy settings without comments (which would typically be most of them).

Requirements Filters

If you click Enable Requirements Filters (seen in Figure 3.3 earlier), you can determine if you want to show policy settings that are meant for particular client types. Again, a Group Policy "client" can be anything that "receives" Group Policy. So, a Group Policy client can be Windows XP, Windows Vista, Windows Server 2003, Windows Server 2008, and so on. The available platforms are listed for you to select, and the list includes various operating system parts that policy settings affect, such as Windows Media Player 10, Windows Installer 3.0, or Net-Meeting 3.0. Just select the appropriate check boxes.

Note that there's a drop-down that changes the Filter results when you've checked multiple items. You can show all or any of the selected platforms.

Figure 3.4 shows a good example of when to use any—that is, if you've got unrelated policy settings you wish to examine at one time. As you can see, all policy settings are for unrelated platforms. Selecting to include settings that match any of the selected platforms will show all the policy settings that match.

FIGURE 3.4   You can select to filter by which platforms are supported

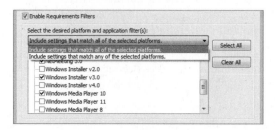

The All function doesn't seem to do much right now. I think the idea is that perhaps you could find a policy that addresses *both* Windows Vista and Windows XP SP2 machines. In that case, the "Include settings that match all of the selected platforms" option seems like a good choice—except Group Policy Administrative Templates aren't coded to work like that. They may be in the future, but not now. If you're able to make this All feature do something useful for you, drop me a line.

Results of Your Filter

Once you've made your selections inside the Filter Options dialog, you're ready to click OK and watch the magic. Let's do a simple filter and look to find any unique Control Panel policy settings that we might want to check out. The filter selections can be seen in Figure 3.5. Here I've made sure to display all policy settings (managed or unmanaged), policy settings that are configured or not configured, and policy settings that are commented or uncommented (more on comments a little later). And for now, I'm just looking for the words *control panel* (in that exact order) to appear in any part of the setting title.

FIGURE 3.5   Here I changed the Keyword Filter modifier to Exact to ensure that my results contained the exact phrase control panel.

Browsing the Results

The results of applying your filter can be seen in multiple places. First, remember that the resulting filter affects both the User Configuration ➢ Policies ➢ Administrative Templates and Computer Configuration ➢ Policies ➢ Administrative Templates. (The old GPMC's View ➢ Filter was independently set, so this is a nice GPMC 2.0 change.)

You can see the policy settings that affect the Control Panel in the user side by clicking User Configuration ➢ Policies ➢ Administrative Templates ➢ Control Panel (and also the folders within Control Panel named Display and Programs). An example is seen in Figure 3.6.

FIGURE 3.6   Browsing results of running the filter

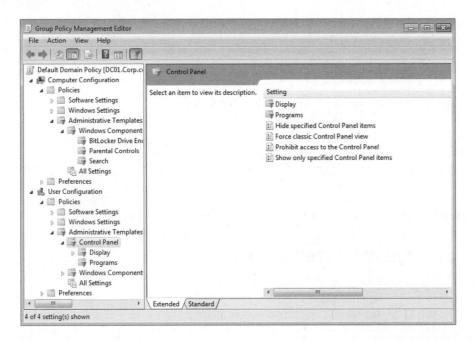

You can also see the policy settings that contain the words *control panel* on the Computer Configuration ➢ Policies ➢ Administrative Templates node (specifically some folders within the Windows Components folder, as seen in Figure 3.7).

Filter Options On/Off

Once the filter is set to On, the icons around the User Configuration ➢ Policies ➢ Administrative Templates and Computer Configuration ➢ Policies ➢ Administrative Templates change. Specifically, the icons take on a "funnel" image to demonstrate that you're looking through the filtered option. In Figure 3.8, I've "blown up" the User Configuration ➢ Policies➢ Administrative Templates section to show you what I'm talking about.

FIGURE 3.7   More results from our filter on the computer side

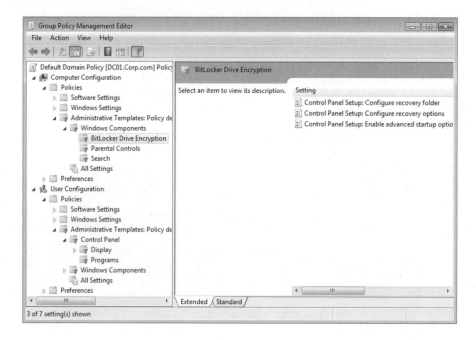

FIGURE 3.8   The funnel image shows you've got filtering enabled.

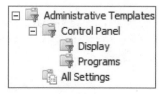

If you ever want to stop looking at only the filtered settings, it's easy. Just right-click any-where within User Configuration ➢ Policies ➢ Administrative Templates or Computer Con-figuration ➢ Policies ➢ Administrative Templates and uncheck Filter On, as seen in Figure 3.9.

When you do, the filter immediately pops off, and you'll be looking at every possible policy setting again.

Reapplying the Filter

In Figure 3.9, you can see the Re-Apply Filter option. Here's how that works: Let's say you apply a filter to show only settings that contain the word *test* in the comment field.

Your results will show you the policy settings that currently match. However, what if you later add more comments to other policy settings that contain the word *test*? Your results won't show that new change immediately. That is, the change won't show until you reapply the filter!

FIGURE 3.9 You can uncheck Filter On to disable the filter.

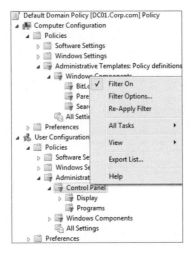

You can see the same result if you choose to show only Not Configured policy settings but then later change one or a few of those to Enabled. Those changes will not be seen until you reapply the filter.

Reapplying the filter really just sets filtering to Off and then turns it back on. Same result (but reapplying the filter is quicker).

The All Settings Node

Along with filters, the All Settings node is a new feature in the updated GPMC. The idea is a little weird, so hang in here with me. There are two ways to leverage the All Settings node: when you're using filtering and when you're not.

Using the All Settings Node in Conjunction with Filtering

The idea is that you can see, at a glance, all the settings that tested "true" for the filter.

Since the results of filtering for *control panel* might exist in various nodes (User Configuration ➢ Policies ➢ Administrative Templates ➢ Control Panel, User Configuration ➢ Policies ➢ Administrative Templates ➢ Control Panel ➢ Display, and User Configuration ➢ Policies ➢ Administrative Templates ➢ Control Panel ➢ Programs), there are a lot of places you'd have to click to see all of your results.

Instead, you can just click the All Settings node (and there's one for each side: User Configuration and Computer Configuration). There you'll see all the matches at a glance. Check it out in Figure 3.10.

In Figure 3.10, you'll also see some other interesting tidbits of information, like whether the policy has been configured (Enabled or Disabled) or if there's a comment within that policy setting (I promise you, we're getting to comments). Finally, it also shows the file path to the policy setting, in case you wanted to show others where to find this policy setting.

FIGURE 3.10   The All Settings node shows 100 percent of the returned filter results in one view.

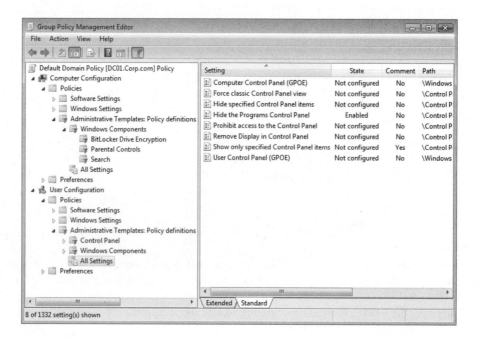

The file path is always relative to User Configuration ➢ Policies ➢ Administrative Templates or Computer Configuration ➢ Policies ➢ Administrative Templates because that's the only place filtering is valid.

Using the All Settings Node without the Use of Filtering

There's another interesting way to use the All Settings node—when the filter is off. There are zillions of policy settings inside User Configuration and Computer Configuration.

What if you just wanted to quickly locate the policy settings with comments?

Or the policy settings that are configured?

Or quickly find a policy setting based on its name?

You could set up a filter (as previously discussed), but that takes several whole seconds! You don't have time for that! You're a busy IT professional!

You can be a speed demon and just click the All Settings node, then click on the column you wish to sort. In Figure 3.11, I've turned off the Filter, then clicked on User Configuration ➢ Policies ➢ Administrative Templates ➢ All Settings, and finally clicked the State column heading.

I can immediately see which policy settings have been configured in this particular GPO. No need to click, click, click my way through filters. This is life in the fast lane.

FIGURE 3.11   Using the All Settings node with filtering turned off

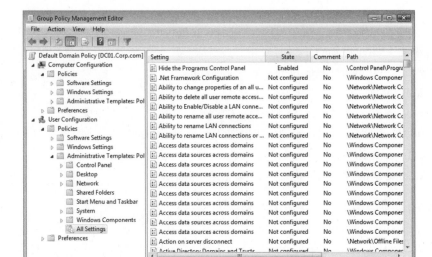

Comments

Imagine for a moment that you're in a large company—maybe you already are and it doesn't require much imagination. Perhaps there are 2, 5, or 50 other administrators. Wouldn't it be nice to be able to leave little messages inside GPOs and particular GPO settings for other administrators who might happen to find a GPO you create?

That's what this section is all about: the Comment feature.

> Again, you'll only be able to leave comments and read others' comments if you use the GPMC 2.0. Admins using Windows XP, Windows 2000, or even Windows Vista *without* the GPMC 2.0 won't be able to read your comments. It only works with the GPMC 2.0.

You can leave and read comments in exactly two places: in the GPO itself and inside a GPO's settings. We'll explore these two here.

Comments about a Specific GPO

In the real world, life moves fast. As a result, sometimes administrators don't always spend the time they would like when crafting the name of a GPO. For instance, you might see a poorly named GPO like "Our Desktop Settings." It's poorly named because it doesn't really explain what those settings are. Is that the Desktop background settings? Or the Control Panel settings? Both? Neither? You get the idea.

Fortunately, now you can choose to leave a comment inside a GPO. Here are some ideas as to what to include when you choose to leave a comment:

- Who's in charge of the GPO

- Who to call if there's a problem with this GPO

- Backup contact information

- Who is supposed to be affected by this GPO

- Detailed information about what the GPO is supposed to do

- Your favorite chocolate chip cookie recipe

Just kidding about that last one. But you get the idea.

Leaving a Comment inside a GPO

Leaving a comment is pretty easy to do, but the problem is that it's not super-duper obvious where to go to leave a comment. (And, as we'll see in the next section, not super-duper obvious where to pick them up, either.)

To leave a comment, you must first have rights to edit the GPO. Then, while you're actually editing the GPO, right-click the topmost node with the name of the GPO, then click Properties, as seen in Figure 3.12. Then you can type in your comment and click OK, as shown in Figure 3.13.

 Windows Vista includes some assistance for right-to-left languages like Arabic and Hebrew. You can find these while right-clicking inside the text field. Things like "Right to Left Reading Order," "Show Unicode Characters," and more are there for that kind of input.

FIGURE 3.12   Leave comments while editing a GPO by going to its Properties dialog.

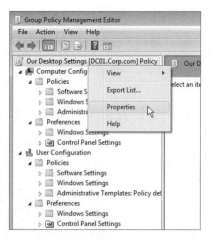

FIGURE 3.13 Entering a comment inside a GPO

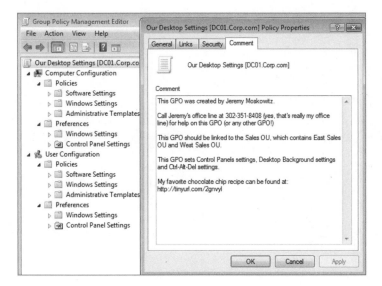

Reading a Comment about a GPO

Reading comments sounds as if it should be easy, but for the uninitiated, they're not easy to find. If you're editing the GPO, you can right-click over the top node, select Properties, and click the Comment tab, as just seen in Figure 3.13. Then, instead of leaving a comment, you can just read the existing comment.

But a better option is found within the GPMC itself. Simply click on the GPO (or the link to the GPO), then click the Details tab, seen in Figure 3.14. You'll see the results in the Comment field below. The formatting is mostly kept the same as when the comment was typed into the Comment editor. And what's more, Unicode characters (like Japanese, Hebrew, etc.) are supported in the editor and the resulting display.

For more information on the Details tab, see Chapter 2 and Chapter 6.

Comments about a Specific GPO Setting

In the last little section you learned how to leave a comment about a particular GPO. Now let's explore the ability to leave comments about a particular Group Policy setting.

Like filters, comments about a specific GPO setting are available only to the Administrative Templates section. You cannot leave comments in other areas, like Security settings (which would be very useful) and the like.

FIGURE 3.14   The Details tab within the GPO shows the comments.

Leaving a Comment inside a Specific GPO Setting

For instance, let's say you wanted to explain why a particular policy setting was Enabled (or Disabled). Simply traverse to the policy setting, get to its properties, then select the Comment tab. Leave a comment like the one you see in Figure 3.15.

FIGURE 3.15   Comments are available on a particular Group Policy setting.

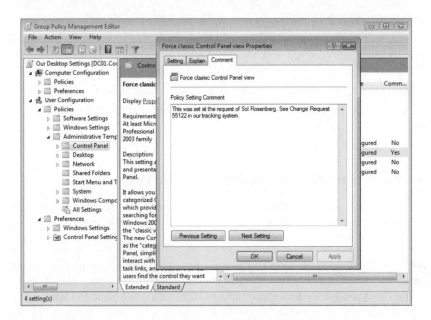

Where and What Are the Comments Anyway?

Behind the scenes, comments are really plain text or XML files placed in SYSVOL.

General GPO comments are placed in a plain text file located here:

`\\<domain>\SYSVOL\<domain>\Policies\<GPO GUID>\CPO.cmt`

Individual comments for GPO settings are placed in two XML files for each GPO, one for Computer Configuration comments and another for User Configuration comments. The files are placed here:

`\\<domain>\SYSVOL\<domain>\Policies\<GPO GUID>\Machine\Comment.cmtx`
`\\<domain>\SYSVOL\<domain>\Policies\<GPO GUID>\User\Comment.cmtx`

Reading a Comment inside a Specific GPO Setting

There are two techniques to quickly read any comments inside particular GPO settings. First, while you're editing the GPO, you can quickly check to see which policy settings (if any) contain comments. You can also see them while tooling around inside the GPMC.

Quickly Spying Comments While Editing the GPO

Remember from my discussion of the All Settings node that if the filter is off, you can then just click either User Configuration ➢ Policies ➢ Administrative Templates ➢ All Settings or Computer Configuration ➢ Policies ➢ Administrative Templates ➢ All Settings and then click the Comment column to sort the ones with comments, which bubble to the top. You can see this in Figure 3.16. Then it's a simple matter of double-clicking the policy setting in question and clicking on the Comment tab to read it.

FIGURE 3.16   The All Settings node (and, actually, all nodes) within the GPME displays a Comment column that can be sorted.

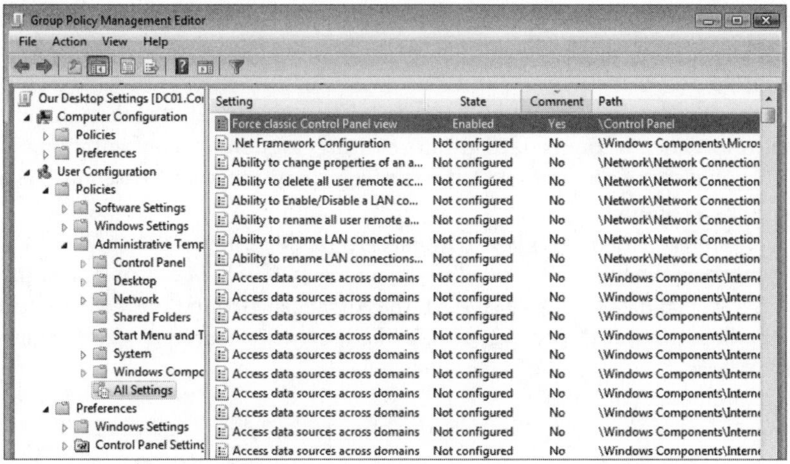

Looking at All Comments While inside the GPMC

The alternative way to see all comments about the policy settings inside the GPO is to view the settings report. Simply click on the GPO (or the link to a GPO) and click the Settings tab. When you do, any comments about any policy settings are displayed inline, as seen in Figure 3.17.

FIGURE 3.17   The comments can be seen inside your GPMC settings reports.

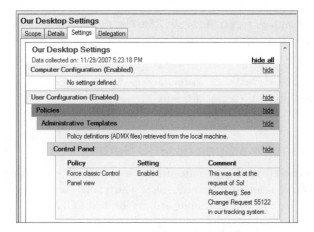

Starter GPOs

The last big, new GPMC feature is called Starter GPOs. In big companies, there are often just a handful of people at the top who really "get" Group Policy. But there are a whole lot of people in the company who have to implement it. Not everyone can take a master class on Group Policy (hint, hint: www.GPanswers.com/workshop) or spend the time reading this book and working through all the examples.

With that in mind, Microsoft created Starter GPOs. The idea is that someone can create a GPO with some baseline settings, including comments, and make them available for others as a jumping-off point.

For instance, if you were the Domain Administrator and wanted to make sure that all your OU administrators got a recommended group of settings for desktop configuration, that would be easy. You would create a Starter GPO, then let them know they had a baseline to use directly, or to edit as they so desired.

You could think of Starter GPOs as templates for making new policies. That way, you're not back to nothing whenever you need to create a new GPO. The problem is, the word *template* has a special meaning with AGPM, the Advanced Group Policy Management tool, which we'll talk about in Chapter 12. That's likely why this feature is called Starter GPOs and not Templates.

When you create your first Starter GPO, a new directory is created in the domain, specifically, the <Domain>\SYSVOL\<Domain>\StarterGPOs folder. During creation, any new Starter GPOs are added underneath this folder and get named the same as their GUIDs, just like any other GPO.

Creating a Starter GPO

The GPMC 2.0 has a new node called Starter GPOs. Simply right-click it and select New. When you do, you'll be prompted to give it a name and make some comments, as you see in Figure 3.18.

FIGURE 3.18 Add a useful comment when creating a new Starter GPO.

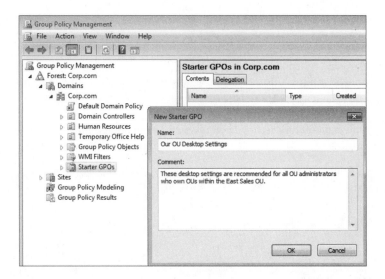

You'll edit this GPO in a minute, but first, take a look at the Details tab of the Starter GPO, which you can see in Figure 3.19. Inside it, you'll see your comment and a field labeled "Starter GPO type." All Starter GPOs that you create will be type Custom. Microsoft might be providing some additional guidance by releasing some of its own Starter GPOs. For instance, I wouldn't be surprised if Microsoft suggests some Lockdown and Security Starter GPOs to help people get a grip on some common problems.

When they're released, they will have a "Starter GPO type" of System.

Be sure to join the www.GPanswers.com newsletter and you'll receive updates when information about new Starter GPOs is released. You can sign up at www.GPanswers.com/newsletter.

FIGURE 3.19   The two types of Starter GPOs are Custom and System.

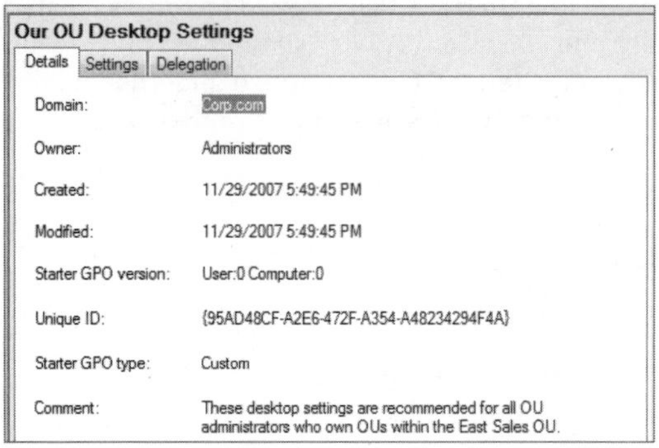

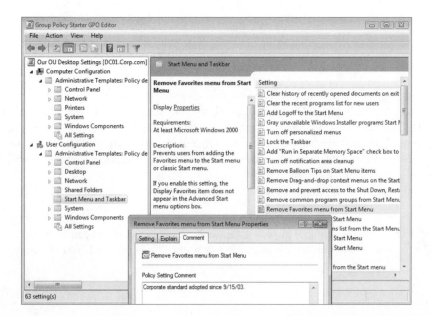

Editing a Starter GPO

Editing a Starter GPO is almost like editing a regular GPO. Just right-click the Starter GPO and select Edit. However, when you do, you'll notice it doesn't look exactly like what you're used to. In fact, only Computer Configuration ➢ Policies ➢ Administrative Templates and User Configuration ➢ Policies ➢ Administrative Templates are available as starter policy settings. You can see this in Figure 3.20.

At this point, you can edit any settings you wish and even add comments about any particular policy settings.

FIGURE 3.20   Starter GPOs allow for Administrative Templates settings along with comments inside any Administrative Templates settings.

Once you're finished, close the GPME.

A keen eye will spot that the Group Policy Object Editor title bar name has changes to "Group Policy Starter GPO Editor" when you edit a Starter GPO.

It's a real bummer that the idea of Starter GPOs wasn't extended to other areas like security. That way, a nice baseline could be generated in all areas of Group Policy, not just Administrative Templates. However, if you're licensed for the Advanced Group Policy Management Tool (AGPM), which we talk about in Chapter 12, you'll see how to leverage an AGPM feature called Templates, which is a lot like Starter GPOs, except that all areas within the GPME are available to use.

Of course, AGPM costs money, and Starter GPOs are free with the new GPMC 2.0. So, the free tool has at least something.

Leveraging a Starter GPO

Now that you've created a Starter GPO, it's time for others to leverage your creation. To do that, an OU administrator (or Domain Admin, etc.) has two options: using the Starter GPOs node or just creating a new GPO as they normally would.

Using the Starter GPOs Node

Right-click the Starter GPO in the Starter GPOs node, and select New GPO From Starter GPO (as seen in Figure 3.21).

FIGURE 3.21   You can spawn a new GPO from the Starter GPOs node.

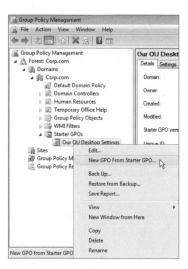

Next, the New GPO dialog appears, and it auto-fills the Source Starter GPO field, as seen in Figure 3.22.

FIGURE 3.22   The source Starter GPO is preset when you are modifying a Starter GPO.

Creating a New GPO and Selecting a Starter GPO

The other way to use a Starter GPO is to simply create a new GPO. This can be done either by right-clicking the Group Policy Objects node and selecting New or by clicking over the Domain or OU levels and selecting "Create a GPO in this domain, and link it here." Regardless of which you do, you'll see the New GPO dialog, shown in Figure 3.23. At this point, you can select Source Starter GPO and choose the Starter GPO you wish to use.

FIGURE 3.23   If you're creating a GPO normally, you can select a Source Starter GPO.

Backing Up and Restoring Starter GPOs

Backing up and Restoring GPOs is covered in Chapter 2. However, it should be noted that the backup that you normally do to protect yourself from GPO deletion, corruption, and plain ol' stupidity doesn't protect you here regarding Starter GPOs.

You'll have to occasionally right-click on the Starter GPOs node and select Backup. When you do, you'll be able to back up the Starter GPOs quite like backing up normal GPOs. You can see an example in Figure 3.24.

Other functions like Restore are completely analogous to what you learned in Chapter 2, so be sure to refer back to that chapter for more information about backup and restore in general.

WARNING   Right now, there's no published scriptable interface for backing up and restoring Starter GPOs. Microsoft tells me that it is possible to do this via scripts, so stay tuned to the www.GPanswers.com newsletter and blog for updates when this occurs.

FIGURE 3.24 Backing up Starter GPOs is very similar to backing up regular GPOs.

Delegating Control of Starter GPOs

Windows 2008, as it ships from the factory, has an issue with Starter GPOs such that they appear to have a bug. That is, right now, they cannot be delegated (beyond the Domain Administrators who already have access).

Hopefully, this will be fixed by the time you read this book.

Stay tuned for an update at www.GPanswers.com in this chapter's resources section for a free Starter GPO update when it's available.

Wrapping Up and Sending Starter GPOs

One of the neat things about Starter GPOs is that you can give them to your friends—even if they belong to other domains. It's sort of like backing up a GPO, except all the guts are wrapped up into one file.

It's simple to do: Just click on the Starter GPOs node in the GPMC. Then find the Starter GPO you want to send to a friend. Then click Save as Cabinet. This will save the file as a CAB file.

When your friend gets it, they simply click the Load Cabinet button to reverse the process. You can see the "Load Cabinet" and "Save as Cabinet" buttons in Figure 3.25.

Inside the CAB files are the guts, as seen in Figure 3.26.

FIGURE 3.25 You can save and load Starter GPOs from CAB files

FIGURE 3.26 The guts of the Starter GPO are in a CAB file.

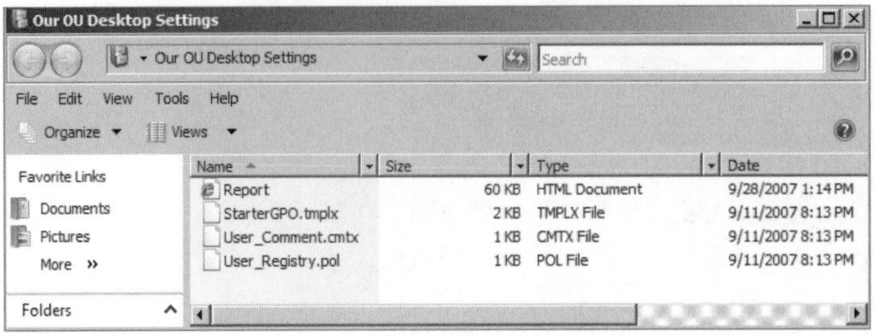

There doesn't seem to be a way to wrap up multiple Starter GPOs into a single CAB file. That would make transporting them enormously easier, but, alas.

Final Thoughts

In this chapter you learned what the GPMC 2.0 can do. Again, these features are only available if one of the following is true:

- You're editing and managing your GPOs from a Windows Server 2008 management station

- You're editing and managing your GPOs from a management station that is Windows Vista + SP1 + newly downloadable GPMC 2.0, which is part of the RSAT tools.

There's one more big thing the updated GPMC brings to the table that bears mentioning. That is that the new Group Policy Preference Extensions are built into Windows Server 2008 (and will also be available as a download for Windows XP and Windows Vista clients—more on this in Chapter 10). And the new GPMC is updated to support the reporting of those features. You'll be seeing sample reports in Chapter 10, so no need to show them to you here.

In the beginning of the book, I pushed hard for you to consider using a Windows Vista management station (or Windows Server 2008) to create and manage your GPOs. If this chapter isn't enough, there's more excruciating detail about why in Chapter 7 and 10.

So, in short, that message doesn't change. Be sure you're using the GPMC 2.0 so you'll get these new filters, comments, and Starter GPO features.

4

Group Policy Processing Behavior Essentials

After you create or modify a GPO in the domain, the policy "wishes" are not immediately dropped on the target machines. In fact, they're not dropped on the target machines at all; they're requested by the client computer at various times throughout the day. GPOs are processed at specific times, based on various conditions. You could basically say that GPOs are "pulled" by the client but originate at the server.

It's likely that you have Windows 2000, Windows XP, Windows 2003, and now Windows Vista and Windows Server 2008 machines in your environment. Each operating system that receives Group Policy instructions processes Group Policy at different times in different ways. With different operating systems requesting different things at different times, the expected behaviors can really get confusing quickly.

Additionally, other factors determine when and how a GPO applies. When users dial in over slow links, things can be—and usually are—different. And you can instruct the Group Policy engine (on a specific computer or all computers) to forgo its out-of-the-box processing behaviors for a customized (and often more secure) way to process.

Often, people throw up their hands when the Group Policy engine doesn't seem to process the dictated GPOs in an expected manner. Group Policy doesn't just process when it wants to; rather, it adheres to a strict set of processing rules. The goal of this chapter and the next chapter is to answer this question: *When* does Group Policy apply?

Understanding the processing rules will help you better understand when Group Policy processes GPOs the way it does. Then, in Chapter 6, you'll get a grip on *why* Group Policy applies. Between these three chapters, your goal is to discover how Group Policy can apply under different circumstances and how you can become a better Group Policy troubleshooter.

Group Policy Processing Principles

For you to best understand how Windows XP or Windows Vista processes GPOs, I'll first describe how Windows 2000 does its thing. Then, we'll better understand how and why Windows XP's and Windows Vista's processing is different. Sure, Windows Server 2003 and Windows Server 2008 also process GPOs as a Group Policy client. We'll pepper in that information when necessary. But, as you're reading along, try to focus on the typical client computer.

To get a feel of how GPO processing works, we're going to walk through what happens to three users:

- Wally, who uses only a Windows 2000 Professional machine
- Xavier, who uses only a Windows XP machine
- Victoria, who uses only a Windows Vista machine

By using Wally, Xavier, and Victoria as our three sample users (on our three sample computers), we can see precisely when Group Policy applies to them—when they're using Windows 2000 machines, Windows XP machines, and Windows Vista machines.

Before we go even one step further, let me debunk a popular myth about Group Policy processing. That is, Group Policy is never *pushed* from the server and forced upon the clients. Rather, the process is quite the opposite. Group Policy occurs when the Group Policy engine on a Windows client requests Group Policy. This happens at various times, but at no time can you magically declare from on high, "All clients?! Go forth and accept my latest GPOs!" It doesn't work like that. Clients request GPOs according to the rules listed in this chapter.

 On www.GPanswers.com, in the "Solutions Guide" I have pointers to two free downloads that can perform a "remote" Group Policy refresh. One is a command-line tool (rGPrefresh), and the other is a graphical snap-in to Active Directory Users and Computers (Specops GPUpdate). You can also check out Jakob Heidelberg's "How to Force Remote Group Policy Processing" solutions here: http://www.windowsecurity.com/articles/How-Force-Remote-Group-Policy-Processing.html. (Shortened to http://tinyurl.com/2opez6).

In a nutshell, Group Policy is potentially triggered to apply at four times. Here's a rundown of those times; I'll discuss them in grueling detail in the next sections.

Initial Policy Processing   For Windows 2000, Windows 2003, and Windows Server 2008 machines, processing occurs when the computer starts up or when the user logs on. By default, in "daily life" there is no initial policy processing for Windows XP machines or Windows Vista machines.

However, later we'll note an exception to this rule: when a user has never logged in before a computer first joins the domain.

Background Refresh Policy Processing (Member Computers)   For Windows 2000, Windows 2003, Windows 2008, Windows XP, and Windows Vista member machines, processing occurs some time after the user logs on (usually at 90-minute intervals or so). A bit later, you'll see how Windows XP and Windows Vista leverage the background policy processing mechanism to a distinct advantage.

Background Refresh Policy Processing (Domain Controllers)   Domain Controllers need love too, and to that end, all Domain Controllers perform a background refresh every 5 minutes (after replication has occurred).

Security Policy Processing   For all operating systems, only the security settings within all GPOs are reprocessed and applied every 16 hours regardless of whether they have changed. This safety mechanism prevents unscrupulous local workstation administrators from doing too much harm.

> You can change the default behavior of certain nonsecurity policy settings so they are enforced in a manner similar to the way that security settings are automatically enforced. But you have to explicitly turn this feature on, and you have to do so correctly. In the section "Security Policy Processing" later in this chapter, I describe how to do this and give you several examples of why you would want to do so.

Special Case: Moving a User or Computer Object   Although all the previous items demonstrate a trigger of when Group Policy applies, one case isn't trigger-specific; however, it's important to understand a special case of Group Policy processing behavior. You might think that if you move a user or computer around in Active Directory (specifically, from one OU to another), then Group Policy is set to reapply—the system would "know" it's been moved around in Active Directory. But that doesn't happen. When you move a user or a computer from one OU to another, background processing may not immediately understand that something was moved. Some time later, the system should detect the change, and background processing should start normally again.

Don't Get Lost   There are definitely nuances in the processing mechanism among the various operating systems. The good news, if your head starts to swim a bit, is that you can dog-ear this page and highlight this little area for quick reference. If you remember one takeaway from this chapter, it should be this: There are three behavior types for target computers:

- Behavior type 1: Windows 2000 Professional workstations, Windows 2000 member servers, Windows Server 2003 member servers, and Windows Server 2008 member servers

- Behavior type 2: Domain Controllers of all sorts: Windows 2000 and Windows Server 2003 and Windows Server 2008

- Behavior type 3: Windows XP and Windows Vista

It's important to understand the difference between these three behavior types. And, once you understand the difference between them, you can decide if you want to take the machines which are in Behavior type 3 (Windows XP and Windows Vista) and make them act like machines which are in Behavior type 1 (Windows 2000 and Windows Server 2003 and Windows Server 2008).

By now, you might have expunged Windows 2000 systems from your domain. However, I would strongly encourage you to read about how all systems are processed.

This is for three reasons:

1. The behaviors described in the following sections are all based upon the original Windows 2000 behavior.

2. It's easier to understand the Windows XP and Windows Vista behavior if you understand the original Windows 2000 behavior.

3. Later in the chapter I'm going to encourage you to "Make your Windows XP and Windows Vista machines act like Windows 2000." So, if you don't understand the Windows 2000 behavior, you won't know what I'm talking about.

Initial Policy Processing

Recall that each GPO has two halves: a Computer half and a User half. This is important to remember when trying to understand when GPOs are processed. Windows 2000 and Windows 2003 perform what is called *initial policy processing*. Windows XP and Windows Vista are also capable of initial policy processing, but it doesn't work quite the same as its Windows 2000 counterpart.

Windows 2000 (and Windows Server 2003 and Windows Server 2008) Initial Policy Processing

Our sample computer user Wally walks into his office and turns on his Windows 2000 Professional machine. The computer half of the policy is always processed at the target machines upon startup as his machine reboots. When a Windows 2000 or Windows 2003 machine starts up, it states that it is "Processing security policy." What this really should say is "Processing Group Policy" (but it doesn't).

 Actually, Windows Server 2008 sometimes goes the extra mile and shows you the name of the Group Policy that is actually applying at that second, which is nice. Except it's not consistent, which is annoying.

At that time, the workstation logs onto the network by contacting a Domain Controller. It finds the Domain Controller by looking up DNS records which say, "Hey, here's the name of a Domain Controller." The Domain Controller then tells the workstation which site it belongs to, which domain it belongs to, and which OU it is in. The system then downloads and processes the computer half of Group Policy in that order. When the processing is finished, the "Press Ctrl+Alt+Delete to begin" prompt is revealed, and Wally can log on by pressing Ctrl+Alt+Delete and giving his username and password.

After Wally is validated to Active Directory, the user half of the GPO is downloaded and then processed in the same precise order: site, domain, and then each nested OU.

Wally's Windows 2000 Desktop is manipulated by the policy settings inside any GPOs targeting Wally's user or computer account. Wally's Desktop is displayed only when all the user-side GPOs are processed.

If you look at how all this goes, you'll see it's a lock-step mechanism: the computer starts up and then processes GPOs in the natural order: local, site, domain, and each nested OU. The user then logs on, and Group Policy is processed, again in the natural order: local, site, domain, and each nested OU. This style of GPO processing is called *synchronous processing*. That is, in order to proceed to the next step in either the startup or the logon processes, the previous step must be completed. For example, the GPOs at the OU level of the user are never downloaded before the GPOs at the site level. Likewise, the GPOs at the domain level for Windows 2000 (and Windows Server 2003 and Windows Server 2008) are never downloaded before the site GPOs that affect a computer.

Therefore, the default for Windows 2000 (and Windows Server 2003 and Windows Server 2008) for both the computer startup and the user logon is that each GPO is processed synchronously. This same process occurs every time a user booting a Windows 2000 (or Windows Server 2003 or Windows Server 2008) machine turns on the machine and then logs on.

Windows XP and Windows Vista Initial Policy Processing

Xavier walks into his office and turns on his Windows XP machine. For a moment, let's assume this is the *first time* that this Windows XP machine has started up since joining the domain. Perhaps it just landed on Xavier's desk after a new desktop rollout of Windows XP. If this is the case, the Windows XP machine will act just like Windows 2000 (as described above). It will look to see which site, domain, and OUs the computer account is in and then apply GPOs synchronously. Likewise, let's assume this is the first time Xavier is logging into this Windows XP machine with his user account, which lives in Active Directory. Again, imagine that this machine just arrived after a desktop rollout. In this case, again, Windows XP will act like Windows 2000 (and synchronously process GPOs based on the site, domain, and OU Xavier is logging on from).

So far, so good. However, Windows XP performs this initial synchronous processing only in this special case described here. That is, either the computer has never started in the domain before or the user has never logged onto this particular Windows XP machine before. To understand Windows XP's normal default processing mode, take a deep breath and read on.

Victoria's experience on Windows Vista will be the same as Xavier's. That is, if Victoria walks into her office and turns on her Windows Vista machine for the first time and logs into the machine for the first time, it will act like Windows 2000 and process GPOs synchronously for both the computer (during startup) and the user (during login).

Background Refresh Policy Processing

Once Wally is logged onto Windows 2000 (or Windows 2003 or Windows Server 2008), and Xavier is logged onto Windows XP, and Victoria is plugging along on Windows Vista, things are great—for everyone. As the administrators, we're happy because Wally, Xavier, and Victoria are all receiving our wishes. They're happy because, well, they're just happy, that's all.

But, now, we decide to add a new GPO or to modify a policy setting inside an existing GPO. What if something is modified in the Group Policy Management Editor that should affect a user or a computer? Aren't Wally, Xavier, and Victoria already logged on—happy as clams? Well, a new setting is destined for an already-logged-in user or computer, and the new changes (and only the new changes) are indeed reflected on the user or computer that should receive them. But this delivery doesn't happen immediately; rather, the changes are delivered according to the *background refresh interval* (sometimes known as the *background processing interval*).

The background refresh interval dictates how often changed GPOs in Active Directory are pulled by the client computer. As I implied earlier, there are different background intervals for the different operating systems' roles (that is, member versus Domain Controller).

When the background refresh interval comes to pass, GPOs are processed *asynchronously*. That is, if a GPO that affects a user's OU (or other Active Directory level) is changed, the changes are pulled to the local computer when the clock strikes the processing time. It doesn't matter if the change happens at any level in Active Directory: OU, domain, or site. When changes are available to users or computers after the user or computer is already logged on, the changes are processed asynchronously. Whichever GPOs at any level have changed, those changes are reflected on the client.

> Standard *application rules* still apply, and the precedence order is still reflected: site, domain, OU. In other words, even though a new GPO linked to a site is ready, it isn't necessarily going to trump a GPO linked to the OU.

When does this happen? According to the background refresh interval for the operating system (discussed next).

Background Refresh Intervals for Windows 2000/2003/2008 Members

It stands to reason that when we change an existing GPO (or create a new GPO), we want our users and computers to get the latest and greatest set of instructions and wishes. With that in mind, let's continue with our example. Remember that Wally is on his Windows 2000 machine and Xavier is on his Windows XP machine.

By default, the background refresh interval for Windows 2000 workstations and for Windows 2000 and Windows 2003 member servers is 90 minutes, with a 0–30 minute positive random differential added to the mix to ensure that no gaggle of PCs will refresh at any one time and clog your network asking for mass GPO downloads from Domain Controllers. Therefore, once a change has been made to a GPO, it could take as little as 90 minutes or as long as 120 minutes for each user or workstation that is already logged onto the network to see that change.

> Microsoft documentation isn't consistent in this description. Often, Microsoft documentation will say the offset is 30 minutes (which could be interpreted as positive or negative 30 minutes). Indeed, in the first edition of this book, I incorrectly reported that "fact." However, since then, I have verified with Microsoft that the refresh interval is (and has always been) 90 minutes plus (not minus) 0–30 minutes.

Again, this is known as the background refresh interval. Additionally, the background refresh interval for the Computer half of Group Policy and the User half of Group Policy are on their own independent schedules. That is, the Computer half or the User half might be refreshed before the other half; they're not necessarily refreshed at the exact same moment because they're on their own individual timetables. This makes sense: the computer and user didn't each get Group Policy at the precise moment in time in the first place, did they?

You can change the background refresh interval for the computer half and/or the user half using Group Policy, as described later in this chapter in the section cleverly titled "Using Group Policy to Affect Group Policy."

You can set individual policy settings to prevent specific areas of Group Policy from being refreshed in the background, such as Internet Explorer Maintenance and Administrative Templates. See the section "Using Group Policy to Affect Group Policy" later in the chapter.

How Does the Group Policy Engine Know What's New or Changed?

The Group Policy engine on Windows 2000 and Windows XP can keep track of what's new or changed via a control mechanism called *version numbers*. Each GPO has a version number for each half of the GPO, and this is stored in Active Directory. If the version number in Active Directory doesn't change, nothing is downloaded. Since nothing has changed, the Group Policy engine thinks it has all the latest-greatest stuff—so why bother to redownload it (which takes time) and reprocess it (which takes more time)?

By default, when a background refresh interval arrives, a time-saving mechanism, "checking the GPO version numbers," is employed to minimize the time needed to get the latest-greatest GPOs. You'll learn more about GPO version numbers in Chapter 6.

To reiterate, when the background refresh interval arrives, only the new or changed GPOs are downloaded and processed.

Background Refresh Intervals for Windows 2000/2003/2008 Domain Controllers

Even though neither Wally nor Xavier are logging onto Domain Controllers, other people might. And because Domain Controllers are a bit special, the processing for Domain Controllers is handled in a special way.

Because Group Policy contains sensitive security settings (for example, Password and Account Policy, Kerberos Policy, Audit Policy), any policy geared for a Domain Controller is refreshed within 5 minutes. This adds a tighter level of security to Domain Controllers. For more information on precisely how the default GPOs work, see Chapter 8.

You can change the background interval for Domain Controllers using Group Policy (as described later in the section "Using Group Policy to Affect Group Policy"). However, you really shouldn't mess with the default values here. They work pretty well.

You'll learn more about affecting Domain Controllers' security in Chapter 8.

Background Refresh Exemptions

Wally has been logged onto his Windows 2000 machine for 4 hours. Xavier has been logged onto his Windows XP machine and Victoria has been logged onto her Windows Vista machine for the same amount of time. Clearly, the background refresh interval has come and gone—somewhere between two and three times.

If any GPOs had been created or any existing GPOs had changed while Wally, Xavier, and Victoria were logged on, both their user accounts and their computer accounts would have embraced the newest policy settings. However, four policy categories are exceptions and are never processed in the background while users are logged on:

Folder Redirection (Explored in Detail in Chapter 3 of the Companion Book)   Folder Redirection's goal is to anchor specific directories, such as the My Documents folder, to certain network shared folders. This policy is never refreshed during a background refresh. The logic behind this is that if an administrator changes this location while the user is using it (and the system responds), the user's data could be at risk for corruption. If the administrator changes Folder Redirection via Group Policy, this change affects only the user at the next logon.

Software Installation (Explored in Detail in Chapter 4 of the Companion Book)   Software Installation is also exempt from background refresh. You can use Group Policy to deploy software packages, large and small, to your users or to your computers. You can also use Group Policy to revoke already-distributed software packages. Software is neither installed nor revoked to users or computers when the background interval comes to pass. You wouldn't want users to lose applications right in the middle of use and, hence, lose or corrupt data. These functions occur only at startup for the computer or at logon for the user.

Special Operations Software has a great third-party tool called Specops Deploy that will permit the deployment of software while the user is logged on. Check out www.GPanswers.com in the "Third-Party Solutions Guide" section for more information.

Logon, Logoff, Startup, and Shutdown Scripts (Explored in Detail in Chapter 8)   These scripts are run only at the appointed time (at logon, logoff, startup, or shutdown). These are not run again and again when the background processing interval comes around. Note that script updates (for example, location and path changes) are updated while the user is already logged on. It's just that, of course, they won't run again until the appointed time.

Disk Quotas (Explored in Previous Editions of the Book)   These are not run when the background processing interval comes around. They are run (changed, really) only at computer startup.

Windows XP/Windows Vista and Background Processing

As I stated in the introduction to this section, Windows XP and Windows Vista do not process new Group Policy updates in the same way that Windows 2000, Windows Server 2003, and Windows Server 2008 do. Let's get a grip on how Windows XP and Windows Vista work.

Now that Xavier has logged onto his Windows XP machine for the first time and Victoria has logged onto her Windows Vista machine for the first time, their sessions will continue to process GPOs in the background as I just described: every 90 minutes or so if any new GPOs appear or any existing GPOs have changed. Xavier now goes home for the night. He logs off the domain and shuts down his machine. When he comes in the next morning, he will not process GPOs the same way that Wally will on his Windows 2000 machine.

When Xavier (or Victoria) logs on the second time (and all subsequent times) to a Windows XP or Windows Vista machine, initial policy processing will no longer be performed as described in the section "Initial Policy Processing" earlier in this chapter. From this point forward, at startup or logon, Windows XP and Windows Vista will not process GPOs synchronously like Windows 2000; rather, GPOs will be processed only in the background.

If you're scratching your head at this point as to why Windows 2000 is different than Windows XP and Windows Vista, here's the short answer. When Windows XP was in development, all the stops were pulled to make the "XPerience" as fast as possible. Both boot times and logon times were indeed faster than ever, but the trade-off came at a price.

By default, Windows XP and Windows Vista process GPOs asynchronously—both at computer startup and at user logon. Upon startup, the computer doesn't wait for the network interface to initialize before starting to process computer GPOs. Windows XP and Windows Vista use the last-known downloaded GPOs as their baseline, even if GPOs have changed in Active Directory while the Windows XP or Windows Vista machine was turned off.

While the network card is still warming up and finding the network and the first Domain Controller, the last-used computer GPOs are already being used. Then, the "Press Ctrl+Alt+Delete to begin" prompt is presented to the user. While this prompt is presented, Windows XP downloads any new computer GPOs. These new computer GPOs are not applied until a bit later.

Assuming the user is now logged on, the Desktop and Start menu appear. Again, the system will not synchronously download the latest site, domain, and OU Group Policy Objects and apply them before displaying the Desktop. Instead, other activity is happening while the latest-greatest Group Policy is being downloaded, so the user might not see the latest-greatest Group Policy effects right away.

Once the computer has started, the user is logged on, and any previously known computer and user GPOs are applied, newly downloaded GPOs (and the policy settings inside) are then processed asynchronously in the background. This net result is a bit of a compromise. The user feels that there is a faster boot time (when the GPO contains computer policy settings) as well as faster logon time (when the GPO is contains user policy settings). The most important policy settings, such as updated Security settings and Administrative Templates (Registry updates), are applied soon after logon—and no one is the wiser. Microsoft calls this Group Policy processing behavior *Fast Boot* (sometimes called *Logon Optimization*). Yes, it does speed things up a bit, but at a cost.

To keep things simple, we just walked through what would happen for Xavier on his Windows XP machine. However, the exact same behavior would occur for Victoria on her Windows Vista machine. There is no difference between Windows Vista and Windows XP in this respect.

Windows XP/Windows Vista Fast-Boot Results

Fast Boot affects two major components: Group Policy processing and user-account attribute processing. The (sometimes strange) results occur for both Xavier on his Windows XP machine and Victoria on her Windows Vista machine when they have previously logged onto it. On his Windows 2000 machine, Wally is spared the Fast Boot behavior.

WINDOWS XP/WINDOWS VISTA FAST BOOT GROUP POLICY PROCESSING DETAILS

The immediate downside to the Windows XP and Windows Vista Fast Boot approach is that, potentially, a user could be totally logged on but not quite have all the GPOs processed. Then, once they are working for a little while—pop! A setting takes effect out of the blue. This is because not all GPOs were processed before the user was presented with the Desktop and Start menu. Your network would have to be pretty slow for this scenario to occur, but it's certainly possible.

The next major downside takes a bit more to wrap your head around. Some Group Policy (and Profile) features can potentially take Windows XP and Windows Vista several additional logons or reboots to actually get the changes you want on them. This strange behavior becomes understandable when we take a step back and think about how certain policy categories are processed on Windows 2000. Specifically, we need to direct our attention to Software Distribution and Folder Redirection policy. I mentioned that on Windows 2000 these two types of policy categories *must* be processed in the foreground (or synchronously) to prevent data corruption. That is, if there are Software Distribution or Folder Redirection edicts to embrace, then they can happen *only* during startup or login.

But we have a paradox: If Windows XP and Windows Vista only process GPOs asynchronously, how are the Software Distribution and Folder Redirection polices handled if they must be handled *synchronously*?

Windows XP and Windows Vista fake it and tag the machine when a software package is targeted for the user or system. The next time the user logs on (or the computer is rebooted for computer-side policy), the Group Policy engine sees that the machine is tagged for Software Distribution and switches, just for this one time, back into synchronous mode. The net result: Windows XP and Windows Vista machines typically require two logons (or reboots) for a user or computer to get a software distribution package.

Again, note that Windows 2000 Professional machines only require one logon (for user settings) or one reboot (for computer settings).

Folder Redirection is a wonderful tool. It has two modes: Basic Folder Redirection (which applies to everyone in the OU) and Advanced Folder Redirection (which checks which security groups the user is in). Windows XP and Windows Vista machines won't get the effects of Basic Folder Redirection for two logons! And Windows XP and Windows Vista machines won't get the effects of Advanced Folder Redirection for a whopping three logons. The first logon tags the system for a Folder Redirection change; the second logon figures out the user's security group membership; and the third logon actually performs the new Folder Redirection—synchronously for just that one logon.

We don't cover Folder Redirection in this book. For details on Folder Redirection, check out Chapter 3 of the companion book.

Again, remember that Fast Boot is automatically disabled the first time any Windows XP or Windows Vista machine is started as a member of the domain. It is also disabled the first time any new user logs onto a Windows XP or Windows Vista client. In these situations, Windows XP and Windows Vista assume (correctly) that no GPO information is known and therefore must go out to Active Directory to get the latest GPOs. The net effect is that if settings for either (or both) Folder Redirection policy and Software Distribution policy already exist, the user will not require additional logons or reboots *the first time* they log onto a Windows XP or Windows Vista machine or when the computer is started for the first time after joining the domain.

FAST BOOT USER-ACCOUNT ATTRIBUTE PROCESSING DETAILS

Group Policy is only one of two areas affected by the Windows XP and Windows Vista Fast Boot mechanism. Some Microsoft documentation claims that other parts of the user's information could require several logons or reboots to take effect.

The idea is that certain attributes are cached and assumed to be accurate at logon. If, after a background download, the information is actually changed, it would only be on the next logon that the change will take effect.

Microsoft says Windows XP takes two logons or reboots to process the following attributes:

- Roaming profile path (discussed in Chapter 2 of the companion book)
- The home directory
- Old-style logon scripts

I have observed this behavior, but I cannot figure out a strict set of rules for when it takes two logons or reboots and when it only takes one. However, in my testing, the aforementioned attributes almost never do take two logons or reboots to apply. But it is possible.

So, under certain circumstances (with Fast Boot enabled), the preceding will hold true. If the user is using Windows XP or Windows Vista, and any of these properties are changed in Active Directory, it *could* take two logons for these changes to actually take effect.

Turning off Windows XP/Windows Vista Fast Boot

If you want your Windows XP and Windows Vista computers to start up a teeny-weeny bit faster (and have your users' Desktops pop up a teeny-weeny bit faster), by all means leave the default of Fast Boot on.

If you're doing some no-no's in Group Policy (namely setting up cross-domain Group Policy links or processing a lot of site-based GPOs), leaving Fast Boot on will, in fact, serve its purpose and likely make each and every startup and logon a wee bit faster.

My recommendation, however, is to get all your machines—Windows XP, Windows Vista, and Windows 2000 Professional—to act the same. That is, I suggest that you force your Windows XP and Windows Vista machines to act like Windows 2000 machines and perform synchronous policy processing during their startup and logon. To do this, you need to create a Group Policy that contains a setting to revert Windows XP and Windows Vista machines back to the old behavior. It might be a smidgen slower to log on, but no slower than your Windows 2000 machines already are.

This will make your Windows XP and Windows Vista machines perform initial policy processing at startup and logon—just like your Windows 2000 machines. That is, the computer will start up, locate all GPOs, and then process them—before displaying the "Press Ctrl+Alt+Delete to begin" prompt. Once the user is logged on, all GPOs are processed before the Desktop is displayed.

Troubleshooting Group Policy is now a heck of a lot more predictable because you're not trying to guess when Software Distribution, Folder Redirection, or when even some settings from Administrative Templates are going to be processed. Since your Windows 2000 machines already act this way (and you can't make Windows 2000 Fast Boot like Windows XP), it probably would be a good enterprise supportability practice to have all machines in your environment act as similarly as possible—even if they are different operating systems.

To set Windows XP and Windows Vista to the Windows 2000 synchronous behavior, for Initial Policy Processing, create and link a GPO (preferably at the domain level) to simply enable the policy setting named **Always wait for the network at computer startup and logon**. This policy can be found in the Computer Configuration ➢ Policies ➢ Administrative Templates ➢ System ➢ Logon branch of Group Policy. The name of this policy setting is a bit confusing. It would have been better, in my opinion, to name it **Make All Client Machines Process GPOs Like Windows 2000**. But they didn't.

Don't give the name of the policy setting **Always wait for the network at computer startup and logon** too much contemplation, even though it's confusing. It does not mean that the machine will just "hang" there until it sees the network during startup and logon. Its job is really only to make Windows XP and Windows Vista machines act like Windows 2000.

Remember, to force Windows XP and Windows Vista machines to receive this computer policy (or any computer policy), the computer account must be within the site, domain, or OU where you set the policy. If you set this policy at the domain level (and enforce it to ensure that it cannot be blocked), you're guaranteed that all Windows XP and Windows Vista machines in your domain will get the policy.

By performing this at the domain level and enforcing the link, all your machines—Windows XP, Windows Vista, Windows 2000, and Windows 2003—will receive the message. But remember that policy settings meant for Windows XP or other operating systems won't affect Windows 2000 machines.

Forcing Background Policy Processing

You get a phone call from the person who handles the firewalls and proxy servers at your company. He tells you that he's added an additional proxy server for your users to use when going out to the Internet. Excitedly, you add a new GPO that affects Wally and Xavier's user objects so they can use the new proxy server via Internet Explorer Maintenance Settings. But you're impatient.

You know that when you make this setting, it's going to take between 90 and 120 minutes to kick in. And you don't want to tell Wally or Xavier to log off and log back on to get the policy—they wouldn't like that much.

In cases like these, you might want to bypass the normal wait time before background policy processing kicks in. The good news is that you can run a simple command that tells the client to skip the normal background processing interval and request an update of new or changed GPOs from the server right now. Again, only new GPOs or GPOs that have changed on the server in some way will actually come down and be reflected on your client machines.

Initiating a Manual Background Refresh for Windows 2000

The command-line tool used to encourage your Windows 2000 machines to kick off a manual background refresh is `secedit`. `secedit` can request the refresh of GPOs (and the settings therein) from the User Configuration node, the Computer Configuration node, or both, but you'll need to run the command once for each half.

As I've mentioned, there is no way from on high to say, "Go forth and refresh, all ye users or computers affected by this recent change in policy!" To utilize `secedit`, you must physically be present at the Windows 2000 machine and execute the command. Otherwise, you must simply wait for the background refresh interval to kick in.

> You can independently change the background refresh interval of both the user and computer. See the section "Using Group Policy to Affect Group Policy" later in this chapter.

But, because you're impatient, you want to see Wally on his Windows 2000 machine start using that new proxy server setting that you plunked into that GPO right away. So you physically trot out to his machine, log on with administrator-level authority, and enter the following commands to manually refresh the GPOs.

For Windows 2000, follow these steps to request a refresh of GPOs from the User Configuration node:

1. Choose Start ➢ Run to open the Run dialog box, and in the Open box, enter **cmd** to open the command-line window.

2. At the prompt, type `secedit /refreshpolicy user_policy`.

For Windows 2000, follow these steps to request a refresh of GPOs from the Computer Configuration node:

1. Choose Start ➢ Run to open the Run dialog box, and in the Open box, enter **cmd** to open the command-line window.

2. At the prompt, type `secedit /refreshpolicy machine_policy`.

See Chapter 8 for additional uses of the `secedit` command.

> You might want to create a batch file called `s.bat` or even `gpupdate.bat`, which runs `secedit` to initiate machine and user policy settings to apply. Then, if you place this batch file on all your workstations, you can perform both in one stroke!

Initiating a Manual Background Refresh for Windows XP and Above

You now want to initiate a manual refresh for Xavier on his Windows XP machine and Victoria on her Windows Vista machine. All operating systems from Windows XP and above refresh GPOs using a different command called `gpupdate`. The `gpupdate` command is similar to `secedit` in that it can refresh either the user or the computer half of a GPO or both. The syntax is `gpupdate /Target:Computer`, `/Target:User`, or just `gpupdate` by itself to trigger both.

Running `gpupdate` while Xavier is logged onto his Windows XP machine immediately gives him the new settings in the GPO you just set. This is, of course, provided the Domain Controller that Xavier and his Windows XP machine are using has the replicated GPO information. Ditto for Victoria on her Windows Vista machine.

Additionally, `gpupdate` can figure out if newly changed items require a logoff or reboot to be active. Since Windows XP and Windows Vista's default behavior is to enable Fast Boot, Software Distribution and Folder Redirection settings are processed only at future logon times. Therefore, specifying `gpupdate` with a `/Logoff` switch will figure out if a policy has changed in Active Directory such that a logoff is required and then automatically log you off. If the updated GPO does not require a logoff, the GPO settings are applied and the currently logged-on user remains logged on.

Similarly, with Windows XP's and Windows Vista's Fast Boot enabled, GPOs that have Software Distribution settings will require a reboot before the software will be available. Therefore, specifying `gpupdate` with a `/boot` switch will figure out if a policy has something that requires a reboot and automatically reboot the computer. If the updated GPO does not require a reboot, the GPO settings are applied, and the user remains logged on.

The `/Logoff` and `/boot` switches are optional.

> For information about how to turn off Windows XP's and Windows Vista's Fast Boot and make it act like Windows 2000, refer to the section "Turning Off Windows XP/Windows Vista Fast Boot" earlier in this chapter.

Security Background Refresh Processing

Even before Microsoft had the big, internal security hurrah, some modicum of security was built into the Group Policy engine. As I've stated, all Group Policy clients process GPOs when the background refresh interval comes to pass—but only those GPOs that were new or changed since the last time the client requested them.

GPUpdate /force Command for Windows XP and higher versus Windows Vista (and Windows Server 2008)

There is one peculiarity about the gpupdate /force command when run in Windows XP. If there's a GPO that deploys software to your user or computer and you run the gpudate /force command, sometimes it gets confused and thinks that the underlying GPOs have changed—even though they haven't. So, when it gets confused, gpupdate will express that a reboot (or logoff) is needed to get the full set of GPOs. However, this isn't strictly correct.

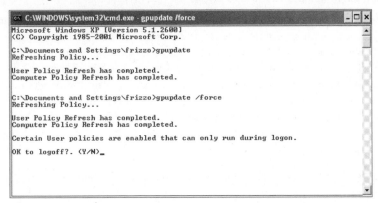

Windows Vista and Windows Server 2008 have apparently cured this inconsistency. Their gpupdate does something different. The newer GPupdate command will inform you that during the next foreground refresh, it will occur synchronously to ensure that all policy is applied.

Wally is on a Windows 2000 machine, and he's been logged on for 4 hours. Likewise, Xavier has been logged onto his Windows XP machine for 4 hours and Victoria has been logged onto her Windows Vista machine for 4 hours.

Imagine for a second that there was a GPO in Active Directory named "Remove Run menu from Start Menu" and its function was to do just that. The client would certainly do so according to the initial policy processing rules and/or the background refresh processing rules.

Assuming that the underlying GPO doesn't get any policy settings modified or any new policy settings or that the GPO itself doesn't get removed, the client already knows to accept this edict. The client just accepts that things haven't changed and, hence, keeps on truckin'. Only a change inside the GPO will trigger the client to realize that new instructions are available, and the client will execute that new edict during its background policy processing.

Now, let's assume that we anoint Wally, Xavier, and Victoria as local administrators of their Windows 2000, Windows XP, and Windows Vista machines, respectively. Since Wally, Xavier, and Victoria are now local administrators, they have total control to go around the Group Policy engine processes and make their own changes. These changes could nullify a policy you've previously set with a GPO and allow them to access and to change features on the system that shouldn't be changed. In this case, there are certainly going to be situations in which the GPOs on the Domain Controllers don't change, but certain parts of the workstation should remain locked down anyway.

Of course, the right answer is to only give people you absolutely trust access to local Administrator accounts. You should never give regular users Administrator accounts if you can possibly help it.

But, with that being said, let's examine two potential exploits of the Group Policy engine if a local administrator does choose to do so.

Group Policy Exploit Example #1: Going around an Administrative Template   Consider the calc.exe program we forced to run every time someone uses a computer in Human Resources. We created a GPO named "Auto-Launch calc.exe" and enabled the policy setting named **Run these programs at user logon** within it. We linked the GPO to the **Human Resources Computers** OU. Our edict affected all users on our computers (including our administrators) such that calc.exe ran for everyone (because the GPO was linked to an OU containing the computer). Imagine, then, that someone with local administrative privileges (such as Wally) on the workstation changes the portion of the Registry that is affected, as shown in Figure 4.1.

FIGURE 4.1   A simple deletion of the Registry entry will nullify our policy setting.

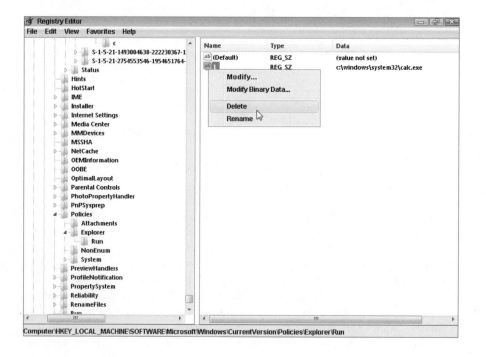

After the local administrator changes the setting, `calc.exe` simply won't run. (Again, only local administrators can make this change. Mere mortals do not have access to this portion of the Registry.) We're now at risk; a local administrator did the dirty work, and now all users on this workstation are officially going around our policy. Ninety minutes or so later, the background refresh interval strikes, and the client computer requests the background refresh from the GPOs in Active Directory. You might think that this should once again lock down the "Auto-Launch calc.exe" ability. But it doesn't. This ability won't get relocked down on reboot, either. Why? Because the Windows client thinks everything is status quo. Because nothing has changed in the underlying GPO in Active Directory that is telling the client its instruction set changed.

In this example, the Group Policy processing engine on the client thinks it has already asked for (and received) the latest version of the policy; the Group Policy processing engine doesn't know about the nefarious Registry change the local workstation administrator performed behind its back. Windows clients are not protected from this sort of attack by default. However, the protection can be made stronger. (See the section "Mandatory Reapplication for Nonsecurity Policy" later in this chapter.) Okay, this example exploit is fairly harmless, but it could be more or less damaging depending on precisely which policy settings we are forcing on our clients (as seen in this next example).

Group Policy Exploit Example #2: Going around a Security Policy Setting   Via Group Policy, we use the material in Chapter 8 to create a security template (and corresponding security policy) that locks down the `\windows\repair` directory with specific file ACLs (for Windows XP machines). For this example, imagine we set the `\windows\repair` directory so that only the Domain Administrators have access. Then, behind our backs, Xavier, now a local administrator, changes these file ACLs to allow everyone full control of these sensitive files. Uh-oh, now we could have a real problem on our hands.

Windows offers protection to handle cleanup for exploits of these two types. Let's see how that works.

In the first example, we went around the **Run these programs at user logon** policy setting by forcefully modifying the Registry. Running `calc.exe` for every user on a particular computer isn't considered a security setting. So, *by default* there is no protection for Exploit #1 (note the emphasis on "by default"). But, before you start panicking, let's examine Exploit #2, which attempts to go around a security policy we set.

Background Security Refresh Processing

The Group Policy engine tries to clean up after examples such as Exploit #2 by asking for a special background refresh—just for the security policy settings. This is called the *background security refresh* and is valid for every version of Windows.

Every 16 hours, a Group Policy client asks Active Directory for all the security-related GPOs that apply for it (not just the ones that have changed). This ensures that if a security setting has changed on the client (behind the Group Policy engine's back), it's automatically patched up within 16 hours.

You can manually change this security refresh interval in two ways. First, you can edit the local workstation's Registry at HKEY_LOCAL_MACHINE\SOFTWARE\ Microsoft\Windows NT\CurrentVersion\Winlogon\GPExtensions\{827D319E- 6EAC-11D2-A4EA-00C04F79F83A}\MaxNoGPOListChangesInterval and leverage a REG_DWORD signifying the number of minutes to pull down the entire security policy (by default, every 16 hours, so 960 minutes). You can also use the Security Policy Processing policy, which is described in the section "Using Group Policy to Affect Group Policy" later in this chapter. For more information, see Microsoft Knowledge Base article 277543 at http://support.microsoft.com/ kb/277543.

To reiterate, background security refresh helps secure stuff on the client only every 16 hours and only if the setting is security related. So, within a maximum of 16 hours, the \windows\repair directory would have the intended permissions rethrust upon it. Okay, great. But in Exploit #1, our evil administrator went around the **Run these programs at user logon** policy setting. And the background security refresh would *not* have re-enforced our intended will upon the system. Running calc.exe is not considered a security policy setting. "How do we secure *those* exploits," I hear you cry? "Read on," I reply. (Hey, that rhymed.)

Mandatory Reapplication for Nonsecurity Policy

Your network is humming along. You've established the GPOs in your organization, and you've let them sit unchanged for several months. Wally logs on. Wally logs off. So does Xavier. And Victoria. They each reboot their machines a bunch. But imagine for a moment that the GPOs in Active Directory haven't changed in months.

When your users or computers perform initial Group Policy processing or background policy processing, a whole lot of nothing happens. If GPOs haven't changed in months, there's nothing for the clients to do. Since the engine has already processed the latest version of what's in Active Directory, what more could it possibly need?

True, every 16 hours the security-related policy settings are guaranteed to be refreshed by the background security refresh. But what about Exploit #1 in which Wally (who was anointed as a local workstation administrator) went around the **Run these programs at user logon** policy setting by hacking his local Registry?

Well, running calc.exe isn't a security policy. But it still could be thought of as a security hole you need to fill (if you were running something really important every time a user logged in). With a little magic, you can force the nonsecurity sections of Group Policy to automatically close their own security holes. You can make the nonsecurity sections of Group Policy enforce their settings, even if the GPOs on the servers haven't changed. This will fix exploits that aren't specifically security related. You'll learn how to do this a bit later in the section "Affecting the Computer Settings of Group Policy."

The general idea is that once the nonsecurity sections of Group Policy are told to mandatorily reapply, they will do so whenever an initial policy processing or background refresh processing happens.

You can choose to (optionally) mandatorily reapply the following areas of Group Policy, along with the initial processing and background refresh:

- Registry (Administrative Templates)
- Internet Explorer Maintenance
- IP Security
- EFS Recovery Policy
- Wireless Policy
- Disk Quota
- Scripts (By Scripts I mean the notification of changes to scripts, not the actual rerunning of scripts after the appointed time.)
- Security
- Folder Redirection
- Software Installation
- Wired Policy

Note that most of the new CSEs for Windows Vista (like Printers and Windows Search) aren't in that list. But Wired (new for Windows Vista) and Wireless Policy (updated for Windows Vista) made it. Why some and not others? Beats me. I think someone just forgot to add them in during the rush-rush to get Windows Vista out the door. Maybe the rest will return in a Windows Vista or Windows Server 2008 service pack or something, but for now, they're not available.

As you'll see in the section "Affecting the Computer Settings of Group Policy," you can use the GUI to select other areas of Group Policy to enforce along with the background refresh.

To recap, if the GPO in Active Directory has *actually* changed, you don't have to worry about whether it will be automatically applied or not. Rather, mandatory reapplication is an extra safety measure that you can choose to place upon your client systems so your will is always downloaded and re-embraced, not only if an existing GPO has changed or a new GPO has appeared. And, you can specify specific Group Policy sections that you wish to do this for.

 As you'll see in Chapter 6, a bit more is going on between the client and the server. Underneath the hood, the client keeps track of the GPO *version number*. If the version number changes in Active Directory, the GPO is flagged as being required for download; it is then redownloaded and applied. If the version number stays the same in Active Directory, the Group Policy isn't redownloaded or applied. Stay tuned for more on GPO version numbers in Chapter 6.

Manually Forcing Clients to Process GPOs (Revisited)

In "Forcing Background Policy Processing," I talked a bit about what happens if you set up a new GPO (or change an existing one) and get impatient. That is, you want to force your client systems to embrace your new settings.

As I've said, there's no way (with the tools in the box) from on high to shout to your client computers and proclaim, "Accept my latest GPOs, ye mere mortals and puny systems!"

If you want to kick off policy processing on a client, you need to trot on over to it to kick it in the shins. You use secedit on Windows 2000 machines and gpupdate on Windows XP, Windows Vista, Windows 2003, and Windows 2008 machines. But the command-line tools have slightly different switches and behaviors.

Windows 2000 *secedit* with the */enforce* Switch

Recall that you must run the Windows 2000 secedit command-line tool on the client that you want to refresh. secedit has an additional switch, /enforce, that ensures that all policy-related settings are processed by the Windows 2000 workstation—regardless of whether the underlying GPO has changed in Active Directory. Instead of waiting 16 hours, you can rush the hands of time and force the background policy refresh processing to strike.

The commands to refresh both sides of Group Policy would be

```
secedit /refreshpolicy machine_policy /enforce
```

and

```
secedit /refreshpolicy user_policy /enforce
```

Windows XP (and Above): *gpupdate* with the */force* Switch

Recall that you must run the Windows command-line tool gpupdate on clients other than Windows 2000. And that you must be on the machine that you specifically want the refresh to occur. The /force switch looks similar to the /enforce switch for the Windows 2000 command-line tool secedit, but it's not the same—it's better.

The gpupdate /force command ensures that all settings in all GPOs are processed by the Windows XP (or higher) machine—regardless of whether the underlying GPO has changed in Active Directory.

The command is typically specified as

```
gpupdate /force
```

Other options are available in conjunction with /force, such as the ability to log off the user or to reboot the machine should a foreground policy be required (in the case of, say, Software Distribution).

The Windows Vista (and Windows Server 2008) /force switch is a little bit smarter than previous operating system versions. This is because in previous versions of the operating systems (like Windows XP), it might suggest a reboot or a logoff when one wasn't specifically needed. Here in Windows Vista, it seems to know better than to make these suggestions when not needed.

Special Case: Moving a User or a Computer Object

When you move a user or a computer within Active Directory, Group Policy may not immediately apply as you think it should. For instance, if you move a computer from the **Human Resources Computers** OU to another OU, that computer may still pull GPOs from the **Human Resources Computers** OU for a while longer. This is because the computer may get confused about where the accounts it's supposed to work with are currently residing.

The `userenv` process syncs with Active Directory every so often to determine if a user or a computer has been moved.

This happens, at most, about every 30 minutes or so.

Once resynced, background processing continues as it normally would. Only this time the user and computer GPOs are pulled from the new destination. If you move a user or a computer, remember that Group Policy processing continues to pull from the old location until it realizes the switch.

And, don't forget that replication takes a while within your site, and also, potentially *between* Active Directory sites.

Altogether, the maximum wait time after a move to get GPOs pulled from a new location is as follows:

- 30 minutes (the maximum Active Directory synchronization time) *and*

- 90 minutes (the maximum Group Policy default background refresh rate) *and*

- 30 minutes (the maximum Group Policy default background refresh rate offset)

So that's the time it takes to replicate the change, plus a maximum of 150 minutes.

It could and usually does happen faster than that, but it can't take any longer. This behavior is important to understand if you move an entire OU (perhaps with many computers) underneath another OU!

Windows Vista and Windows Server 2008 have a special trick, however. If you know the computer or user account has been moved (and, hence, would get different Group Policy settings), you can just run `gpupdate /force`, which double-checks where both the user and computer account live in Active Directory. Once the location is found, it applies GPOs specifically for that new location.

 Windows XP/SP2's gpupdate /force was supposed to have the same behavior as Windows Vista. That is, it should have been able to figure out if the user or computer account had moved. But in my testing, it did not work as well as Windows Vista's. There's an XP/SP2 hotfix (which is theoretically included in XP/SP3) that will make it recheck. Check out Microsoft Knowledge Base article 891630 for the hotfix. You can find it at http://support.microsoft.com/kb/891630.

Policy Application via Remote Access, Slow Links, and after Hibernation

You will certainly have situations in which users take their Windows machines on the road and remote-access your Active Directory and servers via dial-up or VPN.

All versions of Windows, by default, will detect the speed of the connection and make a snap judgment about whether to process Group Policy. However, different operating systems determine the speed differently.

Windows 2000 and Windows XP Group Policy via RAS Speed Determination and Policy Reapplication

If the Windows 2000 or Windows XP machine uses TCP/IP to connect to RAS (Remote Access Service) and the connection is 500 kilobits or greater, it is considered fast enough to process Group Policy.

However, Windows 2000 and Windows XP sometimes have trouble figuring out what the speed actually is. Windows 2000 and Windows XP use ICMP (the same protocol as Ping) to figure out the speed. However, many router administrators have turned off ICMP at the routers. When this happens, and Windows 2000 and Windows XP can't ping their Domain Controllers, they just give up and don't process Group Policy.

And this is bad—because the whole point in figuring out the speed of the link is to help hone in on exactly which portions of Group Policy will apply over a slow link.

And what happens if your user's Windows 2000 or Windows XP laptop is off the network for three days? When they connect back, their Windows 2000 or Windows XP laptop will have tried and tried and tried to refresh policy. However, since a Domain Controller wasn't available, it just keeps on trying.

However, when the user finally does reconnect, Windows 2000 or Windows XP will finally find a Domain Controller. But, this could take (you guessed it) up to 120 minutes (90 minutes, plus the 30 minute offset) for the refresh interval to finally come to pass. Vista improves on this (see next section).

For the record, Windows Server 2003 acts the same way Windows XP does. But, it's really unlikely you're going to have Windows Server 2003 on a laptop that VPNs in from a hotel room.

Windows Vista Group Policy via RAS Speed Determination and Policy Reapplication

Windows Vista uses a different mechanism than Windows XP (or Windows 2000 or Windows Server 2003) to determine if the link is slow. Windows Vista's Group Policy speed detection mechanism depends on an updated Windows component called *Network Location Awareness 2*, or *NLA 2* for short.

NLA 2 is pretty simple (and there's nothing you need to configure). NLA 2 for Windows Vista has two jobs:

1. NLA checks to see if the link is slow or not. This test doesn't use ICMP, so if router administrators have turned off ICMP, the calculation will still work. (See the next section, "What Is Processed over a Slow Network Connection?" for why you should care about what is processed over a slow network connection.)

2. NLA calls out to the universe every so often and asks, "Is there a Domain Controller available NOW?" If the answer is "No!" then Group Policy cannot be updated. Pretty simple. However, if the answer is "Yes!" updated Group Policy could, theoretically, be processed, right?

This might be useful when a user has been working at the beach, disconnected for several days, then finally dials up or comes into the office. However, before actually doing anything, the Group Policy engine kicks in and asks one more question: "Did I miss the last background refresh interval?" (for instance, if the computer was hibernated, and therefore turned off, for three days).

If the answer is "Yes," then the Group Policy engine immediately performs (what amounts to) a gpupdate (no /force) to refresh Group Policy since the last time the user and computer made contact.

Why is the Group Policy engine so specific about finding out whether it missed the last background refresh interval? The Group Policy engine asks this question because NLA could have determined that the computer was ever-so-briefly off the network—and then back on again. And, if that's the case, there was nothing to miss, so nothing is updated. You wouldn't really want it to trigger every time it went off and back on the network. That would be a veritable flurry of Group Policy updating! In other words, the Group Policy ensures that the Windows Vista machine was off the network for a goodly amount of time before asking for a refresh.

Again, Windows Server 2008 acts the same way Windows Vista does. But, it's really unlikely you're going to have Windows Server 2008 on a laptop and VPN in from the beach.

What Is Processed over a Slow Network Connection?

So, if the connection is deemed fast enough, *portions* of Group Policy are applied.

Surprisingly, even if the connection is deemed "not fast enough," several sections of Group Policy are *still* applied. Security settings, Software Restriction Policy settings (Windows XP and higher), and Administrative Templates are *guaranteed* to be downloaded during logon over an RAS connection—regardless of the speed. And there's nothing you can do to change that (not that you should really want to). Additionally, included in security settings are EFS (Encrypting File System) Recovery Policy, and IPsec (IP Security) policy. They are also always downloaded over slow links.

 WARNING The Group Policy interface suggests that downloading of EFS Recovery Policy and IPsec policy can be switched on or off over slow links. This is not true. (See the note in the section "Using Group Policy to Affect Group Policy" later in this chapter.)

If the user connects using RAS before logging onto the workstation (using the "Log on using dial-up connection" check box as seen in Figure 4.2), the security and Administrative Templates policy settings of the Computer node of the GPO are downloaded and applied to the computer once the user is authenticated. Then, the security and Administrative Templates policy settings of the User node of the GPO are applied to the user.

FIGURE 4.2 If you select "Log on using dial-up connection," you first process GPOs in the foreground (when Fast Boot is disabled).

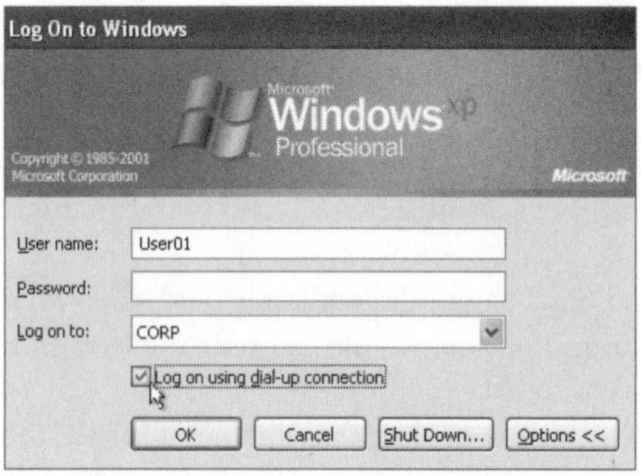

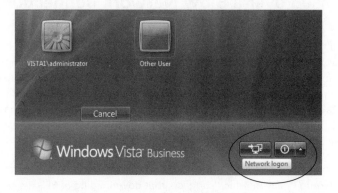

If you've got a Windows Vista machine handy, you'll notice there is no "Log on using dial-up connection" available by default. It's a process and a half to turn it on, if you want it. For more information, see http://tinyurl.com/ypgw8n. It might be worth it; however, in doing so, you can enable users to achieve a foreground policy process. You can see the result of doing so in Figures 4.3 and 4.4.

FIGURE 4.3 You can enable Vista to present a Network Logon icon to connect via VPN at logon time. This will generate a foreground policy processing event.

If the user connects using RAS after logging onto the workstation (say, via VPN using the "Network Connections" icons), the security policy settings and the Administrative Templates policy settings for the user and computer are not applied right away; rather they are applied during the next normal background refresh cycle (every 90–120 minutes by default).

FIGURE 4.4   You can "dial up" using a VPN link only if configured. See http://tinyurl.com/ypgw8n for the procedure in how to enable this.

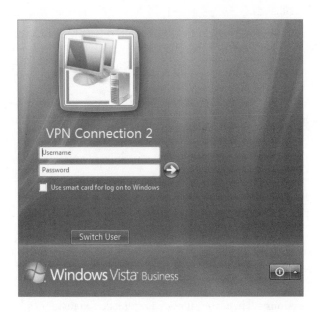

Other sections of Group Policy are handled as follows during a slow connection:

Internet Explorer Maintenance Settings   By default, these are not downloaded over slow links. (You can change this condition using the information in "Using Group Policy to Affect Group Policy" later in this chapter.)

Folder Redirection Settings   By default, these are not downloaded over slow links. (You can change this condition using the information in "Using Group Policy to Affect Group Policy" later in this chapter.)

Scripts (Logon, Logoff, Startup, and Shutdown)   By default, script updates are not downloaded over slow links. (You can change this condition using the information in "Using Group Policy to Affect Group Policy" later in this chapter.) Also see the sidebar "Processing and Running Scripts over Slow Links" later in this chapter.

Disk Quota Settings   By default, these are not downloaded over slow links. (You can change this condition using the information in "Using Group Policy to Affect Group Policy" later in this chapter.) The currently cached disk quota settings are still enforced.

Software Installation and Maintenance   By default, these are not downloaded over slow links. More specifically, the offers of newly available software are not shown to users. Users do have the ability to choose whether to pull down the latest versions of applications at their whim. You can torture your dial-in users by changing the behavior of how offers are handled and by permitting the icons of new software to be displayed. They will hate you after you do this, but that is for you and them to work out. See the corresponding setting described later in this chapter in the section "Using Group Policy to Affect Group Policy." More information about Group Policy Software Installation can be found in Chapter 4 of the companion book.

Software Restriction Policy (Windows XP and Higher)   These are guaranteed to download over slow links. You cannot turn off this ability. More information about Software Restriction Policy can be found in Chapter 8.

802.11 Wireless Policy (Windows XP and Higher)   By default, these are not downloaded over slow links. (You can change this condition using the information in "Using Group Policy to Affect Group Policy" later in this chapter.) The currently cached 802.11 policy settings are still enforced.

802.3 Wired Policy (Windows Vista and Windows Server 2008 Only)   By default, these are not downloaded over slow links. (You can change this condition using the information in "Using Group Policy to Affect Group Policy" later in this chapter.)

Administrative Templates   These are guaranteed to download over slow links. You cannot turn off this ability.

EFS Recovery Policy   These are guaranteed to download over slow links. You cannot turn off this ability. The interface has an option that makes it appear as if you can turn off this ability, but you can't.

IPsec Policy   These are guaranteed to download over slow links. You cannot turn off this ability. The interface has an option that makes it appear as if you can turn off this ability, but you can't.

Group Policy Preference Extensions   The Group Policy Preference Extensions, which we'll explore in Chapter 10, are all guaranteed to download and process over slow links. You cannot turn off this ability.

What is considered fast enough for all these policy categories can be changed from 500Kb to whatever speed you desire (independently for the computer half and the user half). This is detailed in the section "Using Group Policy to Affect Group Policy" later in this chapter.

Processing and Running Scripts over Slow Links

If your users try to run scripts while using slow links, they (and you) might notice some interesting behavior. First, computer startup scripts will not run over slow links. This just isn't supported by the Group Policy engine.

However, one enterprising customer of mine had a service written to explicitly do this after the user was logged on. That said, logon scripts are currently still fair game. However, many factors play into whether the scripts will run.

When a user is dialed in over a slow link, the scripts policy itself will not process. That is, it will not receive information about new or updated scripts. The actual *running* of the scripts is a different matter altogether and is irrespective of whether the user has a slow connection. Therefore, if you applied the script policy while on a high-speed connection (for example, a home office LAN) and then a user should log on over a dial-up connection, scripts will run; the script policy has already been downloaded and set for takeoff. Indeed, your script policy might tell the client to execute the script from the server, which may or may not be available.

But until your users come back to the headquarters, they won't get updates to that script policy if any have occurred. For instance, if the script policy states that the script should be run from an alternate server location, this information won't be downloaded until they come back into headquarters.

Windows 2000 and Windows XP have slightly different behaviors for the actual running of the scripts. Windows 2000 requires that the SYSVOL (NETLOGON share) be accessible for the scripts to even attempt to run. If the machine cannot see SYSVOL, no scripts will run.

Windows XP and above have addressed this problem, but it's thorny. If the machine is 100 percent offline (and, hence, SYSVOL isn't available), the scripts will indeed run. But if the system determines it's on a fast connection and SYSVOL is unavailable, scripts won't run.

Using Group Policy to Affect Group Policy

At times, you might want to change the behavior of Group Policy. Amazingly, you actually use Group Policy settings to change the behavior of Group Policy! Several Group Policy settings appear under both the User and Computer nodes; however, you must set the policy settings in each section independently.

Affecting the User Settings of Group Policy

The Group Policy settings that affect the User node appear under User Configuration ➢ Policies ➢ Administrative Templates ➢ System ➢ Group Policy. Remember that user accounts must be subject to the site, domain, or OU where these GPOs are linked in order to be affected. Most of these policy settings are valid for any Windows machine, although some are explicitly designed and will operate only on Windows XP, Windows Vista, and so on.

The following sections list the policy settings that affect the user side of Group Policy.

Group Policy Refresh Interval for Users

This setting changes the default User node background refresh rate of 90 minutes with a 0–30 minute positive randomizer to almost any number of refresh and randomizer minutes you choose. Choose a smaller number for the background refresh to speed up Group Policy on your machines, or choose a larger number to quell the traffic that a Group Policy refresh takes across your network. There is a similar refresh interval for computers, which is on an alternate clock with its own settings. A setting of 0 is equal to 7 seconds. Set to 0 only in the test lab.

Group Policy Slow Link Detection

You can change the default definition of *fast connectivity for users* from 500Kbps to any speed you like. Recall that certain aspects of Group Policy are not applied to machines that are determined to be coming in over slow links. This setting specifies what constitutes a slow link for the User node. There is an identically named policy setting located under the Computer node (explored later in this chapter) that also needs to be set to define what is slow for the Computer node. Preferably set these to the same number. Note that you can set this to zero to disable Slow Link Detection.

Group Policy Domain Controller Selection

GPOs are written to the PDC emulator by default. When users (generally Domain Administrators or OU administrators) are affected by this setting, they are allowed to create new GPOs on Domain Controllers other than the PDC emulator. (See Chapter 6 for more information on this setting and how and why to use it.)

Create New Group Policy Object Links Disabled by Default

When users (generally Domain Administrators or OU administrators) are affected by this setting, the GPOs they create will be disabled by default. This ensures that users and computers are not hitting their refresh intervals and downloading half-finished GPOs that you are in the process of creating. Enable the GPOs when finished, and they will download during their next background refresh cycle.

Default Name for Group Policy Objects

If a user has been assigned the rights to create GPOs via membership in the Group Policy Creator Owners group and has also been assigned the rights to link GPOs to OUs within Active Directory, the default name created for GPOs is "New Group Policy Object." You might want all GPOs created at the domain level to have one name, perhaps "AppliesToDomain-GPO," and all GPOs created at the **Human Resources** OU level (and all child levels) to have another name, maybe "AppliestoHR-GPO." Again, in order for this policy to work, the user's account with the rights to create GPOs must be affected by the policy.

Enforce Show Policies Only

When users (generally Domain Administrators or OU administrators) are affected by this setting, the "Only show policy settings that can be fully managed" setting (explored in Chapter 7) is forced to be enabled. This prevents the importation of "bad" ADM templates, which have the unfortunate side effect of tattooing the Registry until they are explicitly removed. (See Chapter 7 for more information on using all types of ADM templates.) Note however, that the GPMC 2.0 will always show "bad" ADM templates and hence, this isn't needed when using the GPMC 2.0 on your management station.

Turn Off Automatic Update of ADM Files

You'll learn all about ADM files (and this particular policy setting) in Chapter 7. But, in essence, ADM template files are the underlying "definitions" of what's possible in Group Policy land (when you use pre-Vista machines). On Vista machines or Windows Server 2008 machines, a new mechanism called ADMX files is used.

These ADM files are updated by service packs. The default behavior is to check the launching point—that is, the \windows\inf folder—to see if the ADM template has yet been updated. By default, this check for an update occurs every time you double-click the Administrative Templates section of any GPO as if you were going to modify it. However, if you enable this setting, you're saying to ignore the normal update process and simply keep on using the ADM template you initially used. In other words, you're telling the system you'd prefer to keep the initial ADM template regardless of whether a newer one is available. (See Chapter 7 for critical information on updating ADM templates when service packs are available for Windows XP or Windows 2003.)

Disallow Interactive Users from Generating Resultant Set of Policy Data

Users affected by this setting cannot use the Group Policy Modeling or Group Policy Results tasks in the GPMC. Enabling this setting locks down a possible entry point into the system. That is, it prevents unauthorized users from determining the current security settings on the box and developing attack strategies.

Note that this policy doesn't affect Windows 2000 machines.

Affecting the Computer Settings of Group Policy

The Group Policy settings that affect the Computer node appear under Computer Configuration ➢ Policies ➢ Administrative Templates ➢ System ➢ Group Policy. Once computers are affected by these policy settings, they change the processing behavior of Group Policy. Remember that the computer accounts must be subject to the site, domain, or OU where these GPOs are linked in order to be affected.

Turn Off Background Refresh of Group Policy

When this setting is enabled, the affected computer downloads the latest GPOs for both the user and the computer, according to the background refresh interval—but it doesn't apply them. The GPOs are applied when the user logs off but before the next user logs on. This is helpful in situations in which you want to guarantee that a user's experience stays the same throughout the session.

Group Policy Refresh Interval for Computers

This setting changes the default Computer node background refresh rate of 90 minutes with a 30-minute randomizer to almost any number of refresh and randomizer minutes you choose. Choose a smaller number for the background refresh to speed up Group Policy on your machines, or choose a larger number to quell the traffic a Group Policy refresh causes across your network. A similar refresh interval for the User node is on a completely separate and unrelated timing rate and randomizer. A setting of 0 equals 7 seconds. Set to 0 only in the test lab.

Group Policy Refresh Interval for Domain Controllers

Recall that Domain Controllers are updated regarding Group Policy changes within 5 minutes. You can close or widen that gap as you see fit. The closer the gap, the more network chatter. Widen the gap, and the security settings will be inconsistent until the interval is hit. A setting of 0 equals 7 seconds. Set to 0 only in the test lab.

User Group Policy Loopback Processing Mode

We'll explore this setting in detail in the next chapter.

Allow Cross-Forest User Policy and Roaming User Profiles

This policy is valid only in cross-forest trust scenarios. I'll describe how these work and how this policy works in Chapter 5 in the section "Group Policy with Cross-Forest Trusts."

This policy setting is valid only when applied to Windows XP + SP2 systems and above.

Group Policy Slow Link Detection

You can change the default definition of *fast connectivity* from 500Kbps to any speed you like. Recall that certain aspects of Group Policy are not applied to those machines that are deemed to be coming in over slow links. Independently, an identically named policy setting that exists under the User node (explored earlier) also needs to be set to define what is slow for the User node. Preferably, set these to the same number.

Turn Off Resultant Set of Policy Logging

As you'll see in Chapter 5, users on Windows XP can launch the Resultant Set of Policy (RSoP) snap-in by typing **RSOP.MSC** at the command prompt. Enabling this policy setting doesn't prevent its launch but, for all intents and purposes, disables its use. This policy setting disables the use for the currently logged-on user (known as the interactive user) as well as anyone trying to get the results using the remote features of the RSoP snap-in.

This policy setting is valid only when applied to Windows XP workstations and Windows 2003 servers.

In my testing, this setting did not affect Windows Vista or Windows Server 2008 machines. Your mileage may vary.

 On Windows Vista, regular users can only see the user half of the RSoP by default. They must be delegated the "Read Group Policy Results data" right over the Windows Vista computer they want to gather the information for. We talked about this in Chapter 2's "Special Group Policy Operation Delegations" section.

Remove Users Ability to Invoke Machine Policy Refresh

By default, mere mortal users can perform their own background refreshes using gpupdate, as described in the section "Initiating a Manual Background Refresh for Windows XP and

Above." However, you might not want users to perform their own gpupdate. I can think of only one reason to disable this setting: to prevent users from sucking up bandwidth on Domain Controllers by continually running gpupdate. Other than that, I can't imagine why you would want to prevent them from being able to get the latest GPO settings if they were so inclined. Perhaps one user is performing a denial of service (DoS) attack on your Domain Controllers by continually requesting Group Policy—but even that's a stretch.

Even if this policy is enabled, local administrators can still force a gpupdate. But, again, gpupdate only works when run locally on the machine needing the update.

This policy setting is valid only when applied to Windows XP and newer.

Disallow Interactive Users from Generating Resultant Set of Policy Data

This policy is similar to the **Turn off Resultant Set of Policy logging** setting but affects only the user on the console. Enabling this setting might be useful if you don't want the interactive user to have the ability to generate RSoP data but you still want to allow administrators to get the RSoP remotely. Again, RSoP and its related functions are explored in Chapter 6.

Registry Policy Processing

This setting affects how your policy settings in the Administrative Templates subtrees react (and, generally, any other policy that affects the Registry). Once this policy setting is enabled, you have two other options:

Do Not Apply during Periodic Background Processing   Typically, Administrative Templates settings are refreshed every 90 minutes or so. However, if you enable this setting, you're telling the client not to ever refresh the Administrative Templates in the GPOs that are meant for it after the logon. You might choose to prevent background refresh for Administrative Templates for two reasons:

- When the background refresh occurs, the screen may flicker for a second as the system reapplies the changed GPOs (with their policy settings) and instructs Explorer.exe to refresh the Desktop. This could be a slight distraction for the user every 90 minutes or so.

- You might choose to disable background processing so that users' experiences with the Desktop and applications stay consistent for the entire length of their logon. Having settings suddenly change while the user is logged on could be confusing.

My advice is to leave this setting alone unless you're seriously impacted by the background processing affecting your users' experience.

Process Even If the Group Policy Objects Have Not Changed   If this setting is selected, the system will update and reapply the policy settings in this category even if the underlying GPO has not changed when the background refresh interval occurs. Recall that this type of processing is meant to clean up should an administrator have nefariously gone behind our backs and modified a local setting.

You cannot turn off Registry policy processing over slow links. They are always downloaded and applied.

Internet Explorer Maintenance Policy Processing

Once enabled, this policy setting has three potential options:

Allow Processing across a Slow Network Connection Check this check box to allow Internet Explorer Maintenance settings to download when logging on over slow links. Enabling this could cause your users to experience a longer logon time but they will adhere to your latest Internet Explorer wishes.

Do Not Apply during Periodic Background Processing If this option is selected, the latest Internet Explorer settings in Active Directory GPOs will not be downloaded or applied during the background refresh.

Process Even If the Group Policy Objects Have Not Changed If this option is selected, it updates and reapplies the policy settings in this category even if the underlying GPO has not changed. Recall that this type of processing is meant to clean up should a user or an administrator have nefariously gone behind our backs and modified a local setting.

Software Installation Policy Processing

Once enabled, this policy setting has two potential options:

Allow Processing across a Slow Network Connection As I stated, by default, software deployment offers are not displayed to users connecting over slow links. This is a good thing; allowing users to click the newly available icons to begin the download and installation of new software over a 56K dial-up line can be tortuous. Use this setting to change this behavior.

 If you have already distributed software via Group Policy and an offer has been accepted by a client computer (but perhaps not all pieces of the application have been loaded), setting this selection will likely not help, and your users may experience a long delay in running their application over a slow link. For more information on how to best distribute software to clients who use slow links, see Chapter 4 of the companion book.

Process Even If the Group Policy Objects Have Not Changed For Software Installation, I cannot find any difference whether this option is selected or not, though Microsoft has implied it might correct some actions should the software become damaged. Since software deployment offers are only displayed upon logon or reboot (otherwise known as foreground policy processing), in my testing, this setting seems not to have any outward effect.

 Users can still get caught in a trap regarding Group Policy Software Installation and slow links. That is, if they accept a "partial offer" while connected over a fast link, then try to request more of the same application, the computer will attempt to download that part over a slow link. This happens regardless of how the "Allow Processing across a Slow Network Connection" policy setting is set. See the Software Installation settings described in detail in the companion book in Chapter 4.

Folder Redirection Policy Processing

Once enabled, this policy setting has two potential options:

Allow Processing across a Slow Network Connection   Recall that the Folder Redirection policy is changed only at logon time. Chances are you won't want dialed-in users to experience that new change. Rather, you'll want to wait until they are on your LAN. If you want to torture your users and allow them to accept the changed policy anyway, use this setting to change this behavior.

Process Even If the Group Policy Objects Have Not Changed   I cannot find any difference whether this setting is selected or not, though Microsoft has implied it might correct some folder-redirection woes should the user name get renamed.

Folder Redirection settings are discussed in detail in Chapter 3 of the companion book.

Scripts Policy Processing

Once enabled, this policy setting has three potential options:

Allow Processing across a Slow Network Connection   Recall that, by default, new or changed startup, shutdown, logon, and logoff scripts are not downloaded over slow networks. Change this option to allow the download over slow links. The actual running of the scripts is a different process, as discussed earlier in the sidebar "Processing and Running Scripts over Slow Links."

Do Not Apply during Periodic Background Processing   This option will not allow the newest script instructions to be downloaded. See the sidebar "Processing and Running Scripts over Slow Links" earlier in the chapter.

Process Even If the GPOs Have Not Changed   This option will allow the newest script instructions to be downloaded even if the GPOs have not changed. See the sidebar "Processing and Running Scripts over Slow Links."

Security Policy Processing

Once enabled, this policy setting has two potential options:

Do Not Apply during Periodic Background Processing   Recall that the security settings are refreshed on the machines every 16 hours, whether they need it or not. Checking this option will turn off that refresh. It is recommended to leave this as is. However, you might want to consider enabling this setting for servers with high numbers of transactions that require all the processing power they can muster.

Process Even If the GPOs Have Not Changed   Recall that after 16 hours, this policy category is always refreshed. With this option enabled, the security policies will be reprocessed during *every* refresh cycle.

IP Security Policy Processing

Once enabled, this policy setting has three potential options:

Allow Processing across a Slow Network Connection   When selected, this setting does nothing. IP Security settings are always downloaded, regardless of whether the computer is connected over a slow network. So, you might be asking yourself, what happens when you select this check box, which is shown in Figure 4.5? Answer: nothing—it's a bug in the interface. To repeat: IP Security is always processed, regardless of the link speed.

FIGURE 4.5   The "Allow processing across a slow network connection" setting is not used for IP Security or EFS settings (all versions of Windows).

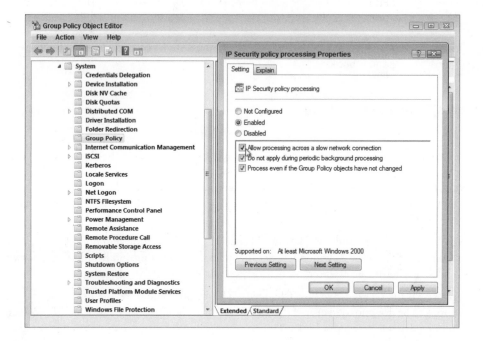

 IPsec policies act slightly different from other policy setting categories. IPsec policy settings are not additive. For IP Security, the last applied policy wins.

Do Not Apply during Periodic Background Processing   If this option is selected, the latest IP Security settings in Active Directory GPOs will not be downloaded or applied during the background refresh.

Process Even If the Group Policy Objects Have Not Changed   If this option is selected, it updates and reapplies the policy settings in this category even if the underlying GPO has not changed. Recall that this type of processing is meant to clean up should a user or an administrator have nefariously gone behind our backs and modified a local setting.

EFS Recovery Policy Processing

Once enabled, this policy setting has three potential options:

Allow Processing across a Slow Network Connection   When this option is selected, it does nothing.

Like IP Security, the EFS recovery settings are always downloaded—even over slow networks. Once again, this is the same bug as shown in Figure 4.5. To repeat, EFS recovery policy is always processed, regardless of link speed.

> EFS recovery policies act slightly different from other policy setting categories. EFS recovery policies are not additive; the last applied policy wins.

Do Not Apply during Periodic Background Processing   If this option is selected, the latest EFS recovery settings in Active Directory GPOs are not downloaded or applied during the background refresh.

Process Even If the Group Policy Objects Have Not Changed   If this option is selected, it updates and reapplies the policy settings in this category even if the underlying GPO has not changed. Recall that this type of processing is meant to clean up should a user or an administrator have nefariously gone behind our backs and modified a local setting.

Wireless Policy Processing

If this policy setting is enabled, it has three potential options:

Allow Processing across a Slow Network Connection   Check this option to allow the latest wireless policy settings to download when the user is logging on over slow links. Enabling this could cause your users to experience a longer logon time.

Do Not Apply during Periodic Background Processing   If this option is selected, the latest wireless policy settings will not be downloaded or applied during the background refresh.

Process Even If the Group Policy Objects Have Not Changed   If this option is selected, it updates and reapplies the policy settings in this category even if the underlying GPO has not changed. Recall that this type of processing is meant to clean up should a user or an administrator have nefariously gone behind our backs and modified a local setting.

Wired Policy Processing

If this policy setting is enabled, it has three potential options:

Allow Processing across a Slow Network Connection   Check this option to allow the latest wired policy settings to download when the user is logging on over slow links. Enabling this could cause your users to experience a longer logon time.

Do Not Apply during Periodic Background Processing   If this option is selected, the latest wired policy settings will not be downloaded or applied during the background refresh.

Process Even If the Group Policy Objects Have Not Changed   If this option is selected, it updates and reapplies the policy settings in this category even if the underlying GPO has not changed. Recall that this type of processing is meant to clean up should a user or an administrator have nefariously gone behind our backs and modified a local setting.

This policy setting is valid only when applied to Windows Vista or Windows Server 2008.

Disk Quota Policy Processing

If this policy setting is enabled, it has three potential options:

Allow Processing across a Slow Network Connection   Check this option to allow the latest disk quota policy settings to download and apply when the user logs on over slow links. Enabling this could cause your users to experience a longer logon time.

Do Not Apply during Periodic Background Processing   If this option is selected, the latest disk quota policy settings will not be downloaded or applied during the background refresh.

Process Even If the Group Policy Objects Have Not Changed   If selected, this option updates and reapplies the policy settings in this category even if the underlying GPO has not changed. Recall that this type of processing is meant to clean up should a user or an administrator have nefariously gone behind our backs and modified a local setting.

Always Use Local ADM Files for Group Policy Object Editor

This policy is valid only when applied to Windows 2003 servers and Windows Vista management stations. This is strange, as you might expect it to affect Windows XP management stations as well. But it doesn't. It only affects Windows Server 2003 and Windows Vista management stations. It didn't seem to do anything in my testing on Windows Server 2008 management stations (GPMC 2.0), and it is unknown if this policy setting will affect Windows Vista + SP1 + GPMC 2.0 management stations.

ADM files are the underlying language that creates policy settings in pre–Windows Vista versions. I'll talk more about ADM files and how to best use them in Chapter 7. However, for reference, if a computer is affected by this policy setting, the Group Policy Object Editor attempts to show the text within the ADM files from your local %windir%\inf directory (usually c:\windows\inf). If the ADM file is different on the Domain Controller than on your local c:\windows\inf directory, you could end up seeing different settings and Explain text than are really inside the Domain Controller.

Indeed, if this policy is enabled, you might now see totally different policy settings than were originally placed in the GPO. However, you might want to enable this policy setting if you know that you will always be using one specific management station. Stay tuned for Chapter 7 to see how to use this function.

Turn Off Local Group Policy Objects Processing

If a Windows Vista computer is affected by this policy setting, then whatever is set within the local GPOs is ignored.

This can be useful if a machine is originally used in a workgroup (nondomain joined environment) and then it's joined to the domain. In that case, you might want to ensure that no user has any lingering policy settings that will specifically affect them. Hence, your desire would be to control everything from Active Directory and not anything from the local level.

Of course, this policy setting only works when being delivered from Active Directory (not when it's set locally).

This policy setting affects only Windows Vista machines (and Widows Server 2008 machines).

Startup Policy Processing Wait Time

 This policy setting affects only Windows Vista machines (and Windows Server 2008 machines).

This policy setting helps with timeouts when processing Group Policy. The policy setting only exists for Windows Vista and Windows Server 2008 machines; however, the facility to control these timeouts exists in other operating systems (like Windows XP/SP2 with a Registry hack).

Check out KB article 840669 (found here: `http://tinyurl.com/88tbo`) if you want to implement this setting for Windows XP/SP2 and earlier machines.

Final Thoughts

Group Policy doesn't just pick and choose when it wants to apply. Rather, a specific set of rules is followed when it comes time to process. Understanding these rules is paramount in helping you prevent potential Group Policy problems.

Many other things can affect the Group Policy engine, including loopback policy processing and how users connect over slow links. So be sure you really get these concepts before you run out and try them in real life.

Here are a few things to keep in mind:

Remember initial policy processing.   Windows 2000 (Workstation and Server), Windows Server 2003, and Windows Server 2008 machines process all GPOs when the computer starts up or when the user logs on. That is, by default, XP and Vista perform initial policy processing only when a user has never logged in on the machine before (or if the computer has just joined the domain).

Remember background refresh policy processing (member servers).   For all machine types, regular member computers refresh some time after the user is logged on (usually 90 minutes or so).

Remember background refresh policy for Windows Vista and Windows XP. By default, Windows Vista and Windows XP are unique and process GPOs *only* in the background (asynchronously). Some features, such as Software Distribution, Folder Redirection, and other functions, can take two reboots or logons to take effect. Advanced Folder Redirection can take three logons to see an effect. This is because these special functions can be processed only in the foreground. You can turn off this feature as described earlier in this chapter.

Remember background refresh policy processing (Domain Controllers). All Domain Controllers receive a background refresh every 5 minutes (after replication has occurred).

Security policy processing occurs every 16 hours. For all operating systems, just the security settings within all GPOs are reprocessed and applied every 16 hours, regardless of whether security settings have changed. This ensures that all security functions in all GPOs are reprocessed if someone has manually gone around the security on the system.

Leverage "Process Even If the Group Policy Objects Have Not Changed." You can force other Group Policy areas (such as Administrative Templates) refresh during the background refresh interval. This will make those categories more secure and less susceptible to attack.

Upgrading a Windows XP Machine to Windows Vista

It's not likely that you'll do this often, but should you choose to do a mass-upgrade of machines (or even a one-off upgrade of a particular Windows XP machine to Windows Vista), you should know what happens with regard to Group Policy. Don't worry, it's not much:

- Any local Group Policy settings are upgraded to the Windows Vista Layer 1 local GPO (see Chapter 1).

- Any special ADM template settings are retained (see Chapter 7).

- RSoP "calculation data" is expunged. However, it is re-created the first time the computer logs onto the domain and when each user logs on.

- If your Windows XP machine happened to have the downloadable version of the GPMC installed, it's removed. Remember, the GPMC is now part of Windows Vista RTM, so that version is used instead. The GPMC preferences are retained, however. Don't forget that the GPMC is ripped out when Windows Vista + SP1 is installed.

Even though a huge number of Windows XP settings are valid on Windows Vista, some settings could have a slightly different outcome when run on Windows Vista. To that end, all policy settings are regrabbed from Active Directory and applied as if the computer had just joined the domain and the user logged on for the first time.

5

Advanced Group Policy Processing

In the last chapter, we talked about basic Group Policy processing principles along with some special cases, including what happens over a slow link and also how to manage the Group Policy engine itself—using Group Policy.

In this chapter, we'll explore some advanced scenarios. Here's the quick breakdown of what they are and why I think you'll be interested:

- If you've ever wanted to decide *when* a particular Group Policy should be applied, you're going to love WMI filters.

- If you've thought to yourself, "How do I get user-side settings to affect my computers?" you're going to love Loopback policy processing.

- And, if you've got multiple Active Directories tied together with cross-forest trusts, you'll want to understand how and when Group Policy applies.

- Finally, if you have any Windows NT machines kicking around out there, you might have old-school `NTCONFIG.POL` files, and you'll want to be sure to know how those fit together with modern Group Policy.

So, let's get started with our advanced Group Policy processing.

GPO Targeting with WMI Filters

In Chapter 2, I alluded to a power called WMI filters. I like to think of WMI filters as adding laser-sighting to the gun of Group Policy. With WMI filters, you can dive into and inspect the soul of your client machines, and if certain criteria are met, you can then apply the GPO to them.

While WMI filters can be used with any GPO, I find that people usually use them for targeting software via Group Policy Software Installation. I explore Group Policy Software Installation in Chapter 4 of the companion book, *Creating the Secure Managed Desktop*.

Before we jump headlong into ferreting out the power of WMI filters, let's make sure we have the machinery necessary to wield this power:

- The domain is at least a Windows 2003 domain or a Windows 2000 domain with an updated Windows 2003 schema. You update a Windows 2000 Active Directory domain's schema to the Windows 2003 domain schema via the command prompt. This is performed with the command `ADPREP /Domainprep`.

- Your target clients are at least Windows XP.

 Windows 2000 clients ignore WMI filters; for Windows 2000 clients, the GPO is always applied—regardless of the evaluation of the WMI filter.

WMI is a huge animal, and you can choose to filter on thousands of items. Hot items to filter on typically include the following:

- The amount of memory
- The available hard-drive space
- CPU speed
- A hotfix
- OS version or service pack level

But you don't have to stop there. You can get creative and filter GPOs on obscure items (if they exist and are supported by the hardware) such as the following:

- BIOS revision
- Manufacturer of the CD drive
- Whether a UPS is connected
- The rotational speed of the fan

The potential esoteric criteria you can query for, and then filter, goes on and on.

An easy example would be "Only apply the 'Hide Desktop Settings Option' GPO on client machines that have at least 128MB of memory or more."

Okay, perhaps it's a silly example. You likely wouldn't care about showing or hiding desktop settings depending on the amount of RAM a computer has. But you can take the ideas here and use them in real examples. You can do things like this:

- "Only deploy Office 2007 when I have these hotfixes installed."
- "On Tuesdays at logon time, start up Excel."
- "Only install an operating system service pack when I have 256MB of RAM and 3GB of free hard drive space."

The idea is that either Group Policy will apply the GPO if the WMI filter evaluates to True or it will not apply the GPO if the WMI filter evaluates to False.

To give this a try, we'll first need some tools to help us figure out which pieces of WMI to query. We'll then take what we've learned and use the GPMC to create a WMI filter to specifically target the systems we want.

Unfortunately, I don't have room to dive into how or why WMI works on a molecular level. If you're unfamiliar with WMI, take a peek at www.microsoft.com/whdc/system/pnppwr/wmi/default.mspx and other documentation at www.dmtf.org.

Tools (and References) of the WMI Trade

To master WMI, you have to do a lot of work. You'll have to read up on and master four crucial pieces of WMI documentation, which are found at the following websites:

- http://msdn2.microsoft.com/en-us/library/ms974579.aspx (shortened to http://tinyurl.com/yt4jlu)

- http://msdn2.microsoft.com/en-us/library/ms974592.aspx (shortened to http://tinyurl.com/2bjfkb)

- http://msdn2.microsoft.com/en-us/library/ms974547.aspx (shortened to http://tinyurl.com/2f464f)

And you'll have to get the accompanying "Windows 2000 Scripting Guide" from Microsoft— the de facto (and very large-o) book on scripting—and work through all the hundreds of examples (at Amazon at http://tinyurl.com/7yypc). Yes, it's a Windows 2000 book, but it's awesome.

What? You don't have time for that? No problem! You can do the next best thing and "wing it." We'll use two tools to create WMI queries, and then we'll manually bend them into WMI filters.

- WMI CIM Studio is available on Microsoft's website. At last check, it was at www.microsoft.com/downloads/release.asp?releaseid=40804 (shortened to http://tinyurl.com/8zot).

- The WMI Scriptomatic version 1 tool download and tutorial is also available from Microsoft. At last check, it was at www.microsoft.com/technet/scriptcenter/tools/wmimatic.mspx (shortened to http://tinyurl.com/cmcd1).

- And there's also the Scriptomatic version 2 tool available at http://tinyurl.com/5wdup.

My choice is to use one of the two Scriptomatic tools, made by my pals the "Microsoft Scripting Guys." Both versions of the Scriptomatic tool basically do the same thing. That is, they zip through all the available WMI classes and then make them available for an easy-breezy query.

In Figure 5.1, the WMI class Win32_PhysicalMemory is selected. Then, scriptomagically, all the WMI attributes in that class are exposed in a ready-to-run VBScript application. You can see them in Figure 5.1, including FormFactor, HotSwappable, and the one we're after, Capacity. Just click the Run button and you can see the output with the values on *this* machine.

FIGURE 5.1 The Scriptomatic version 2 tool from the "Microsoft Scripting Guys"

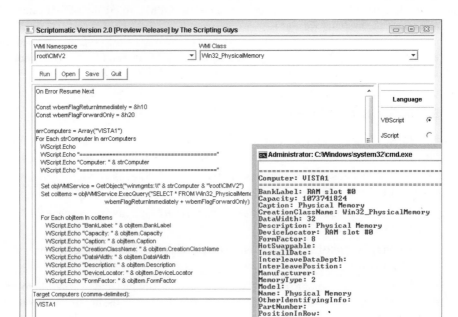

When you click Run, the script runs in a little prompt window. You can see that the Capacity of this box is 1073741824, which is 1GB. The point here, however, is that the unit measurement and expected output of this field is expressed in thousands of bytes. We'll leverage this information when we bend this WMI query into a WMI filter.

WMI Filter Syntax

You can start nearly all the WMI filters you'll create using Scriptomatic. All that's left is to wrap a little logic around the output. All the WMI filters we'll create have the following syntax:

```
SELECT * from Win32_{something}
WHERE {variable} [=,>,<,is, etc] {desired result}
```

Now, all we have to do is plug in the stuff we already know, and we're off and running. In this example, we're using Win32_PhysicalMemory. We know the variable we want is *Capacity*, and we know that we want it to be greater than 128MB, which we can represent as > 128000000. Yes, I know 128000000 isn't exactly 128MB of memory, but it's close enough. Anyway, when you put it all together, you get

```
SELECT * from Win32_PhysicalMemory WHERE Capacity > 128000000
```

Easy as pie. However, not all WMI filters are this easy. Some WMI variable entries have text, and you must use quotes to specifically match what's inside the string to what's inside the WMI variable.

Creating and Using a WMI Filter

Once your WMI filter is in the correct syntax, you're ready to inject it into an existing GPO. Again, this can be any GPO you want.

Creating and using a WMI filter is a two-step process: creating and then using. (I guess that makes sense.)

WMI Filter Creation

Before you can filter a specific GPO, you need to define the filter in Active Directory. Follow these steps:

1. Fire up the GPMC, then drill down to Forest ➤ Domains ➤ WMI Filters node.

2. Right-click the WMI Filters node and select New as seen in Figure 5.2.

3. When you do, you'll be presented with the New WMI Filter dialog box, seen in Figure 5.3. You'll be able to type in a name and description of your new filter. Then, click the Add button, and in the Query field, just enter in the full SELECT statement from before.

FIGURE 5.2   Right-click the WMI Filters node to create a WMI filter.

FIGURE 5.3 This WMI query will evaluate to True when the machine has greater than 128MB memory.

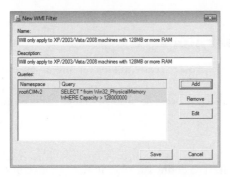

4. When you're done, click Save. Your query is now saved into Active Directory and can be leveraged for any GPO you want. We'll explore how to do that next.

WMI Filter Usage

Using the GPMC, it's easy to find the GPO you want and then leverage the WMI filter you just made. Follow these steps:

1. Locate the "Hide Desktop Settings Option" GPO you created (which should be linked to the domain level).

2. Click the Scope tab of the GPO.

3. In the WMI Filtering section, select the WMI filter you just created, as shown in Figure 5.4.

4. At the prompt, confirm your selection.

FIGURE 5.4 Choose the GPO (or GPO link) and select a WMI filter.

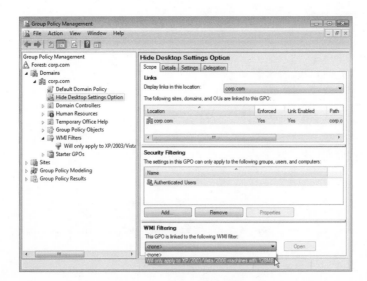

Now this GPO will only apply to Windows XP and higher machines with 128MB of RAM or more. Windows 2000 machines simply ignore WMI filters, and this GPO still applies to them.

Final WMI Filter Thoughts

WMI filters can be a bit tough to create, but they're worth it. You can filter target machines that meet specific criteria for GPOs that leverage GPSI or any other Group Policy function. But keep two things in mind:

WMI Performance Impact   WMI filters take some percentage of performance away each and every time Group Policy processing is evaluated. That is, at every logon, at startup, and every 90 minutes thereafter, you'll take a little performance hit because WMI filters are re-evaluated. So, be careful and don't link a GPO to the domain level or else every single Windows Vista, Windows XP, Windows 2003, and Windows 2008 machine works hard to evaluate that WMI query.

So, my example where I used the WMI filter on a GPO for the whole domain *isn't such a hot idea*. I did it only for the sake of the example, and you should try to avoid that kind of use in the real world.

The upshot: Be careful where you link GPOs with WMI queries. You could seriously affect GPO processing performance. You'll definitely want to test your WMI filters first in the lab for performance metrics before you roll them out companywide.

WMI Filters Don't Apply to Windows 2000   Windows 2000 machines are left out of the mix. They simply ignore the WMI filters placed on GPOs. When a Windows 2000 machine processes a GPO that leverages a WMI filter, it's as if the query always evaluates to True. However, with a little downloadable magic, you can hack Windows 2000 machines to play in the WMI filter game. A free, quasi-supported download, called WMI Filtering for Windows 2000, is available at www.mml.ru/WMIF2K/, and it can inject the necessary code to support WMI filters. It's a little unwieldy to set up, but afterward you should be able to have a unified WMI scheme across your environment. My pal and another Group Policy Guru, Darren Mar-Elia, adds: "While this solution is 'neat,' it's pretty hokey—basically adding users and computers to groups on-the-fly. Not only is it kind of scary but, of course, also requires reboots or relogons to pick up new tokens." In short, use at your own risk.

Return to Chapter 2 some time when you can review how to back up and restore WMI filters as well as how to delegate their creation and use. Also, don't forget about Chapter 11, which also discusses how to script the backup and restore of WMI filters.

Group Policy Loopback Processing

As you know, the normal course of Group Policy scope is local computer, site, domain, and then each nested OU. But sometimes it's necessary to deviate from the normal routine. For instance, you might want all users, whoever they are, to be able to walk up and log onto a specific machine and get the same User node settings. This can be handy in public computing environments such as libraries, nurses' stations, and kiosks as well as manufacturing and production assembly environments. This is also critically necessary for Terminal Server environments, as discussed in the section "Group Policy Loopback—Replace Mode for Terminal Services" later in this chapter.

Wouldn't it be keen if you could round up all the special computers on which users need the same settings for an OU and force them to use these settings? Whoever logs onto those computers would get the same Internet Explorer settings (such as a special proxy) and logon scripts or certain Control Panel restrictions—just for those workstations.

Reviewing Normal Group Policy Processing

Recall that sometimes computers and users can each be relegated into different OUs. Indeed, any user from any other portion of the domain, say the Domain Administrator, could log onto VISTA1 located under the **Human Resources Computers** OU.

When a user account contained in one OU logs onto a computer contained in another OU, the normal behavior is to process the computer GPOs based on the site, domain, OU hierarchy and then process the user GPOs based on the site, domain, OU hierarchy. This is true just by the rules of time: computers start up, their GPOs are processed, users log on, and their GPOs are processed.

 Even when Windows Vista's or Windows XP's default of Fast Boot is turned off, that's generally the way things happen.

So, if the Domain Administrator were to sit down at the VISTA1 machine in the **Human Resources Computers** OU, the normal course of events would apply the policy settings in the Computers node from the Default-First-Site, then the Corp.com domain, and then, finally, the **Human Resources Computers** OU. Next, the policy settings in GPOs linked to the user account would apply; first from the Default-First-Site and then only from the Corp.com domain (as the administrator account is not sitting under any OU in our examples).

With Group Policy Loopback processing, the rules change. There are two Group Policy Loopback modes: Merge and Replace. In both, the computer is tricked into forgetting that it's really a computer. It temporarily puts on a hat that says, "I'm a user," and processes the site, domain, and organizational unit GPOs as if it were a user. Kooky, huh? Let's take a look at the Merge and Replace modes.

Group Policy Loopback—Merge Mode

When computers are subject to Group Policy Loopback—Merge mode, GPOs process in the normal way at startup (and at background refresh time): Computer node for site, for domain, and then for each nested OU. The user then logs on, and policy settings meant for that user are applied in the normal way: All GPOs are processed from the site, the domain, and then each nested OU.

But when computers are affected by Group Policy Loopback—Merge mode, the system determines where the computer account is and applies another round of User node settings—those contained in all GPOs that lead to that computer (yes, User node settings). This means that the logged-on user gets whacked with two different sets of User node policy settings. Here's the timeline:

- The computer starts up and gets the appropriate Computer node policy settings.

- The user logs on and gets the appropriate User node policy settings.

- The computer then puts on a hat that says, "I'm a user." Then all *User* node policy settings apply to the *computer*. Again, this happens because the computer is wearing the "I'm a user" hat.

The net result is that the user settings from the user's account and the user settings from the computer (which temporarily thinks it's a user) are equal to each other; neither is more important than the other, except when they overlap. In that case, the computer settings win, as usual.

The Group Policy Loopback—Merge mode is rarely used unless you need to modify a property in the user profile, but do it per computer.

Group Policy Loopback—Replace Mode

When computers are subject to Group Policy Loopback—Replace mode, Group Policy processes in the normal way at startup (and at background refresh time): Computer node for site, domain, and then each nested OU. The user then logs on, and GPOs meant for the user are totally ignored down the food chain for the logged-on user. Instead, the computer puts on an "I'm a user" hat, and the system determines where the computer account is but applies the User node settings contained in all GPOs that lead to that computer. Therefore, you change the balance of power so all users are forced to heed the User settings based on what is geared for the computer. Confused? Let's generate an example to "unconfuse" you.

By and large, Group Policy Loopback—Replace mode is more useful than Merge mode and works well in public computing environments such as labs, kiosks, classrooms, training machines, libraries, and so on. So let's work though an example to solidify our understanding of Replace mode. In this example, we'll perform a variety of steps.

1. Create a new OU called **Public Kiosk**.
2. Move a Windows Vista machine into the **Public Kiosk** OU.
3. Create a new GPO for the **Public Kiosk** OU that performs two functions:
   - Disables the Display Properties dialog box.
   - Performs Group Policy Loopback—Replace mode processing so that all users logging onto the computers in the **Public Kiosk** OU will be unable to use the Display Properties dialog box.

For our examples, we'll pretend to have another machine called VISTA2. This is a new machine, just for this set of examples. It is not listed in Chapter 1 in the section "Getting Ready to Use this Book."

Setting All Who Log onto a Specific Computer to Use a Specific Printer

You might want to use the Group Policy Loopback—Merge mode to create a printer and apply it to anyone who uses a particular machine. For instance, you might want anyone who logs onto a machine on the fourth floor to automatically connect to the printer on the fourth floor. One way to do this is to run around to every machine on the fourth floor, log on as the user, and manually connect to the printer on the fourth floor.

If you've ever attempted this feat, you might have also tried to create a Group Policy startup script for a computer to try to connect everyone to a printer on the network; but it won't work. There is no user environment in which to house this newly created printer. So you have a paradox: How do you run a computer startup script for every user who sits down at a machine but run this startup script after the user is logged on? Group Policy Loopback—Merge mode comes to the rescue.

In both Loopback Processing modes, the computer doesn't think it's a computer. It temporarily puts on a user hat and processes the site, domain, and organizational unit GPOs as if it were a user.

With that in mind, you'll need to do several things:

1. Create a VB script that connects you to the printer you want. (Later in this sidebar, you'll see an example, ASSIGNHP4.VBS.)

2. Create an OU, say, **4th Floor Computers**, and move the computers on the fourth floor into it.

3. Create a new GPO on that OU and name it, say, "All computers get HPLJ4 Printer."

4. Drill down into the new GPO to Computer Configuration ➢ Policies ➢ Administrative Templates ➢ System ➢ Group Policy ➢ User Group Policy Loopback Processing mode, and specify that it be in Merge mode.

5. Drill down into User Configuration ➢ Windows ➢ Scripts ➢ Logon. Click Add to add a new file, click Browse to open the File Requester, copy the ASSIGNHP4.VBS script, and add it to the list to run.

Remember, in Loopback Processing mode, the computer thinks it's a user, so use User/Logon scripts, not Computer/Startup script.

Now, whenever you log on as any user to a computer in the **4th Floor Computers** OU, the GPOs meant for the user will be evaluated and run. The computer will then put on a user hat and run its own logon script, and you will get the printer assigned for every user on a computer.

Here is the ASSIGNHP4.VBS VB script you can use for the preceding example:

```
Set wshNetwork = CreateObject("WScript.Network")


    PrinterPath = "\\server1\HPLJ4"
    PrinterDriver = "HP LaserJet 4"
    WshNetwork.AddwindowsPrinterConnection PrinterPath, PrinterDriver
    WshNetwork.SetDefaultPrinter "\\server1\HPLJ4"
    Wscript.Echo "Default Printer Created"


Set wshNetwork = Nothing
```

Thanks to Richard Zimmerman of ABC Computers for the inspiration for this tip. Before you go implementing this tip, be sure to read Chapter 10 in this book and Chapter 9 in the companion book, *Creating a Secure Managed Desktop*, where we'll show you how to use ordinary Group Policy to get the same job accomplished. That is, we'll show you how to zap printers down to specific machines in a more efficient way. However, I'm leaving this example here because it's a firm demonstration, in general, of what Merge mode does.

Creating a New OU

To create a new OU called **Public Kiosk,** follow these steps:

1. Log onto the Domain Controller DC01 as Domain Administrator.

2. Choose Start ➢ All Programs ➢ Administrative Tools and select Active Directory Users and Computers.

3. Right-click the domain name, and choose New ➢ Organizational Unit. Enter **Public Kiosk** as the name in the New Object—New Organizational Unit dialog box.

 You are creating this new OU on the same level as **Human Resources**. Do not create this new OU underneath **Human Resources**.

Moving a Client into the Public Kiosk OU

In this case, we'll move a different computer, say VISTA2, into the **Public Kiosk** OU. Follow these steps:

1. In Active Directory Users and Computers, right-click the domain and choose Find to open the "Find Users, Contacts and Groups" dialog box.

2. In the Find drop-down, select Computers. In the Name field, type **VISTA2** (or the name of some other computer) to find the computer account of the same name. Once you've found it, right-click the account, and choose Move. Move the account to the **Public Kiosk** OU.

Repeat these steps for all other computers you want to move to the **Public Kiosk** OU.

Creating a Group Policy Object with Group Policy Loopback— Replace Mode

We want the Display Properties dialog box disabled for all users who log onto VISTA2. To do this, we need to set two policy settings within a single GPO: **Remove Display in Control Panel** and **User Group Policy Loopback Processing Mode**. Follow these steps using the GPMC:

1. Right-click the **Public Kiosk** OU, and choose "Create a GPO in this domain, and Link it here."

2. In the "New GPO" dialog box, name the GPO something descriptive, such as "No Display Setting—Loopback Replace."

3. Highlight the GPO and click Edit to open the Group Policy Management Editor.

4. To hide the Settings tab, drill down to User Configuration ➤ Policies ➤ Administrative Templates ➤ Control Panel ➤ Display and double-click the **Remove Display in Control Panel** policy setting. Change the policy setting from Not Configured to Enabled, and click OK.

5. To enable Loopback processing, drill down to Computer Configuration ➤ Policies ➤ Administrative Templates ➤ System ➤ Group Policy and double-click the **User Group Policy Loopback Processing Mode** policy setting. Change the setting from Not Configured to Enabled, select Replace from the drop-down box, as shown in Figure 5.5, and click OK.

6. Close the Group Policy Management Editor.

FIGURE 5.5 Choose the Loopback Processing mode desired, in this case, Replace.

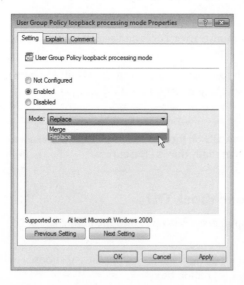

Verifying That Group Policy Loopback—Replace Mode Is Working

You'll want to log onto VISTA2, but you'll need to restart it because Loopback processing doesn't seem to ever take effect until a reboot occurs. Since we're using Loopback Policy processing in Replace mode, you can choose any user you have defined—a mere mortal or even the administrator of the domain.

Right-click over the Desktop and select Personalize and note that no one can access the Display settings, as shown in Figure 5.6.

FIGURE 5.6   With Group Policy Loopback—Replace Mode processing enabled, all users are affected by a computer's setting.

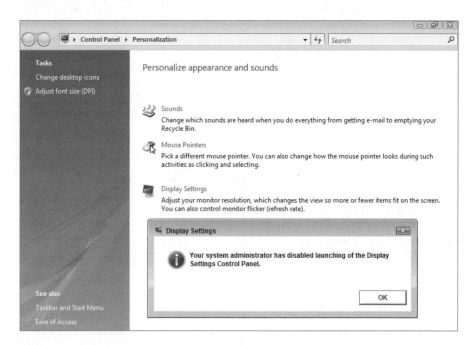

Group Policy Loopback—Replace Mode policy processing is powerful but really is only useful for specialty machines. Additionally, you'll need to use it sparingly, because Loopback processing is a bit more CPU intensive for the client and servers and quite difficult to trouble-shoot should things go wrong.

Group Policy Loopback—Replace Mode for Terminal Services

Group Policy Loopback—Replace mode has one other major use: Terminal Services. If you have lots of servers and lots of users logging onto them, chances are you want everyone who logs onto your Terminal Services machines to have precisely the same settings, regardless of who they are.

The process of establishing these settings is straightforward:

1. Create an OU for your Terminal Services computers and give it an appropriate name, such as **Terminal Services Computers** OU.

2. Set Loopback Replace mode to apply to that OU.

3. Stuff your Terminal Services computer objects into the OU and reboot them.

Now any user policy settings within GPOs set on the **Terminal Services Computers** OU and everyone logging onto the Terminal Services computers will get the exact same settings.

Windows 2000 servers, Windows 2003 Terminal Services, and Windows Server 2008 computers respond just fine to Loopback—Replace mode. Just be sure to stuff your Terminal Services computer objects into your designated OU, too, and then manually configure the policy settings on those computers as desired.

As an administrator, you might want to log onto Terminal Services machines, but you don't want the same settings as everyone else. To configure this, simply use the techniques found in Chapter 2 and filter the GPO containing the policy that performs the lockout for, say, Domain Administrators.

Yet Another Practical Use for Group Policy Loopback Mode

I don't know about you, but I just hate it when I walk up to a server and log on. Usually, I have no idea what the server's name, function, IP address, and so on could possibly be. In the NT 4 days, I used the following trick:

1. Fire up Windows Paint.

2. Create a BMP file that detailed the name, function, and IP address and save it as, say, `c:\winnt\background.bmp`.

3. Modify the `.default` user profile so that when no one was logged on at the console, the `.bmp` file was displayed. To do this, open the Registry of the local server and change `HKEY_USERS\ .DEFAULT\Control Panel\Desktop\Wallpaper` to a path of `c:\winnt\background.bmp`.

But there was one major problem—as soon as I logged onto the server, the background went away (because my local profile took over), and 20 seconds later, I forgot what the machine's name, function, and IP address were. With Windows 2003 and the Group Policy Loopback—Replace Mode policy, I've discovered a cool trick; you can now force the same background BMP for every user who physically logs onto any given machine.

The idea is simple:

- Create the BMP file as explained earlier, and store it once again, locally, as `c:\windows\ background.bmp`.

- Create a new GPO on the Domain Controllers OU or on your own OU for your servers. Call the policy "Forced Background Wallpaper—Loopback Replace."

- Modify the User node of the policy as follows:

1. Drill down through User Configuration ➢ Policies ➢ Administrative Templates ➢ Desktop ➢ Active Desktop ➢ **Enable Active Desktop**, and set Enabled.

2. Drill down through User Configuration ➢ Policies ➢ Administrative Templates ➢ Desktop ➢ Active Desktop ➢ **Desktop Wallpaper**, and set Enabled. Set the wallpaper name to c:\windows \background.bmp.

3. Drill down through User Node ➢ Administrative Templates ➢ Desktop ➢ Active Desktop ➢ **Allow Only Bitmapped Wallpaper**, and set Enabled.

4. To modify the Computer node of the policy, drill down through Computer Configuration ➢ Policies ➢ Administrative Templates ➢ System ➢ Group Policy ➢ and enable **User Group Policy Loopback Processing Mode**. Set to Loopback—Merge.

Now whenever anyone logs onto that server, they will get the exact same background BMP! This is still true even if they usually get a background dictated via some other Group Policy for their own personal account!

There is one more accompanying tip to seal the deal. If you've enabled Terminal Services Administration mode, by default you cannot see the wallpaper when coming in over Terminal Services. Change the default behavior of Terminal Services by using the Terminal Services Configuration application, right-clicking the RDP protocol, and selecting the Environment tab. Choose to view the wallpaper by deselecting the Disable the Wallpaper check box.

A similar ability is available from the BGINFO tool, which you can download from Microsoft's Sysinternals site at http://tinyurl.com/u6yy2. And it's dynamic, so if something changes on the server, the background changes with it. However, this tip is a useful example of how to use the Group Policy Loopback—Replace mode.

Additional Terminal Services Tips

As a little side note, if your Terminal Services run at least Windows Server 2003, at your disposal is an arsenal of policy settings designed to manage Windows 2003 Terminal Services. You'll find two sets of Terminal Services policy settings for Windows 2003: one for users and one for computers:

- To manipulate Terminal Services computers, drill down through Computer Configuration ➢ Policies ➢ Administrative Templates ➢ Windows Components ➢ Terminal Services.

- To manipulate Terminal Services clients, drill down through User Configuration ➢ Policies ➢ Administrative Templates ➢ Windows Components ➢ Terminal Services.

Including information on how best to use the policy settings that configure Windows 2003 Terminal Services (and Windows Server 2008) is beyond the scope of this book. To that end, I recommend Christa Anderson's *Windows IT Pro Magazine* article "Using GPOs to Configure Terminal Services." You can find it at http://tinyurl.com/2ojbyw.

One final parting tip regarding Terminal Services: Microsoft has a nice document that has a lot of tips and tricks for Terminal Services administrators vis-à-vis Group Policy. The document is named "Step-by-Step Guide for Configuring Group Policy for Terminal Services" and can be found here: `http://tinyurl.com/3dsydv`.

Group Policy with Cross-Forest Trusts

Windows 2003 domains brought a new trust type to the table, a forest trust (also known as a cross-forest trust). The idea is that if you have multiple, unrelated forests, you can join their root domains with one single trust; then, anytime new domains pop up in either forest, there is an automatically implied trust relationship.

To do this requires a large commitment from all parties involved. All domains must be in at least Windows 2003 Functional mode, and all forests must be in Windows 2003 Functional mode. Only then is it possible to create cross-forest trusts via the Active Directory Domains and Trusts utility. For an example of an organization that might use this, see Figure 5.7.

In this example, all domains trust all other domains via the cross-forest trust. Indeed, a user with an account housed in bigu.edu, say, Sol Rosenberg, could sit down at a computer in either Corp.com or Widgets.corp.com and log onto his user account, which is maintained in bigu.edu.

When Sol (srosenberg) from bigu.edu logs onto any computer in domains below Corp.com (that is, Widgets.corp.com), the logon screen will not present BIGU as an option. To log on, Sol will need to type **srosenberg@bigu.edu** as his logon id along with his password. This is one of the limitations of cross-forest trusts.

What Happens When Logging onto Different Clients across a Cross-Forest Trust?

So what happens when Sol from bigu.edu has access to various computer types in the Corp.com forest? Let's find out.

Logging onto Windows XP (with no Service Pack or with SP1) across a Cross-Forest Trust

For users logging onto Windows XP machines in Windows 2003 domains, Group Policy across forests acts as if it were one big forest. For instance, if Sol Rosenberg logs into WIDGETS-XPPRO6 at Widgets.corp.com or VISTA1 at Corp.com, he would get the GPOs that affect his user account and the user policy settings that affect him. The Windows XP computer Sol uses will get the GPOs meant for it. (The computer would embrace the policy settings based on the site, the domain, and the OU it's in.)

FIGURE 5.7   Here's one example of how a cross-forest trust can be used.

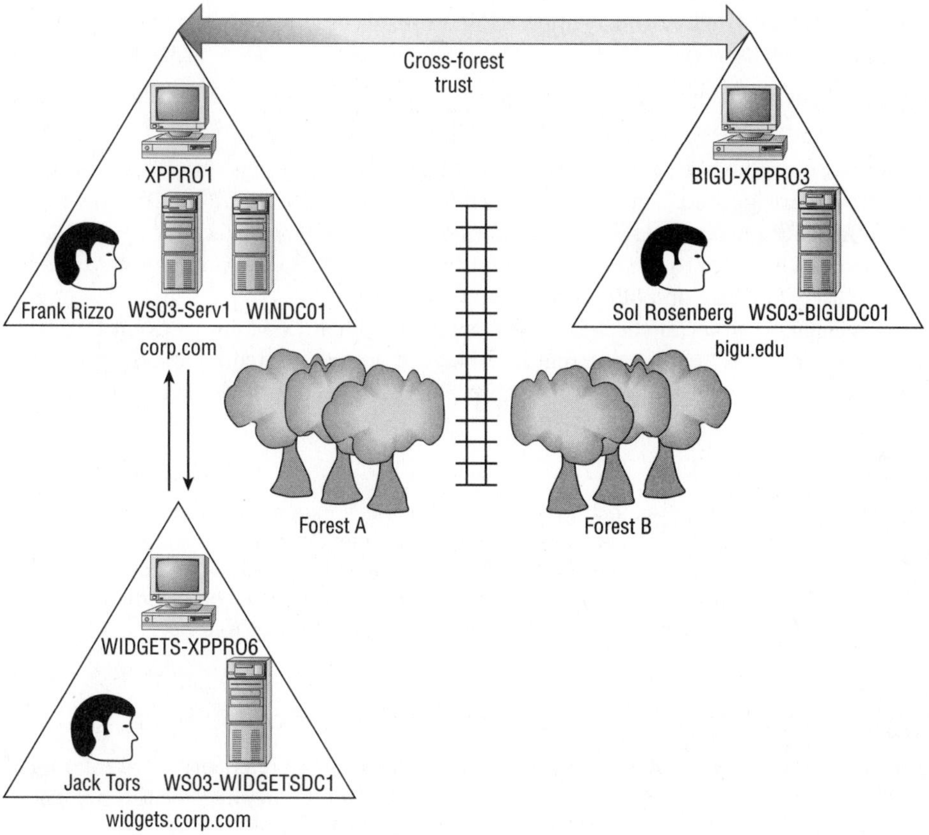

Makes sense. Take a deep breath, and then read the next section.

> **WARNING**   What about Windows XP's SP2 or Windows Vista? They're different, so keep reading.

Logging onto a Windows 2003 Server across a Cross-Forest Trust

Here's where things get weird, so try to stay with me. Imagine that Sol Rosenberg in bigu.edu is also the SQL database administrator for a server named WS03-Serv1 over in Corp.com in the **Human Resources SQL-Servers** OU. From time to time, Sol gets in his car and travels from the BigU campus over to the WS03-Serv1 computer sitting at the Corp.com headquarters. He sits down, logs on locally to the console (where he's been granted access), and he doesn't get the GPOs meant for him (and therefore doesn't get his own policy settings).

Instead the server processes GPOs as if it were using Group Policy Loopback Processing—Replace mode. What does this mean?

- The GPOs that would normally apply to Sol's user account in bigu.edu are ignored by the Windows 2003 server.

- The computer puts on an "I'm a user" hat and says, "Give me the GPOs that would apply to me if I were a user."

So, in our example, we can see that when Sol from bigu.edu logs onto WS03-Serv1, his policy settings are ignored. The computer then looks at the GPOs that would apply to users in the **Human Resources SQL-Servers** OU (where the WS03-Serv1 account resides).

Since no GPOs linked to the **Human Resources SQL-Servers** OU contain policy settings geared for users, Sol gets no policy settings applied.

After logging on, you can check out the Application Event Log and see Event ID 1109, which states that Sol is "from a different forest logged onto this machine. Cross forest Group Policy processing is disabled and Loopback processing has been enforced in this forest for this user account."

For your own testing and to solidify this concept, you might wish, just for now, to link an existing GPO (that has user policy settings) to the **Human Resources Computers** OU. For instance, link the "Hide Desktop Tab" GPO to the **Human Resources Computers** OU, then log back on as Sol. Sol's user account will be affected by the GPO with the policy setting.

Logging onto Windows 2000 across a Cross-Forest Trust

Logging onto a Windows 2000 system with SP4 across the trust—either Server or Professional—is just like logging onto Windows 2003 Server. That is, the GPOs that affect the user are ignored, and the computer processes Group Policy Loopback—Replace mode.

Logging onto a Windows 2000 system that doesn't have SP4 (SP3 and earlier) across the trust—either Server or Professional—will not cause Loopback to be performed. The user will get the expected user settings, and the computer will get the expected computer settings.

Logging onto Windows XP/SP2, Windows Vista, or Windows Server 2008 across a Cross-Forest Trust

Logging onto Windows XP with SP2, Windows Vista, or Windows Server 2008 installed across the trust is just like logging onto Windows 2003 Server (or Windows 2000 Professional with SP4). That is, GPOs that would normally affect users are ignored, and the computer processes Group Policy Loopback—Replace mode.

Event ID 1109 will be generated in the Application Event log stating that a user is "...from a different forest."

The Big Question: Why Loopback across Cross-Forest Trusts?

At this point, you're likely scratching your head in disbelief. Why would Sol not get the GPOs that should affect him? The answer is simple: if Sol were assigned software (see Chapter 4 of the companion book), logon scripts, or other potentially dangerous settings, our machine's stability could be affected.

This mechanism protects our systems from stuff that we might not want to happen to it. Since we're not administrating Sol, we don't know what potential harm Sol's settings might do. Then, we need to examine what might happen if the folks at Microsoft decided to do things differently, say, have no GPOs affect Sol when he uses our Corp.com machines. That might be really bad too, because then Sol would have free reign to do whatever he wanted.

So what does Loopback buy us? Loopback makes us think about what happens when users from afar use our systems. Even though, as you know, user policy settings don't affect computers, you can start to design your OUs and GPOs for this occasion. That is, if you set up user policy settings in OUs that just contain servers and someone in a foreign domain logs on, they'll at least get the user policy settings you intend for them to—not what their administrator wanted.

Strange? Yes, but it works, and this becomes strangely more logical the more you think about it.

What about workstation machines? This is a less-critical problem on workstation machines, because, well, it's just a workstation. If someone is assigned an application (see Chapter 4 of the companion book) that maybe does evil stuff, at least it's affecting only a workstation, not a server that a whole team might have access to.

I have more advice on how to manage this in the section "Disabling Loopback Processing When Using Cross-Forest Trusts."

Microsoft has additional documentation about times when you might not want GPOs applied on Windows 2000 systems. See Knowledge Base article 823862 for more information. Check out http://support.microsoft.com/kb/823862 for the article.

Disabling Loopback Processing When Using Cross-Forest Trusts

If you do not want the default behavior, which is that Loopback Replace processing is enabled for the computer, you can set a specific Group Policy to apply to the computers you want to be normal again. Here are my recommendations:

- Keep the default behavior for all servers: Windows 2000 Server + SP4, Windows 2003 Server, and Windows Server 2008. You want them to process in Group Policy Loopback—Replace mode.

- Return the "normal" behavior for all workstations: Windows Vista, Windows 2000 + SP4, and Windows XP + SP2. Windows 2000 + SP3 (and earlier) and Windows XP + SP1 (and no service pack) are already at the "normal" behavior. You want them to process GPOs using regular processing rules.

To do this, you need to locate the **Allow Cross-Forest User Policy and Roaming User Profiles** policy setting. Drill down through Computer Configuration ➢ Policies ➢ Administrative Templates ➢ System ➢ Group Policy. Note that the policy setting says "At least Windows Server 2003" but it will affect Windows XP/SP2 machines as well.

To set it up, follow these steps:

1. Create a new GPO at the domain level, say, "No Loopback for Cross-Forest." Enable the policy setting named **Allow Cross-Forest User Policy and Roaming User Profiles.** This will initially affect all computers, including servers.

   However, I suggest that you filter out your server machines so that they keep the default Loopback behavior. I suggest you do this as shown in the following steps.

2. Create a security group called AllMyServers.

3. Add all the Windows 2000 and Windows 2003 servers (regardless of service pack) in the domain to the AllMyServers group.

4. Deny the AllMyServers group the ability to process this new GPO.

> In an environment that has no Windows 2000 clients, you can optionally set up a WMI filter to apply the policy just to the servers.

This will maintain the Loopback behavior for servers but go back to normal processing for absolutely all workstations in the domain. This way your servers are protected from other users in trusted forests potentially doing bad stuff to your servers. But those same users are free to have normal processing on all your workstations.

> Be careful when using the Deny attribute to deny a group the ability to apply Group Policy. The GPMC will not show you that you are passing over specific users or computers from applying the GPO in the Settings tab. I discussed this earlier in Chapter 2.

Cross-Forest Trust Client Matrix

If your head is spinning about what happens to users when they use a specific client across a cross-forest trust, Table 5.1 is for you. This table also shows which client systems can be set back to normal processing by enabling the **Allow Cross-Forest User Policy and Roaming User Profiles** policy setting.

TABLE 5.1 Cross-Forest Trust Client Matrix

Client	What Happens When a User Logs on across the Cross-Forest Trust	Can be Changed by the Allow Cross-Forest User Policy and Roaming User Profiles Policy Setting
Windows 2000 Server or Professional, with no service pack, SP1, SP2, or SP3	User gets user settings. Computer gets computer settings.	No
Windows 2000 Server or Professional, with SP4	User settings are ignored. Computer gets settings as if it were a user (that is, Group Policy Loopback—Replace mode).	Yes
Windows XP with no service pack or SP1	User gets user settings. Computer gets computer settings.	No
Windows XP with SP2	User settings are ignored. Computer gets settings as if it were a user (that is, Group Policy Loopback—Replace mode).	Yes
Windows 2003 Server with or without any service pack	User settings are ignored. Computer gets settings as if it were a user (that is, Group Policy Loopback—Replace mode).	Yes
Windows Vista	User settings are ignored. Computer gets settings as if it were a user (that is, Group Policy Loopback—Replace mode).	Yes
Windows Server 2008	User settings are ignored. Computer gets settings as if it were a user (that is, Group Policy Loopback—Replace mode).	Yes

Understanding Cross-Forest Trust Permissions

Windows 2003 cross-forest trusts have two modes: Forest-wide Authentication and Selective Authentication, as shown in Figure 5.8. To view the screen shown in Figure 5.8, open Active Directory Domains and Trusts, locate the properties of the trust, click the Authentication tab.

FIGURE 5.8 You can set Forest-Wide Authentication or Selective Authentication.

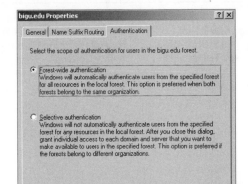

In a Windows 2003 Active Directory domain, Full Authentication mode permits Group Policy across forests to act as if it were one big forest. That is, GPOs are processed according to Table 5.1.

We already know that Sol is the SQL database administrator over at Corp.com, and we saw what happened when he logged onto the Windows 2003 member server WS03-Serv1. Twice a week, however, Sol works at Widgets.corp.com on the WIDGETS-XPPRO3 for some CAD work. Then, the unthinkable happens.

An attack originating at bigu.edu upon Corp.com's computers gets the two Domain Administrators in a heated battle. The Corp.com Domain Administrator decides he wants to prevent attacks from bigu.edu, so he enables Selective Authentication. Now no one from bigu.edu can log onto any of the machines in Corp.com or Widgets.corp.com. Ergo, Sol will not be able to log onto either his WS03-Serv1 Windows 2003 member server in Corp.com or his WIDGETS-XPPRO3 machine in Widgets.corp.com. Sol needs the "Allowed to Authenticate" right on the computer objects he will use. In this example, you can see what is done for WIDGETS-XPPRO3, in Figure 5.9.

Additional computers in Corp.com and Widgets.corp.com need these explicit rights if anyone else from bigu.edu is going to use them. Then, Group Policy will process as described earlier and summarized in Table 5.1.

See Chapter 2 of the companion book for a description of how profiles react in conjunction with cross-forest trusts.

FIGURE 5.9   You need to specifically grant the "Allowed to Authenticate" right in order for Sol to use this machine.

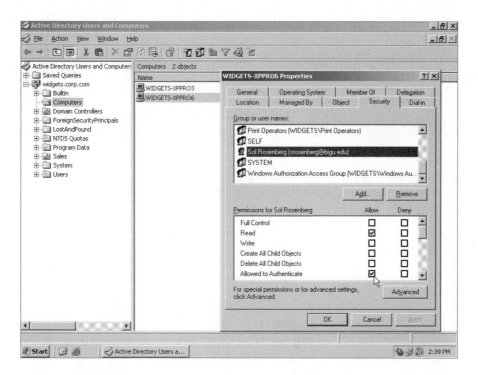

Intermixing Group Policy and NT 4 System Policy

I've already discussed how Group Policy cannot apply to Windows 9x or Windows NT clients. Group Policy applies only to Windows 2000 clients and newer. However, the opposite is not true. That is, NT 4 System Policy (whose filename is `NTCONFIG.POL`) is perfectly valid and accepted on Windows 2000 and newer. You might have an occasion to use both at the same time—typically if you're in the middle of an NT 4–to–Active Directory migration. If this happens, it's likely you'll have both Active Directory Group Policy and legacy NT 4 System Policy on the same network.

If you're trying to migrate from NT to Active Directory, you basically have four major scenarios:

1. Both computer and user accounts in a Windows NT domain

2. A computer account in Windows NT and a user account in an Active Directory domain

3. A computer account in an Active Directory domain and a user account in Windows NT

4. Both computer and user accounts in Active Directory

You could, if you wanted, have an NT 4 System Policy file (named NTCONFIG.POL) in each and every domain—NT 4 or an Active Directory domain. Hopefully, you won't be taking your NTCONFIG.POL files with you when you go to Active Directory, but if you do, you'll need to know how that calculates into the final RSoP. Additionally, it's important to remember that NT 4 System Policy "tattoos" the machines it touches, meaning that even if you're eventually going to phase out NT 4 System Policy, you'll need a battle plan to specifically reverse the settings in NTCONFIG.POL so that your clients can phase out the settings.

Let's briefly examine what will happen in each of these cases, which are illustrated in Figure 5.10.

FIGURE 5.10 There are four main cases when dealing with NT 4 System Policy and "modern" (Windows 2000, Windows Server 2003, Windows XP, or Windows Vista) clients.

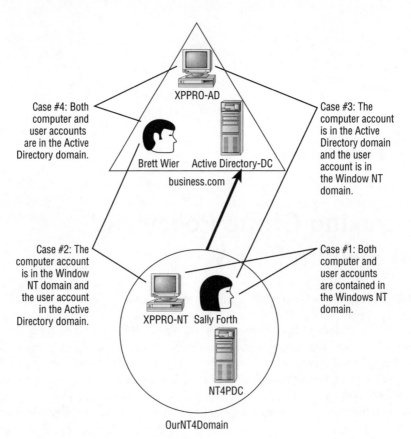

Case 1: Both computer and user accounts are contained in the Windows NT domain.
When the computer starts up, it first applies any settings in the computer side of the local
GPO. Next, the user logs onto the NT 4 domain and obtains the user-side settings from the
NTCONFIG.POL file. If present, the user side of the local GPO applies after the NTCONFIG.POL
settings. These settings are added cumulatively, except if there is a conflict. If there is a conflict,
most often the NTCONFIG.POL settings win.

**Case 2: The computer account is in the Windows NT domain, and the user account is in the
Active Directory domain.** When the computer starts up, it logs onto the NT 4 domain. If
present, the computer side of the local GPO applies. When the user logs onto Active Directory,
two things happen:

- The computer downloads and applies NTCONFIG.POL (from the NT 4 domain).
- The user processes GPOs normally. First, user-side local GPO settings apply, followed by
  the user-side Active Directory GPOs. As expected, these Active Directory GPO settings
  are added cumulatively to the local GPO settings, except if there is a conflict. If there is
  a conflict, the last written Group Policy setting wins. If there is any NTCONFIG.POL file
  in the domain where the user's account is located, that old System Policy is ignored for
  the user.

 In some circumstances, it appears that the local Group Policy wins, such as
when you set a background Desktop image. As usual, you'll want to test to
make sure that what you want is what you get when you intermix NT 4 System Policy and local GPOs.

**Case 3: The computer account is in an Active Directory domain, and the user account is in the
Windows NT domain.** When the computer starts up, it first applies any settings in the computer side of the local GPO. Then, after the computer logs onto Active Directory, it receives
the computer-side GPOs from the site, domain, and OUs.

As expected, these Active Directory GPO settings are added cumulatively to the local GPO settings, except if there is a conflict. If there is a conflict, the last-written Group Policy setting
wins. If there is an NTCONFIG.POL file in the domain where the computer's account is located,
that old System Policy is ignored for the computer.

Upon logon, if present, the user side of the local GPO applies to the user. Then, the user downloads
and applies user-side settings from the NTCONFIG.POL file on the NT domain. These settings are
added cumulatively, except if there is a conflict. If there is a conflict, NTCONFIG.POL wins.

Case 4: Both computer and user accounts are in Active Directory. Most of this book is
about this scenario. Both the computer and user apply local GPO settings first, followed by the
GPOs from Active Directory: site, domain, and OUs. These Active Directory GPO settings
append the local GPO settings, except if there is a conflict. If there is a conflict, the Active
Directory GPO settings win over the local GPO settings. No System Policy (NTCONFIG.POL)
is downloaded. However, clients that have been tattooed by NTCONFIG.POL will stay tattooed,

and it's likely that at least some Registry entries will have to be manually scrubbed. Therefore, it's best to reverse the NTCONFIG.POL settings while you still can—before both the computer and the user accounts have been migrated. After the migration, neither the user nor the computer will read from the NTCONFIG.POL file.

Final Thoughts

In this chapter, you learned ways to utilize Group Policy in some interesting cases.

WMI filters are great; just be careful when you use them. They do take a little while to process on each machine, so be careful in the number of WMI filters you're asking your machines to process.

Loopback processing is great too; its job is to help you ensure that the same set of user settings affects a machine. It can be confusing to understand and use at first, so be sure to really test this out in a test lab before running it in your production environment.

If you have cross-forest trusts, consider what happens over the trust. You can decide if you want to revert back to "standard" behavior (that is, you can retrain the system to allow Group Policy Objects to affect your user accounts) or stay with (Loopback) behavior. Group Policy processing with a cross-forest trust can be tricky because different operating systems and the roles they play in the domain dictate when Group Policy applies. And, sometimes, a service pack will change the behavior of some of the processing. But hopefully the text, examples, and Table 5.1 can help you with any problems.

Finally, if you have any Windows NT machines kicking around out there, you might have old-school NTCONFIG.POL files. You'll want to be sure to know how those fit together with modern Group Policy. Let's hope you've been able to move away from any NT 4 System Policy. Remember that they tattoo and are difficult to fully scrub out of your environment. If you're still migrating from NT 4 to Windows 2000 or Active Directory, you'll need to understand the reaction when user and/or computer accounts still have a foot in NT 4. With that in mind, test, test, test before you deploy.

6

Troubleshooting Group Policy

Working with Group Policy isn't always a bed of roses. Sure, it's delightful when you can set up GPOs with their policy settings from upon high and have them reflected on your users' desktops. However, when you make a Group Policy wish, a specific process occurs before that wish comes true. Indeed, the previous chapter discussed *when* Group Policy applies. Now you understand the general rules of the game and when they occur.

But what if the unexpected happens? More specifically, it's difficult to determine *where* a policy setting comes from and *how* it's applied. Or, if Group Policy isn't working, *why* not, and *what's* going on? Additionally, you're usually after *whom* to blame, but that's actually something that auditing (discussed in Chapter 8) can help with. Additionally, check out our information on third-party tools in the appendix.

A user might call the help desk and loudly declare, "Things have just changed on my Desktop! I want them back the way they were!" Okay, sure, you want things better too. But a lot of variables are involved. First, there are the four levels: Local Group Policy (and potentially multiple local GPOs in Windows Vista and Windows Server 2008), site, domain, and each nested OU (so perhaps even more levels). Then, to make matters worse, what if multiple administrators are making multiple and simultaneous Group Policy changes across your environment? Who knows who has enabled what Group Policy settings and how some user is getting Group Policy applied?

Additional factors are involved as well. For instance, if you have old-style NT 4 System Policy, things can be particularly complex. Or perhaps you have a Windows 2003 forest, with cross-forest trusts to another Windows 2003 forest, and users are logging in all over the place. Not to mention a whole litany of things that could possibly go wrong between the time you make your wish and the time the client is expected to honor that wish.

Here's a foretaste of what to expect while troubleshooting GPOs:

Disabled GPOs   If the GPO is disabled or half the GPO is disabled, you need to hunt it down. Maybe someone decided to disable a GPO link and didn't tell you?

Inheritance Troubles and Trouble with WMI Filtering   Between local, site, domain, and multiple nested OUs, it can be a challenge to locate the GPO you need to fix. Also, introducing WMI filters can make troubleshooting even harder.

Special thanks to Darren Mar-Elia for his additional contributions to this chapter.

GPO Precedence at a Given Level   With multiple GPOs linked to a specific level in Active Directory, you might have some extra hunting to do.

Permissions Problems   Ensuring that users and computers are in the correct site, domain, and OU is one battle; however, ensuring that they have the correct permissions to access GPOs is quite another.

Windows XP and Windows Vista Processing   Windows XP and Windows Vista change the way GPOs are processed. And cross-forest trusts can be somewhat confusing as well.

Replication Problems   The health of the GPO itself on Domain Controllers is important when hunting down policy settings that aren't applying.

Infrastructure Problems   Group Policy processing requires that all pieces of your infrastructure are healthy, including such seemingly unrelated pieces as DNS, the services running on the client, and the ability to pass network protocols between clients and domain controllers. Additionally, healthy Active Directory design is where your Domain Controllers are all part of specific Active Directory sites (that is, don't create sites without Domain Controllers). Good Active Directory design equals good (consistent) Group Policy processing. The first place to look when Active Directory (or replication) behaves strangely is DNS. As my good friend Mark Minasi likes to say, "The second place to look for replication problems is DNS too."

Loopback Policy Processing   Sometimes, by mistake, an administrator has enabled loopback policy processing for a computer (or multiple computers). When this happens, the user sees unexpected behavior because the GPOs that would normally apply to him are suddenly out of the ordinary. Just understanding how loopback policy processing works can be a tricky matter. Not only do we have two different modes (Replace or Merge), on top of that you can have complex permission settings on the GPOs themselves, making it hard to calculate which settings a given user will take on.

Slow Links   You've rolled out your RAS (Remote Access Service). Now how and when are your clients going to process GPOs?

These are just a few places where you might encounter trouble. Between various client types with different processing behavior, these problems and the occasional solar flare make things crazy. Troubleshooting can get complicated. Fast.

In this chapter, we'll first dive into *where* Group Policy "lives" to give you a better sense of what's going on. We'll then explore some techniques and tools that will enable you to get an even better view of *why* specific policies are being applied.

Under the Hood of Group Policy

As stated in Chapter 1, Group Policy scope really has four levels: Local Group Policy (including Multiple Local Group Policy Objects) and then the three levels of Active Directory–based Group Policy—site, domain, and OU. When troubleshooting Group Policy, one approach is to first get a firm understanding of what's going on under the hood. As a kid, I took things apart all the time. My parents went mental when they came home and the dishwasher was in pieces all over the kitchen floor. It wasn't broken; I just wanted to know how it worked. If you're like me, this section is for you.

Inside Local Group Policy

Remember that a GPO is manipulated when someone walks up to the machine, runs the Local Group Policy Object Editor (GPEDIT.MSC), and makes a wish or three. Remember that in all versions of Windows prior to Vista, there was only one local GPO on a machine and local GPOs affected everyone who logged on to that machine.

Enterprise Admins, by default, do not have local administrator rights on individual client machines. Domain Admins, but not Enterprise Admins, have rights to Local Group Policy Objects (LGPOs)

Where Local Group Policy Lives

Once wishes are made with GPEDIT.MSC and a Local Group Policy is modified, the Local Group Policy lives in two places. The first part is file based, and the second part is Registry based:

The File-Based Part of Local Group Policy (all Versions of Windows)   The file-based part of the default local GPO can be found in C:\windows\system32\grouppolicy.

The File-Based Part of Local Group Policy for MLGPOs (Vista and Windows Server 2008 Only)
Remember that in Windows Vista (and Windows Server 2008 for that matter), there are now Multiple Local GPOs (MLGPOs). Because of this, the storage of those user-specific and group-specific GPOs is in a different location than the default local GPOs. Namely, they are stored in a new subfolder of \Windows\SYSTEM32 called GroupPolicyUsers, as shown in Figure 6.1.

FIGURE 6.1   Viewing the directories of Vista local GPOs

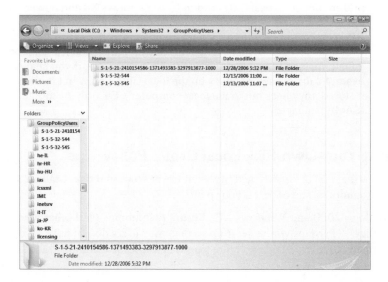

As you can see in the figure, there are three SID-named folders that contain the user-specific portion of the local GPO. (Remember that the computer portion applies to everyone, and, hence, there is no computer portion represented here.) You might actually have more than three folders here. In my example, the first SID you see in the list (with a SID of S-1-5-21-2410154586-1371493383-3297913877-1000) is the SID of a user account for whom I created a user-specific local GPO.

And, again, as you know from Chapter 1, I could have any number of user-specific local GPOs defined. And, for each of those user-specific GPOs, each one would have its own SID-based folder.

In addition, the two other folders that you see in Figure 6.1 are ones you will find on your Vista systems if you decide to define local GPOs specific for the Administrators group. And, still, another folder that holds LGPO information for nonadministrators. The folder called S-1-5-32-544 defines the Administrators GPO (and not coincidentally, that is the SID of the built-in Administrators group). Likewise, the folder named S-1-5-32-545 is the SID of the built-in Users group, which represents the nonadministrators local GPO.

Again, you should notice one major difference between the default local GPO and these user-specific local GPOs. That is, the default local GPO includes a computer-specific Machine folder in addition to the default User folder. However, any user-specific local GPO only contains a User folder (since it only contains user-specific policy settings).

The files and folders found in the local GPO mirrors, for the most part, are the way the file-based portion of an Active Directory–based GPO stores its stuff. This is good news, as it makes understanding the two types of GPOs (local versus domain-based GPOs) nearly equal.

Feel free to inspect the C:\windows\system32\grouppolicy folder, and then jump to the section "Group Policy Templates" later in this chapter to get the gist of the file structure. Note, however, that not all the structure may be present until the local GPO is edited. For Windows XP and newer operating systems, one major difference between local and Active Directory–based GPOs is that, when you make a policy change to the security attributes within the local GPO, that change is made directly to the workstation you're editing instead of being stored in the file system. So, if you change, for example, the password policy on the local GPO, you won't find evidence of it stored anywhere but in the local computer's Security Accounts Manager (SAM) database.

Three Use-at-Your-Own-Risk Local Group Policy Tips

Here are three tips that you are welcome to try—but use at your own risk. I cannot vouch for their validity or soundness, so you're on your own.

Tip #1 (for Windows 2000 and Windows XP): Ensure that admins (and other users) avoid Local Group Policy.   Perhaps you've set it up so that your users do not have access to the Start ➢ Run command. However, when you're logged in as the local administrator, you want the Run command. Then, check out `support.microsoft.com/kb/293655`. This tip shows you how admins (and other users) can override Local Group Policy for Windows 2000, XP, and Server 2003. Note that in Windows Vista, with the Multiple Local GPO feature, this tip is no longer required to segregate administrative policy from nonadministrative policy. However, this tip is valid only when the workstation isn't a domain member.

Tip #2: Reset Local Group Policy to the defaults. If you've set up a Local Group Policy and want to restore it to its default configuration, there's no easy way. However, my good pal Mark Minasi has a newsletter (#32) on the subject. Track it down at `www.minasi.com/archive.htm`. Even Mark admits that this solution might not be totally complete.

Tip #3: Copy a local GPO from one computer to another. This tip works in all versions of Windows, including Windows Vista. If you have the need to replicate a local GPO from one machine to another, it's possible (but not advisable). In fact this tip is expressly untested, unverified, and unsupported by the Group Policy team. Anyway, if you choose to proceed, you could simply copy the files contained within `%systemroot%\system32\GroupPolicy` from the source machine to the target machine. But note that not everything will come over. Scripts and Administrative Templates will come over, but other stuff like security will not, because as I mentioned earlier, security policy settings on the Local GPO are not stored within the file system. In short, if you try this trick, be sure to test the results to make sure all the stuff you want to come across does come across.

As you're performing this tip, be sure that you also hand-modify the `gpt.ini` found in the root of this directory. In short, make sure the number present here is greater than the number found in the `gpt.ini` of your target machines. As you'll learn later, the `gpt.ini` houses the *version number* of a GPO. If you don't set the version number higher than what is already present on the target computer, the local GPO engine doesn't know anything has changed, and hence you won't see the updated settings. And it's not just a matter of setting the version number to the same number plus 1. Version numbers are a bit more complicated than that. So, before you run off and try this tip, you'll also need to learn more about how version numbers work. See the sidebar later in the chapter entitled "Understanding Group Policy Version Numbers," which should give you the data you need.

With Windows Vista you can copy the user-specific MLGPOs from the `%systemroot%\system32\GroupPolicyUsers` directory on the source system to the same location on the target system. But, you will need to rename the directory to the correct SID of a user on the target system, and you will need to change the security permissions on the copied folder too.

Likewise, you can copy the administrators' and the non-administrators' specific MLGPOs by copying the appropriate folders (`S-1-5-32-544` and `S-1-5-32-545`). However, this is not supported in any way, and I recommend that you test this thoroughly if you should need it in a production environment.

Inside Active Directory Group Policy Objects

Here's the strange part about Group Policy (as if it weren't already strange enough). Chapter 1 discussed how creating a GPO really involves two steps. First, the GPO is written in the Group

Policy Objects container, and then it is *linked* to a level—site, domain, or OU. So, we know that GPOs don't really "live" at the level where they're linked. Specifically, all GPOs live inside the Group Policy Objects container in the domain. That is, they're always kept nestled inside this container yet are logically linked (but not stored) to the other levels to which they point. I referred to the GPOs we created as swimming around in a virtual pool within the domain.

So far in our journey, we created four new GPOs that affect our storyline:

- "Hide Screen Saver Option," which we applied to the Default-First-Site Name site

- "Hide Desktop Settings Option," which we applied to the Corp.com domain

- "Hide Display Settings Option/Restore Screen Saver Option," which we applied to the **Human Resources Users** OU

- "Auto-Launch Calc.exe," which we applied to the **Human Resources Computers** OU

We can check in with our concept of these GPOs as floating in a swimming pool within the Group Policy Objects container as shown here.

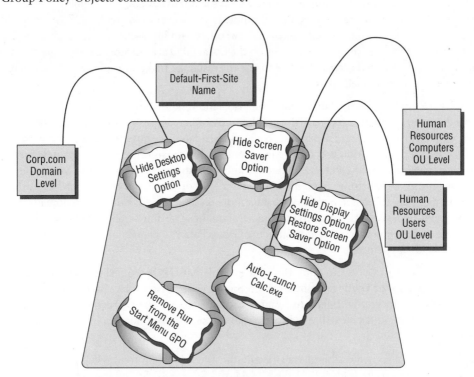

The Corp.com GPO Swimming Pool

As you can see, the GPOs never "live" at any level in Active Directory. They aren't really stored at any particular level, although it might appear (using the old-school interface) that they are.

To reiterate, if you leverage a GPO that is supposed to affect a site, an OU, or even a domain, the GPO itself is not stored directly at that level. Rather, the GPO is simply linked to the level in Active Directory. When a GPO is called to be used, it has to request a Domain Controller to fetch it from the Group Policy Objects container (and from its parts in SYSVOL) and pull the information out.

Each time you create a new GPO, it's born and placed into the swimming pool within the domain—ready for action if linked to a level in Active Directory. You can reuse a GPO at multiple levels in Active Directory simply by linking it to another level of Active Directory.

So, when GPOs are created for use at the site, domain, or OU level, they're always created within the domain swimming pool, the Group Policy Objects container, where we just link to the GPOs we need when we need them.

We're going to continue this discussion a littttle out of order here. We'll be talking about domain-linked GPOs, OU-linked GPOs, then round out with site-linked GPOs. Yes, yes, we all know the "right" order is site, domain, OU—so bear with me here (I think you'll understand why we're going out of order by the time this little section is complete).

Group Policy Objects from a Domain Perspective

Since we know that all GPOs are just hanging out in the Group Policy Objects container waiting to be used, we can take this one step further. That is, even those GPOs linked to the domain level aren't exempt from having to be "fetched." When clients use domain-linked GPOs, they have to make the same requests and "ask" the Domain Controller for the GPOs that apply to them.

This is usually not a problem; the Domain Controller doesn't have far to go to get the GPO in the swimming pool to apply it to the domain. But this is precisely why doing *cross-domain* GPO linking is so slow and painful.

For instance, in an environment with multiple domains, it might appear to be easier to recycle an existing GPO that lives in another domain. But when it comes time to grab the information inside the GPO, it needs to be brought back all the way from Domain Controllers in the originating domain. Again, this cross-domain GPO linking is very, very painful and should be avoided at all costs. In the appendix, I describe how to copy GPOs from one domain to another. This avoids the problem altogether because there's no "penalty" for creating a copy from a source domain and then having the copy live in your domain. Sure, it takes up a wee bit of storage in the new domain's swimming pool. But it's better than cross-domain linking.

Group Policy Objects from an OU Perspective

Since GPOs live in the Group Policy Objects container at the domain level, a distinct advantage is associated with the way Group Policy does its thing: it's tremendously easy to move, link, and unlink GPOs to the domain and/or its OUs. You could, if you desired, simply unlink a GPO in the domain or OU and link it back to some other OU. Or you could link one GPO to the domain and/or multiple OUs.

It's typical and usual that you'll use OUs to apply most of your GPOs. If GPOs live in the Group Policy Objects container swimming pool, it's easy for multiple, unrelated OUs to reuse the same GPOs and just create new links to existing GPOs.

Group Policy Objects from a Site Perspective

Site-level GPOs are a bit unique. If you used (or continue to use) the old-school interface via Active Directory Sites and Services to dictate a site-based GPO, you might be in for a world of pain. By default, all site-level GPOs created using the old-school interface will live in the

Group Policy Objects container of the Domain Controllers of the *root* domain—and only the root domain, that is, the first Active Directory domain brought online. Then, every time a GPO meant for a site is called for use by a client system, a Domain Controller from the root domain must fetch that information. If the closest Domain Controller from the root domain is in Singapore, so be it. You can see where the pain could get severe.

The GPMC basically forces us to create site-based GPOs in a thoughtful way. Specifically, you need to create the GPO in the domain swimming pool of your choice. Then, you need to link the GPO from the domain to the site you want. As you saw in Chapter 1, we first create the GPO in the Group Policy Objects container.

The idea is to create the GPO in the domain that makes sense and is closest to where the site-linked GPO will be used. Then, once we expose the site, we just add a link to our existing GPO, which is already in the domain swimming pool. In short, we get the site GPO to leverage the closest domain's swimming pool. Sure, it takes a little extra planning to think about which swimming pool is closest to the users and computers in the site—but it's worth it. That way, we're not asking some Domain Controller in Singapore to serve our New York users.

Remember, by default, only members of the Enterprise Administrators group (or members of the Domain Admins group in the root domain) can create new site-level GPOs or link to existing GPOs from the site level. Optionally, this right can be delegated.

The Birth, Life, and Death of a GPO

Now that you understand where GPOs actually live, we can take the next step: understanding the "journey" of a GPO. Specifically, a GPO is born and must stay healthy if it's going to stay alive. If its usefulness becomes depleted, you can call in the Sopranos boys to whack it—never to be seen again.

How Group Policy Objects Are "Born"

Before you can give birth to GPOs, you need rights to do so, and you can get these rights in two ways. First, you can be a member of the Group Policy Creator Owners or Domain Admins security group.

If you're a member of the Group Policy Creator Owners group, you have rights to create but not link GPOs. Domain Administrators can create GPOs and link them to where they want.

You can also be granted explicit rights via the Delegation tab in the Group Policy Objects container via the GPMC (as you saw in Chapter 2).

A new Group Policy Object is born when you right-click the Group Policy Objects container and choose New. Now you're setting into motion a specific chain of events.

First, by default, the PDC emulator is contacted to see if it's available for writing. If not, the user is prompted about how to proceed, as shown in Figure 6.2.

GPOs are initially born in the PDC emulator, and then, a bit later, they are replicated to the other Domain Controllers within the site and then between sites. Assuming the PDC emulator is available, you can give your GPO a friendly name, say "Hide Display Settings Option/ Restore Screen Saver Option," as we did in Chapter 1.

FIGURE 6.2 If the PDC emulator is not available for writing, the user is prompted for an alternate location.

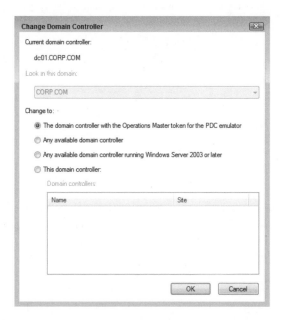

Once that happens, your GPO is officially "born." The PDC emulator has already performed certain functions on your behalf:

- The GPO was given a unique ID that takes its form as a globally unique identifier (GUID).

- It created a *Group Policy Container (GPC)* object in the Policies folder of the system container in the Active Directory domain partition. Think of this as a reference in Active Directory for your new GPO.

- It created a *Group Policy Template (GPT)* folder in the SYSVOL Policies directory of the PDC emulator. This is where the real files that make up your GPO live. They're replicated to every Domain Controller for quicker retrieval.

- Additionally, if "Create a GPO in this domain, and Link it here" is used when focused on the domain or OU level (or the old-school interface is used), the new GPO you just created is automatically *linked* to the current level you were focused at—domain or OU.

When you inspect the properties of any new GPO, you'll see the unique ID it is automatically given, as shown in Figure 6.3.

So, every GPO is made up of two components (the GPC and GPT), and those components are split between two places on that Domain Controller. The good news, though, is it all ties back to the GPO's GUID. We'll explore each of these components in the next two sections.

FIGURE 6.3   Every GPO gets a unique name.

How a GPO "Lives"

A GPO in Active Directory is made up of two constituent parts. One part isn't enough, and the GPO cannot live without both parts. Both parts are required in order to communicate the GPO message.

As you'll see in a bit, the GPO derives its life from these two parts.

Group Policy Containers (GPCs)

The Active Directory database contains the first half of a GPO. Not to get too geeky, but these are just objects (of class `groupPolicyContainer`), which we refer to as the Group Policy Containers, or GPCs. Each GPO defined in a domain has exactly one GPC object defined for it. Then, it's this GPC object that can hold multiple properties related to the Group Policy Object—for instance, version and display information and some policy settings. A GPC has a unique name that takes the format of a globally unique identifier (GUID)—see the sidebar "GPC Attributes." The GUID is *not* the friendly name we use when administering the GPO. The friendly name is stored as an attribute—called `displayName`–on that GPC object in Active Directory.

You can see the GPCs for every Group Policy you create by diving into the Active Directory Users and Computers console.

To view the GPCs and their GUIDs, follow these steps:

1.   Log on to the server DC01 as Administrator of the domain.

2. Choose Start ➢ All Programs ➢ Administrative Tools ➢ Active Directory Users and Computers.

3. Choose View ➢ Advanced Features, as shown in Figure 6.4, to display the Policies folder.

4. Expand the System folder to display the Policies folder along with the GPCs, as shown in Figure 6.5.

FIGURE 6.4   Turn on the Advanced Features setting to see the Policies folder (and a whole lot more).

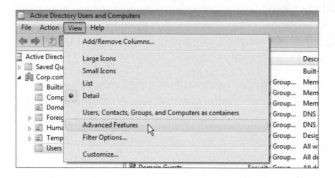

FIGURE 6.5   Expand the Policies folder to expose the underlying GPC objects.

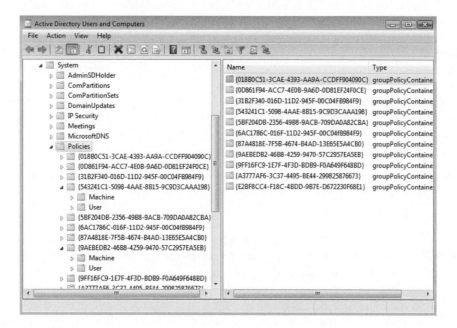

GPC Attributes

When a GPC object is created, it is given several attributes:

Common Name (CN) In Active Directory, you'll see that this attribute is really called cn. An LDAP (Lightweight Directory Access Protocol) designation for the name is assigned to an object. GPC names use the GUID format to ensure uniqueness throughout a forest—for example, CN=2C53BFD6-A2DB-44AF-9476-130492934271.

Distinguished Name (DN) In Active Directory, you'll see an attribute called distinguishedName. This is the object's common name plus the path to the object from the root of the LDAP tree. For example, CN=2C53BFD6-A2DB-44AF-9476-130492934271, CN=Policies, CN=System, DC=corp, DC=com.

Display Name In Active Directory, you'll see an attribute called displayName. This is the friendly name assigned to the Group Policy in the user interface, for example, the Hide Screen Saver Tab GPO.

Version In Active Directory, you'll see an attribute called versionNumber. This is a counter that keeps track of updates to a GPC object (more on this topic a little later).

GUID In Active Directory, you'll see an attribute called objectGUID. This is the GUID assigned to the object itself.

You might find it a little confusing for the GPC object to have a GUID that refers to the object itself and a name that uses a GUID format. For an important reason, Microsoft needed a way to make the underlying, real name of GPOs unique, independent of their friendly names. Suppose two administrators create two (or more) GPOs with the same friendly name on their own Domain Controllers. When these GPC objects replicate, one of them has to be discarded, overwritten, or renamed, depending on the exact circumstances of the replication collision. That could be a bad thing. Therefore, Microsoft solves this problem by using underlying unique names formatted with the GUID format. There is a negligible chance of identical GUIDs being created, not only within one Active Directory but also across the entire world, should the need arise to coexist with GPOs in other forests (such as with cross-forest trusts).

To see the major attributes for the GPC objects in your domain, take a look at Chapter 11. You'll find a PowerShell script that lets you see (and document) these objects.

Up until this point, we've been using the GPMC interface to create GPOs. When we use the GPMC to create GPOs, we've made reference to the Group Policy Objects container within the GPMC as a representation of the swimming pool. But the GPMC isn't showing you the real swimming pool—it's showing you a *representation* of the swimming pool. What it's showing you is the GPC part of the swimming pool. The other "half" of the swimming pool is the GPT (which we'll talk about next), the files that live in the replicated SYSVOL folder that exists on every domain controller in an Active Directory domain. The exact path to the GPT is \\<domain name>\sysvol\<domain name>\policies.

When you drill into a GPC container in Active Directory, you should see one GUID-named folder for every GPO you have created, plus two more for the two default GPOs—the Default Domain Policy and the Default Domain Controllers Policy (which we'll explore in Chapter 8).

In Figure 6.5, I have lots of GPOs already created; therefore, I have lots of containers. You might have fewer.

Those two default GPOs, in fact, have what are referred to as "well-known GUIDs." That is, the GUID for each of those two GPOs will be the same no matter what AD domain you look at. They are the same in your AD domain as mine! That makes it easy to find them. When you're used to seeing those two GUIDs time and again, you will know right away which GPOs they represent.

When you try to drill down into the subcontainers, some will and some will not expand past the {*GUID*}\Machine and {*GUID*}\User levels. Those that do expand do so because you have set up policy settings in that specific GPO that Active Directory needs to maintain information on, such as when you Publish or Assign applications. We'll look at where each policy area stores its settings after the section on the GPT.

We explore how to Publish and Assign applications in Chapter 4 of the companion book, *Creating the Secure Managed Desktop: Group Policy, SoftGrid, Microsoft Deployment Toolkit and Management Tools*.

Don't be surprised if, at this stage in working through the book, you do not have any fully expandable subfolders as shown in Figure 6.5. The subfolders that don't expand simply don't have any Group Policy settings stored within them. Most everything else the GPO needs to be useful is stored in the GPT, which is explored in the next section.

Who Really Has Permissions to Do What?

In Chapter 2, we applied various permissions on the GPO, including who had "Read" and "Apply Group Policy" permissions, as well as who could see the settings or edit the stuff inside the GPO. The locking mechanism for "Who really has what permissions" on a specific GPO is found right here, at the Policies folder:

- On the one hand, the locking mechanism on the Policies folder itself dictates who can and cannot create GPOs. However, it should be noted that these permissions are not inherited to the GUID-named GPT folder itself.

- See the note following Figure 6.8 for specific information on how to change the default permissions.

- On the other hand, the locking mechanism on the GUID-named GPT folders underneath the Policies folder dictates which users have access to "Read" and "Apply Group Policy," or can change the GPO itself.

In reality, the permissions that you see in GPMC for a given GPO reflect the permissions of *both* the GPC and GPT. While the permissions that you can grant to an Active Directory object do not map one-to-one to the permissions that you can grant to a file system folder like those found in SYSVOL, they roughly translate into the same permissions. For this reason, it's very important that you *not* try to directly modify the permissions on a GPO by simply modifying the permissions on either the GPC or the GPT independently. The best tool for this task is the GPMC's security filtering and delegation features.

However, in my GPanswers.com newsletter #13, (found at www.GPanswers.com/newsletter), you will find a tip that does walk through how to expressly change the underlying permissions in an emergency. Note that in that article, it's a special case and, again, should only be performed as described in that particular emergency.

Who Can Create New Group Policy Objects?

Right-click the Policies container, select Properties, then click the Security tab to display several names, some of which should be familiar, including the Group Policy Creator Owners and Domain Administrators groups. Additionally present will be anyone you explicitly added via the Delegation tab upon the Group Policy Objects container in GPMC. You saw how to do this in Chapter 2. At that time, we added a user named Joe User from our domain.

If you examine the properties of the Policies container (as shown in Figure 6.6), you'll see the Group Policy Creator Owners group. Joe is also listed (because he was expressly granted permission via the GPMC). Note also that the Domain Admins and Enterprise Admins groups are also present, but those names are at the top of the list, so you can't see them in Figure 6.6.

FIGURE 6.6   Expand the Policies folder to expose the underlying GPC objects.

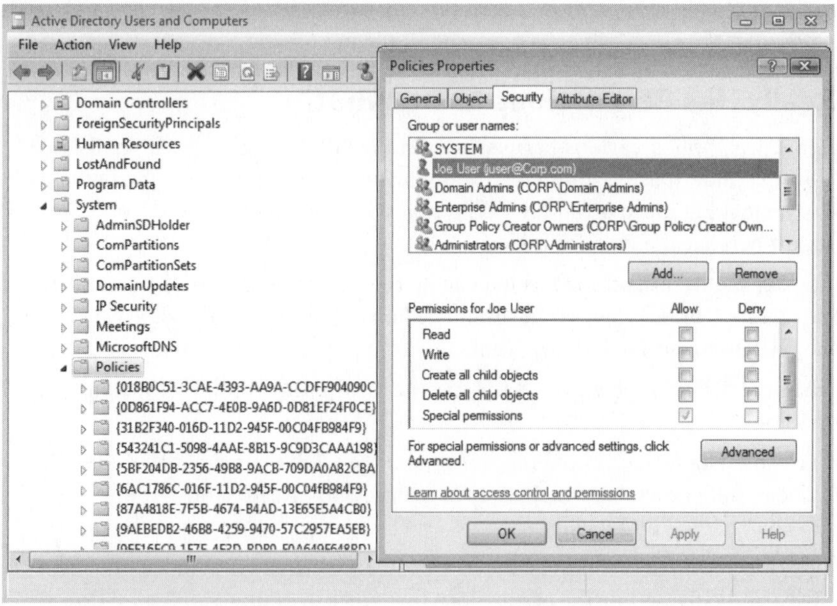

![Active Directory Users and Computers window with Policies Properties dialog showing the Security tab.](image)

You can click the Advanced button to display Joe's precise "Special Permissions." Indeed, Joe has only one permission, and it's called "Create groupPolicyContainer Objects." Once he has this right, the system permits him to create GPC folders and populate them with Group Policy information when he creates a new GPO.

The Group Policy Creator Owners group has many, many more unnecessary permissions on the Policies folder, including "Create all child objects," "Create User Objects," and a whole lot of stuff that, really, doesn't have anything to do with Group Policy. Indeed, if you log on as someone in the Group Policy Creator Owners group and right-click the Policies folder, you can do some things you really shouldn't do, as you can see in Figure 6.7.

The system (thankfully) won't let you do *all* the functions listed here, but it does let you do *some* of them. And, again, you really shouldn't be poking around like this. Of course, the "right" thing to do is to set permissions only via the GPMC. However, I show you these things for demonstration purposes so you can get a better feeling for what is different between someone in the Group Policy Creator Owners Group versus someone who has been explicitly delegated rights via the Delegation tab upon the Group Policy Objects container in GPMC.

The Domain Administrators group and the Enterprise Administrators group also have explicit permissions here. When they create new GPOs, they do so because of their explicit permissions, not because they are members of the Group Policy Creator Owners group.

FIGURE 6.7   For the love of Pete, please don't do this.

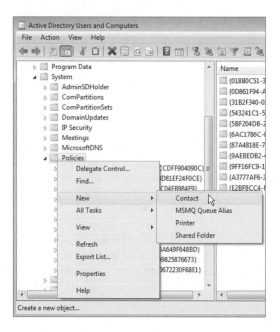

Who Can Manipulate and Edit Existing Group Policy Objects?

Right-click a GPO folder (with the name of a GUID) under the Policies folder and choose Properties to display the Security tab (see Figure 6.8), which will show the same information as when, in Chapter 2, you used the "Deny" attribute to pass over certain security groups. That is, the same information is shown here as when we clicked the Advanced button in the Delegation tab when focused on the GPO (or GPO link, because it's using the same information taken from the actual GPO).

FIGURE 6.8   Each GPC can display the underlying permissions of the GPO.

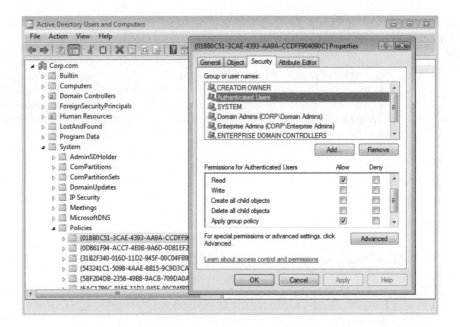

 The permissions that a new GPO gets when it's created are controlled by the `DefaultSecurityDescriptor` attribute on the `groupPolicyContainer` class within the Active Directory schema. If you want your GPOs to get different default permissions when they're created, you can modify the schema instance of this attribute. The Microsoft Knowledge Base article at `http://support.microsoft.com/kb/321476/en-us` describes how to do that.

Unless otherwise delegated, the person or group who created the GPO is the only one other than Domain Admins and Enterprise Admins who can modify or delete the GPO. However, this may be a particularly sensitive issue if you have many Domain Administrators—as they all have "joint ownership" of the GPOs they create. There is a serious potential risk in one administrator taking the reins and modifying another administrator's GPOs.

However, as you saw in Chapter 2, you can also grant someone explicit rights via the Delegation tab upon the GPOs container via the GPMC. In this example, I have done this for Joe. Figure 6.9 shows the properties of a GPO that Joe has created.

Since Joe has explicit permissions to create GPOs, he becomes the owner of the GPOs he creates. You can clearly see that Joe created it, and now he owns it. Hence, Joe doesn't have to worry about other explicitly anointed users or groups changing the GPOs he creates and owns. Note, however, that the Domain Administrators and Enterprise Administrators group will, in fact, be able to change any GPOs that Joe creates. Additionally, note that other users within Group Policy Creator Owners cannot dive in and edit Joe's GPOs. Again—Joe owns it; it's his.

FIGURE 6.9   If Joe creates a GPO, he owns the GPO. No one else (other than Domain Admins or Enterprise Admins) can edit it.

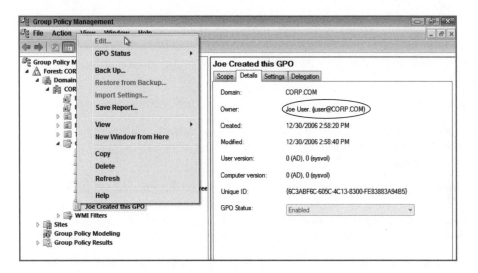

Using LDP to See the Guts of a GPC

The GPC object itself holds even more critical attributes for GPOs:

gPCFileSysPath   The physical path to the associated Policies folder, or GPT, stored in SYS-VOL. The Policies folder has the same name as the GPC, which is another reason that uniqueness is so important. The GPT is discussed in the next section.

gPCMachineExtensionNames This is a list of GUIDs of the computer-related CSEs (*client-side extensions*)—and the MMC snap-in that manages them—that will be called for this particular GPO. For instance, if a GPO has policy set on the Administrative Templates node under the Computer Configuration node in the Group Policy Object Editor, the gPCMachineExtensionNames list includes the GUID of the Registry client-side extension and the GUID of the MMC snap-in for the Administrative Templates node. CSEs are discussed later in this chapter in the section "How Client Systems Get Group Policy Objects."

gPCUserExtensionNames This is a list of the GUIDs of the CSEs and their MMC snap-ins, called by a user-related Group Policy. Again, I'll discuss CSEs a bit later in this chapter.

When you try to dive in and view these attributes using Active Directory Users and Computers, you cannot see them. The only way to see them is to use either the ADSIEdit MMC snap-in or the LDP tool, which is an LDAP browser tool. Both tools are found by loading the support tools from the SUPPORT\TOOLS folder on the Windows Server 2003 CD (Windows Server 2008 has the tools built in).

LDP lets you perform LDAP queries right into the actual guts of Active Directory. Using LDP, you can see these attributes. Normally, you wouldn't want or need to go poking around in here, but taking the time to learn just where attributes are can help you understand what constitutes a GPO.

To query a specific GPO to see its underlying attributes, follow these steps:

1. After loading the Support tools on the Domain Controller, choose Start ➢ Run to open the Run dialog box, and in the Open field, type **LDP** and press Enter to select the domain of your choice.

2. Choose Connection ➢ Bind, and in the dialog box type the administrative credentials to the domain. In the Domain field, you'll need to type the DNS name of the domain, for example, **Corp.com**. If you successfully connect, you'll see your first query results in the right pane of the LDP window.

3. Choose View ➢ Tree to open up a dialog that lets you specify the distinguished name of the domain. If your domain is Corp.com, enter **dc=corp, dc=com**. If you do that correctly, your left pane will show the domain name with a plus (+) sign. You should be able to double-click the plus sign and expand the contents within the domain.

4. Find the System container and double-click it to expand it.

5. Find the Policies container and double-click it to expand it.

6. Find the unique name of the GPO you want to inspect and double-click it to expand it. (For information about how to find a specific unique name of a GPO, see the earlier section "How Group Policy Objects Are 'Born.'") In the following illustration, the attributes are highlighted.

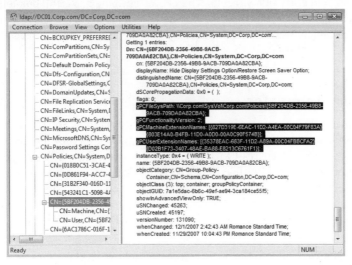

Once you find the unique name, the resultant LDP query will show you the properties on that GPO.

There is one more important attribute to inspect by using LDP: gPLink. Recall that a GPO can be linked by one level, multiple levels, or no levels. If a GPO is to be linked to a site, a domain, or an OU, that level needs to have a *pointer* or *link* to the GPO. When clients log on (computer and user), they use LDAP to query to each level they are a part of (site, domain, OUs) to find out if the level has the gPLink attribute set. If so, the client makes an LDAP query to find out what GPOs are meant for it. With the information in hand, it determines what files to download from the SYSVOL share on its logon server. (You can see these queries happening for yourself, when you inspect Userenv.log, explored later in the section "Turning On Verbose Logging.")

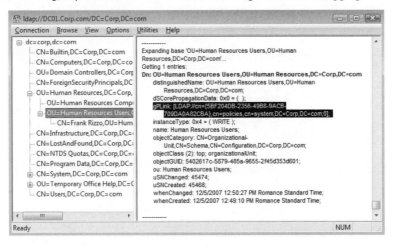

> To see the `gPLink` attribute, you can simply click the level you want to inspect. In this case, click the **Human Resources Users** OU you created in Chapter 1.
>
> In the right pane, find LDP's query results. The `gPLink` attribute has LDAP pointers to the unique names of the GPOs. In this case, the **Human Resources Users** OU has links to the "Hide Display Settings Option/Restore Screen Saver Option" GPO, in my case, 5BF204DB-2356-49B8-9ACB-709DA0A82CBA.

Group Policy Templates

As we just learned, GPCs are stored in the Active Directory database and replicated via normal Active Directory replication. A Group Policy Template (GPT), on the other hand, is stored as a set of files in the SYSVOL share of each Domain Controller. Each GPT is replicated to each Domain Controller through FRS (File Replication Service).

When we used the Properties tab of the GPO, we were able to find its unique name (as we did earlier in Figure 6.3). We can use the unique name to locate the GPC in Active Directory, and it's the same unique name we can use to locate the GPT in the SYSVOL.

To see the GPTs in SYSVOL, follow these steps:

1. On a Domain Controller in the domain, open Windows Explorer.

2. Change the directory to the SYSVOL container. Its usual location is `C:\Windows\SYSVOL\SYSVOL\<domain name>` (in this case, `C:\Windows\SYSVOL\SYSVOL\corp.com`).

3. Change into the Policies folder. You'll see a list of folders. The folder names match the GPC GUID names stored in Active Directory (seen in the previous exercise). Figure 6.10 shows a Policies folder containing many GPOs.

FIGURE 6.10   The unique names of the GPOs are found as folder names in SYSVOL. This is the unique name for the "Hide Display Settings Option/Restore Screen Saver Option" you saw in the last graphic in the sidebar entitled "Using LDP to See the Guts of a GPC" Figure 6.4 earlier.

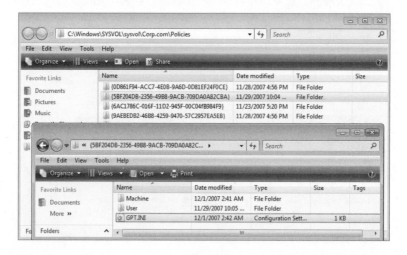

Double-clicking a Policies folder inside SYSVOL displays the contents of the GPT. Inside, you'll see several subfolders and a file. The first entry on this list is the file (`gpt.ini`); the rest are subfolders.

gpt.ini   The one file you will always find under the GUID folder. It holds the version number of the GPT as well as the equivalent information to the `gpcMachineExtensionName` and `gpcUserExtensionName` attributes found on the GPC object in Active Directory. Namely, these two keys within the `gpt.ini` list the GUIDs of the Client-Side Extensions and their associated MMC snap-in extensions that have been implemented within the GPO. This lets the client know which CSEs need to be called when GPOs are processed. (You'll read about version numbers in the next section.) You'll also see a little text snippet in every `gpt.ini` that says "displayName=New Group Policy Object." This snippet of text is the same for every GPO and is currently unused at this time.

\Adm   If you create your GPOs using a Windows Vista management station (as we discussed in Chapter 1 and we'll drive home in Chapter 7), you won't see an ADM directory in any of your newly created GPOs. However, if you create GPOs from pre-Vista machines, this directory is created to house policy settings called Administrative Template files. In short, when you create or edit a GPO from a pre-Vista machine, the Administrative Templates (`.adm` files) are copied from the `\Windows\INF` folder. Again, this happens from the machine where you're editing that GPO, into the GPT's `\Adm` folder.

By default, those `.adm` files are `Conf.adm`, `Inetres.adm`, `System.adm`, `wmplayer.adm`, and `wuau.adm`.

Hang tight. You'll find more info about this as you hit Chapter 7. Double-clicking the `\Adm` folder displays the templates. Note that the `\Adm` folder will not exist until the GPO is opened for the first time from a pre-Vista machine and you click either the Computer or the User Administrative Template node.

Note that the presence of the `\Adm` folder in the GPT is an artifact of pre-Windows Vista operating systems. When you create and edit a new GPO using Vista, no `\Adm` folder is created because Vista no longer copies the ADM files up to the GPT—they are held locally in `C:\windows\policydefinitions` or in the "Central Store." However, if you edit a GPO that was created with Vista using a "down-level" operating system (for example, XP, 2003, and so on), the `\Adm` folder will get created and populated in the GPT. Note that this behavior—editing a Vista GPO from a down-level version of Windows—is generally not a good idea. Once you've gone Vista from a GP perspective, it's best to edit those GPOs using Vista from then on. The next chapter describes the Central Store and ADMX files in great detail.

\Machine   This folder contains the settings for the computer side of the GPO, including startup and shutdown scripts (though there's nothing requiring them to live here; they could be located in other places as well), pointers to applications that are assigned, and Registry settings (among other settings). The actual contents of the \Machine folder depend on the computer options specified in the GPO. The potential contents include the following:

The Registry.pol File   Holds the Registry settings set in Computer Configuration ➢ Policies ➢ Administrative Templates as well as settings for Software Restriction Policy under Computer Configuration ➢ Policies ➢ Windows Settings ➢ Security Settings ➢ Software Restriction Policies.

The \Applications Folder   Stores pointer files called Application Advertisement Scripts, or AAS files. These files are used in conjunction with Group Policy Software Deployment. These are the instructions that the client computers use to process Software Installation. Software Installation is further discussed in its own chapter, Chapter 4, in the companion book, *Implementing the Secure and Managed Desktop*. But AAS files are described further in the sidebar entitled "Inside .aas Files."

Inside *.aas* Files

The .aas file serves a specific role in the context of Software Installation Policy. This file is created when you first deploy an MSI package. It contains information related to the advertisement of the package.

Advertisement is an MSI feature that allows you to deploy part of an application (you can think of it like a shortcut or file extension association) to a computer or user. The whole application is not installed right away; instead, when the user first clicks the shortcut or activates a file extension associated with the advertised package, the installation proceeds at that time. This feature is known as *Install-On-First-Use*.

The .aas file holds that advertisement information specific to the package you've deployed. It also contains the hard-coded path to the package you've specified. This is why you cannot easily change the path to a package once you've deployed it via Software Installation Policy. This .aas file must be regenerated and the path to the package that is referenced in the GPC portion of the GPO must also be updated.

The \Microsoft\Windows NT\Secedit Folder   Stores a file called GptTmpl.inf. This file holds various computer security settings, defined under the Computer Configuration ➢ Policies ➢ Windows Settings ➢ Security Settings portion of the GPO. You can also set up these settings in advance and deploy them *en masse* using the techniques described in Chapter 8.

The \Scripts\Shutdown Folder   Contains the instructions for which shutdown scripts to run and, optionally, the actual files used for computer shutdown scripts. The instructions as to which scripts will run and where the scripts are stored are held in a file called scripts.ini, within this folder. Can be of any scripting file type (that the ShellExecute process can run), including .bat, .cmd, .vbs, .js, and others. You'll see how to use this in Chapter 8.

The **\Scripts\Startup** Folder   Contains the instructions for which startup scripts to run and, optionally, the actual files used for computer startup scripts. The instructions as to which scripts will run and where the scripts are stored are held in a file called `scripts.ini`, within this folder. Can be of any scripting file types (that the `ShellExecute` process can run), including `.bat`, `.cmd`, `.vbs`, `.js`, and others. You'll see how to use this in Chapter 8.

\User   This folder contains the settings for the user side of the Group Policy coin, including logon and logoff scripts, pointers to applications that are published or assigned, and Registry settings. Depending on the options used on each GPO, it represents what is in the `\User` folder under the computer side of the GPT.

The **Registry.pol** File   Holds the Registry settings set in User Configuration ➢ Policies ➢ Administrative Templates as well as settings for Software Restriction Policy under User Configuration ➢ Policies ➢ Windows Settings ➢ Security Settings ➢ Software Restriction Policies.

The **\Applications** Folder   Stores pointer files called `.aas` files for applications deployed with Group Policy Software Installation.

The **\Documents and Settings** Folder   Contains a file called `Fdeploy.ini`, which stores applicable Folder Redirection settings. You can learn more about Folder Redirection in the companion book, *Creating the Secure Managed Desktop*, in Chapter 3.

The **\Microsoft\IEAK** Folder   Stores files to represent the changes made in User Configuration ➢ Policies ➢ Windows Settings ➢ Internet Explorer Maintenance.

The **\Microsoft\RemoteInstall** Folder   Stores `Oscfilter.ini`, which specifies Group Policy Remote Installation Services settings. Remote Installation Services isn't used anymore. We set up its successor, Windows Deployment Services, in Chapter 1 of the companion book, *Creating the Secure Managed Desktop*.

The **\Scripts\Logon** Folder   Contains the instructions for which logon scripts to run and, optionally, the actual files used for user logon scripts. The instructions as to which scripts will run and where the scripts are stored are held in a file called `scripts.ini`, within this folder. Can be of any acceptable file type, including `.bat`, `.vbs`, `.js`, and others. You'll see how to use this in Chapter 8.

The **\Scripts\Logoff** Folder   Contains the instructions for which logoff scripts to run and, optionally, the actual files used for user logoff scripts. The instructions as to which scripts will run and where the scripts are stored are held in a file called `scripts.ini`, within this folder. Can be of any acceptable file type, including `.bat`, `.vbs`, `.js`, and others. You'll see how to use this in Chapter 8.

Group Policy Settings Storage

As I've indicated, Group Policy settings, the things that you set when you're editing a GPO, are stored within one half of the GPO—either the GPC or GPT. The decision as to which is used to store a given setting varies with the size of the data being stored. Typically, because Active Directory is not designed for storing large blocks of data, those settings that require big chunks of stuff are stored in the GPT instead of the GPC.

But it really does vary by each Client Side Extension. Table 6.1 indicates where each Client Side Extension, up to and including Windows Vista, stores its settings.

TABLE 6.1 Client Side Extensions and Their Storage Locations

Client-Side Extension	Storage Location	Comments
Wireless	Stored in AD, under the GPC container for a given GPO, within the path CN=wireless,CN=Windows, CN=Microsoft,CN=Machine.	Wireless policies are stored in AD as objects of class msieee80211-Policy. This class is supported only in Active Directory domains of Windows Server 2003 and newer AD domains. So, even though this CSE is on Windows XP, the policy must still be defined in domains that have that minimum schema level. Note that there is also a required schema update to support the enhanced Wireless policy that's only supported on Windows Vista clients. This is further explained in Chapter 9.
Folder Redirection	Stored in SYSVOL, under the GPT container for a given GPO. Folder Redirection policy is stored in a file called fdeploy .ini in the subfolder User\ Documents and Settings within the GPT.	
Administrative Template Policy	Stored in SYSVOL, under the GPT container for a given GPO. Administrative Templates policy is stored in a file called registry .pol, which can be defined per user and per computer. Within a given GPT, if you've defined both user and computer Administrative Templates policy, you will see a registry.pol file under both the user and machine subfolders.	ADM files that are in use by a given GPO are stored with the GPO in the GPT. You'll find them in a folder called ADM, off the root of the GPT for a given GPO. Thus, each GPO that sets Administrative Templates policy will store its own copy of the ADM files used to edit it, even if they are the same as another GPO. Again, this has particular ramifications when adding your own ADM templates or using operating systems earlier than Windows Vista. See the next chapter for all the gory details.

TABLE 6.1   Client Side Extensions and Their Storage Locations *(continued)*

Client-Side Extension	Storage Location	Comments
Disk Quota	Stored in SYSVOL, under the GPT container for a given GPO. Disk quota policy is also stored in `registry.pol`; however, you'll only find it in the copy of `registry.pol` stored under the machine folder, as this is a per-machine policy only.	
QoS Packet Scheduler	Stored in SYSVOL, under the GPT container for a given GPO. QoS policy is also stored in `registry.pol`; however, you'll only find it in the copy of `registry.pol` stored under the machine folder, as this is a per-machine policy only.	
Startup/Shutdown and Logon/Logoff Scripts	Stored in SYSVOL under the GPT container for a given GPO. Machine-specific scripts are stored in the `machine\scripts\startup` and `machine\scripts\shutdown` folders. User-specific scripts are stored in the `user\logon` and `user\logoff` folders.	Note that script files themselves do not have to be stored in SYSVOL. You can reference scripts located anywhere on your network, as long as they are accessible to the computer or user. The `scripts.ini` file found in the `computer\scripts` folder and `user\scripts` folder in SYSVOL contains the actual references to any scripts that you've defined.
Internet Explorer Maintenance and Zonemapping	Stored in SYSVOL under the GPT container for a given GPO. Specifically, IE Maintenance settings are stored in the GPT under the `\User\Microsoft\IEAK` folder.	Basic "branding" settings are stored in a file under this folder called `install.ins`. Security zone settings are stored in a subfolder called Branding and are stored as `.inf` files.
Security Settings	Stored in SYSVOL under the GPT container for a given GPO. Security settings are stored in the `Machine\Microsoft\Windows NT\SecEdit` folder in a file called `GptTmpl.inf`.	The format of this file is identical to those created when you use the MMC Security Templates editor to create a Security Template. The exception to this is Software Restriction Policy, which is stored in the `registry.pol` file.

TABLE 6.1   Client Side Extensions and Their Storage Locations *(continued)*

Client-Side Extension	Storage Location	Comments
Software Installation	Stored in both the GPC and GPT. Within the GPT, deployed package information is stored under the container machine (or user) \Applications, within an Application Advertisement File or AAS file. Within the GPC, a special object of class packageRegistration is created for each application deployed. This object can be found in the GPC for a GPO under machine (or user)\Class Store\ Packages.	packageRegistration objects found in the GPC contain information such as the path to the MSI file, any transforms (modifications) that have been selected, and whether the application is published or assigned. (See the companion book's Chapter 4 for more details.)
IP Security	IPsec policy is a special case. Settings are stored as special objects strictly in Active Directory but *not* within the GPC. Namely, IPsec policy settings are stored under the CN=IP Security, CN=System container within a domain. Therefore, IP Security settings are stored domain wide and can be referenced by any GPO in the domain. When you *assign* a particular IPsec policy to a GPO, an additional object is created within the GPC of the GPO—specifically, an *ipsecPolicy* object is created under the Machine\ Microsoft\Windows container under the GPO. This object stores the association between the available IPsec policies in the domain and that GPO.	
Windows Search (Vista only)	Stored in SYSVOL, under the GPT container for a given GPO. Windows Search policy is also stored in registry.pol; however, you'll find it only in the copy of registry.pol stored under the machine folder, as this is a per-machine policy only.	

TABLE 6.1   Client Side Extensions and Their Storage Locations *(continued)*

Client-Side Extension	Storage Location	Comments
Offline Files (Vista only)	Stored in SYSVOL, under the GPT container for a given GPO. Offline Files policy is also stored in `registry.pol`, within both the machine and user folders, depending upon which side is being set.	
Deployed Printer Connections (Vista only)	Stored in AD, under the GPC container for a given GPO, within the path `CN=PushedPrinterConnections`, `CN=Machine (or CN=User)`.	Deployed Printer Connection policies are stored in Active Directory as objects of class `msPrint-ConnectionPolicy`. This class is only supported in Windows Server 2003 R2 (and Longhorn Server) domains. Therefore, this feature, Deployed Printer Connection policy, can be defined only in domains that have that minimum schema level.
Enterprise QoS Policy (Vista only)	Stored in SYSVOL, under the GPT container for a given GPO. Enterprise QoS policy is also stored in `registry.pol`, within both the machine and user folders, depending upon which side is being set.	
802.3 and Vista Wireless Policy (Vista only)	Both of these policy areas are stored in AD in the GPC but require a schema update.	See Chapter 9 for the required schema update to support both Wired and Wireless schema policy.

Understanding Group Policy Version Numbers

If you take a peek at any GPO's `gpt.ini`, you'll see its version number. You can see the same number if you dive in to the GPC using the directions found in the sidebar (in this chapter) entitled "Using LDP to See the Guts of a GPC."

So, how is that version number constructed? Here's the formula:

Version = (Number of user section changes * 65536) + (Number of computer section changes)

So, when you create a new GPO, the version number is 0. Click Edit over a GPO and start editing, and then the numbers start going up. Enable a policy on the computer side and click OK. Then set it back to Not Configured. That'll add 2 to the version number. Edit a policy on the user side and click OK. That'll add 65536. Change it back to Not Configured and it'll add another 65536. The version number's largess isn't super important here. That is, it doesn't matter how huge the number gets.

So, how do we, in our daily lives, see the version number? In the Details tab of any Group Policy, as seen here.

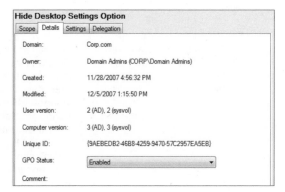

In this example, we can see that the user side has been modified twice (2 * 65536) and the computer version has been modified three times (add 3 to that). So, if we peek in the gpt.ini of this GPO, the version number should be 131075.

Again, both the GPC and the GPT store the version number for the GPO. Buuut, as we've described, there could be situations where replication hasn't finished and the GPC and GPT version numbers don't agree. With that case, the GPMC (which shows the version numbers via the Details tab of a GPO) will *always* use the GPC version number as the final reference but will give you a message if these are not in sync.

The Group Policy team at Microsoft has an interesting blog entry on the subject. Check it out at http://tinyurl.com/2gfmmg.

Verifying That GPCs and GPTs Are in Sync

The two pieces of information that make up a GPO are GPCs and GPTs:

- GPCs are stored in the Active Directory database and are replicated via normal Active Directory replication.
- GPTs are stored in the SYSVOL folders of every Domain Controller and are replicated using FRS replication.

Here's the trick: For Windows 2000, for Group Policy to be applied, both the GPC and the corresponding GPT need to be synchronized. *Synchronization* simply means that the `versionNumber` attribute on the GPC object for a given GPO needs to be the same as the `versionNumber` key found in the GPT's `gpt.ini` file for that same GPO.

For all versions of Windows after Windows 2000, the GPC and GPT no longer need to have the same version for Group Policy processing of that GPO to proceed.

Recall that both the GPC and GPT are originally written to the PDC emulator by default. Once they're written, the goal is to replicate the GPC and GPT to other Domain Controllers. With just one Domain Controller in a domain, there are no replication issues because there are no other Domain Controllers to replicate to; it's all happening on one system. But when multiple Domain Controllers in a domain enter the picture, things get a little hairier. This is because normal Active Directory replication and FRS replication are on completely independent schedules (though under normal circumstances, they take the same path).

An administrator can create or modify a GPO, and the GPC might not replicate in lockstep with the files in the GPT. This isn't normally a problem because, over time, all Domain Controllers end up with exactly the same information in their replicas of the Active Directory database and in their SYSVOL folders. But during a given replication cycle, there may be intervals when the GPC and GPT *don't* match on a particular Domain Controller.

Additionally, the GPC and GPT share a *version number* for each half of the GPO—computer and user. The version numbers are incremented each time the GPO is modified and are included in the list of attributes that are replicated to other Domain Controllers. Remember in Chapter 1 I stated that if a specific GPO doesn't change, the default for the client is to not process the GPO. After all, if nothing's changed, why should the client bother? The client uses these version numbers to figure out if something has changed. The client keeps a cache of the GPOs it last applied along with the version number within the Registry. Then, if the GPO has been touched, say, by the modification of a particular policy setting or the addition of a policy setting, the version number of the GPO in Active Directory changes. The next time the client tries to process GPOs, it will see the change, and the client will download the entire GPO again and embrace the revised instruction set! So, version numbers are important for clients to recognize that new instructions are waiting for them.

So far, so good. Now, there's a bit more to fully understanding version numbers. According to Microsoft, here's the secret to figuring out whether a GPO is going to process on a workstation:

- Both the GPC and GPT parts of the GPO must be present on the Domain Controller the workstation uses to log on.

- If the client processing Group Policy is Windows 2000, then the GPC and GPT must have the same version number.

- If it's XP, Server 2003, or Vista, then the GPC and GPT can have different version numbers and Group Policy processing will still occur.

- In all cases, if the version number held in the GPC or GPT is different than the version number held in the Registry from the last time that GPO was processed, then Windows considers that a change has occurred and goes ahead and processes policy.

The main point here is that for early versions of Windows (Windows 2000), Group Policy processing would fail if the version numbers didn't match up. It's still important for the two pieces to synchronize at some point. If they aren't synchronized at some point, this implies that one piece doesn't have the latest information for settings. At some point, the replication should complete and all Domain Controllers will have the same Group Policy data; then, machines and users will get the latest version of Group Policy settings. If this *never* happens, then you have a problem with your domain and should follow up with the tools and techniques in this section.

 Version numbers aren't the only thing that would constitute a "change." A change could also be a removed GPO (or added GPO), a change in security group membership, and a new or removed WMI filter. Also, it's important to point out that if one GPO changes, the CSEs that process that GPO must reprocess *all* GPOs in the list, not just the one that changes.

Changing the Default Domain Controller for the Initial Write of Group Policy Objects

GPOs are, by default, created and edited using the Domain Controller that houses the PDC emulator. Of course, over time, those new and modified GPOs make it to all other Domain Controllers using replication. However, sometimes in large Active Directories, you may not want to leverage the PDC emulator as the "go to" place when creating and editing Group Policy.

Imagine this scenario: There is one domain but two sites—the United States and China. The U.S. site holds the Domain Controller designated as the PDC emulator. Therefore, whenever an administrator in China writes a GPO, they must connect across the WAN to write the GPO and then wait for the entire GPO (both the GPC half and the GPT half) to replicate to their local Domain Controllers.

You can, however, specify which Domain Controller to write the GPO to, which is a two-step process:

1. Select a Domain Controller to be *active*. Open the GPMC, right-click the domain name, select Change Domain Controller, and select the Domain Controller to which you want the Group Policy to apply.

2. Create your GPO and edit it. At the root node of the Group Policy snap-in, choose View ➢ DC Options. Now you have the following three choices:

    ▪   "The one with the Operations Master token for the PDC Emulator." The default behavior, this option finds the PDC emulator in the domain and writes the GPO there. Replication then occurs, starting from the PDC emulator.

- • "The one used by the Active Directory snap-ins." Since you just selected the *active* Domain Controller, this is your best bet because you know exactly which Domain Controller you selected in the first step.

- • "Any available Domain Controller." The odds are good that you will get a local Domain Controller to write to (based on Active Directory site information), but not always.

Therefore, the best course of action is to select the Domain Controller you want to initially write to and then select "The one used by the Active Directory snap-ins" to guarantee it.

Sound like too much work for each GPO? Alternatively, you can create a GPO that affects those accounts that can create GPOs. Use the policy setting located at User Configuration ➢ Policies ➢ Administrative Templates ➢ System ➢ Group Policy setting named **Group Policy Domain Controller Selection**. You'll get the same three choices listed earlier. Set it, and forget it.

Here's a parting tip for this sidebar. Often, GPOs are created with the additional intent to use security groups to filter them. After creating a GPO with the GPMC, an administrator will also create some security groups using Active Directory Users and Computers to filter them. However, after creating the GPO and the security groups, many admins are surprised that the security groups they want to add "now" are not immediately available. This is because the GPMC is using one Domain Controller and the Active Directory Users and Computers tool is using another Domain Controller. Therefore, replication of the group has not yet reached the Domain Controller the GPMC is using! So the tip is to manually focus both the Active Directory Users and Computers and/or GPMCs explicitly on the same Domain Controller (or just the PDC emulator) before creating GPOs where you'll also want to filter using groups.

Using *Gpotool.exe*

If you suspect you're having problems with keeping your GPTs and GPCs in sync, you can use Gpotool.exe, a tool included with the Windows 2000 and Windows 2003 Resource Kits. You can run Gpotool.exe on any Domain Controller to verify that both the GPCs and GPTs are in sync and have consistent data among all Domain Controllers in the domain. At last check the Gpotool.exe (and other Group Policy–related tools) can be downloaded from http://tinyurl.com/ydjmm3.

As of this writing, there isn't an updated Gpotool.exe for Windows Server 2008, and there may not be one. The current version seems to work just fine with GPOs that live on Windows Server 2008 machines.

Running Gpotool without any parameters verifies that all GPCs and GPTs are synchronized across all Domain Controllers in the domain. If you are having trouble with only one GPO, however, you might not want to go through the intense process required to check every GPO's GPC and GPT on every Domain Controller. Instead, however, you can use the /gpo: switch, which allows you to specify a friendly name or GUID of a GPO you are having problems with. For instance, if you suspect that you are having problems with any of the "Hide Screen Saver Option" or "Hide Display Settings Option/Restore Screen Saver Option" GPOs we created in Chapter 1, you can run Gpotool /gpo:Hide to search for all GPOs starting with the word *Hide*, as shown in Figure 6.11.

FIGURE 6.11 Use Gpotool to see if your GPCs and GPTs are synchronized across your Domain Controllers.

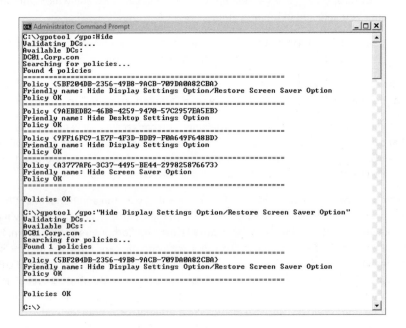

 To specifically verify the "Hide Display Settings Option/Restore Screen Saver Option" setting, you can also run Gpotool /gpo: "Hide Settings Tab / Restore Screen Saver Tab" as seen in Figure 6.11. Note that the /gpo: switch is case sensitive. For instance, running Gpotool /gpo:Hide is different from running GPOTOOL /gpo:hide.

This example shows when things are going right. This next example (see Figure 6.12) shows when things might be wrong.

In this example, we are verifying the synchronization of the GPO named "Broken2." In this case, the versions between the GPC and GPT do not match. You can see this when comparing what the tool calls the DS version with the SYSVOL version. The DS version represents the GPC, and the SYSVOL version represents the GPT.

Before panicking, recall that this "problem" might not actually be a problem. Remember, the GPC and GPT replicate independently. The DC our clients are currently using might have simply received the SYSVOL (GPT) changes before the Active Directory changes (GPC) or vice versa. Wait a little while, and the two versions might converge. If they do not converge, this problem could indicate either Active Directory or FRS replication issues.

FIGURE 6.12   Gpotool has found trouble in paradise.

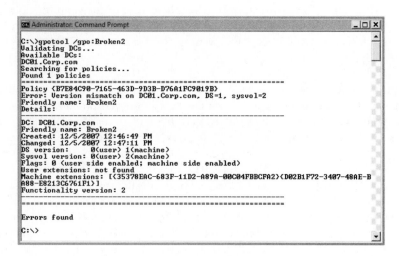

Here are some additional tips about using Gpotool:

- Running Gpotool on a large domain with lots of GPOs can take a looooong time and really bog down your Domain Controller performance. If possible, run Gpotool only after hours, when the fewest number of people will be affected.

- If you must run it during working hours, you might want to specify the /dc: option and specify to check only the GPOs on the PDC emulator (the place where GPOs are initially born and initially modified). If you're going to have a problem, it's quite likely to be initially pinpointed on this key Domain Controller.

- Gpotool has one extra super-power. That is, it can also verify the underlying ACLs of the GPT part of a GPO. Recall that the GPT is the part of the GPO that lives in SYSVOL. To perform this extra check, you need to specifically specify it on the command line of Gpotool as Gpotool /checkacl. By default, this test is not run because it is additionally time and resource intensive. There is one key point about the /checkacl switch: it checks only the ACL inheritance flag on the SYSVOL Policies folder itself, not the ACLs on the individual folders that contain the guts of the GPO. So, if you have a specific permissions problem on the folder containing a GPO, the /checkacl switch won't really help you ferret that out.

- One caveat about Gpotool—it only checks to see if the version numbers are the same between the GPC and GPT. It does not check to see, say, if all of the files that are supposed to be in the GPT are there. If you're having FRS replication problems for example, then only some of the GPT files may have replicated to a given DC, and Gpotool won't tell you that if it finds that the gpt.ini file has the information it needs.

Using *Replmon* to See the Version Numbers

The Replmon (Replication Monitor) tool is available as part of the support tools on the Windows 2003 (or Windows 2000) Server CD. Replmon is one of the most useful free tools Microsoft has ever created. As of this writing, Replmon isn't available for Windows Server 2008. That's okay. You can just run it from a Windows Server 2003 machine on your domain.

For our purposes, we'll use it in a fashion similar to how we used Gpotool; that is, Replmon can tell us if a GPO's GPC and GPT are in agreement with the version numbers.

First, load the support tools in the \SUPPORT\TOOLS folder on a Windows Server 2003. Then, choose Start ➢ Run to open the Run dialog box, and type **Replmon** in the Open box. Right-click the Monitored Servers icon and choose Add Monitored Server. For now, just add the PDC emulator. In my case, I'll add DC01. Once the server is being monitored, right-click it and choose Show Group Policy Object Status to display a screen like that shown in Figure 6.13.

In Figure 6.13, you can see that the GPO named "Broken2" has an X in the Sync Status column. The version numbers are dissimilar in the GPC and GPT. Again, this might not be a real "problem" because the GPC and GPT are being independently replicated. Perhaps this Domain Controller did not yet get the latest updates.

FIGURE 6.13 Replmon can show you the version numbers of all your GPOs.

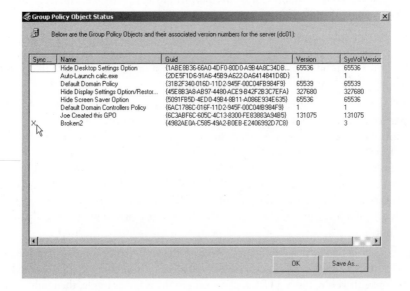

Isolating Replication Problems

You can try to see if Active Directory replication is working (and, hence, if GPC replication is working) by performing several "litmus tests." Here are some examples:

- Create a new GPO in the Group Policy Objects container. Just create it with no policy settings, and don't link it anywhere.

- Create a new OU in Active Directory Users and Computers or the GPMC.

- Add a new user in Active Directory.

In each case, you want to see if these objects are replicated to other DCs. After creating your objects on one Domain Controller, use the Active Directory Users and Computers and/or GPMC to check other Domain Controllers. Simply right-click the domain and choose another Domain Controller.

If these litmus tests fail, you can try to force replication using Active Directory Sites and Services. If you need extra-strength replication, `Replmon` can help force replication in multiple ways.

You can try to see if SYSVOL replication is working via FRS (and, hence, if GPT replication is working) by simply throwing any file—say, a `Readme.txt` file—into the SYSVOL share of any Domain Controller and seeing if it is replicated to the other Domain Controllers' SYSVOL shares. If it is not automatically copied to the other Domain Controllers, test each machine's connectivity using the `ping` command.

Here are some additional tips for troubleshooting FRS replication:

- Microsoft TechNet has an excellent feature-length article, "Troubleshooting FRS," at the TechNet home page at `http://tinyurl.com/yobuf4`. Microsoft has a tool, SONAR (part of the Windows 2003 Resource Kit), that can dramatically help with FRS troubleshooting.

- Microsoft has another tool, ULTRASOUND, which surpasses SONAR's ability to help troubleshoot FRS.

ULTRASOUND and SONAR are available on the Microsoft website. At last check, SONAR can be found at `http://tinyurl.com/5ouk9` and Ultrasound can be found at `http://tinyurl.com/odgu`. General FRS and troubleshooting and information can be found at `www.microsoft.com/frs` as of this writing.

The Microsoft Knowledge Base articles Q221112, Q221111, Q272279, and Q229928 are good starting points to learn more about FRS and how to troubleshoot SYSVOL replication problems by debugging FRS. See Q229896 and Q249256 for details on how to debug Active Directory replication.

Death of a GPO

As you saw in Chapter 2, there are three ways to stop using a GPO at a level in Active Directory. One way is to "Delete the link" to the GPO at the level being used in Active Directory. In the swimming pool analogy, we're simply removing the tether to our child in the pool, but we're leaving the object swimming in the pool should other levels want to use it.

The other is "Disabling the link." This leaves the tether in place but basically prevents the level from receiving the power within the OU.

The final way to stop using a GPO is to delete it. With the GMPC, you can delete a GPO only by traversing to the Group Policy Objects node, right-clicking it, and choosing Delete, as you saw back in Figure 2.6. But, again, be careful; other levels of Active Directory (including those in other domains and forests) might be using this GPO you're about to whack.

> **WARNING**   As we've discussed in previous chapters, cross-domain linking of GPOs is a no-no. And, if you whack the GPO in the source domain, it won't clean up links to *other* (target) domains.

How Client Systems Get Group Policy Objects

The items stored on the server make up only half the story. The real magic happens when the GPO is applied at the client, usually a workstation, although certainly servers behave in the same way. Half of Group Policy's usefulness is that it can apply equally to servers and desktops and laptops. Indeed, with the advent of Windows 2003 and, of course, Windows Vista, the new policy settings they bring to the table mean you can control and configure more stuff than ever. So the details in this section are for all clients—servers and workstations.

When Group Policy is deployed from upon high to client systems, the clients always do the requesting. This is why, when the chips are down and things aren't going right, you'll need to trot out to the system and crack open the Event Log (among other troubleshooting areas) to help uncover why the client isn't picking up your desires.

Microsoft doesn't provide a way to instantaneously "push" the policy settings inside GPOs to clients, even if you think they should get a new change right now. Out of the box, there's no "push the big red button and force the latest Group Policy to all my clients" command to make sure every client gets your will. This can be a little disappointing, especially if you need a security setting, such as a Software Restriction Policy, propagated to all your clients right now. There are several ways, however, to make this a reality:

- In Chapter 11, I'll show you a little scripting magic to forcefully push Group Policy out the door. Note, however, that this script needs to be "prepared" on the client machine before you can leverage it.

- In the Third-Party Group Policy Solutions Guide on www.GPanswers.com is a link to a free tool called RGPrefresh, which also performs this function. (Alternatively, you can download that tool right from my fellow MVP Darren Mar-Elia's website at http://www.gpoguy.com/rgprefresh.htm.)

- Also in the Third-Party Group Policy Solutions Guide on www.GPanswers.com is a link to another free tool called SpecOps GPupdate, which also performs this function. This tool is graphical and hooks in to Active Directory Users and Computers and allows you to perform four functions upon your client machines: Group Policy Refresh, reboot, shutdown, and startup (if the client machine has a wake-on-LAN card).

- These and additional examples are explained in Jakob H. Heidelberg's article "How to Force Remote Group Policy Processing" at `http://tinyurl.com/2opez6`.

But, without these "tricks," unfortunately, Group Policy is processed only when the computer starts up, when the user logs on, and at periodic intervals in the background, as discussed in Chapter 4. In that chapter, you learned "when" Group Policy is processed; in this section, you'll learn both "how" and "why" Group Policy is processed.

The Steps to Group Policy Processing

Group Policy processing on the client is broken down into roughly two parts. The first part is called "core" or "infrastructure" processing. We'll break it down for Windows Vista and pre-Vista machines here, the two types of computers you're likely to have.

Core Processing for Pre–Windows Vista Machines

During the core processing stage of Group Policy processing, Windows tries to accomplish a number of tasks. Chief among those:

- To determine if the connection to the Domain Controller is over a slow link
- To discover all of the GPOs that apply to the computer or user
- To discover which Client Side Extensions have to be called
- To discover whether anything has changed (GPOs, security group memberships, WMI filters) since the last processing cycle
- To create the final list of GPOs that need to be applied

In order to perform these tasks, Windows requires a number of network protocols be successfully passed between the client and the DC that it's paired with. These protocols, and their usages, are listed here:

- ICMP for slow link detection
- RPC (TCP port 135 and some random port that's greater than port 1024) for authentication to AD
- LDAP (TCP port 389) for querying AD to determine the list of GPOs, group membership, WMI filters, and so on
- SMB (TCP port 445) for querying the GPT in SYSVOL

If the client tries to get to the server and any of the protocols listed above are blocked (usually by a firewall), then all Group Policy processing will fail. Thus it's important that Windows clients have unimpeded access to all potential domain controllers that will respond to authentication and Group Policy requests for these protocols. Again, it's not super-common in the Windows world (yet) to turn the firewalls on for Domain Controllers and servers.

Another point to note is that Group Policy processing in Windows versions prior to Windows Vista ran within the privileged Winlogon process. Winlogon is a system service and thus has the highest level of privilege within Windows. For that reason, poorly behaved CSEs could potentially crash Windows. This didn't happen often (or ever, to my knowledge, but it was certainly possible). As we'll see in the next section, the inner workings of Group Policy changes in Windows Vista, as we'll see with the *Group Policy Client service*.

Once the core steps are complete, each CSE DLL is called by the Winlogon process, in the order that they are registered in the Registry under HKLM\Software\Microsoft\Windows NT\CurrentVersion\Winlogon\GPExtensions (with the exception of Administrative Templates Policy, which always runs first), and each CSE processes the GPOs that have been discovered during the core processing cycle.

Core Processing for Windows Vista

So, Microsoft has made a significant change to the Group Policy processing engine in Windows Vista. It has moved the engine from Winlogon into a separate service, called the *Group Policy Client* Service. This service is "hardened" so that even an administrator cannot easily stop it.

This is probably a good thing because there are not too many situations where you'd want to disable Group Policy processing completely. As I mentioned, a normal administrator cannot easily stop the Group Policy Client Service. If you go into the Services MMC snap-in and highlight the service, you'll notice that the options to stop and start the service are grayed out. It takes a bit of work to stop the service, and when you do, it will automatically restart itself after a short period of time. However, if you want to see this in motion, here is the general process.

If you want to try this out (just for fun), you'll need to start the Windows Task Manager and select the Services tab. Locate the service called gpsvc, and note the process ID listed next to it, as shown in Figure 6.14. Next, move to the Processes tab in Task Manager and locate the svchost process with the same process ID as the gpsvc entry. Highlight that svchost process and click the End Process button to end the service.

That's all there is to it!

FIGURE 6.14   Viewing the Group Policy Client Service process

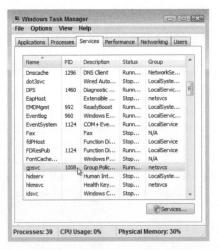

Now, the main difference between core processing for Windows Vista versus the older operating systems is the ICMP slow link detection process. Even though, underneath the hood, there's lots of new stuff for Vista, it acts pretty much like XP. Except in one big respect, and that's the slow link detection process. This is described next.

Windows Vista and Slow Link Detection

Windows Vista uses a completely different mechanism to detect a slow link. Instead of using ICMP pings, Vista relies on the Network Location Awareness (NLA) service that is part of the operating system. The NLA service uses a series of higher-level communications with Domain Controllers to determine when a Domain Controller is available and at what link speed it is available. The NLA process is more dynamic and thus is able to inform the Group Policy engine when a Domain Controller becomes available (where the previous mechanism was not). Because of this, it's important to understand under what scenarios GP processing occurs when NLA detects that a DC is available. We'll discuss this later in the chapter in the section "Troubleshooting NLA in Windows Vista."

If you were to use Windows Server 2008 as your Group Policy client over a slow link, it would detect slow links the same way. But how often are you using Windows Server 2008 to dial up from a hotel room?

Client-Side Extensions

When a Group Policy "clock" strikes, the client's Group Policy engine springs into action to start processing your wishes. The GPOs that are meant for the client are downloaded from Active Directory, and then the client pretty much does the rest.

When GPOs are set from upon high, usually not all policy setting categories are used. For instance, you might set up an Administrative Template policy but not an Internet Explorer Maintenance policy. The client is smart enough to know which policy setting groups affect it.

The client knows which policy setting groups affects it specifically because it asks each GPO which extensions have been set within it through the gpcMachineExtensionName and gpcUserExtensionName attributes in the GPC that we introduced earlier.

This happens during the "core" processing part of Group Policy. During this core processing cycle, the client queries Active Directory to get its list of GPOs, figures out which ones actually apply to it, and makes a list of the CSEs that will need to run for the GPOs found. Once all that core work is done, then each CSE is called in turn to do its thing.

CSEs are really DLLs (Dynamic Link Libraries) that perform the Group Policy processing. These DLLs are called by the system Winlogon process (or the Group Policy Client Service in Windows Vista) and are shipped, out of the box in clients capable of processing Group Policy: Windows 2000, Windows XP, Windows 2003, Windows Vista, and Windows Server 2008.

These CSEs are automatically registered in the operating system and are identified in the Registry by their GUIDs.

Additional CSEs can be created by third-party programmers who want to control their own aspects of the operating system or their own software. See the Sidebar "Group Policy Software Vendors with their own CSEs" for a sampling.

Group Policy Software Vendors with their own CSEs

The whole idea of Client-Side Extensions (CSEs) is that if you have a great idea, and you want to make that idea happen via Group Policy, you can do it. Several vendors have stepped up and created their own CSEs that implement their ideas. Come to www.GPanswers.com for the latest look at products that have their own CSEs. As of this writing, the following companies have the following products with their own CSEs.

- Quest

  Quest Group Policy Extensions for Desktops

  Found here: http://www.quest.com/group-policy-extensions-for-desktops

  This product helps you craft policies in ways that were previously difficult. For instance, you can leverage an existing machine's GPO settings and make it a "template" to zap down to other systems. This also has configurations that manipulate Microsoft Outlook, control the Registry, manage files and folders, and more.

- Special Operations Software

  SpecsOps Deploy

  Found here: http://www.specopssoft.com/products/specopsdeploy

  This CSE enables you to perform several Group Policy Software Installation tasks (discussed in Chapter 4 of the companion book, *Implementing the Secure and Managed Desktop*) that you can't natively perform. For instance, you can distribute software to users and computers that are already logged on as well as get a detailed log of which computers received software.

  SpecOps Inventory

  Found here: http://www.specopssoft.com/products/specopsinventory

  This product performs hardware and software inventory via the Group Policy engine and provides detailed reports of what software and hardware your enterprise is using.

- PolicyPak Software

The PolicyPak family of tools can be found here: www.PolicyPak.com

This is a set of specific CSEs that control applications that aren't natively Group Policy enabled. So, if you wanted to manage Adobe Acrobat Reader or WinZip or the Norton AntiVirus client via Group Policy, PolicyPak has a prepackaged "pak" for you to manage those applications.

Additionally, PolicyPak has a Group Policy Design Studio tool that enables you to create your own paks. Check out PolicyPak.com for more details.

In Windows 2000, the OS shipped with 9 CSEs. In Windows XP and 2003, Microsoft added 2 more, for a total of 11 CSEs. With Windows XP SP2 another CSE was added. Vista adds an additional 5 for a total of 17.

Once the Group Policy Preference Extensions are added to Windows XP or Windows Vista, another 21 are added. Or, since they're in the box for Windows Server 2008, the in-the-box number jumps to a total of 38.

The three Windows XP SP2 and Windows 2003 SP1 CSEs are Internet Explorer Zonemapping, 802.11x Wireless policies, and Quality of Service Packet Scheduler policies. Vista adds the Enterprise QoS, 802.3, Offline Files, Deployed Printer Connections, and Windows Search CSEs. Some additional policy functionality, such as Software Restriction Policies, was added in XP and Windows 2003 but was implemented within an existing CSE.

To take a look at the CSEs on a Windows 2000, Windows XP, or Windows Vista workstation, follow these steps:

1. On Windows XPPRO1 or VISTA1, log on as Administrator.

2. For Windows XP, choose Start ➢ Run (for Windows Vista, just type **regedit** into the Search dialog box) to open the Run dialog box, in the Open box type **Run Regedit**, and press Enter to open the Registry Editor, as shown in Figure 6.15.

3. Drill down into HKLM ➢ Software ➢ Microsoft ➢ Windows NT ➢ Current Version ➢ Winlogon ➢ GPExtensions. Here you will find a list of GUIDs, each representing a CSE.

Let's take a look at the next sections to understand precisely what we're looking at.

CSEs for Pre–Windows Vista Machines

Figure 6.15 shows a sample CSE and the settings for disk quotas. See Table 6.2 for the CSEs listed by Class ID, the functions they perform, and the associated DLLs. Note that a particular DLL can be responsible for more than one function.

FIGURE 6.15 The Client-Side Extension DLLs actually perform the GPO processing.

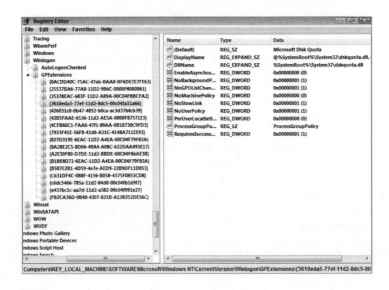

TABLE 6.2 GUIDs, Their Functions, and Their Corresponding DLLs for Pre–Windows Vista Machines

Class ID	Function	DLL
{C6DC5466-785A-11D2-84D0-00C04FB169F7}	Software deployment	appmgmts.dll
{3610EDA5-77EF-11D2-8DC5-00C04FA31A66}	Disk quotas	dskquota.dll
{B1BE8D72-6EAC-11D2-A4EA-00C04F79F83A}	EFS recovery	scecli.dll
{25537BA6-77A8-11D2-9B6C-0000F8080861}	Folder redirection	fdeploy.dll
{A2E30F80-D7DE-11d2-BBDE-00C04F86AE3B}	Internet Explorer settings	iedkcs32.dll
{e437bc1c-aa7d-11d2-a382-00c04f991e27}	IP security	gptext.dll
{35378EAC-683F-11D2-A89A-00C04FBBCFA2}	Registry settings (Administrative Templates)	userenv.dll
{42B5FAAE-6536-11D2-AE5A-0000F87571E3}	Scripts	gptext.dll
{827D319E-6EAC-11D2-A4EA-00C04F79F83A}	Security	scecli.dll

TABLE 6.2   GUIDs, Their Functions, and Their Corresponding DLLs for Pre–Windows Vista Machines *(continued)*

Class ID	Function	DLL
{0ACDD40C-75AC-47ab-BAA0-BF6DE7E7FE63}	Wireless (802.11x) (Windows XP+ only)	gptext.dll
{4CFB60C1-FAA6-47f1-89AA-0B18730C9FD3}	Internet Zone Mapping (Windows XP+)	iedkcs32.dll
{426031c0-0b47-4852-b0ca-ac3d37bfcb39}	Quality of Service Packet Scheduler (Windows XP+ only)	gptext.dll
None	Software Restriction (Windows XP+ only)	None
None	Remote Installation Services (RIS) (Windows Server 2003 and earlier)	None

Why don't all CSEs have DLLs? Neither Remote Installation Services (RIS) nor Software Restriction polices require CSEs to be associated with DLLs. RIS is active *before* the operating system is. Software Restriction policies don't require CSEs because they "tag along" on the functionality of another CSE.

When creating custom ADM or ADMX templates (see "ADM/ADMX Template Syntax" on this book's website, www.GPanswers.com), the CLIENTEXT keyword specifies which client-side extension is needed to process particular settings on the client computer. This is required for some policy features, such as Software Restriction and Disk Quota Policy that use the same file to store their settings as does Administrative Template Policy.

CSEs for Windows Vista Machines

See Table 6.3 for the Windows Vista–specific CSEs listed by Class ID, the functions they perform, and the associated DLLs. Again, all the pre-Vista CSEs are also on Windows Vista, so they're not repeated in this table since they're already listed in Table 6.2. Note that a particular DLL can be responsible for more than one function.

TABLE 6.3 CSE GUIDs, Their Functions, and Their Corresponding DLLs That Exist Only on Windows Vista Machines

Class ID	Function	DLL
{7933F41E-56F8-41d6-A31C-4148A711EE93}	Windows Search	srchadmin.dll
{7B983727-8072-47ea-83A4-39C6CE25BAE6}	Offline Files (see note)	cscobj.dll
{8A28E2C5-8D06-49A4-A08C-632DAA493E17}	Deployed Printer Connections	gpprnext.dll
{B587E2B1-4D59-4e7e-AED9-22B9DF11D053}	802.3 Policy	dot3gpclnt.dll
{FB2CA36D-0B40-4307-821B-A13B252DE56C}	Enterprise QoS	gptext.dll

 Offline Files existed before Windows Vista (in Windows 2000 and Windows XP), but in Windows Vista it became its own CSE.

Additional CSEs for Windows 2008 Machines and Machines with the Group Policy Preference Extensions Loaded

We'll actually explore these new superpowers in Chapter 10.

These are the Group Policy Preference Extensions, which, while they hook into Group Policy, don't always act like the Group Policy that we've come to know and love. (Again, we'll explore it in Chapter 10.)

But it should be noted that they come in two forms: they're already in the box for Windows Server 2008 and they're downloadable for Windows XP, Windows 2003, and Windows Vista. They won't install on Windows 2000.

In Table 6.4, you can see the list of CSEs, their GUIDs, and the corresponding functions that are added once the Group Policy Preference Extensions are loaded.

TABLE 6.4 CSE GUIDs, Their Functions, and Their Corresponding DLLs That Exist Only When You Add the Group Policy Preference Extensions

CSE GUIDs	Function	DLL
{0E28E245-9368-4853-AD84-6DA3BA35BB75}	Group Policy Environment	gpprefcl.dll
{17D89FEC-5C44-4972-B12D-241CAEF74509}	Group Policy Local Users and Groups	gpprefcl.dll
{1A6364EB-776B-4120-ADE1-B63A406A76B5}	Group Policy Device Settings	gpprefcl.dll

TABLE 6.4   CSE GUIDs, Their Functions, and Their Corresponding DLLs That Exist Only When You Add the Group Policy Preference Extensions *(continued)*

CSE GUIDs	Function	DLL
{3A0DBA37-F8B2-4356-83DE-3E90BD5C261F}	Group Policy Network Options	gpprefcl.dll
{5794DAFD-BE60-433f-88A2-1A31939AC01F}	Group Policy Drive Maps	gpprefcl.dll
{6232C319-91AC-4931-9385-E70C2B099F0E}	Group Policy Folders	gpprefcl.dll
{6A4C88C6-C502-4f74-8F60-2CB23EDC24E2}	Group Policy Network Shares	gpprefcl.dll
{7150F9BF-48AD-4da4-A49C-29EF4A8369BA}	Group Policy Files	gpprefcl.dll
{728EE579-943C-4519-9EF7-AB56765798ED}	Group Policy Data Sources	gpprefcl.dll
{74EE6C03-5363-4554-B161-627540339CAB}	Group Policy INI Files	gpprefcl.dll
{91FBB303-0CD5-4055-BF42-E512A681B325}	Group Policy Services	gpprefcl.dll
{A3F3E39B-5D83-4940-B954-28315B82F0A8}	Group Policy Folder Options	gpprefcl.dll
{AADCED64-746C-4633-A97C-D61349046527}	Group Policy Scheduled Tasks	gpprefcl.dll
{B087BE9D-ED37-454f-AF9C-04291E351182}	Group Policy Registry	gpprefcl.dll
{BC75B1ED-5833-4858-9BB8-CBF0B166DF9D}	Group Policy Printers	gpprefcl.dll
{C418DD9D-0D14-4efb-8FBF-CFE535C8FAC7}	Group Policy Shortcuts	gpprefcl.dll
{E47248BA-94CC-49c4-BBB5-9EB7F05183D0}	Group Policy Internet Settings	gpprefcl.dll
{E4F48E54-F38D-4884-BFB9-D4D2E5729C18}	Group Policy Start Menu Settings	gpprefcl.dll
{E5094040-C46C-4115-B030-04FB2E545B00}	Group Policy Regional Options	gpprefcl.dll
{E62688F0-25FD-4c90-BFF5-F508B9D2E31F}	Group Policy Power Options	gpprefcl.dll
{F9C77450-3A41-477E-9310-9ACD617BD9E3}	Group Policy Applications	gpprefcl.dll

There's no mistake in the table. All the new Group Policy Preference Extensions use the *same* DLL, but if you look at the actual Registry entry, you'll see that each one's `Displayname` key notes the DLL name (`gppprefcl.dll`) with an entry point ID.

Inside CSE Values

For each CSE, several values can be set or not. Not all CSEs use these values. Indeed, Microsoft does not support modifying them in any way. They are presented in Table 6.5 for your own edification, but in most circumstances, you should not be modifying them unless explicitly directed to do so by Microsoft Product Support Services (PSS).

Remember, the CSE sets these values—you don't, unless you're directed by Microsoft PSS to help make sure the CSE is working the way it's supposed to.

TABLE 6.5   Client-Side Extension Values

Registry Value	Data Type	Function	Data	Default
DLLName	REG_EXPAND_SZ	Contains the DLL name	CSE DLL	Per CSE
ProcessGroupPolicy	REG_SZ	The name of the callback function within the CSE that processes policy	The function name	Per CSE
NoMachinePolicy	REG_DWORD	Indicates whether this CSE supports per-computer settings	0=Does Not; 1=Does	0
NoUserPolicy	REG_DWORD	Indicates whether this CSE supports per-user settings	0=Does Not; 1=Does	0

TABLE 6.5 Client-Side Extension Values *(continued)*

Registry Value	Data Type	Function	Data	Default
NoSlowLink	REG_DWORD	Enable/disable over slow link	0=Process; 1=Don't process	0
NoBackgroundPolicy	REG_DWORD	Enable/disable background GPO processing	0=Process; 1=Don't process	0
NoGPOListChanges	REG_DWORD	Process if changed or not	0=Always process; 1=Do not process unless changes	0
PerUserLocalSettings	REG_DWORD	Caches policies for user in the machine section of the Registry	0=Don't cache; 1=Cache	0
RequiresSuccessfulRegistry	REG_DWORD	Forces CSE DLLs to be registered with the operating system	0=Don't care; 1=CSEs must be registered	0
EnableAsynchronousProcessing	REG_DWORD	Enable/disable asynchronous GPO processing	0=Synchronous; 1= Asynchronous	Depends on the CSE

Note that many of the options listed in Table 6.5 (for example, NoSlowLink, NoBackgroundPolicy, NoGPOListChanges) can be set within the Computer Configuration ➢ Policies ➢ Administrative Templates ➢ System ➢ Group Policy section of a GPO. When they are set through policy, then the values shown in the Registry value column listed in the table are ignored.

I hope you won't have to spend too much time in here. But I present this information so that if you need to debug a certain CSE, you can go right to the source and see how a setting might not be what you want.

Remember that most of these settings are either established by the system default or can be changed. You can change the settings yourself—such as the ability to process over slow links, the ability to be disabled, or the ability to be processed in the background—using the techniques described near the end of Chapter 4.

Where Are Administrative Templates Registry Settings Stored?

Because one of the most commonly applied policy settings is the Administrative Templates, let's take a minute to analyze specifically how Administrative Templates are processed when the client processes them.

 Here, we're just talking about proper "policies" and not "preferences" (which are discussed in Chapter 7).

I've already discussed how Group Policy is more evolved than old NT 4–style policies. Specifically, one of the most compelling features is that most policy settings do not tattoo the Registry anymore. That is, once a setting is applied, it applies only for that computer or user. When the user or computer leaves the scope of the GPO (for example, when you move the user from the **Human Resources Users** OU to the **Accounting Users** OU), the Registry settings that did apply to them are removed and the new Registry settings then apply.

When an NT 4–style policy was written, the writer could choose to modify any portion of the Registry. Now, as you've seen, when the settings specified in the Administrative Templates section of Group Policy no longer apply (for example, when a new user logs on or the computer is moved to another OU), the settings are removed or applied appropriately for the next user.

Administrative Templates Group Policy settings are usually stored in the following locations:

User Settings `HKEY_CURRENT_USER\Software\Policies`

Computer Settings `HKEY_LOCAL_MACHINE\Software\Policies`

Alternatively, some applications may choose the following locations:

User Settings `HKEY_CURRENT_USER\Software\Microsoft\Windows\CurrentVersion\Policies`

Computer Settings `HKEY_LOCAL_MACHINE\Software\Microsoft\Windows\Currentversion\Policies`

 Microsoft is encouraging third-party developers to write their applications so that they utilize `HKEY_CURRENT_USER\Software\Policies` or `HKEY_LOCAL_MACHINE\Software\Policies` to become Group Policy enabled.

Knowing how this works helps us understand why each version of Windows increases the number of Administrative Templates policy settings that can apply to it. It's quite simple: the specific program that's targeted for the policy setting looks for settings at these two Registry locations. Sometimes that application is one we overlook a lot—Explorer.exe! For Windows XP, Explorer.exe has been "smartened up" and now knows to look in these Registry keys for about 200 new items. Windows XP/SP2's firewall has been smartened up to look for about 20 new items. You get the idea.

This also answers the question of why Windows 2000 machines seem to "overlook" policy settings that are designed only for Windows XP or Windows 2003. In short, "older" operating systems (which are really applications) simply don't know to "look" for new policy settings (even though those settings are written into the target machine's Registry). So, all operating systems (which, again, are really applications) that can download the policy settings *do*. But, who cares? If an older system applies a policy setting, the Registry is modified and then it's generally ignored by the applications running on it. Windows 2000 just doesn't know to look for the new Registry changes that Windows XP, Windows Vista, or Windows 2003 policy settings change. Occasionally, with the release of a service pack, the application in question might get a new lease on life and understand some new policy settings—because the application has now been updated to look for them in the Registry. This has already happened for Explorer, Software Update Services, Windows Media Player, and Office, to name a few.

If you have a mixture of Windows 2000 desktops and member servers and Windows XP, Windows Vista, or Windows 2003 member servers, you might need to keep track of policy settings that affect only XP, for example. It's likely a good idea to create GPOs with names specific to which operating system they apply to: Windows 2000, Windows XP, Windows 2003, and/or Windows Vista.

Because the settings inside Administrative Templates are written to only these four locations, we are free from the bonds of having our Registries tattooed. The Administrative Templates CSE (Userenv.dll) applies the settings placed in any of these four locations to the current mix of user and system.

As you move users in and out of OUs, or change group membership, the settings that apply to them change as well. Under the covers, this process is a bit more subtle. The way the nontattooing behavior works is that when Registry settings are first applied, they are merged into files that are stored on the computer in per-computer and per-user areas—each file is called ntuser.pol. The next time the Administrative Templates CSE runs, it looks into these stored files and makes a list of all of the policy settings that exist in the four "special" keys I mentioned previously (at the beginning of this section). It then deletes all of those settings, as specified by that file. Then, the CSE re-creates that file with all the new Administrative Template settings that currently apply to the computer or user. Finally, it applies those values to the computer or user portions of the Registry.

Any settings that are outside the four "special" locations are *not* covered by this removal process, and thus you have the tattooing behavior.

For information on how to use other Administrative Templates, see Chapter 7, and for information on how to create your own Administrative Templates, see "ADM/ADMX Template Syntax" on www.GPanswers.com in the Book Resources section.

Why Isn't Group Policy Applying?

At times, you set up Group Policy from upon high and your users or workstations do not receive the changes. Why might that be the case?

First, remember how Group Policy is processed:

- The GPO "lives" in the swimming pool in the domain.

- The client requests Group Policy at various times throughout the day.

- The client connects to a Domain Controller to get the latest batch of GPOs. (Group Policy isn't somehow "pushed" from upon high.)

- If it's status-quo, that is

    - Nothing has changed inside the GPO (based on changed version number)

    - The location of the user or computer hasn't changed in Active Directory

    - The user or computer hasn't changed group memberships

    - Any WMI filters set on the GPO haven't changed

    the default behavior is to not reprocess the GPOs (though this can be changed as explored in Chapter 4).

- If there is a change (with respect to any of these previous bullet points), then all applicable CSEs reprocess all applicable GPOs.

That's the long and the short of it.

Now, if you think all this is happening properly, try to answer the questions in the following sections to find out what could be damming the proper flow of your Group Policy process.

Reviewing the Basics

Sometimes, it's the small, day-to-day things that prevent a GPO from applying. By testing a simple application that has normal features, you can often find problems and eliminate them, which allows Group Policy to behave the way you expect.

Is the Group Policy Object or Link Disabled?

Recall from Chapter 1 that there are two halves of the Group Policy coin: a computer half and a user half. Also recall that either portion or both can be disabled. Indeed, a GPO itself can be fully disabled (see Figure 6.16).

Check the GPO itself or any related GPO links. Click the Details tab and check the GPO Status setting. If it is anything other than Enabled, you might be in trouble.

> If you change the status of the GPO, that status changes on all links that use this GPO.

Are You Sure about the Inheritance?

Recall that Group Policy flows downward from each level—site, domain, and each nested OU—and is cumulative. Also recall that in all versions of Windows prior to Vista, there is only one Local Group Policy for a computer, which is applied first.

And, in Vista there are three levels of MLGPOs. See Chapter 1 for the full rundown. Remember, in MLGPOs it's a "last written wins" policy.

FIGURE 6.16   You can disable the entire GPO if desired.

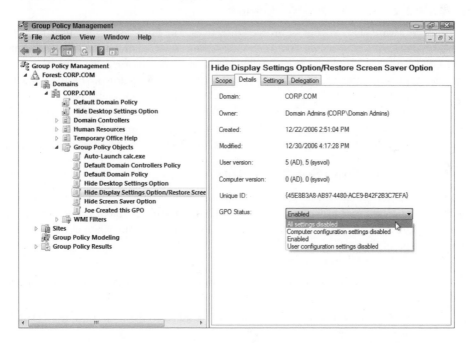

Are You Trying to Apply Policy to a Group Inside an OU?

This bears repeating: You can't just plunk an NT-style/Active Directory group that contains users into an OU and expect them to get Group Policy. Group Policy doesn't work that way; you can only apply Group Policy directly to users or computers in an OU. Not a group.

Multiple Group Policy Objects at a Level

Also recall that there can be many GPOs at any level, which are applied in the reverse order—that is, from bottom to top, as described in Chapter 2. Since any two (or more) GPOs can contain the same or even conflicting settings, the last-applied GPO wins. If you mean for one GPO to have higher precedence, use the Up and Down buttons to manipulate the order. Remember, the GPO with the *lowest* number gets the *highest* priority. Confusing, I know, but that's the deal.

Examining Your Block Inheritance Usage

The GPMC gives you a quick view of all instances of Block Inheritance with the Blue Exclamation Point (!). Remember: once you select to block inheritance, *all GPOs* from higher levels are considered null and void—not just the one policy setting or GPO you had in mind to block. It's as if you were starting from a totally blank slate. Therefore, whenever you block inheritance, you must start from scratch—either creating and linking new GPOs or simply linking to existing GPOs already swimming in the GPOs container.

Examining Your "Enforced" Usage

Conversely, be aware of all of your "Enforce" directives. The Enforce icon is a little lock next to the GPO link. Enforce specifies that the policy settings selected and contained within in a *specific* GPO cannot be avoided at any inherited level from this point forward. Note that Block Inheritance applies to a container in Active Directory (for example, a domain or an OU), while Enforced applies to a GPO link. So if you have a GPO linked to four containers in Active Directory, you could have only one of those links "Enforced," two of them or all of them (or none!). When Block Policy Inheritance and Enforce are seemingly in conflict, Enforce always wins. Recall that Enforce was previously known as No Override in the old-school parlance.

Are Your Permissions Set Correctly?

Recall from Chapter 2 that two permissions—"Read" and "Apply Group Policy"—must be set so that the affected user processes a specific GPO. By default, Authenticated Users have these two rights, but you can remove this group and set your own filtering via the Security Filtering section on the Scope tab of a GPO link.

In Chapter 2, I showed you two ways to filter:

- Round up only the users, computers, or security groups who *should* get the GPO applied to them.

- Figure out who you *do not* want to get the GPO applied to them, and use the "Deny" attribute over the "Apply Group Policy" right.

When all is said and done, users will need both "Read" and "Apply Group Policy" permissions on the GPO itself to apply GPOs. And, you can prevent a GPO from applying by simply setting "Deny" access on one or the other of these two rights. Though, if you're going to use this technique, best practices dictate to always try to deny access on "Apply Group Policy" and not "Read."

> Try to always deny "Apply Group Policy" (and not "Read") because later, that user might need to be able to modify the GPO. And, without read access, they cannot modify it.

Having only one of those permissions means that Group Policy will not apply when processing is supposed to occur. Additionally, make sure to remember that the "Deny" attribute always trumps all other permissions. If an explicit "Deny" attribute is encountered, it is as if it were the only bit in the world that matters. Therefore, if a specific GPO is not being applied to a user or a group, make sure that "Deny" isn't somehow getting into the picture along the way.

> Any use of the "Deny" bit is not displayed in the Security Filtering section of the Scope tab; so you really have no notification if it's being used. I predict this will be a common reason for Group Policy not applying; the old-school way to perform Group Policy filtering involved heavy use of the "Deny" bit, and now the GPMC will not easily display this fact unless you use the Group Policy Results Wizard (or gpresult.exe).

Advanced Inspection

If you've gone through the basics, and nothing is overtly wrong, perhaps a more subtle interaction is occurring. See if any of the following questions and solutions fit the bill.

Is Windows XP/Windows Vista Fast Boot On?

The default behavior of Windows XP and Windows Vista is different from that of Windows 2000. The default behavior of Windows 2000 is to process GPOs in the foreground (at computer startup or user logon) synchronously. That is, for the policy settings that affect a Windows 2000 computer (which will take effect at startup), every GPO is applied—local, site, domain, and each nested OU—even before the user has the ability to press Ctrl+Alt+Del to log on. Once the user logs on, the policy settings that affect the user side are applied—local, site, domain, and each nested OU—before the user's Desktop is finally displayed and they can start working.

This usually isn't too much of a problem for the policy settings within GPOs that affect computers, but it can seriously affect your user's experience if enabled for user policy processing. Even *after* a user is logged on, GPOs can suddenly be downloaded and policy settings start popping up and changing the user's environment.

Moreover, as I stated in Chapter 4, by default, several key items in Windows XP take between two and three reboots to become effective. To that end, I suggest you modify the default behavior. The strongest advice I can give you is to create and link a new GPO at the domain level. Name your new GPO something like "Force Windows XP and Vista machines to act like Windows 2000," and enable the **Always wait for the network at computer startup and logon** policy setting. Then, select Enforced so it cannot be blocked.

To find this policy setting, drill down through the Computer Configuration ➢ Policies ➢ Administrative Templates ➢ System ➢ Logon branch of Group Policy. (For more information, see Chapter 4.)

Therefore, if you have erratic Group Policy application (especially for Software Installation, Folder Redirection, or Profile settings), see if the Windows XP and Windows Vista default of Fast Boot is still active.

Is Asynchronous Processing Turned On in Windows 2000?

Windows 2000 was born with a way to try to act like Windows XP and Vista and process GPOs asynchronously. However, doing so is not recommended, as amazingly unpredictable results can occur. Windows XP was built from the ground up to do asynchronous processing; Windows 2000 really wasn't. So, in a nutshell, don't turn on asynchronous processing for Windows 2000 machines. It's a bad idea.

> Asynchronous processing is independent for both the computer and the user sides.

Are Both the GPC and GPT Replicated Correctly?

As stated in the first part of this chapter, Group Policy is made up of two halves:

- The GPC, which is found in Active Directory and replicated via normal Active Directory replication

- The GPT, which is found in the SYSVOL share of one Domain Controller and replicated via FRS to other Domain Controllers

Both the GPC and GPT are replicated independently and can be on different schedules before converging.

Use the techniques described earlier in conjunction with `Gpotool` and `Replmon` to diagnose issues with replicating the GPC and GPT.

Did You Check the DNS Configuration of the Server and Client?

In order for the GPC and GPT to actually replicate correctly, the DNS structure must be 100 percent kosher at all times—both on the server and at the client. If you suspect that the GPC and GPT are not being replicated correctly, you might try to see if the DNS structure is the way you intend. If it is, I don't specifically recommend you rip it all up and reconfigure it if everything else is working. The Microsoft Knowledge Base article at `http://support.microsoft.com/kb/291382/en-us` provides a good foundation for understanding how to create a healthy DNS infrastructure.

In some cases, one Domain Controller might not be providing Group Policy to your clients. In the next section, I'll show you how to find out if your clients are really logged on and, if so, what Domain Controller the computer and user are using for logon.

Are You Really Logged On?

Windows 2000 doesn't perform the logon process precisely the same way that Windows XP or Windows Vista does. Specifically, when a user logs on to a Windows XP or Vista machine, Windows XP or Vista might or might not have really made contact with a Domain Controller to validate that user and give them a Kerberos ticket to the network. Kerberos is the newer authentication mechanism that has supplanted NTLM. Windows XP and Windows Vista will try its darndest to speed things up (again) and log on with cached credentials. Windows XP and Windows Vista will then try to contact a Domain Controller and get the Kerberos ticket for the user.

In Windows 2000, it is easy to identify the Domain Controller where the local Desktop authenticated. You issue a `set` command at a command prompt and look for the contents of the *LOGONSERVER* variable, as shown in Figure 6.17.

FIGURE 6.17 The LOGONSERVER variable shows the Domain Controller where this Windows 2000 client is picking up its Group Policy settings.

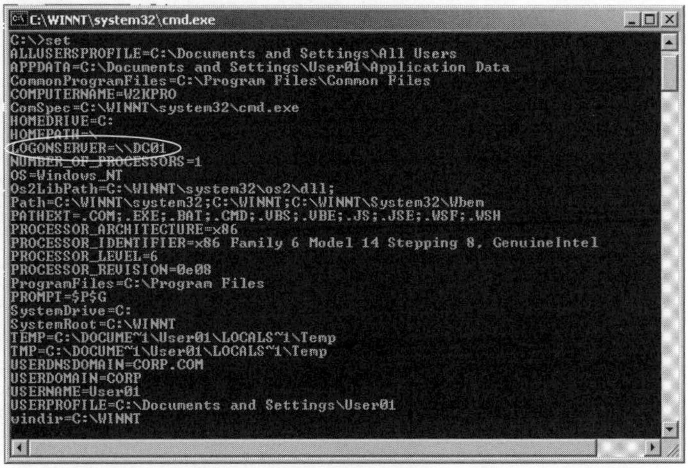

In Windows 2000, if you aren't logged on to a Domain Controller, you see the variable set to the local computer name.

WARNING In Windows XP and Windows Vista, you simply cannot trust this *LOGONSERVER* variable to tell you the truth. Additionally, you cannot trust the Windows XP or Windows Vista SYSTEMINFO utility either, which claims to provide this data.

Just based on the way Windows XP and Windows Vista do their logon thing, you cannot use these aforementioned methods. XP will simply tell a bald-faced lie and say that you are logged on (via the *LOGONSERVER* variable, with the information from the last Domain Controller it contacted).

With Windows XP and Windows Vista, to ensure that your user and computer are really logged on the network, you can count on just one tool—Kerbtray (or the command-line equivalent, `klist.exe`). Kerbtray and `klist` are found in the Windows 2003 Resource Kit and are small enough to be put on a floppy and run on a suspect machine. When you run Kerbtray, it puts a little icon in the notification area. If the computer and user have Kerberos tickets, the icon turns green and you know you're really logged on. However, if the Kerbtray returns a graphic of a bunch of loose keys (that, in my opinion, look like question marks), as shown in Figure 6.18, you know you're not actually logged on and, hence, not downloading the most recent GPOs. Again, if you were really logged on, the graphic would be a green ticket.

FIGURE 6.18 The Windows XP and Windows Vista LOGONSERVER variable cannot be trusted. Use Kerbtray instead, which is shown running in the notification area.

In Figure 6.18, you can see several things:

- The computer's network card is disabled (as shown in the Network Connections window).

- The *LOGONSERVER* variable is set to a Domain Controller (as shown in the CMD prompt window). Feel free to simply say out loud, "If the network card is off, this is bloody impossible."

- Kerbtray, thankfully, returns that icon of a bunch of loose keys verifying that we're not really logged on.

So, to find out if you're really logged on when using a Windows XP or Windows Vista computer, it's "Kerbtray or the highway." Once you've validated with Kerbtray that the computer has really logged on, you can *then* use the *LOGONSERVER* variable to make sure which Domain Controller the Windows XP or Windows Vista machine has used. Because, you'll know the truth: whether or not you're really logged on.

Did Something Recently Move?

If a computer account or a user account is moved from one OU to another, Windows (all versions) can wait as long as 30 minutes to realize this fact. Once it does, it might or might not apply background Group Policy processing for another 90 minutes or more! Running GPUpdate (or SECEDIT for Windows 2000 machines) will not help.

However, if you're expecting a specific setting to take effect on a user or computer that has moved more than 150 minutes ago, you'll then need to figure out if the move has been embraced by the Domain Controller the workstation used to authenticate. (See the previous section for information about how to determine the Domain Controller via the *LOGONSERVER* variable, but make sure you're really logged on!)

You can then fire up Active Directory Users and Computers and connect to the Domain Controller in question, as shown in Figure 6.19.

If the target computer's local Domain Controller does not know about the move, you might want to manually kick off replication using Active Directory Sites and Services. If the target computer's local Domain Controller *does* know about the move, you might want to try logging the user off and back on or restarting the computer. Although using SECEDIT (for Windows 2000 machines) or GPUpdate (for Windows XP, Windows Vista, Windows 2003, and Windows 2008 machines) to refresh the GPO is a good option, it's best to log off and/or reboot the machine to guarantee that the computer will perform the initial policy processing as described in Chapter 4.

I've seen Microsoft documentation that states that running GPUpdate /force on a Windows XP/SP2 machine will "jump-start" the machine and/or user account into recognizing that it has moved around in Active Directory. I've done extensive testing but get inconsistent results. Sometimes it seems to work; other times it doesn't. In short, when a user or computer is moved around in Active Directory, I always re–log in as the user, or reboot the computer. It's slightly better with Windows Vista, but even then, I've seen it work and not work. There's an update for Windows XP/SP2 (which should be included in XP/SP3) that should make this work a little better. Check out MSKB 891630 for more information.

Is the Machine Properly Joined to the Domain?

With Windows 2000, if a device is moved from one OU to another and then the device is rebooted *before* DC replication occurs, sometimes the device can be bumped out of being a domain member because the *computer trust*, also known as a *secure channel*, is broken. To see if the computer trust (secure channel) to the domain is damaged, you can use NLTEST, which is in the Windows 2000 Support Tools on the Windows 2000 CD. The verification syntax is nltest /sc_query:domain_name. If the test passes, then you're kosher. If not, you might need to disjoin and rejoin the device to the domain.

FIGURE 6.19 You can always manually connect to a Domain Controller to see if Active Directory has performed replication.

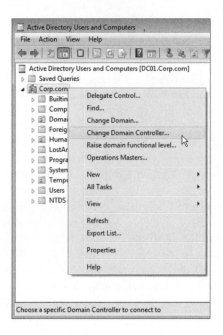

Is Loopback Policy Enabled?

Enabling Loopback policy will turn Group Policy on its ear: loopback forces the same user policy settings for everyone who logs on to a specific computer. If you're seeing user policy settings apply but not computer policies, or if things are applying without rhyme or reason, chances are loopback policy is enabled. Review Chapter 4 to see in depth how it works, when you should use it, and how to turn it off.

In Windows XP, determining you are in loopback mode is difficult.

In Windows Vista, it's a little easier. Look for Event ID 5311 in the Windows Vista Group Policy Event Logs. In the event directly, you'll see if loopback policy processing mode is set to Replace, Merge, or not enabled. We show this a little later in Figure 6.29.

How Are Slow Links Being Defined, and How Are Slow Links Handled?

If you notice that Group Policy is not applied to users coming in over a slow link, remember the rules for slow links:

- Registry and security settings are always applied over slow (and fast) links.

- EFS (Encrypting File System) and IPsec (IP Security) policies are *always* applied over slow links. You cannot turn this behavior off, even though settings found under the Computer Configuration ➢ Policies ➢ Administrative Templates ➢ System ➢ Group Policy branch imply that you can. This is a bug in the interface, as described in Chapter 4.

- By default, Disk Quotas, Folder Redirection, Internet Explorer settings, and Software Deployment are not applied over slow links. Updated and new logon scripts are also not downloaded over slow links. You can change this default behavior under Computer Configuration ➢ Policies ➢ Administrative Templates ➢ System ➢ Group Policy, as described in Chapter 4. Note that there is a difference between processing scripts policy and running scripts. Scripts themselves run only during a foreground processing cycle (computer startup or user logon), but the *updating* of the list of scripts that needs to run can be done in the background. That updating is what I'm referring to here.

Additionally, you can change the definition of what equals a slow link. By default, a slow link is 500Kb or less. You can change the definition for the user settings in User Configuration ➢ Policies ➢ Administrative Templates ➢ System ➢ Group Policy ➢ **Group Policy Slow Link Detection** and for the computer settings in Computer Configuration ➢ Policies ➢ Administrative Templates ➢ System ➢ Group Policy ➢ **Group Policy Slow Link Detection**. Figure 6.20 shows the user settings. If Group Policy is not being applied to your slow-linked clients, be sure to inspect the slow link definition to make sure they fit.

Last, don't forget about your broadband users on DSL or cable modem. Those speeds are sometimes faster than 500Kb and sometimes slower than 500Kb. This could mean that your broadband users might get GPOs on weekends but not when logged on during peak usage times. Therefore, if this happens, set the definition of slow link up or down as necessary.

Finally, it should be noted that if you set the slow link threshold to 0, the client will always assume it's on a fast link.

FIGURE 6.20   Make sure you haven't raised the bar too high for your slower-connected users to receive Group Policy.

Troubleshooting NLA in Windows Vista

If you're working on a Windows Vista client, you may need to determine if an NLA refresh has occurred. As I mentioned earlier, NLA is the service that replaces ICMP slow link detection when determining link speed and Domain Controller availability in Windows Vista.

If the Domain Controller is not available to the client, either because the client is remote and not connected to the company network or because the Domain Controller is simply not available, then Group Policy processing will fail.

When the Domain Controller becomes available again, NLA will detect its presence and trigger an immediate request to perform a background refresh of Group Policy. But, here's the trick: NLA will actually perform this refresh *only* if the previous refresh of Group Policy has failed. If the previous Group Policy refresh succeeded, and *then* the Domain Controller becomes unavailable and *then* available again (before the next Group Policy processing cycle), then NLA will not trigger a background refresh. You will be able to see NLA-based Group Policy refresh by looking at the Group Policy Operational Log, described in the section entitled, "Verbose Logging in Windows Vista and Windows Server 2008." The event will look identical to that shown in Figure 6.21.

FIGURE 6.21   Viewing an event indicating an NLA-based Group Policy refresh

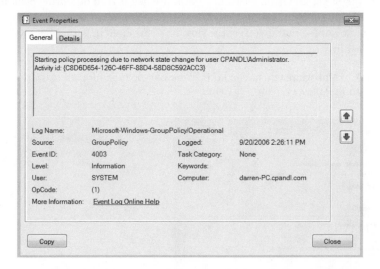

Note that it took as much as 10 minutes for NLA to complete its detection of the Domain Controller and trigger a background Group Policy processing cycle in my testing. So, don't expect an NLA-based Group Policy refresh to happen immediately after your DC becomes available. Depending upon your system and network, your mileage may vary.

Is the Date and Time Correct on the Client System?

Time differences greater than 5 minutes between the client system and the validating Domain Controller will cause Kerberos to simply not permit the logon. If you don't have Kerberos, you've got a logon problem, and that's going to yield a Group Policy problem.

Are Your Active Directory Sites Configured Correctly?

Sometimes Group Policy won't apply if your client isn't in a properly defined Active Directory site (that has IP information associated with it). With that in mind, check the subnet the client is on, and verify that it is correctly associated to an Active Directory site and that the site has Domain Controller coverage.

Did You Check the DNS Configuration of the Client?

One of the most frequently encountered problems with Windows 2000 and above is that things just "stop working" when DNS gets out of whack. Specifically, if you're not seeing Group Policy apply to your client machines, make sure their DNS client is pointing to a Domain Controller or other authoritative source for the domain. If it's pointing to the wrong place or not pointing anywhere, Group Policy will simply not be downloaded. As a colleague of mine likes to say, "Healthy DNS equals a healthy Active Directory."

Moreover, in the age of Windows 2003 with its multiple forests with cross-forest trusts, Group Policy could be applying from just about anywhere and everywhere. It's more important than ever to verify that all DNS server pointers are designed properly and working as they should. For instance, if clients cannot access their "home" Domain Controllers while leveraging a cross-forest trust, they won't get Group Policy.

Finally, to put a fine point on it, Group Policy leverages *only* the fully qualified name. It's not enough to verify that you can resolve a computer named XPPRO1 as opposed to XPPRO1.corp.com. The first is actually the NetBIOS name and *not* the fully qualified domain name. The second is the fully qualified domain name. If you find yourself in a DNS resolution situation where resolving the NetBIOS name will work but the fully qualified name will not work, then you have a DNS problem that needs to be addressed.

Are You Trying to Set Password or Account Policy on an OU?

As you'll see in Chapter 8, certain Group Policy items, namely password and account policy, cannot be set at the OU level. Rather, these policy settings are only domain wide. The GUI lets you set these policy settings at the OU level, but they don't affect users or machines. Well, that's not really true, as you'll see in Chapter 8, but, for the purpose of troubleshooting, just remember that you can't have, say, 6-character passwords in the **Sales** OU and 12-character passwords in the **Engineering** OU. It won't work. (You will see in Chapter 8 where password policy affects local accounts in an OU. Stay tuned for that later.)

Did Someone Muck with Security behind the Group Policy Engine's Back?

As you saw in Chapter 3, there are a number of ways to "go around" the back of the Group Policy engine. Remember, though, that these exploits require local administrative access. However, this implies that users with local administrative access can manually hack the Registry and return their systems to just about however they want. Then, as I've described, Group Policy will not reapply upon background refresh, logon, or reboot. It reapplies changes only when something related to Group Policy has changed, as previously mentioned.

Windows 2000 uses the SECEDIT command to refresh Group Policy, but, as I've stated, it still won't forcefully reapply all the settings—even if the /enforce switch is used (which just forcefully reapplies security settings). Windows XP's and Windows Vista's GPUpdate command will refresh changed Group Policy as well, but its /force switch is quite powerful and will reapply all settings—even those that have not changed.

Is the Target Computer in the Correct OU? Is the Target User in the Correct OU?

This is my personal sore point. This is the one I usually check last, and it's usually what's at fault. That is, I've simply forgotten to place the user object or the computer object into the OU to which I want the GPO to apply. Therefore, the object isn't in the "scope" of where Group Policy will apply.

You can configure all the user or computer policy settings on an OU that you like, but, quite obviously, unless that user or computer object is actually *in* the OU, the target computer will simply not receive the message you're sending. And, no, you cannot just move a security group that contains the user or computer objects and plunk it in the desired OU. Group Policy doesn't work that way. That actual user or computer object needs to be in the site, domain, or OU that the GPO applies! And since no two objects can be in any two OUs at the same time, this can be a challenge.

 Security groups are irrelevant—except for filtering.

Is There a Firewall on (or between) Your Domain Controllers?

Windows XP/SP2 and Windows Vista get a lot of press because they ship with the firewall turned on. And now Windows Server 2008 has the firewall turned on.

But Windows 2003 (with and without SP1) *also* has a firewall. It's just that, by default, Windows 2003's firewall isn't turned *on*.

So, whatever your Domain Controllers types are, if someone has misconfigured the built-in firewall, your clients will not be able to make contact to then download the Group Policy Objects.

Note that on Windows Server 2008, your Domain Controllers should automatically open up the correct ports when they're upgraded from a mere server to a Domain Controller. Though I have seen times when they haven't. In that case, you might need to remove the Active Directory "role" and reinstall it to get the ports to open properly.

Likewise, if someone has put up a hardware firewall or some other software firewall barrier between your client and your Domain Controllers and it's blocking some of the core protocols required by the client to communicate with a Domain Controller, you simply won't be able to get the Domain Controller's attention, and hence you can't download Group Policy.

Did You Disable ICMP (Ping) from Your Clients to Your Domain Controllers? (For Pre-Vista Machines)

Once a client system makes contact with a Domain Controller to download its Group Policy Objects, it then immediately does a quick "speed test" to see whether it's on a fast network or a slow network. It does this by using the ICMP protocol, more commonly described as Ping.

Before we get into what happens when clients cannot ping Domain Controllers, let's first examine why they might not be able to ping Domain Controllers:

- There's a firewall between the client and Domain Controller that prevents ICMP.

- There's a firewall on the Domain Controller itself (such as Windows 2003's firewall) that prevents ICMP.

- You have a router between the client and the Domain Controller that doesn't like the size of the ICMP test packets the client is using (2048 bytes is the default ICMP packet size used by slow link detection). Therefore, the ICMP test packets are being discarded, and it's as if they're never reaching the Domain Controller at all. Microsoft has a Knowledge Base article about this specific problem and its resolution at `http://tinyurl.com/df9bx`.

Let's examine the first two issues (which are really the same thing). That is, what if ICMP simply cannot be passed along to the Domain Controller? Perhaps a corporate decision to squash ICMP packets has been passed down, and now you just have to "handle it."

If ICMP is disabled, and slow link detection has not been disabled on the client, then no Group Policy processing will occur. It simply fails. Either you have to disable slow link detection or you need to allow ICMP to pass unrestricted between the client and the Domain Controller. Note that when slow link detection is disabled, a "fast link" is *always* assumed. With that in mind, be sure to consider the impact when software installation and folder redirection comes into play.

You can disable slow link detection by following the instructions in the Microsoft Knowledge Base article at `http://support.microsoft.com/kb/227260/en-us`.

Did Someone Muck with the ACLs of the GPT Part of the GPO in SYSVOL?

There is very, very little reason to ever need to manually dig into the guts of the GPO within SYSVOL (that's the GPT part) and manually manipulate the file ACLs. However, uninitiated administrators will sometimes play—to nasty consequences. And, as stated earlier, `Gpotool /checkacl` won't actually validate the file ACLs on the GPO's GPT parts. In other words, if the ACLs on the GPT are damaged, your best bet is to whack the GPO and restore from backup. The restore process should create the GPO with the correct ACLs upon its re-creation. You can also try using the GPMC to simply make a modification to a damaged GPO's ACLs. Any change will do. By doing so, this can sometimes "re-synchronize" the ACLs on the GPC and GPT, though it depends upon how badly the GPT's ACLs have been modified as to whether this method will work.

Client-Side Troubleshooting

One of the most important skills to master is the ability to determine what's going on at the client. By and large, the Group Policy Results tool, which you run from the GPMC, should give you what you need. However, occasionally, only trotting out to the client can truly determine what is happening on your client systems.

You could be roaming the halls, just trying to get the last Krispy Kreme glazed doughnut from the break room, when someone snags you and plops you in their seat for a little impromptu troubleshooting session. They want you to figure out why Group Policy isn't the same today as it was yesterday or why they're suddenly getting new or different settings.

This section will describe the various means for determining the RSoP (Resultant Set of Policy) while sitting at a client or using some remote-control mechanism such as Microsoft SMS (Systems Management Server), VNC (Virtual Networking Client), or even, in the case of Windows XP or Windows Vista, Remote Desktop (or Remote Assistance).

As you saw in Chapter 4, the GPMC has two tools to help you tap into this data: Group Policy Results and Group Policy Modeling. However, there are other client-side tools at your disposal. Additionally, I'll describe how to leverage a function in Windows XP, Windows 2003, and Windows Vista to determine a target user's and computer's RSoP remotely!

Let me add a word about Group Policy troubleshooting technique before you run off and try to troubleshoot things. There is a good progression to things that is worth following:

- The first step you should take is to use the RSoP capabilities I describe in the next sections to make sure you know what's happening—which GPOs are applying, which aren't, and why.

- Once you've got that under your belt and still can't find the problem, the next step is to dive into the logs—starting with the Application Event Log on the problem client.

- Then proceed to the `userenv.log` file for Windows XP (described in the section "Advanced Group Policy Troubleshooting with Log Files") or the Group Policy Event Logs for Windows Vista (also described in section the "Leveraging Vista and Windows Server 2008 Admin Logs for Troubleshooting" later).

- If `userenv.log` doesn't yield results, and you still can't find the problem, progress to CSE-specific logs.

This approach will minimize the time you spend solving a problem and leaves the most complex troubleshooting tasks as a last resort.

RSoP for Windows 2000

If you're sitting at a Windows 2000 machine, there aren't a lot of options to help you determine the RSoP. However, one particular tool can really bring home the bacon—`GPResult.exe`. This is one of the most important tools for Group Policy troubleshooting. When the going gets tough and I can't figure out what's going on, I look to `GPResult` to help tell me the score. You'll find `GPResult` in the Windows 2000 Server Resource Kit, but it is also built into the Windows 2000 Service Pack 4 and is in `C:\Windows\system32`.

The main goal of GPResult is to expose which GPOs are applied from where and the settings. The Achilles heel of GPResult on Windows 2000 is that it *must* be run on the client experiencing the problem.

GPResult appears only on the Windows 2000 installations on which Service Pack 4 was installed *after* the machine was installed. GPResult will not appear if a slipstreamed Windows 2000 with SP4 was used to create a machine fresh. This is a bug in the definition of the service pack and is subject to change in future service packs. You can just expand GPResult.exe from the service pack files and plunk it in the C:\windows\system32 folder without any penalty.

If you can set up a Telnet server on a client system, you can telnet to the client and then run GPResult as if you were at the client. This could save you a hike or two. However, you'll need to log on with the credentials of the user (not of the local administrator) to get the same results. Note that Telnet passwords are usually cleartext, which can be a bad, bad thing if someone sniffs the wire.

GPResult has three modes—normal, verbose, and super-verbose—and can expose the user settings, the computer settings, or, by default, both. If you don't have Windows 2000 SP4 loaded, you can copy GPResult onto a floppy (from an SP4 installation or from the resource kit) or run it over the network.

Although GPResult is powerful, it has a limited set of options:

- /v displays verbose output. In the next section, you'll see an example of verbose output.

- /s displays super-verbose output. This equates to the new /z option in GPResult for Windows XP, Windows Server 2003, Windows Vista, and Windows Server 2008. Again, I'll discuss how you might use this in the next section.

- /c limits the output to the computer-side policy settings. This equates to the /scope computer option with newer editions of GPResult.

- /u limits the output to the user-side policy settings. This equates to the /scope user option with newer editions of GPResult.

You can mix and match the options. For instance, to display verbose output for the computer section, you can run GPResult /v /c.

We'll explore GPResult in depth in the next section, but, due to space concerns, I'll describe it mostly from a Windows XP and Windows Vista perspective.

The Windows 2000 GPResult isn't nearly as feature rich as its Windows XP, Windows Vista, Windows 2003, or Windows Server 2008 counterpart (for example, it will not show you detailed security policy results), but, as you'll soon see, there is still life in the Windows 2000 version.

RSoP for Windows Server 2008, Windows Vista, Windows 2003, and Windows XP

Windows Vista, Windows XP, and Windows 2003 greatly expand our capacity to determine the RSoP of client machines and users on those machines. In this section, we'll explore several options. The first stop is a grown-up GPResult to help us get to the bottom of what's happening on our client machines. It should be noted that GPResult provides the same information as the GPMC's Group Policy Results Wizard, which can be used to generate the same data if a graphical tool is desired over the GPResult command-line variety.

GPResult for Windows 2003, Windows Vista RTM, and Windows XP

GPResult for Windows Vista, Windows 2003, and Windows XP is more advanced than its Windows 2000 counterpart because it relies on the WMI-based RSoP infrastructure that was added in these newer operating systems. Indeed, you can run GPResult when you're sitting at a user's desktop or at your own desktop, or you can run it remotely and pretend to be that user. If you're running it while sitting at someone's desktop, you'll likely use the following options:

- /v is for verbose mode. It presents the most meaningful information.

- /z is for zuper, er, super-verbose mode. Based on the types of policy settings that affect the user or computer, it displays way more information than you'll likely ever want to see.

- /scope user limits the output to the user-side policy settings, and /scope computer limits the output to the computer-side policy settings.

> There was a change in GPResult.exe for Windows Vista. Namely, as a regular, nonelevated user running GPResult.exe in Vista, you will get only user-side results from the tool. If you attempt to report on computer-side settings, you will get an Access Denied error until you run the command in an elevated context. Note that you could delegate specific users or groups the right to read this data using the GPMC.

You can mix and match the options. For instance, to display verbose output for the user section, you can run GPResult /v /scope user.

GPResult for Windows Vista + SP1 and Windows Server 2008

GPResult for Windows Vista + SP1 and Windows Server 2008 acts a little differently. You can't just type a single gpresult.exe at a command prompt to get data. That's right. One minute you're running plain ol' GPResult on your Windows Vista machine, and now you must run gpresult.exe /R to return the same data.

That's our pals at Microsoft. Just keeping us on our toes.

But the good news is that there are also two new output options.

GPResult /H:File.html will output the results as HTML to a file named File.html and GPResult /X:File.xml will output the results as XML to a file name.

Note at no time will GPResult show the contents of the Group Policy Preference Extensions data. More on this in Chapter 10, the Group Policy Preference Extensions chapter.

GPResult in a Windows Vista World

There is one special note about running GPResult for Windows Vista. That is, if you try to run it as a regular user to get your RSoP data, you'll only be able to see the user-side settings. Why? Because that's all you have access to in this more-secure Windows Vista world. To address this, you have two choices.

Choice 1 Run GPResult twice: once as the user in question, and again as an admin. (You run GPResult as an admin by running a command prompt as an administrative user.) This way, you take the user-side RSoP (that you just ran as the user) and the computer-side RSoP (that you just ran as an administrative user). Then, both of those halves make up the genuine RSoP. Frustrating, but necessary with the way Windows Vista security prevents regular users from seeing this. What makes this more frustrating is that if you've never logged in to a particular client machine as that administrator, you get an error from GPResult that expresses that there is no RSoP data for that admin. So, in the following shot, we're logged in as Joe User trying to get his RSoP data (top window). As stated, the computer side is inaccessible to him by default. So, we perform the runas command to get our own command-line window as the Administrator (bottom window). To counter, we then run GPResult /scope:computer. We still get an error about the *user* side not having data (bottom window), even though we simply want the *computer* side of the equation. Frustrating to the max.

Choice 2 Use the GPMC to delegate users the ability to see their own computer-side RSoP data. Again, this isn't permitted by default in a Vista world. This works just fine for pre-Vista machines. So, in my opinion, there's very little reason not to just permit the user to see it. Assuming you wanted to permit everyone in the domain to see their own RSoP data, we need to review how to perform delegation (discussed in Chapter 4). If we wanted to perform this delegation, we would use the GPMC, click the domain level, click the Delegation tab. In the Permission drop-down, we would select "Read Group Policy Results data," then add in Authenticated Users (or modify the rights over the Domain Users group, which is always already listed) and select to apply to "This container and all child containers."

You can see a screen shot of this here.

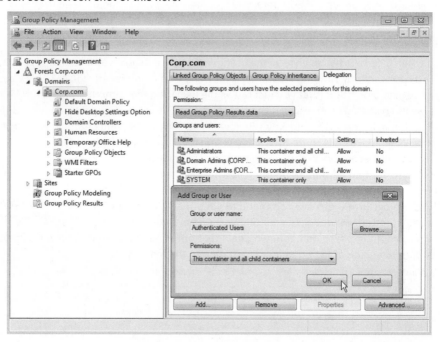

In this little sidebar we talked about what it takes to get the RSoP of a machine if we're physically sitting down at it. It's a totally different story if you're looking to get this data remotely, from another machine. And the equation gets even more intense if you're looking to delegate rights to a nonadministrative user (like someone on the help desk). A little later in this chapter, we review how to successfully retrieve Group Policy Results and Group Policy Modeling data as a nonadmin user. Be sure to read those sections to get the full picture or you'll be left out in the cold wondering why you're getting Access Denied messages.

Those sections are "Remotely Calculating a Client's RSoP (When You've Delegated Permissions to Someone Who's Not a Local Administrator of the Target Machine)" and "Remotely Calculating a Client's Group Policy Modeling Analysis Data (When You've Delegated Permissions to Someone Who's Not a Local Administrator of the Target Machine)."

Here's the result of running GPResult with no arguments while logged on to the XPPRO1 workstation (which is in the **Human Resources Computers** OU) as Frank Rizzo (who is in the **Human Resources Users** OU). I have slightly modified the output for formatting purposes. Note that some of the display might be somewhat different from yours.

```
Microsoft (R) Windows (R) XP Operating System Group Policy Result tool v2.0
Copyright (C) Microsoft Corp. 1981-2001


Created On 12/30/2007 at 10:00:40 PM


RSOP results for CORP\frizzo on XPPRO1 : Logging Mode
-------------------------------------------------------


OS Type:                  Microsoft Windows XP Professional
OS Configuration:         Member Workstation
OS Version:               5.1.2600
Domain Name:              CORP
Domain Type:              Windows 2000
Site Name:                Default-First-Site-Name
Roaming Profile:
Local Profile:            C:\Documents and Settings\frizzo
Connected over a slow link?: No


COMPUTER SETTINGS
------------------
    CN=XPPRO1,OU=Human Resources Computers,OU=Human Resources,DC=CORP,DC=COM
    Last time Group Policy was applied: 12/30/2007 at 9:58:06 PM
    Group Policy was applied from:     dc01.CORP.COM
    Group Policy slow link threshold:  500 kbps


    Applied Group Policy Objects
    ----------------------------
        Auto-Launch calc.exe
        Default Domain Policy


    The following GPOs were not applied because they were filtered out
    ------------------------------------------------------------------
        Hide Desktop Settings Option
            Filtering:  Not Applied (Empty)
```

```
      Hide Screen Saver Option
            Filtering:  Not Applied (Empty)

      Local Group Policy
            Filtering:  Not Applied (Empty)


The computer is a part of the following security groups:
----------------------------------------------------------
      BUILTIN\Administrators
      Everyone
      BUILTIN\Users
      XPPRO1$
      Computers-That-Get-the-Auto-Launch Calc.exe-GPO
      Domain Computers
      NT AUTHORITY\NETWORK
      NT AUTHORITY\Authenticated Users



USER SETTINGS
--------------
      CN=Frank Rizzo,OU=Human Resources Users,OU=Human Resources,DC=CORP,DC=COM
      Last time Group Policy was applied: 12/30/2007 at 9:59:44 PM
      Group Policy was applied from:       dc01.CORP.COM
      Group Policy slow link threshold:    500 kbps


      Applied Group Policy Objects
      ----------------------------
            Hide Display Settings Option/Restore Screen Saver Option
            Default Domain Policy
            Hide Desktop Settings Option
            Hide Screen Saver Option
            Local Group Policy


The user is a part of the following security groups:
----------------------------------------------------
      Domain Users
      Everyone
      BUILTIN\Users
      LOCAL
      NT AUTHORITY\INTERACTIVE
      NT AUTHORITY\Authenticated Users
```

You can redirect the output to a text file with GPResult > filename.txt.

You can glean all sorts of juicy tidbits from GPResult. Here are the key areas to inspect when troubleshooting client RSoP:

- Find the "Applied Group Policy Objects" entries for both the user and computer. Remember that Group Policy is applied from the local computer first, then the site level, then the domain level, and then each nested OU. If a setting is unexpected on the client, simply use the provided information along with the Group Policy Object Editor to start tracking the errant GPO.

- Use the "Last time Group Policy was applied:" entry to check to see the last time the GPO was applied—via either initial or background refresh processing. Use GPUpdate to refresh this, and then ensure that the value is updated when you rerun GPResult.

- Use the spelled-out distinguished name of the computer and user objects (for example, CN=Frank Rizzo, OU=Human Resources Users, DC=corp, and DC=com) to verify that the user and computer objects are located where you think they should be in Active Directory. If they are not, verify the location of the user and computer accounts using Active Directory Users and Computers. You might need to reboot this client machine if the location in Active Directory doesn't check out.

- Use "The user is a part of the following security groups" and "The computer is a part of the following security groups" sections to verify that the user or computer is in the groups you expect. Perhaps your user or computer object is inside a group that is denied access to either the "Read" or "Apply Group Policy" permissions on the GPO you were expecting. Note that if you make a change to a computer's security group membership, Group Policy will not pick up that change unless you reboot the computer. There is no way around this, unfortunately. The same holds true for user group changes—the user will need to re–log on before the security group changes take.

- Find the "Connected over a slow link?" entry for the log and the "Group Policy slow link threshold" entries for both the user and computer. Remember that the various areas of Group Policy are processed differently when coming over slow links. (See Chapters 4 and various chapters in the companion book, *Implementing the Secure and Managed Desktop*.)

- Find the section "The following GPOs were not applied because they were filtered out" for both the user and the computer halves. If you have GPOs listed here, the user or computer was, in fact, in the site, domain, or OU that the GPO was supposed to apply to. However, the GPOs listed here have not applied this user or computer for a variety of reasons. GPResult can tell you why this has happened. Here are some of the common reasons:

Denied (Security)   The user or computer has been explicitly denied "Read" and "Apply Group Policy" rights to process the GPO. For instance, in the previous example, the "Auto-Launch Calc.exe" doesn't apply to XPPRO1 because in Chapter 2, we explicitly denied the XPPRO1 computer object the ability to process the "Apply Group Policy" attribute.

Not Applied (Empty) This GPO doesn't have any policy settings set in the user or computer half. For instance, in the previous example, the "Hide Desktop Settings Option" GPO doesn't have any computer-side policy settings. Hence, this GPO doesn't apply to Frank's computer object. Specifically, here the Group Policy engine is seeing that the number of revisions for either the user or computer half is 0. This is tied to the version number of the GPO, so if the version number is not updated correctly when a GPO change is made, the GPO could be mistakenly viewed as empty.

Not Applied (Unknown Reason) Usually Block Inheritance has been used, or the user doesn't have rights to read the GPO (though other, truly "unknown reasons" could also be valid). In the previous example, the "Hide Screen Saver Option," which is set at the site level, won't apply to Frank because we've blocked inheritance at the **Human Resources** OU.

Three Different *GPResult*s—Three Different Outputs!

If you want to take GPResult to the next level, use it with the /v switch. You can then see which Registry settings are specifically being altered by the GPOs. This could be useful if you want to manually dive into the Registry and perform the same punch the policy setting is doing on a machine that isn't connected to Active Directory and see if you get the same results.

However, running GPResult /v on Windows 2000, Windows XP, Windows 2003, Windows Server 2008, or Windows Vista can return different outputs. For the sake of brevity, here are three comparison snippets to illustrate some additional information possible with GPResult /v. This output has been taken out to show you some specific details and also formatted slightly for readability.

GPResult /v for Windows XP is the least useful. When you run it, you'll get output similar to the following.

```
Administrative Templates
GPO: Hide Desktop Settings Option
Setting: Software\Microsoft\Windows\CurrentVersion\Policies\System
State:   Enabled
```

This output merely tells you that the GPO "Hide Desktop Settings Option" manipulates a Registry key somewhere in the path specified in the Setting field. Whoopie.

When you run the command on a Windows Server 2008, Windows 2003, or Windows Vista computer, you get the following:

```
Administrative Templates
-----------------------
GPO: Hide Desktop Settings Option
KeyName: Software\Microsoft\Windows\CurrentVersion\Policies\
System\NoDispBackgroundPage
Value: 1, 0, 0, 0
State: Enabled
```

This output is more useful, because it shows you that it's the `NoDispBackroundPage` Registry entry with the value of 1 in the Registry that is performing the function. I'm guessing the difference in output between Windows XP and Windows 2003 and Windows Vista is just a `GPResult` bug. But the point is that with `GPResult` on Windows XP, the output displayed is, in fact, not as useful as the output from the other operating systems.

However, the most useful `GPResult /v` output comes from the `GPResult` in the Windows 2000 Resource Kit! (Yes! Windows 2000!)

```
The user received "Registry" settings from these GPOs:
    Hide Desktop Settings Option
        Revision Number:    3
        Unique Name:    {1ABE8B36-66A0-4DF0-80D0-A9B4A8C34DB1}
        Domain Name:    corp.com
        Linked to:    Domain (DC=corp,DC=com)
    The following settings were applied from: Hide Desktop Settings Option
        KeyName:    Software\Microsoft\Windows\CurrentVersion\Policies\System
        ValueName:    NoDispBackgroundPage
        ValueType:    REG_DWORD
        Value:    0x00000001
```

The Windows 2000 `GPResult /v` shows you the `ValueName` (like the Windows 2003 version), but it also shows you the `ValueType` (REG_DWORD). Additionally, it can also easily show you the association between the GPO friendly name (say, "Hide Desktop Settings Option") and the GUID (in my case, {1ABE8B36-66A0-4DF0-80D0-A9B4A8C34DB1}). You might need this information later with other tools such as the Event Viewer, which may or may not use the friendly name.

So my advice? The `GPResult` built into Windows XP, Windows 2003, and Windows Vista is much better for basic troubleshooting. Its output describing *why* specific GPOs are not being processed is excellent. However, keep a copy of the Windows 2000 version of `GPResult` handy. It runs just fine on Windows XP and Windows 2003 and Windows Vista machines, and, because of its additional functions in displaying both the Registry and the GPO GUID, you can get a lot closer to knowing *what* has been changed.

Remotely Calculating a Client's RSoP (Using the *GPResult* from Windows XP+)

The Windows 2000 version of `GPResult` doesn't work the way the Windows XP, Windows Vista, and Windows 2003 version does. The Windows XP, Windows Vista, Windows 2003, and Windows 2008 version of `GPResult` has a secret weapon tucked up its sleeve. You can almost hear it say, "Are you talkin' to me?"

Its weapon is that it can tap into the WMI provider built into those operating systems. `GPResult` is like the GPMC's Group Policy Results Wizard. That is, it can be run from any Windows XP, Windows Vista, Windows 2003, or Windows 2008 machine, and provided the target machine is turned on, the system can collect information about any particular user who has ever logged on locally. It's then a simple matter of displaying the results. You simply run GPResult, point it to a system, and provide the name of the user whose RSoP data you wish to collect.

This magic only works on Windows XP and higher machines, as both source computers and target computers. Windows 2000 computers don't have a tap into this WMI magic, so they can't play.

There are two more important cautions here (which I talked about in the section "*GPResult* for Windows 2003, Windows Vista RTM, and Windows XP,", but they bear repeating). That is, this magic works only if the target user has ever logged on to the target machine. They only need to have logged on just once, and they don't even need to be logged on while you run the test. But if the target user has *never* logged on to the target machine, remotely calculating GPResult for that user will fail. Additionally, remotely trying to get a Windows XP/Service Pack 2 or Windows Vista computer's RSoP via GPResult will fail if the Windows Firewall is enabled.

As described in Chapter 2, either turn off the Windows Firewall or enable the Windows XP/ Service Pack 2 policy setting titled **Windows Firewall: Allow Inbound Remote Administration Exception,** which can be located in Computer Configuration ➢ Policies ➢ Administrative Templates ➢ Network ➢ Network Connections ➢ Windows Firewall ➢ Domain (or Standard) Profile. This setting does affect both Windows XP/SP2 and Windows Vista machines.

Or, for your Windows Vista clients, you can really be gung ho and use the new Windows Firewall with Advanced Security (which you'll learn about in Chapter 9), which of course has an alternate method only for Windows Vista.

This would be found under Computer Configuration ➢ Policies ➢ Windows Settings ➢ Security Settings ➢ Windows Firewall with Advanced Security ➢Inbound Rules.

With that in mind, here are your additional Windows XP, Windows Vista, and Windows 2003 GPResult options:

- /s <target system name or IP address> points to the target system.

- /user <optional domain\username> collects RSoP data for the target user.

You can combine any of the aforementioned GPResult switches as well. If you log on to DC01 and want to see only the user-side policy settings when Frank Rizzo logs on to XPPRO1, type the following:

```
gpresult /user frizzo /s xppro1 /scope:user
```

Again, this command succeeds only if Frank has ever logged on to XPPRO1 (which he has).

GPResult is much better at telling you *why* a GPO is applying rather than *what* specific policy settings are contained within a GPO. For instance, notice that at no time did GPResult tell us what policy settings were contained in the local GPO. And, even when we performed a GPResult /v, we only found out the Registry keys that were modified—not the proper name of the specific policy setting that is doing the work. For these tasks, we'll need to use the GPMC (as seen in Chapter 2) or the RSoP snap-in (described in a bit in the section "Two Antiquated Ways of Getting RSOP Results That No One Should Use (Usually)").

Remotely Calculating a Client's RSoP (When You've Delegated Permissions to Someone Who's Not a Local Administrator of the Target Machine)

In Chapter 2 (and to a lesser extent in this chapter), we talked about the idea of opening up the Windows XP or Windows Vista firewall to **Windows Firewall: Allow Inbound Remote Administration Exception**. Again, this policy setting is located in Computer Configuration ➢ Policies ➢ Windows Firewall ➢ Domain Profile.

The idea is that you can't remotely grab an RSoP using either `GPResult.exe` or the GPMC's Group Policy Results Wizard without being able to communicate to the WMI provider on the target machine. To do this, at minimum you need to open up ports 135 and 445, which is precisely what this particular policy setting will do on a computer.

But, there's a little twist (which we've already discussed). That is, you need rights to view the RSoP data. Now, if you're a local administrator on the target machine, you already have all the rights you need. You just needed to open up that firewall enough to get that data.

But, if you want to delegate rights to, say, the help desk (or another nonadministrative group), you do, in fact, need an extra boost to ensure that they can read the RSoP data. (If you need a refresher on how to delegate the permission in the first place, be sure to read Chapter 2's section entitled "Special Group Policy Operation Delegations.") Again, this area is located in the Delegation tab on the OU (or domain or site) you want to delegate rights to.

Once you've performed the delegation of the "Read Group Policy Results data" right upon the user and/or computer you want, you also need to perform these very important additional delegation steps. (Again, these steps are required only if you've delegated this ability to a non-administrator of the target machine.)

For instance, let's assume that Tom User (from the help desk) needs access to read Group Policy Results data from a computer that Brett Wier is using (Vista1.corp.com). First, you delegate rights over the OU that Vista1.corp.com is in such that Tom can "Read Group Policy Results data." But even if you do that, as soon as Tom tries to run the Group Policy Results Wizard, he gets an "Access is denied" message as seen in Figure 6.22.

FIGURE 6.22   Tom doesn't have access to run Group Policy Results against machines for which he isn't also a local administrator.

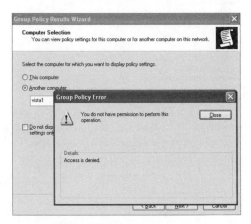

To open it up a little (and decrease your security a little, too), you'll need to create and link a GPO that affects the target computer's OU. Then, make sure the following policy settings are enabled within that GPO:

1. We already covered this one, but just to be sure you have it in place: Computer Configuration ➤ Policies ➤ Administrative Templates ➤ Network Connections ➤ Windows Firewall ➤ Domain Profile ➤ **Windows Firewall: Allow Inbound Remote Administration Exception**. Choose which subnets to allow inbound requests from (or specify * to allow all subnets).

2. Computer Configuration ➤ Policies ➤ Windows Settings ➤ Security Settings ➤ Local Policies ➤ Security Options ➤ **DCOM: Machine Access Restrictions in SDDL syntax**. When you edit the policy setting, you'll first select "Define this policy setting," then click Edit Security, add in Tom User, and specify to allow Remote Access. When you do this, a security descriptor is (thankfully) automatically built, like O:BAG:BAD:(A;;CDCLC;;;) and is usually quite long. You can see a screen shot of this in Figure 6.23 (though the security descriptor isn't in the screen shot, because I haven't hit OK yet).

3. Computer Configuration ➤ Policies ➤ Windows Settings ➤ Security Settings ➤ Local Policies ➤ Security Options ➤ **DCOM: Machine Launch Restrictions in SDDL syntax**. Again, be sure to click "Define this policy setting." Then, add in the same person (Tom User) and grant the "Remote Launch: Allow" and "Remote Activation: Allow" rights.

Since you've changed the computer-side settings, be sure to run `gpupdate /force` on the target machine (or just reboot it).

When you do, you'll give nonadministrative users the ability to read another computer's RSoP data using the GPMC's Group Policy Results Wizard.

FIGURE 6.23 For each DCOM permission, add in the delegated user and specify they have Remote Access: Allow permissions.

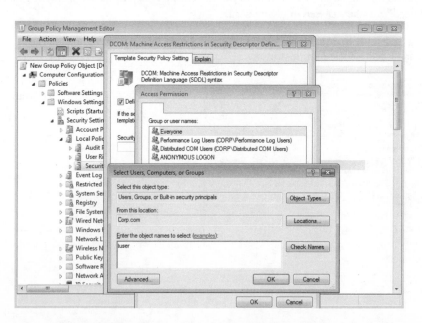

After these steps are performed, you've delegated a user (or group, like the Help Desk) and have now enabled the ability to "reach out" and see what's going on at other machines—even if they're not a local admin. Don't forget about the golden rule here, though: If the target machine's firewall is blocking your incoming request, even though you've now delegated the permission, it still ain't gonna work.

Remotely Calculating a Client's Group Policy Modeling Analysis Data (When You've Delegated Permissions to Someone Who's Not a Local Administrator of the Target Machine)

This is a similar situation to what we encountered before. Imagine you've given Tom User from the help desk the rights to "Perform Group Policy Modeling analyses." If you need a refresher on how to delegate the permission in the first place, be sure to read Chapter 2's section entitled "Special Group Policy Operation Delegations." Be sure to delegate the permission upon both the OUs that contain the user and computer accounts or you'll be stuck with seeing only half the results data. However, just performing the delegation steps aren't enough—you'll still get an Access Denied message from the Group Policy Modeling Wizard as soon as you try to pick the Windows Server 2003 Domain Controller on which to perform the calculations.

So, since Windows Server 2003/SP1, the default security for DCOM permissions has changed, requiring changes akin to what you saw in the previous section. But, here's the trick: You're not modifying the target computer's DCOM settings; you're modifying the Windows Server 2003/SP1's Domain Controller settings. To do this, create and link a GPO on the **Domain Controllers** OU. I suggest you *don't* modify the default Domain Controller for this purpose, though it would work just fine. Then, modify the GPO as follows:

1. Computer Configuration ➢ Policies ➢ Windows Settings ➢ Security Settings ➢ Local Policies ➢ Security Options ➢ **DCOM: Machine Access Restrictions in SDDL syntax**. When you edit the policy setting, you'll first select "Define this policy setting," then click Edit Security, add in Tom User, and specify to allow Remote Access. When you do this, a security descriptor is (thankfully) automatically built, like O:BAG:BAD:(A;;CDCLC;;;) and is usually quite long. You can see a screen shot of this in Figure 6.23.

2. Computer Configuration ➢ Policies ➢ Windows Settings ➢ Security Settings ➢ Local Policies ➢ Security Options ➢ **DCOM: Machine Launch Restrictions in SDDL syntax**. Again, be sure to click "Define this policy setting." Then, add in the same person (Tom User) and grant the "Remote Launch: Allow" and "Remote Activation: Allow" rights.

Now, Tom User from the help desk can see Brett Wier (and Brett's computer) Group Policy Analysis data using the Group Policy Modeling Wizard.

Two Antiquated Ways of Getting RSOP Results That No One Should Use (Usually)

The GPMC or GPResults.exe is going to be the way to get the most out of performing an RSoP. However, there are two older tools, which you can feel free to explore on your own but not use in "real life."

Tool #1: Windows XP's Group Policy "Help and Support System" RSoP Tool

I think the intent behind this tool was good. That is, if a user had some issue with their machine, you could walk them through getting a graphical RSoP and then have them read it back to you over the phone. When you're done laughing at that, give this a try, for old times' sake.

To launch the Windows XP Group Policy "Help and Support System" RSoP tool, otherwise just known as the GUI RSoP tool, choose Start ⮞ Help and Support to open Help and Support Center. Then click "Get support, or find information in Windows XP newsgroups." Next, click "Advanced System Information." Finally, select "View Group Policy settings applied."

You'll see the many sections of user and computer Group Policy in the GUI RSoP tool. On Windows XP, this tool is, in some ways, superior to GPResult because you can see which Registry keys are being modified by Active Directory GPOs and also what's going on inside the local GPO. Although this tool does provide the names of the GPOs that apply, it doesn't address *why* GPOs are or are not applying, as GPResult does. So, a yin and yang approach with both the GPResult and the GUI RSoP tools may be needed to get the whole story.

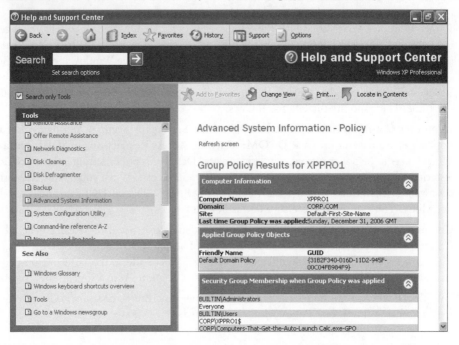

At the bottom of the GUI RSoP, you'll see an option to save the report to an HTML file. The default location is C:\, but nonadministrators cannot save files here. If users save to an HTML file, be sure they have permission for the folder.

I have found that the results data this produces is not always 100 percent accurate.

Tool #2: The RSoP MMC Snap-In

Yet another tool can help you determine the RSoP of the client. Technically, this tool is named the RSoP MMC snap-in. This tool has, more or less, been rendered obsolete by the reports you get from the GPMC.

And, here's a real kicker: The tool ships in the box for Windows Vista and Windows Server 2008, but it hasn't been updated since Windows XP.

I'm showing you how to use the tool here only for reference and completeness. Again, in Vista, this tool is not to be used; it won't work properly and the results you get from it could be bogus.

Here's how to use the RSoP MMC.

1. Choose Start ➤ Run to open the Run dialog box. In the Open box, enter **MMC** and press Enter to open the MMC.

2. Choose File ➤ Add/Remove Snap-in.

3. Click Add to see the list of snap-ins and select Resultant Set of Policy to start the Resultant Set of Policy Wizard.

4. Click Next to open the Mode Selection screen. If you're running Windows XP, or Windows Vista, only Logging mode (the equivalent of Group Policy Results) is available. If you've got at least one Windows 2003 Domain Controller in your forest, Planning mode (the equivalent of Group Policy Modeling) is also listed.

5. You'll then specify to perform the calculation on this computer or another Windows XP, Windows Vista, or Windows 2003 computer.

6. Next, you'll select the user; you can pretend to log on as any user who has logged on to the machine at least one time before. Note that you won't be able to "pretend" to log on as just anyone unless you're *really* logged in as someone with Administrator rights on the target machine.

7. Once the parameters are plugged in (which user on what computer), you can click Next.

Note that you can also simply run RSOP.MSC from Start ➤ Run and get immediate RSoP results of the logged-in user on the computer.

The RSoP MMC snap-in tool does have one goodie that its bigger brother, the GPMC, does not have. That is, besides showing the "winning" GPO, it also lets you know the "losing" GPOs. After you complete the wizard and close the open screens, the RSoP you just calculated will appear in its own window, similar to what is seen in the image below.

Note, alternatively, that you can just run RSOP.MSC instead of just adding in the specific user and computer you wanted. Running RSOP.MSC at a command prompt will show you the current user on the current computer.

The RSoP snap-in will show you only the policy settings that are set and which GPOs they are coming from: local, site, domain, or OU, as shown next.

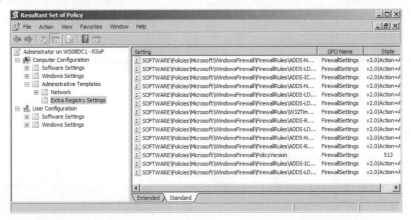

The problem with the RSoP snap-in, is, again, it has not been updated since Windows XP. This means that any new whiz-bang Windows Vista and Windows Server 2008 features aren't reported correctly.

In the screen shot above, you can see what happens if you set Windows Vista firewall settings. The RSoP snap-in doesn't know how to "interpret" them and hence displays them as "Extra Registry Settings." Additionally, the new Group Policy Preference Extensions (which we talk about in Chapter 10) just plain don't show up here at all!

The only good, modern reason to use RSoP is if a third-party tool vendor suggests that you use it to get RSoP data from its tool. In short, most third-party Group Policy tools cannot utilize the settings reports within the GPMC, and the RSoP is the only valid way a third-party tool vendor can hook in to leverage any kinds of results reporting.

Advanced Group Policy Troubleshooting with Log Files

We've already explored some of the techniques to troubleshoot Group Policy application. You can enable some underlying operating system troubleshooting tools to help diagnose just what the heck is going on when the unexpected occurs.

Using the Event Viewer

Quite possibly, the most overlooked and underutilized tool in Windows is the Event Viewer. The client's Event Viewer logs both the successful and unsuccessful application of Group Policy (see Figure 6.24).

Before beating your head against the wall, check the client's Event Log for relevant Group Policy records. The Event Log in Windows XP and Windows 2003 spits out much more information and many more warnings than did the Event Log in Windows 2000—so take advantage of it.

In Windows Vista, the Event Log takes on a whole new importance with respect to Group Policy troubleshooting. In fact, as we talk in this section about logs that are useful in troubleshooting, we'll talk about how this all changes in a Windows Vista world.

In Figure 6.24, the Event Log returned an error code of 1053. Doing a quick search in Microsoft TechNet, you can find a related Windows 2000 article, Q261007, which shows that the client is pointing to an incorrect DNS server. Again, search the Microsoft Knowledge Base when you find an event that might be at fault. You might find a hidden gem there—just perfectly ready to solve your problem.

FIGURE 6.24   The Event Viewer is a terrific place to start your troubleshooting journey.

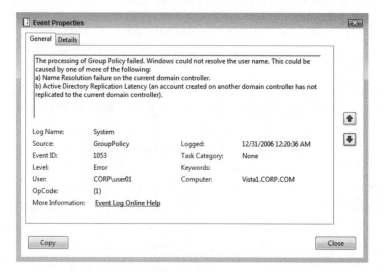

Diagnostic Event Logging (for Pre-Vista Machines Only)

If you really want to go bananas, you can enable *diagnostic logging* to supercharge your Event Log in Windows 2000, Windows XP, and Windows 2003. To do so, a Registry key to the client machine must be created. Traverse to `HKEY_Local_Machine\Software\Microsoft\Windows NT\CurrentVersion`. Create a Diagnostics key, but leave the Class entry empty. You can specify logging types by creating one of two `REG_DWORD` keys:

`RunDiagnosticLoggingGroupPolicy`   Create this `REG_DWORD` to log only Group Policy events. To enable logging, set the data value to 1. Log entries appear in the Application Log.

`AppMgmtDebugLevel`   Create this `REG_DWORD`, but do so with a data value of 4b in hexadecimal. At the next targeted software deployment, you'll find a log in the local `\windows\debug\usermode` folder named `appmgmt.log`, which can also aid in troubleshooting why applications fail to load.

WARNING Some older Microsoft documentation also shows `RunDiagnosticLogging-IntelliMirror` and `RunDiagnosticLoggingAppDeploy` keys as viable options for the Diagnostics key. These entries are apparently documentation bugs and do absolutely nothing in Windows.

When you've finished debugging, delete the Diagnostic keys so your Event Logs don't fill up.

Diagnostic Event Logging (for Vista and Windows Server 2008)

In Windows Vista and Windows Server 2008, Event Log entries related to Group Policy have changed significantly. First of all, Group Policy–related events have moved from the Application to the System Log. The system generates Group Policy events with an event source of (who woulda guessed?) GroupPolicy, as shown in Figure 6.25.

FIGURE 6.25   Viewing the Windows Vista System log and Group Policy Events

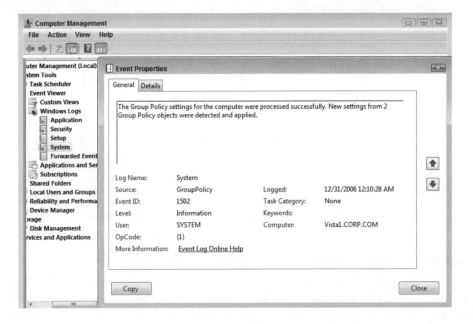

The logging of Group Policy events in Vista and Windows Server 2008 is on by default, so you don't need to enable anything specifically. You can simply filter events in this log with a source of GroupPolicy and get a snapshot of GP Processing. The events recorded in this log related to Group Policy are really a summary of each processing event—they tell you things like whether Group Policy processing proceeded successfully, which Domain Controller was used to process policy, and how many GPOs were processed. They do not provide deep levels of detail. In the next section, we'll talk about how you can get that detail out of the Event Log in Windows Vista.

Turning On Verbose Logging

Sometimes, all the server pieces are working perfectly, but the end result on the client is cock-eyed. You can examine Group Policy step by step by turning on *verbose logging*, which goes beyond the diagnostic Event Log Registry hacks.

Verbose Logging (for Pre-Vista Machines)

When you enable verbose logging by editing the Registry at the client, you are telling the system to generate extra events in a file called USERENV.LOG in the \windows\debug\usermode folder (or \winnt\debug\usermode for Windows 2000). By default, this file is enabled in Windows XP and Server 2003 but is not set to verbose mode. You can then examine the file to see what the client thinks is really happening.

To enable verbose logging, follow these steps:

1. Log on locally to the client system as the Administrator.

2. Run REGEDIT.

3. In the Registry Editor, traverse to HKEY_Local_Machine\Software\Microsoft\ Windows NT\CurrentVersion\Winlogon.

4. In the Edit DWORD Value dialog box, add a REG_DWORD value by entering **UserEnvDebugLevel** in the Value Name box, and in the Value Data box, enter the hex value of **10002**, as shown in Figure 6.26. Click OK.

5. Close the Registry Editor.

The hex value 10002 signifies verbose logging. The hex value 10001 signifies to log only errors and warnings. The hex value 10000 doesn't log anything.

Note that after you make this entry in Windows XP or Windows 2003, verbose logging is enabled right away, but Windows 2000 often requires a reboot for the logging change to take effect. After you modify the entry, log off as the local Administrator, and log on as someone with many GPOs that would affect their user object—say, Frank Rizzo in the **Human Resources Users** OU. After logging on as Frank, you can immediately log off and back on as the Administrator for the workstation and then read the log file.

You can also hack the Registry at a command prompt. You can use the RUNAS command to run the command prompt as the Administrator. For this system, type **runas /user:XPPro1\administrator cmd**, and type the password to log on as the Administrator.

FIGURE 6.26 Verbose logging requires a hack to the Registry.

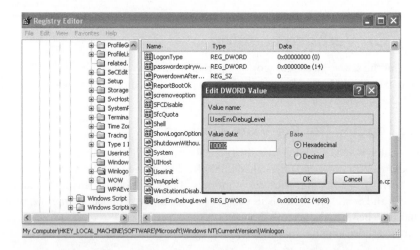

In the Userenv.log file in the \windows\debug\usermode folder, you should come across the following snippet. The output here has been truncated and formatted for better reading and for the sake of example. Additionally, line headers such as ProcessGPOs, AddGPO, and SearchDSObject have all been removed.

```
Starting user Group Policy (Background) processing...
Starting computer Group Policy (Background) processing...
User name is:  CN=Frank Rizzo,OU=Human Resources Users,OU=Human
Resources,DC=corp,DC=com,
Domain name is:  CORP
Domain controller is:  \\DC01.corp.com  Domain DN is corp.com
network name is 192.168.2.0


User name is:  CN=XPPRO1,OU=Human Resources Computers,OU=Human
Resources,DC=corp,DC=com,
Domain name is:  CORP

Domain controller is:  \\DC01.corp.com  Domain DN is corp.com
Calling GetGPOInfo for normal policy mode


No site name defined.  Skipping site policy.

Searching <OU=Human Resources Users,OU=Human Resources,DC=corp,DC=com>
Found GPO(s):
```

```
<[LDAP://cn={45E8B3A8-AB97-4480-ACE9-
B42F2B3C7EFA},cn=policies,cn=system,DC=corp,DC=com;0]>


Searching <OU=Human Resources,DC=corp,DC=com>
Found GPO(s):  < >
<OU=Human Resources,DC=corp,DC=com> has the Block From Above attribute set
Searching <DC=corp,DC=com>


Found GPO(s):
<[LDAP://cn={45E8B3A8-AB97-4480-ACE9-B42F2B3C7EFA}
},cn=policies,cn=system,DC=corp,DC=com;0][LDAP://CN=
{31B2F340-016D-11D2-945F-00C04FB984F9},CN=Policies,CN=System,DC=corp,DC=com;0]>


GPO will not be added to the list since the Block flag is set and this GPO is
not in enforce mode.



Searching
<CN={45E8B3A8-AB97-4480-ACE9-
B42F2B3C7EFA},CN=Policies,CN=System,DC=corp,DC=com>
User does not have access to the GPO and so will not be applied.
Found functionality version of:  2
Found file system path of:
<\\corp.com\SysVol\corp.com\Policies{45E8B3A8-AB97-4480-ACE9-B42F2B3C7EFA} >
Sysvol access skipped because GPO is not getting applied.
Found common name of:  < {45E8B3A8-AB97-4480-ACE9-B42F2B3C7EFA} >
Found display name of:
<Hide Display Settings Option / Restore Screen Saver Option >
Found user version of:  GPC is 2, GPT is 65535
Found flags of:  0
Found extensions:  [{35378EAC-683F-11D2-A89A-00C04FBBCFA2}{0F6B957E-509E-11D1-
    A7CC-0000F87571E3}]
```

You can learn a lot quickly by doing a little sleuthing inside the results. First, the computer is processing in Normal mode (as opposed to Loopback mode). And, while you're here, you can sniff out three back-to-back "errors" that I've detailed below.

The first error occurred due to some Active Directory site misconfiguration error. The text is clear: "No site name defined. Skipping site policy."

The second error occurred when the GPO represented by GUID {45E8B3A8-AB97-4480-ACE9-B42F2B3C7EFA} wasn't applied. This is the "Hide Desktop Settings Option" GPO we created and linked to the domain. The report states that the "GPO will not be added to the list since the Block flag is set and this GPO is not in enforce mode." This indicates that the GPO isn't being enforced while the OU level (**Human Resources**) is blocking inheritance.

The last error occurred when the GPO with the {45E8B3A8-AB97-4480-ACE9-B42F2B3C7EFA} was not applied due to "User does not have access to the GPO." In my case, the GUID matched with the "Hide Display Settings Option/Restore Screen Saver Option" GPO. Back in Chapter 2, one example denied the HR-OU-Admins security group the access to read that GPO, so it would not apply to them. Frank Rizzo is a member of the HR-OU-Admins group and, hence, does not get the GPO.

> You might also want to check out a free tool that can make the job of parsing this log a bit easier. The guys at SysProSoft have a free tool that does the hard work. Check it out at http://www.sysprosoft.com/policyreporter.shtml. It's also listed on www.GPanswers.com in the "Third-Party Solutions" guide.

Some other information you can glean from this file includes the timestamp when the event occurred. Each line of the userenv.log file includes some text that looks like the following:

```
USERENV(2b8.2bc) 09:09:57:250
```

The meaning of this is relatively straightforward. Userenv is the process under which these events are occurring. (2b8.2bc) indicates, in hexadecimal form, the process and thread ID of this particular event, and then the time shown indicates the time that this event is occurring. The time is broken down as hour:minute:second:hundreths-of-a-second. The process and thread ID tag is useful if, for example, you are troubleshooting Group Policy processing after issuing a gpupdate command. Because GPUpdate runs both computer and user processing at roughly the same time, each of these will have unique thread IDs but events will be intertwined with each other. So, you can use the thread ID to distinguish a user processing event from a computer processing one.

Additionally, the one piece of information that userenv.log will tell you (that you can't get very easily elsewhere) is the time interval until the *next* background processing update. This usually comes at the end of a given processing cycle and looks something like this:

```
USERENV(2b8.908) 09:15:41:062 GPOThread:
Next refresh will happen in 105 minutes
```

The downside to userenv.log is that it also logs user profile activity, which can really muddy up your Group Policy troubleshooting. Because of this, I usually just delete or rename the existing userenv.log file in the C:\windows\debug\usermode folder. Then, I'll run GPUpdate. When it's finished, my userenv.log file contains *only* the data from that last Group Policy processing cycle. In short, this process makes it much easier to troubleshoot.

Other Types of Verbose Logging

In addition to userenv.log, some of the individual CSEs provide their own verbose log files that you can enable with Registry tweaks. When you can't get the information you need from the Event Log or userenv.log, your next step is to try to track down the problem with one of these CSE-specific logs. While not every CSE creates its own log file, most of the important ones do, and you can use these logs to get more detailed information about a particular Group Policy area that has gone awry. The following table lists all available CSE-specific logs and Registry values needed to enable them.

Component	Location of Log	Location in Registry	Value
Security CSE	%windir%\Security\ Logs\WinLogon.log	HKLM\Software\ Microsoft\Windows NT\CurrentVersion\ Winlogon\ GPExtensions\ {827d319e-6eac-11d2-a4ea-00c04f79f83a}	ExtensionDebugLevel DWORD 2
Folder Redirection CSE	%windir%\Debug\User Mode\FDeploy.log (Windows XP and 2003 only) Windows Vista and Windows Server 2008 in Application Log.	HKLM\Software\ Microsoft\Windows NT\CurrentVersion\ Diagnostics	FDeployDebugLevel DWORD 0x0B
Software Installation CSE	%windir%\Debug\ UserMode\ AppMgmt.log	HKLM\Software\ Microsoft\Windows NT\CurrentVersion\ Diagnostics	AppMgmtDebugLevel DWORD 0x9b

> See Darren Mar-Elia's website www.GPOguy.com for a great ADM template to help automate these Registry punches, if needed, on your client machines.

Verbose Logging in Windows Vista and Windows Server 2008

Windows Vista introduced major changes to the information that the Group Policy engine provides for you to troubleshoot problems. And that same information is also now available for Windows Server 2008.

This is great news! But in order to best leverage that new data, you're going to need to know where and how to find it. This section is devoted to that task.

Windows Vista and Windows Server 2008 no longer keep verbose Group Policy logging information in userenv.log. Instead, this type of detailed logging has moved to the System Event Log—which in the context of Group Policy is referred to as the *Admin Log*—and into a new place called the *Group Policy Operational Log*.

Both of these logs leverage the new features in the code-named "Crimson" Event Log system. This is a good thing because the events logged here are now clearer and more easily collected than they were in the userenv.log file. Crimson also has some neat features, such as subscription, that I'll introduce here and that can further help with your Group Policy troubleshooting tasks. The Group Policy logs are also enabled as verbose by default, so you don't need to bother with turning on and off Event Logs with Registry hacks.

To find the Group Policy Operational Log, simply open the Event Viewer and drill into Applications and Services Logs ➤ Microsoft ➤ Windows ➤ Group Policy ➤ Operational. What you'll get is a set of events similar to those found in Figure 6.27.

FIGURE 6.27 Viewing the Group Policy Operational Log in Windows Vista and Windows Server 2008

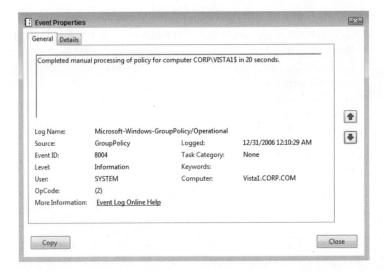

As you can see from the figure, the Group Policy Operational Log has more detailed and useful information than the userenv.log, such as the amount of time it took to process Group Policy for a user. If you're using Windows Vista or Windows Server 2008, then the Operational Log is going to be your best Group Policy friend and will provide almost all the information you need to track down Group Policy problems. I say "almost" because while Windows Vista and Windows Server 2008 made great strides in consolidating the userenv.log file into the Event Logs, the CSE-specific logs that I mentioned earlier for previous versions of Windows still exist in Windows Vista and Windows Server 2008 and are still stored in separate text files that must be explicitly enabled.

Leveraging Vista and Windows Server 2008 Admin Logs for Troubleshooting

Let's look at how you might use the Windows Vista and Windows Server 2008 Admin Log for troubleshooting a Group Policy problem.

The System Log is designed to give you high-level information about the state of the Group Policy engine. So it will tell you things such as if computer Group Policy processing succeeded or failed, but it won't necessarily tell you what happened or why (see Figure 6.28).

One other useful piece of information the Admin Log will give you is the time it took for Group Policy processing to occur. You can see this in the event in Figure 6.28 by clicking the Details tab in the lower preview pane of the Event Viewer, as shown in Figure 6.29.

Note that in Figure 6.29, the ProcessingTimeInMilliseconds field shows 18656 milliseconds, or 18.656 seconds. That is how long it took for computer processing to occur. Also note that the ProcessingMode is listed as 0. That indicates that the computer is working in normal processing mode, as opposed to loopback processing. If the value were 1 or 2, that would indicate that loopback merge mode or replace mode, respectively, was enabled. And, of course, the DCName field indicates which DC serviced the Group Policy engine's request for Group Policy processing during the last cycle.

FIGURE 6.28   Viewing a Group Policy Admin Log event

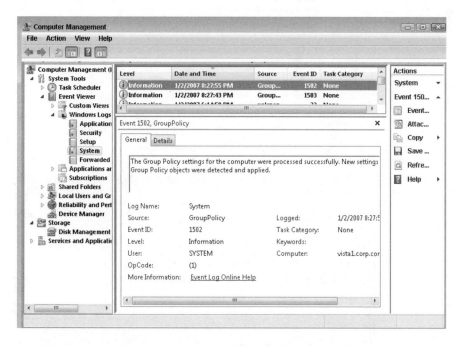

In addition to telling you when things are good with Group Policy, the System Log will also tell you when things aren't so good. And, new to Vista and Windows Server 2008, the failure logs will also try to give you some hints as to why things aren't working. For example, check out the event in Figure 6.30.

FIGURE 6.29 Viewing the Group Policy processing time

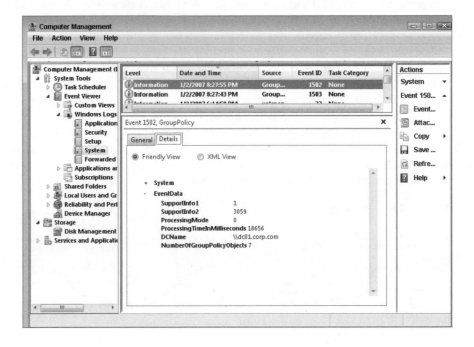

FIGURE 6.30 Viewing a Group Policy failure event

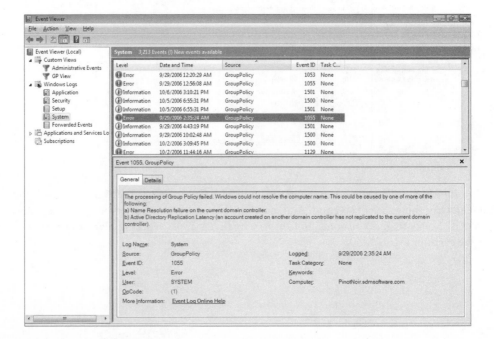

As you can see from Figure 6.30, not only does the event tell you that Group Policy processing has failed because it couldn't resolve the computer name, but it also gives you several possible reasons why that failure occurred. Additionally, if you were to click the hyperlinked "Event Log Online Help" at the bottom of the page, you would be taken to a Microsoft website that contains more detailed information about this event ID.

Leveraging Vista and Windows Server 2008 Operational Logs for Troubleshooting

Assuming that the Vista and Windows Server 2008 Admin Logs don't help you track down the problem, the next step would be the Group Policy Operational Logs. As I mentioned, these logs provide the same level of detail that the userenv.log file provided in prior Windows version, but in a nice Event Log format.

This is great, but how can you really use this data to troubleshoot a problem when there are so many events generated in a given processing cycle? For example, a given Group Policy processing cycle could generate 20 to 30 Operational Log events, and the Operational Log itself could contain hundreds of these events. The goal is to narrow in on *one* Group Policy processing cycle and walk through the steps that it took to either succeed or fail. You can accomplish this task using a custom view, a feature of the Crimson Event Log system.

Each instance of a Group Policy processing cycle is uniquely identified by a field in the event called a *Correlation Activity ID*. This is akin to the thread ID I mentioned earlier when discussing the userenv.log file. By creating a custom view that filters events by this ActivityID, you can get a listing of only those Group Policy Operational events related to a given processing cycle. Let's walk through how to do that.

To filter the Operational Event Logs by a specific Group Policy Activity ID:

1. Start the Event Viewer utility.

2. The first thing you need to do is find the activity ID for the Group Policy processing cycle you're interested in. You can do that by going into the Operational Log, finding an event that is part of the cycle in question, clicking the Details tab in the lower preview pane, and selecting the XML View button, as shown in Figure 6.31. Copy this activity ID someplace safe—we'll need it in a second.

3. On the left-hand pane of the Event Viewer, right-click the Custom Views node and choose Create Custom View.

4. The Create Custom View dialog appears on the Filter pane, but for this exercise, we're going to enter the XML filter directly rather than using the check boxes. So, click the XML tab and check the box that says "Edit query manually."

5. Paste the following XML query string into the filter query box:

```
<QueryList><Query Id="0"
 Path="Application"><Select Path="Microsoft-Windows-GroupPolicy/
Operational">*[System/Correlation/@ActivityID='{INSERT ACTIVITY ID HERE}']
</Select></Query></QueryList>
```

6. Replace the ActivityID you found in step 2 in the spot that says, "INSERT ACTIVITY ID HERE." Once you do that, click OK twice and the upper-right results pane of the Event Viewer will show only a filtered view of your Group Policy events.

FIGURE 6.31   Locating the Correlation ActivityID in a Group Policy Event

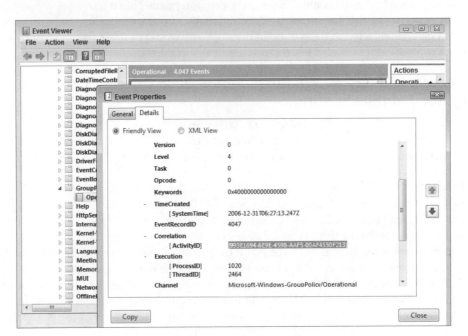

GPLogView

Now that we've filtered the events down to a single Group Policy cycle, you might be saying to yourself, "Gee, that's pretty hard to see what's really going on given that I have to scroll through each event without getting to see them all in a single view." Well, for that reason, Microsoft has created a tool called GPLogView.

This command-line utility lets you output the events of a Group Policy Operational Log to a variety of easy-to-read formats, including straight text and HTML. You can download the tool at `http://go.microsoft.com/fwlink/?LinkId=75004`.

Here is a taste of what it can do. You can use it to do the exact same thing we did in the previous custom view description—output the events associated with a single Activity ID. To do that you would run the `gplogview.exe` command using the following syntax:

```
Gplogview -a 9A867233-04FF-4625-B7D1-6DEB763E2DCA -o ouput.txt
```

This generates a step-by-step listing of all events with the activity ID we've supplied to an output file called `output.txt`. If we open `output.txt` in Notepad, we see a nice listing, similar to what we've got in `userenv.log` but without the clutter and unintelligible references to APIs! Figure 6.32 shows a small sample of the output.

Note that it provides useful information such as the bandwidth detected during slow link detection, the time until the next processing cycle, which GPOs were applied and denied, and why.

Additionally, if you look at the actual events in Event Viewer that correspond to each of the events listed in the output from GPLogView, you can get some additionally useful information. For example, at the start of every policy processing cycle, some useful summary flags are included in each event under the Details tab, such as show in Figure 6.33.

FIGURE 6.32 Viewing the output from GPLogView

FIGURE 6.33 Viewing summary flags for a Group Policy Operational event

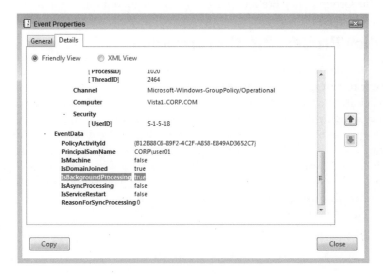

The flags you see in this figure can provide a glimpse into the kind of processing that is occurring. For example, the *isBackgroundProcessing* = true flag indicates that this is a background processing cycle rather than a foreground one. This is important because certain CSEs, such as Software Installation and Folder Redirection, don't run during background processing. This summary view also provides useful information such as whether processing occurred asynchronously (IsAsyncProcessing) and whether it's machine or user processing that is being logged (IsMachine).

Overall, the Group Policy Operational Log is the place to be when it comes to troubleshooting Group Policy problems in Windows Vista and Windows Server 2008.

 Microsoft has an indispensable document on Group Policy troubleshooting and the Event Logs for Windows Vista and Windows Server 2008. It's called (cleverly enough) "Troubleshooting Group Policy with Event Logs." You should be able to find it on www.GPanswers.com in the Microsoft Resources section. Or, just Google for the name of the white paper.

Enabling Tracing for the Group Policy Preference Extensions

We'll be exploring the Group Policy Preference Extensions in detail in Chapter 10. They're big enough to get their own chapter. And in that chapter we'll explore how to troubleshoot them if something goes wrong.

In short, the Group Policy Preference Extensions don't produce any direct log files by default. The assumption is that "they're working fine" unless you want to get more information out of them.

To do that, there are a slew of policy settings that enable tracking logs. Again, we'll explore these and how to use them in Chapter 10. But for completeness, I'm putting a reference to their existence here, in the troubleshooting section, as well.

You can find the Group Policy Preference Extensions tracing policy settings at Computer Configuration ➢ Policies ➢ Administrative Templates ➢ Group Policy ➢ Logging and Tracing.

You can see the Group Policy Preference Extensions tracing options in Figure 6.34.

Group Policy Processing Performance

I often hear the question, Is it better to have fewer, bigger GPOs or more GPOs with fewer settings? The answer to that question is the basis for this section.

The bottom line around Group Policy processing performance is that the time it takes to process Group Policy is highly dependent upon what you're doing within a given set of GPOs and the state of your environment. If you think about all the things we've discussed in this chapter about how Group Policy is stored and processed, then you have probably discovered that there is a lot of variability in the process. For example, setting Administrative Template policy is a lot less time consuming than repermissioning a large file tree using File Security policy. Likewise, installing Microsoft Office using Software Installation Policy is going to take more time than setting users' rights on a given system.

Additionally, the time that Group Policy processing spends during the core processing phase, where the client communicates with AD to determine which GPOs to apply, is typically a small percentage of the overall processing time as compared to the CSE processing part of the cycle. Thus having to enumerate more GPOs or less GPOs will have a negligible effect on the overall processing time as compared to having to perform the more time-intensive CSE processing. And, it's also important to remember that Group Policy processing only occurs if something changes in the Group Policy infrastructure for a given computer or user. So, in most environments, days may go by in between changes to GPOs occurs or a new GPO is created. Given that, the question of performance really gets down to what's acceptable in your environment.

FIGURE 6.34 You use these policy settings to troubleshoot the Group Policy Preference Extensions.

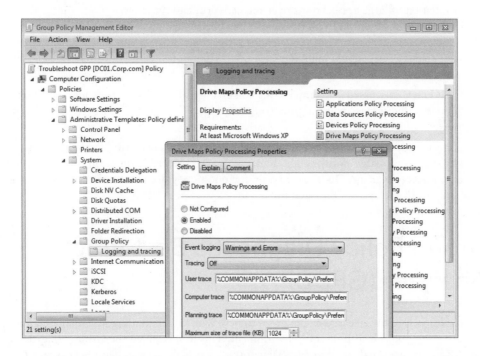

The best thing you can do to optimize processing performance is measure and understand where time is being spent during a given processing cycle. You can do this using any number of the tools we've mentioned in this chapter. For example, the `userenv.log` file in pre–Windows Vista versions of the OS will timestamp each step of the processing cycle, letting you see where time is being spent. Similarly, the Group Policy Operational Log will do the same thing in Vista and Windows Server 2008. In addition, you can download a free command-line utility called `gptime.exe` at `www.gpoguy.com/tools.htm` that outputs the time spent processing Group Policy for either a local or remote computer.

There are a number of factors that can affect Group Policy processing performance more than just the number of GPOs you have applied to a given user or computer. Some of these are highlighted here:

- Keep the number of security groups applied to a GPO to a minimum. The more security groups a client has to read and process to determine if a GPO applies or does not apply, the more time is spent during the core processing phase.

- Make sure that you are not forcing policy application for a given CSE (by enabling the relevant policy under `Computer Configuration\Policies\Administrative Templates\System\Group Policy`) during every refresh cycle unless you absolutely have to.

- Make sure that you minimize the amount of "expensive" operations that your GPOs do. Expensive operations include Folder Redirection of large amounts of user data, Software Installation of large applications over the network, and repermissioning of large file or Registry trees. Additionally, Scripts policy can be problematic if the scripts are performing complex tasks that can hang. The default script timeout in Group Policy is 10 minutes. That means a script could hang there for up to 10 minutes, with your users waiting, until it finally times out.

- WMI Filters (discussed in Chapter 5) also take a biggish chunk of processing time to figure out if the condition is "true" or not. You should use WMI filters if you need them, but not to excess.

So, in the end, the question of whether fewer, bigger GPOs perform better than more, smaller GPOs is probably not the right question to ask. The better question is which configuration is easier to manage. Once you answer that question, you can optimize for performance using the tips I've relayed in this section.

Group Policy Diagnostic Best Practice Analyzer (GPDBPA)

Microsoft has recently released a small tool to help with understanding and managing the overall Group Policy health of your environment. This tool is called the Group Policy Diagnostic Best Practice Analyzer, but the "Diagnostic" is usually silent when I hear others talk about it. So, in practice, it's called the GPBPA, for short. Actually, that isn't very short, but, heck, I'll still call it the GPBPA.

You only need to install the tool on one computer, but there are four potential downloads for the tool, depending on the type of system on which you want install. You can find a full list here of the supported installs: `http://support.microsoft.com/default.aspx/kb/940122`.

Supported installations include the following systems:

- Windows Server 2003 32-bit
- Windows Server 2003 64-bit

- Windows XP 32-bit

- Windows XP 64-bit

> As of this writing there is no version for Windows Server 2008 or Vista, nor do I hear rumors of updating the tool for those operating systems.

You'll need to have the .NET Framework installed if you want to run it on Windows XP. You can find that here: `http://tinyurl.com/6nkqy`.

For these examples, I'll run the GPBPA on Windows Server 2003 (which already has the .NET Framework 1.1 installed.)

The GPBPA is a pretty uneventful download and install. Once it's installed, you can fire up the GPBPA by locating the icon off the Start ➤ All Programs menu as seen in Figure 6.35.

FIGURE 6.35   The GPBPA appears on the root of the Start menu.

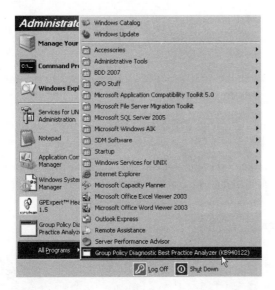

Once you start the program, you'll be brought to the GPBPA's welcome screen where you can select what you want and how you want to scan, as seen in Figure 6.36.

Performing Your Scan

The point of the GPBPA is to help you ferret out any glaring and overt errors that might be causing Group Policy to fail. You can scan three potential areas of concern:

- Domain Controllers: Important because this is where the Group Policy "guts" like the GPC and GPT are stored.

FIGURE 6.36 The GPBPA helps you analyze your GPOs or client systems.

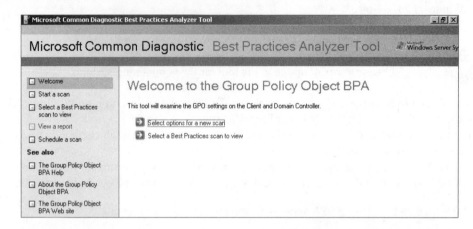

- Managed Node: Could also be called the Group Policy client and can be any type of machine, Windows 2000 onward to Windows Vista, including servers that are members of the domain.

- All nodes: This will test all the Domain Controllers and all the nodes. Not recommended due to the potential network activity this could generate.

Performing an Initial Scan and Remediation for Your Domain Controller(s)

You start a scan by clicking "Start a scan" in the left menu, as seen in Figure 6.36, or by clicking "Select options for a new scan," also seen in Figure 6.36. In Figure 6.37, you can see I've selected to test VMDC02 in the demo domain.

FIGURE 6.37 Use the GPBPA to get a baseline scan.

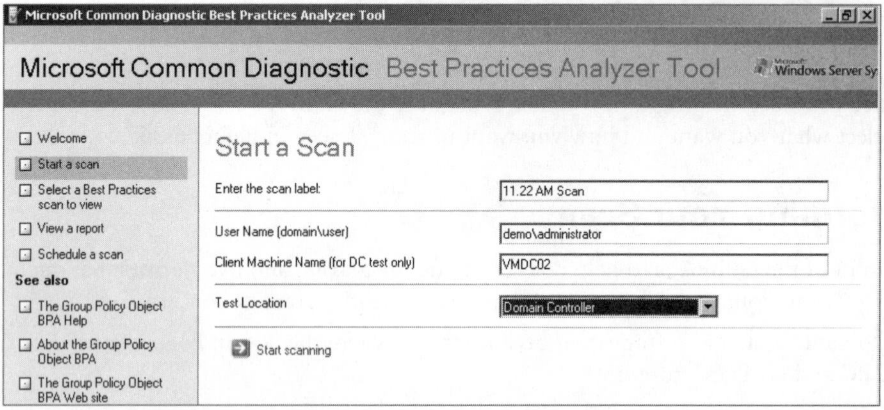

Scanning Your Domain Controllers

The health check takes only a minute, and then the results of the report are available by clicking the "View a report of this Best Practices scan" entry in the Scanning Completed page (not shown). In Figure 6.38, you can see a report of the output.

FIGURE 6.38   The GPBPA reports on critical issues.

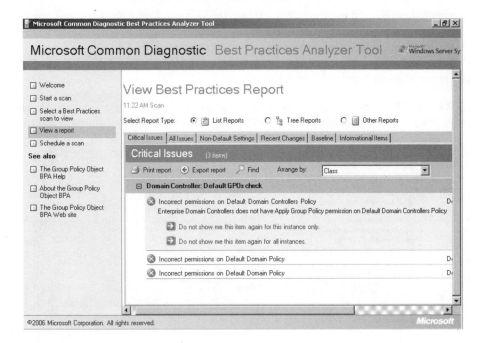

In this example, the GPBPA has returned three errors in the Critical Issues tab. There are other categories of information and errors as well:

- All issues (includes critical issues and noncritical issues): In this tab, you'll get information about anything found in the event logs that should be changed but aren't necessarily required.

- Non-Default Settings: Nothing seems to show up here.

- Recent Changes: Nothing seems to show up here.

- Baseline: Nothing seems to show up here.

- Informational Items: This tab actually shows you what has gone right in your Group Policy world. Full of information that is gleaned from Event Logs that are demonstrating that the correct behavior is occurring.

The reason nothing shows up in those fields is that the Best Practice Analyzer tool is a framework for lots of areas, not just Group Policy. So, these fields aren't valid for Group Policy but may be for other BPA tools.

We'll review the first error, remediate it, and then rescan to make sure our remediation has taken effect.

Remediating Any Errors for Your Domain Controllers

In Figure 6.38, you can see that there are three errors. The first one that's highlighted describes that the built-in group called Enterprise Domain Controllers has not been granted the "Apply Group Policy" permission for the Default Domain Controllers Policy.

To remediate this, we'll use the GPMC to find the **Domain Controllers** OU and inside it, the link to the Default Domain Controllers Policy. After clicking on it, we'll click the Delegation node, then click the Advanced button.

We'll then add in Enterprise Domain Controllers and finally select the Allow "Apply Group Policy" permission, as seen in Figure 6.39.

FIGURE 6.39 You can get closer to best practices by performing the steps the GPBPA suggests, like granting Enterprise Domain Controllers "Apply Group Policy" rights as seen here.

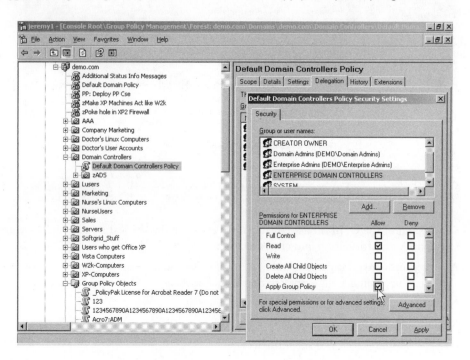

Click OK to close the Default Domain Controllers Policy Security settings.

Rerunning Your Scan

At this point, we'll want to check to see if we properly remediated the issue. Back in the GPBPA, select Start a Scan and enter in the same parameters you did earlier, except this time give the Scan Label a new name, like After Remediation.

Once completed, you should be able to see the report and see that your error has been remediated, as seen in Figure 6.40.

FIGURE 6.40   After remediating your issue, rerun the scan to see if it was addressed.

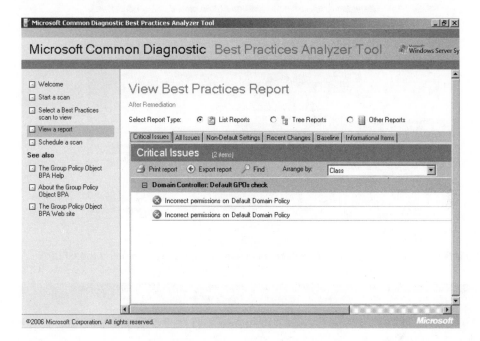

Checking out the Tree Reports

An alternate way to view the reports is by clicking Tree Reports, as seen in Figure 6.41. When you do, you'll get an alternate view of the report, including all the intermediary steps performed to get to the final result shown in Figure 6.41. Here you can see which tests were performed and how the conclusions were generated.

Performing an Initial Scan and Remediation for Your Clients

Now that you've checked out and remediated your Domain Controllers for errors, it's time to do the same for your client machines.

Similar to what you did in Figure 6.37, you're simply going to change the Test Location to Managed Node. But here's something interesting—you don't have to name a node (like XPPRO1 or Vista1) and those machines don't even have to be on!

This test checks the GPO health as if it was being downloaded by a client computer. Again, the most critical issues will appear in the Critical Issues tab, as seen in Figure 6.42.

FIGURE 6.41 The GPBPA tree reports

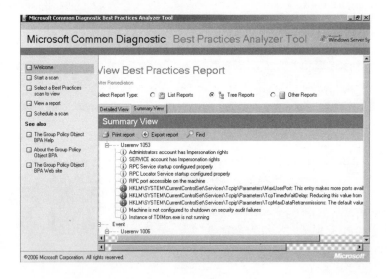

FIGURE 6.42 You can check potential client computer health using the GPBPA.

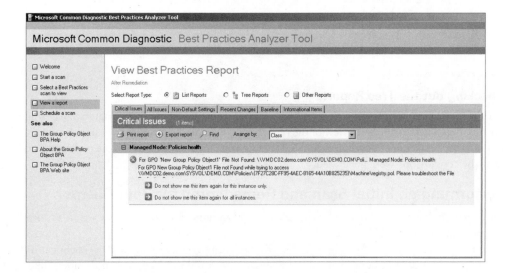

However, in this particular case, the report is obscured because the output it too big. If you look closely, the instructions are to "Please troubleshoot the File" then trails off. What file?

In this case, I suggest you click Export Report, which can save the report out to an HTML page. Once it's seen in full, you can see in Figure 6.43 it's suggesting that you "Please troubleshoot the File Replication Service."

Note, however, that when you do a client scan, the All Issues node can be somewhat overwhelming. There will be lots of noncritical items and repeats of the same issues if they come up multiple times. For instance, in my examples, I have some GPOs that are being Enforced. The GPBPA reports this fact each and every time. Indeed, the GPBPA reports these as a "GPLINK with No Override" (where *No Override* is the old-school parlance for *Enforced*). To me, the Enforced property is a perfectly valid configuration if you know what you're doing. With that in mind, you can click on one of these entries and select "Do not show me this item again for all instances," as seen in Figure 6.44.

FIGURE 6.43   The GPBPA Critical Issues report

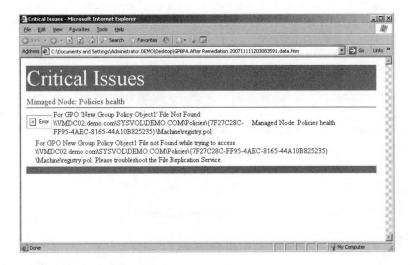

FIGURE 6.44   The GPBPA can present many issues that aren't really issues at all.

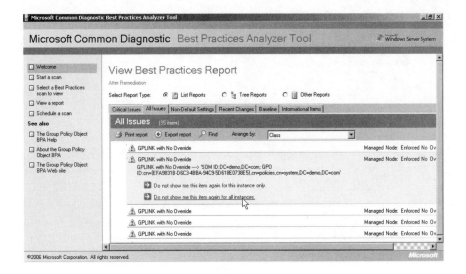

Scheduled Scans

The GPBPA also permits you to set up a scheduled scan by clicking on the Schedule a Scan node, as seen in Figure 6.45.

You can set a scan to run once, daily, weekly, or monthly. The task is only set when three things are true:

- You've entered in some scan parameters in the "Start a scan" step (seen earlier).
- "Enable scan scheduling" is selected.
- You click "Save and Exit this tool."

Only then is the task placed into Task Manager, as seen in Figure 6.46.

Note that the name of the task isn't super-obvious, but you can see that the Run command is specified as the `bpacmd.exe`, shown in Figure 6.46.

FIGURE 6.45 You can schedule scans with the GPBPA.

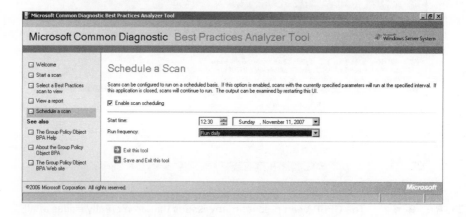

FIGURE 6.46 Scheduled GPBPA scans are placed into Task Manager.

The point is to see change over time between some original snapshot in time (some baseline report) and today. Do note that the reports you auto-generate by scheduling a task will not receive a unique name, and you can easily overwrite a report you might have wanted to keep around.

GPBPA Final Thoughts

A nice list of what the GPBPA scans for is part of the GPBPA help file. It's in the "Overview of Group Policy Diagnostics" section and details what things are checked for on the client computer and the Domain Controllers, as seen in Figure 6.47.

FIGURE 6.47   Check the GPBPA help file for more information for what issues are scanned.

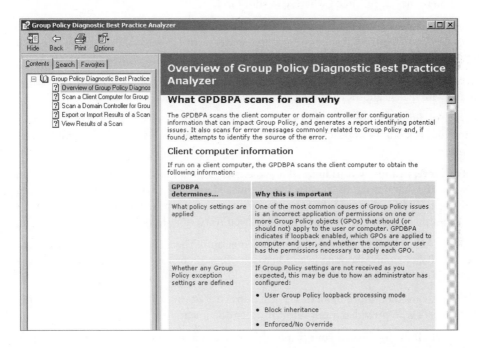

If this tool ever goes through a revision, I would suggest that they try to reduce the overall "noise" it generates as not every message it produces is worthy of an action item.

Indeed, I spun up a new domain and immediately ran the GPBPA tests and was hit with 11 warnings. That seems a little unreasonable considering there's not that much I could have screwed up since rebooting after DCPROMO.

It's a free tool, but you certainly get what you pay for. It's not supposed to be the Grand Poobah of troubleshooting, but it does do a fine job in highlighting true critical errors that might be interfering with your road to Group Policy happiness.

Final Thoughts

You want to be a better troubleshooter for Group Policy issues? You're well on the way.

In the last chapter, you learned when Group Policy is supposed to apply. It doesn't just happen when it wants to; it happens according to a set of precise timings. In this chapter, you learned two more key items to help on your troubleshooting journey. First, you learned the real story about what's going on under the hood. Then, you learned how to take that knowledge and troubleshoot Group Policy. Hopefully, every page in this chapter will help you further troubleshoot Group Policy should something go awry. However, here are some parting tips when troubleshooting Group Policy:

Check the basics.   When troubleshooting, first check the basics. Make sure you're not using Block Inheritance or Enforced where you shouldn't.

Check permissions.   Users need both "Read" and "Apply Group Policy" permissions to the GPOs. Computers do too. If a user (or group the user is in) is "Denied" access to either of these permissions, then the GPO will not apply.

Leverage the built-in tools.   Use the built-in debugging tools, such as the Event Viewer, supercharged with the Diagnostics key to help troubleshoot even tougher problems.

Leverage additional tools.   There are lots of additional troubleshooting tools at your disposal. Be sure to check out the appendix, in which I introduce WinPolicies, GPMonitor, GPInventory, and more.

Verify that replication is working.   If a client isn't getting the GPOs you think they should, it just may be that normal replication hasn't finished yet. GPCs replicate via Active Directory replication. GPTs replicate via FRS replication. They are supposed to take the same path, but sometimes they don't. Use Gpotool and Replmon to troubleshoot.

Check out Microsoft's troubleshooting documentation.   There are two official white papers on Group Policy troubleshooting from Microsoft. One can be found at http://go.microsoft .com/fwlink/?LinkId=14949.

There's also another, more modern version at http://tinyurl.com/3ceraj. I was one of the reviewers who provided input into this later document.

Remember all the log files at your disposal.   In this chapter, we've discussed a few log files. However, there are many more available. As we'll see in other chapters along our journey, there are log files for many processes related to Group Policy. We've just seen UserEnv.log, but additionally, there is FDeploy.log (examined in the companion book's Chapter 3, in the section "Folder Redirection"), Appmgmt.log (examined in the companion book's Chapter 4, in the section "Software Installation"), and others. Reference the two aforementioned Microsoft documents on Group Policy troubleshooting for the additional logs, in areas such as troubleshooting "internal" GPMC or Group Policy Object Editor workings via the Gpmgmt.log and GPedit.log, respectively.

## 7

ADM and ADMX Template Management

You might occasionally wonder, "Where do all those bazillions of policy settings within Administrative Templates come from?" They're not a magical gift from the Group Policy Fairy Godmother—they're encoded inside files within Windows that allow you to do the stuff you want to do. Group Policy has lots of nooks and crannies in which many options can be set. It's likely you'll spend most of your time manipulating the Administrative Templates section. Consequently, you need to know where all these settings come from.

In Windows XP and earlier, the Administrative Templates section is born from ADM files. In Windows Vista and Windows Server 2008, that same section comes from ADMX and ADML files. These templates hold the key to a large chunk of what makes Group Policy great. These settings are so important and powerful because they alter the Registry on the target computer. These ADM and ADMX files describe the Registry settings that can be toggled on or off through the Group Policy Management Editor.

That's where the duality of this chapter comes in. It's not only going to be really important to understand the "under the hood" goings-on of both ADM and ADMX files, it's also important to understand where Windows Vista and Windows Server 2008 bring new features to the table when ADMX files are used.

And, while not strictly necessary, if you want to take your Group Policy game to the next level, you might want to invest some time in understanding the language used to create ADMX files. After you understand the syntax, you can create, modify, and troubleshoot almost any Registry change that is implemented by the Administrative Templates in the Group Policy Management Editor.

Finally, a little later in the chapter, we'll explore a new tool from Microsoft and FullArmor that can take existing ADM files you might already have and convert them into ADMX files.

You'll find the complete reference for creating your own ADMX templates in the "ADMX Template Syntax" download on this book's website. If you still feel you need to create ADM files after reading this chapter, the previous edition's download of a similar reference, "ADM Template Syntax," should still be available on www.GPanswers.com as well.

But before we continue, we need to make absolutely certain we've got down a specific concept that we already nailed in Chapter 3. The idea that there's a new kid in town called GPMC 2.0, and he's only available on Windows Vista and Windows Server 2008. So, to be sure we've got our vocabulary right:

- The GPMC 1.0 works with Windows XP and Windows Server 2003 machines. It's a download from Microsoft that might be removed by the time you read this.

- The GPMC 1.5 is already loaded and waiting for us when we create a new Windows Vista machine from scratch, except the GPMC 1.5 that's built into Windows Vista is automatically *uninstalled* when we load Windows Vista + SP1.

- To get the GPMC back on Windows Vista, we need to download from Microsoft the GPMC 2.0 that is part of RSAT (Remote Server Administration Tools).

- And, the GPMC 2.0 is automatically present on Windows Server 2008 systems. There's nothing new to download.

The GPMC 2.0 isn't available for Windows XP or Windows Server 2003. It can only run on Windows Vista or Windows Server 2008. So, once you have the GPMC 2.0 on your Windows Vista machine or Windows Server 2008, we can just type **gpmc.msc** at the command prompt to fire it up.

 The Help ➢ About properties of the GPMC 2.0 will actually say Version 6.0+. This corresponds to the version of Windows, not really the version of the GPMC. I just like to call it the GPMC 2.0 because it's easy for us to see the progression. So, GPMC 2.0 isn't Microsoft's official term, it's my term.

Here's how we're going to negotiate this chapter: Now that we've got our vocabulary straightened out, we'll be referring to the GPMC 1.0, GPMC 1.5, and GPMC 2.0. Each one has its own underlying Group Policy Editor. Some of you might read this chapter and split hairs as I say things like "This setting displays differently in GPMC 1.0 vs. GPMC 2.0" when I'm really talking about how the setting appears *within* the Group Policy Editor that each GPMC uses. I think talking about the GPMC as a whole "packaged set" (the GPMC and the editor it uses) as a whole "version" will simply make this whole thing easier to understand.

In my vocabulary, your *management station* is the machine from which you're actively creating and editing your Group Policy universe. And my goal is to sweet-talk you into wanting to use a GPMC 2.0 machine as your management station as quickly as possible. If you're still using a Windows XP machine, or even a Windows Vista machine (with the built-in GPMC 1.5), as your management station, I want you to consider using the GPMC 2.0 for your management station after reading this chapter. In Chapter 3, you learned about a slew of new GPMC 2.0 features (Comments, Filters, and Starter GPOs). The rest of the GPMC features are found here, within this chapter. (Though note that, in Chapter 10, we go into the "really supersonic big news": the Group Policy Preference Extensions.)

Finally, I'm going to basically ignore the GPMC 1.5—the one that shipped with Windows Vista. I'm going to assume you've gone the extra mile to load the GPMC 2.0; this means you've got Windows Vista + SP1 and the GPMC 2.0 download, or you've decided to use a Windows Server 2008 machine as your management station. However, it should be noted that when I refer to the GPMC 2.0, most things will be valid for the GPMC 1.5, but not everything.

This will make it easier overall to talk about the GPMC 1.0 vs. the GPMC 2.0—the two most common versions people will use. If there's a special tidbit about the GPMC 1.5 (the version that shipped with Windows Vista in the box), I'll make mention of it.

But otherwise, I'll assume you've installed the GPMC 2.0 on Windows Vista (or have the GPMC 2.0 built into Windows Server 2008) and our focus will be on the distinction between managing Group Policy from a Windows XP or 2003 machine (GPMC 1.0) vs. a Windows Vista + SP1 + GPMC 2.0 or Windows Server 2008 (GPMC 2.0).

Policies vs. Preferences

One of the most heralded benefits of moving away from your old Windows NT 4–based System Policy is the nonpersistence of the Registry changes using Group Policy. Every Windows NT 4 System Policy change was *persistent*. When you enabled a System Policy, it stayed turned on until you set an explicit policy to turn it off. You couldn't just delete the policy and have the setting go away, as is the case with today's Group Policy engine. If you used Windows NT System Policy, you had to fight the same problem over and over.

Versions of Windows since Windows 2000 utilize a new model for policies. Microsoft created special locations in the Registry for Windows 2000, aptly named *Policies*. Microsoft documentation states that four Registry areas are considered the approved places to create policies out of Registry hacks:

- `HKLM\Software\Policies` (computer settings, the preferred location)
- `HKLM\Software\Microsoft\Windows\CurrentVersion\Policies` (computer settings, an alternative location)
- `HKCU\Software\Policies` (user settings, the preferred location)
- `HKCU\Software\Microsoft\Windows\CurrentVersion\Policies` (user settings, an alternative location)

These locations are preferred because they have security permissions that do not allow a regular user to modify these keys. Again, the preferred locations are noted above, if any software developers are reading this book (and you know who you are).

When a policy setting is set to Enabled and the client embraces the Group Policy directives, a Registry entry is set in one of these keys. When the GPO that applied the keys is removed, the Registry values associated with it are also removed. However, it should be noted that the application (or operating system component) needs to look for changes to these keys in order for it to take effect. That is, the Group Policy engine doesn't "notify" the application—the application has to do its own checking. So, with this in mind, if an older operating system receives a policy setting for a newer operating system, nothing "bad" happens. It just gets ignored.

WARNING   It should be noted that local administrators have security permissions to these keys and could maliciously modify delivered GPO settings because of rights within this portion of the Registry.

This is the magic that makes Group Policy shine over old-style NT 4 System Policy; that is, Group Policy won't tattoo because it's being directed to go in a nonsticking place in the Registry. Old-style NT 4 System Policy had no such facility. Today, Microsoft calls these NT-style policies that tattoo *preferences*.

You might want to control a pet application that you have deployed in-house, say, DogFood-Maker 6.1. Great—you've decided you want more control. Now, you need to determine which Registry values and data DogFoodMaker 6.1 understands. That could take some time; you might be able to ask the manufacturer for the valid Registry values, or you might have some manual labor in front of you to determine what can be controlled via the Registry. You'll then be able to begin to create your own templates.

However, after you've determined how DogFoodMaker 6.1 can be controlled via the Registry, you'll find you have two categories of Registry tweaks:

- Values that fit neatly into the new Policies keys listed earlier

- Values that are anywhere else

You'll have some good news and some bad news. If DogFoodMaker 6.1 can accept control via the Registry, you can still create template files and control the application. The bad news is that if you try to utilize a Registry key that isn't part of the Policies keys, then you will not have proper policies. Rather, they become old-style tattooing preferences.

To reiterate, the target applications must be programmed to look for values in the Policies keys. Some applications, such as Word 2000, check the Policies keys (specifically `HKEY_CURRENT_USER\Software\Policies\Microsoft\Office\9.0\Word\`).

Other applications, such as WordPad, do not "understand" the Policies keys. (WordPad looks in `HKEY_CURRENT_USER\Software\Microsoft\Windows\CurrentVersion\Applets\Wordpad`). Hence, WordPad wouldn't be a candidate to hand-create a template file for the purpose of coding for true policy settings. You could, however, still create your own *preferences* for WordPad that modify and tattoo the Registry. Therefore, you will have to do the legwork to figure out if your applications are compatible with the new Profiles keys.

Because preferences and policies act so differently, you will need to quickly identify them within the Group Policy Object Editor interface. You will want to note whether you're pushing an actual new-style policy to them or a persistent old-style policy. You'll see both cases in this chapter.

When viewed with the GPMC 2.0, new-style policies are designated by little "paper" icons. When viewed on Windows XP, new-style policies are designated by little blue dots. Again, these are "proper" because they modify the Policies Registry keys.

Policies that represent Registry punches in places *other* than the preferred Microsoft policies are designated another way. In the GPMC 2.0 editor, they're represented by paper icons with a down arrow. In GPMC 1.0's editor, they're designated by red dots.

Again, you'll see this distinction a bit later as you work through the examples.

Since this is an important distinction in the rest of this chapter, let's recap:

- New-style policies are temporary Registry changes that are downloaded at logon and startup (and periodically in the background). They don't tattoo the Registry (though they are maintained and stay persistent should the user log on while offline). These are set to modify the Registry in specific Microsoft-blessed Policies keys. Applications need to be coded to recognize the presence of the keys in order to take advantage of the magic of policies. In the GPMC 1.5's or GPMC 2.0's editor, these look like little paper icons.

- New-style policies also don't overwrite user preferences if they exist. For instance, if a program like Microsoft Word is policy-enabled and a user specifies to enable "Correct two initial capitals," but later the administrator chooses to disable this setting with a GPO, the original user's desires will just magically "come back." So, when you remove a true policy setting from a GPO (that is, set to Not Configured), the original user preference will be "returned."

- Old-style preferences are persistent Registry changes sent from on high using the Group Policy Management Editor. These typically tattoo the Registry until they're specifically removed. In GPMC 1.5 and GPMC 2.0 editor interface, they look like paper icons with a little down arrow. Unlike new-style policies, if you remove the GPO, you "orphan" the settings on the target computer (no fun at all). They work like old-style NT System Policy. These can be set to modify the Registry anywhere.

Hang tight, dear reader. The differences between preferences and policies will be underscored a bit later when we add in additional templates and you create your own settings to manipulate your clients later in this chapter.

ADM vs. ADMX File Distinction

Because GPMC 1.0 and 2.0 have such radically different ways of presenting (what appears to be) the same stuff to you via the Group Policy Management Editor (or the Group Policy Object Editor), it might be helpful to get a brief rundown of each technology. It's likely you have a mixed environment—of Windows XP and Windows Vista client machines and management stations. So, as we proceed in the chapter, you'll have a feel for what's going on under the hood.

Again, many settings are available in both the Computer and the User Administrative Templates sections of the Group Policy Management Editor. How these settings are displayed depends on what is inside the default ADM templates. Therefore, when you create any new GPO, you start with baseline policy settings.

GPMC 1.0 ADM File Introduction

The default templates are stored in the `%systemroot%\inf` folder, which is usually `c:\windows\inf`, and you'll find the following templates are installed by default on Windows XP+SP2 machines:

- `Conf.adm`
- `Inetres.adm`
- `System.adm`
- `Wmplayer.adm`
- `Wuau.adm`

These five ADM templates create both the Computer and User portion within Administrative Templates of a default Group Policy. Table 7.1 provides information about what each default template is and what lives inside it.

 inetcorp.adm and inetset.adm are two ADM templates that can alternatively be used to manipulate Internet Explorer settings. However, it is not advised, as they don't work well for newer versions of Internet Explorer.

TABLE 7.1 Default ADM Templates

ADM Template	Features	Where to Find in Interface
Conf.adm	NetMeeting settings.	Computer Configuration/User Configuration ➢ Administrative Templates ➢ Windows Components ➢ NetMeeting
Inetres.adm	Internet Explorer settings, including security, advanced options, and toolbar settings. It is equivalent to the options that are available when using the Internet Options menu inside Internet Explorer.	Computer Configuration/User Configuration ➢ Administrative Templates ➢ Windows Components ➢ Internet Explorer
Inetcorp.adm (not used in a GPO by default)	Used for Internet Explorer Maintenance Preference mode settings.	User Configuration ➢ Windows Settings ➢ Internet Explorer Maintenance. We won't be exploring this particular ADM template much. If you want more information on its ins and outs, read http://tinyurl.com/z3cae. It is not suggested to use this unless especially directed by a specific Microsoft document or PSS person.
Inetset.adm (not used in a GPO by default)	"Advanced Settings" for Internet Explorer 6.	User Configuration ➢ Windows Settings ➢ Internet Explorer Maintenance ➢ Advanced. Only visible in Internet Explorer Maintenance Preference mode (in Chapter 9, see the section "Internet Explorer Maintenance (IEM)" section). It is not suggested to use this unless especially directed by a specific Microsoft document or PSS person.

TABLE 7.1   Default ADM Templates *(continued)*

ADM Template	Features	Where to Find in Interface
System.adm	Operating system changes and settings. Most of the Computer and User Administrative Templates settings are in this ADM template.	Everything else under Computer Configuration/User Configuration ➤ Administrative Templates
Wmplayer.adm	Windows Media Player 9 settings.	User Configuration ➤ Administrative Templates ➤ Windows Components ➤ Windows Media Player
Wuau.adm	Controls client's access to Software Update Services servers.	Computer Configuration ➤ Administrative Templates ➤ Windows Components ➤ Windows Update

GPMC 2.0 ADMX File Introduction

As we saw with the GPMC 1.0, there's a mere handful of ADM files that make up the bulk of our settings. With the GPMC 2.0, things change from ADM files to ADMX and ADML files, and what was once a handful is now an entire growler-full.

What's a growler? http://en.wikipedia.org/wiki/Growler.

The GPMC 2.0's ADMX files are stored in the `%systemroot%\PolicyDefinitions` folder, which is usually `c:\windows\PolicyDefinitions`.

There are now about 132 ADMX files, which roughly cover the same settings found in Windows XP. They're generally component specific. For instance, you'll find things like `WindowsMediaPlayer.admx` and `EventLog.admx`, amongst others.

Here's something neat about ADMX files—they're language neutral. That is, the definitions for the Registry values that are controlled are inside the ADMX file. However, the text strings describing the policy and the Explain text are contained within a *separate* file called an ADML file—each ADMX file has a corresponding ADML file. These ADML files are located in specific subdirectories for each language within the `c:\windows\PolicyDefinitions` folder. For instance, U.S. English is contained within the `en-US` directory, which can be seen in Figure 7.1.

The term *en-US* stands for U.S. English. For other locales, visit http://tinyurl.com/223ebg. For instance, HE is for Hebrew, RU is for Russian, DE is for German, AR is for Arabic.

FIGURE 7.1 A quick list of some ADMX files. Note the language-specific directory here for English (en-US).

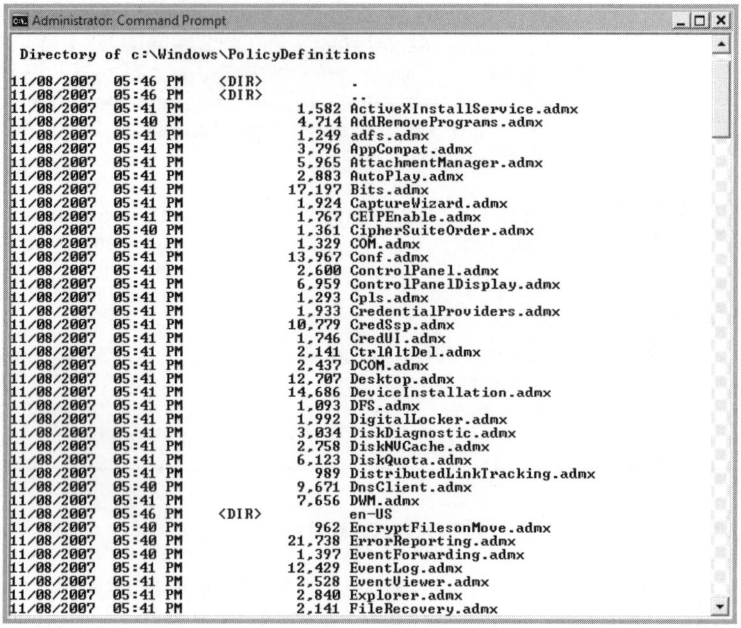

```
Administrator: Command Prompt                                              _ □ x

Directory of c:\Windows\PolicyDefinitions

11/08/2007  05:46 PM    <DIR>          .
11/08/2007  05:46 PM    <DIR>          ..
11/08/2007  05:41 PM             1,582 ActiveXInstallService.admx
11/08/2007  05:40 PM             4,714 AddRemovePrograms.admx
11/08/2007  05:41 PM             1,249 adfs.admx
11/08/2007  05:41 PM             3,796 AppCompat.admx
11/08/2007  05:41 PM             5,965 AttachmentManager.admx
11/08/2007  05:41 PM             2,883 AutoPlay.admx
11/08/2007  05:41 PM            17,197 Bits.admx
11/08/2007  05:41 PM             1,924 CaptureWizard.admx
11/08/2007  05:41 PM             1,767 CEIPEnable.admx
11/08/2007  05:40 PM             1,361 CipherSuiteOrder.admx
11/08/2007  05:41 PM             1,329 COM.admx
11/08/2007  05:41 PM            13,967 Conf.admx
11/08/2007  05:41 PM             2,600 ControlPanel.admx
11/08/2007  05:41 PM             6,959 ControlPanelDisplay.admx
11/08/2007  05:41 PM             1,293 Cpls.admx
11/08/2007  05:41 PM             1,933 CredentialProviders.admx
11/08/2007  05:41 PM            10,779 CredSsp.admx
11/08/2007  05:41 PM             1,746 CredUI.admx
11/08/2007  05:41 PM             2,141 CtrlAltDel.admx
11/08/2007  05:41 PM             2,437 DCOM.admx
11/08/2007  05:41 PM            12,707 Desktop.admx
11/08/2007  05:41 PM            14,686 DeviceInstallation.admx
11/08/2007  05:41 PM             1,093 DFS.admx
11/08/2007  05:41 PM             1,992 DigitalLocker.admx
11/08/2007  05:41 PM             3,034 DiskDiagnostic.admx
11/08/2007  05:41 PM             2,758 DiskNVCache.admx
11/08/2007  05:41 PM             6,123 DiskQuota.admx
11/08/2007  05:41 PM               989 DistributedLinkTracking.admx
11/08/2007  05:41 PM             9,671 DnsClient.admx
11/08/2007  05:41 PM             7,656 DWM.admx
11/08/2007  05:46 PM    <DIR>          en-US
11/08/2007  05:40 PM               962 EncryptFilesonMove.admx
11/08/2007  05:40 PM            21,738 ErrorReporting.admx
11/08/2007  05:40 PM             1,397 EventForwarding.admx
11/08/2007  05:41 PM            12,429 EventLog.admx
11/08/2007  05:41 PM             2,528 EventViewer.admx
11/08/2007  05:41 PM             2,840 Explorer.admx
11/08/2007  05:41 PM             2,141 FileRecovery.admx
```

ADM vs. ADMX Files—At a Glance

Our goal for the rest of the chapter is to give you an in-depth look at both ADM and ADMX files and for you to understand the differences between them. However, before we get going, here's a quick little reference table so you can see where we're going; you can also utilize this table as an ongoing reference.

ADM Files	ADMX Files
Lots and lots of definitions are packed into several large-ish files. The biggest one is SYSTEM.ADM.	Definitions are split logically into much smaller ADMX files, generally by Windows feature area.
Each ADM file contains settings in one specific language.	ADMX files are language neutral. Language-specific information is contained within a corresponding ADML file. Language-specific files live in hard-coded directories. For example, U.S. English language files live in %systemroot%\PolicyDefinitions\en-US.
Live on each Windows XP machine in %systemroot%\inf.	Live on each Windows Vista machine in %systemroot%\PolicyDefinitions.

ADM Files

Every time a GPO is "born," it costs about 3MB on each Domain Controller because the ADM files are placed inside the GPO

Use their own proprietary ADM syntax for describing Registry policy.

ADMX Files

GPOs created from ADMX files never have big space requirements. That's because the ADMX files are never pushed into the GPO themselves (regardless of whether the Central Store is used or not). We'll discuss the Central Store a bit later.

Use standard XML as the syntax for describing Registry policy.

Creating and Editing GPOs in a Mixed Environment

As I noted in Chapter 1, Windows XP and Windows 2003 have about 200 more policy settings available to them than their Windows 2000 pals do. And Windows Vista has about 700 more policy settings than Windows XP.

The good news (as I've previously stated) is that Windows 2000 clients ignore policy settings meant for Windows XP or Windows 2003. And Windows XP clients ignore policy settings meant for Windows Vista. This makes sense: older clients don't have the "moving parts" required to do anything if these policy settings are set.

You're likely to have a mix of client and server systems. It's likely you'll have the following systems:

- Domain Controllers: Windows 2000, Windows Server 2003, and/or Windows Server 2008 servers

- Member servers: Windows 2000, Windows Server 2003, and/or Windows Server 2008 servers

- Client machines (your users' machines): Windows 2000, Windows Server 2003, Windows XP, Windows Vista, Windows Server 2008

- Management stations (your machines, the ones you manage Group Policy from): Windows XP, Windows Vista, and/or Windows Server 2008

It's also possible you might have historically used Windows Server 2003 (and now Windows Server 2008) as a management station. I've seen some of my consulting customers use a server via Terminal Services mode as the single management station in a domain to mitigate multiple administrators making Group Policy changes at the same time.

Figure 7.2 shows a typical Active Directory domain that could be representative of what you might have.

The question is, With all these types of client systems, how do we ensure we've got the maximum power to control them all?

That's what we're going to explore in this next section.

FIGURE 7.2 A typical Active Directory domain with administrative systems, client systems, Domain Controllers, and servers

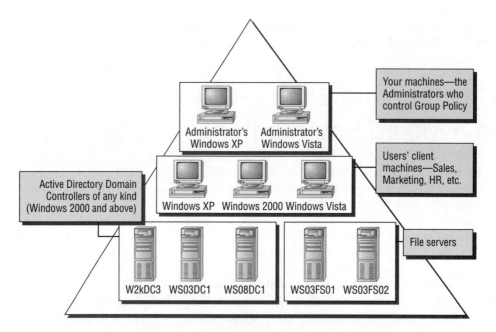

How Do You Currently Manage Your Group Policy Objects?

Before we proceed, you need to answer this question: How do you currently manage, create, and modify your GPOs?

- Do you walk up to a Domain Controller (or use Terminal Services to connect directly to a Domain Controller) to create or modify your GPOs?

- Do you use any machine you happen to be working on that day to create or modify your GPOs? (This could be a Windows 2000 machine, Windows XP machine, server—whatever).

- Do you use a specific machine to manipulate all the GPOs over which you have control? That is, do you have a *management station* you use when you need to manage your GPOs?

If you use either the first or second option, you're likely going to want to change your habits and start working with a strategy that gets you toward a *management station*.

Here's why. Every time a new operating system is released (and again each time a new service pack is released), there's more power to behold. Here's a brief history of increased power and what you can control:

Windows Version	Number of Policy Settings	What Can You Control (out of the Box)?
Windows 2000	About 300 policy settings	Windows 2000
Windows 2000 + SP1	About 20 additional policy settings	Windows 2000, Windows 2000 + SP1
Windows 2000 + SP4	5 additional policy settings	All version of Windows 2000
Windows XP	About 150 additional policy settings	Windows XP and all versions of Windows 2000
Windows Server 2003	About 24 additional policy settings	Windows Server 2003, Windows XP, and all versions of Windows 2000
Windows XP + SP1	About 10 additional policy settings	Windows XP + SP1, Windows XP, and all versions of Windows 2000
Windows XP + SP2	About 600 additional policy settings	Windows XP + SP2, Windows XP + SP1, Windows XP, and all versions of Windows 2000
Windows Server 2003 + SP1	About 5 additional policy settings	Windows Server 2003 + SP1, Windows Server 2003, Windows XP + SP2, Windows XP + SP1, Windows XP, and all versions of Windows 2000
Windows Vista	About 700 additional policy settings	Windows Vista, Windows Server 2003 + SP1, Windows Server 2003, Windows XP + SP2, Windows XP + SP1, Windows XP, and all versions of Windows 2000
Windows Server 2008	About 10 additional policy settings (not including the Preference Extensions, described in Chapter 10)	Windows Server 2008, Windows Vista, Windows XP + SP2, Windows XP + SP1, Windows XP, Windows Vista, Windows Server 2003 + SP1, Windows Server 2003, and all versions of Windows 2000
Windows Vista + SP1 + GPMC 2.0	Same as Windows Server 2008	Same as Windows Server 2008

Additionally, when service packs come out, Microsoft has been known to update the wording of policy settings and the Explain text for clarity (though its underlying actions are usually the same).

So, Microsoft makes updates; you have more power, right? Sure. But the message is clear: if you want to control every client and server machine in your environment using Group Policy, use the latest version of the OS—Windows Server 2008 or Windows Vista + SP1 + GPMC 2.0 (which is part of the RSAT tools). Again, we covered this in Chapters 1 and 3.

What Happens When You Create a New GPO?

The GPMC 1.0 (the one that runs on Windows XP and Windows Server 2003) uses ADM files and the GPMC 2.0 (the one that runs on Windows Vista and Windows Server 2008) uses ADMX files (for editing GPOs)—and different things happen when GPOs are created using these management station types. Figure 7.3 shows the *"Reader's Digest"* version of what we'll be discussing here, and after that will be the in-depth analysis of what's going on.

FIGURE 7.3 What's copied into the GPO when using which type of management station

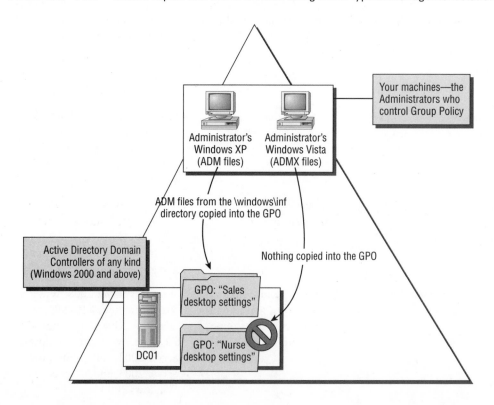

Creating and Editing a New GPO While Using the GPMC 1.0.

In order for us to create GPOs using a GPMC 1.0 machine, we need to have a Windows XP or Windows Server 2003 machine with the GPMC 1.0 console loaded (downloadable at `http://tinyurl.com/q77wx`). Note that the GPMC requires the .NET 1.1 Framework files (downloadable at `http://tinyurl.com/6nkqy`).

Note that the GPMC requires .NET Framework 1.1. If you *only* have the .NET Framework 2.0, the GPMC won't install.

Recall from Chapter 5 that when you use any ADM templates, these templates are added to the file-based Group Policy Template (found in SYSVOL) of the GPO. Unfortunately, there's no master update location where you can just drop the latest ADM files from Microsoft (or other vendors) and universally update the ADM files of existing GPOs and any future GPO that will be created. Indeed, you'll need to understand where new GPOs get their ADM templates from when you create new GPOs or modify existing GPOs.

In all cases, the editor you use (either Active Directory Users and Computers or GPMC) really uses the GPEDIT MMC snap-in (really the `GPEDIT.DLL`) when actually poking around or creating new GPOs. GPEDIT pulls the ADM template files from the computer it is running on. And it yanks these ADM template files from `%systemroot%\inf`—usually `c:\windows\inf`—directly into the GPO. Each time you do this, you're burning about 3MB of disk space—on every Domain Controller. This is because all material inside the GPO is replicated to every Domain Controller.

If you've created 100 GPOs using the GPMC 1.0 (or, heck, the Active Directory Users and Computers interface), you're using about 300 to 500MB of disk space on every Domain Controller to store these ADM files. This problem is called SYSVOL bloat. In Figure 7.4, you can see a sample SYSVOL with several GPOs. Recall that GPOs live on every Domain Controller in the `sysvol\corp.com\Policies` directory underneath their GUID. Each GPO has an ADM directory each containing the same ADM templates at about 3MB each directory.

FIGURE 7.4 Every GPO created with a pre-Vista management station pushes about 3MB into SYSVOL.

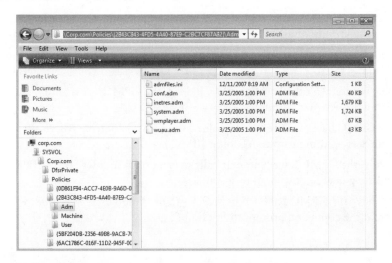

How to Prevent SYSVOL Bloat If You're Still Using Pre-Vista Management Stations

There is a way to avoid copying up the ADM files into the GPO, hence wasting about 3MB on each Domain Controller per GPO. The trick is to use a policy setting entitled **Always use local ADM files for Group Policy Object Editor** (located in Computer Configuration ≻ Administrative Templates ≻ System ≻ Group Policy) and have it affect your management station.

By enabling this policy, you're telling your management station, "I'm not going to push ADM files into the SYSVOL folder." Sounds great, right?

The downside, however, is that if you try to edit the GPO on a machine that doesn't have the same ADM templates as the GPO (or worse, the local machine is just plain missing an ADM template), you simply won't be able to edit the GPO the way you want. You'll have to track down the original machine that had the full complement of ADM templates to properly manage the GPO.

Because of the downsides, this workaround is suggested for only very large environments that have lots of GPOs that are taking a long time to replicate because of all the ADM template data being pushed into the GPO.

Here's the big ol' scary warning about the policy setting: it only works if the GPMC 1.0 application is installed upon Windows Server 2003 (not Windows XP). Why? I have no idea. So, if you want to prevent SYSVOL bloat from ADM files, and you want to utilize this sneaky way to do it, you absolutely must make your GPMC 1.0 management station Windows Server 2003 (and not Windows XP).

Microsoft talks a bit more about this in Knowledge Base article 816662 found at `http://support.microsoft.com/kb/816662`.

Creating a New GPO While Using a GPMC 2.0 Management Station

In order for us to create GPOs using a GPMC 2.0 management station, we need to recall something we already talked about in several chapters and revisited in the chapter introduction:

- The GPMC 1.5 is already loaded and waiting for us when we create a new Windows Vista machine from scratch.

- Except this version isn't the latest/greatest. Indeed, the GPMC 1.5 is automatically uninstalled when we load Windows Vista + SP1.

- To get the GPMC back, we need to download the GPMC 2.0 from Microsoft as part of the Remote Server Administration Toolkit (RSAT).

- Alternatively, the GPMC 2.0 is automatically present on Windows Server 2008 systems. There's nothing new to download or install.

So, once we have the GPMC 2.0 on Windows Vista or Windows Server 2008, we can just type **gpmc.msc** at the command prompt to fire it up.

Once we create a GPO using our GPMC 2.0 management station, we can also take a look at what's generated inside SYSVOL. In Figure 7.5, you can see that the top window was created using a Windows Vista management station. You know this because there's no ADM directory.

And, because there's no ADM directory (and no ADM files inside it), there's no wasted space (SYSVOL bloat) from ADM files.

FIGURE 7.5   The top window shows a GPO's contents when it's created using a GPMC 2.0 management station. The middle window shows a GPO's contents when it's created using a GPMC 1.0 management station. The bottom window shows the contents of the ADM directory for the GPO created using the GPMC 1.0 management station.

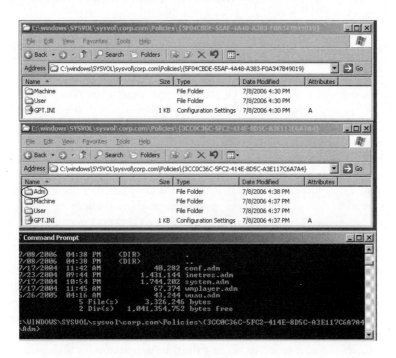

What Happens When You Edit an Existing GPO?

Here's where things get complicated. That is, you could have the four following situations:

- Scenario 1: Start out by creating and editing a GPO on a pre-Vista management station (like Windows 2000, Windows XP, Windows Server 2003, and so on). Edit using another pre-Vista management station. In this scenario, no Windows Vista is involved.

- Scenario 2: Start out by creating and editing a GPO on a pre-Vista management station. Edit using a Windows Vista station or Windows Server 2008 management station.

- Scenario 3: Start out by creating and editing a GPO on a Windows Vista or Windows Server 2008 management station. Edit using another Windows Vista or Windows Server 2008 station.

- Scenario 4: Start out by creating and editing a GPO on a Windows Vista or Windows Server 2008 management station. Edit using a pre-Vista (i.e., Windows XP) management station.

Scenario 1: Start Out by Creating and Editing GPO Using the GPMC 1.0. Edit Using Another GPMC 1.0 Management Station.

Again, here, the new GPMC 2.0 isn't involved. In this scenario, it's all about pre-Vista machines using the GPMC 1.0 with old-school ADM templates and ADM template behavior. And, of course, note that by creating a GPO using a GPMC 1.0 machine, you won't be able to get to any of the Vista or Windows Server 2008 goodies—that's because all the Windows Vista and Windows Server 2008 goodies are available only when you use a GPMC 2.0 management station (which of course runs only on Windows Vista or Windows Server 2008).

So, let's imagine that you've created 128 GPOs using an old and crusty Windows XP machine with the GPMC 1.0 loaded. Of course, all 128 GPOs have the original Windows XP versions of those ADM templates (yes, old and crusty).

Now, you learn about a policy setting in Windows XP/SP2 that requires the corresponding Windows XP/SP2 templates. What are you going to do?

Easy! Jump on a Windows XP/SP2 machine and edit the GPO using the GPMC!

This is because, as we already understand, the ADM template files used to modify and update a GPO are always copied from your management station. Older ADM templates inside GPOs are automatically updated when you re-edit a GPO on a machine that has new ADM templates.

When you edit the GPO on your GPMC 1.0 management station and merely look at the policy settings in the Administrative Templates section, the editor will say, "Ah-ha! I've got Windows XP/SP2 templates available to me! This specific GPO's ADM templates are only the original old and crusty Windows XP templates. I can tell because the date is sooo old. I'll update the underlying ADM templates automatically from `c:\windows\inf` in Windows XP—without even saying a word. That's because I have newer ones!"

And it then proceeds. And it proceeds because the time/date stamp for Windows XP ADM templates your editor has access to is more recent than the time/date stamp for Windows 2000 ADM templates. It's doing you a favor behind your back. You must repeat for every old GPO you want to update. If you want to update all your GPOs with Windows XP/SP2 ADMs, you simply have to open each old GPO and look at the policy settings in the Administrative Templates section. But again, you need to do this from a Windows XP/SP2 management station. Then they'll be updated.

Again, there's no universal master update location where you can just "drop in" your latest ADM templates and be done. However, with a script, you can update all your GPOs at one time (see the sidebar "Automatically Updating All Your Existing GPOs at Once with the Latest ADM Templates").

Automatically Updating All Your Existing GPOs at Once with the Latest ADM Templates

In Chapter 11, you'll get a grip on all the myriad of things you can do with scripting and Group Policy. However, one thing that we won't tackle there (but we do want to tackle here) is how to automatically update all your existing GPOs with the latest ADM templates. As of this writing, the latest ADM templates are Windows 2003/SP2, but you could use this same tip to update all your GPOs with the ADM templates from, say, Windows XP/SP2 or earlier (not that you would really want to). Or, use this tip when XP/SP3 comes out if you cannot (for some reason) commit to a GPMC 2.0 management station (which only runs on Windows Vista or Windows Server 2008).

If you want to update all your GPOs (or just some of them), Microsoft has a downloadable script that will do this for you at http://tinyurl.com/7v4s2. It runs as a command line (as opposed to a GUI-based script). When you're ready to give the script a try, be sure to run it from the command line as cscript admupdate.vbs so it continues to use the command line for output (and not try to push data to the graphical output).

Here's what you need to tell the script:

- You need to tell it which GPOs to update. You can update using the /GUID switch, the /GPOfriendlyname switch, or the very powerful /ALL switch.

- You need to tell it where the latest ADM files reside. You do this with the /ADMSRC switch.

- You need to tell it what domain to update. You do this with the /DNSDOM:<domain> switch.

There are other switches available.

But, if you tell it just this much information, it performs a *simulation* of what it will do.

When you're actually ready for the script to do the deed and perform the upgrade, you need to add the /FILECOPY:ON switch. This actually performs the work. Note that this could take a *long* time and cause a *lot* of replication traffic. So, be sure to do it in the off-hours if possible.

Again, running this script isn't expressly necessary—for two reasons. First, because, as we've discussed, anytime you specifically touch an old GPO with an updated management station, the GPO will be automatically updated. Use this script to simply guarantee that the latest ADM files are pushed to every GPO. Second, by the time this chapter is over, I'm going to have convinced you to use a Windows Vista management station. And then the GPOs themselves won't care about ADM files at all.

But, if you're still in a Windows XP–only environment, where you don't even have one Windows Vista management station, then this tip is still useful for you.

Scenario 2: Start Out by Creating and Editing a GPO with the GPMC 1.0. Edit Using the GPMC 2.0.

This will be the common "upgrade" scenario. That is, you've already got your gaggle of GPOs created. You created them using Windows 2000, Windows XP, or Windows Server 2003 with Active Directory Users and Computers or the GPMC 1.0. Now, you've got Vista or Windows Server 2008 with the GPMC 2.0 installed, and you're ready to use it. What happens?

Not much! If you start to use a Vista management station and edit an existing GPO created by a pre-Vista operating system, nothing happens in SYSVOL. No GPMC 2.0 ADMX files are copied anywhere, and very little happens overall.

However, while you're editing the GPO, you'll have access to all the latest-greatest Vista policy settings, one of which is seen in Figure 7.6.

FIGURE 7.6 Editing an existing GPO with Vista gives you the ability to see updated settings.

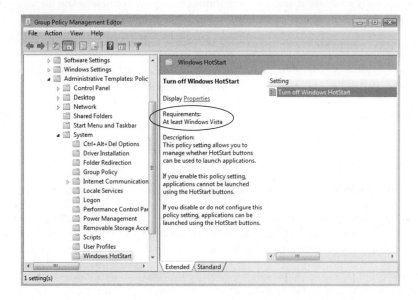

For argument's sake, let's say you decided to enable "Turn off Windows HotStart"—a Windows Vista–only feature.

Now, what happens if you try to edit and/or report on those settings using the GPMC 1.0 using Windows XP? Short answer: It's not good. That's because the GPMC 1.0 doesn't know how to interpret the Vista-only settings you've set within the GPO. If you try to edit the GPO on a GPMC 1.0 machine, you simply won't see the newly available Windows Vista policy setting.

And, if you try to look at it using the GPMC 1.0's Settings Report feature, the Vista-only settings show up as "Extra Registry Settings," as seen in Figure 7.7.

In Figure 7.7 you can see the Settings tab from GPMC running on a GPMC 1.0 machine running Windows XP, which is a report of what's going on inside the GPO.

FIGURE 7.7 Windows XP doesn't know how to interpret Vista-only settings within a GPO. These settings show up as "Extra Registry Settings."

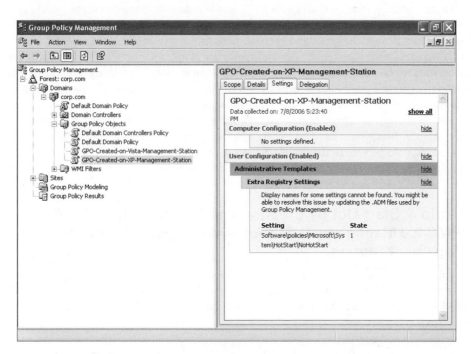

Again, if you were to continue to use your GPMC 1.0 management station to *edit* the GPO, you'd find that you simply wouldn't be able to find the **Turn off Windows Hotstart** policy setting—or any other Windows Vista–specific policy setting for that matter.

While it's clearly not a good idea, there is nothing that technically prevents you from using Windows XP to make a change to a GPO that was created using a GPMC 1.0 management station. In short, you simply can't see the Vista settings.

If a custom ADM file has been added to the GPO (yes, ADM), then Vista will utilize it and present it.

Scenario 3: Start Out by Creating and Editing a GPO Using the GPMC 2.0. Edit Using Another GPMC 2.0 Management Station.

This is the scenario you want to strive for. That is, always use the GPMC 2.0 (Windows Vista + SP1 + GPMC 2.0 or Windows Server 2008) to create and edit your GPOs.

When new settings come out, say, with a Vista or Windows Server 2008 service pack, you'll be all set. You won't have to do a thing (except use the GPMC 2.0 upon the latest and greatest operating system to get the latest and greatest settings).

So, it sounds like the message is, "Always use the latest-greatest operating system and service pack and load the GPMC 2.0 upon it for my management station." But what if you're not ready to personally upgrade your management station to the latest and greatest? Or, what if you had 20 administrators, each with their own management station?

If *only* there were a way to ensure that all your administrators always used the latest and greatest ADMX files, you'd have no issues. That way, anyone who uses the GPMC 2.0 (or GPMC 1.5) would be able to determine the latest and greatest settings.

Sounds like a dream, right? Good news: It's a dream that we'll make a reality in the next big section, with the Central Store. So stay tuned!

Scenario 4: Start Out by Creating and Editing a GPO Using a GPMC 2.0 Management Station. Edit Using a GPMC 1.0 Management Station.

Avoid this scenario whenever possible. This is the worst of all worlds because when you originally created the GPO on your GPMC 2.0 management station, you did so without copying the 3MB of ADM files up (remember, Windows Vista and Windows Server 2008 don't use ADM files to define Group Policy settings).

So, you did good here!

However, by merely *viewing* the GPO using the GPMC 1.0, you end up pushing up the 3MB of ADM files into the GPO. So, every time you do this, you'll see an ADM directory inside the GPO because they were pushed up from your GPMC 1.0 machine.

And it's done "invisibly."

GPMC 2.0 Management Stations and the Central Store

As we discussed, the ideal world is to use only the GPMC 2.0 for your management stations. Sure, that means you'll have to spin up one Windows Vista + SP1 machine (and download the GPMC 2.0) or use a Windows Server 2008 machine.

But remember, if you have even one Windows Vista client machine or one Windows Server 2008 machine out there in sales, marketing, human resources, and so on, you'll need to manage it *from* a GPMC 2.0 machine. That's because the GPMC 1.0 (which runs on Windows XP and Windows Server 2003) won't have the definitions of the policy settings that the GPMC 2.0 clients have.

So, we'll assume from here on that you'll be using only GPMC 2.0 as your management station (either Windows Vista + SP1 + GPMC 2.0 or Windows Server 2008), eschewing GPMC 1.0 management stations.

 If you want the best practices for GPMC 1.0 (i.e., Windows XP management stations), where, again, only if you have zero Windows Vista clients—right?—then you'll have to pick up the third edition of this book (and check out Chapter 5), which has lots of tips, tricks, gotchas, bugs, trials, and tribulations about Windows XP management stations running the GPMC 1.0.

As you're reading this right now, Microsoft has just shipped Vista's first service pack. But let's fast-forward a bit and assume, oh, that we're up to Windows Vista + SP3. Yep, Windows Vista Service Pack 3 has just been released and you need to control the new whiz-bang features that only come with Windows Vista + SP3 client computers. (Again, I'm dreaming a little into the future here; new whiz-bang features might or might not come in service packs or other delivery vehicles, but stay with me through this example anyway.)

"No problem!" you say, "I'll just create a Windows Vista + SP3 machine and put on the GPMC 2.0 as my management station." And you'd be right! Except that you already have a GPMC 2.0 machine as your management station. So you wouldn't want to run out and create a *whole new machine* just for this. You'd want to leverage the GPMC 2.0 management station you already have, right?

Sure!

This is easy! You're a diligent administrator (you bought this book, subscribe to the www.GPanswers.com mailing list, and practice good Group Policy hygiene, after all), and you know you have three ways to update your current GPMC 2.0 management station:

- If your GPMC 2.0 management station is Windows Vista, you would just apply Windows Vista's SP3.That would update the ADMX files that live in `c:\windows\PolicyDefinitions`.

- Or, you could forgo applying SP3 to your Windows Vista management station and simply copy the ADMX (and associated ADML files) from another Windows Vista + SP3 machine to your management station. Again, you'll plunk them in the `c:\windows\PolicyDefinitions directory`.

- Or, if your GPMC 2.0 management station is Windows Server 2008, then you could also just simply copy the ADMX (and associated ADML files) from another Windows Vista + SP3 machine to your Windows Server 2008 management station. Again, you'll plunk them in the `c:\windows\PolicyDefinitions` directory.

So, the message again sounds simple: Whenever Microsoft has new ADMX/ADML files, get them into your GPMC 2.0 management station.

Simple, yes—until you realize you have 20 administrators in your company, each with their own Windows Vista management station. Or you remember those administrators who love to bounce from machine to machine because they have three sites to run. Yikes! How are you going to guarantee that all of these administrators will use the updated ADMX files?

Let's assume you've successfully upgraded *your* Windows Vista management station to SP3, but only some of your 20 administrators successfully upgrade to Windows Vista +

SP3 (or have created custom ADMX files, or jam in the ADMX files into their own local
`c:\windows\PolicyDefinitions`).

This becomes a big problem—fast. Here's why: If you create a new GPO, that GPO will
have the definitions for all the whiz-bang stuff Windows Vista + SP3 has to offer. However,
when another administrator (who doesn't have the latest ADMX files) tries to edit or report
on that GPO, they simply won't see the policy settings for Windows Vista + SP3 available.

> GPMC reports about this newly created GPO would show the new whizbang
> features as "Extra Registry Settings," but actually trying to edit the GPO itself
> will not show them.

What you need is a way to ensure that all administrators who are using GPMC 2.0 management stations have a one-stop-shop way to ensure that they're getting the latest ADMX
files. That way, everyone will be on the same page, and there will be no challenges when one
administrator creates a GPO and another tries to edit it.

The Windows ADMX/ADML Central Store

The GPMC 1.5 (the one that ships with Windows Vista) and GPMC 2.0 (the downloadable
for Windows Vista + SP1 or built into Windows Server 2008) have a trick up their sleeves.

That is, they can use a Central Store for ADMX and ADML files. Recall that the ADMX
files are the definitions themselves, and the ADML files are the language-specific files for each
ADMX file.

The idea is that the Central Store lives on every Domain Controller. So, after the Central
Store is created, your GPMC 2.0 management station simply looks for it—every time it tries
to create or edit a GPO—and it will automatically use the definitions contained within the
ADMX files inside the Central Store.

This means you don't have to worry about running around to each of your 20 management
stations to update them whenever new ADMX files come out. You simply plop them in the
Central Store and you're done. You don't even have to tell the GPMC 1.5 or 2.0 management
stations you did anything; they'll just automatically look and use the latest definitions!

Here's the best part: It doesn't matter what kind of Domain Controllers you have. Doesn't
matter if you have Windows 2000, Windows Server 2003, Windows Server 2008, or a mix of
all three. It's the GPMC 2.0 that is doing the work to look for the Central Store in the place
upon the Domain Controller.

Wait, I'm going to stop here, and take a big deep breath and say it one more time. Because
I know you're reading fast and want to get to the good stuff. So, say it out loud if you have
to: **It doesn't matter if you have Windows 2000, Windows Server 2003, Windows Server
2008, or a mix of all three. It doesn't matter what domain mode you're in. It's the GPMC 1.5
or GPMC 2.0 that is doing the work to look for the Central Store in the prescribed place on
the Domain Controller.**

Got it? You don't have to "sell" your boss on upgrading the whole server back end just to
get this cool Central Store stuff. With one GPMC 2.0 management station, you've basically
got the magic you need.

So, let's read on and make it happen.

Creating the Central Store

Creating the Central Store must be done by a Domain Administrator because only a Domain Administrator has the ability to write to the location we need in SYSVOL. You can do this operation on any Domain Controller, because all Domain Controllers will automatically replicate the changes we do here to all other Domain Controllers via normal Active Directory/SYSVOL replication. However, it's likely best to perform this on the PDC emulator because that's the default location the GPMC and Group Policy Object Editor use by default.

To create the Central Store:

1. On the PDC emulator, use Explorer or the command line to create a directory within `%systemroot%\sysvol\sysvol\`*domain name*`\policies`. You want to create a directory called `PolicyDefinitions` as seen in Figure 7.8.

2. We need a location to store our language-specific ADML files. Within `PolicyDefinitions` you'll create a directory for each locale. Again, U.S. English is en-US. For other locales, visit `http://tinyurl.com/qpomo`.

Note that the directory name must be the same as specified in the locale reference page. If it's not, the ADMX file will not find its corresponding ADML file for that language.

FIGURE 7.8 Create a new directory called PolicyDefinitions in the Policies folder of SYSVOL.

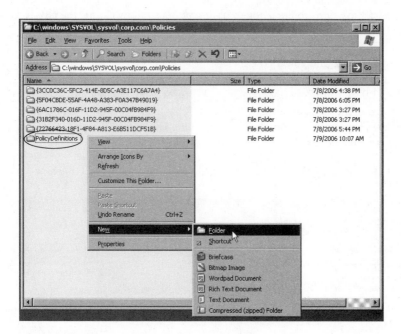

Populating the Central Store

Now, you simply have to get the latest, greatest ADMX and ADML files from your GPMC 2.0 machine into the Central Store.

There are a zillion possible ways to copy the files there. But, the steps are most easily done with two **xcopy** commands. This will work if your Windows Vista management station has access to the Domain Controller and that you have write rights.

To copy the ADMX files into the Central Store from your Windows Vista management station:

```
xcopy %systemroot%\PolicyDefinitions\*
%logonserver%\sysvol\%userdnsdomain%\policies\PolicyDefinitions
```

To copy in the ADML files into, say, the U.S. English directory we created earlier:

```
xcopy %systemroot%\PolicyDefinitions\EN-US\*
%logonserver%\sysvol\%userdnsdomain%\policies\
PolicyDefinitions\EN-US\
```

> You can also get a free graphical utility for creating and populating the Central Store automatically at www.gpoguy.com/tools.htm.

Verifying that You're Using the Central Store

Once you've created the Central Store directories in SYSVOL and copied the ADMX and ADML files to their proper location, you're ready to try it out! Start out by closing the GPMC 2.0 if it's already open, then re-open it. You can fire up the GPMC by clicking Start and in the Run box typing **gpmc.msc**.

And, then just create and edit a GPO.

However, can you be sure you're really using the Central Store?

The GPMC 2.0's Group Policy Management Editor will tell you if you're using local policy definitions or using the Central Store. In Figure 7.9, you can see a GPO where the Administrative Templates are retrieved from the local machine. However, as soon as the Central Store is available, that same notice changes to what's seen in Figure 7.10.

FIGURE 7.9   Policy definitions are originally pulled from the local machine.

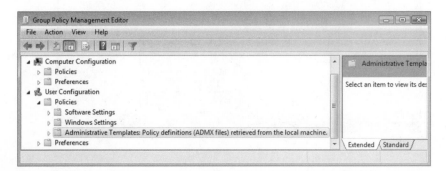

FIGURE 7.10 Policy definitions can be pulled from the Central Store.

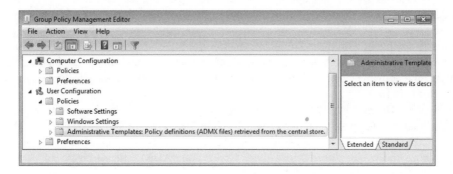

There is a secondary test as well to help you verify that you're using the Central Store. That is, when you create and edit a GPO, then click the Settings tab inside the GPMC, you'll see a line under either Computer Configuration or User Configuration that says "Policy definitions (ADMX files) retrieved from the Central Store." You can see this in Figure 7.11.

FIGURE 7.11 Anytime you click the Settings tab, the impromptu report will demonstrate if you are using the Central Store for your ADMX files.

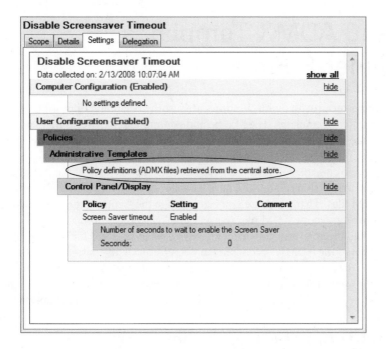

Updating the Central Store

ADMX and ADML files will be updated. If you've got Windows Server 2008, the ADMX and ADML files are newer than the ones in the "out of the box" Windows Vista. Likewise, when Windows Vista's SP2, SP3, and so on comes out, those will be newer still, and so on.

When this happens, you'll need to update the Central Store, which couldn't be easier. Simply copy the latest and greatest ADMX files to the `PolicyDefinitions` directory you created in SYSVOL, and copy the latest and greatest ADML files to the language-specific directory within `PolicyDefinitions`.

Then you're done.

Additionally, other products, like Office 2007, will have ADMX and ADML files. If you wish to make those available to all administrators, just do the same thing. Drop them into the Central Store and you're done. (More about Office 2007 ADMX files a bit later.)

Office 2007 has, confusingly, both ADM templates and ADMX templates. You can find the ADM and ADMX/ADML templates here, `http://tinyurl.com/2rr8c2`, but don't bother putting ADM files in the Central Store because ADM templates and the Central Store don't mix. Again, we'll learn about Office 2007 ADMX files a little later.

ADM and ADMX Templates from Other Sources

The templates Microsoft provides with Windows are just the beginning of possibilities when it comes to Administrative Templates. The idea behind additional templates is that you or third-party software vendors can create them to restrict or enhance features of either the operating system or applications.

If you know what to control, you're in business. Just code it up in an ADM or ADMX file and utilize it. If you're starting from scratch and have a choice, of course you'll want to use ADMX files instead of ADM files. That's because you can leverage the Central Store for ADMX files instead of remembering to copy ADM files to every management station.

However, it should be noted that you might already be using an ADM file or three. If you are, how do you get them to the ADMX "promised land"? A free tool, of course. Before we get into that, I will say that's the best option: get those custom and additional ADM files into ADMX format and leverage the Central Store. However, for completeness, I do want to explain what happens if you try to introduce an ADM file directly into a Windows Vista management station.

Using ADM Templates from Other Sources

Recall that ADM templates are the pre-Vista way to make definitions of what we can control. And, recall that there are both true *policies* and *preferences* that can be defined within an ADM file (or, ADMX file too).

Policies write to the "correct" place in the target computer's Registry. And, when the user or computer falls out of the "scope of management" of the GPO (that is, it doesn't apply to them anymore), the setting should revert back to the default.

Preferences write anywhere in the Registry that the application might be looking for it. Preferences tattoo the Registry. So, when the user or computer falls out of the scope of management of the GPO, the setting just sticks around.

You have the ability to get some ADM files from various sources. These ADM files sometimes have definitions for true policies. Other ADM files have definitions for preferences. How do you know which are which? The good news is, the Group Policy Management Editor interface shows you a difference between the two.

The editor for the GPMC 1.0 shows blue for policies and red for preferences. In the GPMC 2.0, it shows a little paper icon for policies and a paper icon with a down arrow for preferences. That way, you can make an informed decision on whether or not you want to implement a preference.

Indeed, on GPanswers.com (`http://www.gpanswers.com/faq/` in the "Tips and Tricks" section halfway down the page), we have a gaggle of downloadable ADM templates that people have created to control various aspects of applications and of their systems.

Leveraging ADM Templates from Your Windows Management Station

If you want to leverage and load one of these ADM templates into an existing GPO, simply edit it using the GPMC and bringing up the Group Policy Object Editor as seen in Figure 7.12. Then, choose either User Configuration ➢ Policies ➢ Administrative Templates or Computer Configuration ➢ Policies ➢ Administrative Templates, right-click over either instance of Administrative Templates, and choose Add/Remove Templates to open the Add/Remove Templates dialog box.

Click the Add button to open up the file requester, and select to load the ADM template you want. I'll show you in the next section or two where to track down more ADM files, but I wanted to show you this first so you'd know how to use them.

The original default location to start looking for ADM files is from `\windows\inf`; however, in practice you could store your ADM files anywhere. Just remember that every time you use an ADM template, you're actually copying that file directly into the GPO within SYSVOL.

 When you're adding an Administrative Template, the interface suggests that you can choose to add it from either the Computer Configuration or the User Configuration node. In actuality, you can add the ADM template from either section and the appropriate policy settings appear under whichever node the ADM template was designed for.

Once ADM templates are added using a GPMC 2.0 management station, they show up under a special node within the Group Policy Object Editor, called Classic Administrative Templates (ADM), as seen in Figure 7.13. In Figure 7.13, I've loaded an ADM template for Word 2003 (again, I'll show you where to get these templates in a minute so you can experiment, too).

FIGURE 7.12 You can still Add/Remove Templates from a GPO you create with Windows Vista.

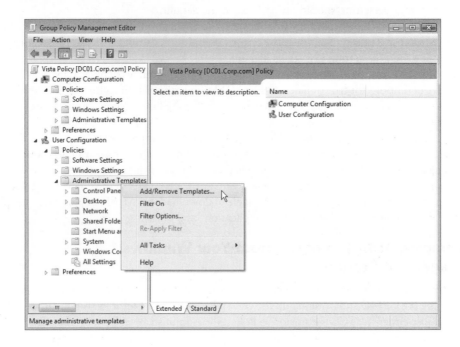

FIGURE 7.13 ADM templates are permitted in GPOs created from Windows Vista management stations. True policy settings are automatically available for use.

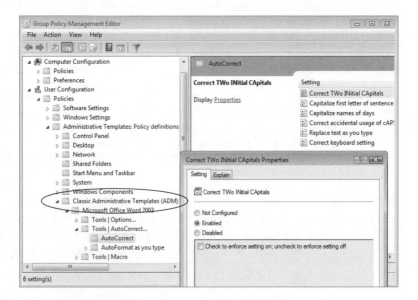

Again, ADM files can have definitions for true policies or for old-style preferences. If you load additional ADM templates into the Group Policy Management Editor (as shown in Figure 7.14) that contain old-style preferences, you will also see these (where they're initially hidden when using the GPMC 1.0 and 1.5). We'll explore this phenomenon in the very next section.

FIGURE 7.14   ADM files containing preferences imported into a GPO using GPMC 2.0 will show the categories and policy settings (and preferences) available.

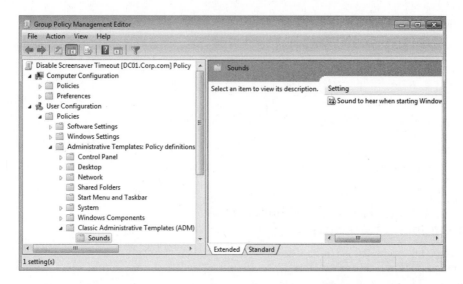

A little later, I'll show you how to "create your own" ADM file that controls the Windows XP start sound. However, that trick won't produce a proper policy; rather, it produces an old-style preference.

Viewing Old-Style Preferences (for GPMC 1.0 and 1.5 Management Stations)

Depending on the version of the GPMC you're using, you may or may not immediately see the ADM settings you just imported. You will however, immediately see the same Classic Administrative Templates (ADM) node and the list of categories contained within the ADM file containing preferences (as seen in Figure 7.14). But, for the GPMC 1.0 (on Windows XP or Windows Server 2003) and the GPMC 1.5 (on Windows Vista out of the box) you won't immediately see any settings. This is because that GPMC edition (and its corresponding Group Policy Editor) automatically prevents you from seeing these "dangerous" preferences—you need to turn on that ability inside the GPO.

If you're using the GPMC 1.0 or GPMC 1.5, to see the preference settings contained within the ADM file, use the menu at the top and select View ➢ Filtering to open the Filtering dialog box, shown in Figure 7.15. By default, the "Only show policy settings that can be fully managed" check box is checked. This is a safety mechanism that prevents old-style tattooing policies from being visible. Uncheck the check box, and you'll be in business.

FIGURE 7.15 For the GPMC 1.5 and GPMC 1.0, to see old-style preferences, clear the "Only show policy settings that can be fully managed" check box. This check box is checked by default to prevent you from seeing old-school preferences.

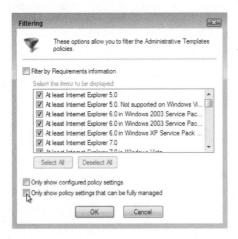

Viewing Old-Style Preferences (for GPMC 2.0 Management Stations)

This step isn't necessary if you're using the GPMC 2.0 (Windows Vista + SP1 + GPMC 2.0 download or Windows Server 2008). You should immediately see the preference setting within the Classic Administrative Templates (ADM) node.

Using Old-Style Preferences

Once you're editing a preference, you'll notice that old-style preferences have a paper icon with a down arrow on them. This is to indicate that this is a preference and not a true policy, and these values will stick around even after the policy no longer applies to the user or computer.

Indeed, the GPMC 1.5 and 2.0 Group Policy Management Editor is nice enough to even tell you this fact, as seen in Figure 7.16. You can see the little down arrow icon for any tattooing preference.

Microsoft Office ADM Templates

If you are also interested in deploying Office 2000, Office XP, Office 2003, or Office 2007, you'll be happy to know that they each come with a slew of customized ADM templates for you to import and use to your advantage.

- For Office 2000, download the Office 2000 Resource Kit tools at `http://office` `.microsoft.com/en-us/ork2000/HA101693191033.aspx`.

FIGURE 7.16   The GPMC 1.5 and 2.0's Group Policy Management Editor warns you about the issues when leveraging preferences and not policies.

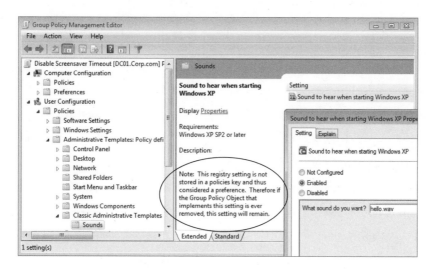

- For Office XP, download the Office XP Resource Kit tools at `http://office .microsoft.com/en-gb/help/HA011362921033.aspx`.

- Office 2003 templates are located in the Office 2003 Resource Kit. Check `www.microsoft .com/office`. At last check, some even newer templates are available in the Office 2003/SP2 Resource Kit at `http://tinyurl.com/4wxxn`.

- Office 2007 ADM and ADMX templates are located at `http://tinyurl.com/2w9qs7`. However, Office 2007 is the first to utilize ADMX templates.

 For information on how to automatically deploy Office 2000, XP, or 2003 (with patches and personalized customizations) to your users, see Chapter 4 in the companion book, *Creating the Secure Managed Desktop*.

The file you're looking for (with either Office 2000 or XP) is called `Orktools.exe` (for Office 2003, it's `Ork.exe`), and it's about 9MB. After you install the corresponding Resource Kit on your management station, the files in the next section are automatically placed in the `\windows\inf` folder for importation like the other ADM files.

Office 2000, Office XP, Office 2003, and Office 2007 ADM Templates

Here is a list of the ADM templates available for Office 2000, Office XP, Office 2003, and Office 2007.

Office 2000 Templates	Office XP Templates	Office 2003 Templates	Office 2007 Templates	Description
access9.adm	access10.adm	access11.adm	access12.adm	Access settings
clipgal5.adm	gal10.adm	gaal11.adm	N/A	Restrict access to media clips
excel9.adm	excel10.adm	excel11.adm	excel12.adm	Excel settings
frontpg4.adm	fp10.adm	fp11.adm	N/A	FrontPage settings
instlr1.adm	instalr11.adm	instalr11.adm	N/A	Windows Installer settings
office9.adm	office10.adm	office11.adm	office12.adm	Common Office settings
outlk9.adm	outlk10.adm	outlk11.adm	outlk12.adm	Outlook 2000 settings
ppoint9.adm	ppt10.adm	ppt11.adm	ppt12.adm	PowerPoint settings
pub9.adm	pub10.adm	pub11.adm	pub12.adm	Publisher settings
word9.adm	word10.adm	word11.adm	word12.adm	Word settings
N/A	N/A	N/A	visio12.adm	Visio Settings
N/A	N/A	aer.adm	N/A	Corporate Windows Error Reporting (See the section "Microsoft Corporate Error Reporting" later in this chapter.)
N/A	N/A	rm11.adm	N/A	Microsoft Relationship Manager File location
N/A	N/A	scrib11.adm	onent12.adm	Microsoft OneNote 2003 settings
N/A	N/A	N/A	cpao12.adm	Calendar Printing Assistant for Outlook 2007
N/A	N/A	N/A	groove12.adm	Groove 2007
N/A	N/A	N/A	ic12.adm	Office InterConnect 2007
N/A	N/A	N/A	inf12.adm	InfoPath 2007
N/A	N/A	N/A	proj12.adm	Project 2007
N/A	N/A	N/A	spd12.adm	SharePoint Designer 2007

Implementing a Customized Office Policy

After the Office templates are on the server, you can simply load them alongside the currently loaded templates. You can load all, some, or none—it's up to you.

In this example, we'll make believe we need to set up a custom Word 2003 policy for a collection of users. Normally, as in this example, Office template settings are meant for users, not computers. However, Office does include computer-side settings that you can use to override user-side settings if you want.

> If you don't want to use the Office 2003 ADM templates in this example, you can substitute Office XP or Office 2000 templates. Just make sure you also have the corresponding Office suite installed on the target machine!

Here, you'll see how to use an additional template. We'll load the word11.adm template alongside our current default templates. Then we'll change the default behavior of our Human Resources users for Word 2003 as follows:

- The grammar checker is turned off while we type in Word.
- The spell checker is turned off while we type in Word.
- Word will ignore words in uppercase during spell check.
- Word will ignore words with numbers during spell check.

To change Word's default behavior for the **Human Resources Users** OU, follow these steps:

1. Log on to your Windows Vista management station as the Domain Administrator.

2. Download the Office 2003 Resource Kit tools and make sure the ADM templates are properly installed in the \windows\inf folder.

3. Fire up the GPMC.

4. Right-click the **Human Resources Users** OU and select "Create and link a GPO here."

5. Create a new GPO called "Word 2003 Settings."

6. Edit the "Word 2003 Settings" GPO.

7. Choose either User Configuration ➤ Policies ➤ Administrative Templates or Computer Configuration ➤ Policies ➤ Administrative Templates, right-click over either instance of Administrative Templates, and choose Add/Remove Templates to open the Add/Remove Templates dialog box.

> When you're adding an Administrative Template, the interface suggests that you can choose to add it from either the Computer Configuration or the User Configuration node. In actuality, you can add the ADM template from either section, and the appropriate policy settings appear under whichever node the ADM template was designed for.

8. Click the Add button to open up the file requester, and select to load the Word11.adm template from the \windows\inf folder. Click Close to close the Add/Remove Templates dialog box to return to the Group Policy Object Editor.

9. To turn off the "Check grammar as you type" feature, drill down to User Configuration ➢ Policies ➢ Administrative Templates ➢ Classic Administrative Templates (ADM) ➢ Microsoft Office Word 2003 ➢ Tools ➢ Options ➢ Spelling & Grammar ➢ Check grammar as you type. Then, enable the setting, but do *not* select the check box. This forces the policy on the user, but clearing the check box forces it off.

10. Repeat step 9 for "Check spelling as you type," "Ignore words in UPPERCASE," and "Ignore words with numbers."

You can try this exercise with the other Office 2003–supplied templates listed earlier. These will affect Excel, PowerPoint, Access, and the like.

To test your new policy on the **Human Resources Users** OU, simply log on to any machine loaded with Word 2003 as a user who would be affected by the new policy. For instance, log on to XPPRO1 as Frank Rizzo, our old HR pal from Chapter 1 (assuming you have Word 2003 loaded).

Then in Word, choose Tools ➢ Options to open the Options dialog box, and make sure the settings reflect the policy settings you dictated.

Now, in this example we just explored, we were using the raw ADM files. Again, you can (as you'll discover a little later) take these ADM files and covert them—lock, stock, and barrel—into ADMX files to be used in the Central Store.

Also note that Office 2007 now has downloadable ADMX files—no need to convert or do anything fancy. Just plop 'em in your Central Store and start using them. We'll talk more about the Office 2007 ADMX files a little later. Check it out in the upcoming section "Using ADMX Templates from Other Sources."

Other Microsoft ADM Templates

Microsoft has two additional applications outside the Office family of products that leverage the Group Policy infrastructure by using ADM templates.

Microsoft Software Update Services (SUS) and Windows Server Update Services (WSUS)

The job of Windows Server Update Services (WSUS) is to ensure that patches are deployed to your Windows 2000, Windows XP, and Windows 2003 client systems. After a server is set up to deploy the patches, the client system learns about the server by way of a custom ADM template.

The template is built into Windows 2003 and Windows 2000 + SP4 as Wuau.adm. However, the template is not built into Windows 2000 + SP3.

You can learn more about WSUS, how to deploy it, and how to use the rather complex ADM templates in Chapter 7 of the companion book, *Creating the Secure Managed Desktop*. Last, Microsoft has an excellent guide to the policy settings with regard to WSUS available at http://tinyurl.com/ytwg39.

Microsoft Corporate Error Reporting

Microsoft has a service that lets corporate IT administrators "trap" error messages to a central server, instead of allowing them to be sent directly to Microsoft; it's called Corporate Error Reporting (CER). CER can help track systems that frequently crash and can provide an easier way to connect with Microsoft if a system does fail often. It can trap information for a lot of

Microsoft's most popular applications, including Office XP, Windows XP, Windows 2003, Project 2002, and SharePoint Portal Server.

Microsoft CER uses the ADM file Cer2.adm. You can get more information on CER at http://tinyurl.com/2n233o. You'll find the ADM file in the "toolbox" section of the web page.

Corporate Error Reporting is built into Office 2003, and more information can be found here: http://tinyurl.com/3bnvlw.

 The MDOP tools (available for Microsoft Software Assurance customers for an extra fee) also comes with a package named Microsoft System Center Desktop Error Monitoring for industrial-strength reporting.

ADM Templates You Shouldn't Use with Windows 2000, Windows XP, or 2003

Both the Office 2000 Resource Kit and Windows 2003 Server itself come with additional ADM templates that are not truly meant for the Group Policy Object Editor. Make a note of them so that you don't use them by mistake.

Office 2000 NT/95 Templates

Additional settings to configure Internet Explorer 5 are included in the Office 2000 Resource Kit, but they are not automatically copied to the \windows\inf folder. These are found, after the Office 2000 Resource Kit is installed, in the \Program Files\IEAK\policies\EN folder. The ADM policies in the ADM templates (located in the following table) are *not* meant for the Group Policy Object Editor. Rather, these are for the old-style Windows NT/95 Poledit.exe program.

Internet Explorer 5 Templates	Description
Aaxa.adm	Data binding settings.
Chat.adm	Microsoft Chat settings.
Conf.adm	NetMeeting settings.
Inetcorp.adm	Dial-up, language, and temporary Internet files settings.
Inetres.adm	Internet properties, including connections, toolbars, and toolbar settings. Equivalent to the Tools ➢ Internet Options command.
Inetset.adm	Additional Internet properties: AutoComplete, display, and some advanced settings.
Oe.adm	Outlook Express Identity Manager settings. Use this to prevent users from changing or configuring identities.
Sp1shell.adm	Active Desktop settings.
Subs.adm	Offline Pages settings.

Some of these templates *can* be loaded into Windows 2000, but you probably wouldn't want to do so; some settings included in these templates include actual policies (nontattooing), and some include only preferences (only tattoo). To review the difference between policies and preferences, see the opening section of this chapter. You can just use the included Internet Explorer template settings found in Windows 2000's `inetres.adm` instead of loading these templates that include both policies and preferences.

Windows NT Templates

Additionally included with a Windows 2000 computer are even more ADM templates. These are not for use within the Windows 2000 Group Policy Object Editor either; rather, they are for use with the old-style NT `Poledit.exe` program.

Windows NT Template	Function
`Common.adm`	User interface options common to Windows NT 4 and Windows 9*x*. For use with System Policy Object Editor (`Poledit.exe`).
`Inetcorp.adm`	Dial-up, language, and temporary Internet files settings. For use with System Policy Object Editor (`Poledit.exe`).
`Inetset.adm`	Additional Internet properties: AutoComplete, display, and some advanced settings. For use with System Policy Object Editor (`Poledit.exe`).
`Windows.adm`	User interface options specific to Windows 95 and Windows 98. For use with System Policy Object Editor (`Poledit.exe`).
`Winnt.adm`	User interface options specific to Windows NT 4. For use with System Policy Object Editor (`Poledit.exe`).

These templates are really not 100 percent compatible with the Group Policy Administrative Template interface if imported directly. Some will indicate that they are unsupported, as shown here.

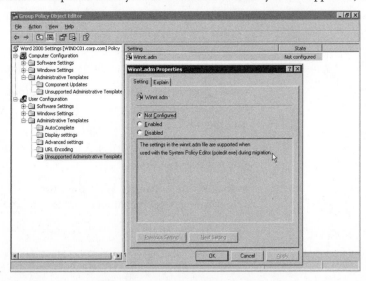

These are to be used with the old System Policy Object Editor (`Poledit.exe`). For instance, if you do end up loading, say, the `Winnt.adm` into the Windows 2003 Group Policy Object Editor, you are informed that it won't work, and the settings will not be displayed.

Using ADMX Templates from Other Sources

You'll get ADMX files the same way you got ADM files: companies like Microsoft will make them available to control the products they support, and enterprising geeks will produce ADMX files which control other parts of the operating system and third-party applications.

The same basic note and warning applies though: ADMX files can contain both (or either) true policies or old-school preferences. And, if they do contain preferences, with the GPMC 1.0 and 1.5, you'll need to explicitly show them in the Group Policy Object Editor. (The newer GPMC 2.0 automatically shows old-school preferences.)

ADMX Templates for Office 2007

As of right now, Office 2007 has been released, and about nine months after Office 2007 was released, so was its corresponding ADMX files. You can download the ADM and ADMX (and a lot of language-specific ADML files) here: `http://tinyurl.com/2w9qs7`.

And, when you download them, you already know what to do. Just chuck 'em in the Central Store (both ADMX and ADML files in the appropriate places) and you'll be golden. Then all the new GPOs that you create will be able to control Office 2007 when you use a GPMC 2.0 management station!

ADMX Templates from Other Sources

Will other Microsoft products have ADMX files? We hope so. So, while I have nothing specific to report now, check in every so often on `www.GPanswers.com` (especially the newsletters, where I'll try to let you know about any new ones that pop up).

Darren Mar-Elia, who runs `www.GPOguy.com` has an ADMX version of his troubleshooting tool, called `GPOLOG.adm`, at `www.gpoguy.com/gpolog.htm`.

Deciding How to Use ADMX Templates

Once you have the ADMX templates, you need to decide how to use them. If you've already created the Central Store, terrific. Just plop them into the Central Store and you're done. However, note that this means that all administrators who have access to create GPOs using Windows Vista management stations will be able to leverage all ADMX files.

You might not want to enable all administrators to leverage all ADMX templates.

If that's the case, you have only one option: put the specific ADMX files you only want some administrators to get upon only the Windows Vista management station you want them to use. The downside, however, is that if another Group Policy administrator (on his Windows Vista management station) tries to edit the GPO or report on it, he won't get the same view of all the settings that you do. That's because his Windows Vista management station doesn't contain the ADMX file you're using.

So, best practice is to use the ADMX file Central Store whenever possible.

ADMX Migrator and ADMX Editor Tools

Since leveraging ADM files directly inside GPOs that also use ADMX files can be fraught with peril, wouldn't it be a better idea to just utilize ADMX files everywhere? That way, you can just plop 'em all in the Central Store and be done. If you already have custom ADM files and need to get them to ADMX land, there's a utility that was written by FullArmor Corporation and licensed by Microsoft to give to you for free.

It's got a silly name: the ADMX Migrator tool. Doesn't it sound like it migrates ADMX files? Well, it doesn't. Maybe it should have been called ADM2ADMX or something, but regardless of the name, it's a cool tool. You can download the tool from Microsoft here: `http://tinyurl` `.com/ydb6ub`. Note that it requires the .NET Framework 2.0 to be currently installed.

Additionally, inside the ADMX Migrator tool package is a neat ADMX editor to help you handcraft your own ADMX files from scratch. The idea is that you don't have to "learn" a new language and hand-code it using, say, Notepad. Just use the tool to create your own ADMX files and you're in business.

For these examples, I'm running the tools on my Windows Vista management station, but they'll work just fine on a Windows XP that has the .NET Framework 2.0 loaded as well.

ADMX Migrator

There are lots of places you can get pre-made ADM files. You might try leveraging some right now—some are at `www.GPanswers.com`, others are found online at various other websites. Here's an example of a simple ADM file if you want to follow along. Just take this text, and copy it into Notepad and save it as `Sounds.ADM`.

```
CLASS USER

CATEGORY "Sounds"
    POLICY "Sound to hear when starting Windows XP"
        KEYNAME "Appevents\Schemes\Apps\.Default\SystemStart\.Current"
        PART "What sound do you want?" EDITTEXT REQUIRED
        VALUENAME ".default"
        END PART
    END POLICY

END CATEGORY
```

Then run the tool named `faAdmxConv.exe` against the ADM file you have. It can be as simple as just pointing to the file, but there are more switches if you have specific requirements.

Once run, it will create an ADMX and ADML file for the ADM. The documentation swears that it will put them in a temporary directory on the running user's profile, but in my tests, the resulting files seem to go to the root of the c:\ drive. Be sure to look for your new ADMX file in c:\ and the ADML file in `c:\en-US`.

To prevent this behavior, you can also just specify an output directory like this:

```
faAdmxConv.exe admname.adm c:\outputdirectory
```

Once you're in the directory of your choice, the resulting files are ready to be put in the Central Store (or, if you're not using the Central Store, then with individual GPMC 2.0 management stations). You can see the program run and its output in Figure 7.17.

FIGURE 7.17   The faAdmxConv.exe tool will take your ADM and convert it into an ADMX and ADML file.

The ADMX Migrator tool sometimes can't handle the SUPPORTED keyword. In this example, I've removed the SUPPORTED keyword to ensure that conversion occurs properly. However, in the conversion you'll see the warning, as seen in Figure 7.17.

Then, if you want to leverage these in the Central Store, put the ADMX file in the \PolicyDefinitions directory within the SYSVOL and the ADML file in the language directory (en-US for English).

The ADMX Migrator tool sometimes appears to be hit or miss during conversion. I've filed several bugs with the Group Policy team to have them fixed. Many issues were corrected in version 1.2, but I'm hoping they clear up the remaining issues soon.

ADMX Editor

In the previous example, we leveraged an existing ADM file that modified Windows XP's startup sound. What if you wanted to create the ADMX file from scratch?

Creating an ADMX template can sometimes be difficult. The hardest part can be figuring out which Registry setting you need to modify on the client system. You can use several tools to help you. One such tool is ProcessMonitor from Microsoft's Sysinternals tools. You can find it at http://tinyurl.com/y45pu7. This tool can help point out what's changing on the client.

Then, armed with that information, you can triumphantly create your own custom ADM or ADMX template and try it. That's where the ADMX editor, also in the ADMX Migrator download, comes in.

Start the ADMX Editor by clicking Start ➤ All Programs ➤ FullArmor ➤ FullArmor ADMX Migrator ➤ ADMX Editor.

Once you fire it up, you'll be able to create a new ADMX file and add categories, like "Misc XP Sounds" as seen in Figure 7.18. Note that it's not easy (at all) to realize you need to click to the right of Display Name to get that field to turn on. Once you do, you can enter in the name.

FIGURE 7.18 Once you create a new ADMX file, you can create your first category, such as "Misc XP Sounds."

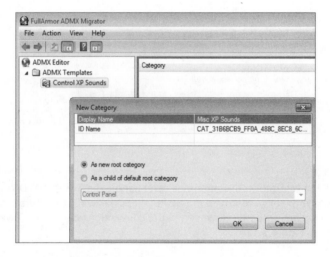

Then, right-click over your new category and enter in your first policy setting. Here, we're only entering one: **Sound to hear when starting Windows XP.** We then give it the Registry key (seen in the previous ADM listing) and the Registry value name (also seen in the previous ADM listing) and finally specify that it's a User-side setting with the pull-down menu next to Class. You can see these all entered in Figure 7.19.

FIGURE 7.19   You can create your own policy settings within the categories you previously created.

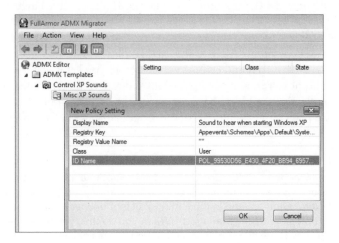

Then, you can add different elements such as a Dropdown List, ComboBox, and more, as seen in Figure 7.20. You can also enter in your own Explain text and Supported On text.

FIGURE 7.20   You can add various elements like TextBox requesters, DropdownLists and more.

When ready, you can right-click over the ADMX file (in my example the node labeled "Control XP Sounds") and click Save As. This will create an ADMX and ADML file. Be sure to (again) move the ADMX into the Central Store and the ADML file into the language directory (en-US) for English.

I really wish there was some kind of "preview mode" to see if you got it right before you went through the motion of copying the ADMX and ADML files to their final location—because there's potentially a lot of trial and error involved before you get it just right.

When you do get it right, however, and fire up the GPO editor, you'll notice that the category is there (in my example it's called Misc XP Sounds) but the settings within it are absent. That's because the keys we're dictating aren't part of the proper Policies keys and hence won't show by default.

If you're using the GPMC 1.5 or 1.0, and you want to expose the settings, remember that you'll need to select View ➢ Filtering from the Group Policy Object Editor window, and in the Filtering dialog, *uncheck* "Only show policy settings that can be fully managed." When you do this, you'll see the setting show up with a little down-arrow designating that it's not a true Policy setting, as seen in Figure 7.14.

Finding the Policy Settings You Need and Cracking the ADM/ADMX Files

I get about ten emails a day that ask me, "Hey Jeremy, how do you X with Group Policy?" (where X is some policy or trick I've never personally tried to do before).

My standard answer is, "I don't know" because I simply don't have all 1,800 Windows XP and certainly not all 2,400 Windows Vista policy settings memorized. So, I immediately follow up my "I don't know" with "But we can find out!"

Use the GPMC 2.0's New Filter

We learned about this in Chapter 3. That is, the GPMC 2.0 has a new filtering mechanism inside the editor that can search for all sorts of details, including policy settings that match your specified keywords in the title, Explain text, or a comment you've left. You can see an example in Figure 7.21. For more information on the filtering capabilities of the GPMC 2.0, see Chapter 3.

FIGURE 7.21   Use the GPMC 2.0's editor to help you filter and find policy settings

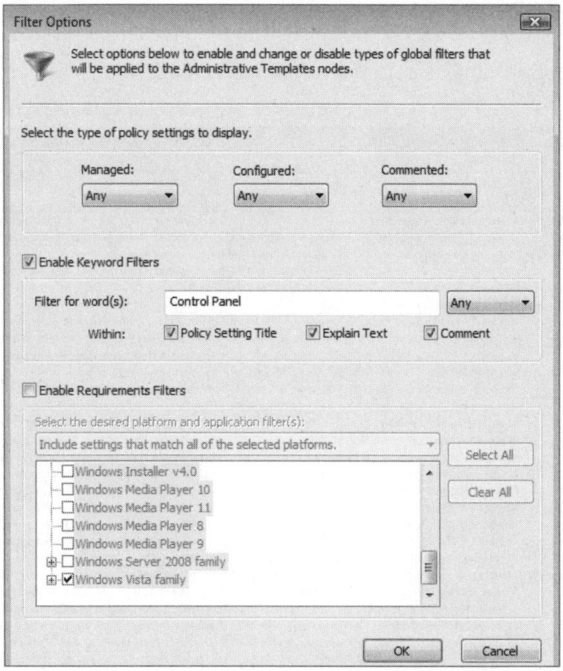

Microsoft's *Policy Settings Spreadsheets* for Windows XP and Windows Vista

Microsoft has created some wonderful documents: one for Windows XP, one for Windows Vista, and now one for Windows Server 2008.

In short, you can download a Microsoft Excel spreadsheet detailing the following:

- Every policy setting

- Every path to every policy setting (User or Computer, Policies ➢ Administrative Templates ➢ etc.)

- Every security setting

- Every Explain text entry for each policy setting

- Every Registry punch for every policy setting

I always keep an updated pointer from my GPanswers.com website in the Microsoft resources to this spreadsheet. Again, at this time, Microsoft has one for Windows XP management stations and one for Windows Vista management stations and one for Windows Server 2008 management stations. I don't know how much longer they plan on keeping the Windows XP version around. You can see what this looks like in Figure 7.22.

Additionally, since it's just Excel, you can perform quick sorts. For instance, by using column E (Supported on), you can limit the view to show you, say, only Windows XP+SP2 settings. This is super handy.

FIGURE 7.22 The PolicySettings.xls settings reference spreadsheet

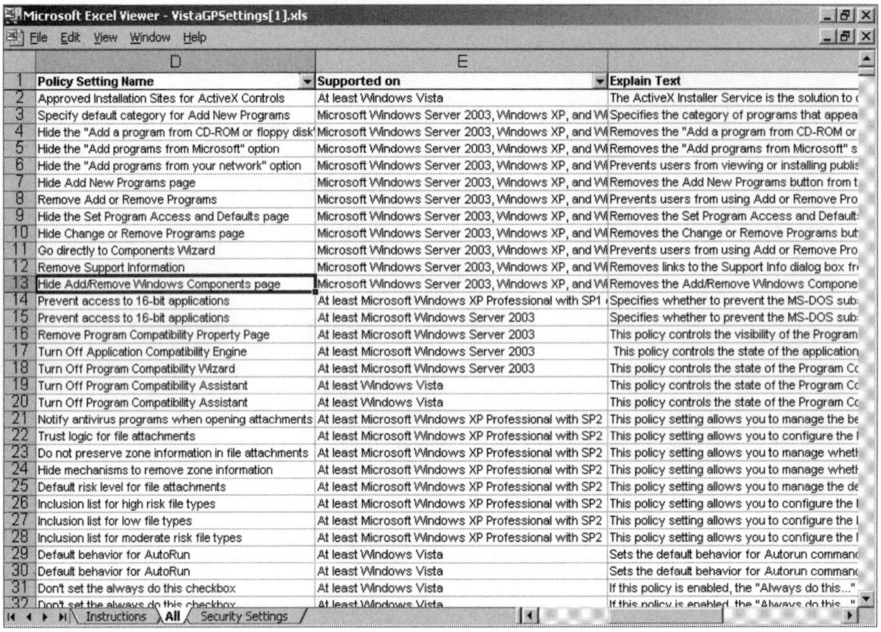

	D	E	
1	Policy Setting Name	Supported on	Explain Text
2	Approved Installation Sites for ActiveX Controls	At least Windows Vista	The ActiveX Installer Service is the solution to (
3	Specify default category for Add New Programs	Microsoft Windows Server 2003, Windows XP, and Wi	Specifies the category of programs that appea
4	Hide the "Add a program from CD-ROM or floppy disk'	Microsoft Windows Server 2003, Windows XP, and Wi	Removes the "Add a program from CD-ROM or
5	Hide the "Add programs from Microsoft" option	Microsoft Windows Server 2003, Windows XP, and Wi	Removes the "Add programs from Microsoft" s
6	Hide the "Add programs from your network" option	Microsoft Windows Server 2003, Windows XP, and Wi	Prevents users from viewing or installing publis
7	Hide Add New Programs page	Microsoft Windows Server 2003, Windows XP, and Wi	Removes the Add New Programs button from t
8	Remove Add or Remove Programs	Microsoft Windows Server 2003, Windows XP, and Wi	Prevents users from using Add or Remove Pro
9	Hide the Set Program Access and Defaults page	Microsoft Windows Server 2003, Windows XP, and Wi	Removes the Set Program Access and Default
10	Hide Change or Remove Programs page	Microsoft Windows Server 2003, Windows XP, and Wi	Removes the Change or Remove Programs but
11	Go directly to Components Wizard	Microsoft Windows Server 2003, Windows XP, and Wi	Prevents users from using Add or Remove Pro
12	Remove Support Information	Microsoft Windows Server 2003, Windows XP, and Wi	Removes links to the Support Info dialog box fr
13	Hide Add/Remove Windows Components page	Microsoft Windows Server 2003, Windows XP, and Wi	Removes the Add/Remove Windows Compone
14	Prevent access to 16-bit applications	At least Microsoft Windows XP Professional with SP1	Specifies whether to prevent the MS-DOS sub
15	Prevent access to 16-bit applications	At least Microsoft Windows Server 2003	Specifies whether to prevent the MS-DOS sub
16	Remove Program Compatibility Property Page	At least Microsoft Windows Server 2003	This policy controls the visibility of the Program
17	Turn Off Application Compatibility Engine	At least Microsoft Windows Server 2003	This policy controls the state of the application
18	Turn Off Program Compatibility Wizard	At least Microsoft Windows Server 2003	This policy controls the state of the Program Cc
19	Turn Off Program Compatibility Assistant	At least Windows Vista	This policy controls the state of the Program Cc
20	Turn Off Program Compatibility Assistant	At least Windows Vista	This policy controls the state of the Program Cc
21	Notify antivirus programs when opening attachments	At least Microsoft Windows XP Professional with SP2	This policy setting allows you to manage the be
22	Trust logic for file attachments	At least Microsoft Windows XP Professional with SP2	This policy setting allows you to configure the l
23	Do not preserve zone information in file attachments	At least Microsoft Windows XP Professional with SP2	This policy setting allows you to manage wheth
24	Hide mechanisms to remove zone information	At least Microsoft Windows XP Professional with SP2	This policy setting allows you to manage wheth
25	Default risk level for file attachments	At least Microsoft Windows XP Professional with SP2	This policy setting allows you to manage the de
26	Inclusion list for high risk file types	At least Microsoft Windows XP Professional with SP2	This policy setting allows you to configure the l
27	Inclusion list for low file types	At least Microsoft Windows XP Professional with SP2	This policy setting allows you to configure the l
28	Inclusion list for moderate risk file types	At least Microsoft Windows XP Professional with SP2	This policy setting allows you to configure the l
29	Default behavior for AutoRun	At least Windows Vista	Sets the default behavior for Autorun command
30	Default behavior for AutoRun	At least Windows Vista	Sets the default behavior for Autorun command
31	Don't set the always do this checkbox	At least Windows Vista	If this policy is enabled, the "Always do this..."
32	Don't set the always do this checkbox	At least Windows Vista	If this policy is enabled, the "Always do this..."

Last-Ditch Effort Troubleshooting via Registry Punch

Chapter 5 discussed many ways to troubleshoot if Group Policy doesn't seem to be applying. However, if you've verified that you're getting the policy setting via GPRESULT or the Group Policy Results Wizard and you're certain you should be getting a specific policy you set, perhaps the problem is elsewhere.

Occasionally, there are bugs in the help text definitions of some policy settings in the ADM/ADMX templates. Sometimes the policy setting states that "Enable" does one thing and "Disable" does another—and, really, it doesn't work that way at all. Other times, the actual underlying definition of the policy setting is incorrect and the Registry location it's set to modify doesn't really do anything. In all honesty, these problems are few and far between, but it is precisely what service pack updates to existing ADM files try to correct.

So, if you're 100 percent convinced you're getting the GPO laid down on the client system, yet you're still not seeing the result of a specific policy setting, take it to the next step. That is, crack open the spreadsheet (or ADM/ADMX file itself), locate the policy definition, find the portion of the Registry that the policy will be setting, and manually enter that hack into your client system. After you do, verify it against what the policy setting says it's supposed to do.

Is it actually doing what it says it's supposed to do? For instance, if you suspected that the **Force Classic Control Panel View** policy setting wasn't doing what it says it was going to do, simply crack open `ControlPanel.admx` using Notepad, and locate the **ForceClassicControlPanel** policy setting (as shown in Figure 7.23).

FIGURE 7.23   Open the ADMX template to locate the policy and the corresponding Registry hack.

As you can see, the policy setting modifies `Software\Microsoft\Windows\CurrentVersion\Policies\Explorer`. It adds a value of `ForceClassicControlPanel` and sets it to 1 to force the XP Control Panel to revert back to the older Windows 2000 style.

You can plunk this into the Registry yourself and see this actually happen; you don't need to set a GPO to try it. After you verify the results, you're closer to knowing precisely what's going on.

Final Thoughts

Managing ADM and ADMX files can be a little tricky. And this whole notion of GPMC 1.0, GPMC 1.5, and GPMC 2.0 can be kind of confusing too. (And it doesn't really help that the *real* name of the GPMC 2.0 is version 6.0; but I digress.)

The key message to take away is always use a GPMC 2.0 management station if possible to do your editing. Again, that means you'll need to get a Windows Vista + SP1 + downloadable GPMC 2.0 (within the RSAT tools) or a Windows Server 2008 machine. Then commit to using that as your management station.

If you bounce around using various operating system types, you'll be back in "SYSVOL bloat" hell again because the GPMC 1.0 isn't trained (by default) to stop pushing old-school ADM templates into the GPO.

It's easy to use Microsoft and third-party, vendor-supplied ADM templates to control your applications or to make your own ADM modifications. But remember—only applications coded to read Registry settings from the Policy keys will be true policies. They will be applied and removed when different users log on or off. They will not tattoo. They will appear with a paper icon (in the GPMC 2.0) or a blue dot (in the GPMC 1.0) in the Group Policy Object Editor. Most applications are not yet Policy key–aware, which means if you want to create your own modifications, you'll likely need to make them preferences. Preferences do not modify the Policy keys. They tattoo the Registry. They will appear with a down arrow (in Windows Vista) or a red dot (in pre–Windows Vista versions) in the Group Policy Object Editor.

 If you want an application that can truly policy-enable your existing applications, check out www.PolicyPak.com.

Be wary of downloading ADM templates you find online. They'll usually work as advertised, but the problem, again, is that they're likely chock-full of irritating tattooing preferences, not lovely nontattooing policies. Of course, I have some free ADM templates to download at www.GPanswers.com/faq.

If you have an ADM file you want to use in the Central Store, you'll have to convert it to ADMX first. Use the downloadable ADMX Migrator tool to perform that magic. Additionally, use the ADMX Editor (part of the ADMX Migrator download) to hand-create your own ADMX files if you like.

If you're interested in hand-creating ADMX files, we will have tips and tricks and a forum on www.GPanswers.com. We will also maintain the previous edition's "ADM Template Syntax" section if you need that as well. Last, check out Microsoft's document Step-by-Step Guide to Managing Group Policy ADMX Files.doc at http://go.microsoft.com/fwlink/?LinkId=55414.

And for the truly geeky, you can check out the ADMX schema, located at http://tinyurl.com/28k56v.

8

Implementing Security with Group Policy

There is a little aphorism that's grown on me over time. It's a simple mantra, which hopefully you can agree with:

> If you don't know Group Policy, you don't know security.

That's because Group Policy and security are so intrinsically linked. Not only are you setting configuration items (which will make you more secure), not only are you setting security items (which will make you more secure), but you also need to know the ins and outs of where Group Policy applies, who it applies to, and when that magic is going to happen.

That's what previous chapters were all about. In this chapter, and the next, we'll check out all of the actual security goodies Microsoft has built into Windows and the controllable aspects therein.

But, Group Policy is a big, big place, and we simply don't have room to go over *all* the stuff you can do with Group Policy. So I'm picking the most important things to show you in the next remaining chapters with the amount of room I have.

In this security chapter we've got just an enormous amount to cover. Here's the list:

Default GPOs   We'll first look at the two default GPOs: the "Default Domain Policy" GPO and the "Default Domain Controllers Policy" GPO and how they help tighten security.

Local vs. Effective Permissions (sidebar)   Why do security settings sometimes show up differently on our client machines? You'll find out.

Auditing Servers and Group Policy Usage   Who is using our clients and servers? You'll find out how to find out. You'll also find out what's changed for Windows Server 2008.

User and Computer Scripts   Old-school logon scripts were never like this. Find out why.

Internet Explorer Settings   With the advent of Internet Explorer 7, things get a little confusing. There are several different areas to control Internet Explorer, and we'll check out where those are.

Restricted Groups   You'll find out how to force group membership and nested group membership.

Software Restriction Policies   Put the smackdown and allow/disallow specific applications to run.

Last, but certainly not least, we'll harness and focus our Group Policy power in two ways: using Security Templates and the Security Configuration Wizard.

Security Templates give someone else the ability to decide what settings might be useful for you. They'll edit these settings offline, and you'll leverage them on your systems. This method works well for workstation security.

However, if you want a new way to get to the heart of server security, the final thing we'll talk about is a way to secure your servers using Group Policy. This technique came with Windows 2003/SP1 and it's called the Security Configuration Wizard, or SCW for short. It's been updated for Windows Server 2008 a little bit.

Don't let the fact that it's a "wizard" fool you into thinking it's got limited power. It's a superstar, and you'll see how to use it and how to make your Group Policy world rock with new power.

While we'll mention some Windows Vista–specific and Windows Server 2008 tidbits here, the new Windows Vista–only and Windows Server 2008–only goodies are in the next chapter. Note that you'll still see our screen shots from Windows Vista—because, as we've already discussed, to get the most out of Group Policy, you'll want to use a Windows Vista management station.

Combined, these two chapters on Group Policy and security are biiig. So don't try to read them both at once. Watch a ballgame and get a beer about halfway through each chapter.

Then come back, ready to rock. I'll be here for you.

Windows 2003/SP1 and Windows Vista bring some new additions to the table. As you're plunking around some of the special security policy settings, the newer Group Policy editors will give you a "heads-up" pop-up style message if you're about to modify a security setting that could do some harm. Microsoft calls these "soft barriers" because they don't prevent you from shooting yourself in the foot but they do warn you first. You can check out Microsoft Knowledge Base article 823659 at http://support.microsoft.com/kb/823659 for specific security policy settings that are affected. The pop-ups warn about anything that could be considered a risky configuration and alert you to known compatibility problems.

The Two Default Group Policy Objects

Whenever you create a new domain, three things automatically happen:

- The initial (and only) OU, named **Domain Controllers**, is created automatically by the DCPROMO process.

- A default GPO is created and linked to the domain level, called "Default Domain Policy."

- A default GPO is created for the **Domain Controllers** OU, called "Default Domain Controllers Policy."

This section helps answer the question, Why are these GPOs different from all other GPOs?

These two GPOs are special. First, you cannot easily delete them (though you can rename them). Next, it's a best practice to modify these GPOs only for the security settings that we'll describe in this section. Too often, people will modify the "Default Domain Controller Policy" GPO or "Default Domain Policy" GPO only to mess it up beyond recognition. So, these special default GPOs shouldn't be modified with the "normal stuff" you do day to day. In general, stay clear of them, and modify them only when a setting prescribed for them is actually required.

Instead of modifying the "Default Domain Controller Policy" GPO or "Default Domain Policy" GPO for normal stuff, you should create a new GPO and link it at the level you want, then implement your policy settings inside that new GPO. And, it's a best practice to always be sure that the defaults are highest in the link order (that means they're the most powerful if anything should conflict in another GPO at the same level).

WARNING   The "Default Domain Policy" GPO and "Default Domain Controllers Policy" GPO can actually be deleted, but I strongly recommend that you DON'T EVER DELETE THESE. If you truly want to delete either of the default policies, you'll need to add back in the "Delete" access control entry to a group you belong to—Domain Administrators, for instance. Even then, I can't see why you would want to delete them. If you want to disable their link for some reason (again, I can't imagine why), do that, but leave the actual GPOs in place. If you do run into a situation where these are deleted, then use the command dcgpofix.exe (described in detail later) to get them back.

It's not that the GPOs themselves are really all that different, but rather that their location is special, as you'll see later in this chapter. The locations in question are the domain level and the **Domain Controllers** OU.

GPOs Linked at the Domain Level

If you take a look inside the domain level, you'll see one GPO that was created by default: the "Default Domain Policy." The purpose of this GPO is to set the default configurations for the Account Policies branch in the Group Policy Object Editor. These Account Policies encompass three important domain-wide security settings:

- Password policy
- Account Lockout policy
- Kerberos policy

You can see these settings in Figure 8.1.

FIGURE 8.1 The "Default Domain Policy" GPO (linked to the domain level) sets the domain's default Account Policies, Kerberos policy, and Password policy. If you link GPOs containing these policy settings anywhere else, they are essentially ignored when Active Directory is being used.

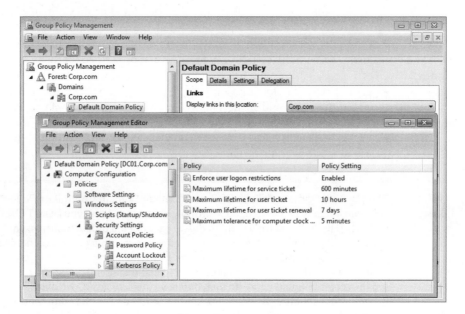

Again, the default policy settings are set inside the "Default Domain Policy" GPO and linked to the domain level. However, you can change the defaults of the Account Policies in one of two ways:

- By modifying the "Default Domain Policy" GPO directly
- By creating your own GPO linked to the domain level and changing the precedence order within the domain level

You'll see how shortly.

Again, the special part about the domain level of Group Policy is that this is the only place these three Group Policy settings can be set for the domain, and the default settings for the domain are prespecified in the "Default Domain Policy" GPO.

If you try to set Password policy, Account Lockout policy, or Kerberos policy anywhere else in the domain (say, at any OU or on any site), the settings are ignored when users log on to the domain; they don't matter, and only those linked to the domain level take effect.

Microsoft has taken a lot of heat for the fact that Account Policies must agree for all the accounts in the domain. Up until recently, that meant if two administrators of two OUs couldn't agree on equal Account Policies (usually things like password length), they would have needed to split those users between two domains—a major administrative overhead nightmare.

So they changed it in Windows Server 2008. It's not a light-year improvement, but it does do the job. We'll explore that here as well.

Special Policy Settings for the Domain Level

In addition to Password policy, Account Lockout policy, and Kerberos policy, five additional policy settings take effect only when a GPO is linked to the domain level. They are located under Computer Configuration ➤ Policies ➤ Windows Settings ➤ Security Settings ➤ Local Policies ➤ Security Options:

Network Security: Force logoff when logon hours expire (was "Automatically Log Off Users When Logon Time Expires" in Windows 2000)   You can set up accounts so that users logged on to Active Directory must log off when they exceed the hours available to them.

Accounts: Rename administrator account (was "Rename administrator account" in Windows 2000)   You can use this policy setting to forcibly rename the Administrator account. This works only for the Domain Administrator account when set at the domain level. This is useful as a level of "extra protection" so that no matter what the Administrator account is renamed to in Active Directory Users and Computers, it will "snap back" to this name after Group Policy refreshes. The "display name" in Active Directory Users and Computers won't actually change, but the underlying "real" name of the account will be changed.

Accounts: Rename guest Account (was "Rename guest account" in Windows 2000)   You can rename the domain Guest account using this policy setting. This works only for the Guest account when set at the domain level.

Accounts: Administrator account status   This setting is valid only for Windows 2003 domains (and higher). You can forcibly disable the Administrator account using this setting. See this tech note for more information: `http://tinyurl.com/y36ths`.

Accounts: Guest account status   This setting is valid only for Windows 2003 domains (and higher). You can forcibly disable the Guest account using this setting. See this tech note for more information: `http://tinyurl.com/y39kqp`.

Setting these five special security settings at any other level has no effect on domain accounts contained within Active Directory. However, if you linked a GPO containing these settings to an OU, the local computer would certainly respond accordingly.

Again, these policies cannot affect domain accounts when a GPO containing these settings is linked to, say, the **Sales** OU or **Marketing** OU. This is because these policies must specifically affect the Domain Controllers computer objects.

Modifying the "Default Domain Policy" GPO Directly

You can dive into the "Default Domain Policy" GPO in two ways. Use the Group Policy Management Console (GPMC) and click the domain name. You'll see the "Default Domain Policy" GPO linked to the domain level. If you try to edit the GPO at this level, you'll see the standard set of policy settings you've come to know and love while inside the Group Policy Object Editor. (Though again, as I've stated, you won't want to add "normal stuff" to this GPO.)

Here, for instance, you can specify (among other settings) that the password length is 10 characters, the user is locked out after the third password attempt, and Kerberos ticket expiration time is 600 minutes. But these values are only valid for the entire domain.

Again, if you want to add more policy settings at the domain level (which would affect all users or computers in the domain)—great! But try to leave the "Default Domain Policy" GPO alone, except when you need to change the "special" policy settings as described in this section.

Creating Your Own Group Policy Object Linked to the Domain Level and Changing the Precedence

Recall that at any level (site, domain, or OU), all the policy settings within all the GPOs linked to a level are merged unless there is a conflict. Then, the GPO with the highest precedence "wins" at a level. I talked about this in Chapter 2. The same is true regarding the settings special to the domain level: Password policy, Account Lockout policy, and Kerberos policy.

The defaults for these three policies are set within the "Default Domain Policy" GPO, but you could certainly create and link more GPOs to the domain level that would override the defaults. That doesn't necessarily mean that you should. Take a look at the example in Figure 8.2.

FIGURE 8.2 If you have a GPO with a higher precedence than the "Default Domain Policy" GPO, it will "win" if there's a conflict.

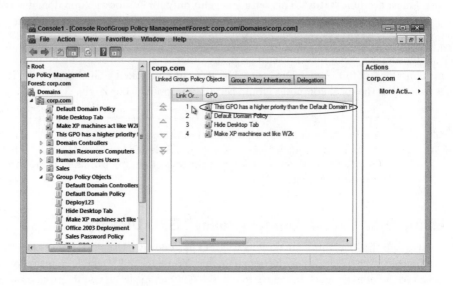

Here, a GPO is higher in priority than the "Default Domain Policy." If you do this, you better know precisely what you are doing! Again, this is because any policy setting within any GPO with a higher priority than the "Default Domain Policy" GPO will "win."

Which Approach Do You Take?

As you've seen, you can either modify the "Default Domain Policy" GPO or create your own GPO and ensure that the precedence is higher than the "Default Domain Policy" GPO. If you need to modify a special domain-wide account policy setting, which approach do you take? Here are the two schools of thought:

School of Thought #1   Modify only the Account Policies settings in the "Default Domain Policy" GPO. Then, ensure that it has the highest precedence at the domain level. This guarantees that if anyone does link other GPOs to the domain level, this one always wins.

School of Thought #2   Leave the defaults in the "Default Domain Policy" GPO. Never modify the "Default Domain Policy" GPO—ever. Create a new GPO for any special settings you want to override in the "Default Domain Policy" GPO. Then, link the GPO to the domain level, and ensure that it has higher precedence than the "Default Domain Policy" GPO (as seen in Figure 8.2).

Various Microsoft insiders have given me different (sometimes conflicting) advice about which to use. So what do I think?

If you want to modify any special domain-wide security settings, use School of Thought #1. This is the simplest and cleanest way. If you do it this way, you'll always treat the "Default Domain Policy" GPO with kid gloves and know it has a special use. And you can check in on it from time to time to make sure no one has lowered the precedence on it. Additionally, some applications, such as Microsoft SMS, will specifically modify the Default Domain Policy GPO. Hence, if you want that application to run smoothly, it's best to let it do what it wants to do.

School of Thought #2 has its merits. Leave the "Default Domain Policy" GPO clean as a whistle, and then create your own GPOs with higher precedence settings. However, I don't think this is a great idea, because you might forget that you set something important inside this new GPO.

Either way works, but my preference is for School of Thought #1.

Group Policy Objects Linked to the Domain Controllers OU

How is the **Domain Controllers** OU different? You can see there is also a default GPO linked, named the "Default Domain Controllers Policy" GPO. But, before we dive into it, let's take a step back. First, it's important to think of all the Domain Controllers as essentially equal. If one Domain Controller gets a policy setting (Security setting or otherwise), they should all really be getting the exact same policy settings. On logon, users choose a Domain Controller for validation at random; however, you want the experience they receive to be consistent, not random. Moreover, when you, as the Domain Administrator, log on to a Domain Controller at the console, you also want your experience to be consistent.

Oh, and did I mention that when servers are finished being promoted into Domain Controllers via DCPROMO, they automatically end up in the **Domain Controllers** OU? So, that's where the "Default Domain Controllers Policy" GPO comes into play. Again, it's easy to find the "Default Domain Controllers Policy" GPO. It's linked to the **Domain Controllers** OU.

Again, since all Domain Controllers are, by default, nestled within the **Domain Controllers** OU, all Domain Controllers are affected by all the aspects inside the "Default Domain Controllers Policy" GPO. Of specific note are the Security Settings, as shown in Figure 8.3.

For instance, you'll want the same Event Log settings for all Domain Controllers. You'll want to set it once, inside a GPO linked to the **Domain Controllers** OU, and have it affect all Domain Controllers. By default, the "Default Domain Controllers Policy" GPO has the following set to specific defaults, which should remain consistent among all Domain Controllers.

FIGURE 8.3   The "Default Domain Controllers Policy" GPO affects every Domain Controller in the Domain Controllers OU.

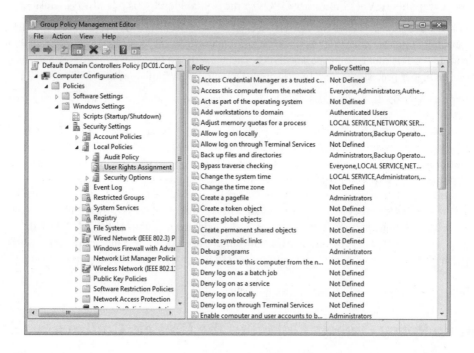

 Right-click any node and choose Export List from the shortcut menu to export to a text file for an easy way to document complex settings, such as User Rights Assignments.

Audit Policies   Located in Computer Configuration ➢ Policies ➢ Windows Settings ➢ Security Settings ➢ Local Policies ➢ Audit Policy. Here you can change the default auditing policies of Windows 2000, Windows 2003, or Windows 2008. Windows 2000 is a little light for my taste, and Windows 2003 is a little strong. We talk about auditing later in this chapter in the section "Auditing with Group Policy."

User Rights Assignment   Located in Computer Configuration ➢ Policies ➢ Windows Settings ➢ Security Settings ➢ Local Policies ➢ User Rights Assignment. Here you can configure which accounts you will "Allow log on locally" or "Log on as a service" among other specific rights.

Domain Controller Event Log Settings   Located in Computer Configuration ➢ Policies ➢ Windows Settings ➢ Security Settings ➢ Event Log. Set them here, and all Domain Controllers in the **Domain Controllers** OU will obey. Settings such as the maximum size of logs are contained here. Note, however, that decreasing the size of an Event log will not take effect on the DCs; you can enforce a log size increase, but not a decrease.

Various Security Options   Located in Computer Configuration ➢ Policies ➢ Windows Settings ➢ Security Settings ➢ Local Policies ➢ Security Options. Here you'll find settings such as "Interactive logon: Do not display last user name," which will affect the behavior of clients, servers, and/or Domain Controllers. Windows 2000 domains have different names for these settings. Note that GPOs created on Windows Vista machines will have more Windows Vista–specific security options available. The Group Policy spreadsheet (found at www.GPanswers.com in the Microsoft Resources section) has a list of all the security options and what target machines can be affected.

The same rules apply to the **Domain Controllers** OU as they do for the domain level. That is, you can put a GPO in at a higher precedence than the "Default Domain Controllers Policy" GPO. However, my recommendation is to use the "Default Domain Controllers Policy" GPO for the "special" things that you set at this level, and ensure that it's got the highest precedence when being processed within the OU.

Oops, the "Default Domain Policy" GPO and/or "Default Domain Controllers Policy" GPO Got Screwed Up!

If you modify the "Default Domain Policy" GPO or "Default Domain Controllers Policy" GPO such that you want to return it back to the defaults, you might just have a shot. The procedure is different for Windows 2000 domains or those with Windows 2003 Domain Controllers. First, you'll need to determine which default GPO got screwed up; then you need to take the appropriate steps. These procedures are among the most popular requests for Microsoft Product Support Services. However, these tools should be performed only as an absolute last resort because it will restore your defaults as if the installation were done "out of the box." So, be careful. If you have a backup of your defaults, you should try to perform a restore first—before using these "emergency-only" tools.

Repairing the Defaults for Windows 2003 Domains

As long as you have even one Windows 2003 Domain Controller, you have it made in the shade. Well, not too made, as you might already be in the doghouse if the default GPOs are screwed up. However, Windows 2003 domains with their Windows 2003 Domain Controllers come with a command-line tool, DCGPOFIX, to make it easy to restore back to the defaults. You can tell DCGPOFIX to restore the "Default Domain Policy" GPO (with the /Target:Domain switch) or the "Default Domain Controllers Policy" GPO (with the /Target:DC switch). Or you can restore both with the /Target:BOTH switch, as in Figure 8.4. The command-line tool has not changed functionality in Windows Server 2008.

FIGURE 8.4 Use DCGPOFIX with Windows 2003 Domain Controllers to restore the defaults if necessary.

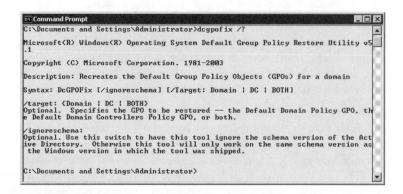

Optionally, you can simply reset the User Rights Assignment for Windows 2003 instead of plowing back the entire "Default Domain Controllers" GPO. To do so, see the Microsoft Knowledge Base article "HOW TO: Reset User Rights in the Default Domain Group Policy in Windows Server 2003" (KB 324800) at http://support.microsoft.com/kb/324800.

However, you might also encounter a strange situation if you're trying to bring back one of the default GPOs but you've updated the schema to some later version. If that happens, DCGPOFIX won't proceed unless you add the /ignoreschema switch in front.

The idea is that it will bring back the default GPO you choose based on the schema it knows (originally), not the one you might have upgraded to. There's a Microsoft Knowledge Base article here on it: http://support.microsoft.com/kb/932445.

This article states that nothing was modified in the schema that would affect Group Policy from Windows Server 2003 to Windows Server 2003 R2, but I don't know what that means in terms of Windows Server 2008.

If you have to restore the default GPOs for some reason, you might be in heap of trouble anyway and might want to call Microsoft Product Support Services for extra guidance.

Repairing the Defaults for Windows 2000 Domains

If the "Default Domain Policy" GPO or "Default Domain Controller Policy" GPO for a Windows 2000 domain get irreparably damaged, you can download and run a tool that was previously available only to customers when they called Microsoft Product Support Services. That is, Windows 2000 now has an equivalent to Windows 2003's DCGPOFIX. Its name is RecreateDefPol, and you have to download it. Here's a (shortened) link to the tool: www.tinyurl.com/3yyr3.

Understanding Local and Effective Security Permissions

The whole point of Group Policy is that when you make a wish from upon high, your client machines will embrace your wish. I've already discussed that Group Policy can be set, if you like, on the local machine. However, GPOs from Active Directory that contain policy settings that conflict with those on the local machine will "win" and override those set at the local machine.

If a local security policy is set on a machine and then a GPO in the domain "wins," you'll want to know, at a glance, which changes are coming from upon high within Active Directory Group Policy. This is the difference between "local" policies and "effective" policies.

With Windows 2000 clients, it was sometimes difficult to tell that your security wishes were being embraced. Windows 2000 local policy has a Local Setting and Effective Setting column to assist; but it wasn't always accurate. An older Microsoft Knowledge Base article (Q257922) described this as "Local Security Policy May Not Accurately Reflect Actual System Settings." However, that Knowledge Base article is no longer available.

The user interface in Windows Vista, Windows XP, Windows 2003, and Windows 2008 member servers has changed a bit since Windows 2000. Specifically, it now clearly distinguishes between security policies that can be changed locally versus security policies that are coming from upon high.

In this screen shot below, you can see a local machine policy via `GPEDIT.MSC`. Many Security Option settings are not being enforced from an Active Directory GPO (say, at the domain level or in an OU that contains the client machine). However, in the screen shot here, I set up one policy setting, the **Devices: Restrict CD-ROM access to locally logged-on user only**, set to Enabled within a GPO linked to the OU that contains the computer. Because Active Directory GPOs trump Local Computer Policy, this security policy setting therefore cannot be adjusted locally.

Setting this security policy setting locally (once it's set from a GPO linked to the OU) is not permitted. Indeed, the icon changes within `GPEDIT.MSC` to show you that the security policy is set within Active Directory:

- The security policies that are being dictated from a GPO in Active Directory have a little scroll icon flanked with two computers.

- The security policies that can still be set locally have "1/0" icons.

- This same "effective setting" icon theme is valid throughout other security settings categories: Account Policy (including Password policy), Audit Policy, User Rights Assignment, and Security Options.

So, you can have Active Directory GPOs restrict the modification of local computer policy. Windows XP and higher have a better way than Windows 2000 to display effective permissions. The icon within the local computer policy has changed from "1/0" icons to a scroll and computer icon.

The Strange Life of Password Policy

If you create a new GPO, link it to any OU, and then edit your new GPO, it certainly appears as if you *could* set the Password policy and Account Lockout policy using a GPO

But does it do anything? Let's find out.

Additionally, we'll talk about a new function in Windows Server 2008 called Fine-Grained Password Policy.

What Happens When You Set Password Settings at an OU Level

For example, I have a **Sales** OU in which I recently placed VISTA1. As you can see in Figure 8.5, I created and linked a GPO, called "Sales Password Policy," to the **Sales** OU. I am setting the Password policy such that the minimum password length is 10 characters.

At first glance this would seem to be counterproductive, because, as already stated, these policy settings only take hold of the accounts in the domain via the "Default Domain Policy" GPO. But administrators might actually want to perform this seemingly contradictory action.

That is, when the user logs on locally to the Windows workstation, the account policy settings contained in the GPO linked to the OU will have been magically planted on their machine to take effect for *local* accounts. In Figure 8.6, I have logged in as the local administrator account on the workstation.

FIGURE 8.5   It might seem counterproductive to set the Password policy at any level but the domain.

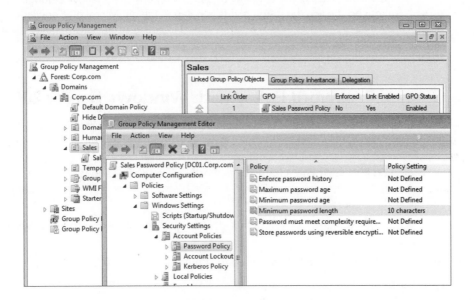

FIGURE 8.6   Setting a Password policy in the domain (other than at the domain level) will affect passwords used for local accounts upon member machines.

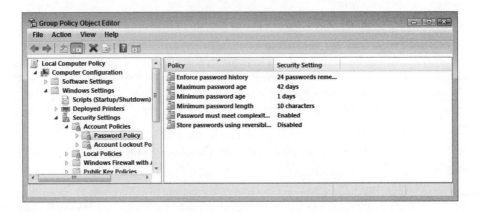

Again, this won't affect users' accounts when users are logging on to the domain; rather, it affects only the local accounts on the targeted computers. This could be helpful if you grant local administrator rights to users upon their workstations or laptops and want to set a baseline.

 If you are still using Windows 2000 machines, Figure 8.6 would show both "Local" and "Effective" settings for Windows 2000 Professional machines. However, because of the behavior described here, the effective settings might not be accurate. Again, this is noted in the old Microsoft Knowledge Base 257922 article "Local Security Policy May Not Accurately Reflect Actual System Settings."

Fine-Grained Password Policy with Windows Server 2008

So if setting Password policy at an OU level doesn't affect your domain users, is there a way to set password policies on specific users in the domain such that they have different password requirements?

Short answer: Yes. It's called Fine-Grained Password Policy (FGPP) and it's built into Windows Server 2008.

Longer answer (here goes):

You can do this with Windows Server 2008 if all Domain Controllers are Windows Server 2008, and...

The domain functional level has been raised to Windows Server 2008, and...

You can accept that you can't set Fine-Grained Password Policy upon OUs, and...

You accept that you can't use Group Policy to do it.

Oh wait, there's more:

Setting it up is a real bear. We'll be going through that in a second, but I just wanted to give you a heads-up now.

And, finally, did I mention that you can't use Group Policy and affect an entire OU?

Wouldn't that be nice? You bet, and it's quite simply not part of the deal here.

Now, this is a Group Policy book, but I'm going to give you the ever-so-brief run-through anyway, because you might want to get a feel for how this works. I'll have some links a little later for you to get super-deep with FGPP if you'd like to.

Let me jump to the end of the story though and say, quite simply, if you want to have

Fine-Grained Password Policy

and you want those policies dictated to specific OUs and specific people

and you want to use Group Policy

you can do so using a third-party add-on option via a company called Specops. Their product is called Specops Password Policy. And you can check it out at http://www.specopssoft.com/products/specopspasswordpolicy/ (http://tinyurl.com/yw8rr9).

A little later, after I've described all the gyrations required to get native Windows Server 2008 FGPP working, I'm also going to talk about a free Specops tool (with a darn similar name) called Specops Password Policy Basic. Stay tuned. We'll be working with that tool to help us with FGPP a little later.

So, with all those caveats behind us, what does FGPP bring to the table? It brings us the ability to dictate a specific password policy for a user account or an Active Directory global security group the user is a member of. The key takeaway here is the word *group* and not *OU*.

Let's check it out to see how it works. You'll want to perform these steps directly on your Windows Server 2008 Domain Controller.

Getting Ready for Fine-Grained Password Policy

Most domains will default to Windows Server 2003 functional level. However, if you're going to make use of this new feature, the domain functional level must be Windows Server 2008. You can check and/or raise the functional level by using Active Directory Users and Computers, right-clicking over the domain name, and selecting "Raise domain functional level," as seen in Figure 8.7.

FIGURE 8.7   Use Active Directory Users and Computers to raise the domain functional level (if needed).

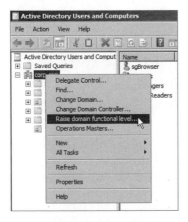

When you do, you can see the current domain functional level and/or change to Windows Server 2008 functional level if necessary, as shown in Figure 8.8. You'll need to do this if you want to proceed.

For a complete list of domain and forest level functionality features, check out http://tinyurl.com/23owaa.

FIGURE 8.8 You must be in Windows Server 2008 Functional Level (which you raise here if necessary) to get Fine-Grained Password Policy.

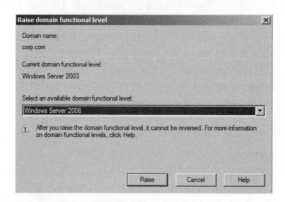

Creating a Password Setting Object (PSO)

Now, most people will run screaming when I mention the tool we'll be using for FGPP. It's (wait for it) ADSI Edit (which is now part of the Windows Server 2008 operating system and not an add-on tool).

ADSI Edit will help us create the unit we need, called a Password Setting Object, or PSO for short. Here's the breakdown of what we need to do to make the magic happen:

1. Create a PSO in the Password Settings Container (PSC) using ADSI Edit.

2. Configure the PSO options by completing the ADSI wizard.

3. Link the PSO to a user account or a global security group.

It's a long road, so let's get started.

Creating a Password Settings Object

Again, the tool we use is (shudder) ADSI Edit. So, start out by clicking Start ➢ Run and typing **adsiedit.msc** into the Run box. When you do, ADSI Edit will appear.

Right-click over the only node available (ADSI Edit) and select "Connect to." At the Connections Settings screen, accept all the defaults and select OK. You should be able to drill down into your Active Directory.

At this point, find Default naming context ➢ <domain FQDN> ➢ CN = System ➢ CN = Password Settings Container. Then right-click and select New ➢ Object, as seen in Figure 8.9.

Next you'll be presented with a crappy little wizard that walks you through the process, as seen in Figure 8.10.

With his permission, I'm borrowing my technical editor Jakob Heidelberg's excellent write-up of this subject from his blog, but also adding some additional items. You'll see this write-up in Table 8.1. (I'll give you a link a little later to his write-up on the subject.) Each item in the table represents a step in the Wizard, so be sure to read my notes carefully if you try to tackle this.

FIGURE 8.9   You start setting Fine-Grained Password policy using ADSI Edit.

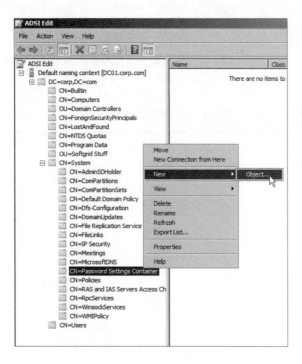

FIGURE 8.10   One screen of the Fine-Grained Password Policy Wizard (if you can call it that).

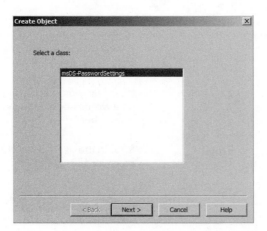

Note that some of the numbers are calculated as negative numbers. Yikes. So, how do you calculate these numbers? With this web page, which has a calculator script, of course:

http://msdn2.microsoft.com/en-us/library/ms974598.aspx
(http://tinyurl.com/yuekhs)

In our example here, we've suggested some values and provide their corresponding meaning as a baseline.

TABLE 8.1 Required Attributes to Set in Fine-Grained Password Policy

Attribute	Value	Meaning
Cn	SalesPasswords	This is the name of the policy. Try to come up with a naming convention for these policies if you will have lots of them.
msDS-PasswordSettingsPrecedence	10	This number is used as a "cost" for priority between different policies in case a user is hit by multiple PSOs. Be sure to leave space below and above for future use. The stronger the PSO password settings are, the lower the "cost" should be. In other words, use low numbers for PSOs you want to "win" if there's a precedence collision. (See more on this subject in the "Resulting Set of PSOs" section a little later.)
msDS-PasswordReversibleEncryptionEnabled	False	Boolean value to select if passwords should be stored with reversible encryption (usually not a good idea).
msDS-PasswordHistoryLength	32	How many previously used passwords should the system remember?
msDS-PasswordComplexityEnabled	True	Should the users use a complex password (Boolean value)?
msDS-MinimumPasswordLength	16	What should be the minimum number of characters in the user accounts password?

TABLE 8.1 Required Attributes to Set in Fine-Grained Password Policy *(continued)*

Attribute	Value	Meaning
msDS-MinimumPasswordAge	-864000000000 (9 zeros) Enter as negative value.	What is the minimum password age? (In this case, 1 day.) Note the minus sign to enter this as a negative value.
msDS-MaximumPasswordAge	-36288000000000 (9 zeros) Enter as negative value.	What is the maximum password age? (In this case, 42 days.) Note the minus sign to enter this as a negative value.
msDS-LockoutThreshold	5	How many failed attempts before the user account will be locked?
msDS-LockoutObservationWindow	-18000000000 (9 zeros) Enter as negative value.	After how long should the counter for failed attempts be reset? (In this case, 6 minutes.) Note the minus sign to enter this as a negative value.
msDS-LockoutDuration	-18000000000 (9 zeros) Enter as negative value.	For how long should the user account object be locked in case of too many bad passwords entered? (In this case, 6 minutes.) Note the minus sign to enter this as a negative value.

When you're finished entering the values in Table 8.1 into the Wizard, you can (get this), continue to optionally enter in even *more* values. But for now, just click Finish at the end of the wizard. At this point, you should see your PSO in the Password Settings Container object.

Double-click it to get its properties. We need to set a filter upon it. In the lower-right corner of the PSO's properties, you'll see a Filter button (not shown in Figure 8.11.) When you click it you'll see the Filtering options appear (seen in Figure 8.11). You can see the various default filter options.

Change the filter so the following options are selected:

- Show attributes: Mandatory, Optional
- Show read-only attributes: Constructed, Backlinks, and System-only

Leave the following two unchecked:

- Show only attributes that have values
- Show only writeable attributes

You can see the desired filter state in Figure 8.12.

FIGURE 8.11 You need to change the filter options.

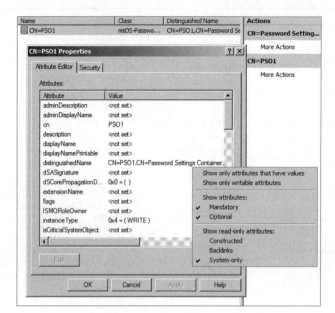

FIGURE 8.12 The changed filter options

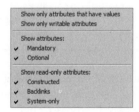

Now, inside the PSO, you should be able to see the msDS-PSOAppliesTo attribute as seen in Figure 8.13. Click Edit, then select Add Windows Account and pick the users and/or groups of your choice to get this particular password policy. In this case, I'm assigning the PSO to EastSalesUser1 and EastSalesUser2.

You'll see the msDS-PSOAppliesTo variable changes to reflect the SIDs of the users and groups you just added.

When you're done losing your mind inside ADSI Edit, close the tool.

Resulting Set of PSOs

In our example above, we created one PSO and linked it to some user accounts. But how can we see the results of our labor?

FIGURE 8.13   You can assign specific PSOs to user accounts.

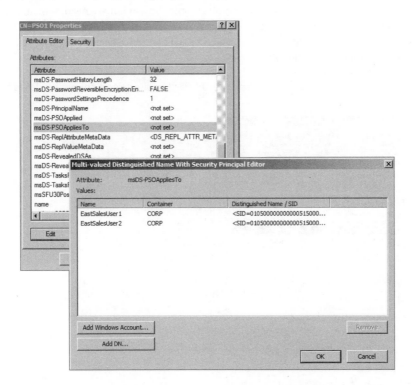

The Active Directory Users and Computer Attribute Editor

You can validate your efforts by firing up Active Directory Users and Computers. But Active Directory Users and Computers needs to be running in a special mode called Advanced Features to see the results of what we just performed. So, after running Active Directory Users and Computers, select View ➢ Advanced Features, as seen in Figure 8.14.

FIGURE 8.14   Use Active Directory Users and Computers Advanced Features to see if your users are receiving Fine-Grained Password Policies.

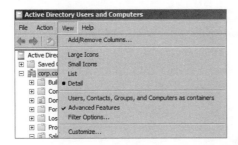

Then, find and open the user account. Click on the new Windows Server 2008 Attribute Editor tab, seen in Figure 8.15. Now, the defaults won't show what we need, which means we need to click Filter and reselect the filter options we selected earlier in Figure 8.12. Once you do that, you should see an attribute called `msDS-ResultantPSO`, seen in Figure 8.16. This is the PSO that is ultimately applied to the user.

FIGURE 8.15   The attribute we need, msDS-PSOApplied, isn't shown by default.

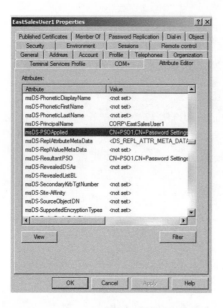

FIGURE 8.16   The attribute we need, msDS-PSOApplied, is shown only when properly filtered.

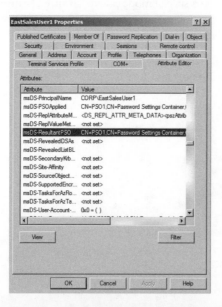

PSO Precedence

Now in all this hubbub of creating a PSO for your users and groups, you might have forgotten all about the Default Domain Policy. Turns out, it's still working for you, behind the scenes in case you never touch PSOs.

Here's the breakdown of what happens now that you have PSOs set up:

1. If a user has a PSO linked directly to him, that PSO automatically wins. If there are multiple PSOs linked to the user, you'll see a warning in the Event log, and the one with the *lowest* precedence value is the resultant PSO. If the user doesn't have a PSO linked directly to him, see #2.

2. If the user is a member of a global security group, he gets a PSO linked to that security group. If the user is a member of multiple groups with PSOs linked to them, see #3.

3. All the global groups of which the user is a member (and has PSOs linked) are compared. The one with the lowest precedence dictates his resultant PSO.

4. If none of these applies (no PSOs on his account or any group he's a member of), the Default Domain Policy is applied.

So one good strategy is to ensure that your Default Domain Policy password settings are really tough by default. That way, if you make some mistake with FGPP, and someone "defaults" to the Default Domain Policy, you've still got nice, tough security on those passwords. Basically, you'll be "secure by default."

Using Specops Password Policy Basic (Free Edition)

So, let me get this straight: you didn't like entering all that data using the crappy wizard, running scripts to calculate negative values, and then linking it over to the user or group accounts?

Right.

If there were only a free GUI tool to help you through that minefield. Well, there is, and it's called Specops Password Policy Basic and is available at www.specopssoft.com (specific link http://tinyurl.com/33s7bt). Note that you'll need to have PowerShell installed on the management station upon which you install this tool.

In Figure 8.17, you can see how easy it is to configure a new PSO, provide parameters, then address which members should get the policy.

Easy!

Specops Password Policy Basic also allows you to see which PSOs "win" if multiple PSOs address a user, a group, or both.

It's free, so positively check it out.

Again, their pay tool, Specops Password Policy (not basic or free) enables you to perform Fine-Grained Password Policy directly to users or OUs, using Group Policy. Ah, joy.

Command Line PSO Management

If you're a command-line freak and don't want to deal with the hassle of the ADSI Edit GUI we saw, Joe from www.Joeware.net has a great tool called PSOmgr that will do just the trick. Just head over to

http://www.joeware.net/freetools/tools/psomgr/index.htm

FIGURE 8.17 Specops Password Policy Basic makes quick work of complicated Fine-Grained Password Policy

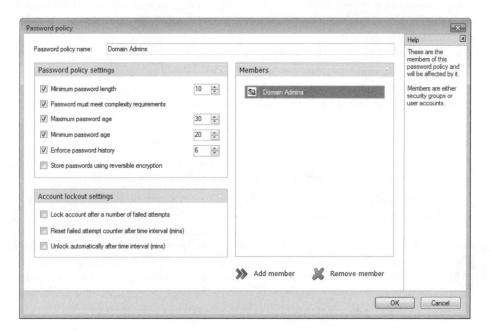

More Information on Fine-Grained Password Policy

Before we leave this section, it should be noted that there are three attributes that, on a per-user basis, can always override the PSO:

- Reversible password encryption required
- Password not required
- Password does not expire

   If any of these attributes are set directly upon a user using Active Directory Users and Computers, they will be honored, and the PSO policy for those attributes will be ignored.

   If you'd like to spend more quality time with FGPP, here are some great links for you to explore.

- Microsoft's documentation on this: `http://tinyurl.com/2xubeo`
- Step-by-step guide from Microsoft: `http://tinyurl.com/28726o`
- Jakob Heidelberg's take on FGPP: `http://tinyurl.com/2xld67` (Jakob is the technical editor for this book, and one really smart dude.)
- And his part II: `http://tinyurl.com/224lyj`
- And Ulf B. Simon-Weidner's blog at `http://tinyurl.com/22h4sf`

Inside Auditing With and Without Group Policy

Auditing is a powerful tool. It can help you determine when people are doing things they shouldn't as well as help you determine when people are doing things they should.

But here's the trick: some auditing occurs when you use Group Policy to turn it on. But apparently someone within the Windows Server 2008 team didn't get that memo. So there's some newly expanded stuff you can audit for in Windows Server 2008, except you don't use Group Policy to turn it on.

Grr.

We'll first examine the auditing possibilities with Group Policy; that is, the stuff you can actually audit when you use Group Policy to enable the auditing. Then, we'll talk about auditing Group Policy itself.

Finally, we'll review the new auditing features that are only available with Windows Vista and Windows Server 2008—except they don't use Group Policy to get enabled. You'll see when we get there.

Auditing with Group Policy

So, Group Policy can be used to turn on many auditable events.

Certain aspects of auditing you'll turn on at the **Domain Controller** OU level, inside the "Default Domain Controllers Policy" GPO. Other aspects of auditing you'll typically turn on at other OU levels (via a GPO linked to the OU containing the systems you want to audit).

In Figure 8.18, you can see the default auditing settings contained within the "Default Domain Controllers Policy" GPO.

FIGURE 8.18   Windows 2003 enables lots of auditable events by default.

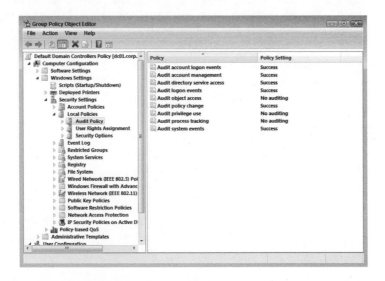

The list of possibilities for auditing are numerous and confusing. Table 8.2 shows what can be audited, along with where you should perform the audit.

> No matter how much you audit, it does you no good unless you're actually reviewing the logs! There is no way out of the box to centralize the collection of logs from your Domain Controllers, servers, or workstations. Consider a third-party tool, such as Microsoft MOM or Event Log Sentry II from www.engagent.com.

TABLE 8.2   Auditable Events

Auditing Right	What It Does	Where You Should Set It	Is It On by Default in Windows 2003 Active Directory?	Notes
Audit account logon events	Enters events when someone attempts to log on to Active Directory.	In the "Default Domain Controllers Policy" GPO to monitor when anyone tries to log on to Active Directory.	Yes.	By default, only successes generate events. Settings can be changed to record logon failures as well.
Audit account management	Enters events when someone creates, deletes, renames, enables, or disables users, computers, groups and so on.	In the "Default Domain Controllers Policy" GPO to generate events for when users, computers, and so on are created in Active Directory. Set at the OU level to generate events on file servers or workstations for when users and groups are created on member machines.	Yes. Enabled on Domain Controllers, which log Active Directory events only. Not enabled on member servers.	By default, only successful object manipulations generate events. Settings can be changed to record failures as well.

TABLE 8.2   Auditable Events *(continued)*

Auditing Right	What It Does	Where You Should Set It	Is It On by Default in Windows 2003 Active Directory?	Notes
Audit directory service access	Enters events when Active Directory objects are specified to be audited.	In the "Default Domain Controllers Policy" GPO.	Yes. In the "Default Domain Controllers Policy" GPO, which will log Active Directory access and GPO creation, deletion, and modification. See the section "Auditing Group Policy Object Changes." Not enabled on member servers.	Works in conjunction with the actual attribute in Active Directory that has auditing for users or computers enabled. Can be used to audit other aspects of Active Directory. See the section "Auditing Group Policy Changes."
Audit logon events	Enters events for interactive logon (Local logon) and network logon (Kerberos).	Set at OU level to generate logon events on servers you want to track access for.	Yes. In "Default Domain Controller Policy" GPO, which affects only Active Directory logons.	Set this setting to determine if UserA touches a shared folder on ServerA. This will constitute an auditable event for "Audit logon events."
Audit object access	Enters events when file objects are specified to be audited.	If you store files on your Domain Controllers, you can set this at the "Default Domain Controllers Policy" GPO. Else, set it at the OU level to monitor specific files within member machines.	No.	Works in conjunction with the actual file on the file server having auditing enabled. See the section "Auditing File Access."

TABLE 8.2 Auditable Events *(continued)*

Auditing Right	What It Does	Where You Should Set It	Is It On by Default in Windows 2003 Active Directory?	Notes
Audit policy change	Enters events when changes are made to user rights, auditing policies, or trust relationships.	In the "Default Domain Controllers" GPO to monitor when changes are made within Active Directory. Set at OU level to monitor when changes are made on member machines.	Yes. In "Default Domain Controllers Policy" GPO, which affects only Active Directory events.	
Audit privilege use	Enters events when any user right is used, such as backup and restore.	In the "Default Domain Controllers Policy" GPO to generate events for when accounts in Active Directory are used. Set at the OU level to generate events on file servers when accounts on member machines are used.	No.	
Audit process tracking	Enters events when specific programs or processes are running.	In the "Default Domain Controllers Policy" GPO to affect Domain Controllers. Set at the OU level to monitor processes on specific servers within the OU.	No.	This is an advanced auditing feature that can generate a lot of events once turned on. Only turn this on at the behest of Microsoft PSS or another troubleshooting authority.

TABLE 8.2   Auditable Events *(continued)*

Auditing Right	What It Does	Where You Should Set It	Is It On by Default in Windows 2003 Active Directory?	Notes
Audit system events	Enters events when the system starts up, shuts down, or any time the security or system logs have been modified.	In the "Default Domain Controllers Policy" GPO to determine when Domain Controllers are rebooted or logs have been modified. Set at an OU level to monitor when member machines are rebooted or logs have been modified.	Yes. In "Default Domain Controllers Policy" GPO, which affects only Domain Controllers.	

Auditing Group Policy Object Changes

You might be asked to determine who created a specific Group Policy and when it was created. To that end, you can leverage Active Directory's auditing capability and use Group Policy to audit Group Policy! Whenever a new Group Policy is born, deleted, or modified, various events such as the 566 Event in Figure 8.19 (for Windows Server 2003) and the 4662 Event in Figure 8.21 (for Windows Server 2008) are generated.

These events are generated on the Domain Controllers because two things are automatically set up by default in Active Directory (since Windows Server 2003):

- **Audit directory service access** is enabled in the "Default Domain Controllers Policy" GPO. You can see this in Figure 8.18, earlier in this chapter. In 100 percent new Windows Server 2008 domains, this isn't set "on" in the GPO; it is just hard-coded "on" by default regardless of the value in the GUI.

- Auditing is turned on for the "Policies" object container within Active Directory. The Policies folder is where the GPC (Group Policy Container) for a given GPO is stored in Active Directory. Auditing is turned on so that events are generated when anyone creates, destroys, or modifies any objects inside the folder.

FIGURE 8.19 Event 566s are generated when GPOs are created or modified (Windows Server 2003).

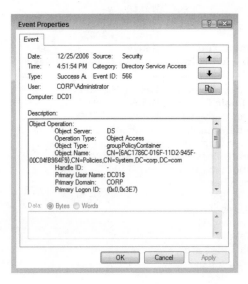

To view the Policies container, follow these steps:

1. Launch Active Directory Users and Computers.

2. Choose View ➢ Advanced Features. This enables you to see some normally hidden folders and security rights within Active Directory Users and Computers.

3. Drill down into Domain ➢ System ➢ Policies.

4. Right-click the Policies folder, and choose the Properties from the shortcut menu to open the Properties dialog box.

5. Click the Security tab.

6. Click the Advanced button to open the Advanced Security Settings for Policies window.

7. Click the Auditing tab, which is shown in Figure 8.20.

If you drill down even deeper, you'll discover that the Everyone group will trigger events when new GPOs are modified or created. It is this interaction that generates events, such as those shown in Figure 8.19 and Figure 8.21.

If you wanted to hone in on who triggered events (as opposed to the Everyone group), you could remove the Everyone group from being audited (shown in Figure 8.20) and plunk in just the users or groups you wanted to monitor.

FIGURE 8.20   Auditing for GPO changes is set on the Policies folder within Active Directory Users and Computers.

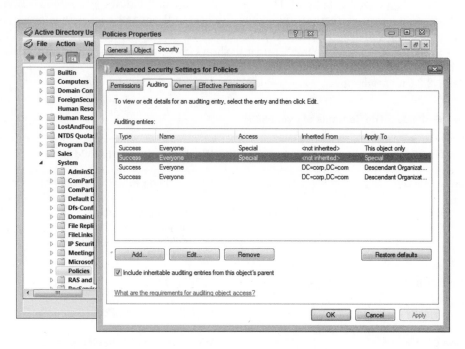

FIGURE 8.21   Event 4662 is generated when GPOs are created or modified (Windows Server 2008).

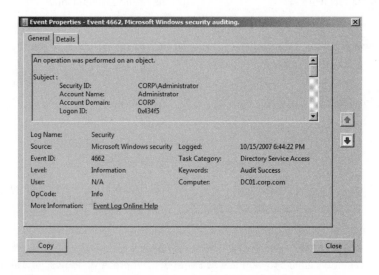

Group Policy Auditing Event IDs for Windows Server 2003

As you saw in Figure 8.19, the Event ID for GPO Auditing on Windows Server 2003 is Event ID number 566. However, there are numerous instances of Event 566, each with information that depends on precisely what you do to the GPO. The bad news is that the audit doesn't show you the GPO's "friendly name"; rather, it shows only the GUID, which is a little disappointing and makes things difficult to track down.

Table 8.3 shows what to expect when looking within Event 566.

TABLE 8.3 The Contents of Event 566

Action That Occurred	Field to Look For	What It Shows in the Field
Create a new GPO	Accesses	Create Child groupPolicyContainer
Modify a GPO	Properties	Write Property—Default property set versionNumber gPCMachineExtensionNames groupPolicyContainer
Remove a GPO	Access	WRITE_DAC
	Properties	WRITE_DAC groupPolicyContainer
Change GPO status	Properties	Write Property—Default property set flags groupPolicyContainer
Remove the Link Enabled status or remove the link from an OU	Properties	Write Property—Default property set gPLink organizationalUnit
Enforce/unenforce a GPO link	Properties	Write Property—Default property set gPLink organizationalUnit (or domainDNS if done at the domain level)
Block/unblock inheritance on an OU	Object Type	OrganizationalUnit
	Properties	Default property set gPOptions organizationalUnit
Change permissions	Properties	WRITE_DAC groupPolicyContainer

NOTE Windows 2000 shows these as Event 565, whereas Windows 2003 shows them as Event 566. The "Field to Look For" column and the "What It Shows" column may not be precisely the same for Windows 2000 domains.

Windows 2000 will also pop up Event 643 whenever the "Default Domain Policy" GPO is processed (whether changed or unchanged). You might see a lot of these, and you can safely ignore them.

Group Policy Auditing Event IDs for Windows Server 2008

The Event ID number changes from 566 in Windows Server 2003 to 4662 in Windows Server 2008. You can see an example in Figure 8.22, which shows that a specific GPO is being changed.

FIGURE 8.22   The GUID of the GPO is listed in the auditing trail.

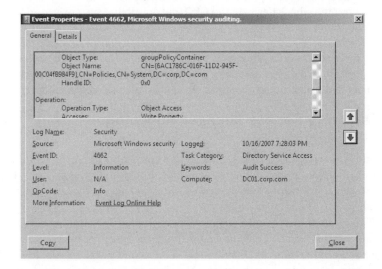

Whoopie.

I'm more than a little disappointed that Windows Server 2008 brings basically zero improvements in figuring out what's changed within a GPO. And, what's more, reading the Event log details of a changed GPO is harder than trying to figure out what's going on in the movie *Pulp Fiction* the first time you watch it.

Auditing Directory Service Changes

So, with Windows Server 2008 come some potentially useful new auditing capabilities. The idea is that you can turn on the ability to show four new Event ID types for when stuff happens in Active Directory. Here are the Event IDs and what they show:

- Event 5136: Show modified attributes
- Event 5137: Show created attributes

- Event 5138: Show undeleted attributes
- Event 5139: Show moved attributes

I was initially excited about these events, thinking that when a Group Policy Object was created or changed it would show me Event 5137 and 5136 and show me the changes *within the GPO*.

It doesn't.

It tells you a new GPO was created (but I knew that from Event IDs 4662). But the problem is that Windows Server 2008 still has no way to "crack in" to the GPO to see what's changed. If that's what you want to do, there are third-party tools listed in the auditing section of the Appendix of this book that can do that.

> Additionally, AGPM, which we talk about in Chapter 12, has the ability to determine who "checked-in" a GPO (but only if that system is used for Group Policy management).

However, what these events do is show you what has changed in Active Directory. Say EastSalesUser9 was renamed Sally. In that case, you'll get multiple 5136 events because there are a gaggle of things that go on under the hood when a simple user rename occurs.

Turning on Directory Service Changes Subcategory

So how do you enable these new gifts?

Not using Group Policy itself, I'm afraid. This one is a command-line-only venture, which you must perform by hand on every Domain Controller. And you do this on every Domain Controller because you don't want some Domain Controllers to log these new items and others missing out.

Again, before I give you the secret sauce here, you need to ask yourself, "How useful is this going to be for me?" Already you could audit if something changed. The question is, "Do you want to see before and after results of the auditing?" The second question you need to ask yourself is, "Am I prepared to perform multiple steps along anywhere in Active Directory I want to actually audit for these special events?" If the answer is "Yes again," then go for it.

The new event IDs fall under a new category, well, subcategory, of features called "Directory service changes." So, to turn them on you'll use the `auditpol.exe` command on your Windows Server 2008 Domain Controller.

The command you need to type is this (as seen in Figure 8.23):

```
auditpol /set /subcategory:"directory service changes" /success:enable
```

FIGURE 8.23   Turn on the new Event IDs.

```
C:\Users\Administrator>auditpol /set /subcategory:"directory service changes" /s
uccess:enable
The command was successfully executed.

C:\Users\Administrator>
```

Auditing the Specific OU

But wait! There's more you have to do. Specifically, you have to turn on auditing at the OU level. At least, it's an OU in my example, you can audit other areas of Active Directory as well. Here's what to do next:

1. Using Active Directory Users and Computers, right-click the organizational unit (OU) (or any object) for which you want to enable auditing, and then click Properties.

2. Click the Security tab, then click Advanced, and finally click the Auditing tab.

3. Click Add, and under "Enter the object name to select," type **Everyone** (or anyone you want to specifically audit for), then click OK.

4. In "Apply onto," click "Descendant User objects" (which is really far down the list). Note that you could also audit other objects if the container you're auditing contains other objects.

5. Under Access, select the Successful check box for "Write all properties."

6. Click OK in all open windows.

The Results

To see your results, just rename a user within that OU you just adjusted for auditing. In Figure 8.24, you can see that I've renamed EastSalesUser9 to Sally.

Is this useful? Well, here's the thing: you'd still get 4662 events that express that something's happened to the account anyway.

FIGURE 8.24 Here you can see that the AttributeValue of Sally is placed upon the ObjectDN of EastSalesUser9.

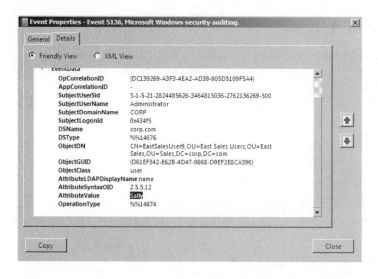

So the jury is out. My pal Randy Franklyn Smith, who really knows auditing and the Event log, has a neat blog entry where he gives his opinion on auditpol.exe here: http://www.ultimatewindowssecurity.com/newauditpol/..

Additionally, if you want more information from the source on this, a Microsoft guide that has lots of Auditpol advice can be found here: http://tinyurl.com/2qwu9e.

AuditPol For Clients

Earlier, we used auditpol.exe to audit for directory services events. Auditpol can also be used to audit for some extra categories of features on client systems as well.

Except that because auditpol.exe is a .exe, and not "command-able" using Group Policy, you have to run around to each machine and run the command or use a script to apply your auditpol.exe wishes to each machine.

Obviously, some scriptable solution is preferred. But of course, that's going to be really, really clunky. First you need to configure one machine with the auditpol.exe settings you want, then export them. Then, you need to set a special policy setting called **Audit: Force audit policy subcategory settings (Windows Vista or later) to override audit policy category settings** so you don't overwrite your client's systems with domain GPOs.

Finally, you run a script to pull the settings from the Netlogon share to each of your Windows Vista clients.

Check out Microsoft KB 921469, which shows you how to do the dirty work.

Auditing File Access

If you want to enable auditing when users attempt to access files on file servers, you could run around to each server and turn on file auditing. Or (insert fanfare music here), you could use Group Policy to do it in one fell swoop.

So, to leverage file auditing on a wide scale, you need to do the following within Active Directory:

- Create an OU.
- Move the accounts of those file servers in the OU.
- Create a GPO linked to the OU.
- Enable the **Audit object access** policy setting inside the GPO linked to the OU.

Once you do this, you then specify which files or folders on the target file server you wish to audit. To do so, follow these steps:

1. At the target file server itself, use Explorer to drill down into the drive letter and directory that you want to audit. Right-click the folder (or just one specific file), and choose Properties from the shortcut menu to open the Properties dialog box.

2. Click the Security tab, and then click the Advanced button to open the Advanced Security Settings for the share.

3. Click the Auditing tab.

4. Click Add to pop up the Auditing Entry dialog, seen in Figure 8.25. This dialog will allow you to add users to the auditing entries.

The simplest and most effective entry you can add is the Everyone group, as shown in Figure 8.25. When anyone tries to touch the file, you can audit for certain triggers, such as the "Read" permission.

FIGURE 8.25   Set auditing for files on the file or folder on the target system.

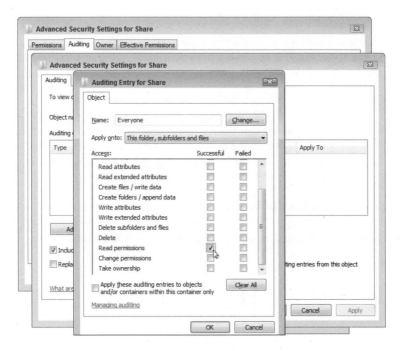

Logon, Logoff, Startup, and Shutdown Scripts

Users have always been able to get logon scripts. NT 4 used User Manager for Domains to assign logon scripts, and Windows 2000, 2003, and 2008 domains may use Active Directory

Users and Computers to assign logon scripts. However, you can step up to the next level using Group Policy and get more than just logon scripts:

- Users can get logon and logoff scripts.
- Computers can get startup and/or shutdown scripts.

And, the best part is, you're not limited to old DOS-style batch files. Scripts deployed via Group Policy can use DOS-style .BAT or .CMD scripts, VBScript (.VBS files), or JavaScript (.JS files), or even executables.

Although logon and startup scripts might be useful to map to network drives and automatically fire up Excel, the scripts can be equally useful when logging off or shutting down. Imagine automatically scripting the cleanup of the Temp folder or the ability to kick off a full-drive sweep of your virus scanner.

To use scripts with Group Policy, users must be in the site, domain, or OU linked to a GPO that contains a logon or logoff script. As the name of the script implies, users execute the script only at logon or logoff. Computers must also be in the site, domain, or OU linked to a GPO that contains a startup or shutdown script, which they run only at startup or shutdown.

> User and computer scripts delivered via Group Policy do not run "visibly" to the user, which prevents users from canceling them. To that end, scripts run silently in the background unless there is a problem. At that point, you have to wait until the script times out (10 minutes by default). I'll show you a bit later how to expose the scripts to run visibly.

In these examples, I'll use basic DOS-style .BAT commands to explain the concept. Here is an example of a script that displays "Hello World" and then pauses for a key press before removing the files from the *%temp%* folder. In Notepad, create the following file:

```
Echo "Hello World."
Pause
Del /Q /S %temp%
Pause
```

> Only your Windows XP, Windows 2000, Windows 2003, and Windows 2008 clients receive scripts from GPOs. If you have down-level clients (such as Windows NT), they can run only old-style logon scripts. The old-style logon script is located as a Logon Script field in the user's Profile tab inside Active Directory Users and Computers.

Startup and Shutdown Scripts

The Startup and Shutdown script settings are found under the Computer Configuration ➤ Policies node in the Windows Settings ➤ Scripts (Startup/Shutdown) branch. You can get your proposed script into the proper GPO in many ways; however, I think I have found the ideal way, as follows:

1. Once you're in the Group Policy Management Editor, drill down to the Scripts (Startup/Shutdown) node and double-click Startup. The Startup Properties dialog box will appear.

2. Click the Add button to open the Add a Script dialog box.

3. In the Script Name field, you can enter a filename or click Browse to open the Browse dialog box, shown in Figure 8.26.

FIGURE 8.26   You can create .BAT or .VBS files on-the-fly with this little trick.

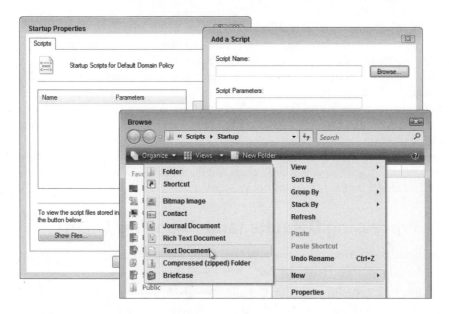

4. To create a new file, right-click in the Browse dialog box, and choose New ➢ Text Document, for example.

5. Enter a name for the file, for example, `myscript.bat`.

6. When asked if you want to change the file extension, click Yes, right-click the file, and choose Edit from the shortcut menu to open Notepad.

7. Type your script, and save the file.

8. Select the new file as the proposed script.

Again, the computer account must be in an OU with a linked GPO that contains a script. However, don't reboot yet. By default, you won't see the script run. And, since our script contains a Pause statement, your users will wait a really long time before the script times out. To allow the script to be visible (and enable you to press any key at the pause), enable a policy setting that also affects the machine. Traverse to Computer Configuration ➢ Policies ➢ Administrative Templates ➢ System ➢ Scripts, and select either **Run startup scripts visible** or **Run shutdown scripts visible,** or enable both options.

Last, it's important to understand the context in which Startup and Shutdown scripts run. Specifically, they run in the LocalSystem context. If you want to connect to resources across the network, you'll need to ensure that those resources allow for computer access across the network (not just user access) because the script will run in the context of the computer account when it accesses network resources (e.g., the Domain Computers group).

Logon and Logoff Scripts

The Logon and Logoff script settings are under the User Configuration ➢ Policies node in the Windows Settings ➢ Scripts (Logon/Logoff) branch. If you're implementing new logon scripts, I suggest you follow the steps in the previous section. Again, the user must be in an OU with a linked GPO with a script. However, don't log off and log back on yet. By default, you won't see the script run. To allow the script to be visible (and enable you to press any key at the pause), you need to enable a Group Policy. Traverse to User Configuration ➢ Policies ➢ Administrative Templates ➢ System ➢ Scripts, and select either **Run logon scripts visible** or **Run logoff scripts visible,** or enable both options.

Logon and Logoff scripts run in the user's context. Remember that a user is just a mere mortal and might not be able to manipulate Registry keys that you might want to run in a logon or logoff script.

For great tip on how to utilize computer startup scripts to manipulate parts of the users' Registry hive (with LocalSystem permissions), check out the article "Efficient Registry Cleanup" by Jakob H. Heidelberg (`http://tinyurl.com/24dm5v`).

Script Processing Defaults (and Changing Them)

One final note about scripts before we move on. Different scripting types run either synchronously or asynchronously. Here's the deal:

Logon Scripts Run Asynchronously by Default   By default, logon scripts run asynchronously. That is, all scripts at a certain level will basically fire off at the same time. There is no precedence order for scripts at the same level, and there is no knowing which script will finish before another. If you want to change this behavior to help "link" one script after another, you have to tell the client computer to run the scripts *synchronously*. If you want to change this (and many times you'll want to), then find Computer Configuration ➢ Policies ➢ Administrative Templates ➢ System ➢ Scripts, and enable **Run logon scripts synchronously.**

Bizarrely, there is also a setting that does the exact same thing located on User Settings ➢ Policies ➢ Administrative Templates ➢ System ➢ Scripts ➢ **Run logon scripts synchronously.** Again, recall that if there's a conflict between these settings, the ones that affect the computer will "win."

Startup Scripts Run Synchronously by Default   By default, startup scripts run synchronously. That is, all scripts are processed from lowest to highest priority order. Then, each script is run—consecutively—until they're finished. This usually makes the most sense, so I tend to leave it as is. However, if you want to change it, then locate Computer Configuration ➢ Policies ➢ Administrative Templates ➢ System ➢ Scripts, and enable **Run startup scripts asynchronously.**

Group Policy Scripts Time Out in 10 Minutes   As stated, if a script just hangs there, you'll have to wait a whopping 10 minutes for it to time out. You can change this with the policy setting found at Computer Configuration ➢ Policies ➢ Administrative Templates ➢ System ➢ Scripts called **Maximum wait time for Group Policy scripts.**

Old-School Logon Scripts Run "Visible"   If you use Active Directory Users and Computers to assign a user a logon script, those scripts will be visible to the user. If you want to hide old-school logon scripts from users while they run, you can change this with the policy setting found at User Settings ➢ Policies ➢Administrative Templates ➢ System ➢ Scripts ➢ **Run legacy logon scripts visible.**

Before we move on, let's take a second to talk about "perceived slow" performance when scripts are used with Group Policy. In previous chapters, I suggested you might want to make your Windows machines act like Windows 2000. That is, use the **Always wait for the network at Startup and Logon** policy setting, which throws Windows into "synchronous" processing mode. There can be one problem with this. It can affect you if you have laptops that are not always "on the network" at bootup. This *can* cause slower performance. Imagine you have traveling users on laptops with startup and login scripts. By default, the scripts are stored on the Domain Controller. So, during bootup or login time, the laptop tries to connect to the Domain Controller for the script. You may want to dictate to the client to use a local path (like `c:\scripts\blah.vbs`) instead of the default, which will go to the server.

Don't Panic: What to Do If Login Scripts with Network Drive Mappings Aren't Working as Expected with Windows Vista

Let's assume you have a share called "share" on DC01. Now, let's assume you have a simple login script within a GPO linked to, say, **Human Resources Users** OU. And this simple script simply

> Cleared out any mapped drives
>
> Said "Hello World"
>
> And mapped a letter (s:) as a network drive to \\dc01\share and
>
> Paused for a keypress before finishing.

It would look like this:

```
net use * /d /y
Echo "Hello World."
net use s: \\dc01\share
pause
```

Try this script as a logon script for a user using a pre-Vista machine and it works great. The drive letter maps at logon time, and the user can use it as long as they want.

Try this script as a logon script for a user using a Windows Vista machine, and, well, you're going to have some issues, as shown in Figure 8.27.

Wait—this gets even weirder. During my testing of the shipping version of Windows Vista, I tried logging out and logging in again, and it totally worked (as seen in Figure 8.28). Here's the thing: The correct behavior is that it's not *supposed* to succeed at all, and I can't explain why it does sometimes succeed on the second login.

FIGURE 8.27 Login scripts run fine on Windows Vista, but a mapped network drive will be inaccessible to the user.

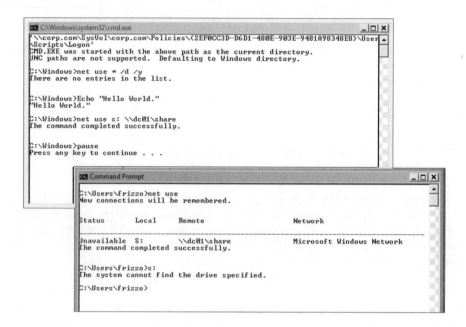

FIGURE 8.28 Second time's a charm when logging in with login scripts.

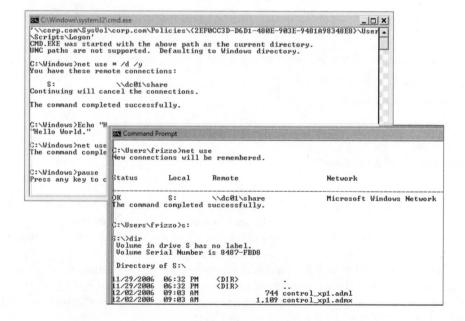

It's not supposed to succeed because User Account Control (UAC is described in detail in the next chapter) is kicking in. So drive mappings from a higher-privilege user shouldn't be able to be leveraged from mere mortal user accounts. (Again, I'm not sure why it succeeds on the second try sometimes. It's not supposed to.)

In short, I'm guessing that you won't ever want it so that the user can't have access to mapped drives. And with these two tips, you can make the behavior act like Windows XP.

Remediation #1

You can set a Registry value on your Windows Vista machines so that it doesn't matter how the network drives are mapped. They'll be accessible by every user. Again, this has to be done on the target machine. Set HKLM ➤ Software ➤ Microsoft ➤ Windows ➤ CurrentVersion ➤ Policies ➤ System ➤ `EnableLinkedConnections` (REG_DWORD) to 1.

Adding this Registry value or changing its value back to 0 requires a reboot. By default, the Registry value doesn't exist on the system and, therefore, the linked connections are *not* added.

Note that creating `EnableLinkedConnections` and setting it to a 1 is not officially supported in Windows Vista. Only the second method (described next) is fully supported.

Remediation #2

We've referenced the Microsoft document entitled "Deploying Group Policy Using Windows Vista" before. It can be found here: `http://tinyurl.com/yenok6`.

Inside, there's a section titled "Group Policy Scripts can fail due to User Account Control." There's a script located in the appendix that you run. This script then calls your login script and, in doing so, will bypass this issue.

But it does so in a, well, not very pretty way. It submits your login script to be run as a scheduled task. So, in short, it'll take a bit (maybe more) for your login script to run. Note that you could edit the script to remove the information messages that the script is being sent to the Task Scheduler.

When I tried to use this method (using the exact provided steps), there was a problem. That's because the document didn't specify to type in the whole path of your login script as a parameter. Therefore, when the Task Scheduler tried to run it, it simply failed. I reported this issue a while ago, but the docs seemingly haven't changed.

Restricted Groups

With a special security-related Group Policy function, you can use Restricted Groups to strictly control the following tasks:

- The membership of security groups that you create in Active Directory
- The security group membership on groups created on member machines (workstations or servers)
- The security groups that are nested within each other

You might want to strictly control these security groups or nestings to make sure that users in other areas of Active Directory, say, other domain administrators, don't inadvertently add someone to a group that shouldn't be there. Here are some practical uses of this technology:

- Ensure that the domain's Backup Operators group contains only Sally and Joe.

- Ensure that the local Administrators group on all desktops contains the user accounts of the help desk and desktop support personnel.

- Ensure that the domain's Sales global group contains the domain's East Sales, West Sales, North Sales, and South Sales local groups.

You set up these Restricted Groups' wishes via a GPO. You might be thinking to yourself that if the domain administrator creates the GPO, can't any domain administrator just delete the GPO and work around the point of the Restricted Groups settings? Yes, but the point of Restricted Groups is additional protection, not ultimate protection.

An analogy might be "museum putty." The idea behind museum putty is that you attach it to your precious objects as extra protection in case an object gets bumped from the shelf. You can see museum putty here: `http://tinyurl` `.com/ycxc78`. The idea is that if someone tries to "bump" users in or out of the group, this will keep just the users you want in place.

My pal Darren Mar-Elia, the previous technical editor for this book, suggests that this could cause problems in Windows 2000 domains because they don't support link-value replication (a feature to help control group membership changes via replication). If you want to read his take on why this feature might not be such a hot idea, check out his blog here: `http://tinyurl.com/yar653`.

Strictly Controlling Active Directory Groups

The ideal way to strictly control Active Directory groups with specific Active Directory users is to create a new GPO and link it to the **Domain Controllers** OU.

You *could* modify the "Default Domain Controllers Policy" GPO directly, but, as stated earlier, it's better to create a new GPO when dealing with "normal" settings such as this one. This keeps the "Default Domain Controllers Policy" GPO as clean as possible. Likewise, you *could* modify the "Default Domain Policy" GPO. But, again, keeping away from the defaults for other than their special uses (as previously discussed) is preferred.

If you set up Restricted Groups policies at multiple levels in Active Directory, there is no "merging" between Restricted Groups policy settings. The "last applied" policy wins. For example, if you set up a Restricted Groups policy, link it to the domain level, create another Restricted Groups policy, and link it to the **Domain Controllers** OU, the one linked to the **Domain Controllers** OU "wins."

To get started with restricted groups:

1. Open the GPO and traverse to Computer Configuration ➢ Policies ➢ Windows Settings ➢ Security Settings ➢ **Restricted Groups**.

2. Right-click Restricted Groups, and choose Add Group from the shortcut menu, which opens the Add Group dialog box.

3. Click Browse to open the Browse dialog box, and browse for a group, say, the domain's Backup Operators; then click OK.

4. When you do, the Backup Operator Properties dialog box, shown in Figure 8.29, appears.

You can now choose domain members to place in the "Members of this group" list. In Figure 8.29, I have already added Sally User's account, which is in the domain, and I'm about to add Joe User's domain account.

FIGURE 8.29 You can specify which users you want to ensure are in specific groups.

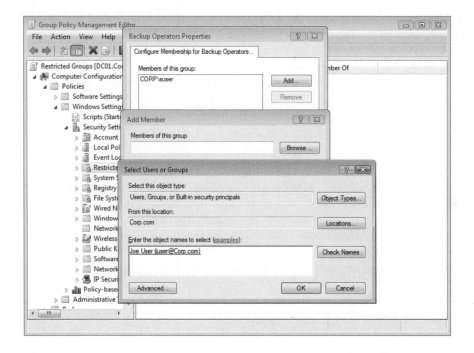

 Be careful about just typing in the user account names without either browsing the domain or manually entering the domain with the DOMAIN\user syntax. Restricted Groups in Active Directory will not apply correctly unless you do this.

When Restricted Groups Settings Take Effect

After you enter the users in the "Members of this group" list and click OK, you can sit back and wait for all Domain Controllers to get the change and process Group Policy. However, if you have only one Domain Controller in your test lab, this change should occur quickly. You can run GPUpdate to make it occur even faster in this case. This happens because any new GPO you create and link to the **Domain Controllers** OU should get picked up and applied right away—about 5 minutes after replication occurs.

Now, take a look inside the Backup Operators group using Active Directory Users and Computers. Sally and Joe's accounts should be forced inside Backup Operators.

When Restricted Groups Settings Get Refreshed

If someone were to *remove* Sally and Joe from Backup Operators in Active Directory Users and Computers, their accounts would be repopulated during the background security refresh, which is every 16 hours.

As described in Chapter 4, you have two choices if you don't want to wait 16 hours for the background security refresh:

- Link a GPO to the **Domain Controllers** OU level, with the **Security policy processing** policy setting with the "Process even if the Group Policy objects have not changed" flag set. Then, the Background Security Refresh will process with the normal background refresh (every 5 minutes for DCs).

- Force a manual refresh by running GPUpdate /FORCE on your Domain Controller. Recall that GPUpdate /FORCE may be used when the underlying GPO hasn't changed and you want your changes reflected immediately.

The users removed from Backup Operators will pop right back in!

There is one caveat with the "Members of this group" section of Restricted Groups. That is, this is an explicit list. If you then add more users using Active Directory Users and Computers, they will also be removed when the Restricted Groups policy is refreshed! Only the users listed in the "Members of this group" section will return.

Strictly Controlling Local Group Membership

You can ensure that specific users are members of specific groups on local machines—workstations or servers. For instance, you can guarantee that Joe and Sally are members of the local Administrators group on all the machines in the **Nurses** OU.

To do this, follow these steps:

1. Create a new GPO, and link it to the **Nurses** OU. Make sure the Nurses computer accounts are in the **Nurses** OU.

2. Dive in to Computer Configuration ➢ Policies ➢ Windows Settings ➢ Security Settings ➢ **Restricted Groups**.

3. Right-click **Restricted Groups,** and select the Add Group option from the shortcut menu to open the Add Group dialog.

4. These initial steps are nearly identical to the previous exercise where we wanted to restrict an Active Directory group. In the last exercise, we clicked the Browse button to locate a security group in Active Directory. However, to signify a local group, we'll just type in the word **Administrators**; *don't click Browse.*

5. You'll then see a Properties dialog box similar to the one seen in Figure 8.29.

6. At this point, you can populate the "Members of this group" list in the same way you did before. Simply click Add and choose the domain members of Sally and Joe, similar to what is seen in Figure 8.29.

When the machine is rebooted or the background policy is refreshed, the local Administrators group is populated with Sally and Joe.

The caveat of the "Members of this group" still applies. That is, this is an explicit list. By default, all workstations have the DOMAIN\Domain Admins listed as members within their local Administrators group. If you don't add DOMAIN\Domain Admins while creating a Restricted Group, they won't be there on the next background refresh.

Strictly Applying Group Nesting

Another trick Restricted Groups can perform is that it can ensure that one domain group is nested inside another. Like the "Strictly Controlling Active Directory Groups" trick, you need a GPO linked to the **Domain Controllers** OU.

The interface is a bit counterintuitive; the idea is that you name a group (say, HR-OU-Admins) and then specify the group of which it will be a member.

To nest one group within another:

1. Open the GPO and traverse to Computer Configuration ➢ Policies ➢ Windows Settings ➢ Security Settings ➢ **Restricted Groups**.

2. Right-click Restricted Groups, and choose Add Group from the shortcut menu, which opens the Add Group dialog box.

3. Click Browse to open the Browse dialog box, and locate the first group.

4. When you do, the Properties dialog box appears, as shown earlier in Figure 8.29.

5. Then, you'll click the Add button in the "This group is a member of" section of the Properties dialog box. You'll then be able to specify the second group name.

When you're finished, and the Group Policy applies, the result will be that the first group will be forcefully nested within the second group. In order for this to really work well, it helps to remember that different domain modes allow for different levels of group nesting. Here's the CliffsNotes version:

- Windows 2000 Mixed mode domains and Windows 2003 Interim mode domains can nest global groups only into domain local groups.

- Windows 2000 and higher Native mode domains can nest global groups into domain local groups. Additionally, global groups can be nested into global groups.

WARNING   While you are creating a Restricted Groups policy, take care. Results can be unpredictable when you mix the "This group is a member of" and "Members of this group" sections. If you have ensured a group's membership using the "Members of this group" setting, don't attempt to further modify that group's membership by feeding the "This group is a member of" users (by lying to the Restricted Groups function) to extend the original group's membership! On occasion, the "This group is a member of" and "Members of this group" will conflict if you try to add users to both headings.

Tricking Restricted Groups So It's Not "Rip and Replace"

Let's assume you have the following scenario: Before you ever even heard of this "Restricted Groups" thing, someone on your desktop design team declared that Fred and Alice would be local admins on all machines. Just add Fred and Alice as local administrators on all desktop machines.

Well, that's great for a small office. But when Fred or Alice leaves—you've got a problem. Sure, you wouldn't mind if Alice was still a local administrator on these machines, but it might even be smarter to keep whoever is a local admin on the machine right now and add in a domain-based group to all computers' Administrators group so you can dictate via Active Directory who is a local admin.

It *is* possible to trick the Restricted Groups function into allowing you to simply add members to a group (and not rip and replace them). As we saw earlier, anytime we try to use "Members of this group," it becomes a "rip and replace" for the members of that group. So, that's precisely *not* what we're going to do.

Instead, if you want to trick Restricted Groups into adding a domain-based group into a local Group Policy (and not rip and replace what's already there), perform the following steps:

1. In Active Directory, pre-create the group you know you'll want to add to the existing local administrators. In my example, I'll use a group called DesktopAdmins.

2. Open the GPO and traverse to Computer Configuration ➢ Policies ➢ Windows Settings ➢ Security Settings ➢ **Restricted Groups**.

3. Right-click Restricted Groups, and choose Add Group from the shortcut menu, which opens the Add Group dialog box.

4. Click Browse to open the Browse dialog box, and locate CORP\DesktopAdmins.

5. Then, you'll click the Add button in the "This group is a member of" section of the Properties dialog box. You'll then be able to specify "administrators" in the second group name. Again, since we're talking about the local Administrators group, you simply *type it in*. Don't browse for it.

Once you're done, you can wait for the Group Policy refresh cycle (or, type **gpupdate.exe** on your target machine) and see the results. In Figure 8.30, you can see two test users (tuser1 and tuser2) added using Restricted Groups.

FIGURE 8.30   You can fool Restricted Groups into specifically adding domain-based groups into your local groups (instead of ripping and replacing). In this example, several local administrators (tuser1 and tuser2) are not removed when this policy is applied.

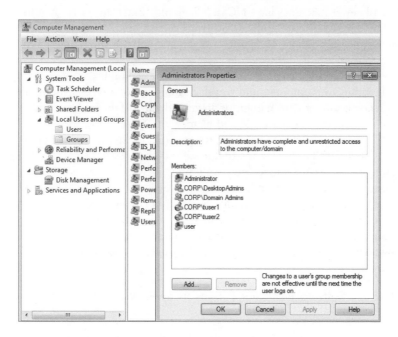

Which Groups Can Go into Which Other Groups via Restricted Groups?

The processing of Restricted Groups can sometimes be picky depending on the scenario. (This is officially documented in the Microsoft Knowledge Base article 810076 at http://support .microsoft.com/kb/810076.) And the "out of the box" processing changes a little bit and becomes more standardized for the most up-to-date clients: Windows 2003, Windows 2000 with SP4, and Windows XP with SP2.

MSKB 810076 now has several tables to help you out during your testing of this feature. Again, to ensure that the tables work for you, you need Windows 2003, Windows 2000 with SP4, or Windows XP with SP2, or you need the hotfix in the Microsoft Knowledge Base article 810076 applied to machines that will receive the forced users or groups.

Neither Windows Vista nor Windows Server 2008 is represented in this table yet, but hopefully it will be. While I haven't tested every combination, I'm told iterations of the operating system from Windows XP/SP2 onward are supposed to also act like Windows XP/SP2.

Software Restriction Policy

Windows XP and newer machines have a CSE (Client Side Extension) that Windows 2000 doesn't have: Software Restriction Policies. Software Restriction Policies enable you, the administrator, to precisely dictate what software will and will not run on your Windows XP desktops.

Many viruses show up in your users' inboxes as either executables or .VBS scripting files. Just one launch within your confines, and you're cleaning up for a week. Additionally, users will bring in unknown software from home or download junk off the Internet, and then, when the computer blows up, they turn around and blame you. What an injustice!

To that end, Microsoft developed Software Restriction Policies, which can put the kibosh on software that shouldn't be there in the first place. You can restrict software for specific users or for all users on a specific machine. You'll find Software Restriction Policies in Computer Configuration ➤ Policies ➤ Windows Settings ➤ Security Settings ➤ **Software Restriction Policies**. Just right-click over the Software Restriction Policies node, and select New Software Restriction Policies, as shown in Figure 8.31, to get started.

Software Restriction Policies is also available as a node under User Configuration ➤ Policies ➤ Windows Settings ➤ Security Settings ➤ **Software Restriction Policies**, which can also be seen in Figure 8.31.

FIGURE 8.31   Software Restriction Policies are available in both the Computer and User nodes.

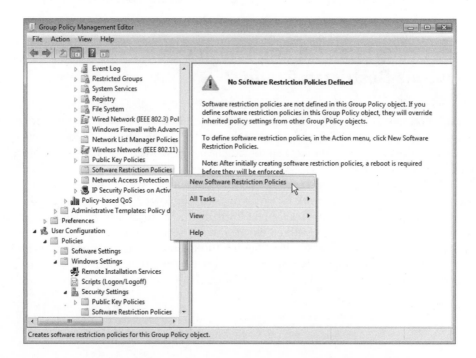

Like other policies that affect users or computers, you'll need an OU containing the user or computer accounts you want to restrict, and you'll need a GPO linked to that OU. Or you can set a GPO linked to the domain level, which affects all machines (or, alternatively, users). Typically, you'll use the computer side branch of Software Restriction Policies. That way, all users on a specific machine are restricted from using specific "known bad" applications.

> Software Restriction Policies are also valid when set upon a local computer within a local policy (via GPEdit.msc). This can be particularly useful for a Windows 2003 or Windows Server 2008 acting as a Terminal Server. Software Restriction Policies are meant to replace the APPSec.exe tool.

GPOs containing Software Restriction Policies might be common in environments that include any variety of Windows machines. However, Windows 2000 machines that are affected by GPOs containing Software Restriction Policies will simply ignore the settings and restrictions contained within.

Software Restriction Policies' "Philosophies"

Using Software Restriction Policies with your Windows users involves three primary philosophies. You can choose your philosophy by selecting the Security Levels branch of Software Restriction Policies, as shown in Figure 8.32.

FIGURE 8.32   The Security Levels branch of Software Restriction Policies sets your default level of protection.

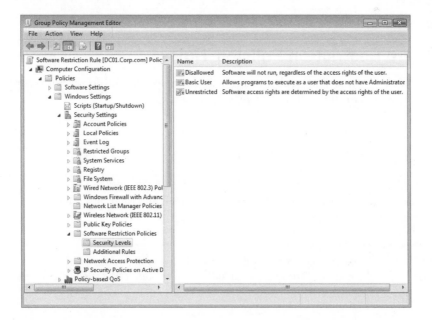

Philosophy #1 (aka "The Black List")   *Allow everything to run except specifically named items.* Here, we've chosen the default that the Unrestricted option is selected. Windows will allow all programs to run, like normal. However, if the administrator names certain applications, such as a virus or a game, it will be prevented from running. It's as if you're putting the things you don't want on the "black list" but allowing everything else to run.

Philosophy #2 (aka "The Doggie Door")   *Don't allow programs of a certain type to run.* Allow only specifically named items of that type to pass. I nickname this one "Doggie Door." The Unrestricted option is selected. You can choose to squelch all files of a certain type, say, all .VBS files. However, you can instruct Windows to allow .VBS files that are digitally signed from your IT department to run.

Philosophy #3 (aka "The White List")   *Nothing is allowed to run but the operating system and explicitly named items.* This is the "Full Lockdown" approach. The Disallowed option is selected. This is the most heavy-handed approach but the safest. Only operating system components will run, unless you specifically open up ways for programs to be run. Be careful when using this method; it can get you into a lot of trouble quickly.

Within these philosophies, you have one extra super-power if you use Windows Vista as your target machine. That is, you can specify that specific software can only be run with Basic User credentials. That is, if you decide that you want to run a specific application but are concerned that in doing so it might run with too many rights, you can specify it to run as a "Basic User."

You cannot select Basic User security level for a Certificate Rule (described next).

Software Restriction Policies' Rules

Once you've chosen your philosophy, you can choose how wide the door is for other stuff. There are four rules to either allow or deny specific software:

- Hash
- Path
- Certificate
- Network zone (or Internet zone on pre-Vista management stations)

To create a new rule, select the Additional Rules folder, and right-click in the right pane to see your choices, as shown in Figure 8.33.

By default, some path rules are set that enable access to critical portions of the Registry. These are enabled so that the operating system can write to the Registry even if the Disallowed option is set in the Security Levels branch.

FIGURE 8.33   The Security Levels branch of Software Restriction Policies sets your default level of protection.

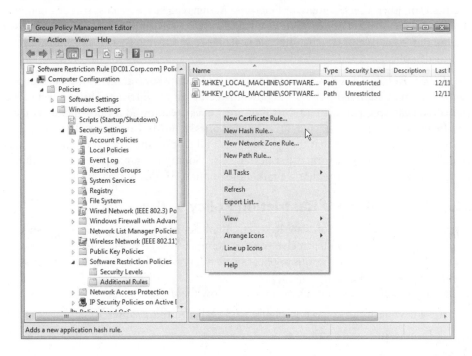

Hash Rule   In computer science terms, a hash value is a numeric representation, or fingerprint, that can uniquely identify a file should it be renamed. It's sort of like a "checksum" value. For instance, if I rename Doom.exe to Gloom.exe, the actual bits, the 1s and 0s, contained within the .EXE file are the same. Therefore, the hash value is the same. However, if any changes are made to the file (even if one bit is changed), the hash value is different. Hash rules are quite useful in containing any application that's an .EXE or a .DLL.

Sure, it's true that a user could use a hex editor (such as FRHED from www.kibria.de/frhed .html) and change just one bit in an .EXE or .DLL file to get a new hash value, but it's bloody unlikely. And that's reasonably good protection for most of us. A little review/tutorial of FHRED can be found here: www.geocities.com/thestarman3/tool/frhed/FRHED.htm.

Path Rule   You can specify to open (or restrict) certain applications based on where they reside on the hard drive. You can set up a path rule to specify a specific folder or full path to a program. Most environment variables are valid, such as *%HOMEDRIVE%*, *%HOMEPATH%*, *%USERPROFILE%*, *%WINDIR%*, *%APPDATA%*, *%PROGRAMFILES%*, and *%TEMP%*. Additionally, path rules can stomp out the running of any file type you desire, say, Visual Basic files. For example, if you set up a Path rule to disallow files named *.vb*, all Visual Basic file variants will be unable to execute.

Certificate Rule   Certificate rules use digitally signed certificates. You can use certificate rules to sign your own applications or scripts and then use a certificate rule to specify your IT department as a Trusted Publisher. Users, admins, or Enterprise Admins can be specified as trusted publishers. Be sure to read the sidebar entitled "Software Restriction Policies and Digital Signatures" before rolling out certificate rules. Note that this rule is unable to specify the Basic User security level as previously described.

Network Zone Rule (on Windows Vista Management Stations) or Internet Zone Rule (on Pre-Vista Management Stations)   Users will download crap off the Internet. This is a fact of life. However, you can specify which Internet Explorer zones are allowed for download. You can specify Internet, Intranet, Restricted Sites, Trusted Sites, and My Computer. The bad news about zone rules, however, is that they simply aren't all that useful. They prevent downloads of applications with the MSI format but nothing else. So, in my opinion, they're not quite ready for primetime use. (Note that we talk more about MSI files in Chapter 10.)

Setting Up a Software Restriction Policy with a Rule

As stated, you can craft your Software Restriction Policies in myriad ways. Space doesn't permit explaining all of them, so I'll just give you one example. We'll test our Software Restriction Policies by locking down a nefarious application that has caused untold distress to innumerable, hapless people: Solitaire!

To restrict Solitaire from your environment, follow these steps:

1.   Create a new hash rule as seen in Figure 8.33 earlier in this chapter.

2.   Click Browse and locate `sol.exe`.

 You might have to type `\\XPPRO1\c$\windows\system32\sol.exe` to point to a copy of Solitaire on one of your Windows XP machines if you're logged on at a Domain Controller (because Solitaire isn't present on Windows 2003 servers). If you have Windows XP/Service Pack 2 loaded on your client system, you can't do this until the SP2 firewall is turned off.

In Windows XP, the "File hash" entry is filled in with the file hash value of `Sol.exe` from the machine, as shown in Figure 8.34.

In Windows Vista, there isn't a file hash that's shown, but it's still doing the work.

 Underneath the hood Windows Vista actually created *two* file hashes. One hash is an MD5 hash (for older Windows XP and Windows Server 2003 clients) and another is an SHA-256 hash for newer XP, Windows Server 2003, Windows Vista, and Windows Server 2008 clients. Windows Vista still reads MD5 hashes created using older Windows XP management stations.

Now let's be super clear: the hash value for `sol.exe` on Windows XP won't equal the hash value for `sol.exe` on Windows Vista. With that in mind, if you wanted to restrict `sol.exe` on both machine types, you'll need to get ahold of each `sol.exe` and add it as a hash value.

FIGURE 8.34   Once you specify the file, the hash value is filled in.

Testing Your Software Restriction Policies

In the previous example, you could create a Software Restriction Policy that affects users or computers. If your policy is for users, for this very first test, log off. If your policy is for computers, reboot the machine. Follow these steps to immediately demonstrate the desired behavior of Software Restriction Policies:

1. Log on the machine that should get the Software Restriction Policies.

2. Choose Start ➢ Run to open the Run dialog box.

3. In the Open box, type **sol.exe**. You'll see the message shown in Figure 8.35.

    If you were to open a command prompt and then type **sol.exe**, you would also be restricted. You'd see the message "The system cannot execute the specified program," which is what you might expect.

FIGURE 8.35   On Windows XP machines, Solitaire is prevented from running.

Software Restriction Policies and Digital Signatures

Note that there is a security policy setting named **System settings: Use Certificate Rules on Windows Executables for Software Restriction Policies** located in Computer Configuration ➢ Policies ➢ Windows Settings ➢ Security Settings ➢ Local Policies ➢ Security Options.

You'll need to enable this policy setting if you create a certificate rule on a *digitally signed* .EXE. You can tell if a file is digitally signed by checking out its properties and looking for a Digital Signatures tab, as seen here in the file's properties. WINWORD.EXE has a Digital Signatures tab, while Sol.exe has none.

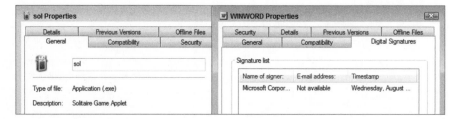

If you were to restrict a digitally signed .EXE, such as WINWORD.EXE, this policy setting would be necessary for the certificate rule to be embraced by your client systems.

As stated, this policy setting is only necessary for digitally signed .EXEs. However, if you only deal with digitally signed .VBS or .MSI files, you don't have to worry about this setting at all.

Understanding When Software Restriction Policies Apply

When you log on to a machine, you're running a shell program that launches other programs. This is sometimes called a "launching process." That shell program (or launching process) is familiar—Explorer.exe. Whenever Explorer.exe (or other launching processes) launches restricted software, it checks a portion of the Registry for any restrictions. How does this help determine when Software Restriction Policies apply?

    Software Restriction Policies are housed in KEY_LOCAL_MACHINE\SOFTWARE\ Policies\Microsoft\Windows\Safer\CodeIdentifiers.

A Software Restriction Policy affects a machine as soon as it's downloaded via the Group Policy engine. After that, no new instances of that application are possible. It doesn't matter if the launching program (i.e., Explorer) has already been started; it doesn't need a refresh. It just restricts the software as specified in the Software Restriction Policies as soon as the Group Policy containing the Software Restriction Policies is applied. Note, however, that programs *already* running don't magically stop running. This will only prevent future instances of the specified application from running. So, if Sol.exe is already running, then a Software Restriction Policy comes down to disable it—as long as Sol.exe is running, it stays running. When you close it, however, it cannot be reopened again because Explorer has checked in with the Registry and prevents it.

Troubleshooting Software Restriction Policies

You can troubleshoot Software Restriction Policies in two primary ways:

- Inspect the Registry to see if the Software Restriction Policies are embraced.
- Enable advanced logging.

Inspecting the Software Restriction Policies Location in the Registry

If Software Restriction Policies aren't being applied, and you logged off and back on, log on again as the administrator at the target machine and check KEY_LOCAL_MACHINE or HKEY_CURRENT_USER\SOFTWARE\Policies\Microsoft\Windows\Safer\CodeIdentifiers. Inside, you'll see numbered branches containing the rules. In Figure 8.36, you can see Sol.exe being restricted by a hash rule.

Do note that operating system files change with service packs—sometimes even innocuous things like Sol.exe! If, after a service pack, your client isn't restricting applications as you expect (because the hash value changes even after a tiiiiny change), make sure the version number of the restricted application matches the version actually located on the client. More specifically, make sure the hash values match.

FIGURE 8.36   The Registry lays out what will be restricted.

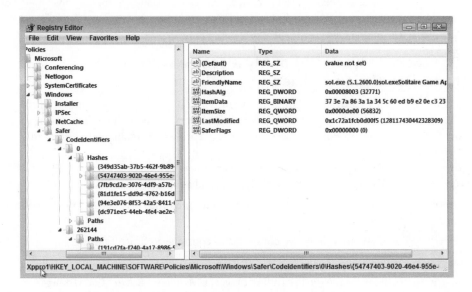

Software Restriction Policies Advanced Logging

You can troubleshoot Software Restriction Policies via a log file. To do so, follow these steps:

1. In the Registry, traverse to KEY_LOCAL_MACHINE\SOFTWARE\Policies\Microsoft\ Windows\Safer\CodeIdentifiers.

2. Create a new string value named LogFileName.

3. In the Data field of the new Registry key, enter the full path and name of a log file—for example, **c:\srplog.txt**.

   Now whenever an application runs, a line is written to the log file explaining why it can or cannot run. Here are two lines from that log file: the first when I run Notepad (which is free to run) and the second when I run the Sol.exe (which is restricted).

```
cmd.exe (PID = 1576) identified C:\WINDOWS\system32\notepad.exe as Unrestricted
    using path rule, Guid = {191cd7fa-f240-4a17-8986-94d480a6c8ca}

cmd.exe (PID = 1576) identified C:\WINDOWS\system32\sol.exe as Disallowed using
    hash rule, Guid = {e669efa3-96d8-4c16-b506-2fec88fbee33}
```

You'll find a great article on Software Restriction Policies in TechNet at http:// technet.microsoft.com/en-us/library/bb457006.aspx. If it's not there, then just search for an article named "Using Software Restriction Policies to Protect Against Unauthorized Software." Also check out this small article series on the subject by Jakob H. Heidelberg called "Default Deny All Applications" (part 1 at http://tinyurl.com/ysb6wu and part 2 at http://tinyurl.com/2hdz7s).

Oops, I Locked Myself Out of My Machine with Software Restriction Policies

If you make a Software Restriction Policy too tight, you can lock yourself right out of the system! Don't panic. If the policy is a GPO in Active Directory, remove the policy setting or disable the GPO. After Group Policy processes on the client, log on again as the user and you should be cleared up.

However, if you make a Software Restriction Policy using the local policy editor (GPEDIT.MSC) and you lock yourself out, you have a slightly longer road to recovery. Follow these steps:

1. Reboot the machine, and press F8 upon startup to open the Advanced Options menu at boot time.

2. Select SAFE MODE and allow the computer to continue to finish booting.

3. Log on as the machine's local administrator.

4. Dive in to HKLM\Software\Policies\Microsoft\Windows\Safer\CodeIdentifiers. Delete everything below the CodeIdentifiers key.

5. Reboot the machine.

You should be out of the woods now.

However, if the policies were set on a given user, the steps are a bit different. Just drill down to that user's HKCU hive file and nuke them there.

More Software Restriction Policies resources can be found at

```
http://www.microsoft.com/technet/windowsvista/security/rstrplcy.mspx
(shortened to http://tinyurl.com/hsthc)
http://www.microsoft.com/technet/security/prodtech/windowsxp/secwinxp/
xpsgch06.mspx
(shortened to http://tinyurl.com/mx96v)
```

Securing Workstations with Templates

In many environments, it's important to ensure that collections of workstations have the same level of security. What good is it if one machine is locked down tight when the bad guys can simply move along to another machine to get on to your network? The "out of the box" security on Windows machines may or may not be adequate for your environment.

You'll need tools to ensure environment-wide security. The Security Templates MMC snap-in and the Security Configuration and Analysis tool are your partners for generating a baseline of security. You can use these tools to "tattoo" the Registry of the computer to make it more difficult to attack—both on and off your network. After you define your security goals with these tools, you can use Group Policy to easily ensure that all affected machines embrace the same baseline for security.

For our examples here, we'll be using Windows XP and not Windows Vista. Why, you ask? Not for any specific reason other than Windows Vista doesn't come with any "starter" templates. Using Windows XP just makes this particular set of examples easier. That way, we're not creating a whole new template from scratch using Windows Vista.

To get started, we'll load the appropriate snap-ins. In this exercise, we'll use one MMC and load the two snap-ins on a Windows XP Professional machine while logged on as a local administrator. After we load the MMC snap-ins, we'll use the tools to become familiar with the predefined templates and start locking down some of our machines.

Before we get too far along in this section, here's the scoop: You'll be using these exercises to lock down your Windows XP (and/or Windows Vista or Windows 2000) machines. Although you *can* perform these procedures for Windows 2003 and 2008, I advise against using this procedure to lock down your Windows 2003 machines. That's because in the next major section, "The Security Configuration Wizard," I'll show you a technique that is faster and works specifically for Windows 2003 and 2008 servers. That is, the procedure in that section won't work for Windows Vista, Windows XP, or Windows 2000 machines, so use the information in this section for them.

This exercise assumes you're loading the snap-ins at a Windows XP Professional machine, though you can certainly perform a similar exercise at a Windows 2000 machine.

1. Choose Start ➢ Run to open the Run dialog box, and in the Open box, enter **MMC** and press Enter to fire up a "naked" MMC.

2. Choose Console ➢ Add/Remove Snap-in to open the Add/Remove Snap-in dialog box.

3. Click Add to open the Add Standalone Snap-in dialog box.

4. Locate and add the Security Configuration and Analysis and Security Templates snap-ins by scrolling through the list and clicking Add. Add each snap-in individually so they'll both be on your MMC palette.

5. Click Close to close the Add Standalone Snap-in dialog box.

6. Click OK to close the Add/Remove Snap-In dialog box.

When finished, your MMC should look like that in Figure 8.37.

FIGURE 8.37   The Security Configuration and Analysis and Security Templates nodes are loaded in the MMC. The available security templates are listed here.

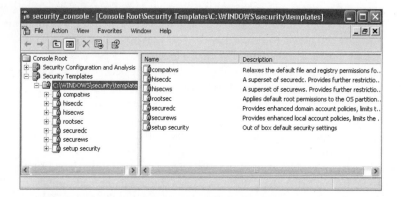

 As I noted earlier, this section demonstrates these techniques with Windows XP and not Windows Vista, and that's because while Windows Vista is perfectly capable of leveraging the examples here, it doesn't ship with any templates. So, I suggest you try this out on your Windows XP machine and, if you love them, create new templates for Windows Vista. Additionally, note that creating fresh templates on Windows XP and leveraging them on Windows Vista could be problematic because not all the security goodies for Windows Vista are present on Windows XP. Again, we're using Windows XP as the examples here so you can get a feel for the interface—then do this when ready for Windows Vista.

Security Templates

To get multiple machines to embrace a collection of security settings, you'll roll your proposed settings into what is called a security template. A security template is nothing more than a collection of security settings wrapped up in an easy-to-deploy, text-based .INF file. Once you have the .INF file locked and loaded the way you want, you can leverage Group Policy to assert your will across your enterprise.

You leverage security templates that come from many sources:

- Some templates are built into Windows. These predefined templates exist for workstations, servers, and domain controllers, and they range in intensity from "default security" to "highly secure."

- Again, note that Vista has no templates included in the box.

- You can create your own security templates from scratch or use the predefined templates as a jumping-off point to create your own.

- Microsoft and other noted third parties have their own collection of security templates for your use. More on third-party templates in a bit.

In these next sections, we'll take a look at the predefined templates and see what they can offer us. We'll then plan a lockdown of our own machines by customizing a template (leveraging one of the predefined templates). Once we actually lock down our machines by applying our templates, we'll see if our lockdown was successful—using both the graphically provided MMC snap-in tools and the command-line interface.

Finally, in the last section, we'll use the template we customized to lock down multiple machines at once using the broad stroke of Group Policy.

Security templates are supposed to help you set a baseline of security upon a gaggle of systems. Let's take a quick look at the available templates within Windows.

 WARNING   I encourage you to not actually do anything with these templates until you read all the way through this section.

Default Security for Windows 2003 and Windows XP

If a machine is a "fresh install," three templates define the default "out of the box" security for a Windows XP or Windows 2003 Domain Controller or a Windows 2003 member server. On Windows XP, you'll find delftwk.inf in the c:\windows\inf folder. The system used this file when it was being born to set the out-of-the-box settings.

On Windows 2003, you'll find defltdc.inf and defltsv.inf in the c:\windows\inf folder. These templates define the baseline security for Windows 2003 Domain Controllers and Windows 2000 servers. The DCFirst.inf template is used to populate the first Windows 2003 Domain Controller with the default Account Policies (Password policy, Account Lockout policy, and Kerberos policy).

Additionally, if a Domain Controller is upgraded from NT 4 or Windows 2000, a different set of security templates is placed on that machine. The templates used by an NT 4 system are called DCup.inf, and the templates used by Windows 2000 are called DCup5.inf. An NT 4 Terminal Server Edition or Windows 2000 machine with Terminal Services/Application mode will run Dsupt.inf to write its default configuration settings. The system automatically uses these files, which are discussed here only for reference. You shouldn't need to touch them again after the system uses them.

Incremental Security Templates

You can use several predefined security .INF template files as a jumping-off point. Rather than use them as is, you can modify them to suit your specific requirements. Indeed, you'll see how to leverage an existing template a bit later in this chapter.

The supplied templates tighten or loosen a workstation, server, or DC (whichever the specific case may be), using the Security Configuration and Analysis MMC snap-in or the secedit command-line tool. (Both are described in detail later in this chapter.) You can see the provided incremental security templates listed in the Security Templates node, as seen in Figure 8.37 earlier in this chapter.

Before we look at how to apply these .INF files to workstations, let's briefly examine each template (based on machine type) and see what it's supposed to do.

This information in this section is specific to Windows 2003 and Windows XP and is not compatible with Windows 2000. When upgraded from NT 4, Windows 2000 machines need to be enhanced with the Basic templates that are not listed here. For more information on Windows 2000 and security templates, see the third edition of this book. Other helpful resources are on TechNet at http:// support.microsoft.com/?kbid=234926. An additional reference to Windows 2000 templates is at the end of this chapter in the section "Final Thoughts."

Domain Controller *.INF* Template Files

These .INF settings apply to Windows 2003 Domain Controllers.

securedc   Increases the security required in the Password policy and Account Policy, bumps up the amount of auditing that occurs on the Domain Controller, and increases some Event log settings, such as the size. This template doesn't modify any file or Registry ACLs (Access Control Lists).

hisecdc   Chokes off all communications with down-level machines by turning off NTLM communication. Only those machines that use NTLM v2 or Kerberos will be able to communicate with any machines to which this template is applied.

You can find certification guidelines for applications at www.microsoft.com/ windowsserver2003/partners/isvs/cfw.mspx.

Applying the Hisecdc.inf template to Domain Controllers is dangerous and can prevent clients from authenticating to your Domain Controllers.

XP Professional *.INF* Template Files

These settings apply to Windows XP Professional machines.

compatws   Applications must pass certification guidelines to be considered "Windows Logo"–compliant. Sometimes, an older application does not follow the new rules once it's up and running. Use this template to allow some older applications (such as Office 97), which are not Windows Logo–certified, to run properly when mere mortals in the Users group run them.

This template elevates the permissions of the Users group by modifying common Registry keys, files, and folders. Often, administrators will give in and grant users who complain about incompatible applications admission into the Power Users group. Applying this template should satisfy their needs without putting them in the Power Users group. Because of this, this template removes all users and groups from the Power Users group.

You can see this behavior for yourself. As an administrator, load Word 97 with the Office 97 spelling check feature onto an NTFS volume on a Windows 2000 or Windows XP machine. Then, log back on as a regular user and, using that Word 97 installation, try to run the spelling utility. As a regular user, you cannot because certain files must be read/writeable to the installation point of Office 97 (usually under Program Files). Apply this template, and your woes disappear. The compatws.inf template modifies NTFS permissions on the Program Files folder so that mere mortals can modify the settings.

securews   These settings increase the security required in the Password Policy and the Account Policy, bump up the amount of auditing that occurs on the workstation, and increase some Event log settings such as the size. This template doesn't modify any file or Registry ACLs.

hisecws   This template turns off NTLM communication and allows only communication with other machines that are running NTLM v2 or Kerberos. NTLM v2 is available on Windows 2000, Windows 2003, and Windows XP machines and on Windows 9x machines and Windows NT 4 machines that have the Directory Services client installed. Kerberos is available only on Windows 2000 machines (and higher). As with the compatsw template, all users and groups are flushed from the Power Users group. A note of caution here: The hisecws.inf template turns off NTLM authentication and allows communication only with other machines that are running NTLM v2 or Kerberos.

Microsoft gives you a nitty-gritty look at the provided templates at http:// tinyurl.com/47e5u and in Knowledge Base article 816585 (for Windows 2003, http://support.microsoft.com/kb/816585) and Knowledge Base article 309689 (for Windows 2000, http://support.microsoft.com/kb/309689).

Other Security Template Sources

There are several places that you locate additional templates to use on your systems.

Security Templates from Uncle Bill   On Microsoft's website, you'll find two publications that work in tandem to help administrators secure both Windows 2003 and Windows XP: "Windows Server 2003 Security Guide" and "Threats and Countermeasures: Security Settings in Windows Server 2003 and Windows XP." At last check, it can be found here: http:// tinyurl.com/dkbu. The download includes several ready-to-use security templates that will go a long way to help you secure your environment. You'll find new templates for Domain Controllers, IIS, IAS, member servers, print servers, client systems, and more! Just three words say it all: Great job, Microsoft.

An older work from Microsoft, the "Windows 2000 Hardening Guide," contains tips as well as security templates. You can find it at `http://tinyurl.com/anm1`.

There are some downloadable security templates for Windows Vista and Windows Server 2008. Check out the following guides and links:

- Windows Vista Security Guide found here: `http://tinyurl.com/22bvwu`
- Windows 2008 Security Guide found here: `http://tinyurl.com/37m3nj`

Special Microsoft Templates

Depending on how a machine was born or upgraded, two templates will be different from machine to machine: `DC security.inf` and `setup security.inf`. The contents of `DC security.inf` are created on-the-fly when you upgrade or create a Domain Controller from scratch. During DCPROMO, a combination of `defltdc.inf`, `dcfirst.inf`, and `defdcgpo.inf` are used to configure the system; then `DC security.inf` is generated. The `setup security.inf` template is created on-the-fly when you upgrade or create a member machine from scratch.

These templates contain a snapshot of some of the security that was configured on the system just prior to performing an upgrade or running DCPROMO. (They'll contain default settings if you performed a fresh install.) This can be particularly helpful if something fails to work after an upgrade or DCPROMO. You can look inside these files to determine what the previously set security was on that system and try to adjust it on the new system.

The templates listed in the previous section won't affect User Rights Assignments that were specifically added to your machine. However, applying the `setup security.inf` and `DC security.inf` templates resets the changed User Rights Assignments to the defaults (or your previous configuration). If you want to do this, my advice is to restore only the specific area you want; don't apply the whole template lock, stock, and barrel. You can see how to do this via the `secedit` command's `/areas` switch (described later in this chapter in Table 8.4). Usually, you don't want to roll back your entire security to the defaults. Rather, you can pick and choose which sections you want to restore.

Security Templates from Uncle Sam   Two U.S. government agencies have each provided its take on some proper security templates:

The National Security Agency has free advice and templates for securing Windows XP and Windows 2000 and even some NT, Cisco, and email server advice at `http://www.nsa.gov/snac/`.

The National Institute of Standards and Technology (NIST) has some templates to help secure Windows XP and Vista:

- For XP: `http://csrc.nist.gov/itsec/guidance_WinXP.html`
- For Vista: `http://csrc.nist.gov/itsec/guidance_vista.html`

Your Own Security Templates

Now that you know which built-in templates perform which functions, you have three options:

- Apply a built-in template as is to a workstation.
- Create your own template from scratch, and apply it to a workstation.
- Modify a built-in template that is already close to what you want to suit your needs, and then apply it to a workstation.

In this section, we'll primarily explore the third option, which essentially covers the skills required to utilize the other two options as well.

You might want to copy the default templates for safekeeping. You can copy them from the %windir%\security\templates folder to a floppy, another folder, a partition, or a computer. However, other Windows XP machines in your environment probably hold the default versions of these files as well, so it is relatively easy to get them back.

Creating a Fresh Template from Scratch

To create your own template, in the Console Root folder just right-click the default folder under Security Templates and choose New Template from the shortcut menu, as shown in Figure 8.38. Then give your new template a name.

When you do this, no security features are defined. This could mean a lot of manual labor handcrafting the template to your heart's desire. The rewards are great, however, as you'll know exactly what is and what is not defined. When you define your own templates, you can either specify a setting on the target or keep the default setting on the target.

FIGURE 8.38 You can create your own security templates if desired.

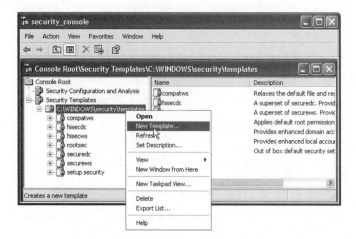

Reusing an Existing Template

Instead of going through the laborious task of handcrafting every Account Policy, Event log setting, and Registry setting (to name a few), you can use one of the existing templates and modify it to suit your needs.

For instance, you might want to increase the security above and beyond what the `hisecws.inf` provides as follows:

- Turn off the Indexing Service. (Only administrators can turn it on.)
- Place the Repair folder (where the Registry backup lives) under stronger lock and key.

In this example, we'll modify the `hisecws.inf` template. To use that template as a jumping-off point, right-click it and save it under a different name—for example, `hisecws_plus.inf`. Your `hisecws_plus.inf` template should show up as an additional entry in the list next to the other templates seen in Figure 8.38.

Modification 1: Stop the Indexing Service

First, we'll disable the Indexing Service at startup. When disabled, this process won't kick off unless an administrator manually turns it on or a process running in the system context turns it on. Follow these steps (which you can also use to disable other services):

1. From the Security Templates MMC snap-in, drill down into `hisecws_plus` ➤ System Services ➤ Indexing Service.

2. Double-click Indexing Service to open the Indexing Service Properties.

3. Click the "Define this Policy Setting in the Template" check box.

4. You can optionally select the Edit Security button to modify the security settings. You don't really have to change anything to enforce this policy. Though, for completeness, you could add the Domain Administrators group to ensure that they always have Full Control. If you want, add the Domain Administrators group, then select Full Control from the list of properties, and click OK.

5. Click the Disabled radio button if it is not already selected.

6. Click OK to close the Template Security Policy Setting dialog box.

The Indexing Service is now set to be disabled, as shown in Figure 8.39.

Modification 2: Tweak the Repair Folder

The Repair folder within Windows contains a backup of your Registry data. The files in this folder need to be well protected to ensure that password-cracking programs and the like are not run against the files, exposing the sensitive passwords.

To protect the Repair folder from prying eyes, follow these steps:

1. Drill down into `hisecws_plus` ➤ File System. Right-click File System and choose Add File from the shortcut menu to open the Security dialog box.

2. Locate the `%systemroot%`\Repair folder (usually `c:\windows\repair`).

3. You'll be prompted to edit security for this folder.

4. You can deny local users and add the HR-OU-ADMINS group, as shown in Figure 8.40.

FIGURE 8.39 The Indexing Service has been set to be disabled.

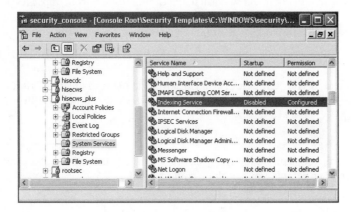

FIGURE 8.40 Use the Security dialog box to allow or deny access to specific folders.

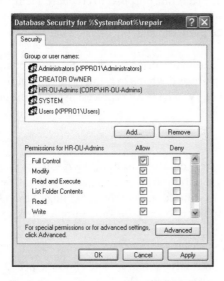

For this example, we want to ensure that the members of our own HR-OU-ADMINS group can access the files at any time. When you click OK in the Security dialog box, you are presented with several choices which appear in the Template Security Policy dialog:

- If you choose "Propagate Inheritable Permissions to all Subfolders and Files," any files or subfolders will receive these NTFS permissions by inheritance only. If there are explicit ACLs on the files or folder, they will not be overwritten.

- If you choose "Replace Existing Permission on All Subfolders and Files with Inheritable Permissions," all current permissions on all affected files and folders are wiped out and replaced with what you have here. This is the default setting.

- If you choose "Do Not Allow Permissions on this File or Folder to Be Replaced," you're asking the operating system not to allow normal inheritance to flow from upper-level folders down to this folder. This option is not valid if an upper-level folder has the "Replace Existing Permission on All Subfolders and Files with Inheritable Permissions" setting.

In this instance, we'll choose the defaults and click OK to exit the Template Security Policy Setting dialog box.

Now that you've created your templates, you can leverage them to create a safer, tighter, more secure computing environment. The next section will show you how to apply your template to a workstation.

WARNING   Be sure, at this point, to right-click the `hisecws_plus.inf` template and select Save. If you don't, your settings could be lost.

The Security Configuration and Analysis Snap-In

The Security Configuration and Analysis snap-in has one purpose: to compare a template with the currently defined settings on a target machine. If the security doesn't match, the Security Configuration and Analysis snap-in can force the settings defined inside the template to be thrust upon the target computer.

The Security Configuration and Analysis snap-in performs an apples-to-apples comparison between the guidelines you set up in the template and what's currently running on the target machine. If there are holes in the target machine, you have two choices: live with the holes, or plug up those holes with the template.

Creating a Baseline

The first step in creating a baseline is to create a database to hold the results of your comparison. You've already loaded the Security Configuration snap-in alongside the Security Templates snap-in on a sample workstation in your domain at the beginning of this chapter, so we're ready to proceed. If you didn't load the two snap-ins on a sample workstation in your domain, do so now.

To create our database, follow these steps:

1. Right-click the Security Configuration and Analysis snap-in, and choose Open Database from the shortcut menu to open the Open Database dialog box.

2. Since we're using the `hisecws_plus.inf` template, you might want to be consistent and enter **hisecws_plus.sdb** in the File Name field, though you're certainly not obligated to. Additionally, it's usually best to house the `.SDB` file in the same location as the `.INF` file so you can find it more easily later. Click Open when you've entered in a name.

3. The Import Template dialog box appears. Select your `hisecws_plus.inf` template file.

WARNING   You will get inconsistent baseline results if you try to run the templates meant for workstations against a server or Domain Controller. Remember, the templates are geared toward specific types of machines.

Once the database is generated, the right pane changes to show you the path of the database, as shown in Figure 8.41.

FIGURE 8.41   The right pane changes to reflect your database path.

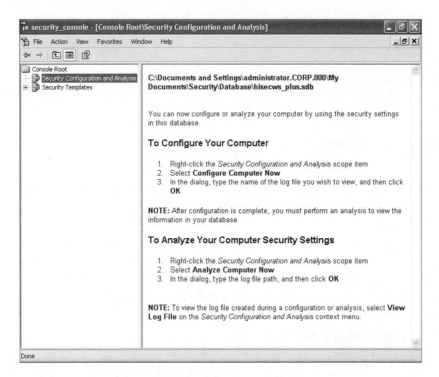

You are now ready to analyze the current computer.

Run the Analysis on the Current Machine

Once you've got your database that houses the sum of the security settings set up, you are ready to analyze the machine against a template. Follow these steps:

1. Right-click the Security and Configuration Analysis snap-in, and choose Analyze Computer Now from the shortcut menu to open the Perform Analysis dialog box. When you do, you'll see what is shown in Figure 8.42, where the analysis will span the six categories of security.

2. A default temporary log location is specified in the Perform Analysis dialog box. It really doesn't matter what the name is. Click OK to run the analysis.

When the analysis is complete, the right pane in the Security Configuration and Analysis snap-in changes to a style similar to that of the Security Templates snap-in.

FIGURE 8.42 The security analysis checks out the six categories of security.

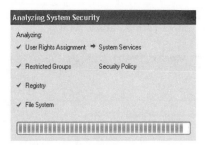

Analyzing the Results

You can analyze the results in two ways:

- You can use the graphical user interface of the Security Configuration and Analysis tool to drill down and double-check that the settings you specified in the template are indeed being applied or not being applied to the current workstation.

- You can paw through the log file by hand and see what it came up with.

The former is much less painful, but there are reasons, described in the section "Using the Log File to Find Differences," that you might want to paw through the log files.

You can check for the changes that were present in the original hisecws.inf template or the modifications you made, such as the NTFS restrictions in the *%systemroot%*\repair folder.

Graphically Displaying Differences

Lots of settings are configured within the hisecws_plus.inf template. For example, in the Security Configuration and Analysis snap-in, drill down to Local Policies ➢ Security Options. You'll see the following possibilities when graphically analyzing the results:

- If the setting has a green check mark, the template you used has a definition and the computer has a setting that already matches. In other words, this computer is compliant with your guidelines for this setting.

- If the results have a big red X, the template has a definition, but the computer you're analyzing either doesn't have a setting or the setting doesn't match.

- If the results don't have either a green check mark or a big red X (only the little 1s and 0s icon), the computer has a setting, but nothing is defined in the template—so there's technically no "problem."

- If the results have a big red exclamation mark, the setting wasn't analyzed. This can happen for one of two reasons:

  - The item was not originally defined in the baseline policy.

  - An error (for example, Access Denied) occurred when the item was queried.

As Figure 8.43 shows, many Security Options have a big red X, meaning that they were defined in the template but the test machine is not compliant.

Using the Log File to Find Differences

You might want to rerun the analysis but save the log file in an easy-to-get-to location, such as the `c:\temp` folder. You can then open and read the log in any text editor, such as Notepad or WordPad. You can, if you're feeling adventurous, paw through the file and manually locate the changes—though this is messy and cumbersome. If you want to go the nongraphical route, you can sometimes speed things up by using your text editor's search feature to find all instances of "Mismatch."

If you're particularly command-line savvy, use the `FINDSTR.EXE` command to sift through the `hisecws_plus.log` and output just those lines that contain the word *Mismatch*.

FIGURE 8.43   A big red X indicates that the machine is not complying with specific settings in the template.

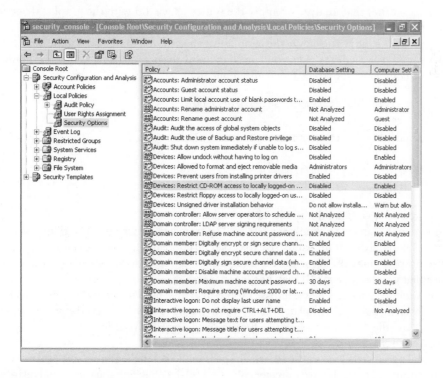

Applying the Template

Now that you know which attributes your target machine does and does not subscribe to, you're ready to apply the template. You can do so in two ways: graphically, via the Security Configuration and Analysis snap-in tool, or via the command-line tool, `secedit`.

WARNING   If you want to heavily armor your test machine, go ahead and apply the template. Else, cancel out now.

Graphically Applying the Template

After you perform the baseline analysis using the Security Configuration and Analysis snap-in tool, you can apply the settings to your test machine. To do so, right-click the Security Configuration and Analysis snap-in tool and choose Configure Computer Now from the shortcut menu. An analysis is not technically required before applying the template, but it's highly recommended so that you know where you currently stand. You'll be prompted for a location to save the log file.

At this point, the computer is configured to the settings you specified in the template. You could, if desired, rerun the analysis phase to see if the application took place. When you see the red Xs change to green check marks, you'll know the application was successful.

Using *secedit* to Analyze and Apply the Template

You can use secedit in Windows 2003, Windows XP, and Windows 2000 if you want to write batch files that analyze or apply the policy as we did with the graphical Security Configuration and Analysis tool.

You can use secedit to analyze the template against the computer's database at any time. To start secedit in analyze mode, you'll need to know the parameters it takes. The following is a sample command line (to be typed all on one line):

```
secedit /analyze /db c:\temp\hisecws_plus.sdb
        /cfg
    c:\windows\security\templates\hisecws_plus.inf
        /log
    c:\temp\hisecws_plus.log
        /verbose
```

Let's break this command into bite-size chunks.

The secedit /analyze chunk requires a /DB parameter, which you must point toward an existing .SDB database. If no database exists, secedit creates a new one on-the-fly. In this case, we're specifying /DB to use the file and path of c:\temp\hisecws_plus.sdb. This assumes that c:\temp exists. (It may not.)

If you want to generate a new database on-the-fly, you'll need to specify the /CFG parameter to point toward your .INF template file, say c:\windows\security\templates\hisecws_plus.inf. Use the /log flag to specify a location and name for your log—for instance, c:\temp\hisecws_plus.log.

Optional parameters are /verbose, which spells out in detail the status, and /quiet, which spits out nothing. The verbose parameter can be useful in debugging situations, and quiet can be useful in batch files when you don't want anyone to know anything is happening.

Now that you understand the command and its parameters, open a command shell and type the **secedit** command, as shown in Figure 8.44.

You can analyze the data in two ways, as discussed earlier. You can do so graphically, using the Security Configuration and Analysis tool, or you can use the log at c:\temp\hisecws_plus.log. To analyze the data graphically, right-click the Security Configuration and Analysis tool, and choose Open Database from the shortcut menu. To analyze the data using Notepad or another text editor, open c:\temp\hisecws_plus.log.

FIGURE 8.44 Use the secedit command to perform batch analysis.

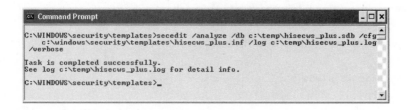

Using *secedit* to Generate a Rollback Template

The Windows 2003 and Vista versions of the secedit command can do something that the Windows XP and Windows 2000 secedit command cannot. It can create a new template that can be used if you want to roll back after a botched template application. Here's the trick though: you must do this *before* you actually apply the template (next step).

To run secedit in this mode, you'll need to know the appropriate parameters. A sample command line using secedit to generate a rollback template on a Domain Controller might be as follows:

```
secedit /generaterollback /db c:\temp\anyname.sdb
        /cfg
    c:\windows\security\templates\securedc.inf
        /rbk
    c:\save_my_bacon
```

In this example, we use the /cfg command to apply the securedc.inf template. And, should we need to roll back, it will create the file rollback_before_securedc.inf to roll back to the state before we applied the securedc.inf template (again, you'll see how to apply templates in the next step).

Here's the big warning though (first of two): if you later decide to apply *another* security template, you'll need to run this command *again*. If you need to perform a rollback, simply apply the security templates back in order such that the most recently created is applied first, and so on back to the first one that was created.

The second big warning is that the resulting template will not have data sufficient to roll back file or Registry ACLs. These templates will roll back everything else though.

Again, note, however, that Windows XP doesn't have the /generaterollback switch, so unfortunately you can't use it here, before the next step.

Using *secedit* to Configure

You can use secedit to configure the machine using the template you defined. To run secedit in configure mode, you'll need to know the appropriate parameters.

The following is a sample command line:

```
secedit /configure /db c:\temp\hisecws_plus.sdb
        /cfg
   c:\windows\security\templates\hisecws_plus.inf
        /log
   c:\temp\hisecws_plus.log
        /verbose
```

Again, let's break the command into bite-size chunks. The `secedit /configure` chunk requires a /DB parameter, which you must point toward an existing .SDB database, say, `c:\templatecopy\hisecws_plus.sdb`.

Use the /CFG `parameter` to point to your .INF template file, `c:\templatecopy\hisecws_plus.inf`. If you don't specify a /CFG entry, `secedit` applies the currently stored template in the database specified in the /DB parameter.

Use the /log flag to specify a location and name for your log—for example, `c:\temp\hisecws_plus.log`.

Use the /overwrite switch to overwrite the current information in the database with the information in the security template.

You can also use `secedit` to surgically replace a specific area in the template to the target machine. Use the /areas switch to isolate and specify one or several areas, as shown in Table 8.4.

TABLE 8.4   Valid Keywords for secedit's /areas Switch

Area	Where to Find
SECURITYPOLICY	Sets all security settings inside the template, except for the Restricted Groups, User Rights Assignment, Registry Keys, File Services, and System Services
GROUP_MGMT	The Restricted Groups branch in the template
USER_RIGHTS	The Local Policy ➤ User Rights Assignment in the template
REGKEYS	The Registry branch in the template
FILESTORE	The File System branch in the template
SERVICES	The System Services branch in the template

To specify multiple areas, you can simply string them together (with a single space between each one), such as /areas REGKEYS SERVICES. To apply all areas, don't specify the /areas switch, since they'll all apply by default. Optional parameters are /verbose, which spells out in detail the status, and /quiet, which spits out nothing at all.

The use of the parameter /cfg c:\temp\hisecws_plus.inf is optional because we already used that .INF file to create our .SDB database in the last step.

Once this process is complete, your system is as secure as the template file dictates.

> If you get an "Access Denied" error, try closing the MMC snap-in in order to close the file lock on the .SDB database.

> You can learn more about the secedit command by opening a command shell and typing **secedit /?**.

Applying Security Templates with Group Policy

You could schlep around to each workstation or server and run secedit with the /configure switch. This works reasonably well in stand-alone environments, if you only need to tie down a handful of machines, or if you're still in an NT 4 domain or a Novell environment and haven't yet upgraded to Active Directory. But a much more common scenario occurs when you want to enforce the same required security setting on multiple machines simultaneously. This requirement is typical at call centers, nursing stations, and public kiosks.

Group Policy's mission is to make broad-stroke enforcement a piece of cake, and this instance certainly qualifies.

Let's say you want to deploy the hisecws_plus.inf template on all the computers in an OU named **Nurses Computers** OU. Follow these steps:

1. Ensure that the **Nurses Computers** OU exists. (We're making it up for the sake of example here.)

2. Move all machines to be affected by this security edict into the **Nurses Computers** OU.

3. Copy the hisecws_plus.inf template from the workstation to a location accessible to the server. You can do this in several ways. The goal is to get the hisecws_plus.inf template that you generated on the workstation over to the server. You can use a network share, email, or even a floppy! When you transfer the file, simply place it into any folder on the server you desire. The best location is the Domain Controller's c:\windows\security\ templates folder.

4. Create a new GPO and link it to the **Nurses Computers** OU. This GPO will be used to import the settings inside the hisecws_plus.inf template you created. Give the GPO a descriptive name, such as Force hisecws_plus.inf.

Once you're editing the GPO, drill down to Computer Configuration ➢ Windows Settings ➢ Security Settings. To utilize any security `.INF` template, simply right-click Security Settings (as shown in Figure 8.45) and choose Import Policy from the shortcut menu.

1. Select the policy you want to use by pointing the file requester toward the `hisecws_plus.inf` file and selecting it. You'll also notice a "Clear this Database Before Importing" check box:

- When this check box is checked, the current Security settings are replaced with those that you defined in the custom `.INF` template.

- When this check box is unchecked, only the attributes you specifically modified are changed. In other words, the state is maintained in those attributes that have no definition.

FIGURE 8.45   Drill down into the Security Settings, right-click, and then import a template.

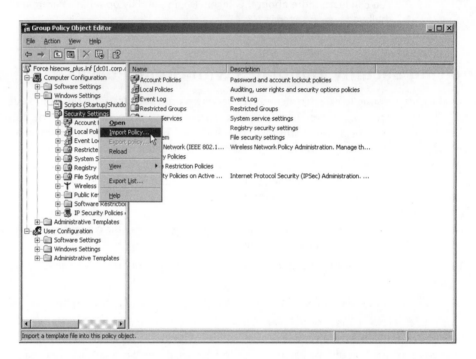

2. You can ensure that the template was imported correctly by verifying that the changes you modified in the `hisecws_plus.inf` template are reflected. For instance, when modifying the `hisecws_plus.inf` template, make sure the `%systemroot%\repair` folder is listed. You can even dive in and inspect the settings.

3. When ready, close the Group Policy Object Editor.

Now, you are ready to reboot the machines affected by the **Nurses Computers** OU, or you can wait until the machines embrace the new security settings you specified in the GPO. Afterward, you can verify that the settings you specified in the `hisecws_plus.inf` template are indeed being reflected and locked down across all machines in the OU.

If you get really gung ho and want to hack the security templates yourself to add your own security settings, it's difficult and ornery but possible. You'll find two excellent references, "How to Customize Security Settings within Templates," at http://tinyurl.com/3n72j, and "How to Add Custom Registry Settings to Security Configuration Editor," at http://tinyurl.com/49p6m. Note that this latter technique is really about modifying the Local Security Options section in the GPeditor and has nothing to do with Security Templates per se.

The Security Configuration Wizard

In the last section, you learned how to leverage security templates and secure your workstations. You then linked a GPO, slurped in the security template, and secured a gaggle of workstations all in one goal.

In this section, the goal is similar.

Except this time, you'll use something called the Security Configuration Wizard, or SCW. I know, I know. You hate wizards. But this one is really super powerful. So powerful, in fact, that it has its own home page at Microsoft.com at www.microsoft.com/scw. Wow!

If you're using Windows Server 2003 or Windows Server 2008, things are somewhat different. Let's start out with Windows Server 2003, then review the changes in Windows Server 2008.

Security Configuration Wizard Primer and Installation

The SCW doesn't exist in Windows Server 2003 RTM. However, with Windows Server 2003 + SP1 and later, it's there if you want it.

It's built into Windows Server 2008, so there's nothing extra to add.

You'll run the SCW on one of your Windows Server machines, say, your Domain Controller. You'll tell the SCW which "roles" the Domain Controller has. For instance, perhaps in addition to being a Domain Controller, it's also a print server and a file server and also maybe a DHCP server. Once you've told it what the machine will be used for, it will pop out a security policy that describes how to secure this Windows 2003 server. Next, you'll convert the policy into a GPO. Finally, you'll link the GPO to an OU in Active Directory, which contains the collection of Windows 2003 servers you want to secure! Hence, all servers in the OU will have the same security policy.

The true goal of the SCW is to "reduce the attack surface." That's the common phrase used when we want to stop all unused services and close up any remaining unused doors. We won't be able to go over all the ins and outs of the SCW. But we will go through a simple example. And, as icing on the security cake, put a Group Policy cherry on top at the end. It'll be sweet.

One note/warning before we get going here: The tasks you perform with the SCW are strictly to secure your Windows 2003/SP1 machines and newer *that are servers*. The output produced by the SCW is not—NOT—meant to secure your Windows Vista, Windows XP, or Windows 2000 machines. Doing so could render your Windows Vista, Windows XP, or Windows 2000 machines wounded and perhaps unrecoverable.

Installing the SCW for Windows Server 2003 (SP1 and Beyond)

As stated, the SCW is available only on Windows 2003 machines after SP1 is loaded. Once it's been loaded, the SCW's help icon should automatically appear on the desktop. However, this does not mean that the SCW is actually installed. To install the SCW, you need to sojourn to Add/Remove Programs and specifically add it. Let's do that now. To install the SCW:

1. Log on to your Windows 2003/SP1 Domain Controller as Administrator.

2. Click Start ➤ Control Panel ➤ Add or Remove Programs.

3. Click the Add/Remove Windows Components button.

4. In the Components list, locate and select Security Configuration Wizard, as seen in Figure 8.46.

5. Click Next to load the component and close Add/Remove Programs.

Once the SCW is loaded, you're ready to rock.

FIGURE 8.46　The Security Configuration Wizard's help file automatically appears on the desktop after SP1 is loaded. However, you need to specifically add in the SCW components via Add/Remove Programs.

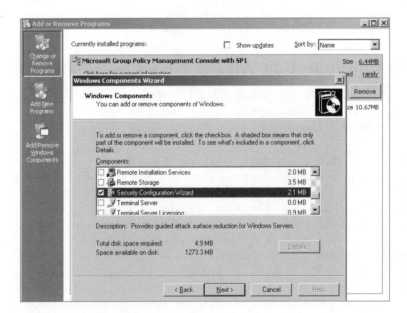

Installing the SCW for Windows Server 2008

The good news for Windows Server 2008 fans is that it's already pre-installed. All you have to do is click Start ➢ All Programs ➢ Administrative Tools and select Security Configuration Wizard as seen in Figure 8.47.

A Practical SCW Example

In this example, we'll produce an SCW policy that turns off all unnecessary services for our Domain Controller. And, we'll additionally leverage this policy for additional Domain Controllers (later) if more come aboard. To create an SCW policy, you'll run the wizard in several big-ish steps.

FIGURE 8.47   The SCW is preloaded and ready to go for Windows Server 2008.

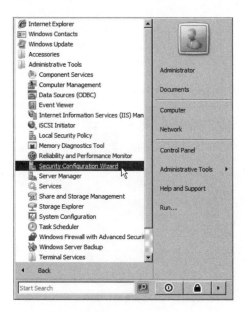

Initial SCW Kickoff

To get started with the SCW:

1. Start the SCW by clicking Start ➢ All Programs ➢ Administrative Tools ➢ Security Configuration Wizard.

2. At the first screen of the wizard, click Next.

3. At the Configuration Action screen, ensure that "Create a new security policy" is selected and click Next, as seen in Figure 8.48.

4. At the Select Server screen, ensure that the DC01 server is selected and click Next. This is the machine that we'll leverage as the baseline machine. That is, the SCW will inspect this machine and see what's running on it so it can make some determinations about which services and such you might want to secure. When you click next, the SCW will inspect this machine and try to determine what its current roles are.

5. After the SCW checks out your system, you'll receive a Processing Complete message and be given the opportunity to "View Configuration Database." The Configuration Database is simply a list of all possible roles the server might play. So, at this time, just click Next.

Role-Based Configuration Section

In this section, you'll have the SCW figure out what roles your server currently has installed. To inspect for roles:

1. Now, you'll be at the first screen of the Role-Based Service Configuration. This section of the wizard helps you add or remove roles this server might be playing. Again, as a Domain Controller, it might also be a print server. Click Next to continue.

FIGURE 8.48 Kick off the SCW by creating a new security policy.

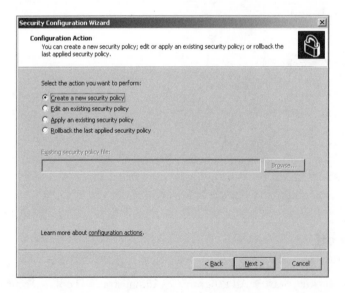

2. When you do, you'll be at the Select Server Roles screen, where you are viewing a list of installed roles, as seen in Figure 8.49. The SCW takes a "best guess" about what it thinks this server is already trying to do and selects those as installed roles. If you have future plans for this machine (or for others later, as you add to the OU) and want to add a role, go ahead at this point. You can select from the list presented here or use the View drop-down list and select to see all roles. Perhaps some day you'll also use certificate services on this machine. In that case, you would need to locate Certificate Server in the list and check it. When you've selected the services you want, click Next.

3. Now you'll be at the Select Client Features screen. Here you'll specify which client components your server runs. Again, by default, it chooses which components it thinks are already in use. Note that for some reason, Group Policy Administrative Client isn't selected, even though the GPMC is detected. I'm not sure why this is overlooked and unselected by default. But, in short, if you plan on running the GPMC on the servers that will get this policy, be sure to also select Group Policy Administrative Client.

4. Choose any additional features you know you are using or want to eventually use and click Next.

FIGURE 8.49   The SCW shows you the roles it thinks are currently running on your server.

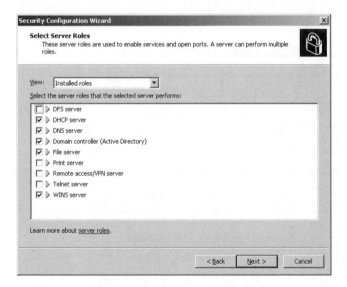

5. You'll be at the Select Administration and Other Options page. Like the pages before it, it makes a best guess about which options you want to use. Choose any additional features you know you are using or want to eventually use and click Next.

6. At the Select Additional Services page, the SCW looks to see if there are any services you might have also loaded. By default, those are checked to continue to run. Click Next to continue.

7. At the Handling Unspecified Services page, you're asked how to handle the services you loaded on the Windows 2003 machine. Select "Do not change the startup mode of the service" and click Next.

8. At the Confirm Service Changes page, you can see what will happen to the myriad of services running on your Domain Controller. In Figure 8.50, you can see that many services, currently set to Automatic, will now be configured to Disabled.

9. When you click Next, you'll proceed to the Network Configuration Section.

Network Security Section

In Windows Server 2003, the firewall is off by default. This means that applications and users can knock on your Windows Server 2003 servers' doors and say "Hi. Is there anyone there who can help me?"

But in Windows Server 2008, the firewall is on by default. This means that applications and users knock on your Windows Server 2008 servers' doors and get no response at all. Ever. Unless that port is open and listening.

FIGURE 8.50 The SCW will make your system less vulnerable to attack by disabling unused services.

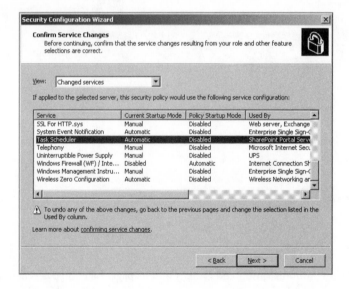

So, here's my advice:

- Skip this section if your interest lies in Windows Server 2003 machines. You're highly unlikely to want to turn on the Windows Server 2003 firewall because it'll be a lot of work trying to ensure which apps are using what ports.

- Use this section if your interest lies in Windows Server 2008. You've already got the Windows Server 2008 firewall on by default. So, if an application doesn't get or give a response, it'll be easy to know that when you install the application and then give it a whirl in your test lab. If the application doesn't respond, you can use this part of the wizard to name the application or open up ports in the various other ways this Add Rule page (seen in Figure 8.51) has to offer.

So, if you choose to continue with this section, you'll encounter the following pages (which are similar in idea to the already-examined pages). That is, the wizard tries to determine what you're already doing on this system and keeps those parts enabled and available for use; it will also close off sections that it thinks are not being used. However, if you zip through this section, you're basically telling the SCW to turn on the Windows firewall for servers that this security policy will affect. That's a risky game because if you fail to open a port, your clients won't be able to access a program running on your server. So, proceed down this section with caution.

If you're doing these exercises on a Windows Server 2008 machine, accept all the defaults and click Next.

If you're doing these exercises on a Windows Server 2003 machine, you can skip this section.

Registry Settings Section

Like the previous section, this section is optional. Here you can make decisions about SMB signing, which operating systems can connect to this server, LDAP signing, outbound and inbound authentication methods, and more.

FIGURE 8.51   You can specify that a specific program has an exception to the firewall rule.

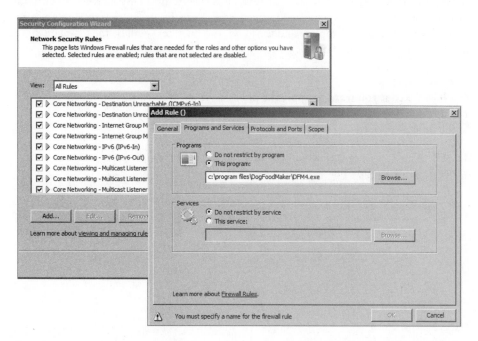

If you're interested in the materials in this section, be sure to read the materials on www.microsoft.com/scw.

For our examples, we're going to skip the Registry Settings Section by selecting "Skip this section" and clicking Next.

Audit Policy Section

Again, this section is optional. And I think you'll likely want to skip it. We examined Audit Policy earlier in this chapter, and it's likely you've already manually configured your audit policy and set it upon the OUs containing the servers you already want to audit.

Moreover, as the warning on this page describes, after these settings are set, they are permanently tattooed.

For our purposes, we'll select "Skip this section" and click Next.

Save Security Policy Section

At this point, you're ready to save your policy. But it doesn't get saved as a GPO. No, no! That would be too easy! Instead, it is saved as an XML file! On the "Security policy file name" line, enter in a legal path on this server and a name for the file, say, `c:\OurSecureDCPolicy.xml`. In the Description field, enter in something useful as well, as seen in Figure 8.52.

However, before you click Next, note that you can also, optionally, choose to "Include Security Templates." Yes! These are the same security templates you could have created in the previous section. Here's the idea: The SCW is easy to use and lets you manipulate a lot of stuff but not everything. Security templates are hard to use but let you manipulate (just about) everything. So, if you created any security templates that additionally increased security for your Windows 2003 servers, you can add them here. Note, however, that if there's a settings conflict between a security template and the SCW, the "winner" will be the template, not the setting contained within the SCW.

Strange, but true..

When ready, click Next.

You'll be asked if you want to apply the policy now or later. At this point, choose "Apply later" and click Next.

At the final page of the wizard, click Finish.

FIGURE 8.52   Here you can add in additional security templates or just save your SCW policy out as an XML file.

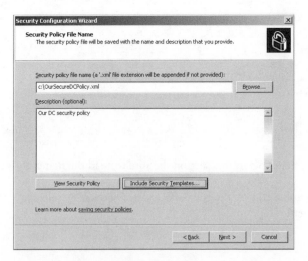

Converting Your SCW Policy to a GPO

At this point, you've got a nice XML file that you, well, can't do a lot with in its current form. However, the goal is to convert this XML file to a bona-fide GPO that you can then link to an OU of your choosing. In this case, you will link it to your **Domain Controllers** OU.

You can covert the GPO with the scwcmd.exe command. The syntax of the command line is as follows:

```
scwcmd transform /p:name_of_xml_file_ /g:name_of_GPO_we_want_to_create
```

So, because you saved the XML file as c:\OurSecureDCPolicy.xml, and you arbitrarily call the GPO "OurSecureDCGPO," the syntax will be

```
scwcmd transform /p:c:\ourSecureDCPolicy.xml /g:OurSecureDCGPO
```

Once the command is performed, you should get a "Command completed successfully" message. A GPO is now created with the name you've provided after the /g (in this case, Our-SecureDCGPO).

WARNING   IIS configuration that is defined in the SCW policy is not parlayed into a transformed GPO. It is lost.

Viewing and Applying Your Transformed GPO

At this point, fire up the GPMC to see if the GPO you just created by transforming the XML file is there. It should be in the Group Policy Objects node but not linked to any site, domain, or OU. Note that you might have to refresh the list of GPOs in the Group Policy Objects node to see the new GPO.

When ready, link the GPO you created to the final destination. In our working example, you would link the GPO to the **Domain Controllers** OU. You don't really need to do this now, but you can do so if you so choose. Again, the GPO will just sit there in the Group Policy Objects node swimming pool—doing nothing—unless it's actually linked to a GPO.

One quick word of warning about the resulting GPO that is created. That is, if you click the Settings tab inside the GPMC to see the resulting GPO that is created, you might not see anything! However, if you edit the GPO, you'll be able to see the settings that are actually contained within the GPO (see Figure 8.53). This is a micro-bug that is there for Windows 2003, but is fixed in 2008.

Note that if you change any settings within the GPO, the problem magically fixes itself, and then you can see the settings contained within the GPO by clicking the Settings tab. Something about editing the GPO inside the Group Policy Object Editor fixes the converted GPO and makes it viewable. Again, this is a bug that never got fixed in Windows Server 2003 but seems to be fixed in Windows Server 2008.

SCW Caveats

There are two additional warnings when using the SCW to create XML policies and then convert them to GPOs.

Don't use the SCW (and corresponding GPOs) to apply settings to machines outside of the type you created it on.   So, the SCW exists for Windows Server 2003 and Windows Server 2008. The current word from my contacts at Microsoft "is to make sure the output of a Windows Server 2003 SCW (and its GPOs) affects only Windows Server 2003 and the output of a Windows Server 2008 SCW (and its GPOs) affects only Windows Server 2008."

FIGURE 8.53   The Settings tab might not show any settings from the transformed GPO. However, editing the GPO will show that the settings are, indeed, changed inside the GPO.

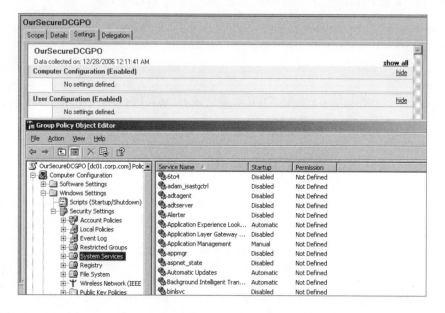

There might be cases where it's okay to "cross the streams" (and I'm working on getting that information to you; be sure to check www.GPanswers.com newsletters). But until then, create GPOs and link them to places that affect only the machine types you created the policy on in the first place.

But in no case should output from the SCW be used to affect and apply to Windows Vista or Windows XP systems. It's only meant for servers.

Don't expect file and Registry ACLs to be able to "roll back."   After you lay down file or Registry ACLs using GPOs), you cannot roll these settings back. They are always permanently tattooed on the target system. It doesn't matter how you lay down those file or Registry ACLs; it can be from the security templates directly, or via GPOs. There's just no way for ACLs to be rolled back.

What I Didn't Cover

Unfortunately, space limitations restrict me from delving into *all* security functions of Group Policy. Of note, two categories are missing from this Group Policy security roundup that can affect all computers (Windows Vista and pre-Vista):

- Certificate Services and Public Key Infrastructure (PKI)

- EFS and the EFS Recovery Policy

For More on Certificate Services and PKI

For getting a grip on Certificate Services and PKI, check out the Microsoft Press book *Windows Server 2008 PKI and Certificate Security* at http://www.microsoft.com/MSPress/books/9549.aspx.

For More on EFS and the EFS Recovery Policy

You'll find information on the Encrypting File System in Windows XP and Windows Server 2003 at http://tinyurl.com/576kx.

Additionally, see the Microsoft Knowledge Base article "Best Practices for the Encrypting File System" (KB 223316) at http://support.microsoft.com/kb/223316.

Final Thoughts

To know security, you need to know Group Policy. To that end, we've toured some of the major sights along the Group Policy security highway. From the "Default Domain Controllers Policy" and "Default Domain Policy" GPOs to Software Restriction Policies to Security Templates—a lot can be accomplished in there.

Walking up to a specific machine and applying local security sounds like a great, straight-forward idea—until you have so many machines you couldn't possibly walk up to them all. This chapter covered some alternate methods for asserting your will across the network.

Use security templates for all types of machines. But if you're configuring Windows 2003/SP1 or newer machines, the new SCW is your new best friend.

Remember that items in the security branch of a GPO will take effect, maximally, every 16 hours—even if the Group Policy doesn't change in Active Directory. This ensures that if a nefarious local administrator changed the policies on his workstation, they'll eventually be refreshed. However, recall that this "Security Background Refresh" will not affect other areas of Group Policy by default. If you want similar behavior, be sure to read Chapter 4 where I discuss the implications of the setting named **Process even if the Group Policy objects have not changed**. You can enable different sections of Group Policy to do this by drilling down in the Group Policy Management Editor within Computer Configuration ➢ Policies ➢ Administrative Templates ➢ System ➢ Group Policy. Again, this was covered in Chapter 4. So, for fullest security and protection, re-read that chapter to understand why and how to enable those settings.

Finally, remember that Fine-Grained Password Policy (FGPP) isn't really related to Group Policy, but there is a tie-in. That is, if no FGPP is assigned to a user or group, then the domain-wide defaults take effect. You might want to consider choosing one or the other: either keep using the Default Domain GPO to store the passwords for everyone in the domain, or alternatively, consider assigning FGPPs for positively everyone in the domain. That way, you only have to really troubleshoot one area if you suspect a problem.

Designing vs. Implementing

This chapter is titled "Implementing Security with Group Policy" because that's what we did. However, an equally challenging project is the *design* of your security policy battle plans *before* you march headlong into implementation. One excellent Microsoft resource, made specifically for the task of working through some examples to design security with GPOs, is the "Common Scenarios" white paper at http://tinyurl.com/4oaks. You can also just search for "Group Policy Common Scenarios Using GPMC" on Microsoft's website.

The "Common Scenarios" white paper includes several "canned" GPOs that help you learn how to design a security policy and includes situations where computers should be Lightly Managed, Mobile, and Kiosk. Once you play with each scenario, you can decide which features you want to keep in your own environment. These GPOs aren't really meant to be deployed as is (you should modify them to suit your own business), but you'll get a better handle on some security design options. A white paper is included to help you work though the scenarios. In all, I think it's an excellent follow-up once you've been through the exercises in this chapter.

9

Windows Vista and Windows Server 2008 Security Enhancements with Group Policy

In the last chapter, we touched upon lots of security goodies. Some enhancements were about Vista systems, some enhancements were about Windows Server 2008 systems, but most were about pre-Vista systems.

In this chapter, it's "The All Vista and Windows Server 2008 Channel." *All Vista and Windows Server 2008, All the Time.* WVST at 102.8 FM!

Okay, I'm done playing around.

The stuff you'll learn here is (mostly) specifically for Windows Vista and (if you like) Windows Server 2008. I'm not going to say "Windows Vista and Windows Server 2008" each time a specific feature works for both Windows Vista and Windows Server 2008. I'm just going to say, "Windows Vista does X," unless there's something specifically different between how a feature works in Windows Vista or Windows Server 2008 that expressly needs to be described. So whenever you read "Windows Vista," you can think "Windows Vista and Windows Server 2008" unless you hear otherwise.

I'm doing this because typically Windows Vista is the client, not Windows Server 2008. It's true you could walk around with Windows Server 2008 on your laptop; you likely won't. So while everything here will work with both Windows Vista and Windows Server 2008, we're going to assume you'll mostly apply these tidbits to Windows Vista.

Here's a foretaste of what we're going to cover:

Vista's Enhanced Wireless and New Wired Ethernet Policy   Windows XP already has Wireless policy. Windows Vista's is better. And it also has a new Wired Ethernet policy that we will check out.

Internet Explorer 7   It's big. It's new. It's Internet Explorer 7. And it's got Group Policy control.

Vista's Updated Windows Firewall with Enhanced Security   Windows XP/SP2 already had a pretty good Windows Firewall, and it was controllable using Group Policy. Windows Vista's is better and more controllable via Group Policy.

User Account Control (UAC)   Or, more specifically, we'll be talking about *controlling* User Account Control.

A quick note about some things that are really important with regard to security but that we won't be covering here.

Device Installation Restrictions   This lets us take control and limit access of hardware being installed on our client machines. Don't want USB sticks to work on your Windows Vista machines? This is the ticket! We'll talk about this in the companion book, *Creating the Secure Managed Desktop*, in Chapter 10, entitled "Finishing Touches with Group Policy: Controlling Hardware, Deploying Printers and Implementing Shadow Copies."

Network Access Protection   This is the how you can quarantine a machine that isn't "healthy enough" to be on your production network so that it doesn't potentially infect others. No up-to-date virus definitions? No love on the network. We'll talk about this in the companion book in Chapter 9, entitled "Network Access Protection using Group Policy."

So, let's roll up those sleeves and get started.

Wireless (802.3) and Wired Network (802.11) Policies

Built-in support for wireless networks was new for Windows XP and Windows 2003 and is now enhanced for Windows Vista. Additionally, Windows Vista has a Wired policy that is new and neat.

You can see two new nodes in Computer Configuration ➤ Policies ➤ Windows Settings ➤ Security Settings ➤ **Wired Network (IEEE 802.3) Policies** and **Wireless Network (IEEE 802.11 Policies)**, as seen in Figure 9.1.

FIGURE 9.1   New nodes for Wired and Wireless policies are now available.

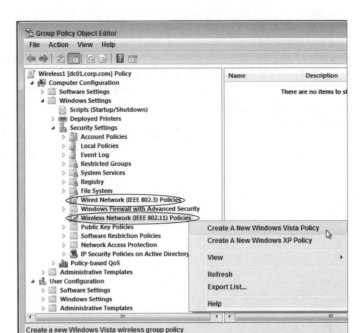

Here's the trick though: to actually make the examples in this section work, you need to have an updated schema. You can get the updated schema in one of three ways:

- If you do a fresh installation of Windows Server 2008 as your first Active Directory domain.

- If you use Windows Server 2008's `adprep /forestprep` command, found in the `\sources` directory on the Windows Server 2008 DVD. To prepare your Windows Server 2003 domain for the introduction of Windows Server 2008 Domain Controllers, you'll also need to run `adprep /domainprep` in each domain (after the `/forestprep`, which takes care of the actual schema update). Additionally, you might also need to run `adprep /domainprep /gpprep`. So please check Microsoft Knowledge Base article 324392 (`http://tinyurl.com/39r59e`) for additional information.

- If you can manually update a Windows Server 2003 domain's schema to just support these attributes. You can find that information here: `http://tinyurl.com/yd7hyy`, in an article titled "Active Directory Schema Extensions for Windows Vista Wireless and Wired Group Policy Enhancements." There are two scripts you must run to make the updates: one for Wired and one for Wireless policy.

To make use of Wireless and Wired Policies, you'll need to commit to one of these three steps or else these policies just won't work. And, it should be noted that you must be an Active Directory Schema Admin to make these changes.

So, instead of reproducing all the steps here, just go there, take the time to do this in your test lab (or get permission to do this in your real world), then come back here when you're finished.

Note that if you try to create new Wireless Network (IEEE 802.11) Policies for Windows XP *without* updating the schema, these policies will succeed, because Windows XP doesn't require the updated schema. Do note, however, that this still requires the Windows Server 2003 Active Directory schema; the Windows 2000 Active Directory schema won't work.

However, if you don't have the schema update, and you attempted to create a new Wireless policy for Windows Vista or new Wired Policy (which is Windows Vista–only anyway), you'll encounter what you see in Figure 9.2.

FIGURE 9.2   What happens if you try to create a new Wired or Wireless policy for Windows Vista without the schema update

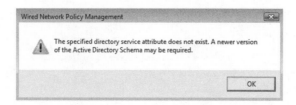

Assuming you've modified the schema as required, you're ready to move on.

802.11 Wireless Policy for Windows XP

When you right-click **Wireless Network (IEEE 802.11) Policies,** you can select "Create a New Windows Vista Policy" or "Create a New Windows XP Policy." For XP, you know which one to pick.

You can set all sorts of wireless parameters for your Windows XP or Windows 2003 computers (though it's unlikely you'll have many Windows 2003 computers with wireless cards). The policy settings themselves are beyond the scope of this book and include options such as WEP, EAP/Smartcard usage, and other scary-sounding wireless settings. However, you can learn about the controllable settings in Chapter 6 of the "Windows Server 2003 Planning Guide." Just search TechNet for "Planning Guide 6—Designing Wireless LAN Security Using 802.1X." At last check it was found here: http://tinyurl.com/yzm3tv.

Note that your users need to be connected to the hard-wired network at least one time and download Group Policy from a Domain Controller to get the appropriate certificates for Wireless policy.

802.11 Wireless Policy and 802.3 Wired Policy for Windows Vista

Windows Vista's Wireless policy adds some new bells and whistles, and the Wired policy is brand spankin' new.

In the new goodies for Wireless you get things like "Mixed Security Mode" (where you can configure several settings to single SSID) and "Allow and Deny Lists" (where you can dictate specifically which SSIDs they can connect and not connect to).

At last check a good starting point for leveraging these policies can be found here:

`www.microsoft.com/technet/windowsvista/network/default.mspx`

shortened to

`http://tinyurl.com/2sferd`

As with the Windows XP version of this policy, your users need to make contact with a Domain Controller to download Group Policy over the wired Ethernet at least one time before this policy can kick in.

The wired policies don't look all that exciting at first blush. But, they're the backbone for Network Access Protection (NAP)—a feature for Windows Server 2008 (with Windows XP/SP3 or Windows Vista and Windows Server 2008 as clients) that will prevent rogue machines from getting on your network.

You can also leverage Wired Policy if your Cisco switch enforces 802.1x authentication. This is common in high-security environments where you want to prevent unauthorized users from plugging laptops into hot network drops. You can learn more about 802.1x authentication with Microsoft's NAP in the Chapter 9, "Network Access Protection (NAP) with Group Policy," of the companion book, *Creating the Secure Managed Desktop*.

Managing Internet Explorer with Group Policy

There's Internet Explorer 6 and now Internet Explorer 7. And you need to know how to control them. And that's where it gets a little confusing because there are lots of areas in Group Policy that look like they can do the job. In this section we'll explore the places you can control Internet Explorer via Group Policy.

Internet Explorer 7 comes with Windows Vista. However, it should be noted that Internet Explorer 7 is technically labeled by Microsoft as a "required" upgrade for your existing Windows XP machines. So this tip might be too late for you. But, if you want to "block" Internet Explorer 7 from being laid down upon your existing Windows XP machines, you can "block" it. It's called the "Toolkit to Disable Automatic Delivery of Internet Explorer 7" and is found here: `http://tinyurl.com/fh3bv`.

The three big things we'll talk about are as follows:

- Internet Explorer Maintenance Policy (which mostly controls Internet Explorer 6)

- Internet Explorer 7's built-in control from Windows Vista management station

- Internet Explorer 7's ADM for Windows XP management stations

Now, a quick note before we get too far into this section. Turns out there are seemingly a zillion different ways to control Internet Explorer using Group Policy. Not only do you have the stuff contained in this section, but in Chapter 10, we'll cover the new Group Policy Preference Extensions, which are yet another way to manage IE. So stay tuned for that as well.

Internet Explorer Maintenance (IEM)

The point of Internet Explorer Maintenance (IEM) settings is to set preferences for things. The definition here for preferences is "suggestions for how a user should use Internet Explorer."

You set Internet Explorer Maintenance settings for users by traversing down to User Configuration ➤ Policies ➤ Windows Settings ➤ **Internet Explorer Maintenance**.

So, if you set a preference for the Internet Explorer home page to be www.GPanswers.com, that's great! You can see IEM settings in Figure 9.3 where I've set the home page URL to www.GPanswers.com.

But here's the trick about IEM settings: There's nothing specifically saying the user can't open up Internet Explorer, go into the options of the browser and set whatever settings they want *in place* of your preferences. In Figure 9.4, a user affected by this policy can just fire up Internet Explorer 7 on Windows Vista and change the home page to whatever they want!

FIGURE 9.3 You can set preferences using Internet Explorer Maintenance.

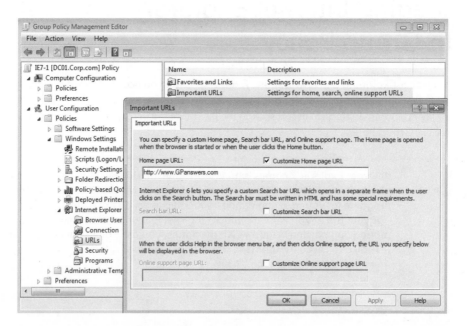

How about this lovely scenario: You spend Friday night at the office putting together a new Internet proxy server. You have 10,000 clients, and now you have to update them. You *could* walk around to each of them to tell Internet Explorer the name of the new proxy server. However, if you use Group Policy with Internet Explorer Maintenance policies, you simply set the name of the new proxy server from upon high and go home for the night.

Again, you'll find all sorts of gizmos to play with that control Internet Explorer: home page settings, proxy settings, security zone settings, favorites, and so on. However, it should be noted that not all IEM settings will affect Internet Explorer 7, as shown in Figure 9.5.

A complete rundown of all the Internet Explorer Maintenance mode settings is beyond the scope of this book; however, there is one "not so obvious" element to this branch of Group Policy: the two modes you can use to deploy Internet Explorer Maintenance settings.

FIGURE 9.4   Users can change the preferences set in Internet Explorer Maintenance to whatever they want.

Mandatory Mode   Acts like other Group Policy settings; that is, your desires are forced upon your client machines. If users change them, the settings are restored. Using this mode is helpful when you want to guarantee important options such as security settings and proxy settings. Additionally, you'll need to locate the **Internet Explorer Maintenance Policy Processing** policy setting (located in Computer Configuration ➢ Policies ➢ Administrative Templates ➢ Group Policy). Inside that setting there's a check box labeled "Process even if Group Policy Objects have not changed." Again, nothing specifically prevents them from changing these values, but once that setting is selected, when a foreground or background refresh is triggered, the values should be returned.

FIGURE 9.5   Some Internet Explorer Maintenance settings are not going to work for Internet Explorer 7.

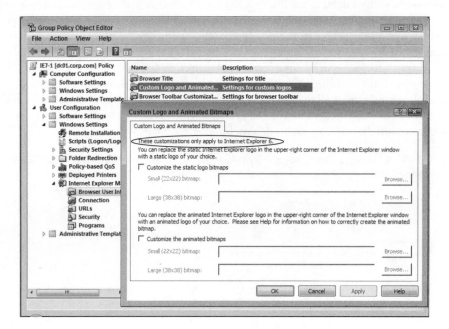

Preference Mode   This is the default and what we just saw. That is, once you make a setting for a user, the change is reflected upon the client. But, it allows users to change them if they desire. This mode is good for users you want to give some degree of liberty to (for example, developers) but want to encourage to use your preferred settings.

If the two modes are confusing, here's the cheat sheet: Preference mode applies only once and then never again, while Mandatory mode will always reapply (like normal policy, but on steroids, because it won't care if the version has changed).

The Internet Explorer Maintenance interface is a little goofy. For some items (such as customized program settings), you'll import the settings from the machine on which the Group Policy Management Editor is actually running. Additionally goofy is that once you make a change to Preference mode, you cannot return to Mandatory mode without wiping out all your settings (via the Reset Browser Settings option).

Windows 2003 allows for what is known as "Internet Explorer Hardening," which is meant to prevent rogue Active X controls and the like from applying. Active X controls are little pieces of code that enhance the Internet Explorer experience but could be used maliciously. Microsoft has a great reference on the subject at `http://tinyurl.com/54wwd`. You can also search Microsoft's website for "Internet Explorer Enhanced Security Configuration."

Internet Explorer Settings Warning

As stated, configuring the Internet Explorer settings can be a bit wacky. There's one more wacky piece that makes them sometimes very difficult to work with. Some policy settings within Internet Explorer are "sticky." That is, they don't act like regular policy settings that just revert to some default when they don't apply.

If you set up Internet Explorer Maintenance policies at multiple levels in Active Directory, you'll want to test to see the "merging" of your policy settings. Some Internet Explorer Maintenance policy settings "merge," and others do not—it depends on what you are setting up. Proxy settings, for instance, do not merge; the last applied policy "wins." However, this is not true for the "Trusted Sites" configuration settings. These policy settings *will* merge. Again, be sure to test your GPOs with Internet Explorer Maintenance policies to verify whether your specific policy settings merge or not.

The one that comes to mind is the Internet Explorer Maintenance proxy server setting (mentioned previously). If you later choose to work without a proxy server and kill the GPO, the proxy setting you set sticks with all your clients. It doesn't peel off the setting. This is a major hassle and one that has no great fix.

I retested this with Windows Vista's Internet Explorer 7, and sure enough, they fixed it. But previous versions of the operating system aren't so fortunate.

I've heard reports of other Internet Explorer settings being sticky, but in my testing, the proxy setting is the only one I've witnessed being sticky. In short, before rolling out Internet Explorer settings (of any kind), you should also ensure that the settings you roll out are nonsticky. Or, if they are sticky, be sure to have a back-out plan to remediate the stickiness if you need to.

Internet Explorer's Group Policy Settings

You're using a Windows Vista management station, right? Of course right, because you read Chapters 1, 2, 3, and 7. But if for some reason you're not (and you're using, say, a Windows XP or Windows Server 2003 management station), you might need to control the new goodies in Internet Explorer 7. If you need to do that, you'll need to get the ADM files for Internet Explorer 7 to load upon your management station. You would go to http://tinyurl.com/ynjyry (expands to a Microsoft download) to get them. Then, use the information in Chapter 7 to import an ADM template.

But wait. You say you are using a Windows Vista (or Windows Server 2008) management station? Then good news for you—the work is already done. The controls for Internet Explorer 7 are already in the box. Nothing to download, nothing to worry about.

The point of the Group Policy settings, found in (User and Computer Configuration) ➢ Policies ➢ Administrative Templates ➢ Windows Components ➢ Internet Explorer ➢ Internet Settings and (User and Computer Configuration) ➢ Policies ➢ Administrative Templates ➢ Windows Components ➢ Internet Explorer, are to guarantee settings.

In other words, preferences (what we just saw earlier) "suggest" a setting; the Group Policy settings "guarantee it." Be sure to read both the Explain text for each Group Policy setting and the requirements. Not every setting is valid for both Internet Explorer 6 and 7, so be sure to read and test.

Do You Know about the Internet Explorer IEAK?

The IEAK (Internet Explorer Administration Kit) is used to set preferences or just to configure a standalone Internet Explorer machine. Sure, you'll usually want to use Group Policy in an Active Directory environment to set true policies (and lock down settings). But the IEAK uses a file type called .INS to set preferences. The IEAK can be downloaded here:

   www.microsoft.com/technet/prodtechnol/ie/ieak/default.mspx

Once your .INS file is created, you can package it in a custom ie7setup.exe, which can be used for deployment. Again, you'll usually not want to use the IEAK for domain-joined machines, as you've got the power of Group Policy to do that for you.

It's true, however, that the IEAK settings and Group Policy settings are darn close in similarity. But, there are a few things that can be done *only* using IEAK that cannot be done through Group Policy. Two examples are the ability to set default feeds and the default search provider, which are only available in the IEAK.

But you might be asking yourself, "Which would 'win' if both applied?" The short answer is "Which ever technology gets applied last."

So, if you start off with IEAK settings, those settings are applied.

If you later change to using Group Policy settings, those are applied.

In short the advice is as follows:

- If you want to guarantee settings, and *can* use Group Policy to do so, you should strive to use Group Policy.

- If you haven't checked out the IE Group Policy Preference Extensions (explored in Chapter 10), you should try that next.

- Finally, only if you must, try the IEAK last.

For more information on the IEAK, check out this swell article in *TechNet Magazine*: http://tinyurl.com/ytuwnt.

Finding Internet Explorer ADM Policy Settings

Windows XP/SP2 and Windows 2003/SP1 added 619 possible Internet Explorer policy settings. Windows Vista adds even more.

Again, you'll find most of these settings at Administrative Templates ➢ Policies ➢ Windows Components ➢ Internet Explorer ➢ Internet Control Panel ➢ Security Page. These settings are under both the User Configuration *and* Computer Configuration nodes.

In Chapter 2, we discussed how Microsoft has an Excel spreadsheet with every policy setting available for download. To get a grip on all that's new here, I suggest you download it (track it down via www.GPanswers.com in the "Microsoft Resources" section) and then click the "Inetresx.admx" column of the spreadsheet. Here you can isolate and check out just the Internet Explorer settings, select to see only the new policy settings for "at least Internet Explorer v6.0 in Windows XP Service Pack 2 or Windows Server 2003 Service Pack 1," and get a feel for what's new and what you might choose to use in your environment.

Additionally, remember that you can filter inside the Group Policy Object while you're editing it. Just use the new Filtering options as described in Chapter 3 and select only "At least Internet Explorer 7.0" and you'll see *only* the new settings, as seen here.

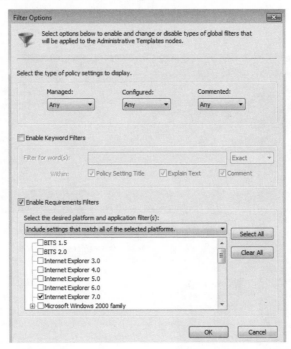

Controlling User Account Control (UAC) with Group Policy

UAC is the User Account Control feature for Windows Vista and Windows Server 2008. You might see it as the "annoying extra pop-up box I need to click in order to do anything useful!" Well, sometimes it might seem that way. But that's not exactly accurate. What's really happening is that you're seeing a prompt for anything that requires administrator rights (that is, that affects the entire computer and all users on that computer) in Windows Vista.

On Windows Server 2008, you might not see the prompts as much because if you log on with the local Administrator account, UAC prompts are largely not presented. However, if you log on as just about anyone else, like a Server Operator, you will see the UAC prompts that we'll discuss here using Windows Vista examples.

In reality, it's not that bad; UAC is designed to put a (small) roadblock in front of administrative tasks and applications so that only administrators can really do anything with these items.

An example of a UAC dialog box that can pop up based on the types of actions and programs you want to run is shown in Figure 9.6, where a mere-mortal user is trying to "Allow a program through Windows Firewall" and is prompted for local administrator credentials.

FIGURE 9.6   Anytime a user clicks on an action with a shield icon, they are prompted for credentials.

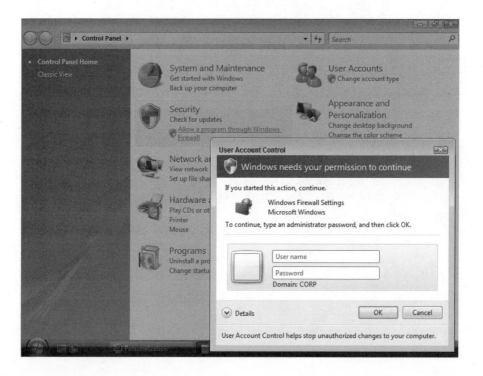

In UAC parlance, a mere-mortal, or regular user, is officially called a *Standard User*. There are three types of prompts you might get when UAC is active:

- Teal bar plus a shield: This program is a part of Windows Vista.

- Gray plus a shield with an exclamation mark: This is signed and trusted by Windows Vista. Trusted means that the certificate used to sign the application "chains" to a certificate in the computer's Trusted Root Certificate Store. Note: the Trusted Root Certificate Store can also be managed via Group Policy.

- Orange plus a shield with an exclamation mark: This program isn't part of Windows Vista and is either unsigned or signed but not yet trusted.

And, at first blush, you might be right. It might be annoying to provide that one extra click or provide alternate credentials. But the underlying idea of UAC is a really good one. That is, regular users need permissions to do the more privileged operations on a Windows Vista machine.

In the short term, you might see the UAC prompts a lot. That's because when you're first configuring Windows Vista, there will be a lot of systemwide changes you'll want to make. But over time, how often are you really making those kinds of changes? Once the computer is configured for your specific environment and the bulk of the software is installed, you will rarely ever see a UAC dialog again.

Additionally, when you log on as an Administrator (local or Domain Administrator), you get "stripped" of your admin rights until you click to say you want to leverage them. UAC's goal is to implement the "Principle of Least Privilege": only use privileged user rights when needed.

The UAC prompts leverage of a technology called UIPI (UI Process Isolation) and another called MIC (Mandatory Integrity Levels). The idea is that the operating system is protected from nonprivileged processes. Only certain types of Windows messages and input are permitted to interact with this dialog. Therefore, previous attacks where the malware would simply click the security dialog before the user ever saw the prompt are thwarted—only privileged processes can interact with the UAC dialogs. This helps prevent what is known as process injection and shatter attacks.

Learn more about process injection and shatter attacks at http://en .wikipedia.org/wiki/Code_injection and http://en.wikipedia.org/ wiki/Shatter_attack.

What's the upshot? Sure, it's one extra click (as an admin) or the fuss of providing admin credentials (for users who aren't admins). But what's the benefit? In short, even admins get the benefit of not doing something potentially harmful because there's one extra click in the way. (How many times have you wished you could have taken an extra "beat" before doing something potentially harmful?)

The other big goodness is that all applications run without admin privilege by default; therefore, scenarios like web browsing and email become much more secure without any changes to the applications. You cannot have "Protected Mode IE" without UAC.

So I encourage you to find it in your heart to try to love this feature. Here's the idea: you want all your users to run as Standard User (or, as they're sometimes called, mere-mortals). That is, they are in the local Users group of the workstation or in the Domain Users group and not in the local Administrators group of the workstation or the Domain Admins group in the domain. In short, they're just users. Additionally, if you want to throw some numbers at the managers in your corporations, the Gartner Group states that running your desktops as a Standard User can reduce TCO by as much as 40 percent versus running that same Desktop with administrative credentials. The idea is that if the user, I mean, administrator of that local machine could just stop making all those darned changes, you would be at their desk fixing their computer a whole lot less. Get it?

Take a quick gander at the general UAC document on Microsoft's website here:

www.microsoft.com/technet/windowsvista/security/uac.mspx

Then come back and learn about the nine different Group Policy controls you have at your disposal to configure it the way you want it to work.

Finally, we'll wrap up our talk on UAC with some prescriptive guidance for certain scenarios to help you configure users based on what they're trying to accomplish.

 If you're starting to develop for Windows Vista, here's a tip. In the past versions of Windows, we ran by default as admin and therefore developed and tested as admin, the manifestation being applications developed this way tended to not work for the Standard User. Now, the idea is that your developers will be developing and testing as Standard User by default.

Just Who Will See the UAC Prompts, Anyway?

The point of UAC is to have "administrative" type users run as mere-mortals until they need to use their superpowers. To that end, you'll likely want to get a handle on just who is going to be affected by UAC prompts and have to run as mere-mortals on Windows Vista (until they elevate their credentials and use that superpower).

There are two categories of folks: anyone who's a member of some special Active Directory or SAM groups and anyone who has one of eight special rights.

Which Groups Are Affected by UAC

There are 16 accounts and related SIDs that are affected by UAC:

- Built-in Administrators
- Power Users
- Account Operators
- Server Operators

- Print Operators
- Backup Operators
- RAS Servers Group
- NT 4 Application Compatibility Group
- Network Configuration Operators
- Cryptographic Operators
- Domain Administrators
- Domain Controllers
- Certificate Publishers
- Schema Administrators
- Enterprise Administrators
- Group Policy Administrators

UAC sometimes call these users Split Token Users or Hybrid Users as they have two user tokens (nonadmin and admin). See the sidebar "How Token Filtering/Split Token Works."

Elevated Rights and SE Privileges

If the user does not belong to any of the groups listed in the preceding section but has any of the privileges listed in Table 9.1, a filtered token will be created for the user with these privileges removed. These privileges are found in the Group Policy Management Editor in Computer Configuration ➤ Policies ➤ Windows Settings ➤ Security Settings ➤ Local Policies ➤ User Rights Assignment.

 You can get these rights from any level: local, site, domain, or OU. Additionally, many rights are predefined in the default Group Policy Objects (discussed in the previous chapter).

TABLE 9.1   Rights and SE Names That Generate a Filtered Token User Experience

Right	SE Name
Create a token object	SeCreateTokenPrivilege
Act as part of the operating system	SeTcbPrivilege
Take ownership of files or other objects	SeTakeOwnershipPrivilege
Back up files and directories	SeBackupPrivilege

TABLE 9.1 Rights and SE Names That Generate a Filtered Token User Experience *(continued)*

Right	SE Name
Restore files and directories	SeRestorePrivilege
Debug programs	SeDebugPrivilege
Impersonate a client after authentication	SeImpersonatePrivilege
Modify an object label	SeRelabelPrivilege
Load and unload device drivers	SeLoadDriverPrivilege

You can check to see if a currently logged-in user has one of these privileges by typing `whoami /priv` at a command prompt.

How Token Filtering/Split Token Works

If you log in with Domain Administrator rights to a Windows XP machine, you can "do" just about anything you want, including shooting your foot off, easily. This is because if you're assigned rights at some level of Active Directory or SAM, Windows XP just lets you use them. Sounds good, until you start making a mistake while web surfing or using email.

In Windows Vista, things get a little more cautious. Again, the idea in Windows Vista is that if you're a member of one of the special groups, listed in Table 9.1, you will get a "split token." That means that in your daily life, you're running around as a mere-mortal. When you need to rip off your shirt and become Superman, you can do that too—but you have to find a close phone booth, er, UAC prompt to help you with that.

So, for instance, if a user is a member of the Administrators group, the filtered token will have the Administrators group membership set to DENY ONLY. Yep, you read that right. As they're running around as a mere-mortal, anything they try to do on the system is expressly Denied.

Meanwhile, a second protection mechanism kicks in. All the machine-impacting privileges are removed from the token. Therefore, as the Domain Administrator is going about his daily life on a Windows Vista machine, when he starts up things like `explorer.exe`, it's using a nonelevated process token.

You can look at this token using whomai.exe, which is included in Windows Vista. First run whoami /groups in a command window when logged in as Domain Administrator, as shown here.

```
C:\Users\a>whoami /groups

GROUP INFORMATION

Group Name                          Type            SID
                   Attributes
================================================================================
Everyone                            Well-known group S-1-1-0
                   Mandatory group, Enabled by default, Enabled group
BUILTIN\Users                       Alias           S-1-5-32-545
                   Mandatory group, Enabled by default, Enabled group
BUILTIN\Administrators              Alias           S-1-5-32-544
                   Group used for deny only
NT AUTHORITY\REMOTE INTERACTIVE LOGON Well-known group S-1-5-14
                   Mandatory group, Enabled by default, Enabled group
NT AUTHORITY\INTERACTIVE            Well-known group S-1-5-4
                   Mandatory group, Enabled by default, Enabled group
NT AUTHORITY\Authenticated Users    Well-known group S-1-5-11
                   Mandatory group, Enabled by default, Enabled group
NT AUTHORITY\This Organization      Well-known group S-1-5-15
                   Mandatory group, Enabled by default, Enabled group
LOCAL                               Well-known group S-1-2-0
                   Mandatory group, Enabled by default, Enabled group
CORP\Domain Admins                  Group           S-1-5-21-1493004638-2222
30367-1098060478-512 Mandatory group, Enabled by default, Enabled group
Mandatory Label\Medium Mandatory Level Unknown SID type S-1-16-8192
                   Group used for deny only

C:\Users\a>_
```

If you look closely you'll see that the BUILTIN\Administrators and the CORP\Domain Admins groups both have a special Deny token—just for them. Kooky! Again, this is reinstated once UAC prompts are satisfied.

Additionally, you can see what privileges are being used at any time with whoami /priv, as shown here.

```
C:\Users\a>whoami /priv

PRIVILEGES INFORMATION

Privilege Name                  Description                           State
================================ ==================================== ========
SeShutdownPrivilege             Shut down the system                  Disabled
SeChangeNotifyPrivilege         Bypass traverse checking              Enabled
SeUndockPrivilege               Remove computer from docking station  Disabled
SeIncreaseWorkingSetPrivilege   Increase a process working set        Disabled
SeTimeZonePrivilege             Change the time zone                  Disabled

C:\Users\a>_
```

Compare this to the whoami /priv command when run on a Windows XP machine shown here.

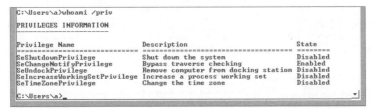

```
C:\WINDOWS\system32\cmd.exe                                        _ □ ×

C:\Documents and Settings\a>whoami /priv

(X) SeChangeNotifyPrivilege        = Bypass traverse checking
(O) SeShutdownPrivilege            = Shut down the system
(X) SeUndockPrivilege              = Remove computer from docking station
(O) SeSecurityPrivilege            = Manage auditing and security log
(O) SeBackupPrivilege              = Back up files and directories
(O) SeRestorePrivilege             = Restore files and directories
(O) SeSystemtimePrivilege          = Change the system time
(O) SeRemoteShutdownPrivilege      = Force shutdown from a remote system
(O) SeTakeOwnershipPrivilege       = Take ownership of files or other objects
(O) SeDebugPrivilege               Debug programs
(O) SeSystemEnvironmentPrivilege   = Modify firmware environment values
(O) SeSystemProfilePrivilege       = Profile system performance
(O) SeProfileSingleProcessPrivilege = Profile single process
(O) SeIncreaseBasePriorityPrivilege = Increase scheduling priority
(X) SeLoadDriverPrivilege          Load and unload device drivers
(O) SeCreatePagefilePrivilege      = Create a pagefile
(O) SeIncreaseQuotaPrivilege       = Adjust memory quotas for a process
(O) SeManageVolumePrivilege        = Perform volume maintenance tasks
(X) SeImpersonatePrivilege         = Impersonate a client after authentication
(X) SeCreateGlobalPrivilege        = Create global objects

C:\Documents and Settings\a>_
```

> So, Windows XP doesn't "filter" anything. Windows Vista goes the extra mile to strip out unused rights until you actually need them. Note that the whoami tool isn't built into Windows XP as it is in Windows Vista. You can load the whoami tool from the Windows XP support tools here: http://tinyurl.com/4uhnu.

Understanding the Group Policy Controls for UAC

There are 10 Group Policy controls for UAC. They are all found within Computer Configuration ➢ Policies ➢ Windows Settings ➢ Security Settings ➢ Local Policies ➢ Security Options and all start with the words "User Account Control:" as seen in Figure 9.7.

Let's examine each policy setting so you can decide if you want to change the default behavior.

FIGURE 9.7 The User Account Control entries are all found under Security Options.

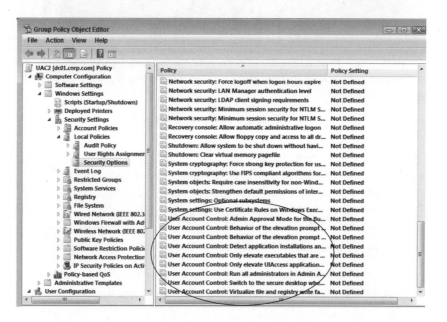

User Account Control: Admin Approval Mode for the Built-in Administrator Account

As we've already discussed, both users and administrators have to "say yes" or provide administrator credentials.

What? No Usable Local Administrator Account on Windows Vista?

By default, the Windows Vista built-in Administrator account is disabled. Yep, you read that right—there is no usable built-in Administrator account on Windows Vista. It's there, it's just disabled. Indeed, check out the following figure, where I'm simply typing `net user administrator` at a Windows Vista command prompt. Note that the "Account active" flag is set to No.

However, if you create a new Windows Vista machine (that isn't joined to the domain), the first user you create by default has the equivalent permissions to a local administrator and all subsequent users are Standard Users—see the following figure where my first user on this fresh Windows Vista installation is named User. Confusing, right?

So, be careful when you give that first local user account's name and password. That first user account really has administrator rights! Yikes!

However, if, during setup, you join the domain directly, you won't have any local user accounts created, and hence, you won't have any accounts you can log on to as a local administrator. Of course, you could always log on to the Enterprise or Domain Administrator accounts (but we're talking about local accounts here).

So, what about that disabled local Administrator account? Well, again, you need to ask yourself if you really need it. In a domain environment, you could always just log in as a Domain Administrator. And, if the machine wasn't joined to the domain during setup, you could log in with that first user. So all bases are covered.

But, if you really felt like you wanted to bring back that local Administrator account, you could do so. Historically, this account has been used for pure maintenance. That's why, by default, it's not enabled and has special behavior once enabled. So before I tell you how to enable the local Administrator account, I want to pass on a big ol' cautionary note: that is, the local Administrator account is exempt (by default) from all UAC prompts.

The behavior is the same on Windows Server 2008 if you log on with the local Administrator account or Domain Administrator account.

You won't see any prompts. If you enable Vista's Administrator account and romp around within Windows Vista while using it, there are absolutely no safety checks. If you wanted to change this behavior, you would manipulate the User Account Control: Admin Approval Mode for the **Built-in Administrator account** policy setting.

Again, it's not recommended that you enable the local Administrator account, but if you wanted to, the command line you would type is this:

```
net user administrator complexp@ssw0rd /active:yes
```

And again, I'm not suggesting you should run out and enable all your local Administrator accounts. But if you do have some "corporate-wide" reason to do this, it would be wise to set a complex password during machine creation time (with an answer file).

But there's another way to enable the local Administrator account. Assuming the password is set on the local Administrator account (say, via the answer file at machine creation time), you can use Group Policy to just "turn it on." You'll find the setting to turn this on in Computer Configuration ➢ Policies ➢ Windows Settings ➢ Security Settings ➢ Local Policies ➢ Security Options ➢ **Accounts: Administrator account status**.

By the way, you might be wondering what happens if your Windows XP machine is upgraded to Windows Vista? The short answer: If you have no other enabled accounts except Administrator, it will leave the Administrator account there but force it to use UAC prompting like all other accounts.

Before we finish talking about the local Administrator account, there is one more local Administrator–related change you need to be aware of. In pre-Windows Vista, you could, if you wanted to, boot into Safe Mode logon with the *disabled* built-in Administrator account. Don't know why you'd want to, but it was possible.

Because Windows Vista is trying to encourage Standard Users on desktops (in businesses) and engaging parental controls (in the home), Safe Mode had to go under some security changes:

On Workgroup or Nondomain Joined Computers If there is at least one active local Administrator account, Safe Mode will not allow logon via the disabled built-in Administrator account. But there's no issue logging in with any active Administrator account. If there are no other active local Administrator accounts, Safe Mode will allow the disabled built-in Administrator account to log on for disaster recovery. From that point, it is suggested that a new Administrator account is created before rebooting the computer.

On Domain Joined Computers The disabled built-in Administrator account cannot log on in Safe Mode under any circumstances. Here's where it gets tricky: If a user whose account is also in the Domain Administrators group has ever logged onto that machine before, they can log on again using Safe Mode, no problem. But what if no one from the Domain Administrators group has ever logged onto that machine? Then the computer must be started in "Safe Mode with Networking" since the credentials will not have been cached. Hopefully, Windows Vista will not be "so broken" that networking support won't work in this case. If the machine is disjoined from the domain, it reverts back to the nondomain joined behavior.

Only admins can "say yes." Standard Users must obtain administrator credentials. Standard Users cannot just "say yes."

This prevents them from doing things that could be potentially harmful to the machine. So, this setting dictates the "Admin Approval mode" for the built-in Administrator account. What built-in Administrator account? Check out the sidebar titled "What? No Usable Local Administrator Account on Windows Vista?"

If you choose to enable this built-in Administrator account, this policy setting affects this account.

Enabled By enabling this setting, the built-in Administrator will be forced to honor UAC prompts.

Disabled (Default) By default if you choose to leave this feature disabled (the default) and log in with the local Administrator account, then that account is exempt from UAC prompts.

User Account Control: Allow UIAccess Applications to Prompt for Elevation without Using the Secure Desktop

This policy setting is new to Windows Vista/SP1 and Windows Server 2008.

UIAccess, or UIA, is a category of features designed to make using Windows easier for persons with disabilities. The problem is that applications that interface with the desktop might need to ask the user about security credentials, and any user needs to be able to enter the answer to UAC security prompts.

And, as it turns out, one application that many people often use is categorized as a UIA application. That's the Windows Remote Assistance application.

What happens if you try to provide remote assistance to a user by default? Well, the UAC prompts will appear on the interactive user's desktop (the person needing help) instead of the secure desktop (the person providing the help).

Buuut, if the person needing the help has the forethought, they can set up Remote Assistance with the "Allow IT Expert to respond to User Account Control prompts" option.

But here's the rub: even that check box requires the user to provide administrative credentials at that moment. So if the user is a Standard User, they can't choose to avoid seeing the credentials.

Oh, the Catch-22 of it all!

That's what this policy setting is meant to help with.

Enabled (Default)   If you enable this setting, the person needing help will see the UAC prompt, but the person providing help will see what the person needing help is doing. This means that the person needing help (Joe User) will need to know a local administrator account's password to get through this prompt.

Disabled   If you disable this policy setting, then you don't have to worry about Joe User knowing a local administrator password in order for him to get remote help.

User Account Control: Behavior of the Elevation Prompt for Administrators in Admin Approval Mode

As stated, even if you log on as a Domain Admin to a local Windows Vista box, you're still going to get UAC prompts.

Actually, if you log on with any of 15 different privileged SIDs, you'll get UAC prompts as an Admin. Or, if you log in with any of 8 user rights, you're also going to see the prompts.

We saw these accounts in a list earlier in this chapter and the user rights in Table 9.1.

This policy setting controls how, when logging in as a member of one of those groups or with one of those rights, you'll see prompts.

If you're an admin, the system already knows you're an admin. It won't (by default) re-ask you to supply credentials. It will, however, ask you (essentially) to acknowledge you're about to do a potentially harmful or impactful thing, like installling an application or creating a new user.

Prompt for consent (default)   Because you're already an admin, by default you don't need to resupply your username and password; you just have to click the Continue button or use Alt+C.

Prompt for credentials   This requires an admin to reenter their username and password or provide the username and password of any other Administrator account.

Elevate without prompting   Use with caution: this will silently "say yes" to any prompt if you're logged in as an admin. Microsoft suggests that this only be used in the most secure (they call it *constrained*) environments.

User Account Control: Behavior of the Elevation Prompt for Standard Users

As expected, mere-mortals have to supply some additional credentials to perform administrative tasks. When will mere-mortals be asked for administrative credentials?

Prompt for credentials (default)   Users logging into nondomain joined machines will always be prompted for administrative credentials. If the user enters valid administrative credentials, the user will be permitted to continue. Note that the policy setting Explain text says, "Default for home," but it's really default for everyone.

Automatically deny elevation requests   If users shouldn't access stuff that they shouldn't, why even prompt for credentials? If you set this policy setting to "Automatically deny elevation requests," the user will simply get an "Access Denied" anytime they try to do something privileged. I discuss this a bit later in the section "UAC Policy Setting Suggestions."

This setting's Explain text says, "Default for enterprise," but it's really a "strong suggestion" for the enterprise. See the scenarios a little later for more information about why this is recommended.

User Account Control: Detect Application Installations and Prompt for Elevation

This security setting determines the behavior of application installation detection for the entire system.

Enabled (default)   Applications that start with the words *setu* (yes, that's right, *setu*, as in `setup.exe`, `setupnow.exe`, and others), *instal* (yes, again, it's *instal*), or *update* will be automatically detected by UAC and prompted for credentials. Note that the policy setting Explain text says, "Default for home," but it's really default for everyone.

Disabled   If you're using GPSI or SMS to deploy your software, this feature isn't needed. It's really only required when Junior or Grandma tries to run `setup.exe` for EvilApp6. GPSI and SMS automatically work around this, so you can safely set this to Disabled here if you want to.

This policy setting says, "Default for enterprise," but it's really a "strong suggestion" for the enterprise. See the scenarios a little later for more information about why this is recommended.

User Account Control: Only Elevate Executables That Are Signed and Validated

You can set up UAC such that applications only run if they are digitally signed via a PKI (Public Key Infrastructure) and Trusted. Enterprise administrators can control the allowed applications list by populating certificates in the local computer's Trusted Root Store.

Population of this store is supported by Group Policy.

Enabled   Only applications signed by a trusted PKI certificate are permitted to run.

Disabled (default)   Doesn't matter if the application is signed via PKI.

User Account Control: Only Elevate UIAccess Applications That Are Installed in Secure Locations

We talked about UIAccess (UIA) programs when we checked out the **User Account Control: Allow UIAccess applications to prompt for elevation without using the secure desktop** setting earlier.

Again, UIAccess is a category of features designed to allow persons with disabilities to more easily use Windows. The problem is that these same applications have the potential to be places where an attacker can gain a toehold in the system and do nefarious things. So, this policy setting manages UIAccess programs and ensures that they can be run only in secure locations. This policy setting takes advantage of IL (Integrity Levels) and MIC (Mandatory Integrity Control).

IL (Integrity Level) and MIC (Mandatory Integrity Control Infrastructure) are whole new concepts in Windows Vista and Windows Server 2008 (and one that's simply too deep to go into here). In short, it lets certain users and programs have certain rights to files based on their "trust level." An ever-so-brief overview of MIC can be found at http://tinyurl.com/y8753w, though decent online information on this subject is kind of hard to come by. (One such decent, but not online, source is Mark Minasi's book *Administering Vista Security: The Big Surprises*, also by Sybex.)

Enabled (default)   Specifies that an application will only launch with "UIAccess integrity" if it resides in a secure location in the file system. The secure locations in Windows Vista are limited to the following directories:

- \Program Files\, including subdirectories
- \Windows\system32\
- \Program Files (x86)\, including subdirectories for 64-bit versions of Windows

Windows enforces a PKI signature check on any interactive application that requests execution with UIAccess integrity level regardless of the state of this security setting.

Disabled An application will start with UIAccess integrity *even if it does not* reside in one of the three secure locations in the file system.

User Account Control: Run All Administrators in Admin Approval Mode

This is the "master switch" for UAC.

Enabled (default) If this setting is Enabled, all UAC prompts are possible (although they might not all happen, based on other things you set). However, at least this switch needs to be Enabled. Changing this setting requires a system reboot.

Disabled If you Disable this policy, UAC and all of its supporting functionality just goes away. Not suggested.

The Security Center feature in Windows Vista will demonstrate that the overall security of the operating system has been reduced.

User Account Control: Switch to the Secure Desktop When Prompting for Elevation

When you try to perform any administrative task, including taking remote control of a PC, you are prompted for authorization. This security setting determines whether the elevation request will prompt for the interactive users desktop or the Secure Desktop.

You might be wondering what the difference is between prompting for the *Secure Desktop* versus the *Interactive Desktop*. The Secure Desktop only allows trusted SYSTEM processes to run on it, which means that an application must have already been approved by an Administrator to be installed and run with SYSTEM privilege. The Interactive Desktop allows USER processes to run (such high-level approval isn't required to install and run USER processes). The interesting part of all this is that it only requires USER-level privilege to spoof the user into believing they are seeing and/or clicking on something that really is being generated, legitimately, from Windows Vista. Therefore, by placing the elevation dialog on the Secure Desktop, only a highly privileged process can hope to run there, which means that the dialog the user is seeing and interacting with is a genuine dialog that Windows Vista has generated (not some bad guy hoping you'll press OK).

 The Secure Desktop protects against input and output spoofing when a user interacts with the UAC elevation dialog.

Enabled (default) All elevation requests by default will go to the Secure Desktop. The Secure Desktop is used here as an "anti-spoofing" technology, so it is recommended that you leave this on.

Disabled   All elevation requests will go to the user's Interactive Desktop. In some specific cases (e.g., an enterprise that leverages Remote Assistance and doesn't allow their Standard Users the ability to approve an elevation request), it may be alright to disable this policy.

Virtualize File and Registry Write Failures to Per-User Locations

Windows Vista and Windows Server 2008 have a new feature called File and Registry Virtualization. The idea is that for years programmers have been told "It's okay to dump your garbage anywhere in Windows." Now, in Windows Vista and Windows Server 2008, it's not. But what about those poor applications? They need to keep working, too. This feature will redirect potentially harmful file and Registry writes to "okay" locations.

The idea is that some applications might try to write to profile and Registry locations they really don't have access to, so a Windows Vista system will redirect (or, as Microsoft calls it, *virtualize*) these writes to writable places in the profile and Registry. So, if an application tries to write application data to `%ProgramFiles%`, `%Windir%`, `%Windir%\system32`, or `HKLM\Software\`, this virtualization feature kicks in and gently places the data into the kosher places in the file system and Registry.

NOTE   We discuss file and Registry virtualization in detail in Chapter 2 of the companion book, *Creating the Secure Managed Desktop*.

This will happen automatically when anyone is logged in as a Standard User.

An administrator may choose to disable this feature—if she's sure she's running all Windows Vista–compliant applications. But how would you really be sure?

Enabled (Default)   Facilitates the runtime redirection of application write failures to defined user locations for both the file system and Registry.

Disabled   Applications that write data to protected locations will simply fail as they did in previous versions of Windows.

TIP   While virtualization is fully configurable, it is not usually required to change the defaults. The default settings for virtualization handle most applications' behaviors correctly. For more information see `http://tinyurl.com/hqmh5`.

UAC Policy Setting Suggestions

There are 10 UAC settings, which we just explored. That means you've got a lot of power to control UAC. As we stated, you really don't want to just "turn it off." You want to tune it based on your situation.

Let's examine some cases, the default behavior, and some suggested remediations.

Case 1: Enterprise Desktop: Standard User (Who Gets Help Remotely When Needed)

This is the type of user who will never need to perform an elevated or privileged administrative task. This is the majority of users. If you need to help them, how will you? Likely, you'll simply use Remote Desktops and perform desktop management remotely.

Suggestion 1: Set "**UAC: Behavior of the elevation prompt for Standard Users**" to **Disabled** If the user should never perform an administrative task, then why present them with the opportunity? If you perform this simple change, they simply won't see the UAC prompts, and it will be denied. By performing this step, you're reducing the overall "attack surface."

Additionally, if users see the credential dialog, it can motivate them to call the help desk and beg, beg, beg for a valid Administrator account. You don't want to get caught in this trap. You can eliminate this type of support call.

Suggestion 2: Set "**UAC: Switch to the Secure Desktop when prompting for elevation**" to **Disabled** The Secure Desktop can be disabled if the logged-on Standard User never elevates. The technology is designed to protect elevations; if the logged-on user never elevates, the Secure Desktop protection is not needed.

Case 2: Enterprise Desktop: Standard User (Who Gets "Over the Shoulder Help" When Needed)

Some environments are such where the user puts in a request, and the administrator walks over to the desk and, while the user is logged in, helps adjust or install applications. This is sometimes called "Over the Shoulder" (OTS) assistance. This can be in places like doctor and lawyer offices and other smaller places that occasionally need tuning.

Main Suggestion: Set "**UAC: Behavior of the elevation prompt for Standard Users**" to "**Prompt for credentials**" In smaller organizations it may be preferable to leave this policy enabled to facilitate administrative help without requiring the administrator to perform a Fast User Switch and log on as himself.

Case 3: Enterprise Desktop: Protected Administrator

This is the case where you've been forced into giving Sally local administrative privileges on her own machine. You don't want to do it, but you have to for some reason. This can happen if Sally is already an administrator of her Windows XP machine before you upgrade it to Windows Vista.

In UAC parlance, Sally would be called a *Protected Administrator* because she is a user who is either directly or indirectly a member of the local administrators group of the client workstation.

Main Suggestion: All UAC policies at default Windows Vista UAC policy defaults are optimized for the Protected Administrator user account type. Simply upgrade Sally's XP Desktop to Windows Vista, and the default UAC policies will enforce that the applications that previously ran on XP with administrative privileges now run with the equivalent privilege of a Standard User.

So now, your email editor and web browser will no longer run with administrative privileges unnecessarily. Rejoice in attack surface reduction!

Case 4: Enterprise Desktop (Running Only Windows Vista "logo'd" Software)

I'm not holding my breath for this one in the near or mid term, because I know you're going to have lots of old and crusty software that isn't "Ready for Windows Vista."

Suggestions: Set **"UAC: Behavior of the elevation prompt for Standard Users to Automatically deny elevation requests"** to **Disabled.**

Set **"UAC: Switch to the secure desktop when prompting for elevation"** to **Disabled.**

Set **"Virtualize file and registry write failures to per-user locations"** to **Disabled.**

If you are running applications that are designed for the Standard User, you will not use nor require the virtualization feature. This feature was designed as legacy application compatibility mitigation but comes with a price.

Applications that leverage virtualization perform a "double read" when accessing data that could potentially be in a virtualized location.

So, if the application was installed to `%ProgramFiles%\ApplicationX\` and under that folder are `FileX` and `FileY`, if during runtime ApplicationX modifies and saves `FileY`, this forces `FileY` to be virtualized to `%userprofile%\..\..\VirtualStore\Program Files\ApplicationX\FileY`.

The next time ApplicationX tries to access `FileX`, it must first look in the user "VirtualStore" as `FileX` could have potentially been virtualized. If `FileX` is not found, it will then query the "real" `%ProgramFiles%\ApplicationX\FileX`.

That's going to be a performance hit. But with these settings, you would increase performance. Again, only a good idea if all the applications are Windows Vista-ized.

Case 5: Enterprise Desktop: Protected Administrator (All Applications Are Signed)

Again, this is a long-term goal for you to reach in your environment. The goal is that all applications are signed by the organization and only a restricted set of "Application signing certificates" are trusted by the client computer.

Main Suggestion: Set **"Only elevate executables that are signed and validated"** to **Enabled** This configuration will ensure that only those applications that either ship with Windows Vista or are explicitly signed and trusted by the organization will be allowed to run with administrative rights.

WARNING If you invoke an elevated `cmd.exe` "command host," you can then launch most applications from within the command host environment, thus bypassing this policy check.

Case 6: Power User–Style User Who Shares Computers with Standard Users

In this case, you would want the power user to be prompted when they do an administrative action. Give the right credentials, then, poof! They're in. But you also want to silently deny the regular user. Don't let them even see what they shouldn't play with.

Main Suggestion: Set "Behavior of the elevation prompt for administrators in Admin Approval Mode" to "Elevate without prompting" If the user wants to gain the benefits of the "Split Token" but never see a UAC elevation dialog, then this configuration is better than disabling UAC all together.

Remember that when UAC is disabled, all of its supporting technologies are also disabled. In almost all cases this is not desirable.

Case 7: Your Users Request Assistance with Windows Remote Assistance

In this case, you would want to ensure that users don't have to know a local administrator password to get help.

Main Suggestion: Utilize the default and ensure the Allow UIAccess applications to prompt for elevation without using the secure desktop is set This way, it's a clear path for them to ask for help and for you to provide help.

Configuring Windows Firewall with Group Policy

Windows XP/SP2 and onward all have a firewall that you can enable if you want to. Actually, Windows XP/SP2, Windows Vista, and Windows Server 2008 already have that firewall enabled.

But really, what's the point? The point of a firewall on your machine (whatever kind it is) is to allow certain kinds of traffic to pass through and certain kinds of traffic to be prevented. That's it. Nothing mysterious here about a firewall.

Windows XP/SP2, Windows Vista, and Windows Server 2008 turn on their respective firewall by default, filtering inbound communication. We saw this phenomenon in Chapter 2 when we tried to perform a "Group Policy Results" to our Windows XP or Windows Vista client system and got an RPC error (which is the same error we'd get if the machine were off). Note that Windows Server 2003/SP1's and Windows XP/SP2's firewalls are functionally equivalent. However, Windows Server 2003/SP1's firewall is not turned on by default when the system is running. (It is, however, turned on by default, initially, if you're performing an integrated [also known as *slipstreamed*] Windows Server 2003/SP1 installation, but that's another story.)

But Windows Vista's and Windows Server 2008's firewalls are on by default, and thankfully, those operating systems have a brand-spankin'-new firewall and a killer updated way via Group Policy to control it. This technology is dubbed WFAS: Windows Firewall with Advanced Security.

Let me declare right now that it's simply not possible for us to go into every single thing you can do with WFAS. That's (at least) a whole book in and of itself.

My goal is to acquaint you with the Windows XP, Windows Vista, and Windows Server 2008 versions of the firewall vis-à-vis Group Policy. That way, when you know the underlying geeky firewall technology, protocols, encryption, certificates, and so on, you'll be ready to implement it all because your Group Policy knowledge will be solid enough to allow you to do what you want.

The other big part is helping you understand precedence order. With a lot of things in Group Policy–land, understanding why a policy (Group Policy or IPsec policy or Connection Rule Policy, and so on) takes effect is paramount to being a master troubleshooter.

Again, the Windows Firewall is a big, big topic, and you should read everything you can here: www.microsoft.com/windowsfirewall.

Before you go headlong into manipulating and changing the default firewall settings for Windows XP or Windows Vista/Windows Server 2008, I recommend that you use caution. In other words, the firewall is, in fact, turned on by default in these operating systems for a reason.

It provides the most protection from the bad guys trying to infect and hack your Windows machines. And it makes sure you'll be mindful about opening up just the ports you want to use, even on a server, well, Windows Server 2008 server by default, anyway.

So, if you're going to start opening up ports on your machines (or kill the firewall altogether), please use these policy settings with caution.

Know what you're changing and why you're changing it.

Again, the defaults are there for a reason!!!

Everything Old Is New Again: The Windows XP vs. WFAS Firewall Controls

Before we get too far down the pike here, do let me describe one potential pitfall about what's happened here in Windows Vista. That is, because Windows XP (and Windows Server 2003 for that matter) already had a firewall (with one set of Group Policy controls), and now Windows Vista and Windows Server 2008 have an updated firewall (with an updated set of Group Policy controls), it can sometimes be a little confusing just what you're controlling and where you're supposed to go in the Group Policy Management Editor in order to control it.

Now there are two sets of firewall settings:

- The "older" Windows XP firewall settings (where both Windows XP and Windows Vista machines can embrace most of these settings)

- The "newer" WFAS settings for Windows Vista and Windows Server 2008 (which Windows XP may not know how to handle)

Indeed, in Chapter 2, we used the policy named **Windows Firewall: Allow inbound remote administrative exception** when we wanted to allow the required ports on both Windows XP and Windows Vista to open up so we could perform a Group Policy Results analysis.

Yep, that one worked! But, I haven't tested all the Windows XP policy settings against a Windows Vista or Windows Server 2008 firewall. And, indeed, there's a more specific, targeted way to achieve the same goals with the WFAS firewall, which is found on Windows Vista and Windows Server 2008.

So, my humble suggestion, before you start creating lots and lots of GPOs with Windows Firewall policies in them, is to name them as such based on which operating system they're supposed to target. Then, you have a very clearly named GPO that you can link to proper places in your hierarchy.

Therefore, I suggest you keep your GPOs separate. Have GPOs that affect only the Windows XP firewall, GPOs that affect only the Windows Vista firewall, and maybe others that affect only the Windows Server 2008 firewall. In this example, you can see two GPOs linked to two OUs. We have "Sales Windows XP Firewall Policy" and "Sales Windows Vista Firewall Policy," and they're only affecting the specific type of computers inside the OUs. I think, in the long run, this is the cleanest and least-confusing path.

This might not always be possible, but it is by far the cleanest implementation

The other way to specify which GPOs affect which machines is via WMI filtering (explored in detail in Chapter 5). With WMI filters you can "target" a machine based on various characteristics. Once you've read that chapter and are comfortable, then come back here when ready. Here are the WMI queries you'll need to target a specific GPO to a specific machine type.

For Vista

```
Select * from Win32_OperatingSystem Where BuildNumber=6000
```

For Windows XP

```
Select * from Win32_OperatingSystem Where BuildNumber =2600
```

For Windows Server 2008 and Windows Vista/SP1 (expected)

These two operating systems are both set to build number 6001. You can use the same query to address both Windows Server 2008 and Windows Vista/SP1 machines as:

```
Select * from Win32_OperatingSystem Where BuildNumber = 6001
```

Manipulating the Windows XP and Windows Server 2003 Firewall

Most of the discussions in this particular section will revolve around trying to manipulate the Windows XP firewall (or Windows Server 2003 firewall, if you've enabled it).

Again, as stated, most of the techniques we'll perform here should work just fine if the target machine is a Windows Vista or Windows Server 2008 machine with its new WFAS. But I haven't specifically tested each of these settings against Windows XP or Windows Server 2008. We'll explore the ins and outs of manipulating those operating systems' WFAS in the next section.

Domain vs. Standard Profiles for Windows XP and Windows Server 2003

If you dive down into the new firewall policy settings, contained within Computer Configuration ➤ Policies ➤ Administrative Templates ➤ Network ➤ Network Connections ➤ Windows Firewall, you'll notice two branches: Domain Profile and Standard Profile. You can see this in Figure 9.8.

FIGURE 9.8   The Domain Profile is used when the machine can make contact to a Domain Controller. The Standard Profile is used when the machine is in a hotel room or at Starbucks, etc.

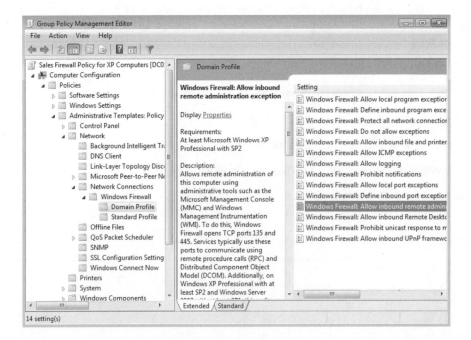

Inside each branch, you'll see a gaggle of settings that are exactly the same. So, what gives?

When policy settings within the Domain Profile are enabled, they affect the firewall when they make contact with the Domain Controller. This is usually when a computer is at the central office and a normal logon occurs.

 In Windows XP the computer didn't actually need to authenticate to a Domain Controller for Domain Profile policy settings to kick in. In Windows Vista, authentication to a Domain Controller is required.

When policy settings within the "Standard Profile" are enabled, they affect the firewall when Windows *cannot* authenticate to a Domain Controller. This might happen when the user is in a hotel room, an Internet cafe, or other areas with public connectivity.

You might set up your Domain Profile settings to have additional port exceptions to be used by the central office administrative team for scanning and remote administration. And, you can leverage your "Standard Profile" settings to ensure that the firewall is at its maximum enforcement. In short, you get to choose how strong the firewall will act in each of these circumstances.

Microsoft has a great little article on how the computer fundamentally determines if it should use the Domain Profile or the Standard Profile. Check it out here: `http://tinyurl .com/cao73`.

Again, these settings here are meant for the Windows XP/SP2 firewall, but they should also work if a Windows Vista firewall gets these settings from a downloaded Group Policy. However, I haven't personally tested each and every one. Here are some tips if you choose to affect Windows Vista machines with Windows XP/SP2 settings:

- Standard Profile settings apply to both the private and public profiles for Windows Vista.

- If you configure the Windows Vista–specific firewall policy, then the Standard Profile settings will stop applying. The assumption is that if the computer is getting a new policy, you must have started using the new policy model.

- There's a known bug in the "allow local port" and "allow local program" settings when applied to Windows Vista. It might not always work when it should. It should be fixed in Windows Vista/SP1.

Killing the Firewall for Windows XP and Windows Server 2003

There might be times when you just want to outright kill the Windows XP or Windows Vista firewall. Additionally, you can prevent an inadvertent mishap should someone try to enable it on Windows Server 2003/SP1!

In Chapter 2, I explained how to kill Windows XP's firewall (which has the same process for Windows Server 2003's firewall, though it isn't even on by default) or Windows Vista's firewall. Again, though, the recommended course for manipulating Windows Vista's firewall will be discussed later, even though this technique will, in fact, work.

To kill the XP/SP2 or Windows Vista firewall, drill down to Administrative Templates ➢ Network ➢ Network Connections ➢ Windows Firewall ➢ Domain Profile and select **Windows Firewall: Protect All Network Connections**. But here's the thing. You don't choose to *Enable* this policy. No, no. You *Disable* it. Yes, you read that right—you Disable it. Read the Explain text help inside the policy for more information on specific usage examples.

Before you do this though, remember that it's a better idea to leave it on and just filter based on the traffic you know you want. Only kill the firewall as a last resort.

Opening Specific Ports, Managing Exceptions, and More for Windows XP and Windows Server 2003

Microsoft did a lot of the hard work for me. That is, they've put together a stellar document about how to fully manage all aspects of your Windows XP/SP2 (and Windows Server 2003/SP1) firewall with Group Policy. By using the techniques Microsoft provides, you'll be able to have very granular control over how the firewall is used in your company (and when users are away from your company).

You can learn how to open specific ports, make specific program exceptions, turn on logging, and more.

For more information about deploying Windows Firewall, see "Deploying Windows Firewall Settings for Microsoft Windows XP with Service Pack 2" on the Microsoft Download Center website at `http://tinyurl.com/a8bfc`. An additionally excellent article can be found here: `www.microsoft.com/technet/community/columns/cableguy/cg0106.mspx` (shortened to `http://tinyurl.com/ujg25`).

Windows Firewall with Advanced Security (for Windows Vista and Windows Server 2008)—WFAS

In this section we'll take a bite-sized tour of what we can do with the updated Windows Firewall with Advanced Security. This new item runs on both Windows Vista and Windows Server 2008—we'll call it WFAS for short.

WFAS's two "prime directives" in life are to

- Block all incoming traffic (unless it is requested or it matches a configured rule)

- Allow all outgoing traffic (unless it matches a configured rule to prevent it)

As you go along in these examples, you'll see UI references to "Location" type, which can be "Domain Location," "Public Location," and "Private Location." To help you understand Network Location Types, read this article: `www.microsoft.com/technet/community/columns/cableguy/cg0906.mspx` (`http://tinyurl.com/ykmp9r`). Because the Windows Vista and Windows Server 2008 machines we'll be manipulating are joined to the domain, they will be considered a part of the "Domain Location" where we can control the WFAS via Group Policy.

Additionally, the IP security (IPsec) function (discussed in more detail next) is also part of WFAS (where it was a separate node of the UI in the Group Policy Management Editor for pre-Vista management stations). We'll see how this all fits together as we work through this section.

Holy Cow! Three Ways to Set WFAS Settings!

There are actually three different *stores* for Windows Firewall for Advanced Security policies and four different ways to make that happen:

- The Active Directory–based Group Policy you know and love

- Local Group Policy accessible via gpedit.msc

- By running WF.MSC, which opens a GUI to the "local WSAF store"

Here's where it gets confusing, so stay with me here: the store hosting rules from WF.MSC and from Local Group Policy are in fact *separate*.

If you crack open WF.MSC, you'll see that there are a number of default rules in WF.MSC (as seen here).

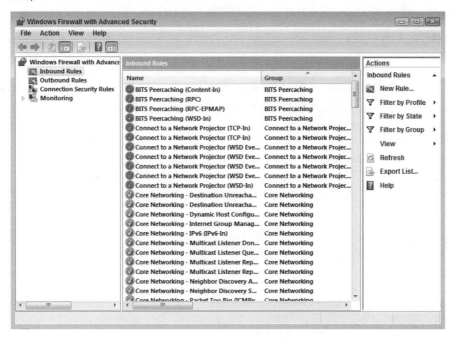

But open the Local Group Policy Editor, and you won't see those rules at all!

You can also see this behavior via the command line. The command is Netsh (then press Enter) advfirewall (then press Enter). Once inside, you can poke around. This is the command-line interface for all the goodies you're looking at in the Group Policy Editor.

> By default you're poking around the "local Windows Firewall store" (the same thing you'd see when you use WF.MSC), but you can use the `set store` command to change focus to, say, the local GPO or even an Active Directory–based GPO. The idea is that once you've "set store" to another place, say a particular GPO, you can do everything via the command line you could do via the GUI.
>
> Nice touch!

Getting Started with WFAS "Properties"

The first place you might want to check out on your WFAS journey is the "Properties" of the WFAS node. Now, I say "Properties" with quotes because there isn't a precise name for them. But, I'll call them "WFAS Properties" for our purposes. You find them by right-clicking over the "Windows Firewall with Advanced Security" node (with the little brick and the world icon) and selecting Properties, as seen in Figure 9.9.

FIGURE 9.9   The Windows Firewall with Advanced Security has "Group Policy–like" properties inside.

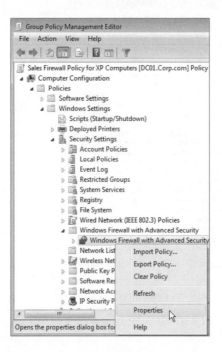

Once there, you'll have lots of settings to play with. These settings specify certain behavior types based on how the machine is connected and some IPsec settings. You can see this in Figure 9.10. However, the trick about *all* of the WFAS Properties settings is that they act exactly like regular Administrative Templates policies. So, recall how in all Administrative Templates policy settings there is an "Enabled," "Not Configured," and "Disabled" ability? Well, all the settings contained here work exactly the same way across multiple GPOs if configured. You can see an example of a subproperties page in Figure 9.10 where it demonstrates "Yes," "No," and "Not Configured." Each setting also displays the default setting if you do nothing (which is a nice touch).

FIGURE 9.10   Imagine that all the settings in the WFAS Properties are just like Administrative Templates settings in other areas of Group Policy.

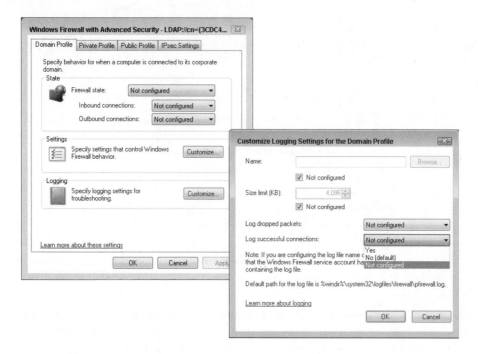

Again, the point is that all the settings contained at this level are just like normal, everyday, garden variety Group Policy. If stored at the Local or domain-based levels, the regular Group Policy precedence rules will apply.

What we'll learn about *next* is a little different, because, while it uses the Group Policy interface, it's not exactly got the same "Group Policy rule precedence" that you've come to know and love with the kinds of settings in here. Stay tuned—I'll try to explain it as we learn more and more, and then wrap up our discussion about WFAS with an overall cheat sheet to help you get which rules come from where and what will win.

Creating New Inbound and Outbound Rules with the WFAS

WFAS is updated to support a neat-o keen new UI as well as some amazing under-the-hood features. Again, we simply don't have room to go over everything, so we'll have to make due with a brief tour. One important point to note is that WFAS has both inbound and outbound rules (where Windows XP's firewall had only inbound rules). You can see where to create rules in Figure 9.11 and simply right-click over the rule type to create a New Rule.

FIGURE 9.11 Once you locate the Inbound and Outbound Rules nodes, you can right-click to select New Rule.

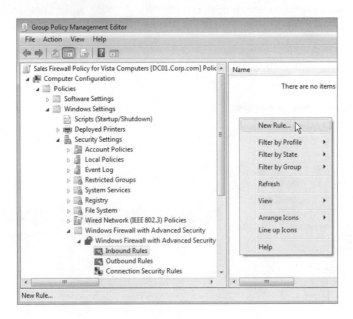

Inbound Rules The goal of inbound rules is to prevent the bad stuff from reaching your machine and allow only traffic you request to reach you. This is the kind of thing most firewalls are used for.

Outbound Rules At first blush, outbound rules seem counterintuitive. Why would you ever want to restrict outbound communication, right? Well, you might want to lock down a workstation from opening connections outbound to particular services. For example, you might have a specialty workstation that is only supposed to be used as a web-browser machine. Well, you can then lock out all outbound remote ports except port 80 (HTTP) and 443 (SSL/HTTPS). This would potentially allow you to squelch a virus or malware program that was trying to "phone home" or otherwise be a baddie. (Note that this works only if you lock out remote ports. If you locked out the local ports, this trick won't work.)

Connection Security Rules These rules dictate if this machine is going to be able to talk to other machines at all. You can create all kinds of rules here, including only being able to talk with machines that are on the same domain, or just enable specific machine-to-machine contact. This is the new way to perform IPsec rules, though there's little mention of the word *IPsec*, actually. Additionally, there are settings here that work in conjunction with an advanced feature (which we cannot cover here) called Network Access Protection (or NAP). The idea is that if your machine doesn't meet certain criteria, then it shouldn't be allowed to talk with its other brothers and sisters. This is configured via the NAP MMC snap-in. Learn more about NAP at www.microsoft.com/nap and in Chapter 9, which is wholly dedicated to NAP, of the companion book, *Creating the Secure Managed Desktop*.

Inbound and Outbound Rule Types

Once you've elected to create a rule, there are four rule types to choose from, as seen in Figure 9.12.

Program   You can actually dictate which programs (specified by path and executable name) you want to allow traffic to flow between. You need to also specify an action (Allow, Block, or "Allow the connection if it is secure"). Note that the "Allow the connection if it is secure" setting requires a valid connection security configuration as well as IPsec rules deployed to handle the IPsec portion of the enforcement.

Port   This is a specific rule based upon TCP or UDP ports. You must also specify which ports (separated by commas). Specific ranges, say, 80–100, won't work unless individually listed with commas separating them.

Predefined   This will likely be where most people spend their time. This is a collection of "well-known" services and which ports to open up if you want traffic to flow.

Custom   This is the kitchen sink. If you want to go whole hog and tweak until you're blue in the face, this is the place for you. If you couldn't configure the settings using one of the other three ways, this is where you do it.

If you want to try this out for a WFAS machine, select Predefined, then use the pull-down to see the various Predefined options, as seen in Figure 9.13. If we want to parallel the example in Chapter 2 (which Allowed Remote Inbound Administration Exception), we could simply select "Remote Administration," as seen in Figure 9.13.

By clicking Next in the wizard, you'll zip past all the predefined rules, saving you oodles of time. Once the wizard is complete, you'll see the new inbound rule and its name, as seen in Figure 9.14. To see what that rule is really doing, just check out the Properties for each line item.

Connection Security Rules

In the previous example we leveraged an inbound rule to open up WFAS to allow a remote administration exception. And the procedure would be pretty similar if we wanted an outbound rule as well.

However, Connection Security rules are different. Connection Security rules define how and when computers authenticate using IPsec or Authenticated IP. Connection Security rules are used in establishing server and domain isolation, as well as in enforcing NAP policy.

These allow for you to specify which other computers you can talk with. Again, the idea here is to prevent your target machines from talking with the bad guys.

You can see the list of available Connection Security rule types in Figure 9.15.

FIGURE 9.12 After creating an inbound or outbound rule, you must select the type. Most often, you'll select Predefined.

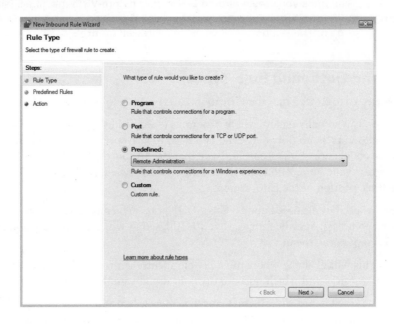

FIGURE 9.13 Use the Predefined rules to allow the kinds of "well-known" traffic your people might need.

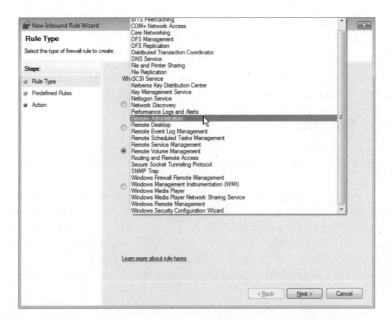

FIGURE 9.14   When the rule is complete, you'll see the results in the right pane.

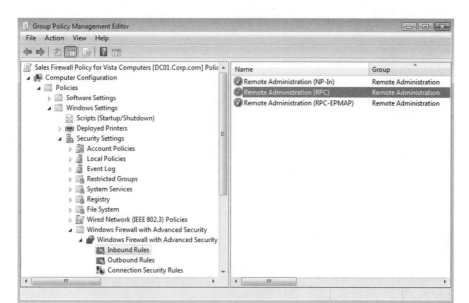

 More info on Authenticated IP at http://tinyurl.com/yelj7a. More information on rule types at http://tinyurl.com/yx4rkk.

Rule Precedence

What if you have multiple WFAS rules applying? Which WFAS rule is going win to restrict
the traffic?

Additionally, what if you have multiple GPOs that affect this target machine with multiple
rules? Turns out, it doesn't matter. All rules are simply "additive" amongst all GPOs—for the
type of rule it is.

So, all inbound rules are all added up. All outbound rules are all added up, and so on. What
you might care about is what if there's a conflict between, say, an inbound rule and an outbound rule. Which will win there?

Again, the list of WFAS rules is merged from all sources and then processed in the order
shown below from top to bottom. This rule process ordering is always enforced, regardless of
the source of the rules:

Windows Service Hardening   This rule restricts services from establishing connections.
These are generally automatically configured out of the box so that Windows Services can
only communicate in specific ways (that is, restricting allowable traffic through a specific
port). However, until you create a firewall rule, traffic is not allowed.

FIGURE 9.15 There is lots of flexibility in WFAS Security Rules.

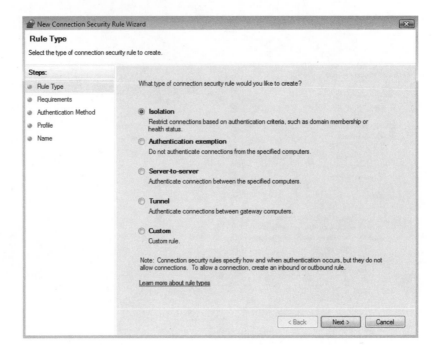

Connection Security rules This type of rule defines how and when computers authenticate using IPsec. Connection Security rules are used in establishing Server and Domain Isolation, as well as in enforcing NAP policy.

Authenticated bypass rules This type of rule allows the connection of particular computers if the traffic is protected with IPsec, regardless of other inbound rules in place. Specified computers are allowed to bypass inbound rules that block traffic. For example, you could allow remote firewall administration from only *certain* computers by creating an "Authenticated bypass" rule for those computers. Or, you could enable support for Remote Assistance by the help desk *only* from the help desk computers.

Block rules This type of rule explicitly blocks a particular type of incoming or outgoing traffic.

Allow rules This type of rule explicitly allows a particular type of incoming or outgoing traffic.

IPsec (Now within Windows Firewall with Advanced Security)

The Internet Protocol security function, or IPsec for short, has a big job: secure the exchange of packets on your TCP/IP network. Its primary mission is host-to-host authentication. However, you can additionally choose to encrypt the traffic via Tunneling or Network Encryption so others can't "spy" on the data flying by.

Maybe you have one super-important Human Resources server. And you want to ensure that no one except the Human Resources people can talk with that server. That's IPsec's job: ensuring that only the right people on the right computers can talk with the other computers you specify.

> IPsec is based on IKE. The RFCs on IKE only support the concept of "*computer authentication*. Microsoft, however, has gone the extra mile and introduced an extension to IKE called Authenticated IP (AuthIP). This new ability introduces the ability to support *user* authentication *as well as* computer authentication. Additionally, the administrator can choose to use *both* user and computer authentication if desired.

IPsec General Resources

IPsec is a big, big topic, and not one we can cover in enormous detail here. However, my job for this section is to get you up to speed on the WFAS implementation of IPsec and explain how "legacy" IPsec interacts with the "new" IPsec. So, if you're not familiar with IPsec and want to follow along, you'll have to spend some quality time at the following websites:

- www.microsoft.com/ipsec (http://tinyurl.com/c7vuf)
- www.microsoft.com/sdisolation
- A great document from Microsoft entitled "Introduction to Windows Firewall with Advanced Security" found at http://tinyurl.com/yx4rkk
- www.microsoft.com/technet/itsolutions/network/evaluate/new_network .mspx (http://tinyurl.com/ydzhad)
- www.microsoft.com/windowsserver2003/techinfo/overview/netcomm.mspx (http://tinyurl.com/4x5y)

I also recommend this excellent webcast from TechEd 2006 by Microsoft's Steve Riley that covers both the firewall and IPsec improvements: http://tinyurl.com/yl4bw3.

Server and Domain Isolation with IPsec

IPsec, at its core, restricts who is talking to whom. Okay, great. So, armed with that knowledge, you can take it to the next level and make sure that machines you know nothing about can't talk to machines you do.

For instance, imagine a consultant comes into your business with a laptop and plugs in. Chances are, with enough poking around, he could figure out your IP address scheme. Now he's able to ping servers and see what's going on over there on machines without a firewall. And, what if he brought a virus in with him from the cold, dark, outside world? Oops, you've got a problem.

To combat this, let's assume instead you want to create "rings of protection" amongst machines you trust and machines you really really trust. That's the idea of Server and Domain Isolation with IPsec. You can see the general idea here in this graphic.

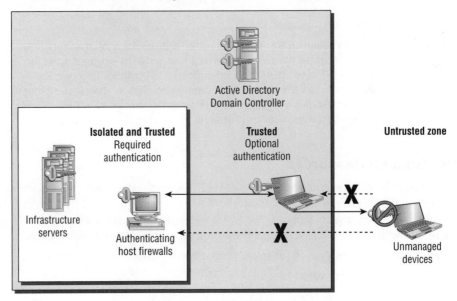

What sounds like a swell idea (and it is) can be a b-i-g project. Indeed, to protect your Windows XP, Windows 2000, and Windows Server 2003 machines from outside invaders (so they'll talk only with other machines you trust) takes about 300 pages of reading and implementing. You can find the big guide for this here:

www.microsoft.com/technet/security/guidance/architectureanddesign/ipsec/default.mspx
(http://tinyurl.com/yywxas)

However, you can find a more general "clearinghouse" of Server and Domain Isolation goodies at Microsoft's website here: www.microsoft.com/sdisolation (http://tinyurl.com/zc74p).

Again, it's something like 300 pages to do this for pre-Vista.

But if you check out http://support.microsoft.com/default.aspx/kb/914841, you'll find information on the Simple Policy Update that actually adds more Windows Server 2003 and Windows XP IPsec support—specifically to reduce the amount of IPsec filters you need to pull this off.

In Windows Vista and Windows Server 2008 it's simpler. There's a great new Microsoft document called "Step-by-Step Guide to Deploying Policies for Windows Firewall with Advanced Security," which is found at http://tinyurl.com/2rmd7u and covers this specific topic in depth.

Getting Started with IPsec with WFAS

Here's where it starts to get a little confusing. That's because there are two types of IPsec rules. I don't know if they have "proper" names, so we'll just call them "older" and "newer" rule types.

Older rule types are found in the node Computer Configuration ➤ Policies ➤ Windows Settings ➤ Security Settings ➤ **IP Security Policies on Active Directory**.

Newer rule types are found inside the new WFAS. Specifically, again, it's Computer Configuration ➤ Policies ➤ Windows Settings ➤ Security Settings ➤ **Windows Firewall with Advanced Security**. You can see both nodes highlighted in Figure 9.16.

To configure "old" IPsec policies, you right-click **IP Security Policies on Active Directory** and select "Create IP Security Policy."

To configure "new" IPsec policies, you right-click **Connection Security rules** and just get started with "New Rule." If IPsec is required it will just automatically be part of that rule.

Note that advanced IPsec configurations may require some additional "global" settings. To do this, right-click **Windows Firewall with Advanced Security** and select Properties, then click the IPsec Settings tab as seen in Figure 9.16. Then, when you click the Customize button in the IPsec Settings tab, you'll have the range of additional IPsec options to play with, as seen in Figure 9.17.

WARNING Note that the "old" IPsec policies' "Default Response Rule" is not valid for Windows Vista or Windows Server 2008 machines. It will warn you of this if you try to create an IPsec policy using a Windows Vista or Windows Server 2008 management station. In short, don't mix old and new policies on the same computer.

FIGURE 9.16 You can see both the "old" and "new" places to configure IPsec policies.

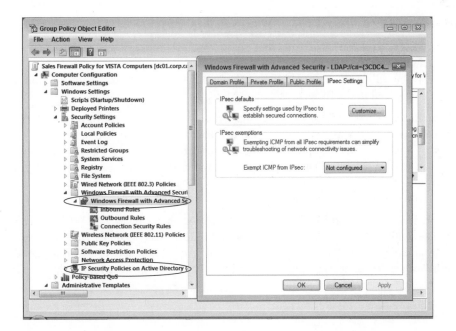

FIGURE 9.17 Some "base" IPsec settings for a GPO can be found in the "Windows Firewall with Advanced Security" properties.

Understanding How WFAS IPsec Rules Work

There are now two types of IPsec rules that can be applied to a machine with WFAS (Windows Vista and Windows Server 2008).

Again, we're calling these the old IPsec rules and the new IPsec rules here. The old IPsec rules are configured in the IP Security Policy Management MMC snap-in.

Old IPsec Rules These are IKE rules that support only machine-based Kerberos, x.509 certificates, and preshared key authentication. Old IKE-based rules are applied in the same way to Windows Vista as they were in pre–Windows Vista operating systems. That is, while multiple policies can be applied to a given machine, the last writer wins and there is no merging of IKE policy settings. So, if you had a policy set at the domain level and another set at the OU level, the OU level would win because there is no merging of any old IPsec rules.

New IPsec Rules Again, the new IPsec rules are created on machines with WFAS and applied to machines with WFAS (for Windows Vista and Windows Server 2008). These rules are supported by an extension to IKE called Authenticated IP (AuthIP). As stated, a seriously good read on AuthIP can be found here: http://tinyurl.com/yelj7a. Here are some helpful tidbits as you explore the new WFAS IPsec. These (really geeky) tidbits are coming (nearly verbatim) from the IPsec team at Microsoft, so, thank them (not me) if you get a nice tip here.

- You can now leverage Interactive user, Kerberos/NTLMv2 credentials, User x.509 certificates, Machine X.509 certificates, NAP Health Certificates, and Anonymous Authentication (optional Authentication) for authenticating an IPsec connection.

- When configuring GPOs for connection security and firewall policies, you could disable the use of local firewall and Connection Security rules. That way, only the Group Policy linked to the site, domain, or OU GPOs could control the Windows Firewall behaviors. You can see where to do this in Figure 9.18 a bit later.

- Like other firewall and Group Policy rules, connection security rules are merged from all applicable GPOs (and processed according to the Rule Precedence list previously discussed).

- Connection Security policies can be configured to create "old" (compatible) policies as well as Windows Vista and Windows Server 2008 systems (see the sidebar entitled "Super-Geeky Note from the Microsoft IPsec Team #1: What's Going on Under the Hood").

- Only AuthIP policy is created for Windows Vista to Windows Vista (or Windows Vista to Windows Server 2008) because IKE doesn't support User Authentication. Again see the sidebar entitled "Super-Geeky Note from the Microsoft IPsec Team #1: What's Going on Under the Hood."

- As noted earlier, Connection Security rules are merged from all applicable GPOs. However, there is a related group of settings for IPsec/Authenticated IP that manage the default IPsec behaviors that are not additive. The settings include the global authentication sets, Quick Mode and Key Exchange settings, and ICMP exemptions.

- On a WFAS client, Connection Security and IPsec rules can come from multiple GPOs. That is, all Connection Security rules on the client that make use of default auth/crypto sets will use the sets from the highest precedence GPO. If you need more flexibility, you have the three options: For authentication sets, configure the authentication through the Connection Security rule instead of using the default authentication. For Quick Mode crypto, use the command line `netsh advfirewall` to configure Quick Mode crypto settings on a per–Connection Security rule basis as needed. For Main Mode, only one set is supported per policy. In the case where multiple Main Mode crypto sets are received, the one from the highest precedence GPO will be applied to all Connection Security rules in the policy. There is unfortunately no way to customize the rules to use different Main Mode crypto sets.

Honestly, these tips are more for the IPsec "superstars" out there than us normal people (me included), so don't panic if it's not 100 percent evident or relevant to your situation.

How Windows Firewall Rules Are Ultimately Calculated

Hopefully by now you understand that there are two categories of "things" that can be set by WFAS policy: properties and rules.

Super-Geeky Note from the Microsoft IPsec Team #1: What's Going on Under the Hood

With WFAS, an admin can create IKE-based IPsec policies through the IP Security Policy Management snap-in. An admin can also create Connection Security rules that will be compatible with down-level IKE-based policies.

So, when the policy is created, here's what's happening under the hood:

- If no WFAS-specific features are required, the policy will be created with both a set of AuthIP (Vista and Windows Server 2008) rules and a set of IKE rules for when the Vista/2008 system needs to connect to IKE-based 2000, XP, and 2003 systems.

- If there are WFAS-specific features (like requiring the use of a second User Authentication), then the system will *not* create pre–Windows Vista IKE rules.

What? Why not?

Simple: Since IKE on XP can't do User Authentication, there's no need to create extra policies where only Windows Vista and Windows Server 2008–specific features are used.

See! Told you this was geeky!

Super-Geeky Note from the Microsoft IPsec Team #2: Get the Right Certs to Do the Right Job

There is a particular nuance with regard to certificates that you'll need to know about before you go headlong into using IPsec and AuthIP. Again, the IPsec/AuthIP policies that are created by WFAS will use AuthIP by preference.

- If both machines are Vista or Windows Server 2008, then they'll use AuthIP to negotiate and authenticate.

- If one of the two talking machines is pre–Windows Vista, then the system will use IKE-based functionality.

- AuthIP uses SSL certs with client and/or server authentication settings configured.

- SSL certs can be client authentication or client and server authentication certs. And, either should work.

What this means is that if you are constructing policies to use certificate authentication for Vista or Windows Server 2008, you'll need certificates that will work with AuthIP. That means the certificates you deploy to the clients need to be SSL certs with client and/or server authentication (depending on if you want one-way or mutual authentication).

It should be noted that these certs differ from the standard digital certs used in Win XP/2003.

Precedence Order for Properties

Properties are found in three ways:

- Running WF.MSC and right-clicking over the Windows Firewall with Advanced Security node (topmost node) and selecting Properties. This is the "local WFAS" store.

- Editing the local GPO of the machine and right-clicking over the Windows Firewall Advanced Security node and selecting Properties.

- Creating a new Active Directory–based GPO, then right-clicking over the Windows Firewall Advanced Security node and selecting Properties.

Again, these properties all act like regular Group Policy Administrative Template settings.

Now, the one thing I waited to explain until now is this: You can "block" the local WFAS store from being added to the calculations. To do this, in any GPO that has Windows Firewall settings that apply to the computer, right-click the Windows Firewall Advanced Security node, and select Properties. Then, in, say, Domain Profile (or the other profiles), click Customize. Locate the Rule Merging section and select No, as seen in Figure 9.18.

This will only block a rule merge. Or, additionally, you could choose No in the "Apply local connection security rules" to block those.

However, it should be noted that you could prevent a local admin from being able to control a property just by setting it in the GPO.

Again, the default is "Yes" that local WFAS store settings (and rules) would apply. Change this only if you do not want local rules to apply. However, do note that WFAS has a zillion built-in firewall rules. And, if you set this to "No," then all those rules suddenly—poof!—turn off. And WFAS's default action would be to block all incoming traffic. And, to change this you would need to set specific rules (I suggest "Predefined rules") to allow which inbound traffic you would allow through.

 You could export the local WFAS store first, and then import it into a domain-based one if you so choose.

Precedence Order for Rules

We've already discussed rule precedence (see the section "Rule Precedence" earlier). Even though the specific "what rule will win" aspect is pretty complicated, the overall Group Policy "rules" are pretty simple.

FIGURE 9.18 You can block the application of the local WFAS firewall rules or local connection security rules by setting it in any Group Policy linked to the computer.

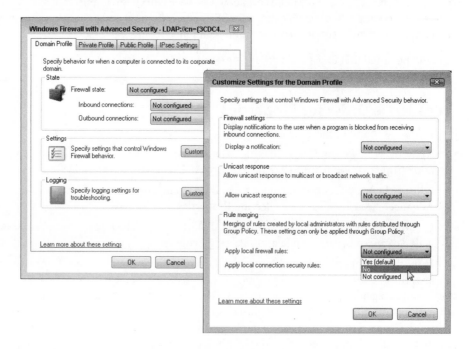

Basically, all Group Policy Objects that contain any WFAS rules are simply added up. There isn't even really a concept of a "conflict" with WFAS rules, because the rules are just "separated" into buckets:

- So, all the inbound rules are added up from the local store, then all GPOs.

- Then, all the outbound rules are added up from the local store, then all GPOs.

- And all the Connection Security rules are added up from the local store, then all GPOs.

- If there's a Deny/Block policy for *any* rule, that's always going to win for that rule type.

You can, if you want, disable the local WFAS store and ignore those rules. That way, you just guarantee that Group Policy is doing all the dirty work to configure everything. In my opinion, this seems like a good way to go, so you don't have to remember if there even is a local WFAS store.

Again, you can see how to kill the WFAS local store's rule application in Figure 9.18.

One final parting WFAS tip. If you check out the local WFAS editor by clicking Start and then typing **WF.MSC** in the Start Search dialog, you'll also have the ability to see the WFAS "monitor," which can be useful for troubleshooting.

Final Thoughts

Windows Vista brings a lot more new security goodies to the table. But it's Group Policy that's the delivery vehicle.

Let's review some fine points before we say *au revoir* to Group Policy and security (for now, anyway):

- Windows XP has a wireless policy you can use right away. However, to use Windows Vista's wireless and wired policy, you need to upgrade the schema.

- Internet Explorer 7 has a lot of goodies to play with. And, they fixed my (least) favorite aspect of Internet Explorer. That is, when you clear out the proxy server setting, Internet Explorer 7 will recognize this and accommodate. Nice.

- User Account Control is a good thing. Don't turn it off entirely. However, use the information here to tweak it based on your situation so both you and your users can live with it.

- Windows XP and Windows Server 2003 have a built-in firewall. So does Windows Vista and Windows Server 2008. But the integration of both the firewall rules and IPsec together make a powerful combination and a real winner when it comes to setting up your networking rules.

See you in the next chapter, where we talk about the greatest thing to hit Group Policy since Group Policy was born. In the companion book, we dedicate a lot of time to additionally increasing your security posture with Group Policy as your main weapon of choice. Topics in the companion book include:

- Scanning and patching your systems with WSUS 3.0 and MBSA (Chapter 8)

- Ensuring that only healthy systems can join your network with Network Access Protection (NAP) and Group Policy (Chapter 9)

- Restricting hardware (like iPods and USB keys) from your network (Chapter 10)

- Total Lockdown of your machines (you know you want it!) in Chapter 11

Learn more about the companion book at www.GPanswers.com/book.

10

Group Policy Preference Extensions

Group Policy, when it was originally born with Windows 2000, was a really big deal. It came with a lot of exciting new features to tinker with. To me, that was the birth of Group Policy, or "Group Policy 1.0."

The next revolution was when the GPMC was added to the power of Group Policy, making the ease of deployment and use of Group Policy skyrocket. To me that was "Group Policy 1.5."

This chapter welcomes what I like to think of as "Group Policy 2.0."

And it's built into Windows Server 2008 and available for Windows Vista, Windows XP, and Windows Server 2003 (but sadly, not Windows 2000). The new tool is called Group Policy Preference Extensions, and it was born from Microsoft's recent acquisition of DesktopStandard Corporation (formerly AutoProf).

Recall that an extension is a way to "do more stuff" with Group Policy. Windows XP does more stuff than Windows 2000, and Windows Vista does more stuff than Windows XP because of Client Side Extensions, which you learned about in Chapter 4. If you'll remember, they're just DLLs that process the directives contained in GPOs.

The Group Policy Preference Extensions are simply that: DLLs; really, one DLL that does a *lot* of stuff. Because Group Policy Preference Extensions is kind of long to say, I'll abbreviate the Group Policy Preference Extensions (the concept) as *GPPEs*, and a specific Group Policy Preference Extension as *a GPPE* or, just *an extension*—for instance, *the Registry preference extension* or *the Registry extension*.

The first question you may have is, "What is all the awesome new power I'm gonna get?" Hang tight. That will be the first thing I show you.

But then the next question you may have is, "Why the heck are they called *preferences* if they hook into Group Policy?" And, yes, I'll explain that in detail, too, I promise, but in short, they act like, well, preferences. That is, they don't "clean up" after themselves, like normal Group Policy settings do, and they don't "lock out" or restrict the user interface (under most circumstances). So, in short, they're not policies—they're preferences.

Again, we're going to go into these details coming up, but it's going to take a lot of pages to actually answer both of these questions thoroughly. So I'll ask you to please hold your horses before running out and trying all these new superpowers. You'll really, really be glad you waited and read this whole chapter to truly understand the powers you have rather than doing something you really wish you didn't do.

Microsoft calls the Group Policy Preference Extensions the *Group Policy preferences* or *GPPrefs,* which I think is a confusing term. That's because Group Policy has *always* been able to deliver preferences (heck, just see Chapter 7 for how to deliver preferences using ADM or ADMX files). So, with that in mind, I'll call them *Group Policy Preference Extensions*, or *GPPEs* for short, so you'll know specifically what I'm talking about and there won't be any ambiguity.

The technology is powerful and awesome; it extends Group Policy's reach and capabilities an astronomical amount. However, it must be fully understood and used with caution to get the most out of it, and so you don't shoot yourself in the foot as you're using it.

That's what this chapter is all about: the nuts, bolts, general use, and troubleshooting of the Group Policy Preference Extensions. We won't be going over each and every new setting. That could be a whole book in and of itself. However, I will have more information about GPPEs in Chapter 9 of the companion book, *Creating the Secure Managed Desktop*, with some interesting examples of how to use them.

In this book, you'll learn the nuts and bolts (and see some working examples). In the companion book's Chapter 9, you'll learn how to utilize the GPPE technology to produce a sexier, er, I mean more managed desktop.

G'bye Logon Scripts, Hello Group Policy Preference Extensions

One takeaway, which you should start thinking about as you're reading through this chapter and the chapter in the companion book, *Creating the Secure Managed Desktop*, is, "Is there anything in my logon or startup process that I script today but could now start using Group Policy for?"

Indeed, almost everyone sets environment variables and maps drive letters using scripts. So, start thinking of pulling those things out of the logon scripts and making them more Group Policy-ish using the Group Policy Preference Extensions.

And, as you'll learn, since the GPPEs can leverage variables, you'll have a lot more flexibility with GPOs and GPPEs than you usually do with logon scripts.

What Is the New Power of the Group Policy Preference Extensions?

Once you run the GPMC and edit a GPO from Windows Server 2008 (or install the RSAT tools on a Windows Vista + SP1 machine, then run the GPMC, and edit a GPO), you'll notice that the normal Group Policy Editor (the GPME) you've come to know and love for years has changed.

The original nodes inside the GPME have been moved under their own node called Policies. So within that node, Policies, is the original stuff you've come to know and love, and not much has changed there. Except that all the original stuff is tucked inside of Policies now.

The new superpower stuff is stored within its own new node called Preferences. That's right, there's a new node in the Group Policy Management Editor, and it's called Preferences. You won't see it until you perform the installation of the Group Policy Preference Extensions management station components, as specified in the next section.

The new Preferences node has lots of new categories on both the user and computer side— and some even overlap! Indeed, not just overlap with itself (i.e., the same preference extension on both the computer and user side), but also overlap with original Group Policy settings (which now live in the Policies nodes.). Yikes! See the section entitled "The Overlap of Group Policy vs. Group Policy Preference Extensions and Associated Issues" a little later for more information on this particular issue.

Here you'll find 21 new categories of fun new toys to play with. (Remember, I said I'd describe the powerful new abilities first, then we'll work on the understanding of that power second.)

You'll also see that these new Group Policy options are split between Windows Settings and Control Panel Settings.

Most GPPEs work when users are first logging on (in the foreground) or while they're already logged on (in the background). However, two GPPEs do not: one is Drive Maps and the other is Printers. For those two categories to take effect, the user needs to log off and back on.

Computer Configuration ➢ Preferences

Again, this node is split in two: Windows Settings and Control Panel Settings. Let's check out each new superpower (in brief).

Computer Configuration ➢ Preferences ➢ Windows Settings

The Windows settings are settings you can make that, well, directly affect Windows. I know that's a little vague, but the other big category is Control Panel, which is also a little vague. In short, it doesn't really matter why they're broken up this way; they just are.

Environment Extension

You can do two big things with the Environment preference extension:

- You can set user and system environment variables.

- You can change or update the special Windows system Path variable.

You can best utilize this extension by using it to set specific environment variables based on certain conditions. Then, in other GPPEs, you can call these variables. For instance, you can define a variable like the one seen in the following image where we're defining NURSEFILES as C:\NURSEFILES. Then, later, you can recycle this variable when you want to use other GPPEs to copy or utilize files based on this variable.

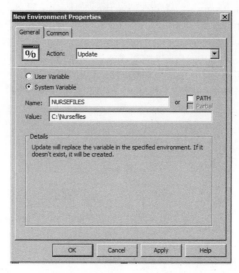

 In the companion book, *Creating the Secure Managed Desktop*, we show you how to leverage a SoftGrid server to distribute applications to your users. You can use the Environment extension to set the %SFT_SOFTGRIDSERVER% system variable to quickly enable users to find the closest SoftGrid server they should use.

Files Extension

The Files preference extension lets you copy files from Point A to Point B. Point A can be a UNC path or the local machine, and so can Point B, though Point B usually is the local machine. The most common scenario is to copy a file (or three) from a share on a server to a user's My Documents folder, the desktop, or C:\ drive.

You can see a screen shot of the Files preference extension in the section "Environment Variables" a little later.

Folders Extension

This extension lets you create new folders and delete existing folders or wipe out their contents. In this example, I'm deleting the contents of the %NURSESFILES% folder, but only if the folder is empty.

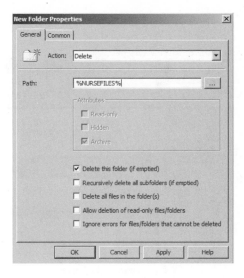

.INI Files Extension

This extension allows you to perform a search and replace within existing .INI files. I have an example in the section "Environment Variables" a little later.

Registry Extension

This is a very powerful extension that can also be a little hard to handle. We'll use this a little later in some examples, but the idea is simple: Punch in a particular Registry setting to your client machines.

You can see in the example here that I'm dictating a particular Registry setting to good ol' Notepad.

What's neat about the Registry extension is that you can send Registry punches normally designed for Users to both HKLM and HKCU. And you can send Registry punches normally designed for Computers to both HKLM and HKCU.

The Registry extension also allows you to set any type of Registry key, like REG_BINARY values, which has traditionally been impossible using ADM and ADMX files.

However, this extension needs to be handled with caution (as do others), especially when the "Remove this item when it is no longer applied" setting is chosen (which we'll discuss when we explore the Common tab a little later).

There are there several ways to utilize the Registry extension:

- **Registry Item:** This lets you specifically set an individual Registry setting. Again, all the major Registry types are supported (REG_SZ, REG_DWORD, REG_BINARY, REG_MULTI_SZ, and REG_EXPAND_SZ), and you can dictate to HKEY_LOCAL_MACHINE, HKEY_CURRENT_USER, HKEY_CLASSES_ROOT, HKEY_USERS, or HKEY_CURRENT_CONFIG.

- **Collection Item:** This is a fancy way of saying "A folder of stuff I want to lump together as a group." In short, by using this item, you can guarantee that groups of Registry settings will affect the machine at the same time. You'll use Item Level Targeting (ILT), which we'll discuss later, to ensure that your criteria is met *before* making the group of changes. For instance, you can check that the machine is a laptop before delivering all the Registry items in this group.

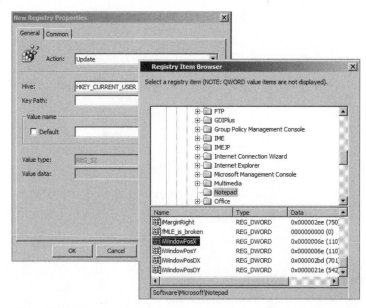

- **Registry Wizard:** This is a great way to take a sample machine's Registry, find a particular setting you want to manage, then manipulate and ultimately deliver the setting. You can select individual Registry settings or a whole Registry branch, change values if you want, then deliver all the changed values.

Network Shares Extension

This extension allows you to create new shares on workstations, or more commonly, servers. Or, alternatively, you can delete those shares.

You can also turn on Access-based Enumeration (ABE), available on Windows Server 2003 and Windows Server 2008, which will prevent someone who doesn't have proper rights from even seeing the shared directory.

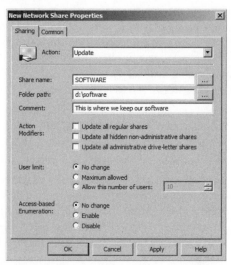

TIP

Learn more about ABE at `http://tinyurl.com/cwa8z`.

Note that this extension won't actually create the directory for the share. The directory has to already exist. But, you can easily create the folders you need using the Folders extension, which we just explored.

Shortcuts Extension

This extension allows you to plunk both program and URL shortcuts on Desktops, in the Startup folder, in the Programs folders, and in a lot of other locations. In this example, I'm plunking a link to `www.GPanswers.com` on the user's Desktop and selecting the little World icon.

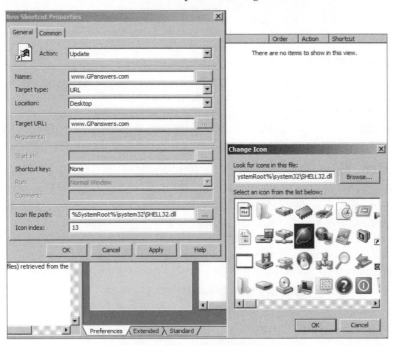

Note that you can also create shortcuts to shell objects. For instance, you can put a link to the Recycle Bin in the folders that users utilize most and even in the "Send to" flyout menu.

Computer Configuration ➢ Preferences ➢ Control Panel Settings

Again, it's a little arbitrary that some settings are considered Windows settings and others are Control Panel settings, but here are the ones listed within Control Panel.

Data Sources Extension

The Data Sources extension lets you set Open Database Connectivity (ODBC) data sources via Group Policy. Typically, this can be a 12-step process that you would normally have to run around and perform on every machine. Now it can be done via Group Policy in a snap.

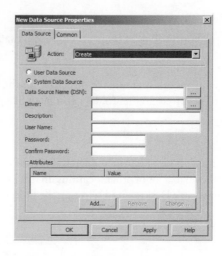

Devices Extension

This extension can disable a specific device or device class. There are similar original Group Policy settings that seemingly conflict with these. Indeed, we talk about these original Group Policy settings in Chapter 8 of the companion book, *Creating the Secure Managed Desktop*.

Check out the section "Group Policy Device Installation Restrictions vs. Devices Preference Extension" for more information about which one does what and which ones are best to use.

Folder Options Extension

This extension exists in both the user and computer sides. However, on the computer side, it has only one possible function (where in the user side it has three functions). That is, you can associate a file extension with a particular class.

This part of this extension corresponds to Explorer's Tools ➤ Options ➤ File Types ➤ Advanced dialog. Personally, in all my years working with Windows, I've never needed to modify anything in there, but clearly someone needed to or they wouldn't have put it in here.

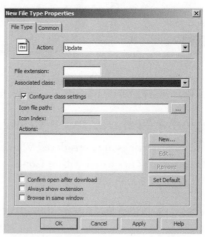

Local Users and Groups Extension

In Chapter 8, we explored restricted groups. That's a toy compared with the Group Policy Preference Extensions' Local Users and Groups. Here, you can jam users into groups, remove specific users from specific groups, change users' passwords, lock out accounts, and set password expirations.

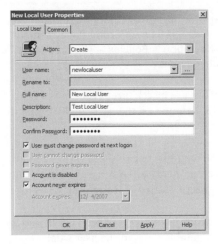

Network Options Extension

The Network Options extension allows you to configure the following connection types:

- **VPN Connections:** This is the "Cadillac" way to go. Previously, setting Virtual Private Network (VPN) connections was tedious, arduous work. Now it's a snap.

- **DUN Connections:** Ditto for Dial-Up Networking (DUN) connections.

Instead of running around to all your laptops and specifying these settings, you can be finished configuring an army of machines before breakfast.

Power Options Extension

This preference item allows you to create new power schemes and control existing ones in Windows XP. You can set things like the hard disk spin down time, how long until the monitor goes into stand-by mode, and what happens to laptops when you hit the power button.

 The settings for the Power Options extension don't apply to Windows Vista. Windows Vista has its own Group Policy settings, and they're found in Computer Configuration ➢ Policies ➢ Administrative Templates ➢ System ➢ Power Management.

Again, because these settings are merely preferences, users can still change the settings if they want to. So, be careful banking on the users maintaining the settings you wanted.

Printers Extension

The Printers extension option might be one of those things you just fall in love with. But, you have to contend with the fact that there's already a way to zap printers down via Group Policy, and we'll talk about it in the section titled "Group Policy Deployed Printers vs. Printers Preference Extension."

In short, the Printers extension allows you to set TCP/IP and local and shared printers (though shared printers are available only on the user side).

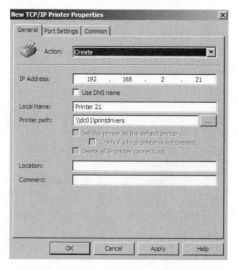

Scheduled Tasks Extension

You can set Version 1 scheduled tasks using this preference extension. Version 1 tasks are valid for Windows XP, Windows Server 2003, Windows Vista, and Windows 2008 machines.

However, Windows Vista and Windows Server 2008 have more features available via Version 2 scheduled tasks, like interfacing with the Event log and such.

So, you can use the Scheduled Task preference extension to deliver tasks to all operating systems (Windows XP and higher), but you cannot use this to take advantage of the Version 2–specific tasks that are available only on Windows Vista and Windows Server 2008.

You can set scheduled tasks and immediate tasks. Scheduled tasks are valid on all supported clients. Immediate tasks are not supported on Windows Vista and Windows Server 2008. That is, immediate tasks only work for Windows XP and Windows Server 2003.

Immediate is kind of a misnomer because in Group Policy, nothing is really "immediate." In reality, you'll have to wait until Group Policy refreshes on the client. When it does, the task is scheduled to run, and then poof, that's it.

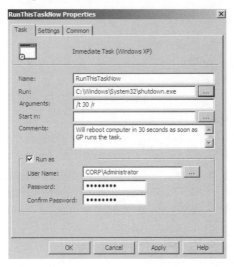

Services Extension

You can manage just about every aspect of a client computer's services. This is especially useful if the target is a server machine and you have a pesky service that's running on multiple machines but you haven't gotten around to changing the service account in, well, years.

Simply change the password in Active Directory first, then deliver a Group Policy containing the Services item with your password change.

The password is stored in encrypted form within the Group Policy's GPT. The password is 256bit AES encrypted. However, there is theoretically an embedded key available so a determined hacker could crack it if necessary.

You can change the following items:

- **Startup:** If you like, you can change the startup type to Automatic, Manual, or Disabled.

- **Service action:** When the Group Policy runs, you can have it start, stop, or restart a service.

- **Log on as:** You can configure the account that the service uses as well as change the password, as noted earlier.
- **Recovery:** What will happen if the service fails on first, second, and subsequent failures. This equates to the Recovery options in the normal services dialog.

Note that original Group Policy has some ability to work with System Services. Be sure to check out the section "Group Policy System Services vs. Services Preference Extension" a little later for a breakdown on how each compares, head to head.

User Configuration ➢ Preferences

On the User Configuration ➢ Preferences side of things, there are lots of preference extensions that overlap. In this section, we'll detail only ones that *don't* specifically overlap (or specific major features that don't overlap).

See Table 10.1 a little later on for the bird's-eye view of where the overlaps are and to see what can specifically be accomplished on either the computer or user side.

User Configuration ➢ Preferences ➢ Windows Settings

Let's explore the GPPEs on the User ➢ Windows Settings side.

Applications Extension

This node is special because there are no configurable items available by default. The node's purpose is to allow you to configure some popular Microsoft applications in a flash: Office XP, Office 2003, Outlook 2003, and more.

However, the required bits do not ship in the box for Windows Vista and are not available as part of the RSAT download. To use this section, be sure to read "Application Extensions: Completing Your Management Station for Windows Server 2008 and Windows Vista" a little later.

Drive Maps Extension

Congratulations. You can finally get out of the "I have to map another network drive via logon scripts" business. It's *finally* come to Group Policy land.

The Drive Maps preference extension is like the Swiss Army knife of drive mappings, and you can create and delete drive mappings and assign letters with ease.

When this extension is combined with item-level targeting (which we talk about later), you'll be able to specifically dictate drive maps to users based on the specific circumstances they're in.

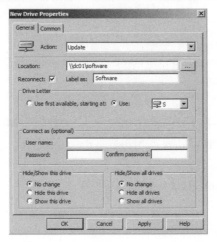

Folder Options Extension

While this exists on both the user and computer side, they have different options. On the user side, you can right-click New ➤ Folder Options and see three options:

- **Folder Options for Windows XP:** This option is shown in the following screen shot. While you could do a lot of these little tweaks by editing the Registry directly, there's a lot of "quick power" available in the Folder Options configuration item. These items mostly equate to Explorer's Tools ➤ Folder Options items that you would normally find inside every Explorer window. You can quickly turn on the ability to have Windows Explorer show hidden files, display full path in the address bar, and show NTFS compressed files with a different color.

- **Folder Options for Windows Vista:** Very similar items to what's available for Windows XP, but specific to Windows Vista.

- **Open With:** This enables you to associate (or de-associate) applications from their extensions. So you can quickly configure a specific application on a machine to handle a particular document file.

The only option on the computer side for Folder Options is File Type.

User Configuration ➤ Preferences ➤ Control Panel

This is the final group of GPPEs. Here we'll discuss the items that are available only on the user side of the house.

Internet Settings Extension

You can set either of the following:

- Internet Explorer 5 and 6 settings (that's *one* kind of setting)
- Or Internet Explorer 7 settings

You can see Internet Explorer 5 and 6 settings here.

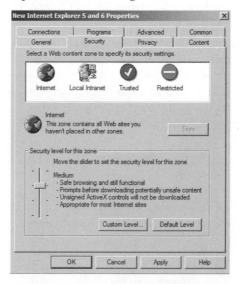

What's strange is that there are lot of user interface elements that seemingly do, well, nothing. There are lots of buttons that are permanently grayed out and entire tabs (like Privacy) that are entirely grayed out.

Other than that, this is a stellar way to set Internet settings. However, it should be noted that there are already two ways to set Internet Explorer settings via Group Policy. So, be sure to read "Group Policy Internet Explorer and Group Policy IE Maintenance Configuration vs. the Internet Settings Preference Extension" a little later to figure out which one to use and when.

Printers Extension

While this category exists on both the computer and user side, when settings are dictated to users, an additional option is available for managing shared printers. Again, be sure to read the section "Group Policy Deployed Printers vs. Printers Preference Extension" a little later for more information.

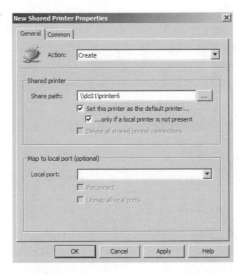

Regional Options Extension

This has always been something I wanted to set via Group Policy. It just seems obvious: depending on who the user is, you can immediately change their local settings. Now you can just do that, quickly and easily, using Group Policy.

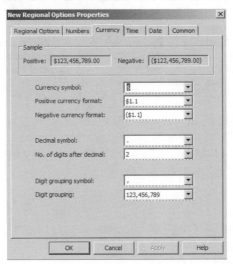

Start Menu Extension

While there are existing settings for controlling the Start menu, this Extension brings a very easy way to make your changes. There are Start menu configurations for Windows XP and Windows Vista.

However, you might not want to try to change any of these settings until you read the section titled "Group Policy Start Menu Policy Settings vs. Start Menu Preference Extension."

Table 10.1 shows you where to find each Group Policy Preference Extension.

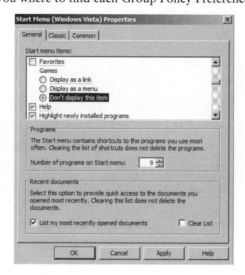

TABLE 10.1 Where to Find Group Policy Preference Extensions

	Computer Configuration ➤ Preferences ➤ Control Panel	Computer Configuration ➤ Preferences ➤ Windows Settings	User Configuration ➤ Preferences ➤ Control Panel	User Configuration ➤ Preferences ➤ Windows Settings
Applications				X
Data Sources	X		X	
Devices	X		X	
Drive Maps				X
Environment		X		X
Files		X		X

TABLE 10.1 Where to Find Group Policy Preference Extensions *(continued)*

	Computer Configuration ➢ Preferences ➢ Control Panel	Computer Configuration ➢ Preferences ➢ Windows Settings	User Configuration ➢ Preferences ➢ Control Panel	User Configuration ➢ Preferences ➢ Windows Settings
Folder Options— Folder Options			X	
Folder Options— Open With			X	
Folder Options— File Type	X			
Folders		X		X
.INI Files		X		X
Internet Settings			X	
Local Users and Groups— Local Group	X		X	
Local Users and Groups— Local User	X		X	
Mail Profiles			X	
Network Options—VPN Connection	X		X	
Network Options—DUN Connection (Dial-up)	X		X	
Power Options— Power Options	X		X	
Power Options— Power Scheme	X		X	

TABLE 10.1   Where to Find Group Policy Preference Extensions   *(continued)*

	Computer Configuration ➤ Preferences ➤ Control Panel	Computer Configuration ➤ Preferences ➤ Windows Settings	User Configuration ➤ Preferences ➤ Control Panel	User Configuration ➤ Preferences ➤ Windows Settings
Printers—Shared Printer			X	
Printers—TCP/IP Printer	X		X	
Printers—Local Printer	X		X	
Regional Options			X	
Registry		X		X
Scheduled Tasks	X		X	
Services	X			
Shortcuts		X		X
Start Menu			X	

Group Policy Preference Extensions Architecture and Installation Instructions

As you'll recall from previous chapters, the magic of Group Policy happens in three steps:

1. You use a management station, which has the GPMC, and the Group Policy Editor, which has a snap-in for the tool you want to use.

2. A GPO is created and lives on your Domain Controllers.

3. The directive you put into the GPO (from your management station) is processed by a particular CSE on the target system.

First things first: Your management station needs to have the updated capability of creating and managing new features. You saw this, for instance, when you upgraded to Windows Vista and you got the ability to do cool new stuff like manage the Windows firewall with advanced security and set wired settings. If you'll recall, you simply can't do these magic tricks from a

Windows XP or Windows 2000 machine because that capability isn't contained within the power of that older Group Policy Object Editor.

Second things second: The directive is stored within the GPO. That mechanism doesn't change.

Third things third: Your target machine must have a Client Side Extension (CSE) that implements the magic you created and stored within the GPO. That is, a moving part (a .DLL, actually) parses the GPO and performs the magic you want done. These could be settings like Disk Quotas, Folder Redirection, Internet Explorer settings, and so on. And, now, the GPPEs.

So, let's figure out what it's going to take to get both our management station and our target machines up to speed.

To get our management station up to speed (to create and manage the new settings):

- Your management station *must* be a Windows Vista or Windows Server 2008 machine. To use Group Policy Preference Extensions, your management station cannot be anything else.

  - Windows Server 2008 has the management station components built in. Well, *not all* of the management station components, actually. Confusingly, there are some pieces you must still reach out and download to be "complete."

  - For Windows Vista, you have to download *all* the management station components. This will be in two steps (we'll see each of these in a moment).

To get our target systems up to speed (to embrace GPOs with the new changes):

- Your target system *may* be Windows XP with at least SP2, Windows Server 2003 with at least SP1, Windows Vista, or Windows Server 2008.
- Only Windows Server 2008 already has the GPPE CSEs built in.
- Windows XP, Windows Server 2003, and Windows Vista need to have the GPPE CSEs installed on them to embrace the new functionality.

It's these two big items we're going to tackle in this section. That way, you're all set when you're ready to start using these new superpowers.

Installing the Client Side Extensions on Your Client Machines

So, as you just learned, we'll need to get the GPPE CSEs on our target machines (except for Windows Server 2008) to rock and roll with GPPEs. Let's explore what we need to do on each machine to make sure they have the "set of instructions" required to embrace the GPOs we're about to create.

The CSEs for Windows Server 2008

Again, everything you need to take advantage of the Group Policy Preference Extensions is already installed here. Both the management station pieces (where you define what you want to control) and the CSE piece (the .DLLs that process the GPOs).

So, if you wanted to get started using Group Policy Preference Extensions, you can do so immediately.

Note that the Group Policy Preference Extensions are not available as Local Group Policy Objects. The Group Policy Preference Extensions appear only when you use the GPMC and manage Active Directory GPOs.

The CSEs for Windows Server 2003, Windows XP, and Windows Vista

Again, for Windows Server 2003, Windows XP, and Windows Vista you need to download pieces to make the magic happen. Let's examine each operating system, where to get the downloads, and how to install the pieces by hand.

The Group Policy Preference Extensions can be downloaded from http://tinyurl.com/2za5zz. You can also track them down by heading over to http://www.microsoft.com/downloads and searching for the word "Preference."

Windows XP and Windows Server 2003 machines also need a prerequisite called XMLlite, and it can be found at http://support.microsoft.com/default.aspx/kb/914783.

Here's the trick. Neither the XMLlite prerequisite nor the GPPEs themselves are MSIs. Nope, they're *patches*. So, for Windows XP and Windows Server 2003, they're .EXE patches, and for Windows Vista they're a newfangled format called .MSU for Microsoft Update patch.

And, if you'll recall, Group Policy Software Installation cannot install patches. You need a big tool like an SCCM 2007 or WSUS which expressly handles patch management. Or, you'll need a script to install them for your systems.

Ugh, what a nightmare!

You'll always be able to install each piece by hand (which we'll explore first), but you'll also want a mass-deployment recipe to start really rolling this out. I'll provide a script that helps you roll this all out to all your machines at once, so you're not running around from machine to machine doing all the dirty work.

Microsoft might choose to make these MSIs in the future, so stay tuned using the GPanswers.com newsletter. At that point you would be able to use Group Policy Software Installation to deploy the MSIs to your client machines.

Installing the Prerequisites and CSEs for Windows Server 2003 and Windows XP by Hand

So, we'll just want to make sure that our existing Windows Server 2003, Windows XP, and (in the next section) our Windows Vista machines have the CSEs ready to accept our instructions from our management stations.

If you're installing the CSEs on Windows Server 2003, you'll likely do each one by hand. This makes sense, as mass deploying and mass rebooting live servers can be, well, not good for your users. However, if you wanted to do a mass rollout of the CSEs, check out the section "Installing the Prerequisites and CSEs for All Operating Systems Automatically."

Again, both Windows XP and Windows Server 2003 have the prerequisite of XMLlite. You can see the available command-line switches in Figure 10.1, if you want to be fancy, or you can just double-click the downloaded .EXE and kick off the installation.

FIGURE 10.1 The XMLlite command-line options

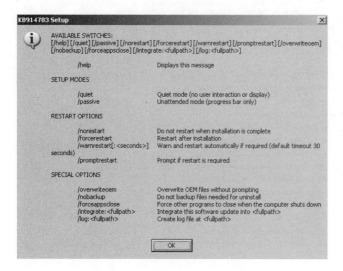

In my testing, the XMLlite components didn't require a reboot (but your mileage may vary). Knowing this fact will come in handy when we try to automate the whole thing using a script.

Next, I simply double-clicked the .EXE that contained the CSE.

Once again, it didn't even require a reboot and it appeared to be ready to go. You might want to reboot once just to be on the safe side.

You can verify the Group Policy Preference Extensions installed on Windows Server 2003 or Windows XP in "Add or Remove Programs" and checking the "Show updates" checkbox, as seen in Figure 10.2. When you do, you'll see the hotfixes, like GPPE installation.

Installing the CSEs for Windows Vista by Hand

The Windows Vista CSE ships as an MSU, a Microsoft Update package, as seen in Figure 10.3. Just double-click it and then click OK to install—you're off to the races.

Again, in my testing there was no need to reboot after completion, but it certainly couldn't hurt. You can verify that the Group Policy Preference Extensions were properly installed by looking at Control Panel ➤ Programs ➤ Uninstall a program and then clicking "Turn Windows features on or off" as seen in Figure 10.4.

Note the Group Policy Preference Extensions are on by default, and it's not such a hot idea to turn them off. Note you can also see the KB update number as an installed update.

FIGURE 10.2   You can verify that the Group Policy Preference Extensions were installed on Windows XP and Windows Server 2003 by selecting "Show updates."

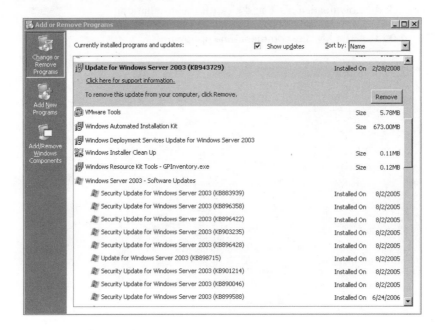

FIGURE 10.3   Installing the Windows Vista MSU file is like installing an executable.

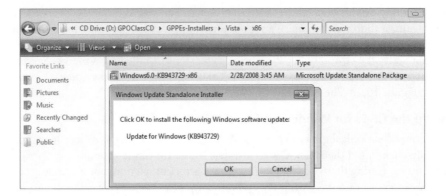

Installing the Prerequisites and CSEs for All Operating Systems Automatically

This gets a little trickier. And it takes a giant script to make it happen.

Fortunately, for you, we've put together that giant script and it's waiting for you at www .GPanswers.com in the Book Resources section. Go grab it, then, if you don't want to use WSUS or a larger management tool like SCCM 2007, use the script to get the GPPEs installed to all your clients.

FIGURE 10.4   You can verify that the Group Policy Preference Extensions were
properly installed.

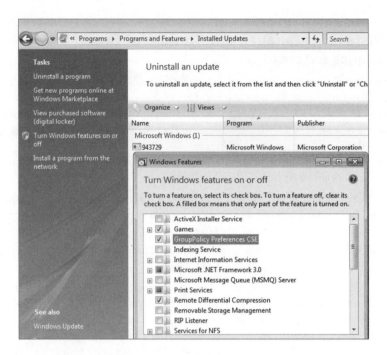

Installing the Group Policy Preference Extensions Management Station Components

At this point, we'll make sure our management stations are prepared to produce the GPOs that contain the new superpowers the Group Policy Preference Extensions provide.

Windows Server 2003 and Windows XP operating systems can't be management stations. That's okay. You'll just use Windows Vista or Windows Server 2008 management stations instead. (You did read Chapter 7, right?)

Let's figure out what it takes to prepare a Windows Server 2008 or Windows Vista machine to be your Group Policy Preference Extensions management station.

Windows Server 2008 as a Management Station for Group Policy Preference Extensions

As I stated earlier, most but not all of the management station components are already installed. What's missing is the Application extension add-ons, which I'll talk about installing in the next section.

The Application Extension add-ons help you craft configurations for Microsoft Office 2003, Office XP, and others. They're a separate download for legal reasons and aren't automatically installed.

Windows Vista as a Management Station for Group Policy Preference Extensions

Using Windows Vista as a management station is your other choice if you don't wish to make Windows Server 2008 your management station. This makes sense. This is likely what you already have on your desk, so it makes sense to keep using it. By this point, you've already got Windows Vista and SP1 and the GPMC 2.0 installed. (I know you already read Chapters 1, 3, and 7 and followed them diligently. Am I right?)

Now, all you need are the Group Policy Preference Extensions management station components. And there are two parts here:

- Group Policy Preference Extensions management station core components. This provides the ability to craft about 80 percent of what's possible with the Group Policy Preference Extensions.

- Application Extension add-ons. Again, this allows you to manage specific Microsoft applications like Microsoft Office 2003 and Office XP.

Right now, we'll install the Group Policy Preference Extensions management station core components, and in the very next section we'll install the Application Extension add-ons.

To get the Group Policy Preference Extensions management station components, you install the Remote Server Administration Tools (RSAT) on Windows Vista. As of this writing, the RSAT tools aren't available. Be sure to go to www.GPanswers.com to learn when they'll be ready for download.

Then, simply install on your Windows Vista + SP1 + GPMC 2.0 machine, and you'll be (almost) ready to rock. At this point you've done 80 percent of the installation. Heck, you should have done this way back in Chapter 1 or Chapter 3.

In the next section, I'll show you how to install the last 20 percent of the Group Policy Preference Extensions management station components that need to be installed for both Windows Vista and Windows Server 2008 management stations.

Application Extensions: Completing Your Management Station for Windows Server 2008 and Windows Vista

If you take a look at one particular node, User Configuration ➤ Preferences ➤ Windows Settings ➤ Applications, you'll curiously note that you can select New ➤ Application, but strangely it doesn't allow you to select any applications. You can see this in Figure 10.5.

This is because, for legal reasons, the DLLs that make up this part of the world aren't installed by default. I don't really comprehend (or really care to comprehend) the legal reasons here, but in short, you (and I) need to download them. The link to grab them is http://go.microsoft.com/fwlink/?LinkId=90745. And then follow the installation instructions.

Once you do, you'll have the applications available to you, as seen in Figure 10.6.

FIGURE 10.5 The applications for the Applications extension need to be downloaded separately.

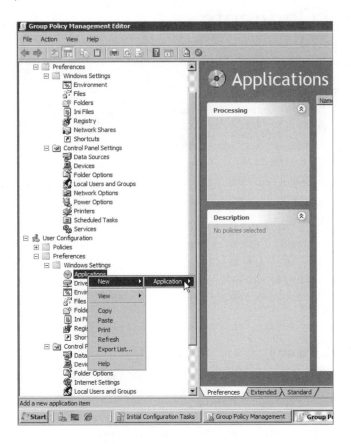

FIGURE 10.6 This is what the Applications extension looks like when the download is installed.

No matter what your management station is (Windows Vista or Windows Server 2008), there is still a need to download another element to be complete—the Application Extension add-on components, which allow you to manage specific Microsoft applications.

Group Policy Preference Extensions Concepts

The Group Policy Preference Extensions look "different" than the rest of the Group Policy universe. That's because they *are* different. They were born at Desktop Standard and integrated into Microsoft technology.

And there are a lot of holdovers, which can be a little confusing.

Those confusing (but powerful) elements we'll cover here are as follows:

- The idea that they aren't really policies but rather preferences. (Don't worry, we'll get to this bit of confusion right away.)

- The multicolored and dashed lines that are in the interface.

- The strange concept called the *CRUD method*.

- The Common tab, which allows you to do some high-power tricks.

- Using Group Policy Preference Extensions "targeting" to further hone your wishes.

In all, it's a cool, cool brave new (or rather *updated*) world. But it does have tricks and pitfalls, and that's what we're going to explore here in this chapter. However, because we can't explore all 21 goodies in this book, we'll explore more in the companion book, *Creating the Secure Managed Desktop*.

Preference, Not Policy

This is a quote from the Group Policy Preference Extensions help file within the GPMC that pretty much sums it up:

> Unlike policy settings, by default preference items are not removed when the hosting GPO becomes out of scope for the user or computer.

Let's spend a little time breaking this apart, really understanding the implications of getting our new superpowers before we proceed to do something we'll later regret.

Let me be really, really clear: please don't mass-deploy Group Policy Preference Extensions settings to your clients until you really understand the Preference vs. Policy issues.

Why Group Policy Works—a Review

Let's recall a little more about what Group Policy does for you. Group Policy delivers settings. And the running application, say Explorer, or Office 2003, or the WSUS client, or Windows Media Player, will pick up the settings and change their behavior based upon what you want the application to do. For instance, if you use Group Policy and enable a setting like User Configuration ➤ Policies ➤ Administrative Templates ➤ Control Panel ➤ **Prohibit Access to the Control Panel**, your expectation is that Explorer will do the dirty work for you and, well, prohibit access to the Control Panel.

Because that directive is written to a protected part of the Registry—in fact, to the "proper" Policies keys—the user cannot edit the Registry and "scoot" out of getting the setting. Again, we covered this in Chapters 3 and 7.

Why ADM/ADMX Files Are and Aren't So Awesome

The whole idea that Group Policy is a massive "settings delivery machine" is great. And also recall how we extended this capability in Chapter 7—for instance, where we created ADM and ADMX files, and one of those ADM templates (which we converted to ADMX for fun) was where we directed Windows XP to play a specific startup sound.

And it worked.

But if you go back to Chapter 7 (in the section "ADMX Migrator and ADMX Editor Tools"), you'll see this ADM template. If you reread that section (or just look closely at the structure of the ADM template), you'll notice that the Registry key doesn't plunk anything into the protected Policies keys. So, if you were to implement this ADM file (or converted ADMX file), something unexpected happens. That is, even though you push the startup sound to Windows XP, users can still continue to make changes to the startup sound. That's because Explorer doesn't know to protect that part of the world; it's not contained within the Policies keys.

And that's the same issue with the new GPPEs. The GPPEs don't write their magical setting to the Policies keys. And you might be asking yourself why. While this sounds bad on the surface, it's really not all that bad. The answer is simple: The applications they control (Explorer, drive settings, ODBC settings, etc.) don't know to look in the Policies keys to pick up settings.

Group Policy Preference Extensions Are Like ADM/ADMX Files (Mostly)

So, the GPPEs specify where these applications should look for their settings. But the downsides in this scheme are the same downsides you would get when you create ADM and ADMX files:

- Settings you dictate with ADM/ADMX and GPPEs can usually be changed, unset, or deleted by the end user (though there are some exceptions).

- If a user moves from one OU to another (or performs in some other way such that they fall out of scope of management), the setting will just stick there; tattooing the machine.

Hence, these new goodies are called Group Policy *Preferences*. And that's because they act more or less like the preferences we created when we created our own ADM and ADMX files.

Group Policy Preference Extensions Advantages over ADM/ADMX Files

However, there is one additional distinction: ADM and ADMX files aren't usually "rewritten" after a user changes settings that are directed for them (though this can be changed via settings located within Computer Configuration ➢ Policies ➢ Administrative Templates ➢ System ➢ Group Policy, as we explored in Chapter 4 in the section "Affecting the Computer Settings of Group Policy").

GPPEs are different. They hook into the "timing" of the Group Policy engine. So, even if a user changes the underlying settings (like, they delete a shortcut that is supposed to affect them using GPPE), the next time Group Policy refreshes, that shortcut will pop right back as if nothing had happened! Keen!

Now, as we'll see a little later, the GPPEs have some extra superpowers available. These superpowers can all be found in the Common tab, and we'll cover these superpowers in detail a little later on.

Some options go above and beyond the original ADM/ADMX preferences:

- "Remove this item when it is no longer applied" can help "peel off" settings when the user or computer falls out of scope of management. But this doesn't always work as you might expect, and we'll explore this a little later.

- "Apply once and do not reapply" changes the GPPE default behavior. So instead of hooking into the timing of the Group Policy engine, settings are simply deployed once and never again—even if the user changes the settings the administrator wanted.

- "Item-level targeting" is sort of like WMI filters on steroids, and it's only available for GPPE settings, not original policy settings.

There are some more options where GPPEs go above and beyond the original ADM/ADMX preferences, but these are the big ones.

The Overlap of Group Policy vs. Group Policy Preference Extensions and Associated Issues

One of the strangest parts of the GPPEs is that they bring totally new superpowers to the table yet overlap some existing areas. This is confusing to say the least, because how will you know which one to use?

Classic vs. Group Policy Preference Extensions Overlap Areas

Some items cursorily overlap with other areas of Group Policy. For instance, drive mappings and Environment variables can also be set with login scripts, as could shortcuts and some other areas if you really put your mind to it. But in some instances, there really is brand-new GPPE functionality that competes with existing classic Group Policy functionality.

It's a classic Rocky Balboa vs. Clubber Lang battle. The new guy has strength, but the original fighter has heart! (Give me some leeway here with this analogy; I live in Philadelphia.)

 More on Rocky Balboa and Clubber Lang in Rocky III here: http://en.wikipedia.org/wiki/Rocky_III.

In this match, er, section, we'll do a quick breakdown of the original Group Policy feature versus the new GPPE feature.

And, since there's overlap, I'll weigh in about which one you should use: either the original Group Policy feature or the new GPPE feature.

Group Policy Deployed Printers vs. Printers Preference Extension

This feature debuted with Windows Server 2003/R2 and then made its way as a mainstream Windows Vista feature.

Check out www.GPanswers.com's Newsletter #17 for more information about deployed printers with Windows Server 2003/R2 and Windows Vista.

This feature is found by traversing to Computer Configuration ➢ Policies ➢ Windows Settings ➢ Deployed Printers and User Configuration ➢ Windows Settings ➢ Deployed Printers.

Note that this feature isn't available by default on a Windows Server 2008 machine until you load the print management components. This is under the Feature section as an add-in within Remote Server Administration Tools ➢ Role Administration Tools ➢ Print Services Tools. Once you load this tool, you'll be able to see that node in the GPME.

The new Printers Extension feature is found in two places: in Computer Configuration ➢ Preferences ➢ Control Panel Settings ➢ Printers and User Configuration ➢ Preferences ➢ Control Panel Settings ➢ Printers.

The Group Policy feature only allows for shared printers, requires Windows Server 2003/ R2 or greater, and only deploys "cleanly" to Windows Vista and Windows Server 2008. You can jury-rig it with the R2 executable PushPrinterConnections.exe (as detailed in www.GPanswers.com Newsletter #17).

This new Printers extension allows for TCP/IP, local printers, or shared printers (user side only), requires no schema changes, and, as long as the Group Policy Preference Extensions are installed on the target machine, makes deploying printers a dream.

This one is a no-brainer: The Printers extension really just clobbers the original Group Policy Printers capability. Start using it right away.

Group Policy Internet Explorer and Group Policy IE Maintenance Configuration vs. the Internet Settings Preference Extension

There was already an overlapping message in Group Policy-land when configuring Internet Explorer (IE). The original policy settings can be found here:

- Computer Configuration ➢ Policies ➢ Administrative Templates ➢ Windows Components ➢ Internet Explorer.

- User Configuration ➢ Policies ➢ Administrative Templates ➢ Windows Components ➢ Internet Explorer. Inside, you'll see original policy settings for IE 5 and 6 and, more recently, IE 7.

But then there are also the IE Maintenance settings, which are found at User Configuration ➢ Policies ➢ Windows Settings ➢ Internet Explorer Maintenance.

So, before we even add the GPPEs, we have triple overlap.

Now, by adding the GPPEs, there's a quadruple overlap. The new GPPE for the IE settings can be found at User Configuration ➤ Preferences ➤ Control Panel Settings ➤ Internet Settings, as seen in Figure 10.7.

FIGURE 10.7 This is the IE preference extension.

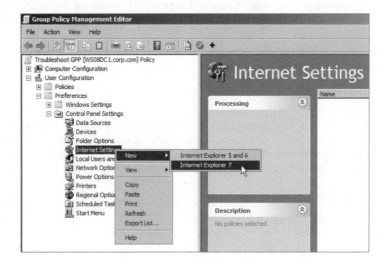

With the overlap in IE, things get really confusing, really fast. What if you have IE settings contained within three or four areas? See the section "How Does the Group Policy Engine Deal with Overlaps?" where we discuss that problem.

But, my advice about which one to use and which one to dump is as follows:

- Abandon older IE 5 and 6 settings on the user side of things and use the Internet Explorer extension instead.

- However, the Internet Explorer extension for IE isn't available on the computer side. So, in that case, see if you can use Computer Configuration ➤ Policies ➤ Administrative Templates ➤ Windows Components ➤ Internet Explorer and, only if you must, User Configuration ➤ Policies ➤ Windows Settings ➤ Internet Explorer Maintenance.

Group Policy Power Management vs. Power Options Preference Extension

Original Power Management options were found in Computer Configuration ➤ Policies ➤ System ➤ Power Management (and the various subnodes within). These settings deal with sleep options, what happens when you push various power buttons, spinning down the hard drive, and more. These power management settings are only usable for Windows Vista (though some may work on Windows Server 2008, but I haven't tested them).

There is also one lone user side setting at User Configuration ➤ Policies ➤ System ➤ Power Management that deals with passwords when the laptop comes back from hibernation.

The new Power Options extension settings are found within Computer Configuration ➤ Preferences ➤ Control Panel Settings ➤ Power Options and User Configuration ➤ Preferences ➤ Control Panel Settings ➤ Power Options, as seen in Figure 10.8.

FIGURE 10.8   The Power Scheme settings are valid only for Windows XP.

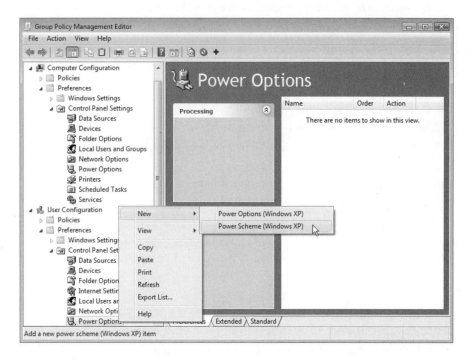

In fact, there is no real overlap here. The original settings deal with Windows Vista settings, and the GPPE settings deal with Windows XP. So, use whichever branch controls the machine type you want to manage.

Group Policy File Security vs. Files Preference Extension

Group Policy has a way to set security on files. But until the Files extension came along, there was no way to actually use Group Policy to get files on the Desktop or into folders (short of using a logon script to do it).

So, this situation is a little weird. It's like two halves that have always wanted to be together. So now with the Files extension (Computer Configuration ➢ Preferences ➢ Windows Settings ➢ Files), you can push a file to a client. And with Group Policy File Security (located within Computer Configuration ➢ Policies ➢ Windows Settings ➢ Security Settings ➢ File System), you can set the ACLs on those files.

What a magic combination!

Group Policy System Services vs. Services Preference Extension

The original way to control services is located in Computer Configuration ➢ Policies ➢ Security Settings ➢ System Services.

The GPPE way to control services is located in Computer Configuration ➢ Preferences ➢ Control Panel Settings ➢ Services.

Both have the ability to change the startup mode of a service to Automatic, Manual, or Disabled. However, here are the differences between the two tools:

- The original way can also set the security on the account (who can start, stop, and pause the service).

- The GPPE way can do the following things that cannot be done the original way:

  - Change the local system account password

  - Start or stop the service once the Group Policy applies

  - Change the recovery options if a service fails

  - Change the program to run if a service fails and/or restart the computer if the service fails

So, while there is overlap here, you should ideally use the original way to change the security on the service if necessary but then use the Services extension to manage the rest of the properties, like local system account password and recovery options.

 Note that the management station needs to be running on a machine with the services you want to manage. This is the same behavior as the original Group Policy services node.

Group Policy Administrative Templates and ADM/ADMX Files vs. Registry Preference Extension and Application Preference Extension Settings

There's a great new tool available within User Configuration ➢ Preferences ➢ Windows Settings ➢ Registry and Computer Configuration ➢ Preferences ➢ Windows Settings ➢ Registry. This tool lets you jam new Registry values into just about any application, just about anywhere in the Registry.

This sort of competes with the idea of ADM and ADMX files whose goal is to let you craft a basic user interface and jam Registry values into your applications.

Additionally, another new GPPE node found at User Configuration ➢ Preferences ➢ Windows Settings ➢ Applications seems to bump up against the ADM and ADMX prime directive. That is, the Applications node provides several common Microsoft applications and their user interfaces and jams new Registry values into their corresponding applications. (You can see a picture of this in Figure 10.6.)

So, which one do you use where? Here's my advice:

- If your ADM/ADMX file has only one or two settings, and you don't change the values within those settings very often, consider reimplementing these settings using the Registry extension. However, if you do so, it might not be super obvious to another administrator precisely what you've done within the Registry extension because the user interface is simply about the Registry *value* and has no framework to describe the user interface of the target application.

- If your ADM/ADMX file has lots of settings, continue to use it. It might be hard to translate an ADM/ADMX file with lots of settings over to the Registry extension, and it might be more trouble than it's worth. However, if you love, love, love what you read in the section "Targeting Your Preference Items" (coming up a little later) and you think you might want to take advantage of that new superpower, then you might want to bite the bullet and reimplement as Registry extension punches.

- If you've been using Office 2003/Office 2007 ADM or ADMX files, consider abandoning them for the Applications extension, which also manages these applications. The Outlook configuration within the Applications extension is simply stellar and has all sorts of smarts that help you dictate Outlook profiles to users—whatever machine they happen to sit down at. This one feature alone is worth the price of converting. Again, you won't see these applications in the Applications node by default. You must install them separately via the download located at `http://go.microsoft.com/fwlink/?LinkId=90745`.

For completeness, I'll mention one other option: It is possible, though not easy, to take an application's user interface and code it such that you can create your own Applications extension for your own application. It should be noted that this code must be hard-coded in C++ and this is, well, in one guy's opinion "really freakin' hard." You can learn more about this option via the Group Policy Software Development Kit at the link `http://go.microsoft.com/fwlink/?LinkId=144`.

> Not to sound like a commercial, but if you're looking to extend your reach to applications using Group Policy, you might want to consider the third-party software called PolicyPak Design Studio, which implements its own form of the Applications node in a much simpler, more approachable, and more extendable way (with more options for your application). In short, there's no C++ involved. Just a GUI editor tool where you "draw" your application's interface and then describe the behavior for each check box and drop-down. There's both a free version and a for-a-fee version. For more information, check out www.PolicyPak.com. Note that the author is a part owner in Policy-Pak Software.

Group Policy Device Installation Restrictions vs. Devices Preference Extension

The original Device Installation Restrictions are found at Computer Configuration ➤ Policies ➤ System ➤ Device Installation ➤ Device Installation Restrictions, and we discuss them in detail in Chapter 8 of the companion book, *Creating the Secure Managed Desktop*.

The new Devices Preference Extension node is found in Computer Configuration ➤ Preferences ➤ Control Panel Settings ➤ Devices and User Configuration ➤ Preferences ➤ Control Panel Settings ➤ Devices.

The original way works for only Windows Vista. The new way works for all operating systems.

However, the two technologies work fundamentally differently. The original technology's job is to prevent users from installing drivers for new hardware. So when you restrict a specific device from your Windows Vista machines, the driver is actually blocked from being installed. And this strategy works great if the device is unplugged and plugged back in a lot because during the next check, it will block the device. So, it works well for things like USB memory sticks and other things that are unplugged and plugged back in. However, the original technology didn't do such a hot job on devices that were already installed on the machine, such as CD-ROMs, SCSI cards, and scanners. Those device drivers are already installed, and you don't usually unplug them and put them back in. So the driver isn't ever rechecked.

The Devices Extension technology works differently. Its job is to disable the actual device or port, not prevent the driver from loading. So at first blush it would seem like the Devices Extension is the way to go. Except there are two flaws with GPPE Devices:

- With the Devices Extension, you cannot dictate a specific piece of hardware that you don't already have on your management station. So if you're looking to just ban 30GB color video iPods, you have to actually track one down and get it hooked into your management station so you can restrict that specific device type. If you can't find one, you can restrict an entire class that links to that, such as USB ports.

- Because it only disables the device (and doesn't prevent the device driver from installing), any user with appropriate rights can simply re-enable the device, as seen in Figure 10.9. However, regular users don't have access to this ability; so be sure to test this in your environment to see if it is good fit.

FIGURE 10.9 If the Devices extension has disabled a device, any user with rights can re-enable it.

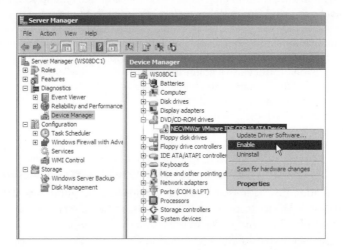

The original technology lets you specify GUIDs of specific hardware IDs. So all you need is to locate the hardware ID of the device you're after and plunk it into the policy setting and you're golden. Moreover, the original Group Policy settings genuinely prevent the drivers from loading, so there's no way they can just re-enable a device if the drivers aren't even installed.

So, which one do you use where? Here's my advice:

- Use the Group Policy Device Installation settings when you have all Windows Vista or Windows Server 2008 machines. Preventing the driver is a better way to go overall. And, because you always use the Hardware ID when implementing the setting, you can be as specific or generic as you want.

- Use the Devices Extension settings when you have anything other than Windows Vista (like Windows XP). Sure, it's not as industrial strength as preventing the driver from loading, but most users won't know to go around it anyway (and if they don't have rights to, this isn't a problem anyway).

- You might want to use Devices Extension with Windows Vista machines *anyway*, because don't forget, the Group Policy Device Installation really only works when devices are removed and reintroduced. Devices Extension works great with devices when they're already used with the machine, such as CD-ROMs and SCSI cards, and so on. But again, it doesn't prevent users with rights from simply enabling these devices if they want to.

- Finally, in my testing, Devices Extension worked perfectly when I used Computer Configuration ➢ Preferences ➢ Control Panel Settings ➢ Devices. I restricted the hardware and did a `gpupdate` command, and my hardware was disabled. However, when I did the same thing using User Configuration ➢ Preferences ➢ Control Panel Settings ➢ Devices and restricted the same hardware, it didn't always take effect right away.

For more on the Devices preference extension vs. Group Policy Device Installation settings, be sure to check out Chapter 9 of the companion book, *Creating the Secure Managed Desktop*, where we have additional information on both solutions.

Group Policy Start Menu Policy Settings vs. Start Menu Preference Extension

The original Group Policy Start Menu policy settings are in User Configuration ➢ Administrative Templates ➢ Start Menu and Taskbar.

The Start Menu extension is located within User Configuration ➢ Preferences ➢ Control Panel Settings ➢ Start Menu.

While there is a lot of overlap, we need to revisit the idea of policy versus preference. Since a policy is going to actually restrict the operating system (and force the user to accept the change), the policy settings can be heavy handed. Heck, that may be just what you want.

On the other hand, the Start Menu extension settings are preferences, which means that they're more like suggestions for the user. So, if the user doesn't like your Start Menu preference settings, they can just reverse them if they so choose.

So, there's not one unified answer about which one you would always use.

Choose the Group Policy Start Menu policy settings when you want to guarantee your settings, and use the Start Menu extension settings when you want to set a baseline but permit the user to change them.

It should be noted that this GPPE (heck, all GPPEs) will refresh every 90 minutes or so by default and wipe out their changed settings. But you can change this behavior later using information found in the sections about the Common tab, specifically in the section "Apply Once and Do Not Reapply."

Group Policy Restricted Groups vs. Local Users and Groups Preference Extension

The original Group Policy Restricted Groups is located within Computer Configuration ➢ Policies ➢ Security Settings ➢ Restricted Groups.

The GPPE Local Users and Groups is located within Computer Configuration ≻ Preferences ≻ Control Panel Settings ≻ Local Users and Groups and User Configuration ≻ Preferences ≻ Control Panel Settings ≻ Local Users and Groups.

We checked out Restricted Groups in Chapter 8, "Implementing Security with Group Policy" In that section, we explored how you could affect both domain-based groups and local groups.

However, the Local Users and Groups extension is meant for, well, just local users and groups.

But, Group Policy Restricted Groups does have some downsides. As we saw, its main goal is to strictly control the group membership, which might not be what you're looking to do. While it's possible to use Group Policy Restricted Groups to simply add a user to a group, it's not intuitive and it's a lot of work.

Moreover, the Local Users and Groups extension is on both the user and computer sides (which means it's more flexible), and you can also use it to add a new user account (complete with all account settings) to the computers of your choice. The Local Users and Groups extension can also delete local groups and cherry-pick specific users to delete from groups (super useful if you just want to pluck just one user out of, say, the local Administrators group).

So, the advice is simple:

- If you want to affect domain-based groups (like Backup Operators, Domain Admins, etc.), stick with Group Policy Restricted Groups.

- Use the Local Users and Groups extension for everything else. It's much easier to understand and implement and you'll likely be happier overall.

 You can also use the Local Users and Groups extension to just change the target machines' local Administrator password. Sweeeeet!

How Does the Group Policy Engine Deal with Overlaps?

Well, there's the short answer, the middle-length answer, and the long answer. Let's go over all of them. (We're old friends now—you knew I would anyway, right?)

The Short Answer: Policy Wins over Preferences

The short answer is that if there's a conflict between a policy setting and a preference setting, the policy setting will win. (So, for instance, items in Computer and User Configuration ≻ Policies should always win over Computer or User Configuration ≻ Preferences.)

Why?

Because only policies actually lock out the user interface of the application they manage (Explorer, Office 2003, etc.).

Preferences don't.

Remember, preferences are suggestions that you can give to the user's application, but the user can usually just wipe them out if they want. (Although, GPPEs will re-apply again at policy refresh time by default.)

Here's a quick example to prove the point. In the example in Figure 10.10, I'm clicking Help to ensure that the Help menu is on the Start Menu for all Windows Vista machines using GPPEs. True, this is the default anyway, but by selecting it here, I'm laying down a preference that is always put on the machine.

However, if I use the policy setting User Configuration ➢ Policies ➢ Administrative Templates ➢ Start Menu and Taskbar ➢ Remove Help menu from Start Menu, as seen in Figure 10.11, the Help option disappears in the Windows Vista Start Menu.

But the general case here is that policies always beat preferences. Rock always beats scissors. Or does it? Can the rock crumble when it's hit by the scissors? Let's continue onward to see at least one interesting case where it doesn't work that way.

FIGURE 10.10   By using GPPEs, you're putting a preference on the client.

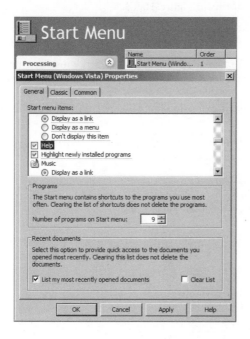

FIGURE 10.11   This policy will positively remove Help from the Start Menu.

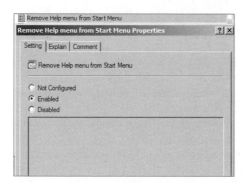

The Middle-Length Answer: Sometimes Preferences Win over Policy

Microsoft's documentation expresses that policy *always* wins over preference. But in fact, that's not always true. Here's an example we can use to prove it:

1. Create a single GPO and link it to a Windows Vista or Windows Server 2008 machine that uses the Internet Settings preference extension to set the Internet Explorer 7 proxy server to 10.1.1.1 with port 8080. You can see a shot of this in Figure 10.12.

2. Then, use Group Policy's Internet Explorer Maintenance to set the proxy to 10.2.2.2 with a port of 8282. You can see a shot of this in Figure 10.13.

3. Then, refresh your client via GPupdate and fire up Internet Explorer 7.

Which home page wins?

The preferences proxy server and port setting (10.1.1.1, port 8080) wins over the policy's 10.2.2.2 with port 8282!

FIGURE 10.12 The Internet Settings extension lets you set preferences for users.

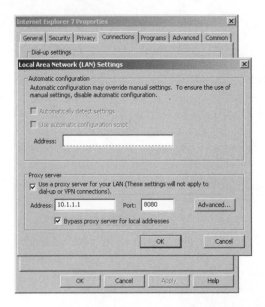

 If you haven't ever run IE 7 because you are usually first prompted to go to www.microsoft.com. But if you check out Tools ≻ Internet Options ≻ General and look at the Home page setting, you'll see the delivered setting.

Uh oh. This seems to break the laws of nature! How can preferences win over policy? Because Internet Explorer Maintenance policy isn't really policy. Indeed, by setting the IE Home page using Internet Explorer Maintenance, the value goes to HKCU\Software\Microsoft\Windows\CurrentVersion\Internet Settings in a value called ProxyServer, as seen in Figure 10.14. And since this is not a place for a true policy, it must actually be a preference.

FIGURE 10.13 Setting the home page via IE Maintenance policy

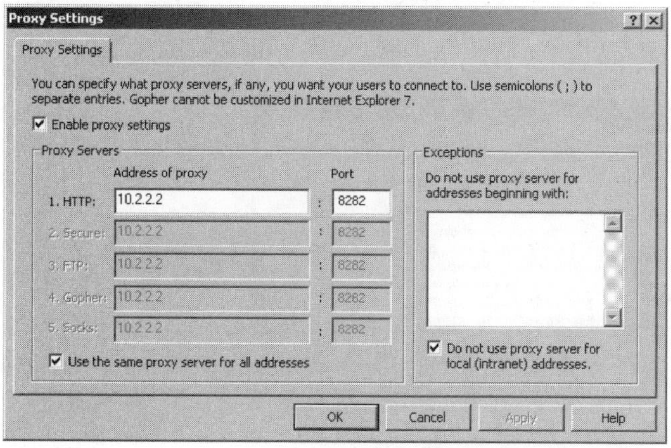

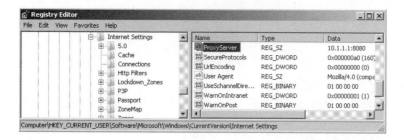

FIGURE 10.14 The value set by both Internet Explorer Maintenance and the IE Group Policy Preferences is the same. The Group Policy Preferences "wins" in this case.

Indeed, the value that's being set is exactly the same for both the IE Group Policy Preference and Internet Explorer Maintenance.

Why does one win over the other? I'll show you the nuances of why in the next section.

But for now, it turns out there is a clever way to attain our goal; which is to force an IE proxy server and lock it down so users cannot change it.

Check out an obscure Administrative Templates policy setting named **Disable changing proxy settings** (located in User Configuration ➢ Policies ➢ Administrative Templates ➢ Windows Components ➢ Internet Explorer). A-ha! That's true policy, so hopefully that will perform some kind of lockdown, as shown in Figure 10.15!

But why then does that Administrative Templates setting named **Disable changing proxy server settings** work in a way the other guys don't? Because IE 7.0 (and 6.0 and 5.0) are all coded to look in the proper policies keys. And if there's a value there that IE recognizes, then IE makes sure to honor that.

And it does.

The end result is that true policy wins. You can see this in Figure 10.16 where the proxy server entry's values are taken from the preferences, but it's locked down via the policy.

FIGURE 10.15 This policy performs a lockdown of IE.

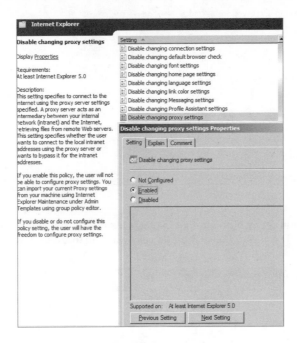

FIGURE 10.16 True policy wins, and the user interface is locked out.

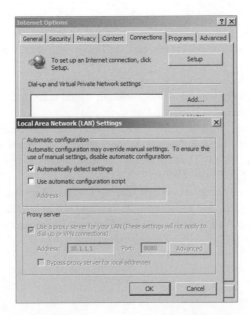

For most people, the medium-length answer will be good-enough.

But you're not most people. You're looking for the most detailed knowledge you can get. So if you're curious to know why the Internet Explorer GPPE won against the Internet Explorer Maintenance Group Policy settings, read on for The Longer Answer.

The Longer Answer: Understanding CSE Timing and Overlap

To get to the bottom of this mystery, we need to understand when Group Policy applies. Recall that the Group Policy system is a last-written-wins technology. So, if you have an overlap between, say, the domain level and the OU level, the default is that the OU level will win because it was written last.

But now things become markedly more confusing. Not only is there overlap between Active Directory levels (site, domain, OU) for some of the features above, there's overlap at the *feature* level, where two or three CSEs compete to write their data last.

Ow.

There is some order in this chaos. But to understand it you'll need an intimate understanding of what happens when the CSEs process (in the foreground and in the background). In short, the CSEs process in the order seen in Figure 10.17. This is a script you can download from `http://tinyurl.com/23xfz3` called `FindGPOsByPolicyExtension.wsf`.

This exposes the same information as if you went to the following Registry key on a machine with the GPPE extensions loaded: `HKEY_LOCAL_MACHINE\SOFTWARE\Microsoft\Windows NT\CurrentVersion\Winlogon\GPExtensions`.

There, you'll see the registrations for all CSEs. The GUID of each CSE dictates the order in which things will process. They'll process alphabetically, by GUID. So, Wireless Group Policy fires off first (that's a classic Group Policy setting), then Group Policy Environment (that's a new GPPE CSE), then Group Policy Local Users and Groups (another new GPPE CSE), then Folder Redirection (a classic Group Policy CSE), and so on.

So on the surface, it appears that if you had a conflict with both classic Group Policy settings and newer GPPE settings, you could just see which one ran last and bank on that setting always "winning."

But that's only true if the two CSEs end up writing to the exact same places.

While this is precisely what we encountered with the Internet Proxy server setting, usually two technologies don't write to exactly the same place. The tie will be broken when an application is coded to look in the proper policies keys. And, if there's a policy setting in those keys, the target application will honor the policy, not the preference.

In our mystery, it's now easy to understand why the Internet Explorer GPPEs (listed as Group Policy Internet Settings) in Figure 10.18 "won" over the IE Maintenance settings (listed as Internet Explorer Zonemapping and Internet Explorer Branding). The new Internet Explorer GPPE CSE (Group Policy Internet Settings) applies *after* the original Internet Explorer CSEs.

But in neither case are we actually applying policy.

We're really just applying preferences—using two different kinds of technology.

We finally got it to work the way we wanted when a true policy was applied, and Internet Explorer saw the policy in the policies keys and acted accordingly.

Whew. All this stuff can give you a headache. This "who will win" stuff is really confusing, and I haven't tested every case. Be sure to test all interactions in a test lab before you roll out settings into production.

FIGURE 10.17 All CSEs process in alphabetical order based upon GUID.

Other Items That Can Affect Group Policy and GPPE Processing

Recall that in Chapter 4 you learned about various policy settings found at Computer Configuration ➤ Policies ➤ Administrative Templates ➤ System ➤ Group Policy that have the configuration option to "Process Even If the Group Policy Objects Have Not Changed." (You can get a refresher back in Chapter 4 in the section "Using Group Policy to Affect Group Policy.")

If this option is turned on for a particular CSE, then that CSE will always try to rewrite its configuration data—upon every single refresh. Again, that's not the default for classic Group Policy, but it is an option on a CSE-by-CSE basis.

However, this same "always try to rewrite configuration data" mantra is held by the GPPE CSEs *by default*, but it can also be set such that the data is laid down once and never rewritten.

So knowing this information, you might have to do a little mental math to figure out which one is going to win if you have conflicting policies *plus* the wildcard settings.

The Group Policy Results reports, as seen in Chapter 2, are going to be helpful in figuring out *which* settings ultimately applied, but they're not going to be helpful in your understanding of *why* the setting ultimately applied.

Hopefully, this section helps you out.

The Lines and Circles and the CRUD Action Modes

By this time, you might have spent a little time plunking around the new Group Policy Preference Extensions (but you haven't really deployed them yet, because you haven't finished the chapter, right?). And, indeed, you can see that they're really, really different than the original Group Policy settings. Many of them (gasp!) kind of look like the thing they actually manage in the Windows user interface! Mon Dieu!

> If you haven't yet tried out GPPEs and want to follow along with these examples, this would be a really good time. That's because you'll learn about both the "lines and circles" and Action modes at the same time. I strongly suggest that you try these settings in a test lab and not in production until you've got a real grip on how everything works.

You'll note that many GPPEs have an action item, and you can set it to Create, Update, Replace, or Delete. This is called the *CRUD method* for short. You'll also notice many GPPEs have these thin solid green lines or thin dashed red lines underneath certain settings. These colorful lines express which settings can possibly affect your client.

We can use the Power Options preference extension in our examples because it has both CRUD ability *and* contains solid green lines for many options. To create a Windows XP power option for your users, dive down to User Configuration ➤ Preferences ➤ Control Panel Settings ➤ Power Options and select New Power Scheme (Windows XP). Alternatively, the same node exists on the computer side if you wanted to play with that. When you do, you'll create a Power Options Preference item and see something similar to what I've got in Figure 10.18.

So both the lines and circles and CRUD action-item features can really bite you in the butt—if you don't know what they mean and how they work. Let's explore those now. We'll tackle the colored lines first, then the CRUD. (That's it, I'm trademarking that phrase: www.GPanswers.com: *We Tackle the CRUD*.) Microsoft doesn't like to call it the CRUD method for obvious reasons. But I do. So that's what I'll be calling it.

The Lines and the Circles

Original Group Policy doesn't have any solid and dashed lines, but many of the new GPPE items do.

So, what's the deal with those solid and dashed lines? It's a way to craft which policy settings within a GPPE you want to affect a client machine.

Here's an example.

Let's say a user has gone in and made some settings they like to use. In our example, we'll assume users on laptops have created their own power schemes for when they're using the batteries on their laptops. And we trust that these laptop users have the scheme they need for their battery because they set it themselves.

However, we want to make sure they save power when they're plugged into the power outlets. No problem! We can use the Power Options extension to define what the Portable/Laptop scheme is and how it uses power. You can see in Figure 10.10 that I've changed the scheme to Portable/Laptop and I'm about ready to make changes.

FIGURE 10.18   Many GPPEs have action items, like this one.

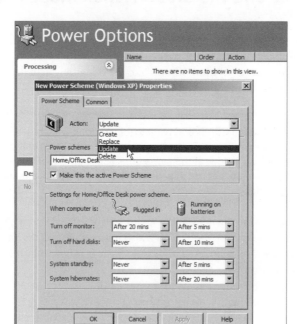

But even though we're changing the "Plugged in" settings, we already said we don't want to disrupt any settings that might have already been made to the "Running on batteries" section of the scheme.

So, what are we going to do? By default *every* setting on this page has a thin green line beneath it. This means that if you update this power scheme, all green underlined settings will be delivered to the client machine. But, ouch! That's exactly what you *don't* want.

You want a way to update *some* of the settings, and not *all* of the settings. You need a way to prevent the processing of some of the settings on the page. To do this, highlight the setting (actually, pull down the pull-down) and then press the F7 key. This will change the thin green line to a thin dashed red line.

Now this setting is exempt from being applied within the edict.

So here's the thing that's really misleading and potentially full of misunderstanding: It doesn't matter what you configure the values to within the settings that now have the red dashed underline. Because your client systems will never, ever pick those values up. This same behavior will hold true for check boxes, fill-in-the-blanks, and radio buttons. If there's a red dashed underline beneath the setting, your clients simply ignore the setting upon refresh.

Microsoft calls this "disabling the policy," but I don't love that term because I don't want to get mixed up in thinking somehow that I'm disabling the functionality the setting provides. By *disabling*, Microsoft really means "disabling the processing of that particular setting."

So, in Figure 10.19, I've selected all the "Running on batteries" settings and disabled them by selecting each setting I wanted to skip the processing for, and then I pressed F7.

FIGURE 10.19   You can enable and disable individual settings using the function keys.

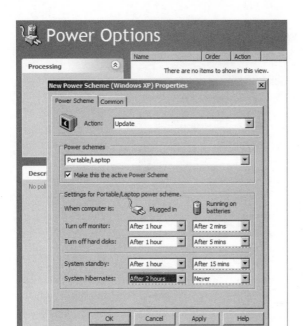

There are other function keys that have meaning in the interface as well. Here are all the function keys and what they do:

- F5: Enables the processing of *all* settings on the page that need to be honored. Useful if you disabled some settings from being honored and want to reset the form.

- F6: Enables the processing of one setting on the page that needs to be honored. Useful if you disabled one setting using F7 and want to change it back. Again, merely changing the value will not reset it to a green underline.

- F7: Disables the processing of one setting on the page. Useful if you want to keep one setting from being updated or changed on the client.

- F8: Disables the processing of all settings. Useful if you want to prevent all the settings on one tab from being honored on the client. Most useful when using the Office Application settings because there are multiple tabs that hold a massive amount of settings. Perhaps you want to disable all settings (which means none will apply) but enable just one tab with two settings.

You'll also see that some settings in the extension have green circles (equivalent to the solid green underline) or red circles a la the "no" sign (which are the equivalent of the thin red dashed line). You can see an example in Figure 10.20, where I've explicitly disabled the processing of two settings within IE 7's Advanced tab. To disable the processing of those items, I simply selected the item and pressed F7. Again, it doesn't matter if the check box is actively checked or not: the value in the check box doesn't get processed if there's a little "no" sign next to it (or it has a red dashed underline).

FIGURE 10.20 The red and green circles in some areas of a preference extension are analogous to the red and green underlines.

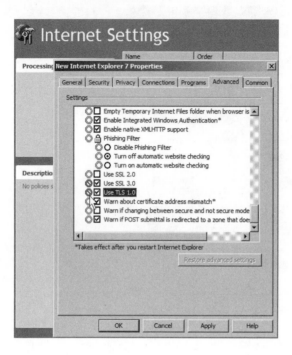

Circles and Lines for the Applications Extension

There are colored circles and lines for the applications within the Applications extension, and they basically act the same as the other colored circles and lines.

However, because each application has *so many* tabs, the Applications extension does a little helpful trick for you. If you visit any tab, you'll see that most settings have a green underline. Now, that means that any setting that has a green underline will have its value placed on the client (check box checked, radio button pushed, etc.).

But, most tabs have lots of stuff that *already* have green lines on most of the tabs! Does that mean that all those settings (even ones you likely don't care about) will be delivered to the client?

Well, *possibly*. There are the three cases to consider. We'll use the Office 2003 properties from the Applications extension as our example.

Case 1: Nothing actually created Let's say you just want to poke around and see what's underneath the hood in the tabs. Of course you'll want to; you're naturally curious.

So you open up a Group Policy Object and create a new Office 2003 Applications Extension item and start poking around.

You can see it has a gaggle of tabs like Assistant, Tools, Web Appearance, and so on. Some tabs have green underlines, and others have red underlines. You know that green-underlined properties are going to be set on the target machine.

Except, you haven't changed anything yet, have you? You're just exploring and poking around.

When you click Cancel, nothing's changed, because the Applications Extension item isn't actually created.

Case 2: Quick visit to existing item, but no changes   Let's say you stumbled across someone else's Office 2003 Applications Extension item, and you wanted to know what was set within the item.

So, you edit the item, and start exploring and poking around *but not changing anything*. You can click the Assistant tab and see what's there or click the Application tab and see what's there. And, you can see what changes were made.

But, again, this is just a quick visit, and you've changed nothing.

When you click Cancel, nothing's changed. That's because you didn't change anything.

Case 3: A visit with a change on any tab   Let's say you stumbled across someone else's Office 2003 Applications Extension item, and you want to know what's set in some tabs (like Assistant), *and* you want to change an item yourself in another tab (like Tools).

So you edit the Applications Extension item and check out the Assistant tab. You can see that in the image below, and you can see that there are no check boxes and no other values have been changed by the previous admin. You do see how there are green lines underneath the values, however.

Now you visit the tab you really need to make changes on—the Tools tab—and you click in one place, say, the "Menus show recently used commands first" check box, as seen in the second screen shot.

Here's the big warning: Because you initially clicked on a tab (Assistant) and that tab has colored settings, then you visited a different tab (Tools) to make a change, all the green underlined settings as now specified on the Assistant tab *will be set* (as well as all the settings in Tools, because they're all green too!).

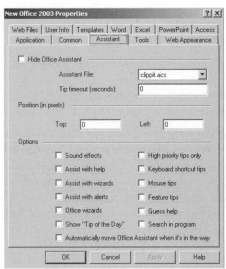

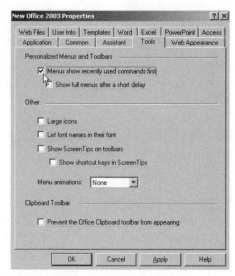

This is very counterintuitive because, well, you didn't make any settings changes to Assistant! You just visited one tab but made your changes in another tab.

But it doesn't matter. In this case, just looking at the tab (then making changes anywhere) does the damage.

The rule is simple: If you visit a tab (and the tab has green underlines) and you make any changes anywhere within the preference item, any tabs you visited will change the properties of their green underlined values.

The CRUD Method: Create, Replace, Update, or Delete

Let's continue with our power scheme for XP example as we work through the next area: the CRUD method.

CRUD stands for Create, Replace, Update, or Delete. You'll notice these settings in the Action drop-down of many extensions, like the Power Scheme extension seen in Figure 10.21.

Here's what happens when an action mode is chosen:

Create Create the setting, but only if it does not already exist. Check out Figure 10.21, where I'm creating a new power scheme for my whole company. Selecting Replace or Update (next options) wouldn't make sense because I'm not trying to modify an existing scheme. Only Create makes sense, because the whole scheme doesn't yet exist.

Replace Delete the setting if it already exists. Then push down new settings. For this, the Power Options preference extension, the whole scheme "Our New Companywide Scheme" would be deleted. Then it would be re-created from scratch. A useful scenario might be after some company-wide power scheme was defined but perhaps defined wholly incorrectly. In this case, choosing Replace would delete *any* settings if they exist. Then, you can reconfigure the GPO with exactly the settings you want to manage (and get it right this time).

Update (Default)   This is the default action. This will create any new settings if they don't exist on the client. And, if any settings do exist on the client, those with thin green underlines will also be updated with the values in the settings.

Delete   Delete the settings. In our example, Delete would delete the whole scheme. Poof.

Use this CRUD action item with caution. You can delete all sorts of things you wish you hadn't: power schemes, drive mappings, the local Administrators group, and more.

So really watch out, and especially test this action before you implement.

There is also a Migrate action, but it's available only for the Outlook profile section inside Applications. Migrate is the same as Update. Except if the profile doesn't exist, it won't create it.

FIGURE 10.21   You use Create to dictate settings that you've never dictated before.

For many GPPEs, you won't see the Action drop-down. In this case, that means there is only one way for these settings to work. It's usually Update.

Common Tab

If you notice back in some of the figures in this chapter, there's a tab that keeps showing up over and over again. It's called the Common tab, and it's full of many of the superpowers the GPPEs provide.

If you click on any Common tab, you'll see that they all have exactly the same options, as follows:

- Stop processing items in this extension if an error occurs
- Run in logged-on user's security context (user policy option)
- Remove this item when it is no longer applied
- Apply once and do not reapply
- Item-level targeting

You can see the Common tab in Figure 10.22, with a little extra note when one of the items is selected. (We'll get to that note in this section as well.)

The idea is that each and every Group Policy preference you make can choose to leverage one or more of these options. Let's examine each of these items now in this section.

FIGURE 10.22   Be super, extra careful when you select the "Remove this item when it is no longer applied" option in the Common tab.

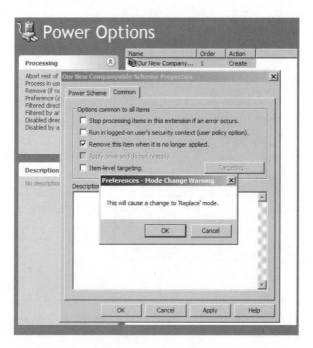

"Stop Processing Items in This Extension If an Error Occurs"

We'll start out with the least-used item of the bunch. The idea here is that if, when you're plunking down multiple preference items (within the same extension), there's a problem, then stop when the system encounters that problem. One situation where this might be helpful is when you use the Files extension. Perhaps you didn't want any files to be copied if, for some reason, the source file suddenly didn't exist. So, as soon as the GPPE engine realized one source file wasn't available, the whole Files preference extension CSE would stop. Other GPPE CSEs, like Drive Maps, Power Options, and Printers would keep on chuggin'.

Again, this isn't the most-used option in the bunch.

"Run In Logged-on User's Security Context (User Policy Option)"

By default, the Group Policy engine runs all commands as SYSTEM, even though it's the user who's really logged in. This is awesome because it means you have some crazy superpowers, like the ability to zap any Registry key to anywhere in the Registry, restrict hardware regardless of who is logged on, and schedule tasks to run *right now*, even if no one is logged in.

There might be a time when you want to use this setting, but in my experience the times are few and far between. One example would be if you want to copy files in the user context, and not the SYSTEM context.

There might be other times where GPPEs just don't seem to take effect. One quick GPPE troubleshooting tip is to flip this setting on within the Common tab. There might be some occasion when trying to perform the action as the SYSTEM doesn't make the magic happen but performing the same action as the logged-in user does.

The other main use for this setting comes with the use of environment variables, which we'll talk about in the next section, so hang tight.

Here are some quick notes about some behaviors of this policy:

- Note that this setting is grayed out when dealing with GPPEs on the computer side, and the behavior is then to *always* use the SYSTEM account.

- Drive Mappings and printers (network printers and TCP/IP printers only) ignore this setting. They *always* use the user context, so checking this check box here shouldn't produce any discernable effect. Note that new drive mappings don't take effect until the next logon and aren't related to this discussion.

"Remove This Item When It Is No Longer Applied"

This is my favorite option because it's full of interesting opportunities, behaviors, and pitfalls. You can see in Figure 10.22, when you click on "Remove this item when it is no longer applied," you'll immediately get a pop-up saying, "This will cause a change to 'Replace' mode." If you click back over to, say, the Power Scheme tab (or whatever tab your GPPE uses that has a CRUD action item), you'll see that the action has automatically been set to Replace and is grayed out to stay that way.

Even though it sets it to Replace mode, you can think of this setting as Delete, and not Replace. Heck, Delete isn't strong enough, really. Think of it as Nuke.

That's because it will nuke the settings if the preference goes out of the scope of management. If you'll recall from Chapter 4, a scope change can happen when any of the following are true:

- Group Policy security filters are used and the user/computer is filtered out (see Chapter 2).

- The Group Policy is deleted.

- The Group Policy is unlinked.

- The Group Policy's link is disabled.

- The preference is deleted.

- WMI filter evaluates to false.

- And now, as we'll learn a little later, if the Item-Level Targeting (ILT) evaluates to false.

If any of these things happens, the target item is Nuked. Let's work through an example with one of my favorites, the Registry extension.

Finding a Value to Change with the Registry Extension

In this example, we're going to change the DoubleClickSpeed entry for all users in the **Human Resources** OU. That includes Sol Rosenberg and everyone else who's logged on. (Again, this is a working example to illustrate a point.)

In Figure 10.23, you can see the Mouse properties on the right and the underlying Registry entry HKEY_CURRENT_USER\Control Panel\Mouse\DoubleClickSpeed and its value of 500. If you move the Mouse properties slider to the right by two notches, the result is 340. Knowing this tidbit, if we use the Registry extension to dictate the DoubleClickSpeed value of 340, we'll be forcing our users to double-click slightly faster.

FIGURE 10.23   We can figure out how the DoubleClickSpeed value works by playing with Explorer.

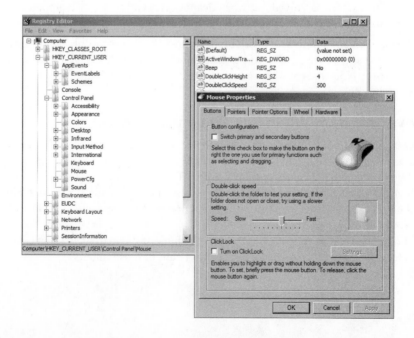

Using the Registry Preference Extension to Dictate the Setting to the Human Resources Users OU

Create and link a GPO over **Human Resources Users** OU. Then edit the GPO and dive into User Configuration ➤ Preferences ➤ Windows Settings ➤ Registry. Click New ➤ Registry Item.

- For Action, make sure Update is selected.
- For Hive, make sure you've chosen HKEY_CURRENT_USER.
- For Key Path, make sure you've selected (or typed in) Control Panel\Mouse.
- For Value name, make sure DoubleClickSpeed is entered (you can leave the Default check box unchecked).
- For Value type, make sure REG_SZ is selected.
- For Value data, enter in 340 (the value we know we want to set).

You can see all of this in Figure 10.24.

Testing the Delivery of Our Settings

At this point, log on as Sol Rosenberg to any machine, then check the double-click speed. You can check the slider in the Control Panel Mouse applet, but an even better check is running REGEDIT. Then dive down into HKEY_CURRENT_USER\Control Panel\Mouse and see if DoubleClickSpeed is set to 340.

FIGURE 10.24   We can dictate specific settings using the Registry CSE.

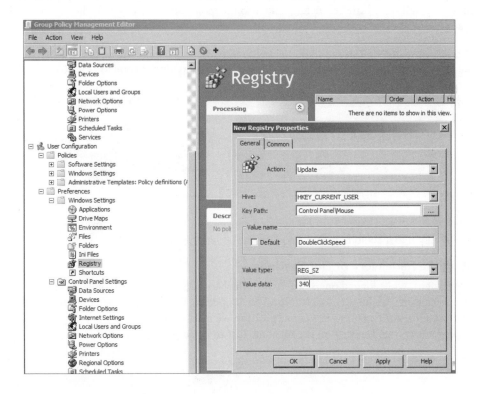

Testing the Default Group Policy Preference Extensions Behavior

At this point, move Sol Rosenberg's account from **Human Resources Users** OU to the **Nurses** OU. (Don't worry, when we're done, we'll move him back.)

Log off, and log back on.

Then run the Registry editor (REGEDIT) and dive down into HKEY_CURRENT_USER\Control Panel\Mouse. What happened to the DoubleClickSpeed settings? Answer: Nothing. They stay put because the Group Policy Preference Extensions' default behavior is to maintain, or tattoo the Registry, even if the user falls out of the scope of management.

Log off as Sol.

Resetting for Our Next Test

At this point, move Sol Rosenberg's account from the **Nurses** OU back to the **Human Resources Users** OU.

Make sure you're logged off as Sol Rosenberg from the target computer.

Now, we're going to see what happens if we change the default behavior.

Turning on "Remove This Item When It Is No Longer Applied"

Now select the Common tab and select "Remove this item when it is no longer applied." You should get a pop-up box saying the mode has been changed to Nuke, er, Replace.

Back on the General tab, you should see that Replace is on, and grayed out so it cannot be changed. Click OK to close the properties page. Now, before we continue, it should be noted that there is a signal of the (potential) devastation to come. If you look at the line item that's produced, you'll see a little red triangle next to the name showing you that the system is in Replace mode, shown in Figure 10.25.

FIGURE 10.25   The red triangle next to the preference item shows we're in Replace mode (and also possibly in "Remove this item when it is no longer applied" mode).

Nothing "bad" will happen until something happens with the scope. Let's examine the normal course of action that could happen up to (and including) that point.

Testing the Redelivery of Our Settings

Just for laughs, while logged on as Sol, reopen the Mouse applet in Control Panel and jam the double-click slider all the way to left. Now run GPupdate. Close and reopen the Mouse applet.

Did the slide jump back to the faster position we dictated?

Indeed, check the Registry on the machine just to be sure if you're not.

That's good: The default behavior of GPPEs is working for you. That is, the default is that it will always reapply the settings, even if someone changes a setting by hand on the target computer.

Seeing the Result of "Remove This Item When It Is No Longer Applied"

At this point, move Sol Rosenberg's account from the **Human Resources** Users OU to the **Nurses** OU a second time.

Log off, and log back on. Then open re-run the Registry editor tool (REGEDIT) and dive down into HKEY_CURRENT_USER\Control Panel\Mouse.

And make a discovery.

That is, the whole DoubleClickSpeed value has been deleted!

You can see this in Figure 10.26. Or, rather, you *can't* see this in Figure 10.26, because it's GONE.

FIGURE 10.26   Once the "Remove this item when it is no longer applied" setting is checked, the DoubleClickSpeed Registry key is deleted. But, thankfully, the Mouse application doesn't seem to mind very much.

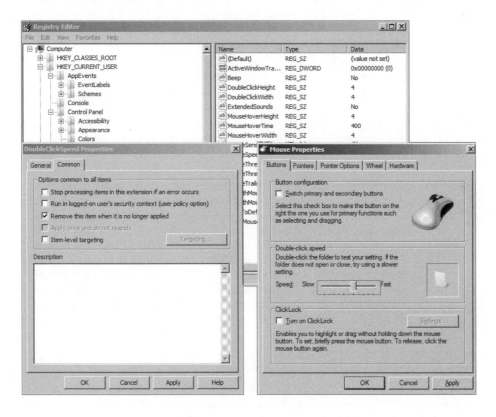

This isn't likely what you expected. You expected it to revert back to 500 or go to 0 or do something else predictable.

Right. Well, it doesn't.

By selecting "Remove this item when it is no longer applied," you Nuke the entry. It literally deletes the whole thing you're working on—in this case, a Registry setting. In other cases, power schemes, local users and groups, data sources, and other things you likely really don't want to *delete*.

Putting the World Right Again for Sol

Put Sol's account back into **Human Resources Users** OU.

Then log out and log back in. You should see the DoubleClickSpeed pop back in place with the value of 340.

Final Thoughts about "Remove This Item When It Is No Longer Applied"

Before we move on to the next topic, I do have some final thoughts about "Remove this item when it is no longer applied."

First, in our DoubleClickSpeed example, we didn't really do any "harm" to the system by deleting the `DoubleClickSpeed` key. In our examples, double-clicking will continue to work because the people who coded Explorer's mouse double-click feature must have said, "Well, if the `DoubleClickSpeed` key suddenly goes missing, we'll assume it's, oh, I dunno, how's 500?" And it keeps on working.

But that's because we're lucky!

If this was some Registry key to a custom application, you could have damaged the application, that's for sure.

Next, it isn't the Replace CRUD action that does this deed. It's positively the "Remove this item when it is no longer applied" check box. Again, think of this as Nuke. But the action item shows Replace, which is kind of misleading.

Additionally, if you want to plunk down Registry values that really don't tattoo and will put back a known value after they fall out of the scope of management, check out PolicyPak Software's PolicyPak. Again, not to sound like a commercial here, but it is the software's claim to fame. It competes with the Registry preference extension and Applications preference extension. Specifically, it will plunk down Registry values and then really, truly, and dearly clean up those values when they fall out of the scope of management, never tattooing the Registry, and never deleting the underlying Registry value. Check it out at www.PolicyPak.com.

"Apply Once and Do Not Reapply"

This is the other setting in the Common tab that I like a lot. This setting does just what it says: it will plunk down the setting, then never reapply. This is good, and it's bad.

On the one hand, you're able to set a true preference for the user. That is, you're suggesting this setting for them, so it's laid down exactly one time. If they want to change it, they can, and your suggestion never "plows down" back on top of their selected setting.

On the other hand, you might have the occasion to want to perform a baseline push of certain values to the system again. And in that case, not even running gpupdate /force will reset the values. Again, the edit is called "Apply once and do not reapply."

> Note that PolicyPak Software has a setting that can overcome this limitation. If you check out PolicyPak at www.PolicyPak.com, be sure to try the setting titled "Treat this setting as a preference (do not reapply, but reapply at GPupdate /force." Additionally, the setting "Revert this policy setting to the default value when it is no longer applied" is another step ahead of the Registry preference extension and Applications preference extension.

Targeting Your Preference Items

The final superpower within the Common tab is titled Item-level targeting, or ILT for short. ILT provides a new way to indicate exactly when a specific preference item should apply. ILT is almost like WMI filters (which we explored in Chapter 5). But ILTs have some advantages over WMI filters:

- They're easier to set up and use immediately. You'll fall in love with the GUI interface of ILTs.

- You can do nested ANDs, ORs, and NOTs within ILTs, making them immediately more flexible than WMI filters.

- They evaluate faster when run on the client. WMI filters really cut into the machine's heart to see what's going on to evaluate the query. ILTs use code within the GPPE CSE to perform the query, so they're much faster. In fact, there's hardly any processing penalty to using them at all.

The categories can be seen in Figure 10.27.

There are all sorts of query-able items, such as amount of RAM, CPU speed, available disk space, and more.

Note that one category within ILTs *is* WMI queries. So, you can leverage WMI queries within ILTs if you wanted to do something that wasn't part of the native ILT queries. The downside is that item-level targeting is only for GPPEs and is simply not available for the other areas of original Group Policy.

How Are Filters Evaluated?

One question you might be asking yourself is, "In what context is the filter evaluated?"

In some cases, the logged-in user might not have rights to determine if a filter is true or not. Likewise, the computer (SYSTEM) might have too much power and inadvertently say that something is true when really it's not true for the user at all.

Thankfully, these scenarios have been thought out. In short, here's what happens:

- Most ILTs are checked in the SYSTEM context. Because the SYSTEM has more rights than the user, this is desirable.

- However, some items should only be determined from the viewpoint of the logged-on user. Here's the breakdown:

  - Security Group Filter: Runs from the point of view of the logged-in user (except if you're checking to see if the computer is a member of a group)

  - Language Filter: Runs from the point of view of the logged-in user

  - File Match Filter: Runs from the point of view of the logged-in user; then, if that fails, runs in the SYSTEM context as a second try

FIGURE 10.27 Item-level targeting lets you specify when specific preferences apply.

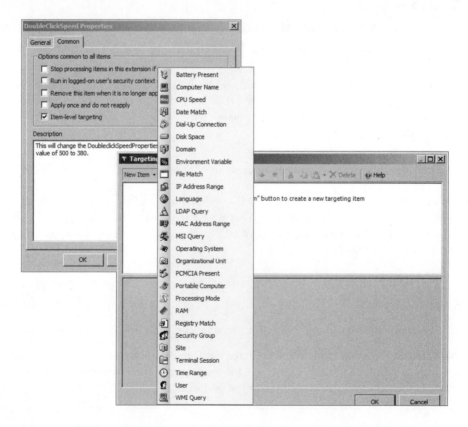

The Targeting Editor

You'll craft your query in the Targeting Editor.

By default, all items are ANDed together. In this way, ILTs can be "banded together" to produce queries where multiple items need to be true for the action to take place.

In Figure 10.28, I've strung together a query to really and truly verify that DogFood-Maker 6.0 is installed on the machine—I'm checking that the MSI product code has been installed on the machine and also that the HKLM\Software\DogFoodMaker hive has a key called Ruff with a value of 6.

FIGURE 10.28   You can string together items in the Targeting Editor with AND.

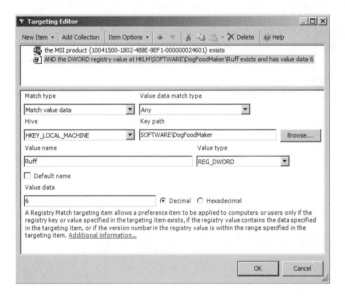

Adding Additional Collections

Alternatively, if you want to do something fancier, you can select the Add Collection button and created nested groups of ILTs. For instance, you can have an ILT apply only when it hits User1 or the Administrator account.

To do that, you'd create two collections (be sure they're at the same level; you don't want to nest one within the other). Then, you'd highlight the second collection and pick Item Options (next to Add Collection) and select OR. Now your second collection is OR.

Now, add your conditions in the first block and in the second block, and they'll be ORed together, as seen in Figure 10.29.

Other Targeting Editor Tricks

You can usually drag and drop things around without thinking about it too much. The ILT editor was rewritten heavily (and heck, renamed!) since the acquisition of the product from DesktopStandard, and they really did a smashing job of cleaning it up and making it easier to use overall.

Be sure to experiment with the cut, paste, and copy items. You'll be able to rapid-fire-create ILTs once you play with these abilities a little more. Additionally, you can add a label to a collection. That way, if you have a complex collection that you're querying for, others can figure out precisely what you were doing. You can see an example of a collection query label in Figure 10.30.

The one thing I really wanted in the ILT editor, I didn't get. I wanted a way to export the potentially rich target I created and import it into another GPPE. But I can't do that. There is no Export/Import feature.

FIGURE 10.29   Using OR, you can ensure that your wishes take place when certain conditions are true.

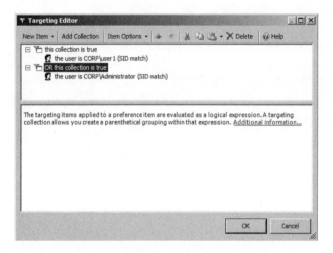

FIGURE 10.30   You can label a Targeting Item.

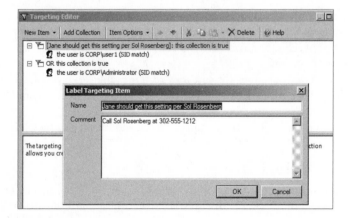

However, a little later, in the section "Drag (or Paste) a Group Policy Preference Extension to a File," you'll learn how to see the underlying XML code for a GPPE. Inside that XML code is also the ILT information for that GPPE.

With that in mind, you could rip out the well-defined Filter section from one preference item and smash it into the preference item (of another type) you needed. Then, drag and drop the XML file back onto the GPPE Editor.

Description Field

This is the final Common entry regarding preference items. Here you're able to put in a simple description of what you're trying to do and notes about ILTs (if any.)

It's within the Common tab, as seen in Figure 10.31.

FIGURE 10.31   Descriptions are GPPE item specific and only appear in the Description field on the left when you finally press OK (not Apply).

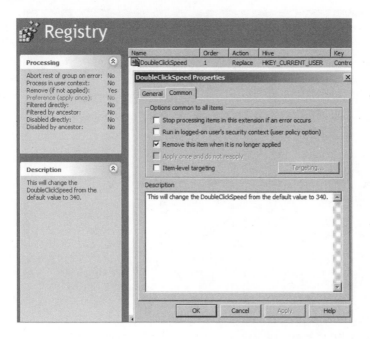

Group Policy Preference Extensions Tips, Tricks, and Troubleshooting

Now that we're past the essentials, we're ready to move on to some very useful tips and tricks to make us more productive with GPPEs. And, of course, if something goes wrong, we'll need to troubleshoot our GPPE universe as well.

Quick Copy, Drag and Drop, Cut and Paste, and Sharing of Settings

I know this heading sounds like a lot of stuff, but it's really only one big thought. That is, the interface which allows you to create GPPE items allows you to basically treat every setting like an object. I like to call this place the "GPPE editor" because it's the place within the Group Policy Management editor that you create GPPE items. So, you can do some neat tricks.

Quick Copy/Paste

In Figure 10.32, I'm about to make a copy of the DoubleClickSpeed Registry punch we dictated in a previous exercise.

FIGURE 10.32   You can right-click a preference item and select Copy (to paste it later).

I can now do several things with this copy.

Right below the current entry, right-click and select Paste from the drop-down menu. You'll see that a copy of the DoubleClickSpeed Registry punch is placed right next to it. We'll explore this in the very next section, so hang tight.

Drag (or Paste) a Group Policy Preference Extension to a File

Go to your Windows Desktop and click Paste. (Yes, leave the Group Policy Management Editor, find the Windows Desktop, right-click, and select Paste.) A new document is automatically created with an XML extension. Alternatively, you can drag the line item from the GPPE editor right to the Desktop or a folder to create a file out of the contents.

You can see my document's icon and the contents of the document within Figure 10.33.

FIGURE 10.33   Each preference item is exportable as a .XML file.

You can see that the file contains the Registry settings as well as the filters built in as one neat little package.

Sharing Your Wisdom with Others (Especially on *www.GPanswers.com*)

At this point, you can email this little gift of a file to a friend and they can drag and drop it into their own Registry Extension preference item list. In Figure 10.34, you can see what your other Administrator friend would do when he drags the corresponding file into his Registry preference extension item list.

FIGURE 10.34   You can share preference items with friends. Have your friend just drag and drop the XML right into the category as a preference item.

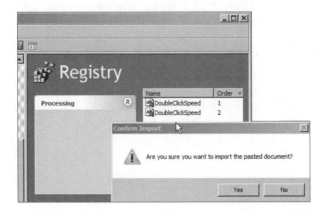

I like this idea of sharing wisdom so much that I'm dedicating a portion of my www.GPanswers.com website to it. If you have a cool tip (for any area of the Group Policy Preference Extensions), just get it into a file and find the "Group Policy Preference Extensions Solutions Repository" on www.GPanswers.com. Then, you'll be able to upload your file, tell us a little about your solution, and share it with the world!

If you're going to share a GPPE XML file with other people outside of your company, be careful to send only XML files that don't have any sensitive information contained within them!

Multiple Preference Items at a Level

So an exercise or two ago, we copied our DoubleClickSpeed Registry entry. You can see this in Figure 10.23. But why would you want to do such a thing?

To be crafty, that's why!

Let's examine how to take advantage of this neat ability.

Filtering Each Preference Item at a Level

If you copy a preference item (which essentially makes two identical items at the same level), you can put a filter on one preference item and another filter on the other preference item. Of course, you'd change each item to act sliiightly differently, so that one item hits one set of users and the other item hits another set of users.

For instance, you could say Administrators get a DoubleClickSpeed of 300, but Users get a DoubleClickSpeed of 480. Just create two preference items (each changed slightly, and each with a different filter).

Again, a silly example, but you get the idea.

But, here's the kicker. GPPEs process multiple preference items at a level by "counting up sequentially." So, if you had three preference items within the same extension, number 1 would be written first, number 2 would be written next, and number 3 would be written last.

If there was a conflict between any levels, the highest number would win.

Changing the Order of Preference Items at a Level

You change the order of the levels by clicking on the preference item you want and then using the menu bar's Up/Down arrows to change the order. So, for instance, in Figure 10.35, you can see that there are two preference items within the Start Menu extension. If you wanted to change the order, click on one of them, then select the menu bar's Up/Down arrows (seen in Figure 10.36). You can also see the full menu bar in Figure 10.36, which we'll refer to throughout the rest of this section.

This business of counting up sequentially within a GPPE extension is a little maddening to a Group Policy guy like me. Especially because I usually have to explain how GPOs *themselves* are processed counting *down* sequentially. See the section "Raising or Lowering the Precedence of Multiple Group Policy Objects" in Chapter 2 for more information.

FIGURE 10.35 You can have multiple, conflicting preference items inside a GPO.

FIGURE 10.36 The menu bar for Group Policy Preference Extensions

Renaming Preference Items at a Level

Since you copied DoubleClickSpeed, you now have what looks like two identical entries. But you don't. You have one filtered one way and another filtered another way. Why not right-click over each entry and rename it, being specific about what each entry now does, as shown in Figure 10.37.

FIGURE 10.37 If preference items within a GPO might potentially conflict, it's easiest to just rename them.

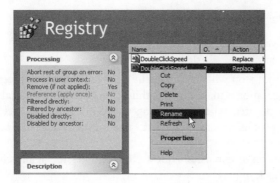

This will come in handy a little later when you learn about preference items and reporting.

Temporarily Disabling a Single Preference Item or Extension Root

Recall that Group Policy has the ability to remove the Link Enabled status from a GPO. When this happens, the GPO configuration stays in place, but it removes the GPO from processing (and usually reverts the setting back to an original setting).

GPPEs have a similar ability, and it can be done at the preference item level or the GPPE extension root level *within* a GPO.

To do this, you can click on a preference item (like DoubleClickSpeed) and click on the red No icon on the menu bar.

Or, if you want to do this on a GPPE extension root level, click on the Extension root, say the Registry extension, and click the No icon on the menu bar.

In Figure 10.38, I've disabled one preference item within the Registry extension, but I've also disabled the whole Registry extension—right at the root as well, just for show.

FIGURE 10.38 Both the first DoubleClickSpeed preference item and the Registry preference extension root are disabled.

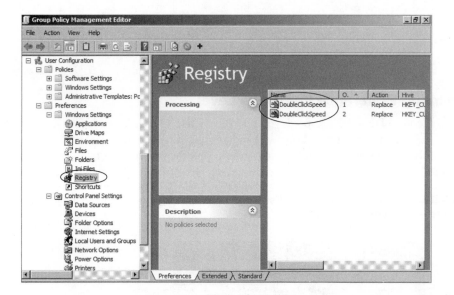

When you select the No icon, that icon will automatically change from red to green.

When either happens, the configuration is maintained within the extension, but it's taken out of processing. And, if the "Remove this item when it is no longer applied" setting is checked, the preference item falls out of the scope of management, so that value is usually deleted. So, again, be careful in using that setting.

To restore the preference extension or extension root itself for processing again, click the green No icon, which will put it back in play.

Environment Variables

One of the other superpowers the GPPEs have is this idea of built-in, addressable variables in addition to the standard environment variables that Windows automatically sets, or ones that you set with logon scripts, or ones that you set using the Environment extension.

The idea is that GPPEs bring these *additional* variables that allow you to specify the relative locations of many, many key items.

Here's a quick example (and there are about a zillion uses, so it was hard to just pick one). Imagine you had a file on a file share, named `Everyone.txt`, and you wanted to get it on everyone's machine. But you didn't just want to copy that file directly, no no! You wanted to rename it in the process to the name of the computer and *also* put it on everyone's Desktop folder. How could you possibly do that? Would you have to create a new GPO for everyone in the company!

Heck no!

With environment variables, you can do this in one step. In Figure 10.30, I've used the Files Preference extension to specify the source file as `\\dc01\share\everyone.txt`. But for Destination File, before typing anything in, I hit the F3 key. When you do, the internal environment variables pop up as a reference and you can select them to be automatically entered for you. For this example, I'll use one internal environment variable (`%CommonDesktopDir%`) and one regular Windows environment variable (`%ComputerName%`).

So, in Figure 10.39, I've specified `%CommonDesktopDir%\%ComputerName%.txt` as the destination filename.

FIGURE 10.39   Hitting F3 when editing a preference item brings up the Select a Variable dialog.

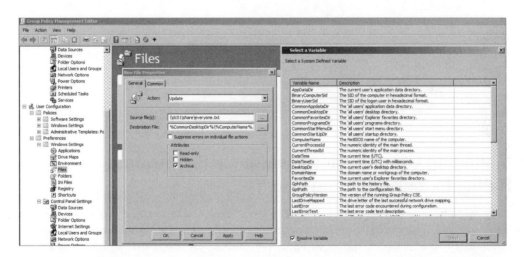

Note the curious Resolve Variable check box when you hit the F3 key, as seen in Figure 10.30. The check box is on, which means variables like `%ComputerName%` resolve to XPPRO1. That's great; this makes sense and meets our goal.

However, strangely, there's also the ability to jam in the words that make up the variables— as variables! So, imagine you had an .INI file you wanted to change, but inside the .INI file, you wanted to jam in an actual variable. For instance, in DogFoodMaker 7.0, you needed to set the `ruffcomputer` property (located within the `[ruffconfig]` section) to actually have the word

%ComputerName% (with percent marks included). You would uncheck the Resolve Variable check box, and what's put into the Property Value field is what's seen in Figure 10.40. That is, the variable name itself is contained within angle brackets (< and >) to signify that the actual variable, %ComputerName%, is jammed into the .INI file.

FIGURE 10.40 It's rare, but you may need to jam in the actual name of a variable, as seen here. Do this by putting angle brackets (< and >) around the variable name.

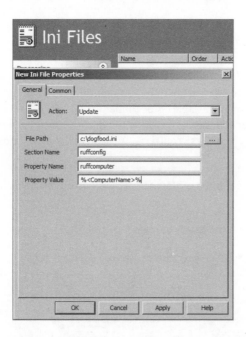

Managing Group Policy Preference Extensions: Hiding Extensions from Use

There might be some times when you'll want to give someone rights to create GPOs but prevent them from utilizing some of the GPPEs. For instance, maybe you didn't want them to be able to manipulate .INI settings or Registry settings. Well, you can take away that power if you want.

There are regular Group Policy settings located at User Configuration ➤ Policies ➤ Administrative Templates ➤ Windows Components ➤ Microsoft Management Console ➤ Group Policy ➤ Preferences that can help you perform the restrictions. You can see these policy settings in Figure 10.41.

The trick is, the Explain text is really awful in these settings. For the ones I've tested, you need to disable the policy setting (yes, disable) to actually prevent the extension from showing.

In Figure 10.41, you can see I've disabled the .INI Files preference extension via its policy setting. In Figure 10.42, you can see the result; the extension to manipulate the .INI files is just—gone (in both the computer and user sides)!

FIGURE 10.41   Use the settings seen here (and select Disable) to prevent the snap-ins from appearing within the MMC.

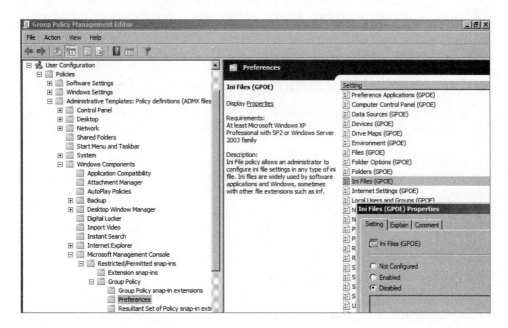

FIGURE 10.42   When admins affected by these policy settings try to create GPOs, the snap-ins are simply hidden.

WARNING   Now, this doesn't mean that GPOs that have any hidden extensions will stop working. It just means that some people (the people affected by these policy settings) cannot manage that part of the world.

Troubleshooting: Reporting, Logging, and Tracing

Sometimes, things don't exactly act as they should. This is normal, because we're not perfect, and the Group Policy Preference Extensions make it easier than ever to do things we might not even really *want* to do.

To that end, we may need to spend some time on troubleshooting the Group Policy Preference Extensions. Here are some quick things to check before you start going crazy and working with detailed logs:

- Before you pull your hair out when you're trying to troubleshoot your clients, the very first question you should ask yourself is, "Do my clients have the Group Policy Preference Extensions installed?" Again, the only client that has it installed by default is Windows Server 2008. You need to download and install the Group Policy Preference Extensions for Windows XP, Windows Vista, and Windows Server 2003.

- Do you have the GPO linked to the correct place (site, domain, OU), and is the computer or user account in the right place?

- Do you have multiple preference items conflicting at the same level?

There are two places to get some dirt about what's going on: The Good Ol' Windows Event log and something new, the Group Policy Preference Extensions Tracing logs.

Importing Group Policy Preference Extensions

In the appendix, you'll learn how to use migration tables to migrate GPOs from one domain to another domain. However, it should be noted that Group Policy Preference Extensions do not seem to honor migration tables. That is, as GPOs that contain preference items are imported, all settings are simply copied straight through, regardless of whether the value is valid in the target domain or not.

Reporting: Settings Tab, GPMC Reporting, and *gpresult*

We have two usual ways of getting Group Policy results data: the Group Policy Results reports and the GPResult command. Let's see how each one responds to the Group Policy Preference Extensions.

The Group Policy Results Reports from the GPMC

In a nutshell, the GPMC settings tab and GPMC HTML reports have all been modified to work with the new GPPEs. The same Group Policy Results and Group Policy Modeling reports you know and love should work just the same with clients that have the Group Policy Preference Extensions installed. There are some differences that need to be accounted for, though. For instance, if more than one preference item is at a level, you can see that within the Settings report of the GPO.

In Figure 10.43, you can see two Start Menu settings that conflicted. Of course, one has to eventually win.

FIGURE 10.43 Group Policy Preference Extensions settings are reflected within the report.

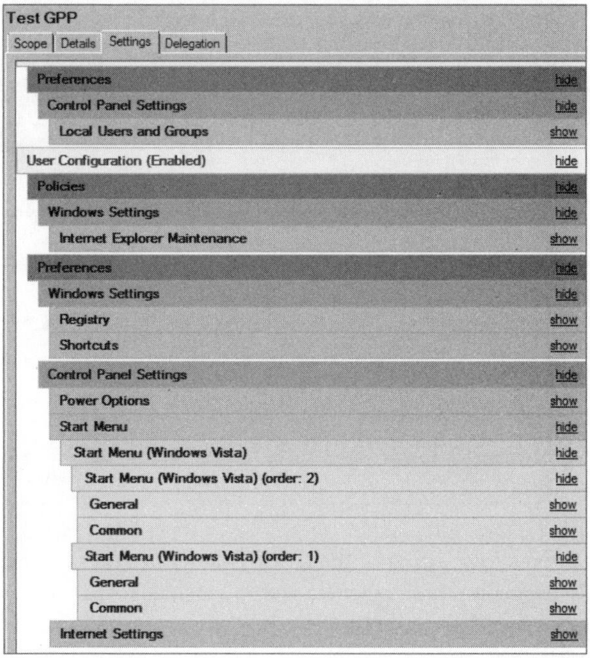

However, when a Group Policy Results report is run, it has to actually figure not only which GPO wins, but also which preference item within a level wins. In Figure 10.44, we can see a Group Policy Results report, and the results are a liiiitle hard to read.

In Figure 10.44, we can see that Test GPP had some "Start Menu (Windows Vista)" settings win on the target machine. That's great. But there's like a billion settings within the Start Menu category. Which ones won? Well, even though the preference items are numbered inside the GPPE interface (remember Figure 10.35 when we talked about the GPPE order?), they're not labeled in the same order within the Group Policy Results reports.

That's a bummer, because that's the kind of thing administrators really want to know: which preference item (within the preference item order) won. But here's a tip. If we had used the rename function to rename a GPPE item, we can easily see which one won because the winning preference item bubbles up to the top by name.

FIGURE 10.44   The winning preference item is the one that bubbles to the top.

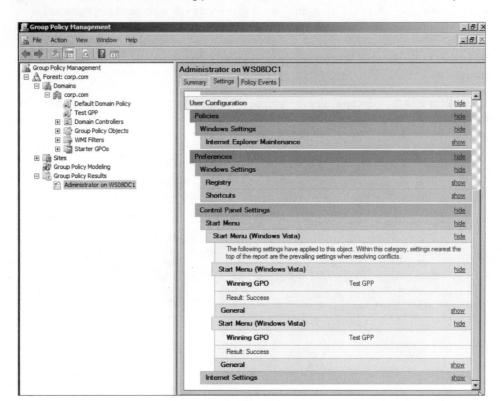

Additionally, there seems to be no reporting of the ILTs. That's not exactly super helpful, as I think I'd like to know why a specific preference item won versus another one. So, again, if a specific ILT was found to be true, there doesn't seem to be any way to discover that from the Group Policy Results reports.

Gpresult.exe

Here, I feel a little let down. I really love the gpresult.exe command line tool. And with it, you can see which GPOs contain GPPEs that apply. But it positively will not show any of the Group Policy Preference Extensions settings.

So, in short, if you want any kind of detailed settings report, you must use the GPMC's Group Policy Results reports as we just saw.

Event Logs

The Windows Application log contains the really bad news about events that the Group Policy Preference Extensions create. In Figure 10.45, we can see that something went wrong on the target machine (WS08DC1) when we attempted to apply Group Policy Shortcuts.

FIGURE 10.45 Group Policy Preference Extensions' bad news can be found in the Application log.

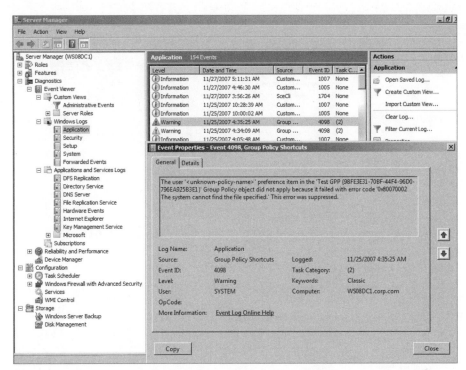

What's interesting is that each and every Group Policy Preference Extension category has its own source, so you can create custom views of the Application log, only showing the source you want (this applies to only Windows Server 2008 and Windows Vista clients). In Figure 10.46, you can see that I'm creating a custom filter where you can select multiple sources (or just one) and show only the errors you want to expose in a single view.

Tracing

In Chapter 4, we talked about the Group Policy operational logs (for Windows Vista and Windows Server 2008) where you can get in-depth information about what's happening with regard to Group Policy. I haven't yet seen any Group Policy Preference Extensions log information ever show up in the Group Policy Operational logs. That's because the Group Policy operational logs are for the processing of the GPOs themselves, not the specific settings *within* the GPO.

And, because the Group Policy Preference Extensions can be also be installed on Windows XP, as well as Windows Server 2003, it wouldn't be a great idea to put detailed Group Policy Preference Extensions logs in a log file *only* for Windows Vista and Windows Server 2008.

FIGURE 10.46   You can create your own Event Log filter to just show the Group Policy Preference Extension that might be having a problem.

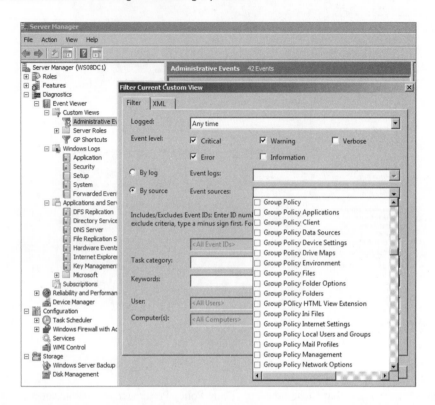

To that end, the Group Policy Preference Extensions have their own detailed logs. The logs are called *traces,* and you turn them on them by enabling specific policy settings within Computer Configuration ➢ Policies ➢ System ➢ Group Policy ➢ Logging and tracing.

You can see the list of policy settings that control Group Policy Preference Extensions in Figure 10.47.

Each Group Policy Preference Extensions log, er, trace, can be set individually. By default they all push information to a shared log for each category.

The shared User log   The idea is that if the Group Policy Preference Extension is on the user side, it will write step-by-step data as to what it's doing within this log. The default location for the shared user log is %COMMONAPPDATA%\GroupPolicy\Preference\Trace\User.log.

The shared Computer log   The idea is that if the Group Policy Preference Extension is on the computer side, it will write step-by-step data as to what it's doing within this log. The default location for the shared user log is %COMMONAPPDATA%\GroupPolicy\Preference\Trace\Computer.log.

FIGURE 10.47 Tracing produces a lot of output. That's why there are two switches to enable it. First, enable the policy setting, and then, select On in the Tracing drop-down or trace logs will not be produced.

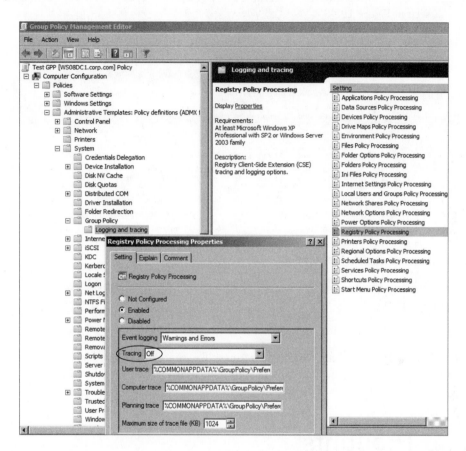

The shared Planning log In ye olden days, when the product was younger (and owned by DesktopStandard), there was no GPMC reports integration. If you wanted to troubleshoot and know what the RSOP was on the client, you needed to run the outmoded RSOP.MSC snap-in on the client system experiencing the problem. Well, those vestiges are still there. You can turn on the Planning log and run RSOP.MSC and see a log generated. There's little reason to do this because you can get reports, as we saw earlier, from GPMC's Group Policy Results reports. The default location for the shared Planning log is %COMMONAPPDATA%\GroupPolicy\Preference\Trace\Planning.log.

The extra trick is that, after you enable the policy setting and ensure that the log files are in a place you can find, you still need to set the logging level, then finally (and here's the kicker) select the drop-down next to Tracing and select On. Yep, that's right. You enabled the policy setting, but that's not good enough. You also need to "double-enable" tracing.

When you do, your log file will appear in C:\ProgramData\GroupPolicy\Preference\ Trace, as seen in Figure 10.48.

FIGURE 10.48 Trace logs can be a bit hairy, but useful.

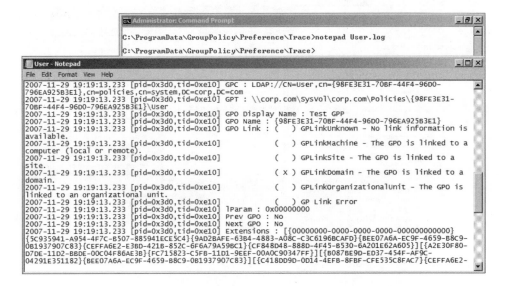

Finally, you might be asking why some settings, like Internet Settings, have both a Computer and a User log when the extension is applicable only on the user side. In short, it shouldn't be there, and it won't do anything.

Final Thoughts

Let's do an ever-so-brief review of the top 10 things we've learned about Group Policy Preference Extensions:

- Management Station Installation: You need a management station that has the Group Policy Preference Extensions loaded. They're built into Windows Server 2008 and available via the RSAT tools for Windows Vista SP1.

- Management Station Installation (part 2): The Applications extension pieces must be downloaded and installed separately on your management station. If you don't install the Applications extension pieces, you won't be able to control items like Office and Outlook. It's a legal thing.

- Client Piece Installation: The client piece is built into Windows Server 2008. There's a download for the Group Policy Preference Extensions for Windows XP (at least) SP2, Windows Vista, and Windows Server 2003 (at least) SP1.

- Group Policy Preference Extensions deliver preferences, where Group Policy (original) delivers policy settings. This usually means that users can undo settings that you deliver via Group Policy Preference Extensions (but not always).

- There is some overlap between Group Policy (original) and Group Policy Preference Extensions. But really, as we analyzed, there is more harmony between the two than overlap.

- Be sure you understand how the red and green lines and circles work in the interface.

- Know your CRUD action modes and what each does. When in doubt, use Update. (When *really* in doubt, try it in a test lab first.)

- The Common tab is available for each preference item you create. Inside this tab are some superpowers like ILT.

- Be super careful using the Common tab element named "Remove this item when it is no longer applied." Remember, it's the equivalent of Nuke.

- Use the Windows Event logs and Group Policy Preference Extensions tracing logs to help you determine if your Group Policy Preference Extensions wishes are being applied or not.

Again, on www.GPanswers.com, my goal is to have a nice way to exchange preference items that you created that are interesting. Because they're just XML files, you can download and then drag and drop them to leverage the knowledge someone else already has. Check out www.GPanswers.com for more information.

Also, if you were an original DesktopStandard PolicyMaker customer, stay tuned on www.GPanswers.com for more information as it happens about how to upgrade from PolicyMaker to the Group Policy Preference Extensions.

## 11

Scripting Group Policy Operations with PowerShell

We've discussed how to perform many of our day-to-day operations using the GPMC. But if we needed to automate those steps, we could be there for a while.

In this chapter, we're going to spend some time discussing how to use PowerShell to document, manage, and interact with Group Policy. PowerShell provides a script interface and an interactive shell that will make day-to-day tasks fun (well, almost fun).

And, for this chapter, we've got a special treat for each little trick we cover. We'll start out handling each task using native PowerShell, but we'll also show you how to do the same tasks using some free snap-ins and PowerShell cmdlets from third-party vendors.

 A cmdlet (pronounced "command-let") is like PowerShell commands in a little, prepackaged snack pack.

While native PowerShell commands are very powerful and can do almost everything we want, the free snap-ins are, well, free, and they make managing Group Policy easier, so we'll definitely want to make use of them.

But wait, there's more. It turns out no fewer than three third-party vendors have seen the Group Policy + scripting light and have designed hooks into the Group Policy system to help with scripting (most via PowerShell). We'll look at those third-party tools as well and see what they have to offer.

This chapter was written by Brandon Shell, PowerShell MVP with Jeremy Moskowitz, Group Policy MVP.

Using PowerShell to Do More with Group Policy

Before we get into heavy lifting with PowerShell, we'll cover some basics to get you up and running. First, we'll talk about installing PowerShell and then discuss the free third-party options available and how to install them.

Then, we'll dive into doing some cool stuff with Group Policy, including automating our documentation and manipulating our GPOs. Next, we'll deal with the sticky business of importing GPOs so we can first utilize them in a test lab before we import them into production.

Preparing for Your PowerShell Experience

PowerShell has some prerequisites, so let's get them out of the way first. You will need at least .NET 2.0, but because there are some classes that act differently in .NET 3.0, we recommend downloading that as well. Although it's unlikely you'll run across a PowerShell script written specifically for .NET 3.0, it is possible, and the script may not act as you intend.

There are different packages for x64 and x86. To install each framework, just download the packages and then run the installers.

Install Type	.NET Framework Version	URL
x86	1.1	http://tinyurl.com/2g5a8
x86	2.0	http://tinyurl.com/wvc3z
x86	3.0	http://tinyurl.com/yjjsra
x64	1.1	http://tinyurl.com/54ore
x64	2.0	http://tinyurl.com/3bqh2e
x64	3.0	http://tinyurl.com/2cpr9f

Installing PowerShell

After you have the .NET Framework versions installed, you're almost there. The next step is to download the appropriate PowerShell package and run the installer.

Fetching and Installing PowerShell

Fetching PowerShell isn't that hard. You can find all the PowerShell packages here: http://tinyurl.com/2j8wue.

There are different packages for Windows XP, 2003, and Vista. Each one also has a separate package for x64. The reason is that PowerShell is shipped as an update and not as an "application." This is good because it makes PowerShell pretty simple to update later, but the negative is that, like a hotfix, it becomes problematic to uninstall after another hotfix is installed.

Next, just run the package installer. This will load the appropriate files and Registry settings.

Windows Server 2008 comes with Windows PowerShell built in as an optional feature. Just open Server Manager, right-click Features, choose Add Features, select Windows PowerShell, and complete the wizard. That way, you're up and running in no time—no downloads needed.

Running PowerShell for the First Time

Before we proceed, let's make sure we have PowerShell installed properly. To run PowerShell, we have two options. When PowerShell is installed, the system path is added so you can simply go to Start ➤ Run ➤ `PowerShell.exe`. Or you can use the shortcut in the Programs menu: Start ➤ All Programs ➤ Windows PowerShell 1.0 ➤ Windows PowerShell.

If PowerShell was installed properly, you should see a PowerShell window like the one shown in Figure 11.1.

FIGURE 11.1   PowerShell is up and running.

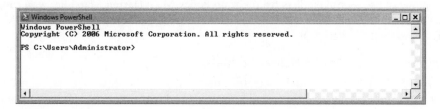

Preparing to Run Our Scripts

Finally, there is one last thing to do. By default, as a security feature, PowerShell will not run any scripts. You can use it as a command-line interface (CLI), but not for scripts out of the box. That's right. It's like having a Ferrari you can't drive unless you have a special set of keys cut. And that's what we're going to do with this next command. We'll be able to drive the Ferrari after we "cut the keys" by running a cmdlet called `Set-ExecutionPolicy`. PowerShell supports several different modes: Unrestricted, RemoteSigned, AllSigned, Restricted, and Default.

- Unrestricted: All scripts will Run.

- RemoteSigned: If a script is downloaded from the Internet or from any site that is considered Internet Zone, it must be signed.

- AllSigned: All scripts must be signed.

- Restricted: No scripts allowed (this is the default).

To change the mode, we need to run a simple command. We recommend setting the mode to at least RemoteSigned. You do that with this command:

```
PS> Set-ExecutionPolicy RemoteSigned
```

We're choosing RemoteSigned because it ensures that we can't inadvertently run scripts downloaded from the Internet. (Because we all know where that might lead.) We'll be writing and running our own scripts, so this is the perfect level of protection.

If you download the chapter's scripts from us at www.GPanswers.com, we'll give you extra direction to make sure they'll run A-OK.

Optional, but Recommended: Downloading and Installing Free Helper Group Policy Cmdlets

These will be helpful as we go over specific examples. We'll show you two ways to do every task. One way will be with straight PowerShell. The second way will be with some free helper cmdlets. Let's check them out, download them, and test them before we go on. Again, this step is optional, but you'll likely want these installed because we do utilize them in some of our examples.

Finding and Downloading the Helper Cmdlets

We are going to use several cmdlets from Group Policy MVP Darren Mar-Elia, who runs www.GPOguy.com. Simply go to www.sdmsoftware.com/freeware and download SDM GPMC PowerShell Cmdlets 1.0.

Installing and Verifying the Helper Cmdlets

The guys at SDM did a wonderful job creating an installer for the SDM cmdlets, so installing is super easy. Simply download the installer from www.sdmsoftware.com/freeware and double-click. That's it! Well, not quite, but pretty darn close. By default, when you install snap-ins they do not get added automatically to PowerShell. You have to specifically add them with the Add-PSSnapin cmdlets:

```
PS> Add-PSSnapin SDMGPOSnapIn
```

This will not return anything, so to verify that it was installed successfully, we need to use another cmdlet, Get-PSSnapin:

```
PS> Get-PSSnapin
```

The results should look like what you see in Figure 11.2.

Adding Our Starter Code (as an Include)

As in all scripting endeavors, we strive to avoid rewriting the same code over and over again. So, we have a script that we'll include with all other scripts.

This script will be our "master" starter script, with the objects, variables, and functions we'll use throughout this chapter. We'll call this script Set-GPEnvironment. This name maintains the verb-noun naming scheme in PowerShell, and while we aren't *required* to do this, it makes it easier to follow the naming patterns in functions and scripts.

We'll have this Set-GPEnvironment script available for download, as well as all the other scripts mentioned in this chapter, in the Book Resources section for this chapter at www.GPanswers.com.

FIGURE 11.2   List of installed snap-ins

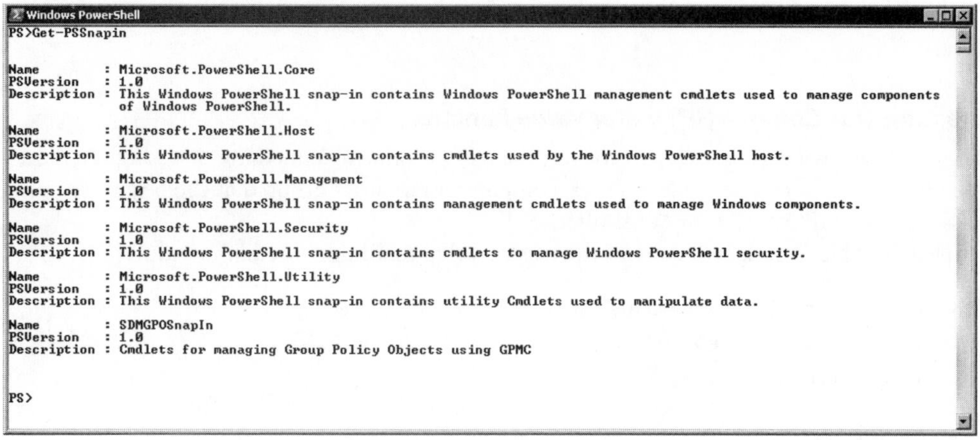

```
Windows PowerShell                                                                    _ □ ×
PS>Get-PSSnapin

Name        : Microsoft.PowerShell.Core
PSVersion   : 1.0
Description : This Windows PowerShell snap-in contains Windows PowerShell management cmdlets used to manage components
              of Windows PowerShell.
Name        : Microsoft.PowerShell.Host
PSVersion   : 1.0
Description : This Windows PowerShell snap-in contains cmdlets used by the Windows PowerShell host.
Name        : Microsoft.PowerShell.Management
PSVersion   : 1.0
Description : This Windows PowerShell snap-in contains management cmdlets used to manage Windows components.
Name        : Microsoft.PowerShell.Security
PSVersion   : 1.0
Description : This Windows PowerShell snap-in contains cmdlets to manage Windows PowerShell security.
Name        : Microsoft.PowerShell.Utility
PSVersion   : 1.0
Description : This Windows PowerShell snap-in contains utility Cmdlets used to manipulate data.
Name        : SDMGPOSnapIn
PSVersion   : 1.0
Description : Cmdlets for managing Group Policy Objects using GPMC


PS>
```

Defining Our Functions within our *Set-GPEnvironment* Include

Because a PowerShell script is really just a group of PowerShell commands run one after another, they are processed from the top down. This means we must first define functions that we'll use elsewhere.

Creating Our *Convert-DNtoDNS* Function

The first function is quite simple. It just translates the distinguished name of the domain to the DNS name so we'll be able to provide more readable feedback. Whenever our script encounters something that looks like dc=corp, dc=com, it'll spit back something more friendly, like corp.com:

```
function Convert-DNToDNS{
    $args[0] -replace "DC=","" -replace ",","."
}
```

Creating Our *Convert-GPSOMtype* Function

This function is used to translate the Scope of Management (SOM) type to a human-readable value. SOM is just a fancy way of saying "a place where a GPO can be linked." And, those locations can only be site, domain, or OU. So with that in mind, our Convert-GPSOMType declaration would look like this:

```
function Convert-GPSOMType {
    Param($SOMType)
    switch ($SOMType)
    {
        $gpmConstants.SOMDomain    {"Domain"}
        $gpmConstants.SOMOU        {"OU"}
```

```
        $gpmConstants.SOMSite    {"Site"}
        Default                  {"Domain"}
    }
}
```

Creating Our *Convert-GPTrusteeValue* Function

The next thing we need is a way to convert the trustee value to something that is a little more friendly to read. A trustee value is a user, computer, or security group that can be granted permissions on a GPO, SOM, or WMI filter.

This little bit of code will convert the trustee value to a human-readable value:

```
function Convert-GPTrusteeValue {
    Param($trusteeValue)
    switch ($trusteeValue)
    {
        1 {"User"}
        2 {"Group"}
        3 {"Domain"}
        4 {"Domain Local Group"}
        5 {"Well Known Group"}
        6 {"Deleted Account"}
        7 {"Invalid"}
        8 {"Unknown"}
        9 {"Computer"}
    }
}
```

Creating Our *Convert-GPPermValue* Function

All GPOs have permissions. And those permissions are the rights that a user or other trustee has to the object. If we understand the permissions set upon a GPO, we can figure out things like which GPO Frank Rizzo owns, which GPOs he has created, or if Domain Admins are denied the "Apply Group Policy" rights somewhere.

 Group Policy permissions can be discovered by gleaning the PermValue function. The PermValue is an enumeration from http://msdn2.microsoft.com/en-us/library/bb540649.aspx.

The PermValue function is a little wacky. It doesn't just say "Johnny has Edit rights to the GPO." It returns integers that we convert to values that make sense to humans. So, that's what we'll do here:

```
function Convert-GPPermValue {
    Param($PermValue)
```

```
    switch ($PermValue)
    {
        $gpmConstants.PermGPOApply                  {"Apply"}
        $gpmConstants.PermGPOCustom                 {"Custom"}
        $gpmConstants.PermGPOEdit                   {"Edit"}
        $gpmConstants.PermGPOEditSecurityandDelete  {"Edit and Delete"}
        $gpmConstants.PermGPORead                   {"Read"}
    }
}
```

Creating Our *Get-GPOBackups* Function

The last function we'll cover here is the `Get-GPOBackups` function. There are several scripts that we'll need to retrieve Group Policy backup files, so we included this function to make retrieval easier. The `Get-GPOBackups` function takes a filesystem folder path and returns all the Group Policy objects that are contained there.

Here is the function:

```
function Get-GPOBackups{
    Param($BackupFolder)

    $gpmSearchCriteria = $gpm.CreateSearchCriteria()
    $gpmSearchCriteria.Add(
      $gpmConstants.SearchPropertyBackupMostRecent,
      $gpmConstants.SearchOPEquals,$True)
    $gpmBackupDir = $gpm.GetBackupDir($BackupFolder)
    $gpmBackupDir.SearchBackups($gpmSearchCriteria)
}
```

Declaring Our Environment Variables

The last section of the `Set-GPEnvironment` script sets up environment variables like Domain, Forest, and GPO info. We'll jam the active values into those variables; then we'll be able to use them over and over again.

```
$gpm = new-object -ComObject "gpmgmt.gpm"
$gpmConstants = $gpm.GetConstants()
$rootDSE = [ADSI]"LDAP://rootDSE"
$ADSIDomain = $rootDSE.defaultNamingContext
$dnsDomain = Convert-DNToDNS $ADSIDomain
$ADSIForestRoot = $rootDSE.rootDomainNamingContext
$dnsForestRoot = Convert-DNToDNS $ADSIForestRoot
$gpmDomain = $gpm.GetDomain($dnsDomain,$null,
                            $gpmConstants.UsePDC)
```

Final Thoughts about Our Include *Set-GPEnvironment* Script

We recommend that you create a folder, C:\Scripts, and place the scripts we're covering in this chapter inside this folder. The first step when actually creating a script would be to just create a normal text file in the script folder, include the functions and environment variables from the sections mentioned earlier, and finally save the file as Set-GPEnvironment.ps1. Of course, this script is also immediately downloadable from www.GPanswers.com in the Book Resources section for this chapter.

Now that we've built Set-GPEnvironment, we have a well-paved road for a successful trip down PowerShell Lane. It provides all the core environment features in a nice, concise, functional manner.

That said, we'll treat the script we just created like a college student treats his parents. We'll just make an occasional call when we need something, and that's it. And just like parents, this script will be there with its wallet open.

Documenting Your Group Policy World with PowerShell

One of the most complicated and annoying parts of managing GPOs is the need to document them. Without clear documentation, troubleshooting can be quite complicated. In this next section, we'll show you how easy it is to create useful documentation with the GPMC and PowerShell.

Listing GPOs

Let's start by creating a script that lists all the GPOs within the domain. And in that list, we will, of course, retrieve some specific information about the GPO. We'll get things like the name, where it's linked in Active Directory, creation time, modification time, and much, much more.

This will be the first script that we cover that will truly show the huge advantage we gain by using PowerShell. This is relatively short script. Heck, it is only three lines long. Here's what it does:

- Calls the include statement of our Set-Environment script.

- Spits out the GPOs.

Dot-Sourcing

You may have noticed how we include the Set-Environment script using a dot (.). This concept is called *dot-sourcing* because all you do is add a dot before you name the script. This is important because by adding the dot before naming the script, you're telling PowerShell to load the script into the same scope as the current environment. This means everything that we defined in the dot-sourced script automatically gets added to the current environment.

You can learn more about scope in the PowerShell help file:

```
PS> Get-Help about_Scope
```

Here is the script; place it in the same folder where you put the other scripts (e.g., `C:\Scripts`):

```
# Get-GPOInfo.ps1
. "$pwd\Set-GPEnvironment.ps1"
$gpmDomain.SearchGPOs($gpm.CreateSearchCriteria())
```

Figure 11.3 shows what the output will look like once the script is completed.

FIGURE 11.3   Output of Get-GPOInfo.ps1

Analyzing the Output of *Get-GPOInfo*

The output doesn't look that impressive, but it is important to understand that the power is *what we can do with* the output.

If this wasn't PowerShell and was, say, just VBScript, and we returned just straight text, then we would be forced to either accept it in whatever form we get it in or write *more* code to parse the output. With PowerShell, this is not the case. We don't really get back text, we get back *objects*. These objects can be molded, formed, and filtered in whatever manner we see fit.

Leveraging Objects for Fun and Profit

We'll talk a lot about objects in this chapter. Let's take a second to discuss the power of outputting an object instead of just text.

What is an object?

An object is a logical representation of a "thing." This thing could have properties and possibly methods. This thing could be anything from a car to a file located on a hard drive. In PowerShell, these things are .NET classes or COM objects.

Why does this matter?

Dealing with objects instead of text gives us a huge advantage. Let's take a car, for example. A car has type, model, tires, color, and a slew of other properties. It also has functions (or methods), like start, stop, drive, and shift. When dealing with text, we could just have

Make   Type   Color

------   ------   ------

Mazda MPV   White

BMW 328i   Gray

Mazda Mazda3 Gray

This is fine if we don't need to do anything with this data, but what if we do? What if we just wanted to see the cars that are gray or cars that are made by Mazda? We would have to search the text and find the lines that have the info we need and manipulate the results to output what we are after.

In PowerShell this is very simple—because each car is an *object* with properties that we can easily filter according to any one individual property. Here is an example.

This line will get all the cars made by Mazda and output only the type:

```
PS> Get-Cars | where{$_.Make -eq "Mazda"} | select-object Type
```

What if we want all the gray cars? We'd simply type this line:

```
PS> Get-Cars | where{$_.Color -eq "Gray"}
```

As we hope you can see, this is much easier to manage and way more powerful than messing with raw text.

Here's an interesting example for us to hang our hats on. In the next section, we'll examine the idea of objects in detail.

Let's say your boss comes in and asks you for a list of every GPO you have in the domain. He doesn't want to see all the fluff, just the names.

You'll have it for him before he leaves the room by running the Get-GPOInfo script you already have (but with a little extra on the end). Here's how to turn his head:

```
PS> C:\Scripts\Get-GPOInfo.ps1 | select-object DisplayName
```

All you're doing is piping the output to the select-object cmdlet and stripping off everything but DisplayName. He is clearly impressed, but he says, "You know... I wonder when they were created?"

You turn around to your computer and you run this command, based on (you guessed it) the same `Get-GPOInfo` script:

```
PS> C:\Scripts\Get-GPOInfo.ps1 | select-object DisplayName,CreationTime
```

This time, you pipe the output through `DisplayName` and `CreationTime`. Again, before he leaves you get him what he asked for. As he picks his jaw off the floor, he says, "I don't suppose you could get me all the GPOs that have been changed in the last week?" You say, "Sure, one sec." Back to the `Get-GPO` script again by running this command:

```
PS> C:\Scripts\Get-GPOInfo.ps1 |
where{$_.ModificationTime -gt (get-date).AddDays(-7)}
```

Your boss is clearly impressed at your speed and agility and he doubles your salary! Okay, maybe not, but he will definitely know who has the information he needs, and he will remember that come review time.

Getting Information about Objects

In the `Get-GPOInfo.ps1` example, we used `select-object` to filter out some properties. Some of you may be curious about how we even knew what properties were available.

The easiest way to get a list of what properties and methods an object has is to pipe the object to a cmdlet called `Get-Member`. `Get-Member` is used to "reflect" the object and list out the properties and methods it finds.

Here is an example:

```
PS> C:\Scripts\Get-GPOInfo.ps1 | Get-Member
```

```
PS C:\scripts> .\Get-GPOInfo.ps1 | Get-Member


   TypeName: System.__ComObject#{8a66a210-b78b-4d99-88e2-c306a817c925}

Name                        MemberType  Definition
Backup                      Method      IGPMResult Backup (string, string, Variant, Variant)
CopyTo                      Method      IGPMResult CopyTo (int, IGPMDomain, Variant, Variant, Va
Delete                      Method      void Delete ()
GenerateReport              Method      IGPMResult GenerateReport (GPMReportType, Variant, Varia
GenerateReportToFile        Method      IGPMResult GenerateReportToFile (GPMReportType, string)
GetSecurityDescriptor       Method      IDispatch GetSecurityDescriptor (int)
GetSecurityInfo             Method      IGPMSecurityInfo GetSecurityInfo ()
GetWMIFilter                Method      IGPMWMIFilter GetWMIFilter ()
Import                      Method      IGPMResult Import (int, IGPMBackup, Variant, Variant, Va
IsACLConsistent             Method      bool IsACLConsistent ()
IsComputerEnabled           Method      bool IsComputerEnabled ()
IsUserEnabled               Method      bool IsUserEnabled ()
MakeACLConsistent           Method      void MakeACLConsistent ()
SetComputerEnabled          Method      void SetComputerEnabled (bool)
SetSecurityDescriptor       Method      void SetSecurityDescriptor (int, IDispatch)
SetSecurityInfo             Method      void SetSecurityInfo (IGPMSecurityInfo)
SetUserEnabled              Method      void SetUserEnabled (bool)
SetWMIFilter                Method      void SetWMIFilter (IGPMWMIFilter)
ComputerDSVersionNumber     Property    int ComputerDSVersionNumber () (get)
ComputerSysvolVersionNumber Property    int ComputerSysvolVersionNumber () (get)
CreationTime                Property    Date CreationTime () (get)
Description                 Property    string Description () (get) (set)
DisplayName                 Property    string DisplayName () (get) (set)
DomainName                  Property    string DomainName () (get)
ID                          Property    string ID () (get)
ModificationTime            Property    Date ModificationTime () (get)
Path                        Property    string Path () (get)
UserDSVersionNumber         Property    int UserDSVersionNumber () (get)
UserSysvolVersionNumber     Property    int UserSysvolVersionNumber () (get)
```

Get-SDMGPO

As we discussed earlier, some of the scripts we are going to write have already been made into cmdlets (think of these as compiled scripts).

We already loaded the third-party (free) `Get-SDMGPO` cmdlet.

Cmdlets are much simpler to deal with because you don't have to deal with scripts at all; we just use the cmdlet! Let's do the same tasks with `Get-SDMGPO`.

To list all GPOs, type this:

```
PS> Get-SDMGPO * | select DisplayName
```

To list all GPOs with `CreationDate`:

```
PS> Get-SDMGPO * | select DisplayName,CreationTime
```

To list all GPOs modified in the last week:

```
PS> Get-SDMGPO * | where{$_.ModificationTime -gt (get-date).AddDays(-7)}
```

Documenting GPO links

In the following sections, you'll learn how to document GPO links. We're going to find all the GPOs and their links. Again, because we're using PowerShell, we have the ability to output objects, not just straight text.

While the power of this may not immediately be evident, you'll soon see why this is such a huge benefit. We're going to show you the code first and then we'll give you a peek under the hood.

It takes three parts to make this script happen:

- Our `include` statement to ensure that we utilize our pre-built `Set-Environment` script

- Setting up the script environment

- And, finally, the body of the script

In Figure 11.4, we'll give you a sneak preview of what the output will look like from our script (once we write it together). We'll run the following command to document our GPO links:

```
PS> C:\Scripts\Get-GPOLinkInfo.ps1
```

FIGURE 11.4 Output of Get-GPOLinkInfo

This output is super useful because it tells us each GPO name, where it's linked, and the type of place it's linked to (site, domain, or OU).

So, let's put the pieces together and tackle this script now.

Include the *Set-Environment* Script

You'll see this in a lot of the scripts we write. This line is where we include the Set-Environment script we wrote earlier:

```
## Getting GP Environment information
. "$pwd\Set-GPEnvironment.ps1"
```

Setup of the Script Environment

Almost every script will need a little setup. These lines are where we set up our search criteria and get the list of GPOs:

```
$gpmSitesContainer = $gpm.GetSitesContainer($dnsForestRoot,
                       "","",
                       $gpmConstants.UsePDC)
$gpmSearchCriteria = $gpm.CreateSearchCriteria()
$somSearchCriteria = $gpm.CreateSearchCriteria()
$GPO_List = $gpmDomain.SearchGPOs($gpmSearchCriteria)
```

The Body of the Script and Putting It All Together

Now we get to the body of the script. This is where we iterate through the GPOs and collect link information. You may also notice we use the output to create a custom object.

We've also tacked on the first two bits and called them out. These were the first two items we just discussed: our include statement (which calls our Set-Environment script) and the code that sets up our script environment. Just plop the body on the end of the script, and there you have it:

```
## Get-GPOLinkInfo.ps1
## Disclaimer info

## Getting GP Environment information
. "$pwd\Set-GPEnvironment.ps1"

$gpmSitesContainer = $gpm.GetSitesContainer
($dnsForestRoot,"","",$gpmConstants.UsePDC)
$gpmSearchCriteria = $gpm.CreateSearchCriteria()
$somSearchCriteria = $gpm.CreateSearchCriteria()
$GPO_List = $gpmDomain.SearchGPOs($gpmSearchCriteria)

Write-Host
```

```
Write-Host "The following list contains GPOs
in the $($gpmDomain.Domain) domain, the containers linked
to them, and their inheritance settings:"
Write-Host

$myCollection = @()

foreach($GPO in $GPO_List)
{
    $somSearchCriteria = $gpm.CreateSearchCriteria()
    $somSearchCriteria.Add(
            $gpmConstants.SearchPropertySOMLinks,
            $gpmConstants.SearchOpContains,$GPO)
    $SOM_List = $gpmDomain.SearchSOMs($somSearchCriteria)
    if($SOM_List.Count -ne 0)
    {
        foreach($SOM in $SOM_List)
        {
            $myobj = "" | Select-Object GPOName,
                                        Location,Type
            $myobj.GPOName = $GPO.DisplayName
            $myobj.Location = $SOM.Name
            $myobj.Type = Convert-GPSOMType($SOM.Type)
            $myCollection += $myobj
        }
        $siteSOM_List = $gpmSitesContainer.SearchSites(
                    $somSearchCriteria)
        foreach($SOM in $siteSOM_List)
        {
            $myobj = "" | Select-Object GPOName,
                                        Location,Type
            $myobj.GPOName = $GPO.DisplayName
            $myobj.Location = $SOM.Name
            $myobj.Type = Convert-GPSOMType($SOM.Type)
            $myCollection += $myobj
        }
    }
}
$myCollection
```

How to Use the *Get-GPOLlnkInfo.ps1* Script

To get the script, you simply traverse to the www.GPanswers.com Book Resources section. Then look for the script named Get-GPOLinkInfo.ps1. Be sure to put this file in the same location as Set-GPEnvironment.ps1.

From the PowerShell prompt, type **<Path To Script>\Get-GPOLinkInfo.ps1** and press Enter. Again, output from this script can be seen in Figure 11.4.

Documenting WMI Filter Links

In the following script, we'll list the WMI filters, their descriptions, and where they are linked. We're going to break this script down into three sections:

- Our include statement from the Set-Environment script
- The processing of the WMI links
- Finding where the WMI filters are linked

Once we have our script put together, you'll be able to run it using the following command:

```
PS> C:\Scripts\Get-GPWMILink.ps1
```

Figure 11.5 shows what the output will look like for our script.

FIGURE 11.5   Output of Get-GPWMILink.ps1

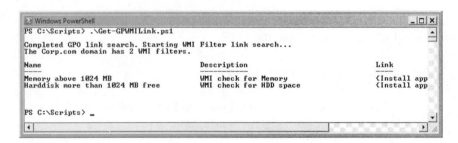

This output tells us each WMI link name, description, and where it's linked. Handy!

The Setup of the Script Environment

As in the previous scripts, we have a little setup to do. This includes dot-sourcing (this is the PowerShell version of include) our master script, creating a search for the WMI filters, and providing an overview of the information we found:

```
## Get-GPWMILink
## Getting GP Environment information
. "$pwd\Set-GPEnvironment.ps1"


Write-Host
```

```
Write-Host "Completed GPO link search. Starting WMI Filter link search..."

$wmiSearchCriteria = $gpm.CreateSearchCriteria()
$wmi_Filter_List = $gpmDomain.SearchWMIFilters($wmiSearchCriteria)

If($wmi_Filter_List.Count -ne 1){$plural = "s"}else{$plural = ""}
Write-Host "The $($gpmDomain.Domain) domain
has $($wmi_Filter_List.Count) WMI filter$($plural)."
```

Iterating through the Filters

Now that we have all the filters, we need to process each one to discover each name and description. We'll also add another property to the Filter object to store the link locations:

```
foreach($WMI_Filter in $wmi_Filter_List)
{
    $WMILink = $WMI_Filter | Select-Object Name,Description,Link
    $gpoSearchCriteria = $gpm.CreateSearchCriteria()
    $gpoSearchCriteria.Add($gpmConstants.SearchPropertyGPOWMIFilter,
                           $gpmConstants.SearchOPEquals,
                           $WMI_Filter)

    $Linked_GPO_List = $gpmDomain.SearchGPOs($gpoSearchCriteria)
    if($Linked_GPO_List.count -gt 0)
    {
        foreach($GPO in $Linked_GPO_List)
        {
            if(!$WMILink.Link){$WMILink.Link = @($GPO.DisplayName)}
            else{$WMILink.Link += $GPO.DisplayName}
        }
    }
    $WMILink
}
Write-Host " "
```

Getting the Link Locations

We've already placed the final piece in the preceding code. But we want to spend some quality time explaining this little piece of code, because it's important to show you specifically where we find the GPOs that have a WMI filter in use. We use the foreach statement to go through each GPO in our list that uses WMI filters. Then we add each one to a collection of GPO display names, which allows us to output them later in a nice list:

```
foreach($GPO in $Linked_GPO_List)
{
```

```
    if(!$WMILink.Link){$WMILink.Link = @($GPO.DisplayName)}
    else{$WMILink.Link += $GPO.DisplayName}
}
```

How to Use the *Get-GPWMILink.ps1* Script

To get the script, you simply go to www.GPanswers.com, look in the Book Resources section for this chapter, and get the script named Get-GPWMILink.ps1. Be sure to put this file in the same location as Set-GPEnvironment.ps1.

Now just type the following command:

```
PS> $pwd\Get-GPWMILink.ps1
```

Again, output from this script can be seen in Figure 11.5.

Listing GPO Permissions

A big part of troubleshooting Group Policy is dealing with permissions on the actual Group Policy Object. In this script, we'll discover how to get the permissions on our GPOs.

This will return a good bit of information like name, user or group, domain, and permission. The following script can be broken into four sections.

- Our include statement for the Set-Environment script
- Getting the GPO
- Getting the permissions
- Creating and outputting the object

Once our script is created, it'll be easy to list the permissions on our GPOs. Just run the command like this against any specific GPO (by name):

```
PS>c:\scripts\Get-GPOPermission.ps1 "Default Domain Policy"
```

Figure 11.6 shows what the output will look like for our script.

This output tells us each user/group name, type, domain, path, SID, permission, if it is denied, if it's inheritable, and if it's inherited.

Setup of the Script Environment

This is the first script that takes input from the user in the form of a parameter. In this section, we set up the parameters, add our include, and set up our search filters:

```
Param($GPOName = (Read-Host "Enter the name of the GPO
to view permissions of"))
# list-GPOPermissions.ps1
. "$pwd\Set-GPEnvironment.ps1"

Write-Host
```

```
#Search for an select a GPO called "General Desktop Settings"
$gpmSearchCriteria = $gpm.CreateSearchCriteria()
$gpmSearchCriteria.Add($gpmConstants.SearchPropertyGPODisplayName,
                    $gpmConstants.SearchOPcontains,$GPOName)
$gpmGPO_List = $gpmDomain.SearchGPOs($gpmSearchCriteria)
```

FIGURE 11.6   Output of Get-GPOPermission

Getting our GPOs

Here we get all the GPOs, and we pick the GUID for the GPO that is passed to the script:

```
$id = $gpmGPO_List | %{$_.ID}
$gpmGPO = $gpmDomain.GetGPO($id)
if(!$?)
{
    Write-Host "Error: $($error[0])"
    break
}
```

Get the Permissions

Now that we have a GPO, we need the permissions. We can get them by calling the GetSecurityInfo() method on the Group Policy Object.

```
$gpmSecurityInfo = $gpmGPO.GetSecurityInfo()
```

Creating and Outputting the Object

In the final part of the script, we'll use the permissions we just collected and create a custom object. Then we can easily parse the output:

```
Write-host  ("The GPO has {0} security entries
on the ACL." -f $gpmSecurityInfo.Count)

foreach($gpmPermission in $gpmSecurityInfo)
{
    $acl = $gpmPermission | Select-Object Name,Type,Domain,Path,SID,
                            Permission,Denied,Inheritable,Inherited
    $acl.Name = $gpmPermission.trustee.trusteeName
    $acl.Type = (Convert-GPTrusteeValue($gpmPermission.trustee.trusteeType))
    $acl.Domain = $gpmPermission.trustee.trusteeDomain
    $acl.Path = $gpmPermission.trustee.trusteeDSPath
    $acl.SID = $gpmPermission.trustee.trusteeSid
    $acl.Permission = (Convert-GPPermValue($gpmPermission.permission))
    $acl.Denied = $gpmPermission.denied
    $acl.Inheritable = $gpmPermission.inheritable
    $acl.Inherited = $gpmPermission.inherited
    $acl
}

Write-Host
```

How to Use the *Get-GPOPermission.ps1* Script

To get the script, you simply go to www.GPanswers.com, look in the Book Resources section for this chapter and get the script named Get-GPOPermission.ps1. Be sure to put this file in the same location as Set-GPEnvironment.ps1.

Now, just call the script with GPO you want to check:

```
PS> $pwd\Get-GPOPermission.ps1 "Default Domain Policy"
```

Again, output from this script can be seen in Figure 11.6.

Another Way to Get a GPO's Security Rights: *Get-SDMgpoSecurity*

Recall that we installed some helper PowerShell cmdlets, which can sometimes make quick work of a Group Policy task. One of those cmdlets is Get-SDMGPOSecurity.

While the output of Get-SDMGPOSecurity is not exactly the same as our script, the information is very similar. This cmdlet provides three pieces of information: the trustee (user or group), permission, and whether or not the permission is inherited. Using Get-SDMGPOSecurity makes quick work of the same task.

The command is similar to the Get-GPOPermission command we created from scratch in the way it runs.

The command is as follows:

```
PS> Get-SDMGPOSecurity "Default Domain Policy"
```

You can see the output of the Get-SDMGPOSecurity cmdlet in Figure 11.17.

FIGURE 11.7 Output of Get-SDMGPOSecurity

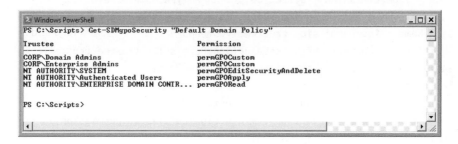

Manipulating GPOs with PowerShell

Another task admins spend a large amount of time on is the actual manipulation of GPOs themselves. But creating, linking, and backing up GPOs are all things we should be able to script.

Now that we have shown you some scripts that enable you to document GPOs, we're ready to take on some of these new challenges.

Creating New GPOs

One of the most common tasks for GPO administrators is creating new GPOs. In the following script, we do just that. This is a pretty straightforward script, so let's first look at the output, then break it down and show you how we got there.

Figure 11.8 shows the output of the script. The command we'll use to create a new GPO is simple. It's just

```
PS> C:\Scripts\New-GPO "MyNewTestGPO"
```

FIGURE 11.8   Output of New-GPO.ps1

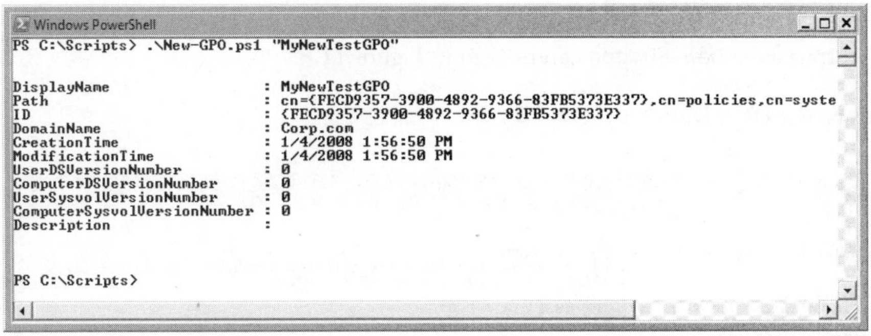

Creating the New-GPO Script

This script is pretty straightforward. We do our normal setup and then we call `CreateGPO()` on the domain GPMC object (`$gpmDomain`) we created in the `Set-GPEnvironment.ps1` script. This call returns the new GPO as the result, so we capture that in `$NewGPO` and set the display name to be the same as the `$GPOName` value. Finally we output the `$NewGPO` object:

```
Param($GPOName = (Read-Host "Enter the Name of New GPO"))
# list-GPOPermissions.ps1
. "$pwd\Set-GPEnvironment.ps1"

$NewGPO = $gpmDomain.CreateGPO()
$NewGPO.DisplayName = $GPOName
$NewGPO
```

How to Use the *New-GPO.ps1* Script

To get the script, you simply go to www.GPanswers.com, look in the Book Resources section for this chapter, and get the script named New-GPO.ps1. Be sure to put this file in the same location as Set-GPEnvironment.ps1.

Now call the script with the name of the GPO you want to create:

```
PS> $pwd\New-GPO "MyNewTestGPO"
```

Again, output from this script can be seen in Figure 11.8.

Another Way to Create a New GPO: Using *New-SDMgpo*

The other SDM cmdlet we'll show you is `New-SDMgpo`. This one acts just like the script we created and is very simple to use.

Here is an example of how to create a new GPO using New-SDMgpo:

```
PS>New-SDMgpo "MySDMTestGPO"
```

The output from New-SDMgpo can be seen in Figure 11.9.

FIGURE 11.9 Output of New-SDMgpo

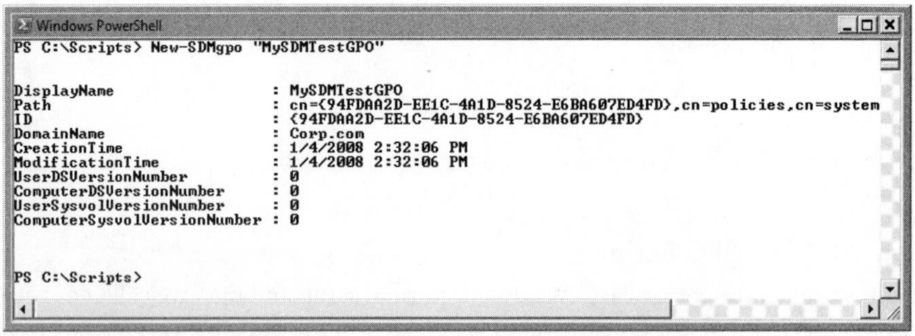

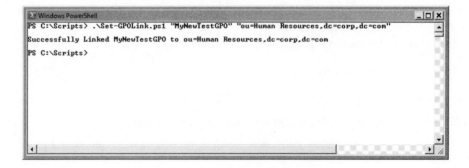

Linking a GPO

We created a GPO, but what good is a GPO if you can't link it? The next script links an existing GPO to a location in Active Directory: either site, domain, or OU.

Our code will simply return a success or failure message. You'll run Set-GPOLink as follows:

```
PS> C:\Scripts\Set-GPOLink.ps1 "MyNewTestGPO"
"ou=Human Resources,dc=corp,dc=com"
```

The output from Set-GPOLink can be seen in Figure 11.10.

FIGURE 11.10 Output for Set-GPOLink

Now, let's look at code. We can break this up into three parts.

- Our `include` statement for the Set-Environment script
- Getting the path and GPO
- Creating the link

Setting up Our *Set-GPOlink* Script

This is pretty much like the previous scripts, but we did add one extra feature. In this script we'll use `$erroractionpreference` to make sure the script runs silently. We then use a little tricky coding magic to check for errors at the end.

```
# Set-GPOLink.ps1
Param($GPOName,
      $GUID,
      $Path = (Read-Host "Enter Path to Link"),
      [switch]$Top)


. "$pwd\Set-GPEnvironment.ps1"
$erroractionpreference = "silentlycontinue"


if(!($GPOName -or $GUID))
{
    Write-Host 'GPOName or GUID is required!' -fore Red
}


if($top){$LinkPrecedence = 1}
else{$LinkPrecedence = -1}
```

Searching Active Directory (the "Path") and Getting GPO Information

Because we create a link between a GPO and a specific location in AD, we have to get both of those ready to establish the link. This includes checking to see if GUID or GPOName was passed and if more than one GPO name that matches was found.

```
$OU = [ADSI]"LDAP://$Path"
if(!$OU.distinguishedName)
{
    Write-Host "Invalid OU supplied." -fore Red
}


if($GUID)
{
    $GPO = $gpmDomain.SearchGPOs(
```

```
        $gpm.CreateSearchCriteria()) | where{
        $_.DisplayName -eq $GPOName}
}
if($GPOName)
{
    $GPO = $gpmDomain.SearchGPOs(
     $gpm.CreateSearchCriteria()) | where{
     $_.DisplayName -eq $GPOName}
    if($GPO.Count -and ($GPO.count -gt 1))
    {
        Write-Host "Found [$($GPO.Count)] GPOs with "
        Write-Host "GPO Display Name of [$GPOName]."
        Write-Host "Please use GUID instead."
        return
    }
}
```

Creating the Link

Finally, we create the link and report the result:

```
$SOM = $gpmDomain.GetSOM($OU.distinguishedName)
$SOM_Link = $SOM.CreateGPOLink($LinkPrecedence, $GPO)
if($?){Write-Host "`nLinked $GPOName to $Path`n"}
else{Write-Host "`nLink Failed, Error:$($error[0])`n"}
```

How to Use the *Set-GPOlink.ps1* Script

To get the script, you simply go to www.GPanswers.com, look in the Book Resources section for this chapter, and get the script named Set-GPOlink.ps1. Be sure to put this file in the same location as Set-GPEnvironment.ps1.

We execute this script by giving it the GPO name (in quotes) and the distinguished name where we want it linked (also in quotes), like this:

```
PS> $pwd\Set-GPOLink.ps1 "MyNewTestGPO" "ou=Human Resources,dc=corp,dc=com"
```

Again, output from this script can be seen in Figure 11.10.

Another Way to Create a New GPO: *Add-SDMGPLink*

If you wanted to leverage a third-party cmdlet, there's an even easier way to do it. If you installed the SDM GPO cmdlet, just type this at the PS> prompt:

```
PS>Add-SDMgplink -Name "MySDMTestGPO" -scope
"ou=Human Resources,dc=corp,dc=com" -location -1
```

Backing Up Group Policy Objects

Another really important, but often overlooked, task is backing up GPOs. Don't be caught without a backup of your GPOs when a disaster hits.

In fact, wouldn't it be nice to have an automated way to back up all your GPOs every night? Well, this script will help you do just that. In a second we'll take a look, but before that let's take a quick peek at the output.

Once we have the script ready to go, we'll run it by specifying the path to which we want to save the output and optionally specify -date as a parameter. (We'll go into the parameters in a minute.) The command will be as follows:

```
PS> c:\scripts\New-GPOBackup.ps1 -path c:\scripts\backups -date
```

We can see the output from New-GPOBackup in Figure 11.11.

FIGURE 11.11   Output of New-GPOBackup.ps1

Even though the output isn't super exciting, we can see that the job is complete. Now, let's take a look at the script. It's composed of four steps:

- Our include statement for the Set-Environment script
- Determining if we want all GPOs, or just one GPO
- Creating a backup folder
- Performing the backup

Setup of *New-GPOBackup*

In the setup, we'll do our normal include of the master GPO script, and we'll also create parameters for backup path and GPO Name and provide a [switch] for the date:

```
# Get-GPOBackup.ps1
Param($Path = $(throw '$Path is Require'),
      $Name,
      [switch]$date)
. "$pwd\Set-GPEnvironment.ps1"
Write-Host
$GPOs = $gpmDomain.SearchGPOs($gpm.CreateSearchCriteria())
```

What is *[switch]*?

This is the second time we have used the [switch] option. A [switch] parameter is a parameter that PowerShell will set to be either $true or $false. It's perfect for checking to see if you want to perform an extra function or not. In this case, we're using it to see if we want to create a subfolder in our backup path for the date.

Backing Up One or All GPOs

We may not want to back up all the GPOs, so we use this code to determine if the -name parameter was passed, which will determine whether we only want to back up one GPO:

```
if($Name)
{
    $GPOs = $GPOs | Where-Object{
            $_.DisplayName -eq $Name}
}
```

Creating a Backup Folder

What would seem to be an easy step turns out to be the biggest piece of code in this script. That is, we need to create a new folder to contain our backups. In this section we have to determine two things:

- Does the user want make a subfolder for date?

- Does the path exist? If not, we create it.

```
if($date)
{
    $backupPath = "{0}\{1:yyyyMMdd}" -f $Path,(Get-Date)
    if(!(test-Path $backupPath))
    {
     New-Item $backupPath -type Directory -force | out-Null
    }
}
else
{
    $backupPath = $path
    if(!(test-Path $backupPath))
    {
     New-Item $backupPath -type Directory -force | out-Null
    }
}
```

Performing the Backup

The last section is fairly straightforward, but it's clearly the most critical part. This is where we actually perform the backup:

```
foreach($gpo in $gpos)
{
    write-Host "Backing Up $($GPO.DisplayName)"
    $gpo.Backup($backupPath,$null,$null) | out-null
}
Write-Host
```

How to Use the *New-GPOBackup.ps1* script

To get the script, you simply go to www.GPanswers.com, look in the Book Resources section for this chapter, and get the script named New-GPOBackup.ps1. Be sure to put this file in the same location as Set-GPEnvironment.ps1.

To use it, we just call the script with backup path and date (optional):

```
PS> $pwd\New-GPOBackup.ps1 -path c:\scripts\backups -date
```

Again, output from this script can be seen in Figure 11.11.

Restoring a GPO

What good are backups if you can't restore them? This next script does exactly that; in fact, not only does it restore a script, it will also list all the backups in a given folder. So, there are two ways to run this script:

- Method #1: Show all GPOs already backed up:

    ```
    C:\Scripts\Restore-GPOBackup.ps1 C:\Scripts\backups\<Insert Date> -list
    ```

- Method #2: Restore the backed up GPO:

    ```
    C:\Scripts\Restore-GPOBackup.ps1
      C:\Scripts\backups\<Insert Date> -name
      "MyNewTestGPO"
    ```

You can see the output from Method #1 in Figure 11.12.
You can see the output from Method #2 in Figure 11.13.
Let's take a look at how we created it. We can break this down as follows:

- Our include statement for the Set-Environment script
- Deciding if we want to see a list of GPOs in the backup
- Performing the restore

FIGURE 11.12 Output of backup list

FIGURE 11.13 Output of Restore-GPOBackup

Setup of *New-GPORestore*

Nothing new here. We include the master script and collect the backups from the folder:

```
# Get-GPInfo.ps1
 Param($Path = $(throw '$path is required'),
      $Name,
      [switch]$list)


. "$pwd\Set-GPEnvironment.ps1"
Write-host
$backups = Get-GPOBackups $Path
```

Do We Want to List the GPOs Contained in Our Backup?

This is a small, but important, section. This is where we check to see if the `list` parameter was passed. If it was, we list the backups and then exit:

```
if($list)
{
    $backups
    return
}
```

Perform the Restore

In this section we actually perform the restore. First, we ask the user if they are sure they want to perform the restore, and then we set the `$erroractionpreference` so we can return the error when we want:

```
$continue = Read-Host "Are you sure you want to restore $Name? (y or n)"
if($continue -ne "y"){return "No Restore Performed"}

$gpo = $backups | Where-Object{$_.GPODisplayName -eq $name}

$erroractionpreference = "SilentlyContinue"
$gpmDomain.RestoreGPO($GPO,0) | out-Null
if($?){Write-Host "Restore Successful"}
else{Write-Host "Restore Failed. Error:$($error[0])"}
Write-Host
```

How to Use the *New-GPORestore.ps1* script

To get the script, you simply go to www.GPanswers.com, look in the Book Resources section for this chapter, and get the script named `New-GPORestore.ps1`. Be sure to put this file in the same location as `Set-GPEnvironment.ps1`.

Now, just call the script with backup path and name or `-list`:

```
PS> $pwd\Restore-GPOBackup.ps1
C:\Scripts\backups\<Insert Date> -name ""MyNewTestGPO""
```

Again, output from the two ways we can use this script can be seen in Figure 11.12 and Figure 11.13.

Importing GPOS

What if you have a GPO from someone else's domain or a test lab domain and want to get it into *your* domain? You can back it up and then import it. We even have the ability to use migration tables in this situation. We discuss migration tables at length in the book's appendix, but in short, a migration table is a mapping for UNCs, SIDs, and other domain-specific information that may be different in the destination domain.

> ## *$ErrorActionPreference*
>
> We have mentioned this once before, but it's important to understand exactly what this does. When PowerShell processes a cmdlet, script, or function, it always checks this variable to see what it should do if the command fails. By default, this is set to Continue, but there are several other settings. Here is the list of the other settings and what they do:
>
> - SilentlyContinue: Don't do or say anything.
>
> - Stop: Stop processing and return an error.
>
> - Continue: Continue processing but return an error.
>
> - Inquire: Ask me what to do.

This will be one of our larger scripts. Importing is actually a multistep process, but before we get into the steps, let's see how we would run the Import-GPO script:

```
PS>c:\scripts\Import-GPO.ps1 -path
C:\Scripts\backups\<Insert Date>
-name MyNewTestGPO -loc "dc=corp,dc=com"
```

The output of the Import-GPO script can be seen in Figure 11.14.

FIGURE 11.14 Output of Import-GPO

Again, the output isn't all that impressive, but when we look under the hood, we will see the V12 this script is packing. As we said, this is a larger script made of several different steps. Let's look at them:

- Our include statement of the Set-Environment script
- Verifying that the parameters are passed and valid
- Creating a new GPO to import to
- Linking the GPO to a specified location
- Checking for a migration table
- Importing the GPO information from backup to the new GPO

Setup

Really nothing new here, just the `include` and the parameters:

```
# Import-GPO.ps1
Param($path = $(throw '$path is required'),
      $Name = $(throw '$Name is required'),
      $Location = $(throw '$Location is required'),
      $MigrationTable,
      [switch]$top)
. "$pwd\Set-GPEnvironment.ps1"
Write-Host
```

Verification

This is a very important part of the script. If we don't have valid information passed, we won't be able to do much. We have to verify that the $path is a valid path, We have to make sure the location is valid in Active Directory, if the migration table was passed we need to validate the file path, and lastly, we set the $linkPrecedence:

```
if(!(test-Path $path)){return "Backup folder is invalid"}
if($top){$LinkPrecedence = 1}else{$LinkPrecedence = -1}
$OU = [ADSI]"LDAP://$Location"
if($migrationtable -and !(test-path $migrationtable))
{
  "Migration Table Path Invalid";return
}
```

Create the GPO

We need a place to import to, so we need to create a new GPO. This is the code that does that:

```
$GPO = $gpmDomain.CreateGPO()
$GPO.DisplayName = $Name
```

Link the GPO

GPOs are of no use if they are not linked to a location in Active Directory:

```
$SOM = $gpmDomain.GetSOM($OU.distinguishedName)
$SOM_Link = $SOM.CreateGPOLink($LinkPrecedence, $GPO)
If($?){
  Write-Host "Successfully linked $Name to $($SOM.Name)"
}
else{
  Write-Host "An error occurred while linking to OU."
}
```

Check for a Migration Table

In this section, we check to see if the user specifies a migration table to use. If they specify one, we create the appropriate object to pass to the Import() method.

```
if($MigrationTable)
{
  Write-Host "Using Migration Table $MigrationTable"
  $GPMMigrationTable = $GPM.GetMigrationTable($MigrationTable)
}
```

Import the GPO

The final step is to import the backup information from the backup path and specify the parameters:

```
$GPOi = Get-GPOBackups($Path) | where-Object{
        $_.GPODisplayName -eq $Name}

$erroractionpreference = "SilentlyContinue"
if($MigrationTable)
{
  $GPO.Import(0,$GPOi,$GPMMigrationTable) | out-Null
}
else
{
  $GPO.Import(0,$GPOi) | out-Null
}
```

What is $?

We've used this variable a few times, so we wanted to explain what is going on here. In Power-Shell, every time you run a command, this variable gets set to $true or $false. If the command did not throw an error, then it returns $true. If the command did result in an error, then this is set to $false. So we can use this variable to see whether or not the last command worked.

How to Use the *Import-GPO.ps1* script

To get the script, you simply go to www.GPanswers.com, look in the Book Resources section for this chapter, and get the script named Import-GPO.ps1. Be sure to put this file in the same location as Set-GPEnvironment.ps1.

To use the script, just add the path that needs to be backed up, the name of the GPO, and the location in AD to link to. You can also add the optional migration table by adding `-migration <PathToTableFile>`:

```
PS>c:\scripts\Import-GPO.ps1 -path
C:\Scripts\backups\<Insert Date> -name MyNewTestGPO
-loc "dc=corp,dc=com"
```

Again, output from this script can be seen in Figure 11.14.

Set-GPPermission

There are few things more useful to script than mass changes to GPOs. One of these mass changes is setting up permissions. Lucky for us, this is pretty simple with PowerShell. With the following script, we can set one of five permissions for a user or group: Read, Apply, Edit, Full Control, and None. The great thing is that this script can not only set the permission for the user, it can do it on multiple GPOs using wildcards or the `-all` flag.

Let's take a quick look at how we run Set-GPPermission:

```
PS>c:\scripts\Set-GPPermission -GPO "MyNewTestGPO"
-User "Corp\Frizzo" -permission FC
```

The `Set-GPPermission` output can be seen in Figure 11.15.

FIGURE 11.15   Output of Set-GPPermission.ps1

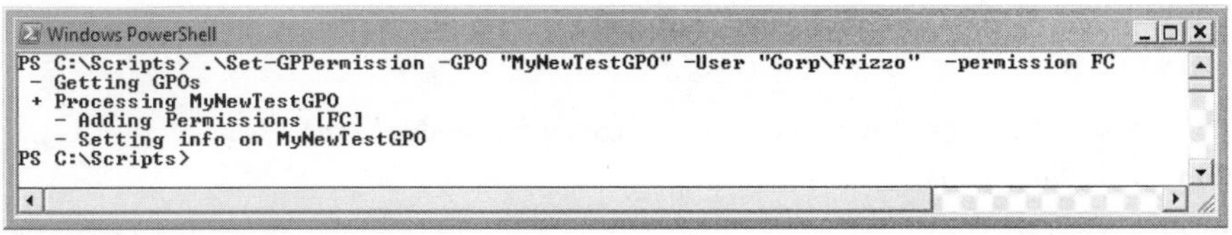

This is one of the larger scripts, but we can break it down into four sections:

- Setup
- Verification
- Filtering GPOs to process them
- Setting permissions

Setup

In the setup section, we have the typical parameters set up and `include` statements for `Set-GPEnvironment.ps1`:

```
# Set-GPOPermission.ps1
Param($GPOName,
      $User,
```

```
        $Permission,
        [switch]$replace,
        [switch]$All,
        [switch]$verbose)

if($verbose){$verbosepreference = "continue"}
else{$erroractionpreference = "SilentlyContinue"}
```

Verification

Because we are dealing with changing permissions here, we need to be careful. In this section we verify that $GPOName or -All is passed. We also validate the $Permission field:

```
if(!($GPOName -or $All))
{
    Write-Host "Please supply GPOName or -All to Set Permissions"
    return
}
. "$pwd\Set-GPEnvironment.ps1"

switch ($Permission)
{
    "Read"  {$Perm = $gpmConstants.permGPORead}
    "Apply" {$Perm = $gpmConstants.permGPOApply}
    "Edit"  {$Perm = $gpmConstants.permGPOEdit}
    "FC"    {
         $Perm = $gpmConstants.permGPOEditSecurityAndDelete}
    "None"  {$Perm = 0}
    Default {Write-Host
              '$Permission should be Read,Apply,Edit,FC, or None'
             return
             }
}
if($perm)
{
    $GPMPermission = $GPM.CreatePermission(
                     $User,$Perm,$false)
}
```

Filtering

We want to be able to set permissions not just on one GPO, but on many GPOs. In this section, we get all the GPOs and then filter out the ones we want:

```
Write-Host " - Getting GPOs"
$GPOs = $gpmDomain.SearchGPOs($gpm.CreateSearchCriteria())
```

```
if($GPOName)
{
    $GPOs = $GPOs | Where{$_.DisplayName -like $GPOName}
}
```

Setting Permissions

In this last section, we get to the meat of the script. We take all the GPOs that we have filtered down and we set the permissions. One important thing to note in this section is the use of $replace. We may want to be able to replace permissions and not just add on to them, so this variable is key. We also use this variable to set the permissions to **None** if no variables are passed:

```
foreach($gpo in $GPOs)
{
    Write-Host " + Processing $($Gpo.DisplayName)"
    $secInfo = $GPO.GetSecurityInfo()
    if($replace -or ($perm -eq 0))
    {
        Write-Host "   - Removing $User Permissions"
        $secInfo.RemoveTrustee($User)
    }
    if($perm -ne 0)
    {
        Write-Host "   - Adding Permissions [$Permission]"
        $secInfo.Add($GPMPermission)
    }
    Write-Host "   - Setting info on $($Gpo.DisplayName)"
    $GPO.SetSecurityInfo($secInfo)
}
```

Operators in PowerShell

In PowerShell there are comparison operators, which are used to compare one object to another object. Understanding the operators' functionality is key. There are about 26 operators that you can use, but we want to cover only a few of them. You can see the use of the -like operator when we filter the GPOs.

- -eq: Equal

- -ne: Not equal

- -ge: Greater than or equal

- -gt: Greater than

- -lt: Less than

- -le: Less than or equal

- -like: Wildcard comparison

- -notlike: Wildcard comparison

- -match: Regular expression comparison

- -notmatch: Regular expression comparison

- -contains: Containment operator

- -notcontains: Containment operator

These are case insensitive by default, so most of these operators have case-sensitive equivalents. You can access these by adding a c in front of the operator, for instance -ceq. You can find more information in the help file by running this command:

```
PS> get-help about_operator
```

Making PowerShell Even Easier with Pay Tools

There are several pay tools that make working with PowerShell a little easier. But not just PowerShell, they makes working with Group Policy easier as well. We are going go over a few of them because we want to make sure you have the best experience when it comes to working with Group Policy and PowerShell.

GPExpert Scripting Toolkit for PowerShell

The SDM team not only provides the free tool we used earlier in the chapter, they also offer a PowerShell snap-in that allows you to actually script GPO settings. Yes, you heard correctly. With this snap-in we can actually script GPO settings. *We're talking about the stuff inside a GPO!*

You can check it out here: http://www.sdmsoftware.com/products2.php.

We have been waiting a long time for something like this, and it is so useful that we had to talk about it.

We will start with installing the snap-in and then verify the install. We will provide an example of getting GPO setting information and then wrap up just one more example: setting some IE settings within GPOs.

Install

The SDM guys are on the ball when it comes to installers, so all you have to do is register and download it from `http://www.sdmsoftware.com/products2.php` or contact `sales@sdmsoftware.com`. After you get the MSI, just double-click on it and the installer does everything for you.

Verify the Install

After we install a snap-in, we want to verify that it was installed properly. If you recall, earlier we used `Get-PSSnapin -reg` to see all the registered snap-ins. We are going to do that again, but this time we are looking for GetGPObjectPSSnapIn.

The output should look something like Figure 11.16.

FIGURE 11.16 Get-PSSnapin after the install

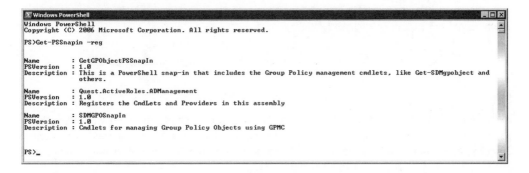

Now that we know it was installed properly, we're ready to get down to business.

Getting Information

After you install and load the snap-in, you get one new cmdlet called `Get-SDMgpobject`. We are going to use this cmdlet to plunk IE settings into a GPO. This script is composed of a couple of sections, listed below. We will go through each one and explain what is going on under the hood.

- Setup
- Getting the GPO
- Getting the section path
- Processing settings

Figure 11.17 shows what the output looks like.

FIGURE 11.17 Output of Get-GPOIESettings.ps1

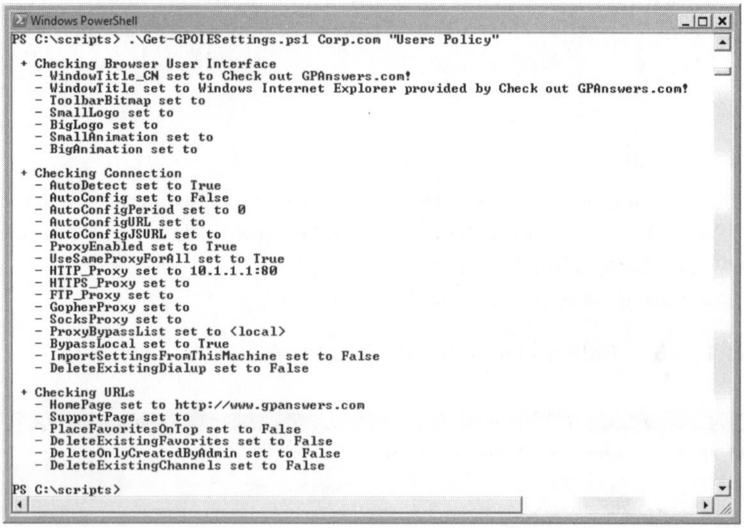

```
Windows PowerShell                                                     _ □ ×
PS C:\scripts> .\Get-GPOIESettings.ps1 Corp.com "Users Policy"

 + Checking Browser User Interface
   - WindowTitle_CN set to Check out GPAnswers.com!
   - WindowTitle set to Windows Internet Explorer provided by Check out GPAnswers.com!
   - ToolbarBitmap set to
   - SmallLogo set to
   - BigLogo set to
   - SmallAnimation set to
   - BigAnimation set to

 + Checking Connection
   - AutoDetect set to True
   - AutoConfig set to False
   - AutoConfigPeriod set to 0
   - AutoConfigURL set to
   - AutoConfigJSURL set to
   - ProxyEnabled set to True
   - UseSameProxyForAll set to True
   - HTTP_Proxy set to 10.1.1.1:80
   - HTTPS_Proxy set to
   - FTP_Proxy set to
   - GopherProxy set to
   - SocksProxy set to
   - ProxyBypassList set to <local>
   - BypassLocal set to True
   - ImportSettingsFromThisMachine set to False
   - DeleteExistingDialup set to False

 + Checking URLs
   - HomePage set to http://www.gpanswers.com
   - SupportPage set to
   - PlaceFavoritesOnTop set to False
   - DeleteExistingFavorites set to False
   - DeleteOnlyCreatedByAdmin set to False
   - DeleteExistingChannels set to False

PS C:\scripts>
```

Setup

In this section, we set up the parameters we will use in the script, and then we'll use Add-PSSnapin to add the snap-in, GetGPObjectPSSnapIn. The parameters for this script are Domain and GPOName. The Domain is the DNS domain name, and the GPOName is the name of the Group Policy you want the settings from:

```
Param($Domain = $(throw '$Domain is required'),
      $GPOName = $(throw '$GPOName is required'))
Write-Host
Add-PSSnapin GetGPObjectPSSnapIn -ea "SilentlyContinue"
```

Getting the GPO

This is where we get the actual GPO. You have two options to load the GPO, by name or by GUID. We used name in this script. You may also notice the path looks a lot like an ADSI path. That was done intentionally to make the cmdlet feel familiar to scripters:

```
$gpo = Get-SDMgpobject -gponame "gpo://$Domain/$GPOName" -openByName $true
```

Getting the Section Path

Now that we have the GPO, we need to specify which part of the GPO we want to look at. In this case, we'll use the following code to look at the IE Maintenance settings:

```
$stng_path = "User Configuration/Windows Settings/IE Maintenance"
$cnt = $gpo.GetObject($stng_path)
```

Pretty much all areas of Group Policy are accessible using the `Get-SDMgpobject`.

Processing the Settings

The final section is where we iterate through the settings in the section we selected. A section is divided into *containers*, or a group of settings, so we need to loop through all the containers and get their respective settings:

```
foreach($container in $cnt.Containers)
{
    " + Checking {0}" -f $container.Name
    $settname = "PROPERTIES"
    $stng = $container.Settings.ItemByName($settname)
    foreach($Prop in $stng.GetPropertyNames())
    {
        $stng.Refresh();
        $result = $stng.Get($Prop)
        "   - {0} set to {1}" -f $prop,$result
    }
    Write-Host
}
```

Setting Group Policy Settings

While getting detailed GPO setting information from a script is totally awesome, being able to actually modify the GPO is really the Holy Grail of scripting GPOs. We would be remiss if we did not demonstrate the ability to set Group Policy settings. In this script, we are going to set the IE proxy settings. Here are the sections:

- Setup
- Getting the GPO
- Getting the section path
- Setting the proxy-specific settings

Figure 11.18 shows what the output looks like

Setup

Here we set up the parameters and use `Add-PSSnapin` to add the snap-in GetGPObjectPSSnapIn. The parameters for this script are `Domain`, `GPOName`, and `Proxy`. The `Domain` is the DNS domain name, the `GPOName` is the name of the policy setting, and the `Proxy` is the name and port number of the proxy server.

```
Param($Domain = $(throw '$Domain is required'),
      $GPOName = $(throw '$GPOName is required'),
      $proxy = $(throw '$proxy is required'))
Write-Host
Add-PSSnapin GetGPObjectPSSnapIn -ea "SilentlyContinue"
```

FIGURE 11.18 Output of Set-GPOIESettings.ps1

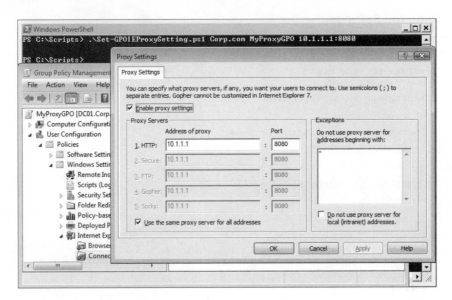

Getting the GPO

Before we can set anything, we need to get the GPO using the following code:

```
$gpo = Get-SDMgpobject -gponame "gpo://$Domain/$GPOName" -openByName $true
```

Getting the Section Path

We retrieved the GPO in the last section, but we need to get the actual container (the folder in the GUI) that has the settings we want to modify. In this case, we want to modify the Connection container in IE Maintenance.

```
$container = $gpo.GetObject(
    "User Configuration/Windows Settings/IE Maintenance/Connection")
```

Setting the Proxy Settings

Now, we get to the meat of the script, the setting of the properties. In this script we are setting the proxy settings, but we also want to enable the proxy and use the same proxy for all protocols. Finally, we want to save the settings:

```
$setting = $container.Settings.ItemByName("PROPERTIES")
$setting.Put("ProxyEnabled",$true)
$setting.Put("HTTP_Proxy",$proxy)
$setting.Put("UseSameProxyForAll",$true)
$setting.Save()
Write-Host
```

FullArmor WorkFlow Studio

This chapter is about scripting Group Policy stuff. And, just because we've used PowerShell to do the scripting doesn't mean we can't also script another way.

FullArmor has a new offering called WorkFlow Studio. This product is very useful for backing up, importing, restoring, and deploying GPOs. It allows you to use a workflow GUI to create a script and share tasks. Some of those tasks might be to create and manage GPOs.

You can check it out at www.fullarmor.com/products-workflow-studio.htm, and you can also see a screen shot in Figure 11.19.

FIGURE 11.19 A Group Policy workflow

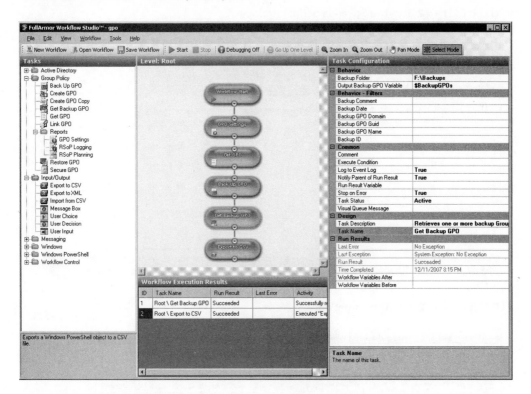

The point of WorkFlow Studio is to get a scriptable, repeatable process. And if you wanted to use that process to create and manage GPOs, you're in the right place!

Specops Software's Specops Command

This company truly has taken Group Policy and PowerShell to the next level. This product not only allows you to use PowerShell for startup, logon, logoff, and shutdown scripts, it allows the scripts to be refreshed at the GPO interval. As if that wasn't enough, it also allows you to target the scripts based on specific criteria.

We don't have space to go through all the things this product can do, but we wanted to provide some ideas and screen shots. You can check out the free product here: `www.specopssoft` `.com/powershell/`.

Figure 11.20 shows what the script assignment interface looks like. You can write the script right here. Specops Command also gives you several other options, like the ability to sign the script or to import a script from a file. Very versatile!

The final thing we want to show is the Targeting tab, shown in Figure 11.21. Gone are the days of wasting dozens of lines of script to make sure the script applies. We can just do it right in the GPO. You can target dozens of different conditions like group, name, IP, and Registry keys, and you can even use WQL (Windows Query Language).

FIGURE 11.20   The Specops Script Interface

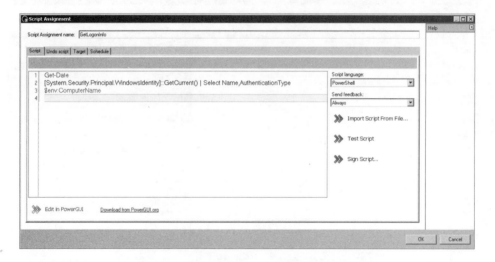

FIGURE 11.21   The Target tab

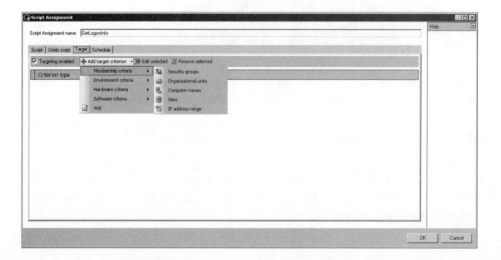

The power Specops provides is huge. There's a pay version that has even more features. Check out their website for more details and to try it for yourself.

Replacing Microsoft's GPMC Scripts with PowerShell Equivalents

Microsoft has an army of interesting VisualBasic scripts that perform many of the functions of the GPMC. And, since they haven't PowerShell-ified them yet, as a service to you, our loyal `www.GPanswers.com` fans, we've written PowerShell equivalents for just about all of the existing Group Policy scripts. You can download the original Microsoft GPMC scripts here: `http://tinyurl.com/23xfz3`.

Then trot on over to the Book Resources section of `www.GPanswers.com` and download the script or scripts you need. Pre-PowerShelled for your convenience.

Table 11.1 shows the original Microsoft script, what it does, and our newly named PowerShell script.

TABLE 11.1   PowerShell Equivalents for Microsoft Scripts

Microsoft Script Name	What It Does	PowerShell Script Name	Notes about Our Power-Shell Script
BackupAllGPOs.wsf	Backs up all GPOs	New-GPOBackup.ps1	Takes parameters -all and -path
BackupGPO.wsf	Backs up a GPO	New-GPOBackup.ps1	Takes parameters -GPOName and -path
CopyGPO.wsf	Copies GPO	New-GPO.ps1	Takes parameters -fromGPO and -GPOName
CreateGPO.wsf	Creates GPO	New-GPO.ps1	Takes parameter -GPOName
DeleteGPO.wsf	Deletes GPO	Remove-GPO.ps1	Takes parameter -GPOName
DumpGPOInfo.wsf	Dumps GPO info	Get-GPO.ps1	Takes parameter -GPOName

TABLE 11.1 PowerShell Equivalents for Microsoft Scripts *(continued)*

Microsoft Script Name	What It Does	PowerShell Script Name	Notes about Our Power-Shell Script
FindDisabledGPOs.wsf	Finds all disabled GPOs	Get-DisabledGPO.ps1	Takes parameter –Domain
FindDuplicateNamedGPOs.wsf	Finds duplicate named GPOs	Get-DupeGPO.ps1	Takes parameter –Domain
FindGPOsByPolicyExtension.wsf	Finds GPOs by policy extension	Get-GPO.ps1	Takes parameter –PolicyExt
FindGPOsBySecurityGroup.wsf	Finds GPOs by security group	Get-GPO.ps1	Takes parameter –Groups
FindGPOsWithNoSecurityFiltering.wsf	Finds GPOs with no security filtering	Get-GPO.ps1	Takes parameter –NoSecurity
findorphanedGPOsInSYSVOL.wsf	Finds orphaned GPOs in SYSVOL	Get-SysVolGPO	Takes parameters –all and –path
FindUnlinkedGPOs.wsf	Finds GPOs with no links	Get-GPO.ps1	Takes parameter –NoLink
GetReportsForAllGPOs.wsf	Get reports for all GPOs	Get-GPOReport.ps1	Takes parameters –all and –path
GetReportsForGPO.wsf	Get reports for a GPO	Get-GPOReport.ps1	Takes parameters –GPOName and –path
GrantPermissionOnAllGPOs.wsf	Grants the permissions for all GPOs	Set-GPOPermission.ps1	Takes parameters –all and –group
ImportAllGPOs.wsf	Imports all GPOs in path	Import-GPO.ps1	Takes parameters –all and –path

TABLE 11.1   PowerShell Equivalents for Microsoft Scripts *(continued)*

Microsoft Script Name	What It Does	PowerShell Script Name	Notes about Our Power-Shell Script
`ImportGPO.wsf`	Imports a GPO in path	`Import-GPO.ps1`	Takes parameters `-GPOName` and `-path`
`ListAllGPOs.wsf`	Lists all GPOs	`Get-GPO.ps1`	Takes parameter `-List`
`QueryBackupLocation.wsf`	Lists all GPOs in backup	`Restore-GPOBackup.ps1`	Takes parameter `-List`
`RestoreAllGPOs.wsf`	Restores all GPOs in path	`Restore-GPOBackup.ps1`	Takes parameters `-all` and `-path` and `-table`
`RestoreGPO.wsf`	Restore a GPO in path	`Restore-GPOBackup.ps1`	Takes parameters `-GPOName` and `-path` and `-table`

Final Thoughts

Here's a great idea! Let's manually configure the permissions on 500 GPOs and adjust them to our needs. Or document them. Or back them up.

If that sounds like a good time to you, then knock yourself out.

But if you want to be able to make massive changes using PowerShell, you can do it with the construction kit we've provided here, with some free cmdlet downloads and with pay tools.

Come to the book resources section of www.GPanswers.com for all the scripts we talked about in this chapter as well as any updates and notes if they're available.

12

Advanced Group Policy Management (AGPM)

Let's start with the bad news. Because there's a lot of good news in this chapter, and I don't want anyone to say, "Hey! I'm 30 pages into this chapter and he didn't tell me [this very important fact I'm about to tell you]."

That is, to use the stuff we're going to talk about in this chapter, you have to pay Microsoft a little extra. That's right. Everything we've talked about in this book so far is "free," inasmuch as it's in the box when you buy Windows and spin up an Active Directory, install your Windows clients, perform some downloads, and so on.

But this chapter is different. In this chapter, we're going to talk about a Microsoft tool called Advanced Group Policy Management, or AGPM for short. And its goal is to help bigger companies with the challenge of GPO management. There's no "Are you sure you really want to do this?" inside the GPMC and Group Policy Object Editor. Everything happens in real time. If you make a mistake, there's no "Group Policy Undo" short of disabling or deleting the GPO and hoping you only have a few desktops to clean up.

AGPM puts a "Change Management" system around Group Policy within the GPMC. Change Management is the art of "not screwing things up." The idea is that some people request changes, others make editing choices, and others approve their changes. AGPM is involved with ensuring that your overall philosophy of Group Policy management is embraced. Here are the main things it's meant to do:

- Ensure that GPOs are configured correctly—before they're placed into production
- Reduce risk of Group Policy deployment errors
- Ensure that Group Policy management is done securely
- Ensure compliancy (i.e., know what's going on, who made the change, and what was changed)

And it's a really cool tool. Which is why Microsoft is making you pay extra for it.

How do you get this tool? First, you must be a Microsoft Software Assurance (SA) customer. Being an SA customer means you pay a little extra insurance money up front hoping that Microsoft produces updates that you want to install. A misconception is that SA customers must be big companies. They don't have to be. You can be an SA customer with as few as 50 seats. You can learn more about becoming an SA customer here: http://www.microsoft.com/licensing/sa/.

Next, you must be willing to buy a pack of products that are bundled into an offering called the Microsoft Desktop Optimization Pack, or MDOP. MDOP contains five big tools, and AGPM is just one of them. We talk about the other really big one, SoftGrid, in the companion book, *Creating the Secure Managed Desktop*.

The idea is that MDOP *today* contains these five big tools. The people who pay *now* get the benefit of using these tools right away. Perhaps in the future, Microsoft might kick a tool out of MDOP, like AGPM, and make it a free download for all customers. Then perhaps they will include a cool new tool in the MDOP to offer those paying to continue their MDOP subscription.

But right now, if you want to use AGPM, the rules are very clear: you need to be an SA customer and you must buy the entire MDOP package for several dollars per seat (usually US$10).

If you want to learn more about the MDOP package, check it out here: `http://www.microsoft .com/windows/products/windowsvista/enterprise/mdopoverview.mspx` (shortened to `http://tinyurl.com/2j38g2`).

This chapter isn't for everyone. But AGPM is a great addition to the possibilities in Group Policy land, so we'll explore what it has to offer.

The Challenge of Group Policy Change Management

Group Policy offers a huge amount of power. (That's why our logo at `www.GPanswers.com` looks like a deity hurling a lightning bolt.) Actually, some could argue that Group Policy has too much power. Not too much power in the hands of someone skilled in the ways of Group Policy kung fu. But rather, it can be too much power for someone who's a mere white belt.

With that in mind, Microsoft's AGPM product seeks to fill in several gaps within the GPMC when it comes to who can do what to Group Policy. In Chapter 2, "Managing Group Policy with the GPMC," you learned about the Group Policy delegation model. Sure, it's possible to say, "Carl can create GPOs," "Ed can edit these GPOs," and "Larry can link GPOs to the Sales OU." But that's not good enough for environments that have multiple administrators who need more granular levels of control.

The other challenge is that, sure, Ed can edit the GPOs. But does he know what he's doing? Wouldn't it be better if Alice approved the GPO that Ed edited? And what if Edward (a different dude than Ed) wanted to edit the same GPO that Ed just edited?

Additionally, with all this creating, editing, and linking, it can be hard to figure out what's happened over time if a problem occurs. If you really wanted to know, could you tell which Ed (Ed or Edward) had edited it, what the edit was, and which Ed edited it last?

So, with that in mind, AGPM brings several change control functionalities to the table to help solve these issues:

- Check In/Check Out workflow management

- Version control

- Difference reporting

- Role-based delegation

- Offline editing of GPOs
- GPO templates (different than Starter GPOs)

The best part is that once it's loaded, AGPM fits right into the GPMC. This means it's not another whole tool to learn (although it does have its ins and outs). In this chapter, we'll explore these major features of AGPM so you can get a feel for how you might use it in your environment.

> It doesn't matter if you're using the Central Store with ADMX files or still using ADM files. AGPM works with GPOs created from any platform, but the best management station platform is a Windows Vista management station with the AGPM client installed. We'll talk about installation in the next section.

Architecture and Installation of AGPM

Actually, the first part of installing AGPM is getting the MDOP media package that contains AGPM. As an SA customer, ask your salesdude or salesdudette, or your Microsoft Technical Accounts Manager (TAM) if you have one, for a copy if you're entitled to it.

AGPM Architecture

The AGPM architecture is, in a word, elegant. It doesn't require any wacky schema extensions. You don't have to touch every DC. You just install two pieces: a server piece and a client piece.

The server piece should be installed on Windows Server 2008 if possible. This is because the server piece (and archive that lives within it) leverages the extensions registered within the machine it's run upon. So, while you can install the AGPM server on Windows Server 2003 (or even Windows Vista, but that's not really a hot idea), it's best to install it on a Windows Server 2008 machine because Windows Server 2008 has the most Group Policy extensions available, so it's the best place to house the archive.

The client part is a misnomer. It's not a client that needs to be installed on every desktop, just a little management piece that needs to be installed on your management stations where you run the GPMC. Since you're likely to use Windows Vista as your management station, this is where you would load your AGPM client.

A little later we'll discuss how to use the AGPM world as the exclusive place to create new GPOs and then manage them. But that means that soon after deployment of the AGPM server, you'll want to get the AGPM client piece out to all your administrators so they can continue managing GPOs (albeit in a new way).

Installing AGPM

Once you have it, the MDOP package contains five big programs. Again, the one we're concerned with is Advanced Group Policy Management, seen in Figure 12.1.

FIGURE 12.1   The MDOP splash and installation screen

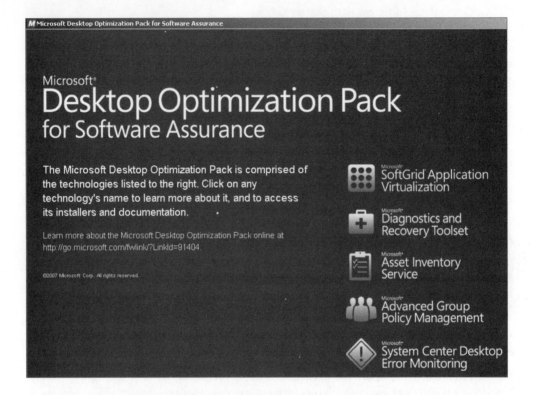

Installing the AGPM Server Service

AGPM performs much of its Check In/Check Out workflow management because it installs a simple service on the server of your choice. There are no schema changes, no Active Directory back-end changes, and no touching all of your Domain Controllers.

It's recommended that you install the AGPM server on a regular server (i.e., not a Domain Controller), but it appears to install and run just fine on a Domain Controller.

However, here's the trick: You'll want to install the AGPM server on a Windows Server 2008 server. That's because AGPM will track 100 percent of the settings only when it's run on the latest operating system. AGPM is a little strange: it relies on the machine it's loaded on as the "backbone" for the CSEs it supports in the archive. So then you need to ask yourself, "Which Windows machines have the *most* CSEs?" And the answer to that is easy: Windows Server 2008. It has the original Group Policy CSEs and the new Group Policy Preference Extensions (GPPEs). And, well, it's a *server*. So, Windows Server 2008 is the ideal candidate (though it is possible to load it on Windows Vista if you needed to in a pinch).

WARNING

Again, if you don't install the AGPM server on a Windows Server 2008 machine, you'll lose the ability to store the new Vista Folder Redirection items, Vista's new Wireless Network 802.11 policies, Vista's new Wired Network 802.3 policies, and Vista's new Deployed Printers policies.

The first piece you'll install is the server piece, and you can do this by clicking on Install Microsoft Advanced Group Policy Management Server, as seen in Figure 12.2.

FIGURE 12.2 Start out by installing the AGPM Server.

At this point, you'll see a wizard-driven Server Setup screen. You'll need to accept the license terms and give it a directory to install the AGPM server in (the default is usually A-OK). The tricky question is when you're asked about the Archive Path, as seen in Figure 12.3. The default for this is a little baffling to me, as it puts the Group Policy archive underneath the All Users\ Application Data directory (also seen in Figure 12.3), and on Windows Server 2008 it puts the path as C:\ProgramData\Microsoft\AGPM (which is a little better). The files that AGPM puts here are just regular files. And, although you shouldn't need to poke directly around the archive (like, ever), if you did need to, it might be nice to have the archive set in a place that's obvious. So I like to change the default to C:\AGPM-ARCHIVE (as seen in Figure 12.4) or something similar where I know I can easily get to it.

FIGURE 12.3 The original path to store AGPM data is a little obtuse.

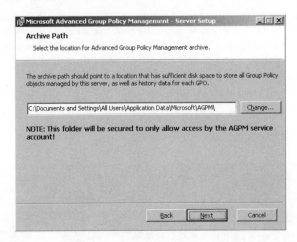

FIGURE 12.4 This is my suggested path for storing AGPM data.

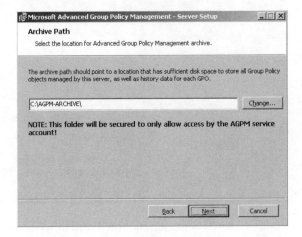

Next, you'll be asked about the AGPM service account, as seen in Figure 12.5. If you have one domain and you install AGPM on a Domain Controller, I suggest you choose Local System. If you have multiple domains or install on a member server, then select User Account and provide an account that you trust. This account will have rights over the AGPM system.

The next screen is the initial Archive Owner account, as seen in Figure 12.6. You can choose a regular user account here, or a security group (e.g., AGPM-OWNERS). This account doesn't need to have Domain Administrator rights. But note that this person will initially own all the material inside the archive. Later, this person will then be able to delegate the stuff contained within the archive to other users of the AGPM system. More users or groups can be delegated these rights later.

I suggest using a new, neutral account. I'm calling mine AGPM-OWNER. I created this account in Active Directory Users and Computers, then selected it, as seen in Figure 12.6.

Finally, you'll be at the final screen and can click Install to install AGPM.

FIGURE 12.5   If you're installing on a Domain Controller, choose Local System.

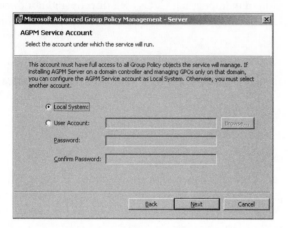

FIGURE 12.6   If installing AGPM on a member server, choose an Active Directory user account with a name reflective of what you're using. We suggest AGPM-OWNER or AGPM-SERVICE or something similar. In my examples, I'll use AGPM-OWNER.

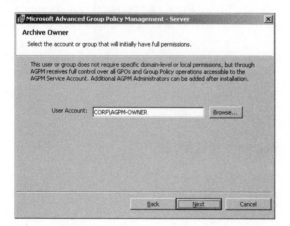

WARNING   Sometimes, using a domain account like AGPM-OWNER can add some headaches because the AGPM-OWNER may not be able to access the original GPOs. If you start to have permissions issues that look unsolvable, read the section "Advanced Configuration and Troubleshooting of AGPM" toward the end of the chapter for some remediation.

When finished, you can install the next piece: the "client" piece that installs within the GPMC.

Right now, the AGPM service can be seen as a single point of failure. That is, if the computer that the service is running on dies (or the service dies), the AGPM system will obviously fail to work. However, right now AGPM is not an officially "clusterable" service, meaning you cannot (right now) officially spin up Microsoft Cluster Services and get failover if the primary server dies. However, the "regular" method of manipulating GPOs (i.e., directly and not through the AGPM system) will still work and can be used as an alternative until the AGPM system or service is back up and running.

We at www.GPanswers.com tested AGPM in a clustered environment and it seemed to work A-OK. Because it's not officially clusterable, your mileage and official support may vary.

Installing the AGPM Client

Since we learned in Chapters 1 and 3 that the best management station is either a Windows Server 2008 machine or, more likely, a Windows Vista + SP1 + updated GPMC machine, that's precisely where we'll load our AGPM client. You load the AGPM client on the machine from which you typically manage your Group Policy.

You saw the AGPM client installation option back at Figure 12.2, so we'll select it now.

The original shipping AGPM's client piece does not install on Windows Server 2008. Be sure you have the latest AGPM before proceeding if you want to install the client piece on a Windows Server 2008 management station.

After you accept the license terms, you'll be prompted for the installation directory. The defaults are fine for this. You'll then have to tell the AGPM client which server the AGPM server is running on, as seen in Figure 12.7.

FIGURE 12.7 Specify the server and the server port for AGPM clients.

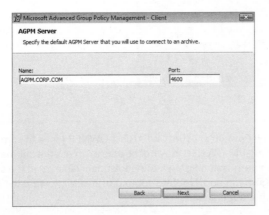

You're then presented with a warning that you're required to open up port 4600 completely as a firewall exception. This is required, so click Yes to continue, as seen in Figure 12.8.

FIGURE 12.8   The AGPM client requires that port 4600 be open.

At this point, the client will install and you'll be done. You'll need to install the AGPM client on each Group Policy administrator's computer or else they won't be able to participate in the Check In/Check Out system.

You can also deploy the AGPM client using Group Policy Software Installation. See Chapter 4 in the companion book, *Creating the Secure Managed Desktop*, for more information.

What Happens after AGPM is Installed?

Once AGPM is installed, you might want to start it up. But you'll notice there isn't any AGPM icon anywhere on the server. The server is just silently running the AGPM service, waiting as a "storage vault" for GPOs we're about to feed it.

Firing Up GPMC the First Time

When you next run the GPMC on your Vista management station, you'll immediately be prompted with what you see in Figure 12.9. That is, the GPMC, now loaded with AGPM's client, is trying to connect with the AGPM server over port 4600—and in doing so raises Vista's hackles. You need to unblock the restrictions to ensure smooth communication between the client and the server. I would have thought answering the question we saw in Figure 12.8 would have been enough to open up the ports, but Vista is kind of picky that way.

GPMC Differentials

Next, if you start to plunk about in the GPMC, you'll see some subtle, but powerful, changes. First, note that if you click on a GPO or a link to a GPO, there's now a new tab, called History, as seen in Figure 12.10. Indeed, you might also get an error similar to what's also seen in Figure 12.10.

FIGURE 12.9   Windows Vista helps you unblock the correct port.

FIGURE 12.10   By default anyone without rights will be denied access to the archive.

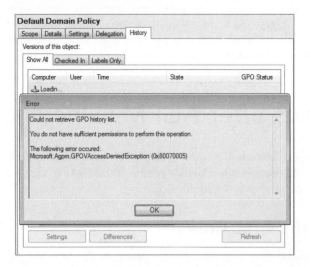

We'll get to that error in a second. But for now, let's finish the quick tour. You'll also notice a whole new node underneath Group Policy Objects called Change Control.

WARNING   Sometimes the Change Control node mysteriously "floats" up to the domain level. So, be sure to check the domain level if you suddenly think, "Where's the Change Control node?"

And within Change Control there are three tabs: Contents, Domain Delegation, and AGPM Server, as seen in Figure 12.11. Indeed, if you click the Contents tab, you might get a similar error to what we just saw (basically, another type of Access Denied, as seen in Figure 12.11).

FIGURE 12.11   Access is Denied for those without rights to the AGPM system.

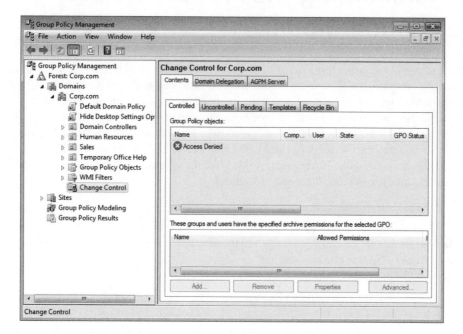

What's With All the Access Denied Errors?

So, why are you being denied? Because you're not logged in as the person you designated to have the initial ability to own the stuff contained within the archive. So on your Windows Vista management station, log on as that user (in my case, I choose AGPM-OWNER).

Once you're logged in with that account (in my case, as AGPM-OWNER) on your Windows Vista management station (which already has the AGPM client installed), fire up the GPMC by selecting Start and typing **GPMC.MSC** in the Search box. Then, see if you still get those Access Denied errors.

You won't, because you own the AGPM archive.

Does the World Change Right Away?

The goal of AGPM is to help you get a better handle on the way you create, approve, and manage GPOs. But installing the AGPM server component doesn't prevent you (immediately) from administrating Group Policy the way you always did. That is, by default, if you've got the ability to create GPOs, you can still create them. And if you've got the ability to link GPOs, you can still link them. Those powers don't go away until they're expressly taken away by the AGPM archive owner (in my example, AGPM-OWNER). By default, every GPO is considered *Uncontrolled*.

What we'll learn next is the delegation model and how to make existing GPOs *Controlled*.

Understanding the AGPM Delegation Model

Again, each GPO can either be Controlled or Uncontrolled. The goal is to move from your current chaotic environment (Uncontrolled) to one that is orderly and neat (Controlled). To that end, we need to understand the roles that are available to us, who can do what. Once we understand that, we'll have a better chance of maintaining order going forward.

The point is to bring order from chaos. To do that, we need an ongoing process to manage our GPOs. You can start to think of the AGPM archive as a big library system. It's been *years* since I stepped into a public library (sorry, but I like the cappuccinos and lemon squares at book stores). But I remember the basic procedure:

- Find a book I want to read.

- Show my library card (which is my credential to "do something" with this book).

- Borrow the book by "checking it out" of the library. At this point I have sole possession of this book. No one else can use it.

- Utilize the book.

- When I'm done, return it to the library in the drop slot. This doesn't mean the book immediately goes back on the shelf; it's just *pending* in the holding pen. The librarian will examine the book to make sure I didn't bend the pages or scribble in the book's margins. The book goes into the "book depository" or "book vault" or "book archive" or whatever that particular library calls it.

- If someone had requested this book while I had it checked out, it wouldn't go back on the shelf. The librarian would call the next book user and let them know the book was waiting for them behind the counter.

- If no one wanted the book, the book is put back on the shelf, sometimes called being "checked in." That way, it's ready to be leveraged by the next person.

So, neat, orderly, and systematic. That's your good ol' public library system. And that's the same idea you'll use when dealing with GPOs in AGPM. Here's the basic framework when dealing with GPOs once you get the hang of AGPM:

- Create a new GPO and put it under control (or control a GPO that was previously uncontrolled).

- Check out the GPO so it cannot be modified by anyone else.

- Edit the GPO (again, only you have access right now).

- Return the GPO to the library by "checking it in." This doesn't mean the GPO is "live" and actively modifying clients. It's *pending* in the "holding pen" until it's approved.

- At this point, others might choose to "check out" the GPO to make more changes.

- Once all changes are made, someone Reviews the changes and makes comments.

- Finally, once all Reviews are made, someone Approves the changes and the GPO goes "live."

AGPM Delegation Roles

Because you can be one administrator in a larger company with dozens of administrators, you can have different roles for different people. You can assign different Active Directory groups to various AGPM roles, or you can assign specific people (without groups) specific roles. Here are the AGPM roles:

Reviewer   You can see the GPO and what's been done to it. Think of this as Read-Only access to the history and settings of the GPO.

Approver   This role should have been called Approver/Reviewer because you automatically get Reviewer rights when you get Approver rights. Approver rights allow you to "check in" GPOs from the archive into the real world. Ultimately, it's the Approver who can take offline GPO copies and make them "live" to affect the user population.

Editor   This role should be called Editor/Reviewer because you automatically get Reviewer rights when you get Editor rights. This allows you to make changes to GPOs. But these changes aren't happening in the real world—they're being changed in an offline archive copy of the GPO, until an Approver performs a "check in," which takes the copy of the GPO and plunks it back down into the live production GPO.

Full Control   You have full ability over all GPOs (and of course rights to Review all GPOs). You can dictate which GPOs are Controlled and Uncontrolled and can perform all roles with any GPOs. By default, only the named account during setup (in my world AGPM-OWNER) is set up as Full Control.

Deeper with AGPM Roles and Rights

The AGPM permissions can be a litttttle mysterious underneath the hood. There are various new levels of security within the AGPM system. On the surface, AGPM adds the following roles: Reviewer, Editor, Approver, and AGPM Administrator.

In the following table, you can see the default permissions for these roles.

	Reviewer	Editor	Approver	AGPM Administrator
List Contents	X	X	X	X
Read Settings	X	X	X	X
Edit Settings		X		X
Create GPOs			X	X
Deploy GPOs			X	X
Delete GPOs			X	X
Modify Options				X
Modify Security				X
Create Templates		X		X

However, occasionally, you need to know exactly which actions a specific role is able to do. In other words, if someone is a Reviewer, Editor, Approver, or AGPM Administrator, which tasks are they able to perform (because of the permissions they have). In the following images, you can see the cross reference of the AGPM Roles, the tasks they can perform, and the required permissions needed to perform that task.

This first set of tables shows the required permissions needed to perform domain-level tasks.

Domain-Level Tasks	Permissions									Roles			
	List Contents	Read Settings	Edit Settings	Modify Options	Create GPO	Deploy GPO	Delete GPO	Modify Security	Create Templates	Reviewer	Editor	Approver	GPOVault Admin (Full control)
Delegate domain-level permissions								X					X
Configure email notification	X			X									X
View mail notification settings	X	X								X	X	X	X
Create a GPO or approve creation	X				X							X	X
Request creation of a GPO	X									X	X		
Control an uncontrolled GPO	X				X							X	X

Domain-Level Tasks	Permissions									Roles			
	List Contents	Read Settings	Edit Settings	Modify Options	Create GPO	Deploy GPO	Delete GPO	Modify Security	Create Templates	Reviewer	Editor	Approver	GPOVault Admin (Full control)
Request control of an uncontrolled GPO	X	X								X	X		
Create a template	X								X		X		X
Set default template for creating new GPOs	X								X		X		X
List GPOs	X									X	X	X	X

The second set of tables shows the required permissions needed to perform Group Policy–level tasks.

GPO-Level Tasks	Permissions									Roles			
	List Contents	Read Settings	Edit Settings	Modify Options	Create a GPO	Deploy a GPO	Delete GPO	Modify Security	Create Templates	Reviewer	Editor	Approver	GPOVault Admin (Full Control)
Delegate GPO-level permissions	1							X				X	X
Deploy a GPO or approve deployment	X					X					X	X	X
Change GPO links during deployment	X	X				X						X	X

GPO-Level Tasks	Permissions									Roles			
	List Contents	Read Settings	Edit Settings	Modify Options	Create a GPO	Deploy a GPO	Delete GPO	Modify Security	Create Templates	Reviewer	Editor	Approver	GPOVault Admin (Full Control)
Request deployment of a GPO	X		X								X		
Delete a GPO archive (move to Recycle Bin/uncontrol) or approve deletion	X		2				2				X	X	X
Delete a deployed GPO or approve deletion	X						X					X	X
Request deletion of a deployed GPO	X		X								X		
Delete a template	X						X				X	X	X
Destroy a GPO	X						X				X	X	X

GPO-Level Tasks	Permissions									Roles			
	List Contents	Read Settings	Edit Settings	Modify Options	Create a GPO	Deploy a GPO	Delete GPO	Modify Security	Create Templates	Reviewer	Editor	Approver	GPOVault Admin (Full Control)
Restore a GPO	X		2			2	2				X	X	X
Archive a GPO	X		2			2	2				X	X	X
Check out a GPO	X		X								X	X	X
Edit a GPO	X		4								X	X	X
Rename a GPO	X		X								X	X	X
Label a GPO	X		2			2					X	X	X
Check in a GPO/undo check out	X		3			2					X	X	X
View GPO history	X									X	X	X	X
View reports or GPO links	X	X								X	X	X	X

X—This task requires this permission.
1—Delegating GPO-level permissions requires List Contents permission at the domain level.
2—This task requires at least one of these permissions.
3—This task requires at least one of these permissions. To perform this task, an individual who has only this permission must be the Editor who checked out the GPO.
4—Only the individual who checked out the GPO or a GPOVault Admin can perform this task.

AGPM Common Tasks

In this section, we're going to conquer the big tasks that AGPM can do.

And we're going to do it as if we were the only administrator in the world. This isn't precisely how AGPM is meant to be used. Indeed, it's meant to be used in a multi-domain-administrator environment—that's the point. But to get a grip on what's possible in the AGPM world, for now anyway, we're going to leverage the AGPM-OWNER account and not one of our already-created OU admins from previous chapters.

We'll get to multiple administrator environments just a little later in the section entitled "AGPM Tasks with Multiple Admins." That way, you'll be able to see 100 percent of what's possible with the power of AGPM now. Then in that section, we'll add others to the AGPM system so you can see how multiple administrators might interact with the system as a whole.

But since we know we want to use multiple administrators later, let's get set up for that and become forward-thinking. In those examples, we'll use the Human Resources OU with our trusty admin Frank Rizzo. In previous chapters, Frank was delegated the ability to create GPOs and also link them to the **Human Resources** OU. Figure 12.12 shows what it might look like if Frank created and linked three GPOs to the **Human Resources** OU.

FIGURE 12.12 Three example GPOs created outside of the AGPM system

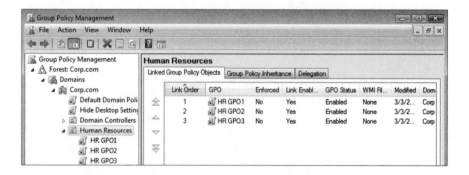

Before we go further, one key point bears repeating: only GPOs that are managed with AGPM can be checked out and checked in. GPOs that were created before AGPM was installed will continue to act as if AGPM *wasn't* installed. We'll see in a minute how to get these GPOs under *Control*.

Now, here's the kicker: even with AGPM installed, it's still possible to shoot yourself in the foot. Using AGPM does not mean you've suddenly invested in a failsafe method to prevent screw-ups. That's because, as we're about to learn, the only time GPOs cannot be edited is when they're Checked Out. We're about to work through these examples, so don't worry if you're a little confused.

Understanding and Working with AGPM's Flow

The point of AGPM is that it provides a way to wrap "history" around the birth, life, and death of a GPO. The AGPM system doesn't care as much about live GPOs as it does about

GPOs that it has in its Archive. Once AGPM has Control of a GPO (which really means a GPO has the ability to be manipulated by AGPM), *that's* when the magic happens. With Control, you're basically saying, "I give in, O great and powerful AGPM system!"

But, even with Control, that doesn't mean the original creator/owner of the GPO can't modify the live GPO. Au contraire. The original owner can still modify the live GPO, affecting the GPO and making changes everywhere it's linked. We'll see a little later how the Deploy function (i.e., actually putting the archive copy into production) will change the live GPO's permissions. But until that point, you're in a danger zone with original, uncontrolled GPOs that are just being brought into the AGPM system.

Figures 12.13 and 12.14 help express the flow of the Birth and Life of a GPO. Note there are two paths to a GPO being "born"—outside of AGPM control (topmost circle) and inside AGM control (leftmost circle).

We're going to go over all the points of this flowchart now, but if you have 120 seconds, really read the flowchart to get a feel for where we're going before you continue.

FIGURE 12.13   The first part of the AGPM "flow."

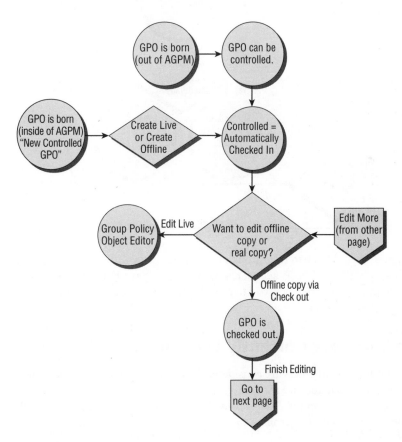

FIGURE 12.14 The second part of the AGPM "flow." More detailed graphic available at www.GPanswers.com in this chapter's resources.

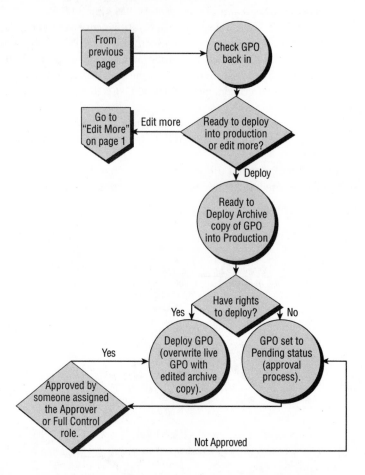

At this point, if you'd like to run through these procedures with me, my suggestion is to be logged into the AGPM-OWNER account. That way, you have Full Control rights to everything we're about to try. Then, a little later, we'll see how to deal with multiple admins with various rights to the system.

Controlling Your Currently Uncontrolled GPOs

After AGPM is loaded, all GPOs are considered *Uncontrolled*. That just means that copies of the GPOs haven't been made into the archive for offline editing. And that's an important point to drive home here: The point of AGPM is to allow you to create a copy of your GPOs offline and edit the offline copies. Controlling those original uncontrolled GPOs is the first step in that process.

So, to that end, I can't see any reason not to control all GPOs. That way, you've got the ability to use the AGPM system to then Check Out GPOs (which will then prevent people from editing them) and do all sorts of awesome things.

However, for our examples, let's Control the three GPOs within Human Resources that we saw earlier in Figure 12.12. To do that we'll click the Change Control node, make sure we're on the Contents tab (at the top), then click the Uncontrolled tab in the middle. All the GPOs in the domain should appear here. Find HR GPO1, HR GPO2, and HR GPO3. Then multiselect (by using the Ctrl key and left-clicking with the mouse) the three GPOs. Finally, rightclick over them and select Control, as seen in Figure 12.15.

FIGURE 12.15 To get started with GPOs within AGPM, you need to take Control.

When you do, you'll be asked for a comment. You can put in anything you like here; it's just a comment for this point in time. Perhaps "Taking control on [insert date here] by [your name]." When you do, you'll be presented (hopefully) with a Succeeded message, similar to what's seen in Figure 12.16.

 If you don't get a Succeeded message, read the section "Advanced Configuration and Troubleshooting of AGPM" later in this chapter for a tip that could help you out.

Now, click on the Controlled tab within the Change Control node. You'll see these three GPOs are now Controlled. And because they're Controlled, they're automatically Checked-In. You can see this status in Figure 12.17.

Now that they're Controlled and Checked-in, you have the ability to make offline copies; it's the offline copies you can edit using AGPM.

FIGURE 12.16 You can see the GPOs you just controlled.

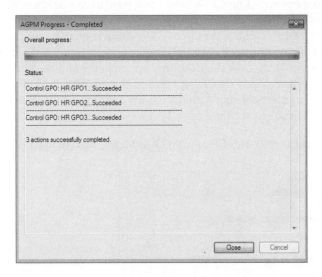

FIGURE 12.17 Checked-in GPOs are now active within AGPM. But they aren't yet protected from the original owner.

Again, just to be super-duper clear, here's a big ol' warning. Just because you've Controlled this GPO doesn't mean that Frank Rizzo, who originally created these GPOs outside of the AGPM system, cannot edit them. You can prove this in one of two ways (or you can try both). First, you can log onto another management station with the GPMC loaded and see if he can edit HR GPO1. Believe me, he can. And the reason he can is that the owner of the live GPO is still Frank. You can see the owner by clicking on the GPO, then clicking the Details tab and checking out the Owner field, as seen in Figure 12.18. There you can see that, indeed, Frank is still the owner. And the owner can always edit the GPO.

FIGURE 12.18 Even though the existing GPO is now Controlled, the original owner can modify it.

Frank will eventually lose his rights as owner of the GPO. But that only happens in the final step of the process when the GPO archive copy is Deployed back on top of the live GPO. It's only during that Deploy process that Frank will finally lose ownership control of that original live GPO. More on this later.

Creating a GPO and Immediately Controlling It

We just learned how we can take *existing* live GPOs and Control them. It's also possible to create brand-new GPOs directly within the AGPM system and immediately control them. To do so, right-click over Change Control, and select New Controlled GPO. When you do, you'll be prompted with what you see in Figure 12.19.

FIGURE 12.19 Creating a new, Controlled GPO.

Next, you can add a comment, and select to "Create live" or "Create offline."

"Create live" will create the GPO in the archive and put it in the Group Policy Objects node (the swimming pool). It's not linked anywhere, which means it's not affecting any levels of Active Directory yet. But note that GPOs created in this way are automatically protected from harm via a special status. That is, GPOs created directly via AGPM show the owner as SYSTEM, or depending on install options, the AGPM service account, as seen in Figure 12.20. This means only administrators who are part of the AGPM system can eventually edit them. That's because AGPM is now "in charge" of this GPO and it cannot be edited in the old (regular) way.

FIGURE 12.20 The Owner of new, Controlled GPOs will automatically be either SYSTEM or the AGPM service account. In our examples, our AGPM service account is named AGPM-OWNER.

And this is what you want to strive for: ensuring that all administrators in your domain are consciously using the AGPM system for all Group Policy creation and editing functions (instead of the "live" native way directly). We'll see how to forcefully require compliance of your administrators a little later to ensure that they're using AGPM and not the native tools to manage your Group Policy universe.

Check Out of a GPO

At this point, let's take AGPM for a real test drive. Our goal is to take an original live GPO, then make a copy of it to work with offline, via Check Out. Once it's Checked Out, we'll be able to edit the offline copy. During this time, the following things are true:

- If the GPO was originally created outside AGPM (i.e., normal GPMC GPO creation), nothing prevents the original owner from modifying the live GPO. Similarly, since the GPO is already live, there's also nothing preventing other administrators from linking to this GPO and using it in its current state. This is kind of bad because we want AGPM to be the way we manage GPOs. But we'll see how to address this situation a little later.

- If the GPO was originally created within AGPM (i.e., as a new controlled GPO), the SYSTEM owns the GPO, so the live GPO cannot be edited by anyone not using the AGPM system.

- In either case, an offline copy of the live GPO is created, and it's the offline copy we'll be editing, so as not to disturb the GPO that's already "doing stuff" for us live.

Let's get started. In the Change Control node, select the Contents tab (top), select the Controlled tab (middle), right-click over a GPO (like HR GPO1), and select Check Out, as seen in Figure 12.21.

FIGURE 12.21   You can work on a copy of a GPO if you perform a Check Out.

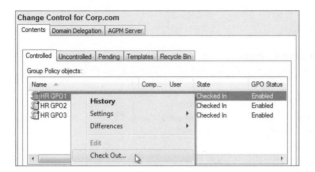

When you do, you'll be prompted for a comment. Perhaps you want to specify why you checked it out, say, to add Control Panel settings. The state now changes to Checked Out and a red outline surrounds the GPO and a red check mark is added, as seen in Figure 12.22.

FIGURE 12.22   Checked-out GPOs can be seen by the outline in the GPO icon (and a little check mark). This is a lot easier to see in color. The GPO is surrounded by a red border nothing that it's checked out.

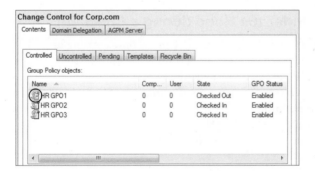

At this point, you'll be ready to edit the offline copy of the GPO that was just created.

Viewing Reports about a Controlled GPO

Now that you've got the GPO in Control, you can examine it a little bit. One of the key things you'll likely want to do is to make sure it has the settings you think it has. By right-clicking over the GPO within the Change Control ➢ Controlled (or other nodes within Change Control), as shown in Figure 12.23, you'll be able to get a quick report of what's going on.

The HTML report is the most useful report here, though there might be some call for an XML report as well. Knowing where the GPO is linked is useful too, of course, and the report is a graphical demonstration of where the GPO is currently linked.

FIGURE 12.23 You can report on GPOs in the archive in multiple ways.

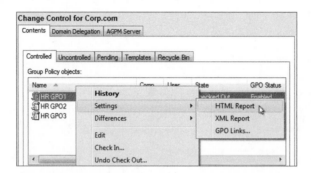

Editing a Checked-Out Offline Copy of a GPO

Again, the person who did the checking out (in our case, the AGPM-OWNER) will be able to Edit the offline copy of the GPO. But before we do that, let's understand why that's possible, and also what's happening to the "real Group Policy world" when we Check-out a GPO and make a copy of it in the archive.

What's Happening Under the Hood during a Checkout

We know that when we Check-out a live GPO, we're really only creating an offline copy to work with. But where does that copy "live"? Turns out, it lives in exactly the same place all other GPOs live—the Group Policy Objects node (the swimming pool).

Here, in Figure 12.24, you can see that a copy of the original GPO (HR GPO1) was created and put in the archive for our editing. This is what we're about to manipulate: the *Checked Out* copy of HR GPO1, not the live HR GPO1 itself.

And now the GPO is Checked Out, only the person who Checked Out the copy of the GPO can edit that offline copy.

> You may have to refresh the Group Policy Objects node to see this new Checked Out copy of the GPO. Additionally, while you're here, click the Details tab of the original GPO to see how Frank is still the owner of that GPO, which is not good. Later, we'll see how and when the ownership of the GPO is revoked from Frank.

And, looking at the Details tab of "[Checked Out] HR GPO1," you can see who owns the GPO: SYSTEM or the AGPM service account. This really means that AGPM is in control of the GPO. And those people with access rights, like AGPM-OWNER or Editors of the GPO, would have the ability to use AGPM to get to this offline copy.

But again, just to make sure we have it in our heads, let's click on the live version of the HR GPO1 and see who owns that. In Figure 12.25, you can see that Frank still owns the *live* HR GPO1.

FIGURE 12.24   A copy of a GPO is created when it's Checked Out.

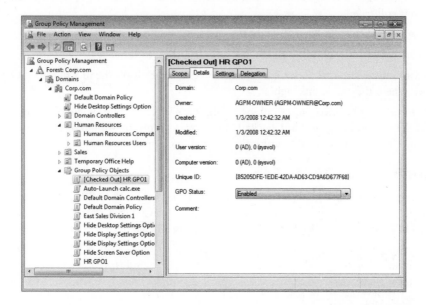

FIGURE 12.25   Frank still owns the original copy of the GPO (which means he can still edit it), so be careful!

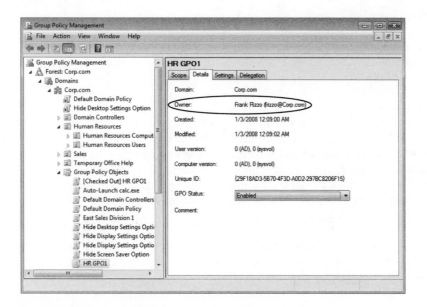

And because he still owns it, Frank could edit the GPO live, which wouldn't be good. Again, we'll see how to control Frank's access to the live GPO soon.

What's Not Controlled During a Check Out

When Check-Out of a GPO is performed, an offline [Checked Out] copy is made. But, the following is still true:

- The owner of the GPO can still edit the real live GPO, not the Checked Out copy.
- Anyone, anywhere with link rights can link or unlink to the real GPO where they want.
- Anyone, anywhere with link rights can Enforce or Un-Enforce the link to the GPO (in the place where they have link rights).

Therefore, don't be lulled into thinking, "Oh, if it's Checked Out, it can't do any harm to anyone." That's just not true. The Checked Out copy is simply an offline *copy* used for editing and is not related to the live GPO until it's checked back in.

Performing Your Offline Edit

Now that you know what's going on under the hood, let's perform an Offline Edit of the copy we made of HR GPO1. To do this, find the Checked Out GPO in Change Control ➢ Contents ➢ Controlled, right-click over it, and select Edit, as seen in Figure 12.26.

FIGURE 12.26 Editing a GPO in the archive

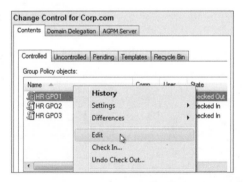

When you do, you'll see the usual Group Policy Editor (or Group Policy Management Editor). Here, let's add some settings for later use. Let's Enable the User Configuration ➢ Policies ➢ Administrative Templates ➢ Control Panel ➢ Display ➢ Hide Desktop tab.

When you're finished, exit the Group Policy Object Editor.

Again, at this point you've edited only the offline copy of the GPO, not the live GPO. This is the point of AGPM—it allows you to perform your proposed changes offline before doing potential harm to the live GPOs.

Check In of a Changed GPO

Remember that the point of performing a Check Out of a copy of a GPO was to make sure that no one else could modify that copy while I had it out. But to do anything else with this GPO (except additional editing), I have to perform a Check In.

Do this by finding the GPO within Change Control ➤ Contents ➤ Controlled, right-clicking over the GPO, and selecting Check In. When you do, you'll be able to make a comment about what you did to the GPO, like "Enabled Hide Desktop Tab."

When you Check In a GPO, the little red band around the GPO icon in the Controlled tab will disappear, because it's no longer Checked Out.

Deploying a GPO into Production

Once the GPO you just edited is Checked In, you can potentially deploy this (modified) copy into production.

The question is, Are you ready? This is where you need to take a deep breath and say, "Okay, I'm ready to overwrite what's currently live in production with the changes I made offline." If you're ready to rock, just right-click over the Controlled GPO and select Deploy, as seen in Figure 12.27.

At this point, you'll be asked if you want to deploy the GPO, as seen in Figure 12.28. Clicking Yes will deploy it immediately, maintaining the link state the link was in at the time that the *archive was created*.

FIGURE 12.27   When you're ready, you can Deploy your GPO's changes into the live network.

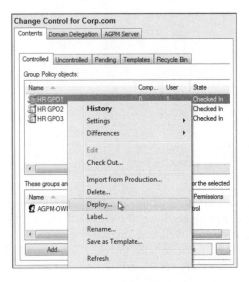

WARNING   Again, if you click Yes, it will deploy the GPO immediately and re-link the GPOs back at the time that the *archive was created*. This is a key point. If the links for the live GPO were changed between the time the GPO was Checked Out (i.e., when the offline copy was made) and *now*, you'll be re-arranging links back to their original configuration.

You can click Advanced to get granular control over link restoration if you'd like.

FIGURE 12.28   You can choose to restore original links if you so desire.

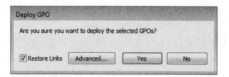

When the deployment is completed, you should get a message similar to Figure 12.29.

FIGURE 12.29   The output from a GPO Deploy command.

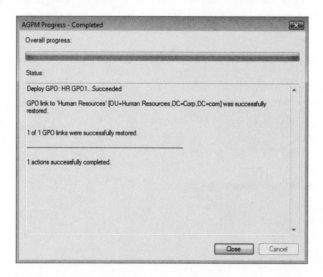

At this point, your GPO and its changes are in production, live, working hard for you! And wait—something extra special happened! Remember how *all this time*, Frank could still go *around* the AGPM system and edit the *live* GPO? Well, not anymore!

As soon as the GPO is Deployed back into production, the Owner changes to SYSTEM (or the specified AGPM service account), and Frank's rights are stripped off the GPO! You can see this in Figure 12.30.

FIGURE 12.30   Original Owners are finally stripped of their rights when the GPO is deployed. Now the AGPM system is in charge of the ownership of the GPO.

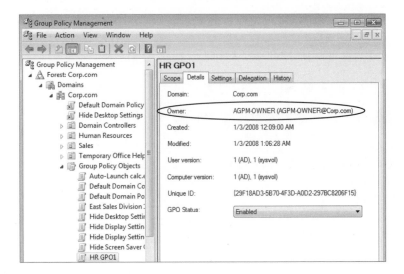

Eventually, we want to get to this state (the SYSTEM or the AGPM service account owning all the live GPOs) for all of our original GPOs. I'll give you some advice for how to do that a little later, so hang tight.

 If you receive errors while Deploying the GPO, check out the section "Advanced Configuration and Troubleshooting of AGPM" for a tip that could help you.

Making Additional Changes to a GPO and Labeling a GPO

At this point, you've got the ability to keep going back and forth. That is, you can Check Out a GPO to make an offline copy. Then, you can edit the offline copy. You can make some changes to that copy. Then, check it back in. Then deploy it on top of the live GPO.

Indeed, to continue with the next exercises, we'll need to have done that so we can inspect some additional features that AGPM provides. We'll be checking out some features like performing a rollback based on older GPOs and doing a comparison of GPOs over time.

With that in mind, let's edit the HR GPO1 by first using Check Out to create an offline copy. Then, we'll use AGPM to edit a change to the GPO copy. For instance, Enable User Configuration ➤ Policies ➤ Administrative Templates ➤ Control Panel ➤ Display ➤ **Hide Settings Tab**.

When you're ready, check in the GPO and then deploy it into production, overwriting the live HR GPO1. Be sure to make comments so you'll know what you did during each step! You can make a comment at any time, without even making any changes to a GPO, by right-clicking the GPO and selecting Label (Figure 12.31).

FIGURE 12.31 You can always add a label to make your actions more clear.

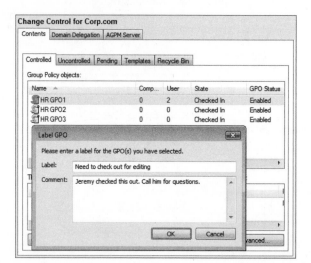

Using History and Differences to Roll Back a GPO

So at this point, you've modified your HR GPO1 twice. Once to Enable the **Hide Desktop Tab** policy setting and another time to Enable the **Hide Settings Tab** policy setting. You did this in three steps: Checking Out (creating a copy), Checking In the copy, and re-Deploying the copy of the GPO on top of the live GPO. So now the GPO is changed and live in the real world.

Now the boss walks into your office and says he wants the Settings tab back.

What are you going to do?

You're going to Roll Back the HR GPO1 GPO back to *before* you enabled the **Hide Settings Tab** policy setting. But lots of changes could have transpired since then. Your job now is to compare GPOs that have passed through the archive and determine which one is the right one. To get started, right-click over the GPO, select Change Control ➤ Controlled, and select History, as seen in Figure 12.32.

FIGURE 12.32 You can look back in time and see a GPO's history.

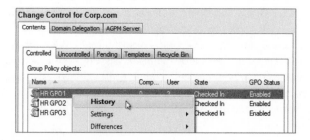

Note that the full History view is added as an additional tab within the GPMC whenever you click on a GPO, even outside the Change Control node.

Inside the History View

The History view shows when the GPO was created, and each time it was Checked In or Deployed plus the comments you added during those steps. Additionally, if you decided to Label your check-ins and -outs while working with the GPOs and their copies within AGPM, you would see an unchanged GPO with a new comment. You can see examples of the History view in Figure 12.33.

FIGURE 12.33   A GPO's history contains timestamps, an indication of who owned the GPO, and comments. If you click on a history item, you can see its settings.

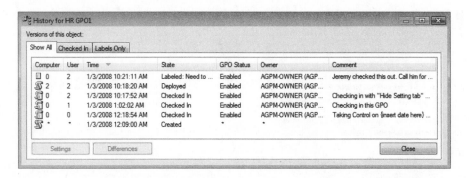

The Computer and User column display version number information. For more information about version numbers, see Chapter 6.

Performing a Difference Report

Assuming the comments weren't clear, this would be the perfect opportunity for you to leverage the History tab to see Difference information. To do that, hold down the Ctrl key, then click two "points in time" to compare. Right-click over one of them, and select Differences ➢ HTML Report, as seen in Figure 12.34.

The report is displayed in a browser window as an HTML document, as seen in Figure 12.35.

When you're comparing two GPOs, you'll see different symbols and corresponding colors to help you decipher the differences between them. Table 12.2 has the breakdown of the meaning of each symbol along with its corresponding Color.

FIGURE 12.34 You can create a History Differences report.

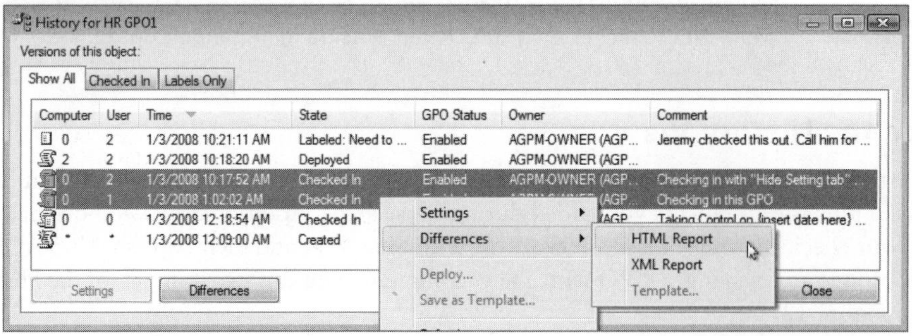

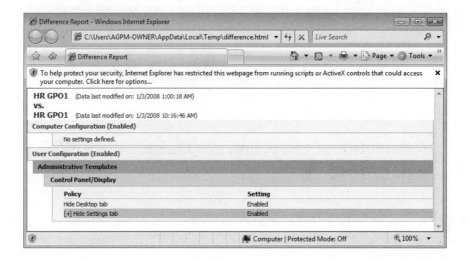

FIGURE 12.35 History reports are color-coded to make differences easy to spot.

TABLE 12.1 AGPM Reporting Symbols, Colors, and Their Meanings

Symbol	Meaning	Color
None	Same settings in both GPOs	Varies
[#]	Item in both GPOs, settings different between them	Blue
[-]	Item exists in first GPO (missing from second GPO)	Red
[+]	Item exists in second GPO (missing from first GPO)	Green

Performing a Rollback Based upon a Difference

Now that you've got a handle on which GPO in the history you want to roll back to (the one that was Checked In after the **Hide Desktop Tab** policy setting was Enabled but before the **Hide Settings Tab** was Enabled), just right-click over it in the History view, and select Deploy, as seen in Figure 12.36.

FIGURE 12.36   You can perform a GPO rollback based on a History item.

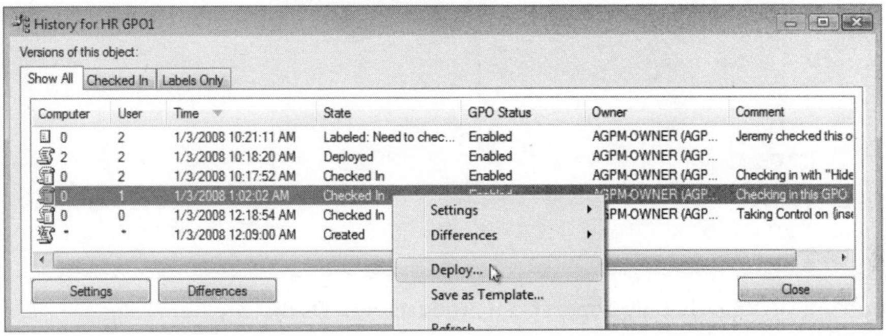

The newest History view should show that archived copy of the GPO as deployed. Just to be safe, inspect the settings of the (now live) GPO to make sure what's deployed is what you expected!

Using "Import from Production" to Catch Up a GPO

Recall that, out of the box, AGPM doesn't prevent original owners of GPOs from making changes to the GPOs they own until the GPO is officially deployed. This can happen when you haven't yet forced all administrators to use the AGPM system and some admins are going around AGPM and creating and editing live GPOs.

So, this could mean you have a real situation on your hands: the good guys are editing the copies of GPOs within AGPM (carefully tracking changes inside the archive), and meanwhile, administrators who didn't get the memo to use AGPM are still editing their GPOs live.

The other case where you might really *have* to use the live version of the GPO (instead of AGPM system) is if the AGPM server or service itself fails. In that instance, you would have to make changes using the Domain Administrator account (which can *always* get into all live GPOs).

In either case, you've still got a problem: The information in the *archive* is different than what is live in *production*. If either of these cases happens, you might want to suck the live version into the archive and compare it to one of the archived GPOs. Then you can use the History tab to do your comparisons as you did earlier and figure out which GPO should live or die: the last known archive copy or the currently live GPO.

To bring a live GPO into the archive, you would select the controlled GPO and select Import from Production, as seen in Figure 12.37.

FIGURE 12.37   Use the Import from Production command if the archive goes offline for a time.

 You can only Import from production GPOs that are Controlled.

Uncontrolling, Restoring, and Destroying a GPO

If for some reason you want to take a GPO out of AGPM's system, you need to delete it, although that's kind of a misnomer. I like to call it "Uncontrol" instead. Let's explore how to delete, I mean, Uncontrol it (and also bring it *back* into the archive if we want to).

Uncontrolling a GPO (Deleting It from the Archive)

To do this, locate the controlled GPO in the Controlled tab and select Delete, as seen in Figure 12.38.

FIGURE 12.38   Deleting a controlled GPO doesn't really delete it.

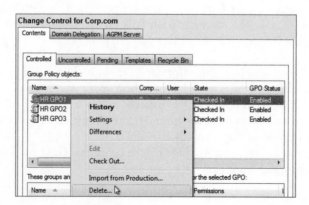

When you do, you'll be prompted with the choice you see in Figure 12.39. That is you can "Delete GPO from archive only (uncontrol)" or "Delete GPO from archive and production."

FIGURE 12.39   You can choose what kind of deletion to perform.

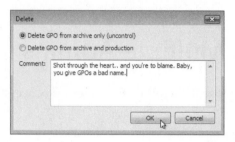

If you select the Uncontrol option, the GPO moves from Controlled to Uncontrolled. All previous history is maintained; it's just not managed (right now) through the AGPM system. If you later want to Control it, just find the GPO (now within) the Uncontrolled tab and re-Control it.

If you select "Delete GPO from archive and production" (the second option in Figure 12.39), the GPO doesn't move to Uncontrolled. This option unlinks it from anywhere it's currently deployed in the live, real world, then moves the archived GPO and its history to the Recycle Bin.

Restoring from the Change Control Recycle Bin

If you use AGPM's facility to Delete archived GPOs or to delete the GPOs from production, you're never far away from a backup. That's because the deleted archives of GPOs (or deleted GPOs themselves) end up in the AGPM Recycle Bin. If you want to recover a deleted GPO from the AGPM universe, just right-click it within the Recycle Bin tab, and select Restore, as seen in Figure 12.40.

Restored GPOs from AGPM are always automatically set to Controlled.

FIGURE 12.40   You can use the AGPM Recycle Bin to recover old GPOs.

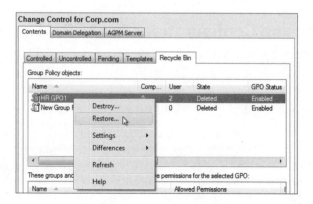

Permanently Deleting a GPO and Its History

In the Recycle Bin, you can also right-click a deleted GPO and select Destroy. This really does delete the GPO and any surrounding history. There is no undo from this operation.

After you perform this, it's dead.

AGPM Tasks with Multiple Admins

At this point, you've now got a grip on all the major AGPM features. Between Check In/Check Out, offline editing, comparison reports, and so on, you're ready to use AGPM.

Well, that would be true if you worked on an island. But you don't. You work with other administrators.

In our previous example in this chapter, we assumed Frank Rizzo, who's in charge of the **Human Resources** OU, originally created three GPOs: HR GPO1, HR GPO2, and HR GPO3. Let's also assume that Frank works with the following people:

- Sammy Cox: Sammy works for Frank. Sammy is the desktop engineer who knows the Human Resources users best. He is a good candidate for the Editor role, so he could request a new GPO (which Frank can create) and then edit the offline copy. He can then request it to go live. But, again, only Frank can approve the GPO and put it in play. (These users weren't created in other exercises; they're new for these examples.)

- Brett Wier: Brett is the IT department manager and is also in charge of quality assurance. He knows his way around GPOs enough to know what he's doing. Brett's a good candidate to be a Reviewer. So, Brett can see the copy of the GPO that's created and what's been done to it that makes it different than the live GPO. So basically, we want to give him "Read-Only" access to the history and settings of the archived GPO. And, of course, because Brett can see what's changed, he can make recommendations to Frank if he thinks the GPO choices made within the **Human Resources** OU are unacceptable.

- Frank Rizzo is the Approver. Since it's the Approver who finally makes GPOs live, Frank will be the guy in trouble if something is put into production that wasn't sanctioned.

Email Preparations and Configurations for AGPM Requests

Requests for Reviewing and Editing are sent to Approvers to say yea or nay. This happens via email. Exchange server isn't *directly* supported as a transport medium. But standard SMTP is, and Exchange Server can be set up to be an SMTP server. If you have an SMTP server set up already, you're almost there. Consult your Exchange admin for how to enable Exchange to honor SMTP requests.

If you really can't get Exchange to be an SMTP server, you might be able to set up your own SMTP server, which we explore how to do in the sidebar "Setting Up an SMTP Server for AGPM Testing." In that same sidebar, we'll set up a test SMTP server to handle our requests in the examples in this chapter.

For our purposes, just fill in the blanks in the Change Control ➢ Domain Delegation node. You can see some example values in Figure 12.41. Just be sure to replace your SMTP server and username with valid names and passwords or no mail will make it to the server.

The most important line is the To: line. Only the people on the To: line will get the emails that the system generates (though the Requester can add people via an optional Cc:). But you'll want to be sure all Approvers are listed (or create an email alias that contains the entire list of Approvers), as well as Editors and perhaps Reviewers. In my example below, just about everyone is notified, but that's my preference.

FIGURE 12.41   You can specify where AGPM emails are sent.

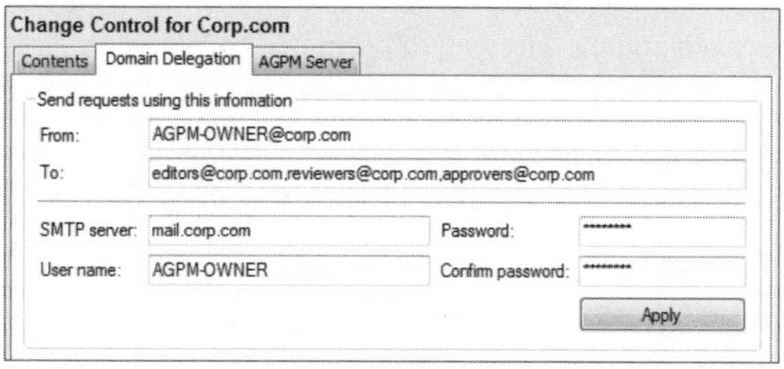

Setting Up an SMTP Server for AGPM Testing

If you don't want to set up an Exchange Server with SMTP support to test out AGPM requests, you can quickly utilize Windows Server 2003 to act as an SMTP server. There is SMTP forwarding in Windows Server 2008, but it cannot host mailboxes, which makes it a poor choice for our tests.

With that in mind, I suggest one of two choices: you can set up a test SMTP server using Windows Server 2003 or download one of about a dozen free SMTP/POP servers that will run on Windows. The one I like is called Office Mail 2.0, by Burrotech.com (www.burrotech.com/om_download.php). I like this one for several reasons:

- It's free.

- It runs on both Windows Server 2003 and Windows Server 2008.

- It works.

- It's small.

- It's super easy to set up.

- It has a Web-based setup tutorial for both the server and mail client (Outlook Express). You can find it at http://tinyurl.com/2y4dll.

- You can see the mail while logged into the server by just clicking on the user's account inside Office Mail. This helps troubleshooting send/receive errors.

- Did I mention it was free?

There is one trick about setting it up when you want to run it on Windows Server 2008. Windows Server 2008 is like Windows XP or Vista. The Windows Firewall is turned on by default. This means if you choose to run your SMTP server (Office Mail or something else) on Windows Server 2008, you need to also tell Windows Server 2008 to open the two mail ports we need: Port 110 for POP and Port 25 for SMTP.

There are multiple ways in Windows Server 2008 to achieve this goal. Perhaps the simplest is by clicking Start and in the search box typing **Firewall** to bring up the Windows Firewall with Advanced Security snap in. Then right-click over Inbound Rules, and select New Rule.

At the Rule Type screen, select Port, then click Next. At the Protocol and Ports screen, ensure that TCP is selected, then in the "Specific local ports" box, type **110,25** as seen here.

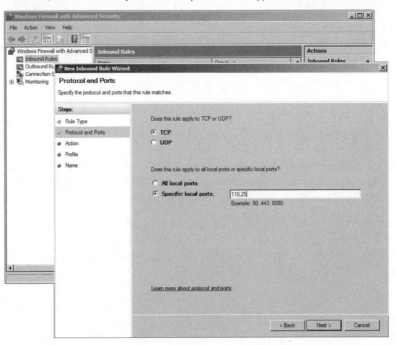

You can accept the rest of the defaults in the wizard, but at the end you must give it a name, like MAIL PORTS.

Once you're finished, mail can be sent to this SMTP server, then picked up with Outlook Express (Windows XP) or Windows Mail (Vista) or another mail client (Outlook, Eudora, etc.). I also like Office Mail as my SMTP server because it puts a test message in each user's inbox, so I know I successfully completed installation and setup correctly.

Adding Someone to the AGPM System

Anyone dealing with the AGPM system needs to be expressly granted access to it. And they also need to have the AGPM client installed. Let's review those pieces now.

Setting Permissions within the AGPM System

The best way to get started is to do what we did earlier. That is, map out who will use the system and which roles they will have. We've decided on the following roles for the following people:

- Frank: Approver
- Sammy: Editor
- Brett: Reviewer

Now, in this chapter, we're going to be dealing with these three people. But you could just as easily create three Active Directory groups, like these:

- AGPM_APPROVERS
- AGPM_REVIEWERS
- AGPM_EDITORS

Then use those groups and just add users to them. We're not going to do that here, but in real life you might want to.

To add people to the AGPM system, you need to go to the Change Control node, and in the Domain Delegation tab, click Add. Once you do, you can add the three user accounts: Frank, Sammy, and Brett.

Adding the Users to the AGPM System

By default, anyone you add using the Add button will have Reviewer and Editor permissions, which is okay for now. And for right now, be sure to use the Add button and not the Advanced button.

In the initial release of AGPM, there's a bug when people are added to the AGPM system and assigned permissions. When I told you how to add people, I said to "click Add." If you use Add, these exercises will work perfectly. If you use Advanced and then add in the user (like Brett, as a Reviewer), these exercises will fail. The bug is that, when you use the Advanced button, the ACLs aren't propagated down to every GPO by default. However, it works fine when you're using the Add button. If you want to, later you can use Advanced to "trim" the settings. But don't initially use Advanced to add the user within the Domain Delegation tab or you'll need to expressly add the admin rights to each and every GPO in the next steps.

In Figure 12.42, I've added all three users to the system, and their default permissions (which are actually set too high right now) are displayed under Allowed Permissions.

You might also want to add the actual domain administrator as Full Control to the system, which would make it equivalent to the AGPM-OWNER. It's just a good idea in case the AGPM-OWNER is unavailable.

FIGURE 12.42   These aren't the final permissions required. You'll need to click each user and select Advanced to fine-tune their security.

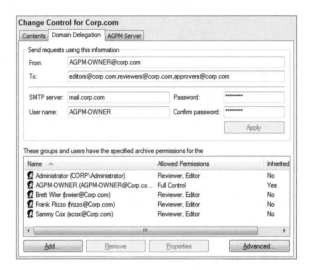

As stated, each user is to get different permissions. And, what's more, the AGPM system doesn't automatically propagate the permissions you set (in the Domain Delegation tab) down to every GPO in the archive.

This is something we need to do manually (and it's a little tedious, so stay with me).

Click on each user, say, Frank Rizzo first, then click the Advanced button.

It's okay to click the Advanced button now and modify the accounts. The bug I told you about in the preceding warning is activated only when you're adding user accounts via the Advanced button.

You can granularly dictate the settings for Frank. Even though we're saying that Frank Rizzo is an Approver, it's likely best in this case to ensure that Frank has Editor rights (and also Reviewer rights) as well. You can see my suggested rights for Frank in Figure 12.43. That way, if Sammy edits a copy of a GPO (offline, of course) that Frank later wants to modify, he can do so.

Modify Sammy's account so he has only Editor rights (and Reviewer rights). You can see Sammy's rights in Figure 12.44.

Finally, modify Brett's account so he has only Reviewer rights. You can see Brett's rights in Figure 12.45.

When you're finished, click OK. The total rights will be seen in Figure 12.46.

FIGURE 12.43   Here you can see Frank Rizzo and his permissions.

FIGURE 12.44   Here you can see Sammy and his permissions.

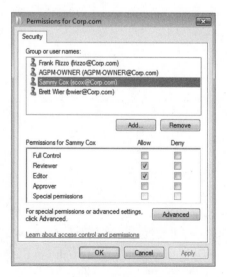

FIGURE 12.45 Here you can see Brett and his permissions.

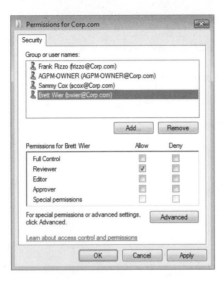

FIGURE 12.46 The finished permissions should look like this.

Ensuring That Your Permissions Apply for All GPOs within the Archive

But here's the caveat: just because you gave Frank, Brett, and Sammy rights in the AGPM system (within the Domain Delegation node), it doesn't mean they'll have rights to every GPO everywhere within the archive.

This really threw me for a loop, so let's break this down, step by step.

In Figure 12.47, which shows the Permissions for the archive for your domain, you need to click Advanced. Then within the Advanced Security Settings for <domain>, click on Frank (again) and notice that the Apply To field only shows "This object only," as you can also see in Figure 12.47.

FIGURE 12.47   Frank doesn't have access to all the GPOs in the archive.

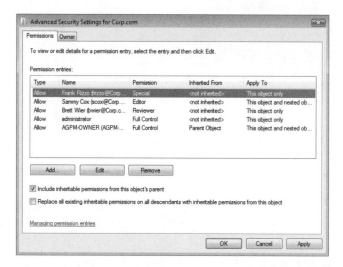

And therein lies the problem. We need to change it so that Frank has access to all GPOs within the AGPM archive. To do this, click the Edit button (seen in Figure 12.47), then change Frank's permissions from "This object only" to "This object and nested objects," as seen in Figure 12.48.

FIGURE 12.48   Frank's permissions need to be propagated to all objects in the archive.

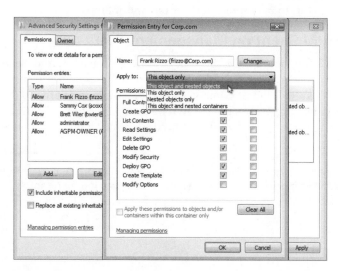

Then Click OK to close the Permission Entry dialog. You should see that Frank's Apply To column changes to "This object and nested objects," as seen in Figure 12.49.

FIGURE 12.49 Frank now has access to everything he needs.

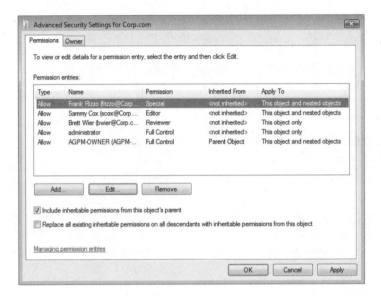

In this section, I modified Frank's access so it applied to "This object and nested objects." Be sure to do the same for Brett and Sammy as well so all these AGPM users have access to "This object and nested objects."

Maybe in real life granting Frank, Sammy, and Brett access across *all* GPOs isn't what you want. In that case, stay tuned for the section titled "Changing Permissions on GPO Archives" where we show you how to get even *more* granular if you had a situation where some AGPM users should have permissions to only some GPOs within the archive.

Installing the AGPM Client on Management Stations

It's likely that the AGPM system was installed by some domain administrator. And the intention, of course, is to start using AGPM as the focus point for all Group Policy management.

Therefore, all parties involved, Frank, Sammy, and Brett, have to install the AGPM client piece as we did earlier in Figure 12.7. Again, the AGPM client needs to be installed on their management station and their management station needs to be a Windows Vista machine.

 Alternatively, you can install the AGPM client on a machine with Windows Server 2003 Terminal Server, then have everyone log on remotely.

Once the AGPM client is installed on all necessary management stations, Frank's, Sammy's, and Brett's GPMC will change so they all have the Change Control node (showing they have the potential ability to use AGPM).

Now that Frank, Sammy, and Brett all have access to the AGPM system, they should no longer get AGPM Access Denied messages as we saw in Figures 12.10 and 12.11.

> If, during your testing, you don't want to set up three Windows Vista management stations (one each for Frank, Sammy, and Brett), you can simply create one Windows Vista management station and install the AGPM client. Then use Windows Vista's Switch User mode to allow each person to log on.

Setting Up Mail Accounts for Each AGPM User

This step has likely already been done in the real world. But if you're following along with the examples, don't forget to also set up email accounts on your SMTP server for Frank, Sammy, and Brett.

In my tests, I set up the following email aliases:

- `approvers@corp.com` to be routed directly to Frank
- `editors@corp.com` to be routed directly to Sammy
- `reviewers@corp.com` to be routed directly to Brett

> Be sure email is working between Frank, Sammy, and Brett before continuing. If mail isn't flowing correctly, your AGPM administrators won't get the signals that anything is waiting for them.

Requesting the Creation of New Controlled GPO

Sammy knows he wants to enable the **Remove Search link from Start Menu** policy setting to affect all the computers in Human Resources.

It's time for Sammy to request a new GPO.

After Sammy logs into his account, he can right-click the Change Control node and select New Controlled GPO, as we did at Figure 12.19.

Except this time the request is coming from Sammy, who's a requestor, really an Editor. At this point Sammy can put in some comments that will go to all the people on the To: line; the most important person being the Approver (Frank Rizzo). You can see this in Figure 12.50.

When Sammy clicks Submit, he'll see something similar to Figure 12.51. That is, the request for a GPO gets sent into the system and an email is sent of pending requests.

Even though Sammy requested a live (but Controlled) GPO, he didn't get that. He got the request submitted for that GPO. Now, it's time for the Approver to verify and approve or reject the request.

FIGURE 12.50 Sammy is requesting a new GPO.

FIGURE 12.51 Sammy's request is emailed via the AGPM system.

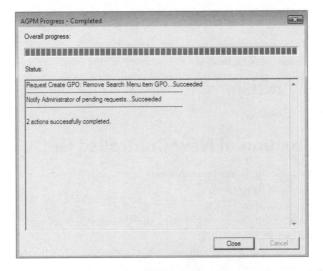

Approving or Rejecting a Pending Request

A pending request is Approved or Rejected in (generally) in two steps. First, the Approver (Frank) receives the email notifying him about a request. Then, the Approver can use the AGPM console to tend to the actual request.

Email Notifications from AGPM

AGPM sends notifications to everyone in the To: line. The emails look like Figure 12.52. It contains the following information:

- Who is doing the requesting (Sammy Cox)
- What he wants (requested creation of a GPO)
- That he doesn't want to use a template (more on this later)
- What he wants to name the GPO
- Any comments left in the request

FIGURE 12.52 Here's what Sammy's email looks like.

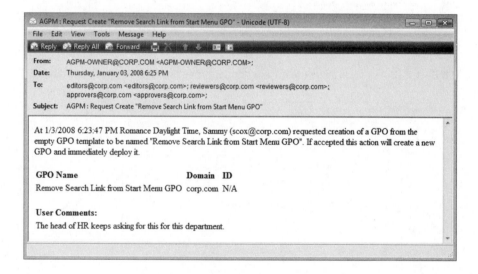

Tending to the Pending Request

At this point, Frank can log onto the GPMC, go to the Change Control node, and click Contents ➢ Pending to see any pending requests. Because Frank is an Approver, he can Approve or Reject the request (as seen in Figure 12.53) and leave comments back to Sammy (which will be logged in the GPO history). Some common comments can be seen in Figure 12.54.

What's odd is that the original requester, Sammy, doesn't get an auto-email response that this request has been tended to. This is just not something AGPM is capable of right now. So, unfortunately, Frank has to manually email Sammy and tell him his request is done. This isn't the ideal workflow, and it's something you have to teach your AGPM admins to do right now.

Note that Frank could also Reject Sammy's request. The GPO is never created, and there is nothing added to the GPO's history.

FIGURE 12.53 Use the Pending tab to handle pending requests.

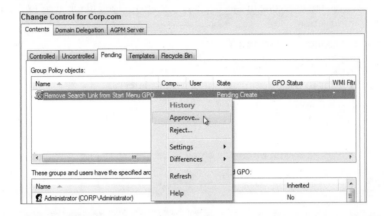

FIGURE 12.54 Include a note during your approval (or rejection) of a pending request.

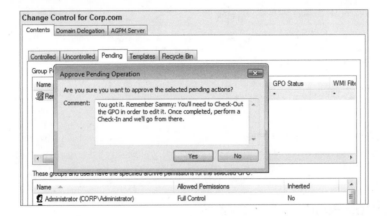

Editing the GPO Offline via Check Out/Check In

As you'll recall, with AGPM, editing the actual GPO never happens live, online. To make proposed changes to the GPO, it must be Checked Out of AGPM first, where a copy is made. Then, during that time, no one else can edit the Checked Out GPO.

This procedure is similar to what we just did. Except this time, Sammy is performing the Check Out, since he was the one who requested the new GPO and who wants to edit the offline copy.

You can see a screen shot showing how to Check Out a GPO earlier in the chapter, Figure 12.21. Once the GPO is Checked Out, Sammy can right-click over the Controlled (and now Checked Out) copy of the GPO and select Edit. Sammy can now Enable the policy setting called **Remove Search link from Start Menu** as he wanted to in his request.

Once the policy setting is enabled, Sammy can then close the Group Policy Object Editor, return to the GPMC ➤ Change Control node, right-click over the GPO, and select Check In. He can leave comments about what he did for others to read, as seen in Figure 12.55.

FIGURE 12.55   You can add a comment while Checking In a GPO.

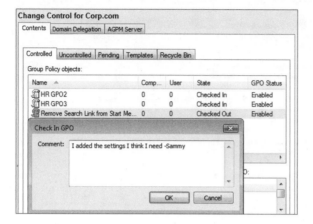

Requesting Deployment of the GPO

Now that Sammy has made his proposed changes to the GPO, he can request deployment. He simply right-clicks over the GPO and selects Deploy. You can see how to Deploy a GPO earlier in the chapter, in Figure 12.27.

When he does this, he can put comments in for the Reviewers, as seen in Figure 12.56. Though, again, the emails always go to everyone on the To: line. The system just isn't granular enough to send the email *only* to Reviewers.

FIGURE 12.56   AGPM users can submit deployment requests.

When Sammy clicks Submit, the emails go out. The example email can be seen in Figure 12.57. Brett, the quality assurance guy, reads the email, so he knows he has something to do.

FIGURE 12.57   Deployment requests get sent to all AGPM users via email.

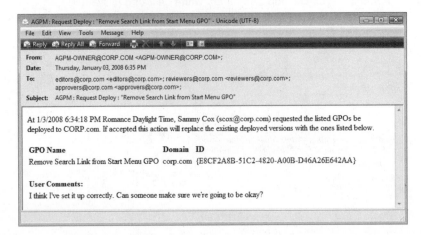

At this point, it's up to someone with Reviewer, Editor, or Approver rights to ensure that Sammy did what he was supposed to in the GPO.

 It's also possible for Sammy to realize he made an error while manipulating the GPO. If he wants to, he can right-click over the GPO again and Withdraw his request. The GPO will return to the Controlled tab.

Analyzing a GPO (as a Reviewer)

Sammy's email made it to all Editors, Reviewers, and Approvers. Who's going to deal with Sammy's request? Well, that depends on who has the ability as a Reviewer over the GPO copy that Sammy has in the archive.

Brett Wier is the Quality Assurance guy, and he is going to ensure that the Group Policy settings are valid before they go into production.

Earlier, we made Brett a Reviewer of all GPOs in the archive, and therefore, Brett should be able to Review Sammy's changes. Brett can now right-click over a GPO that Sammy created and view the HTML report of the settings contained inside, as seen in Figure 12.58.

 If Brett is unable to view the HTML report shown in Figure 12.58, look at the permission on the GPO in the archive. In Figure 12.43, we can see I've specified that Brett has Reviewer rights over this particular GPO in the archive. If you didn't set the security earlier so Brett would have Reviewer rights over "This object and nested objects," then you won't see Brett listed on this GPO's permissions. Be sure to check out the section "Ensuring That Your Permissions Apply for All GPOs within the Archive" earlier in this chapter.

FIGURE 12.58   Brett can review the changes via an HTML report.

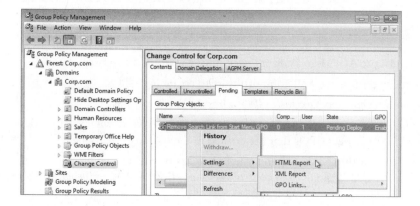

Deploying a GPO into Production

At this point, Frank can log on, find the GPO that Sammy created within the Pending tab, and choose to Approve or Reject it, as seen in Figure 12.59. Approving will re-deploy the GPO into production. Rejecting it will leave it Controlled but not put it into production.

FIGURE 12.59   Frank can Approve the GPO that was created.

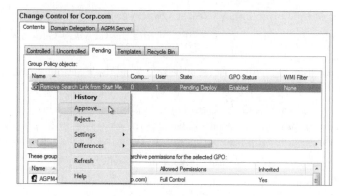

Committing to AGPM via Group Policy Permissions

AGPM is great. But by now, you can see the back door that prevents its immediate usefulness. That is, if someone created a GPO *before* the AGPM system was installed, then, well, that person could just continue to "work around" the AGPM system if they wanted to.

In other words, they can continue to edit the live GPO instead of using the archive. That's not good, because then you would have no record of anything they did because history is recorded only when someone uses the AGPM system to manage copies of the GPO and put them into production.

There are really only a few required steps to guarantee that (under normal circumstances) everyone must use AGPM and not fall back into old habits. Those steps are as follows:

- Removing the ability of all administrators to create live GPOs
- Redeploying (in place) existing GPOs after they're Controlled
- Optionally, changing the Active Directory schema to dictate what security should be defined for any new GPOs that are created in the old way (i.e., outside of AGPM)

Once you've performed these steps, you're essentially forcing all admins to use the AGPM system. This is your big goal: total control of your existing GPOs, and then going forward using only AGPM.

These three steps aren't going to necessarily be easy to implement. But, ultimately, if you really want to ensure that you have a true change-control process around GPOs, you need to do them.

Preventing Admins from Creating Live GPOs

An administrator can create live GPOs if any of the following are true:

- They are a member of the Domain Admins group.
- They are a member of the Group Policy Creator Owners group.
- They have been delegated rights to create GPOs using the GPMC's Group Policy Objects node.

To prevent them from doing so, you must take the following three actions to ensure that no one can create GPOs using the "old" methods:

- Remove all admins who create GPOs from the Domain Admins group. This is going to be hard, and I don't expect many people to do it. But it is the ideal way to ensure that, even you, Mr. or Ms. Admin, don't slip into bad habits and edit live GPOs.
- Remove any listed accounts from Group Policy Creator Owners.
- Remove any listed accounts from the Delegation tab in the Group Policy Objects node within GPMC.

This will prevent *anyone* from having inherent access to do anything in the domain, including creating and editing production GPOs. Once this is done, everyone will have to use AGPM to *create* GPOs.

However, this doesn't stop owners of existing GPOs from editing those live GPOs; we must complete the next step.

> If you remove all users from the Domain Admins group, just be conscious about what you would do if you needed someone back in that group. If you do choose this method, and you really did need to get into the production GPOs in an emergency, you could just add a user back into the Domain Admins group. Note that someone would need rights to be able to add users to groups, but that's an easy right to grant to someone with emergency powers (but be sure to do it in advance!).

Preventing Original GPO Owners from Modifying Their Existing GPOs

Recall that in our previous examples, Frank maintained ownership access to HR GPO1, HR GPO2, and HR GPO3 until we Deployed the GPOs back into production.

Sure, we Checked Out HR GPO1, modified the offline copy, Checked In the copy, then finally Deployed the copy over the live HR GPO1. And when we did this, the ownership changed from Frank Rizzo to the AGPM service account (see earlier Figure 12.30).

But here's the thing: What if you had 500 GPOs? Would you want to click through each one just to strip Frank of his original rights?

The good news is that you can do it, sort of, in a batch style. And it's easy!

All you need to do is this:

- Take Control of the existing GPOs in the domain.
- Multi-select them in the Controlled tab.
- Select Deploy, which will Redeploy them.

You can see the quickest way to do this in Figure 12.60.

FIGURE 12.60 GPOs' ownership is changed when you Deploy them.

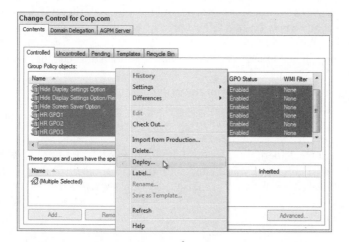

> To select all GPOs, you will have to use Shift or Ctrl+click because Ctrl+A unfortunately doesn't do anything.

When you do this, you'll be asked if you want to Deploy the selected GPOs and optionally Restore Links. Say yes to each, and every GPO you have that's Controlled and now Deployed will do the following:

- Rewrite the GPO copy on top of the live GPO.

- Remove any delegation rights anyone has to the GPO.

- Strip the original owner of ownership rights and replace the ownership with SYSTEM (or the specified AGPM service account).

If you do this as soon as AGPM is installed, you essentially cut off old-school access to the original GPOs. Administrators simply must use the AGPM system and rights you've now set up to manipulate and manage only offline copies of the GPOs and to provide a framework for true Group Policy change management when putting live copies back in place.

However, this doesn't prevent anyone with rights to create GPOs from creating them outside the AGPM system. That's where the next section comes in handy.

Optional: Modifying the Schema to Force New GPOs to Only Be Writeable by AGPM

The last optional piece of Group Policy creation lockdown is to force every new GPO (regardless of how it's created) to basically be noneditable, except by the AGPM system.

To do this, we need to change the underlying permissions of what happens when GPOs (any GPOs) are created. Imagine that GPOs, when they're created, come off the "assembly line" with certain permissions. To do this trick, we have to retool the assembly line.

So, in this example, I'm going to use a new Active Directory security group called AGPM-OWNERS (where I'll put my AGPM-OWNER user account inside to start). That way, from this point forward (after we do this next procedure), only members of the AGPM-OWNERS group will be able to edit any newly created GPOs *directly*. Everyone else should be forced to use the AGPM system to manage GPOs.

The outline for this procedure is found at `http://support.microsoft.com/default.aspx/kb/321476`.

I really think only the most hardcore organizations will want to do this. That's because it's a serious commitment. But then again, you were serious already when you invested in your AGPM system. The downside is that these changes require (gasp!) schema changes. But that's the breaks.

The book team (Jakob Heidelberg, Eric Johnson, and I) has spent a lot of time looking at this solution and wanted to present to you the full solution here in the book. But we ran out of page count for a full walkthrough for all scenarios. Come to `www.GPanswers.com` in the

Book Resources section and look up this chapter's contents. There, you'll find a rundown of the steps to do this. In short, the steps are as follows:

- Preparing for the schema changes
- Finding the SID of the group we want to grant exclusive rights to
- Modifying the schema
- Updating and reloading the schema
- Testing your changes

And, what's more, the walkthrough is better as a downloadable document, because we'll be asking you to copy long strings of characters, like this (all one line):

```
(A;CI;RPWPCCDCLCLOLORCWOWDSDDTSW;;;
S-1-5-21-2281461124-1982115790-1948695546-1113)
```

And that's easier if you have an electronic copy of the document to use.

By the time you've performed this procedure, we'll have driven all the creation and modifications of new GPOs through the AGPM system.

Advanced Configuration and Troubleshooting of AGPM

AGPM is a big place with some big power. In this section, we'll examine some less-often-used features, like templates, and also learn how to set up specific permissions within AGPM, perform some AGPM troubleshooting, and other odds and ends.

Troubleshooting AGPM Permissions

When setting up AGPM, you can either choose to use the SYSTEM account if you're installing it on a Domain Controller, or choose a domain account, like AGPM-OWNER. Picking the latter option can sometimes equal additional headaches, which we'll solve here.

Trouble Deploying Controlled GPOs

Sometimes, it seems that you can't deploy controlled GPOs. You'll get an error stating, "Could not take ownership of the deployed GPO," like what you see in Figure 12.61.

To fix this, you can change the permissions on the GPO itself so that the AGPM service account (e.g., AGPM-OWNER) has "Edit settings, delete, and modify security" on the particular Group Policy Object. You can do this by clicking on the GPO itself and selecting the Delegation tab to edit who has access to the GPO directly. We cover the how-tos in detail in Chapter 2.

FIGURE 12.61   A GPO permissions problem prevents Controlling GPOs.

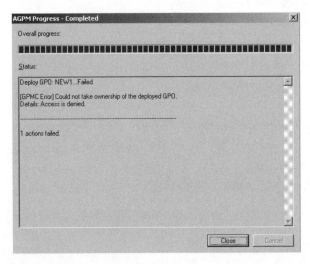

However, you can also use a script we developed in Chapter 11, "Scripting Group Policy Operations with PowerShell." With a quick trip backward to grab that script, we can make the job go quicker. The script is named Set-GPPermission and can be executed with the -all, -user, and -permission switches together. This will append a selected user (the AGPM-OWNER account) to the ACL of all GPOs in the domain, with a chosen permission level: None, Apply, Edit, or Full Control (FC). Here is how to use the script (which we detail in Chapter 11):

```
.\Set-GPPermission.ps1 -all -user "Corp\AGPM-OWNER" -permission FC
```

FIGURE 12.62   Use a script from our scripting chapter to affect all exiting GPOs so the AGPM-OWNER account has rights to the "live" GPOs.

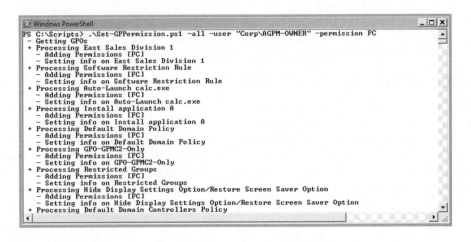

And voilà, the PowerShell script modifies the permissions of all GPOs in the domain, appending the selected user account.

After this, you will be able to deploy your controlled GPOs using AGPM because the AGPM-OWNER account now has permissions to the real GPO.

Trouble Creating New Controlled GPOs

Similarly, you might encounter a situation where you cannot create new Controlled GPOs within AGPM. You might get an error similar to the one you see in Figure 12.63, which is Access Denied.

FIGURE 12.63   An error you might see when creating new Controlled GPOs within AGPM.

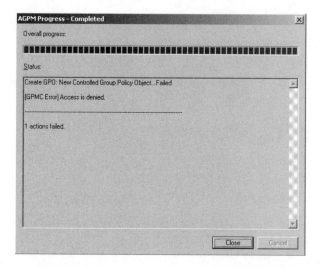

If you encounter this, you likely need to delegate the AGPM service account (e.g., AGPM-OWNER or AGPM-SERVICE) permissions to Create GPOs in the domain.

Again, this is in the Delegation node within the Group Policy Objects container within GPMC. We've described how to set these permissions in Chapter 2.

Leveraging AGPM Templates

In Chapter 3 we learned about the concept of Starter GPOs. Starter GPOs are available when your management station has the GPMC 2.0 loaded (either on Windows Server 2008 or Windows Vista + SP1 + RSAT, which contains GPMC 2.0). However, Starter GPOs are very limited. They only allow you to preserve the settings within Administrative Templates as the starting point when you're creating GPOs.

AGPM's Templates feature goes a lot farther. They allow you to preserve just about every possible setting within a GPO. Then, when a new Controlled GPO is requested, a new GPO is stamped out with all those original settings.

Making a GPO into a Template

The first step in making a template is to make a new Controlled GPO. You might want to give it a name that's indicative of what you want to do with it. In this example, Frank Rizzo, who has Approver rights and therefore can immediately create new Controlled GPOs, can do just that—create a new Controlled GPO as a starting point.

Next, you'll need to Check Out the new GPO. You can't Edit a GPO unless it's Checked Out. Edit the GPO to preserve the template settings. You might want to create templates for all sorts of situations because you can plunk any Group Policy items within the template. Just think about it. You can have templates that consist of the following:

- Administrative templates
- Security settings
- Deployed printers
- Group Policy Preference Extensions
- Or anything else your heart desires

Before you Check In the GPO, right-click over it, and select Save as Template, as seen in Figure 12.64.

FIGURE 12.64   You can create a template from an existing Controlled GPO.

Then, you'll be able to give the template a name and add some salient comments, as seen in Figure 12.65.

FIGURE 12.65   Adding a comment to a new template

Spawning a New Controlled GPO Based upon a Template

At this point, new Controlled GPOs can either be based upon no template (or, really, the default template named <Empty GPO> template), or based on the template you just created.

People making new requests for creating GPOs can choose the template. They can do this during the "Submit New Controlled GPO Request" dialog as seen in Figure 12.66 or, alternatively, by clicking on the Templates tab, locating the template, then right-clicking over it and selecting New Controlled GPO.

FIGURE 12.66 Creating a GPO from an existing template

Setting the Default Template

If you'd like, you may set the default template, which is used whenever anyone creates a GPO, by right-clicking over the template and selecting Set as Default. Note that anyone with Editor rights can set the default template.

Editing a Template

Briefly, once you save a template, you cannot edit it. It's essentially frozen in time forever. However, if you want to, you can do the following procedure, which is almost like editing a template:

1. Create a new Controlled GPO from the template.
2. Edit the GPO.
3. Save it as a template with a darn-similar name (because you can't have two templates with the same name).
4. Put the original template in the Recycle Bin.
5. Destroy the original template in the Recycle Bin.
6. Rename the new template with the original name.

Finding Differences between a Deployed GPO and a Template

One of the great things about templates is that you can do "spot auditing" for differences between a controlled GPO and a template. Indeed, you could consider some templates to be baseline security, depending on how you use them.

With that in mind, to see how far changed HR GPO1 is from a specific template (for instance, the one that created it), just right-click over the GPO and select Differences ➢ Template, as seen in Figure 12.67; then pick the template to compare.

FIGURE 12.67   You can create a Difference report between a GPO and a template to see variations from the original.

The output will be similar to other reports. Blue lines with pound signs (#) designate that the same GPO is in both. Plus signs (+) with green lines designate that some setting was added since the template was made. The minus sign (-) with red lines means that some setting was subtracted since the template was made.

See Figure 12.35 for an example report that will be similar to Difference reports.

Changing Permissions on GPO Archives

In Figure 12.46, we saw how Frank, Brett, and Sammy all had access to the AGPM system. We did this via the Domain Delegation tab. And we made sure they received rights that allowed them to travel through the AGPM system Reviewing, Editing, and Approving requests.

However, you can, if you want, add someone else to a single GPO within the archive. This can be performed only on a Controlled GPO. So, for instance, if someone else (not normally part of the AGPM system) needed rights to manage one GPO in the archive, you could grant it to them. In Figure 12.68, I've added Nurse1 to the Controlled HR GPO2.

By default, when you click Add and select a user, they get Reviewer and Editor rights. But clicking the Advanced button (not shown) brings up the permissions for the Controlled GPO, where you can tailor the permissions to specifically what you need (again, seen in Figure 12.68).

FIGURE 12.68   You can grant permissions to an AGPM user for a single GPO.

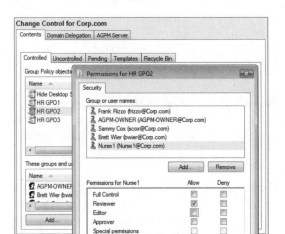

Backing Up, Restoring, and Moving the AGPM Server

Because AGPM is a single point of failure, you need a backup. And this backup can be moved/restored to any server. But, it's certainly easier to bring up a server with the same name as the original AGPM server and restore it to the same location.

In my original example, I installed the AGPM server on DC01 and put the archive within C:\AGPM-ARCHIVE (a change from the defaults, which we talked about earlier). You can see the archive in Figure 12.69.

FIGURE 12.69   The GPOs in the archive are just files in directories.

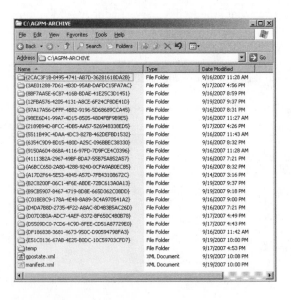

The AGPM archive consists of directories and a handful of files. Just plain old regular directories and files, with backups of Group Policy Objects within them and some pointer files (`gpostate.xml` and `manifest.xml`) to help keep some order to the place.

Backing Up the AGPM Server

To back up the AGPM server, just copy the whole AGPM-ARCHIVE directory to another safe location for easy access. You can schedule this action.

It's likely a good idea to stop the AGPM service running on the server, though, to ensure that no users are currently in the middle of making Group Policy Check Outs/Check Ins.

Of course, the whole process can be scripted and scheduled to happen, say, nightly if desired.

Restoring the AGPM Server

Restoring the AGPM server is really simple: get a new machine to house the AGPM server. Again, this can be Windows Server 2003, Windows Vista (yes, Vista), or Windows Server 2008. Then, install the server as you did earlier. Again, I suggest you specify a directory like `C:\AGPM-ARCHIVE` for the archive. You can specify the same service account you used earlier and the account that will own the AGPM archive (AGPM-OWNER).

Then, once it's fully installed, stop the AGPM service.

Traverse to the directory, and copy in the backed-up files. Make sure the `gpostate.xml` and `manifest.xml` are in the root of the archive.

Finally, once they're all copied, start the AGPM service on the server.

You might have one file in the newly created server called `gpostate.xml`. During a restore, just rename that file `gpostateold.xml`.

Changing the Location of the Clients to the New Server

During this period of restoring (or moving) the AGPM server, your AGPM administrators won't be able to access it. When they click on the Change Control node, they'll get a message similar to what's seen in Figure 12.70.

At this point, if you've restored back to the same server, your clients should be A-OK and seeing the same data in the archive they did before the incident.

FIGURE 12.70   You'll get an AGPM error if you choose to restore to a different server.

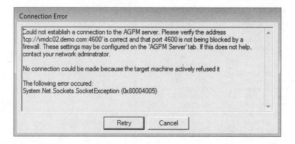

However, if you changed the name of the server, you'll need to change the AGPM client to point toward the new AGPM server. If you don't get the server name correct, you'll see what's in Figure 12.71. Again, to make the change, click in the AGPM Server tab as seen in Figure 12.72.

FIGURE 12.71   You'll get an AGPM client error if it cannot find the AGPM server.

FIGURE 12.72   Be sure the AGPM clients are using the changed AGPM server.

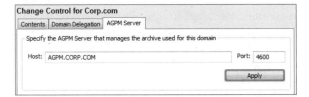

 If you restore your AGPM server to a Windows Vista or Windows Server 2008 machine, you'll also need to explicitly open the AGPM port for inbound communications. The default is port 4600.

Finally, your restore isn't complete until you set the SMTP and email settings, including spelling out who should be on the From: and To: lines as well as setting the SMTP server name and putting back in the password. If you don't finish this step, you might see what's in Figure 12.73. Once those steps are completed, you've successfully restored your AGPM server.

FIGURE 12.73   Another AGPM error regarding SMTP configuration during restore

Changing the Port that AGPM Uses

If for some reason, after AGPM server installation, you need to modify the port that AGPM uses, the procedure is very simple. Just stop the AGPM service, locate the `gpostate.xml` file (in the root of the AGPM archive), locate the line that says `Agpm:port="4600"`, change the port number, then restart the AGPM service, and finally, change the port on the AGPM client to match.

Events from AGPM

I wish I could tell you that AGPM had rich event reporting in the Event Viewer. It doesn't. It seems only to report when the AGPM server has started and stopped and seemingly nothing else.

   If you want detailed reports of what's transpiring between the AGPM client and AGPM server, you need to turn on AGPM Tracing. See the section titled "AGPM Tracing Clients and Servers" a little later.

Leveraging the Built-in AGPM ADM Template

In Chapter 7, you learned about ADM and ADMX files and how ADMX files are the newer technology to control an application's settings. However, strangely, when you load the AGPM client, it also puts an ADM file (the older type of file) on your system in the `\Windows\inf` directory. This file can help you manage both your AGPM servers and your AGPM clients. (Again, an AGPM client means a management station that has the AGPM management piece installed.)

   To use the AGPM ADM template, simply create a new GPO, and link it to the location you want to manage. To leverage the policy settings on the user side, you might want to create an OU called **People who can manage GPOs via AGPM** and link the GPO there.

   Or, to leverage the policy on the computer side, you might want to create an OU called **Our AGPM clients** and/or **Our AGPM servers** and link the GPO there.

   If you fire up the Group Policy Object Editor from Windows Server 2003, you'll need to load the ADM template by hand. But you've moved on to a Windows Vista with the GPMC 2.0 at this point, right? Of course. In that case, if you've loaded the AGPM client on that management station, it will be inside the Group Policy Object Editor ready to use as soon as you're ready.

   You can see the AGPM settings in Computer Configuration ➢ Policies ➢ Administrative Templates ➢ Classic Administrative Templates (ADM) ➢ Windows Components ➢ AGPM and also User Configuration ➢ Policies ➢ Administrative Templates ➢ Classic Administrative Templates (ADM) ➢ AGPM and also another node parallel to AGPM called Microsoft Management Console.

   Let's run down the things the ADM template is capable of performing.

ADM Template Settings That Tell Your AGPM Client which AGPM Server to Use

There are two curiously named settings within User Configuration ➢ Policies ➢ Administrative Templates ➢ Classic Administrative Templates (ADM) ➢ Windows Components ➢ AGPM, as seen in Figure 12.74. They're named **AGPM Server** and **AGPM Server (all domains)**.

   You can choose to use one, both, or neither of these settings.

FIGURE 12.74   The two AGPM settings on the user side

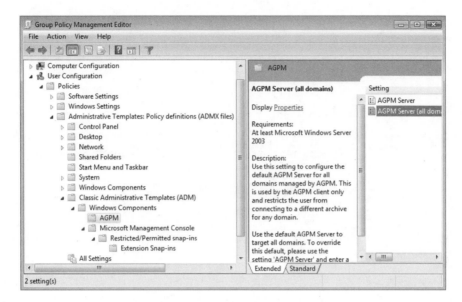

Let's say you had OU administrators who all needed to use the same AGPM server. No problem—you might link a GPO to the domain level (therefore ensuring that every OU administrator got the GPO) and use agpm.corp.com as your AGPM server.

That's great. Except for a small handful of OU admins contained within an OU named **AGPM Testers**. In this OU, they need to use another AGPM server (testagpmserver.corp.com), which is online just for testing purposes.

So, you've got two policy settings. One policy setting, **AGPM Server (all domains)**, would be used to tell the AGPM client which server to use normally (agpm.corp.com.) Buuut, you might consider linking a GPO containing settings within the policy setting named **AGPM Server**, which overwrites any defaults that might be set via the **AGPM Server (all domains)** setting.

You can see how to use the **AGPM Server** policy setting in Figure 12.75.

It's a little counterintuitive, I know. So, here it is in a nutshell: If you have a conflict between **AGPM Server** and **AGPM Server (all domains)**, **AGPM Server** is meant to be the more specific setting, so it will win.

And, a quick warning: In our tests, if the setting was already set locally, this policy setting didn't always apply. So be sure not to set up the AGPM client manually if you're planning on using these Group Policy ADM templates and their settings.

Honing the AGPM Client View

Dive down into User Configuration ➢ Policies ➢ Administrative Templates ➢ Classic Administrative Templates (ADM) ➢ Windows Components ➢ Microsoft Management Console ➢ Restricted/Permitted snap-ins ➢ Extension Snap-ins and there are three policy settings that let you further restrict who can do what within the AGPM client.

You can see these in Figure 12.76.

FIGURE 12.75 Setting the AGPM Server policy setting

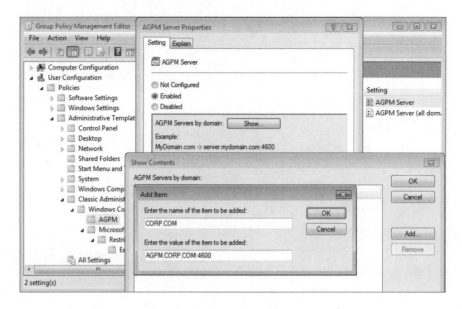

FIGURE 12.76 You can further refine which snap-ins and tabs are shown within the GPMC and AGPM.

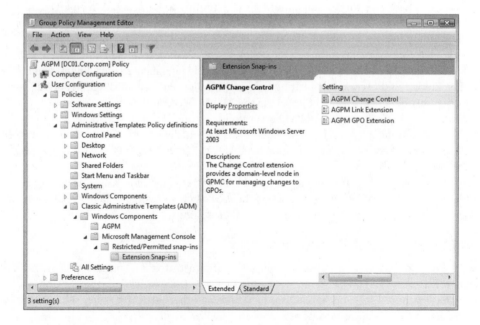

The policy settings are named exceptionally poorly, and the embedded help text really doesn't explain what the policy settings do. So, without further ado, here's the breakdown.

AGPM Change Control

If this policy setting is Disabled (yes, Disabled), the Change Control node will not be shown. Might be useful if anyone *except* the people part of the AGPM cabal in your company inadvertently installs the AGPM client. That way, they won't be tempted to click on the Change Control node and get an Access Denied error message.

AGPM Link Extension

If this policy setting is Disabled (yes, Disabled), the History tab goes away within the GPMC. This occurs for the History tab over linked GPOs and makes History unavailable within the Change Control node.

Might be useful when someone's job is just to request GPOs, and they shouldn't see any history of past GPO implementations.

AGPM GPO Extension

If this policy setting is Disabled (yes, Disabled), the History tab is removed from GPOs that are not linked (just in the swimming pool). That is, you'll see the History tab only on GPOs that are linked.

AGPM Tracing Clients and Servers

In Figure 12.77, you can see the setting for AGPM logging.

FIGURE 12.77   You can set AGPM logging (for both server and client) using Group Policy.

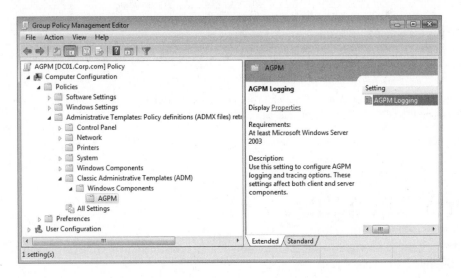

What's interesting about this policy is that the same policy (when Enabled) can affect either AGPM clients or AGPM servers. So, just create the GPO and link it over to the OU containing either AGPM clients or AGPM servers.

Enabling the policy setting and affecting an AGPM client turns on tracing and puts a log in `%LocalAppData%\Microsoft\AGPM\agpm.log`.

Enabling the policy setting and affecting an AGPM server turns on tracing and puts a log in `%CommanAppData%\Microsoft\AGPM\agpmserv.log`.

You can experiment with this to see the logging levels. Indeed, I would recommend you do this before there's an AGPM problem, so you can get a feel for what's possible when logging is enabled.

An Extra Goodie You Get When Running the AGPM Client on Windows Server 2003 (and Not Vista)

Sometimes, you feel as if your work is never done. Well, someone at DesktopStandard, oops, I mean Microsoft, must feel the same way. There's a little leftover piece of technology that isn't used for very much, and it only shows up if the AGPM client is loaded on Windows Server 2003 (and not visible if it's loaded on Windows Vista).

That is, if you click a GPO (and have rights to it) then you'll see a tab that exists only on Windows Server 2003. It's called the Extensions tab. By clicking on it, you can see what CSEs the GPO contains.

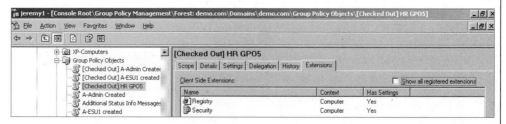

Alternatively, you can click the "Show all registered extensions" check box and see all the extensions the GPO could set and also see which ones have active settings.

Not a big deal, that's for sure. But interesting, nonetheless!

Final Thoughts

AGPM is neat. But it's an investment. Not only is it an investment in terms of money, it's also an investment in terms of time.

Remember that, by default, just because AGPM is deployed doesn't mean that the original owners can't modify the original live GPOs. To prevent that, you'll need to take Control of the

GPO and then Redeploy it (even if that means you're just Redeploying the GPOs back on top of themselves). When you do that, the original owner is changed to SYSTEM or the AGPM-OWNER account (or whatever you called it during setup).

Moreover, consider putting in place the extra "fences" so that no one can create GPOs outside the AGPM system. That way, you won't turn around one day asking, "How come all the machines aren't acting the way we think they should be?" because one administrator didn't get the memo to start using the AGPM system. If you ensure that everyone uses AGPM, you can ensure that you can roll back out of any problem you have.

AGPM is great. It doesn't care if you use technologies like the Central Store, ADM files, custom ADM files, or custom ADMX files (all within Chapter 7) or Group Policy Preference Extensions (Chapter 10). All can be used and all can be rolled back. Just make sure you install AGPM on a Windows Server 2008 machine (or a Windows Vista machine with the Group Policy Preference Extensions loaded) because that archive power relies on the underlying host.

Group Policy Tools

Obviously, the power of Group Policy is awesome, but some aspects of Group Policy and desktop management are better suited to additional tools. In this appendix, we're going to leverage a variety of tools to perform several key duties. We'll also finish discussing what the GPMC has to offer, specifically, migrating existing GPOs between domains. We'll then dive into the other free Group Policy management tools from Microsoft.

Last, we'll round up third-party Group Policy tools, third-party profiles tools, third-party ADM editing tools, and third-party Microsoft Installer (MSI) repackaging tools. However, it should be noted that Group Policy tool manufacturers constantly create and innovate. To that end, some manufacturers choose to show off their products on www.GPanswers.com, so be sure to check out my website for updated information (if available).

Migrating Group Policy Objects between Domains

For years, I stood in front of large audiences and recommended testing the power of GPOs in a test forest. In return, I'd get blank stares because this advice was inherently impractical. Sure, it was safe—safer than testing GPOs in production—but ultimately my advice was doomed. How can you do the hard work in a test domain, test it, debug it, get it all right, and then lift it out of its original test lab universe and put it in production? Answer? Until the GPMC, you couldn't.

These examples will continue with our fictional multidomain environment. You can flip back to Figure 5.7 to see the relationship between our three domains: Corp.com, Widgets.corp.com, and the cross-forest trust between bigu.edu and Corp.com.

Basic Interdomain Copy and Import

Using the GPMC, you can take existing GPOs from any domain and copy them to another domain. The target domain can be a parent domain, a child domain, a cross-forest domain, or a completely foreign domain that has no trusts! Both the Copy and the Import operations transfer only the policy settings; these operations do not modify either the source or the destination links of the GPOs.

The Copy Operation

The interdomain Copy operation is meant to be used when you want to copy live GPOs from one domain to another. That is, you have two domains, connectivity between them, and appropriate rights to the GPOs. To copy the GPO, you need Read rights on the source GPO you want to copy and Write rights in the target domain.

First, you want to tweak your GPMC console so that you can see the two domains you want.

Recall that to add new domains to the GPMC, you simply right-click Domains and choose Show Domains from the shortcut menu to open up the Show Domains dialog box. Then simply select the domains you want to see. To add other forests, right-click Group Policy Management and choose Add Forest from the shortcut menu to open the Add Forest dialog box. You can then enter the name of the forest in the field labeled Domain (yes, domain!).

In this first example, we'll copy a GPO from Corp.com to Widgets.corp.com. An enterprise administrator will have rights in all domains. Since we're logged in as an enterprise administrator, we have rights in both Corp.com (to read) and Widgets.corp.com (to write). Follow these steps:

1. In the Group Policy Objects container, right-click the GPO you want to copy, as shown in Figure A.1. For this example, I've chosen the "Hide Settings Tab/Restore Screen Saver Tab" GPO.

FIGURE A.1 You can copy a GPO from the Group Policy Objects container.

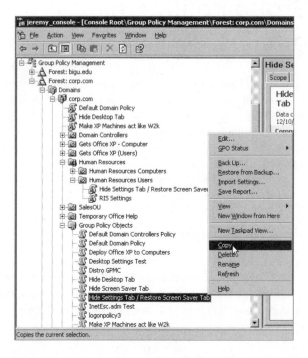

2. Adjust your view of the GPMC so that you can see the target domain. In Figure A.2, I've minimized the view of Corp.com and expanded Widgets.corp.com—especially the Group Policy Objects container.

3. Right-click the target domain's Group Policy Objects container, and choose Paste to start the Cross-Domain Copying Wizard.

4. Click Next to bypass the initial splash screen and open the Specifying permissions screen, shown in Figure A.2.

FIGURE A.2   When you paste a GPO, you can choose how to handle permissions.

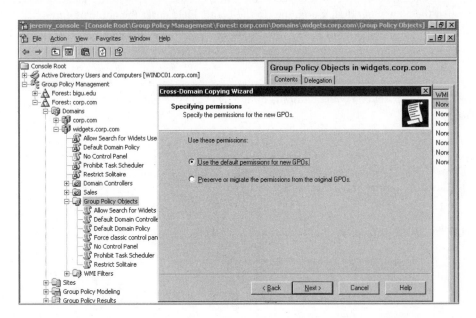

You can now choose to create a GPO with the default permissions or to copy the original permissions to the new GPO. The latter might be useful if you've delegated some special permissions to that GPO and don't want redo your efforts. Most of the time, however, the first option is fine. You can now zip through the rest of the wizard.

 NOTE   You might see a message about Migration Tables. Don't fret; they're right around the corner. For this specific GPO, you won't need Migration Tables, so it won't be an issue.

 WARNING   If you copy a GPO between domains, the WMI filtering is lost because the WMI filter won't necessarily exist in the target domain.

The Import Operation

In the previous scenario, we copied a GPO from Corp.com to Widgets.corp.com. We did this when both domains were online and accessible. But if you are working on an isolated testing network, this won't be possible. How then do you take a GPO you created in the isolated test lab and bring it into production? First, create a backup as described in Chapter 2. You'll then have a collection of files that you can put on a floppy, a CD, and so on and take out into the real world. You can then create a brand-new GPO (or overwrite an existing GPO) and perform the import! Follow these steps:

1. Right-click the Group Policy Objects container, choose New from the shortcut menu to open the New GPO dialog box, and in the Name Field enter the name of a new GPO.

2. Right-click that GPO and choose Import Settings from the shortcut menu, as shown in Figure A.3. This then starts the Import Settings Wizard.

Anyone with Edit rights on the GPO can perform an Import.

You can choose to overwrite an existing GPO, but that's just it. It's an overwrite, not a merge. So, be careful!

FIGURE A.3 You can import the settings and overwrite an existing GPO.

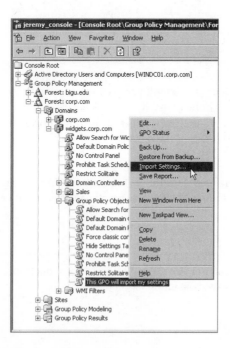

3. The wizard then presents the Backup GPO screen, which allows you to back up the newly created GPO; however, this is unnecessary. This is a safety measure should you decide to overwrite an existing GPO. You can then click Next to see the Backup Location screen.

4. In the Backup Location screen, use the Backup folder field to input the path to where your backup set is and select Next. The Source GPO screen will appear.

5. At the Source GPO screen, select the GPO from which you want to import settings, as shown in Figure A.4, and click Next.

You should now be able to zip through the rest of the wizard. Ignore any references to Migration Tables; they're coming up next.

A Word about Drag and Drop

Dragging and dropping a GPO from one domain into another domain can be hazardous! For example, your intention is to copy a GPO named "Restrict Solitaire" from the GPO container in Widgets.corp.com to the **Human Resources Users** OU in Corp.com. It looks like it's going to make sense: you set up your view in the GPMC to show both domains, you can see the Group Policy Objects container in Widgets.corp.com, and you can see the **Human Resources Users** OU in Corp.com. Then, you drag and drop, and you're asked the following question:

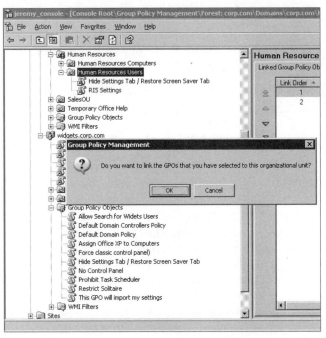

If you click OK, you're not actually copying! Indeed, you're performing a no-no! You are creating a cross-domain link to the GPO, as you can see when you click the Details tab of the GPO:

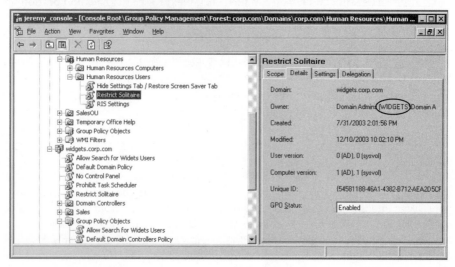

In this example, the Domain field shows that it lives in Widgets.corp.com, even though the GPO is linked to an OU in Corp.com.

Whenever a GPO is linked from across a domain, the GPO must be pulled from a Domain Controller that actually houses it. If it's across the WAN, so be it. And that could mean major slowdowns.

The moral of the story is to be sure you're copying (as described earlier) and not just linking.

Copy and Import with Migration Tables

In the previous examples, we migrated the very simple GPO named "Hide Settings Tab/Restore Screen Saver Tab." That particular GPO contained only Administrative Template settings that affected the Desktop. Nothing fancy, for sure.

However, certain policy settings do perform some fancy footwork. Some GPOs can include references to security groups, such as "Allow Log on Locally." Other GPOs can include references to UNC paths, such as Folder Redirection. Indeed, an Advanced Folder Redirection policy setting contains both security group references and UNC path references! Other possibilities include Restricted Groups, Group Policy Software Installation policy settings, and pointers to scripts.

When you migrate GPOs across domains, you need to take care of these references. Copying a GPO in one domain that redirects folders to the \\DC01\Data share will not likely make much sense when the GPO is used in another domain.

FIGURE A.4   Select a GPO from which you want to import settings.

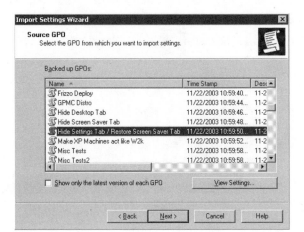

With that in mind, both the Copy and Import functions can leverage *Migration Tables*. Migration tables let you rectify both security group and UNC references that exist in a GPO when you transfer the GPO to another domain. You'll be given the opportunity to use the Migration Tables automatically if your Copy or Import operation detects that a policy setting needs it! After the GPO is ready to be copied or imported, you'll be notified that some adjustments are needed. It's that easy!

In the Migrating References screen of the wizard (shown in Figure A.5), you can choose two paths here:

- Selecting "Copying them identically from the source" can be risky. Again, you won't know what the source is using for security groups or UNC paths. The existing security groups and UNC paths may be valid, but they may not be.

- Selecting "Using this migration table to map them in the destination GPO" gives you the opportunity to choose an existing migration table (if you have one), or you can click the New button to open the Migration Table Editor and create on-the-fly.

To start, use a new blank Migration Table (after pressing the New button) and follow these steps:

1. If you're performing a Copy, choose Tools ➢ Populate from GPO to open the Select GPO screen, then simply select the live GPO. If you're performing an Import, choose Tools ➢ Populate from Backup to open the Select Backup dialog, which allows you to select a GPO from backup.

2. Choose the GPO you're copying or importing to display a list of all the references that need to be corrected.

3. In Figure A.5, you can see both the Source Name and Destination Name fields. The Source Name field will automatically be filled in. All that's left is to enter in the Destination Name UNC path for the new environment and you're done!

FIGURE A.5 A Migration Table can smooth the bumps between domains.

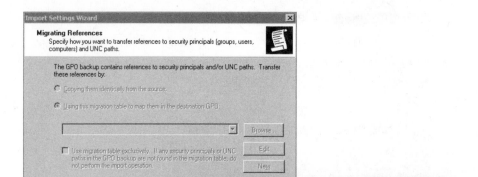

4. Save the file (with a `.migtable` extension), and close the Migration Table Editor—New screen.

5. Back at the Migrating References page, simply click Browse and choose the migration table you just made.

Before clicking the Next button, you can optionally choose the check box that begins with "Use migration table exclusively." In this example, we have but one UNC reference that needs to be rectified. You might have a meaty GPO with 30 UNC paths and another 50 security principles that need to be cleared up. Perhaps you can't locate all the destination names. If you select this check box, the wizard will not proceed unless all the paths in the destination name are valid. Use this setting if you really need to be sure all settings will be verified successfully.

When ready, click Next, click Next again past the summary screen, and you're finished.

Microsoft has a detailed white paper you'll want to check out if you're planning to do a lot of this. You'll find it at www.microsoft.com/windowsserver2003/gpmc/migrgpo.mspx.

WARNING Group Policy Preference Extensions are ignored when migration tables are used. That is, they are copied straight from the source and not adjusted to the target.

Microsoft Tools Roundup

As might be expected, Microsoft has a slew of tools to help manage your Group Policy infrastructure as well as your user profiles. In this section, we'll check out the Microsoft tools and where to find them.

Wholesale Backup and Restore of Your Test Lab (or an Easy Way to Migrate to Production)

One more tip before we leave this section. That is, when you're working in your test lab, you might find it necessary to completely demolish and rebuild your test lab for a variety of reasons. However, as noted in Chapter 2, when a GPO is restored, the links are not restored along with the GPO. Again, this is a protection mechanism for your benefit. However, as they say in the hallowed IT halls, "What you do in the test lab stays in the test lab." So the test lab is a different animal. And, to that end, you might want to back up a whole gaggle of stuff for safekeeping:

- GPOs

- Group Policy links

- Security groups

- OUs

- Users

- Permissions on GPOs

Then, if you need to demolish your test lab and put it back in order, you'll need a way to perform a wholesale restore of all these objects. The GPMC has a built-in script that will back up all these things into one little package. Then, when you're ready, you run another script that takes the package and expands it back into these objects.

The script that does all the backup stuff is called `CreateXMLFromEnvironment.vbs`. The one that does all the restoring is `CreateEnvironmentFromXML.vbs`. Both scripts are located in `C:\Program Files\GPMC\scripts` (with the GPMC 1.0, and available for download for the GPMC 2.0 at `http://tinyurl.com/2quhw5`). The scripts are not present by default on Vista machines; you'll need to download them from the Scripting Center on Microsoft's website.

The other reason to use these scripts is to do a wholesale migration from the test lab into the real production environment. Personally, I'm not all that keen on a wholesale backup and restore of my test lab into the real world, but I guess if you had nothing at all in the real world this could be a useful way to get things over lock, stock, and barrel. These scripts are a little too far reaching for my taste, but perhaps you'll find them just the thing.

Microsoft has various documents about this script, so check out `www.microsoft.com` for some tips about using it. For instance, there's a Microsoft Knowledge Base article on this script at `http://support.microsoft.com/kb/929397`.

Group Policy Tools from Microsoft

Except for Active Directory Monitor and GPInventory, you can download the remainder of the Microsoft tools for free from the Windows 2003 Resource Kit. As of this writing, you can find it at www.microsoft.com/windowsserver2003/downloads/tools/default.mspx under the heading "Windows Server 2003 Resource Kit Tools." After you install the Resource Kit, you'll find the tools in the \Program Files\Windows Resource Kits\Tools folder. Some of these tools are ready to use; others require additional installation.

Active Directory Monitor and GPOTOOL

These tools help to troubleshoot GPOs if the GPC and GPT get out of sync. See Chapter 6 for information.

admX (within *ADMX.MSI*)—ADM Template Comparison Utility

This tool has an unfortunate name; it was born before the advent of ADMX files, so don't be confused and think that admX really has anything to do with ADMX files (which we explored in Chapter 7).

This tool prints (or redirects) an ADM template into a nice readable format for documentation. It will parse an ADM file and list Registry path, Symbolic Policy Name, Full Policy Name, Registry settings, and the Supported on keyword. You can also use it to show the differences between two similar ADM files.

This tool requires additional installation. Be sure the latest .NET Framework is installed (the one built into Windows 2003 is not sufficient). Next, run the ADMX.MSI to install and follow the wizard. After installation, the default location for admX is C:\Program Files\Microsoft\admx. You'll need to execute admX.exe from there.

GPMonitor—Group Policy Monitor Tool

The purpose of GPMonitor, which is shown in Figure A.6, is to perform historical analysis of what has changed between different Group Policy refresh intervals on your clients and servers. This tool requires an armload of additional installation; it unpacks to a set of files that need to stay together. You deploy the MSI (Microsoft Installer) to two locations: the clients you want to monitor and a management station that you'll use to see your results. After you unpack the MSI, you deploy the MSI file via GPSI (Group Policy Software Installation) to the clients. Additionally, this package comes with an ADM template, which you need to import into the Group Policy Management Editor. The point of the ADM file is to push the data about the client's Group Policy application to a central shared folder location.

Once your clients start pushing up the data, you can run the GPMonitorUI at your management station to see what's going on. The clients will upload their historical data every *N* Group Policy refreshes. (The default is every 8.) From your management station, you can then see which GPOs did or did not apply yesterday but are applying today—among other possibilities.

FIGURE A.6   GPMonitor

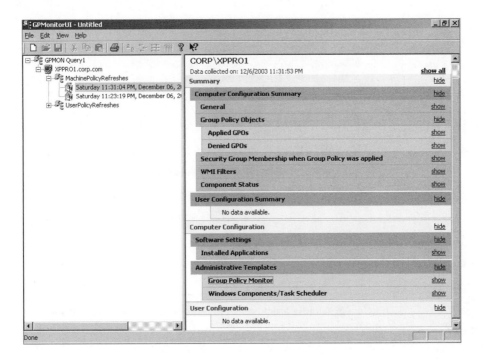

 Your management station needs the GPMC loaded to display the data as seen in Figure A.6, but the clients you want to monitor do not.

GPInventory—Group Policy Inventory Tool

GPInventory is a late addition to the Windows 2003 Server Resource Kit. You must download and install it separately. To find it, search for "Group Policy Inventory" on Microsoft's website. At last check, however, it could be found here: `http://tinyurl.com/b38lu`.

GPInventory can reach across the network and query your clients and servers for a list of attributes you want to document in Excel or a text file. Simply point GPInventory toward a list of clients, select the attributes you want to gather, and then let it do its thing. Afterward, just save the resulting file.

In Figure A.7, I can easily find out how much memory my Windows XP clients have by selecting the WMI: Computer Memory field and documenting the RSoP (Resultant Set of Policy) status of all my clients with some of the other attributes.

You can even change the default attributes that GPInventory will inventory for via the XML file. Read the included documentation for a how-to.

FIGURE A.7 Group Policy Inventory

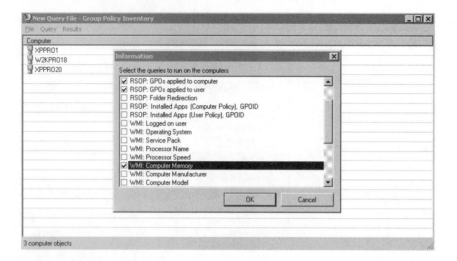

There's a great little article on GPInventory in Microsoft *TechNet Magazine*, found here: http://tinyurl.com/2gw2ry.

The WinPolicies Tool

WinPolicies, which is shown in Figure A.8, is also known as the "Policy Spy." Anyway, Win-Policies can perform lots of the ultra-propeller-head client-side troubleshooting stuff you saw in Chapter 6, without you having to get your fingers too dirty.

Specifically, you can enable verbose logging, perform tracing, refresh policies (enforced or not enforced), and get additional troubleshooting information. Typically, you run this tool on the client system experiencing the problem. You can run it as a mere-mortal user or as an administrator. Several features let you enter alternative credentials so you can use it, mostly, as a mere-mortal but still see log files that are for admins only. That's a nice touch.

WinPolicies doesn't really add any new features to the Group Policy troubleshooting arsenal, but it does consolidate them. And you still need to understand what you're looking at to make heads or tails of the output. Hopefully, the information in Chapter 6 gets you off to the right start.

Note this program may crash if you run it on Windows Vista or Windows Server 2008.

ADMX Migrator

The ADMX Migrator is actually two tools in one: an ADMX Migrator tool and an ADMX Editor tool. We discussed these tools in the section "ADMX Migrator and ADMX Editor Tools" in Chapter 7. Additional information can be found in the online appendix at www.GPanswers.com

FIGURE A.8   WinPolicies

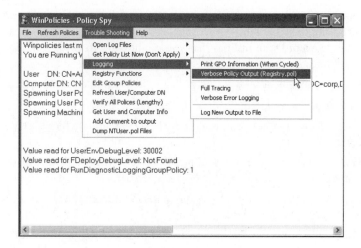

Group Policy Log View (GPLogView)

A new tool for Windows Vista, Group Policy Log View helps you quickly view operational log results and put them in file types of your choice. We saw this tool in Chapter 6. Again, for reference, you can download it here:

> http://go.microsoft.com/fwlink/?LinkId=75004

Profile Tools from Microsoft

Microsoft also has two tools to help manipulate profiles if they need a kick in the pants. Here they are.

The Delprof Tool

You use this utility to bulk-delete profiles—either locally or remotely. An update is available at www.microsoft.com/windowsserver2003/techinfo/reskit/tools/default.mspx. This is a command-line tool, so be careful; you can get in a lot of trouble in a hurry. Microsoft has a nice Knowledge Base article on this tool (315411 at http://support.microsoft.com/kb/315411) that discusses how to eliminate profiles if they are not used in, say, 30 days.

The Proquota Tool

You can use this tool to limit the size that the roaming user profile can become. This isn't a tool you can run, per se. It's part of the operating system. It is invoked whenever the **Limit profile size** policy setting in User Configuration ≻ Policies ≻ Administrative Templates ≻ System ≻ User Profiles is set to Enabled.

Utilities and Add-Ons

There are utilities that pop up all the time to help with Group Policy management and configuration. Instead of listing them here, however, I suggest you go to www.GPanswers.com/solutions, which has a current list of utilities that you might want to check out. Here's a sampling of what you'll find:

- Killpol: Temporarily stops the application of policy to help troubleshoot a system.

- RGPrefresh: Command-line Group Policy refresh utility.

- RegToADM: Tool to convert Registry files (.REG) to ADM template files (http://yizhar.mvps.org).

- GPSIViewer: GUI utility for viewing and printing information on all software installation packages in a domain (www.gpoguy.com/gpsiviewer.htm).

- WMIFTest: GUI utility for testing WMI filters on a given Windows system prior to implementation (www.gpoguy.com/wmiftest.htm).

- Vista Central Store Creator utility: Tool to create and populate the Central Store easily (http://gpoguy.com/cssu.htm).

- PowerShell cmdlets for Group Policy (http://gpoguy.com/powershell.htm).

- Specops GPUpdate: A Group Policy refresh utility that hooks into Active Directory Users and Computers. (www.specopssoft.com/products/specopsgpupdate/).

- Specops Command Basic: A great way to use PowerShell scripts on your Group Policy clients: (www.specopssoft.com/powershell/).

- Specops Password Policy Basic: Helps tame Fine-Grained Password Policies with a nice GUI (http://tinyurl.com/34e3ud).

- PolicyReporter: Helps analyze both Windows XP and Windows Vista logs to help find Group Policy problems (http://tinyurl.com/2ft4nq).

- PolicyPak Design Studio Basic: Create a great Group Policy interface to manage your applications (www.PolicyPak.com).

Third-Party Vendors List

When I wrote the first edition of this book, only one or two vendors were really doing interesting stuff with Group Policy. By the time I wrote the second edition of this book, I had a handful of vendors with a handful of products.

Vendors are now recognizing the power that Group Policy provides. Some vendors are adding to the management capabilities of GPOs, others help in GPO troubleshooting, and still others take the next logical step and extend Group Policy to harness even more power! By the third and fourth editions, the list just kept growing!

In this fifth edition, I'll list all the vendors I know that make third-party products. Do note that names of products change, and features change all the time. To that end, it's better to simply visit a company's websites to get a rundown of its current offerings.

Additionally, some vendors showcase their products on `www.GPanswers.com/solutions`.

Tables A.1, A.2, and A.3 list tools that can help you in your Group Policy journey. In these tables, I provide an incredibly short description of the product.

TABLE A.1   Group Policy Management Tools

Vendor	Product	Company Website	Brief Description
AdventNet	ManageEngine ADManager Plus	`www.adventnet.com`	Web-based product that simplifies Active Directory management from a central point.
BeyondTrust	Privilege Manager	`www.beyondtrust.com`	Helps you set applications to run as admins and users to run with least privilege.
Centrify	DirectControl	`www.centrify.com`	Extends Group Policy to Linux systems.
Configuresoft	Enterprise Configuration Manager	`www.configuresoft.com`	Centralizes and automates the labor-intensive task of planning, auditing, and monitoring changes in Group Policy objects on Windows systems deployed in large enterprise networks or web server farms.
FullArmor	Group Policy Anywhere	`www.fullarmor.com`	Separates Group Policy from Active Directory, allowing you to start using Group Policy today even if you are still planning for Active Directory or Group Policy.

TABLE A.1 Group Policy Management Tools *(continued)*

Vendor	Product	Company Website	Brief Description
FullArmor	PolicyPortal	www.fullarmor.com	Enforces and audits Group Policy on all machines on your network and over the Internet.
FullArmor	Workflow Studio	www.fullarmor.com	Simple yet enterprise-scale data center and business process automation through the power of Windows PowerShell and the flexibility of workflow.
Centeris	Likewise Enterprise	www.centeris.com	Extends Microsoft Group Policy to Unix, Linux, and Mac.
PolicyPak Software	PolicyPak Professional	www.policypak.com	Group Policy enables the applications you already have with your own user interface.
Special Operations Software	Special Operations Suite	www.specopssoft.com	A broad and deeply Active Directory–integrated Desktop Management suite for all sizes of organizations.
Special Operations Software	Specops Deploy	www.specopssoft.com	Enhances the native Group Policy Software Installation functions.
Special Operations Software	Specops Password Policy	www.specopssoft.com	Sets individual password requirements per OU.
Special Operations Software	Specops Inventory	www.specopssoft.com	Provides hardware and software inventory via Group Policy.

TABLE A.1   Group Policy Management Tools   *(continued)*

Vendor	Product	Company Website	Brief Description
Special Operations Software	Specops Command	www.specopssoft.com	Distributed PowerShell solution that enables PowerShell deployment and execution using Group Policy.
SDM Software	GPExpertTroubleshooting Pak	www.SDMsoftware.com	Four products (Health Reporter, Log Analyzer, Status Monitor, and Group Policy Spy) to ensure that Group Policy is functioning across your desktops and servers.
SDM Software	GPExpert Status Monitor	www.SDMsoftware.com	System tray application for desktops that helps desktopadministrators find out when Group Policy is not working.
SDM Software	GPExpert Scripting Toolkit for PowerShell	www.SDMsoftware.com	Automate Group Policy management using PowerShell.
SDM Software	GPExpert Backup Manager for Group Policy	www.SDMsoftware.com	Manages the backup and recovery of GPOs and GPO links in your Active Directory environment.
NetPro	Change Auditor	www.netpro.com	Performs auditing of Group Policy changes.
NetPro	GPOadmin	www.netpro.com	Provides Group Policy version control and Group Policy comparison.
Attachmate/ NetIQ	Group Policy Administrator (Created by FullArmor)	www.netiq.com	Provides change-management capabilities to Group Policy.

TABLE A.1   Group Policy Management Tools   *(continued)*

Vendor	Product	Company Website	Brief Description
Attachmate/ NetIQ	Group Policy Guardian (Created by FullArmor)	www.netiq.com	Performs auditing of Group Policy changes.
SecureVantage	Policy Controls Management Pack for MOM	www.securevantage.com	Performs auditing and discovery of Group Policy inside Microsoft MOM.
SecureVantage	Group Policy Auditor for SCOM	www.securevantage.com	Detailed GPO attribute discovery and auditing, reporting, change alerting, and more.
Scriptlogic	Active Administrator	www.scriptlogic.com	Provides Group Policy auditing and change management.
SysProSoft	Polman	www.SysProSoft.com	A Policy Management tool; more easily interprets policy settings.
Quest	Group Policy Manager	www.quest.com	Provides change management capabilities to Group Policy.
Quest	Group Policy Extensions for Desktops	www.quest.com	A set of Group Policy extensions; performs common administration tasks.
Quest's Vintela	VAS (Vintela Authentication Services)	www.quest.com/unix_ linux/	Extends Group Policy to Linux.

TABLE A.2 Third-Party ADM Template-Creation Tools

Vendor	Product Name	Website	Brief Description
Advanced Toolware	Policy Template Editor 2	`www.advtoolware.com/t4e/pte/pte_default.htm`	Eases the creation of ADM templates.
SysProSoft	ADM Template Editor	`www.SysProSoft.com`	Eases the creation of ADM templates. They may have an ADMX editor by the time you read this.
Microsoft/ FullArmor	ADMX Migrator	Download directly at `http://tinyurl.com/yjnptj`	For migrating from ADM to ADMX and for creating new ADMX from scratch.

TABLE A.3 Third-Party MSI Repackaging Tools

Vendor	Product Name	Website
InstallAware	InstallAware	`www.installaware.com`
Installshield/Macrovision	AdminStudio	`www.installshield.com`
Scriptlogic	DesktopAuthority MSI Studio	`www.scriptlogic.com`
New Boundary	PrismPack	`www.newboundary.com`
Attachmate	WinInstall (many versions)	`www.attachmate.com`
Wise Solutions/Altiris	Wise Package Studio	`www.wise.com`

Index

Note to the reader: Throughout this index **boldfaced** page numbers indicate primary discussions of a topic. *Italicized* page numbers indicate illustrations.

O